Houston Architectural Guide

Third Edition

Stephen Fox
Barrie Scardino Bradley, Editor
Gerald Moorhead, FAIA, Photographer
Minor Design, Design

The Anchorage Foundation of Texas
Architecture Center Houston Foundation

Published by
AIA Houston
and Minor Design

©1990, 1999, 2012, American Insitute of Architects, Houston Chapter

Library of Congress Control Number: 2012913039
ISBN 978-0-615-66959-5

Text by Stephen Fox
Edited by Barrie Scardino Bradley
Photography by Gerald Moorhead, FAIA
Design and Production by Minor Design
Printed in Houston Texas USA

Published by
American Institute of Architects, Houston Chapter
315 Capital Street
Houston TX 77001
USA

aiahouston.org

Front cover: BG Group Place (Picard Chilton and Kendall/Heaton Associates, 2011), a Hines development, reflected in a nearby building.
Photo: Craig Minor, 2012

Back cover: Julia Ideson Building, Houston Public Library (Cram & Ferguson, William Ward Watkin, and Louis A. Glover, 1926) as restored by Gensler, 2011.
Photo: courtesy Gensler.

Typefaces: Rotis Serif, Tarzana Narrow, Trade Gothic, Univers Condensed

Table of Contents

iv	How to Use This Guide	
v	Preface	
viii	Introduction	
1	Tour A-1	Downtown
33	Tour A-2	Downtown
67	Tour A-3	Downtown
85	Tour A-4	Downtown
97	Tour B	Fourth Ward / Midtown / Montrose
149	Tour C	Museum District / Hermann Park / Boulevard Oaks / Southhampton
195	Tour D	Rice University / Texas Medical Center
233	Tour E	The Village / West University Place / Braeswood
263	Tour F	Third Ward / Riverside / Universities
301	Tour G	North Side / East End
333	Tour H-1	The Heights
371	Tour H-2	West End
391	Tour I-1	River Oaks
429	Tour I-2	Kirby
455	Tour J-1	Post Oak
481	Tour J-2	Westheimer / Richmond
497	Tour K	Memorial Villages
517	Tour L	Spring Branch / Energy Corridor / Bear Creek / Addicks
533	Tour M	Hempstead Highway / Garden Oaks / Acres Homes
549	Tour N	Bellaire / Meyerland / Westbury / Sharpstown
569	Tour O	Fifth Ward / Far North Side
579	Tour P	IAH / Kingwood / Humble / Spring
591	Tour Q	The Woodlands
605	Tour R	Klein / Cypress / Fairbanks / Satsuma
619	Tour S	Addicks / Alief / Stafford / Missouri City
637	Tour T	Sugar Land / First Colony
653	Tour U	South / Southwest Houston
663	Tour V	Southeast Houston / Pasadena / Harrisburg
679	Tour W	Bay Area
696	Late Additions	
702	Index	

How to use this guide

This guidebook catalogs extant architecturally significant buildings in greater Houston divided into geographic sections, each of which is prefaced by a map and tour list. Each entry is labeled with a letter designating the tour and a number identifying the site; these labels appear on the maps at their precise location. Within the text of each tour the original name of the building, followed by a current name (in 2012) if applicable. Addresses, dates of completion, and architects follow. When two firms are joined with "and" this signifies a joint venture; two firms joined with "with" signifies the second firm was associate architect. Descriptions of varying length accompany each listing.

Tour Name — Tour A-1

Geographic Location — Downtown

Map Code — **A-31**
Original Name — **RepublicBank Center**
Current Name — [now Bank of America Center]
Address — 700 Louisiana Street
Date — 1983, Johnson/Burgee Architects
Architect — and Kendall/Heaton Associates
Description — RepublicBank tried valiantly to redress the urbanistic shortcomings associated with tall buildings of the 1960s. In an effort to avoid being sterile and unresponsive, it fills its one-block site to the saturation point with elaborate

Preface

The third edition of the *Houston Architectural Guide* has been five years in the making. Completely redesigned with new maps and more legible text, it includes 1,391 entries. The updated guidebook follows the same general pattern of organization as its predecessors: arranged in separate tours based on geography. As in the first (1990) and second (1999) editions, also written by Stephen Fox, this volume aspires to be the definitive word on Houston architecture—not just a tour book, but a reference resource for anyone interested in or seriously studying architecture in the Houston area. The new format created by Minor Design should enhance the ability of the *Houston Architectural Guide* to be useful in a variety of ways.

Houston is the fourth largest city in the United States and therefore a place of countless buildings and sites that might have been included here. The architectural entries chosen for inclusion were at the discretion of the author; AIA Houston and its members had no influence on the selection of sites or architects. This guidebook looks at Houston and its buildings with a critical eye, especially the newest buildings and civic improvements. Criticism is not intended so much to distinguish "good" buildings from "bad" buildings as to identify issues that figure in the design of individual structures and in the process of building in the city. The opinions expressed are not those of AIA Houston. Concerted effort has been made to ensure accuracy, however the author and editor regret inevitable oversights and errors. Readers are encouraged to report any inaccuracies to AIA Houston. The goal of the American Institute of Architects and its many chapters throughout the United States that have produced such guidebooks is to document and make accessible the great architecture of our cities. This book aspires to reveal Houston, one of the greatest of these cities, through the lens of its remarkable architectural heritage.

Barrie Scardino Bradley, *Editor*
Rusty Bienvenue, *Executive Director, AIA Houston*

Acknowledgements

AIA Houston thanks the many individuals and organizations that made preparation and publication of this guidebook possible. The donors who generously underwrote the publication of this book: The Anchorage Foundation of Texas and its officers, especially, Ann Bohnn Brown, and the Architecture Center Houston Foundation (previously the Houston Architecture Foundation); Barrie Scardino Bradley who, after retiring as executive director of AIA Houston, volunteered her time and expertise to edit this book; Gerald Moorhead, FAIA, who donated his services as photographer. Although Moorhead is responsible for the vast majority of the photographs, photographs by Stephen Fox, Craig Minor, and Barrie Scardino Bradley have in some instances supplemented his work.

Members of the Board of Directors of AIA Houston and Board of Trustees of the Architecture Center Houston Foundation, especially those who served as president during the five-year preparation of the manuscript: AIA Houston – Brian Malarkey, FAIA (2008), Daniel Bankhead, AIA (2009), Kathleen English, AIA (2010), Ian Powell, AIA (2011), and Perry Seeberger, AIA (2012); Architecture Center Houston Foundation – Dan Hassebroek, AIA (2008), Michael E. Lewter (2009), Joe Powers, AIA (2010), Wendy Heger, AIA (2011), Randall Walker, AIA (2012).

Staff members of AIA Houston: Rusty Bienvenue, executive director, Matt Wolf, associate director, Mandy Loughman, Jill Sales, Courtney Tutt, Steven Shultz, Morgana Davila, Jeffrey Liao, and Rocio Carlon. Graphic designers and staff of Minor Design: Craig Minor, Suzy Minor, Cheryl Beckett, Kathy Conopio, Rebecca Hamrick, and Anna Peters. Staff of the Houston Metropolitan Research Center at the Houston Public Library: Elizabeth Sargent, acting director, Kemo Curry, retired director, Laney McAdow Dwyer, architectural archivist, Timothy Ronk, archivist, and Joel Draut, photographic archivist. Rice University faculty and staff: School of Architecture: Sarah M. Whiting, Assoc. AIA, dean, Lars Lerup, former dean, John J. Casbarian FAIA, former acting dean; Woodson Research Center and Brown Fine Arts Library, Fondren Library, GIS/Data Center, and the Digital Media Center, Gerald D. Hines College of Architecture,

University of Houston: Patricia Belton Oliver, FAIA, dean, Joseph W. Mashburn, FAIA, former dean, Architecture and Art Library librarian Catherine Essinger. Houston Mod: Steve Curry AIA, 2012 president, Jeff Carowitz, Ben Hill, Russell Howard, Ben Koush, AIA and Karen Lantz, AIA. Rice Design Alliance: Linda Sylvan, executive director. Drivers: Sims McCutchen, Barrie Scardino Bradley, and Rusty Bienvenue.

We would also like to acknowledge the dozens of individuals who helped create the first two editions of the *Houston Architectural Guide*, upon which this third edition is solidly based. And we thank, most of all, the author, Stephen Fox, without whose knowledge and generosity this work would not have been possible.

Introduction

Houston in the second decade of the 21st century suggests that the architectural epoch of the 1970s and '80s—the period of Pennzoil Place and the Menil Collection—was an exceptional highpoint in the city's history rather than marking the attainment of a permanent state of architectural grace. If the architecture produced in Houston during the first decade of the 21st century does not induce the excited expectations associated (at least in retrospect) with the 1970s and '80s, it does represent a significant period of consolidation. An immense volume of new construction that began in the late 1990s has continued, despite economic oscillations at the beginning and end of the 2000 decade. This continuing development is registered by the addition of 353 new sites to this edition. As elsewhere in the U.S. during the 2000s, a significant percentage of new construction involved housing. Houston and Texas did not experience the drastic crisis of foreclosures that afflicted other U.S. cities. Even so, an astonishing amount of new residential construction occurred in the 2000s, with housing built in areas of the city that had never been residential neighborhoods before or that had been dormant for decades. The introduction of light rail public transit in 2004 marked the beginning of a slow but important transformation of Houston's transportation infrastructure. This was complemented by substantial (if also slow) progress on expanding and refitting the public space infrastructure of Houston. Characteristically for Houston, such non-profit organizations as the Hermann Park Conservancy, the Buffalo Bayou Partnership, and the Discovery Green Conservancy took the lead in administering what, in most other U.S. cities, would have been improvement programs conducted by government agencies. Public-private partnerships forged by myriad organizations and the City of Houston have changed the face of Houston's public space. A notable by-product of these improvement projects is that, unlike freeway construction, they have involved distinctive contributions from distinguished landscape architects and architects.

Architectural patronage continues to be exercised by the city's major cultural institutions. Rice University, the Museum of Fine Arts, Houston, and the University of Texas Health Science Center at Houston stand out for the buildings they have constructed in the 21st century, as does a newcomer, the Asia Society. Real estate developers do not perform at the same level that they did when Gerald D. Hines was personally active in Houston. Instead it has fallen to such small-scale developers as Carol Isaak Barden to continue this entrepreneurial tradition of adventurous architectural patronage. Just as often architects have become developers, again at a small scale, as can be seen in the work of MC^2, Intexure, Collaborative Designworks, and Brett Zamore. New corporate patrons have emerged such as the HEB Grocery Company. Yet much of the architecture of consequence built in this new century was designed for individuals who planned to live or work in the buildings they constructed. Such buildings—compact houses or professional buildings—do not reshape the skyline. But over time they have filled out central city neighborhoods (and in Houston this is largely a center city phenomenon) to achieve a density of new architecture most often designed by younger Houston architects, reinforcing past decades of architectural achievement.

A strong trend that has emerged in Houston architecture of the last two decades is sustainable design. Institutional buildings (especially those built by universities—Rice and the UT Health Science Center again stand out) were the pioneers. Their achievements have been echoed in corporate and developer-built designs, which advanced sustainable practices as both socially responsible and competitively advantageous. The urban dimension of promoting sustainable practices is evident in the slow but continuous growth of public support for preserving and reusing Houston's historic architecture (aided by federal tax credits and city tax abatements). As a result, the Main Street-Market Square and Courthouse Square districts in downtown Houston have come back to life. There, late 19th- and early 20th-century buildings have been rehabilitated as live, work, and entertainment places rather than demolished for surface parking lots. The patient efforts of Preservation Houston (formerly the Greater Houston Preservation Alliance) to build consensus and coalitions of support for preserving not just old buildings but entire communities has paid off in many of Houston's inner city neighborhoods. Yet major landmarks still have been lost. Seventy-five buildings listed in the last edition of this guidebook were demolished or defaced between 1999 and 2011. This persistent threat, not only to older buildings but also to modern architecture, led to the formation in 2003 of Houston Mod, Houston's modern architecture preservation group. Houston Mod has conducted surveys to identify and document a broad range of modern architecture in the city. The expanded coverage of architecture of the 1950s and '60s in this edition is a direct beneficiary of their research.

Architectural culture has gained a secure footing in Houston. Architecture schools at Rice University, the University of Houston, and Prairie View A&M provide the foundation for this culture. The Rice Design Alliance, founded in 1972 by the Rice School of Architecture, has been the catalyst for moving this culture beyond academic studios to a public forum by building a devoted public audience for architecture and design, stimulated through lecture series, symposiums, architecture tours, design competitions, and the publication of *Cite: The Architecture and Design Review of Houston*. The American Institute of Architects, Houston Chapter, followed suit in 2006 when it moved downtown and established Architecture Center Houston, now the location of regular architectural exhibitions, lectures, and urban open houses. Houston Tomorrow, founded by David Crossley in 1998, advocates for urban policy and design alternatives that promote socially responsible practices, tasks that can seem Sisyphean in the context of Houston's embedded culture of *laissez-faire*.

Publications document in increasing detail the historical legacy of architecture and landscape architecture in Houston. The Museum of Fine Arts, especially its Bayou Bend and Rienzi collections, the Menil Collection, the Rothko Chapel, the Byzantine Fresco Chapel Foundation, the Gerald D. Hines College of Architecture at the University of Houston, and Rice University have published volumes that address their own institutional architectural histories. Surveys by Ben Koush, Jason Smith, Barry Moore and Anna Mod, and essays by Michelangelo Sabatino and Stephen James document chapters in Houston's modern architectural history. Suzanne Turner and Joann Seale Wilson's book on Glenwood Cemetery, *Houston's Silent Garden*, Jim Parsons and David Bush's *Art Deco Houston*, Erik Slotboom's *Houston Freeways*, David Welling's *Cinema Houston*, and Lars Lerup's *One Million Acres and No Zoning* examine both distinctive and ordinary buildings, landscapes, and infrastructure as well as the urban processes that produce and reproduce Houston.

During the 2000s a new generation of talented young architects joined those who began practices in the 1980s and '90s to pursue architectural exploration and invention. Yet if the pattern that goes back to the 1950s prevails, few will move beyond the arenas of residential and small professional and institutional building types. The extent to which Houston's building economy is rooted in speculative practices, and the preference of developers for profit-proven formulas mean that the most active sectors of the local building economy gravitate to larger architectural firms willing to work within those formulas, not challenge them. Because such public institutions as agencies of city and county government, public school districts, and public universities treat construction expediently, it is rare (although not impossible) for small-scale architectural firms that concentrate on design to receive public commissions.

Through the annual Houston Area Survey, first published in 1982, sociologist Stephen Klineberg has documented the extraordinary diversification of Houston's population as it continues to expand rapidly. What his analyses disclose is the emergence of a new kind of American city not describable in terms of 19th-century urbanism. Klineberg's colleague at Rice University, Lars Lerup, likewise seeks to discern and name the distinctive attributes of what Peter Papademetriou in 1972 called the "city becoming" in his meditations on the forms of urbanism particular to Houston. Houston architecture of the early 21st century is not as radical as the city in which it takes shape. Instead, it engages this emerging city dialectically as architecture seeks to make spatial sense of the confusing, disorienting, and always provocative processes of Houstonization.

Stephen Fox

Downtown

Downtown

Tour A-1

Houston's downtown is the historic center. Like the city at large, though, it is an exploded landscape reorganized frequently with little attention to urbanistic continuity or consistency. Since 1905, when the first steel-framed skyscraper in Houston was built, downtown has undergone an irregular but dependable cycle of change. Each episode created a new skyline, overshadowing that which pre-

ceded it and enlarged the boundaries of what is defined as downtown. The 1970s-'80s manifestation of this cycle produced the gleaming office towers of the Smith-Louisiana corridor on the west side of downtown. These emblems of the city's major economic institutions dominate the landscape, although they are newcomers to the downtown scene. Their shapes, colors, and spaces are audacious and exhilarating. Yet they lack density, their size notwithstanding. Those accustomed to more traditional city centers are apt to find this section of downtown Houston disorienting. It is all new with few traces of even the recent past (pre-1960) to ground the angled, curved, stepped, gridded, reflective towers that rise in proud isolation, one per block. The public way appears eerily under-populated compared to other large cities because the buildings are linked to each other by an extensive, but invisible, network, of pedestrian tunnels beneath the sidewalks and streets. But if this landscape is enigmatic even unnerving, it is not boring. Its modernism is intensified by the presence of public art installations—works by Oldenburg, Nevelson, and Miró—that mediate between pedestrian scale and the engineering scale of the buildings to lend a lyrical quality to the experience of moving through these spacious precincts. East of Louisiana lies what older Houstonians remember as downtown, a composite of department stores, specialty shops, dime stores, cafés, and theaters interspersed with tall office and hotel buildings. The eight blocks of Main between Texas and Clay were the operational and symbolic center of Houston from the 1920s through the 1960s, when the erosion of the Main Street retail district began in earnest.

The ultimate urban consequences of this decay of downtown are visible east of Fannin, where the multi-use Houston Center complex was launched in 1970 by clearing 32 blocks and then rebuilding portions of the site as an enclave of interconnected towers that stands aloof from the city. The opening of Metro's Red Line in 2004 and accompanying urban design improvements have brightened the appearance of Main considerably.

From Texas north to Commerce is what remains of 19th- and early 20th-century Houston. The waterfront at the foot of Main, where barges and shallow-draft steamboats could dock and turn around, was a hub of commercial transport until the 1910s. Behind it, flanked to either side by Courthouse Square and Market Square, was the downtown financial and commercial district. Yet even this small area was successively redeveloped: provisional construction (including large tents) in the 1830s gave way first to wooden, then brick and cast-iron storefronts, then exuberant Victorian commercial buildings, and finally the first generation of skyscrapers.

After the turn of the 20th century, intensification of commercial traffic on both the bayou and numerous railroads that entered Houston transformed the area north of Buffalo Bayou into a district of factories and warehouses. To the east of Main and Courthouse Square, new railroad construction penetrated the middle-income neighborhoods of Second and Third Wards, and residential districts retreated southward up Main, Caroline, and Crawford into the streetcar suburbs of the South End. Downtown is a historic record of Houston's attitude toward growth and development: what is coming will be of more value than what is here already. The result is a dynamic landscape unconstrained by those places, objects, or buildings that evoke memory and are used ritually to bind communities and generations together in loyalty to the city and its culture.

For all its apparent disarray, this landscape does make sense. It is a testament to the priority that Houston's civic culture has always granted to financial speculation and its consequent reluctance to encumber the landscape with monuments whose permanence might obstruct the forward-looking gaze.

1. **Houston City Hall,** 901 Bagby Street
2. **Julia Ideson Building,** 500 McKinney Avenue
3. **Central Library Building,** 400 McKinney Avenue
4. **Heritage Plaza,** 1111 Bagby Street
5. **Sam Houston Park,** 1100 Bagby Street
6. **St. John Church,** Sam Houston Park
7. **San Felipe Cottage,** Sam Houston Park
8. **Yates Homestead,** Sam Houston Park
9. **Staiti House,** Sam Houston Park
10. **Pillot House,** Sam Houston Park
11. **Old Place,** Sam Houston Park
12. **Nichols-Rice-Cherry House,** Sam Houston Park
13. **Castanié-Fromm House,** Sam Houston Park
14. **Kellum-Noble House,** Sam Houston Park
15. **One Allen Center,** 500 Dallas Avenue
16. **Antioch Baptist Church,** 500 Clay Avenue
17. **Four Allen Center,** 1400 Smith Street
18. **Enron Center,** 1500 Louisiana Street
19. **1600 Smith Building,** 1600 Smith Street
20. **500 Jefferson Building,** 500 Jefferson Avenue
21. **Tellepsen Family Downtown YMCA Building,** 808 Pease Avenue
22. **Humble Building,** 800 Bell Avenue
23. **Hyatt Regency Houston,** 1200 Louisiana Street
24. **United Gas Building,** 1000 Louisiana Street
25. **1100 Milam Building,** 1111 Louisiana Street
26. **First International Plaza,** 1100 Louisiana Street
27. **Allied Bank Plaza,** 1000 Louisiana Street
28. **Tenneco Building,** 1001 Louisiana Street
29. **One Shell Plaza,** 910 Louisiana Street
30. **Electric Tower,** 611 Walker Avenue
31. **RepublicBank Center,** 700 Louisiana Street
32. **Pennzoil Place,** 711 Louisiana Street
33. **Texas Commerce Tower,** 600 Travis Street
34. **Auditorium Hotel,** 701 Texas Avenue
35. **Jesse H. Jones Hall for the Performing Arts,** 615 Louisiana Street
36. **Jones Plaza,** 600 block Louisiana Street
37. **Alley Theatre,** 615 Texas Avenue
38. **Gus S. Wortham Theater Center,** 550 Prairie Avenue
39. **Houston Ballet Center for Dance,** 601 Preston Avenue
40. **Sesquicentennial Park,** Buffalo Bayou between Texas and Washington
41. **Albert Thomas Convention and Exposition Center,** 500 Texas Avenue
42. **Federal Office Building and U. S. Courthouse,** 515 Rusk Avenue
43. **Tranquility Park,** 800 block Smith Street
44. **Hobby Center for the Performing Arts,** 800 Bagby Street
45. **Buffalo Bayou Sabine-to-Bagby Promenade,** Sabine to Bagby bridges

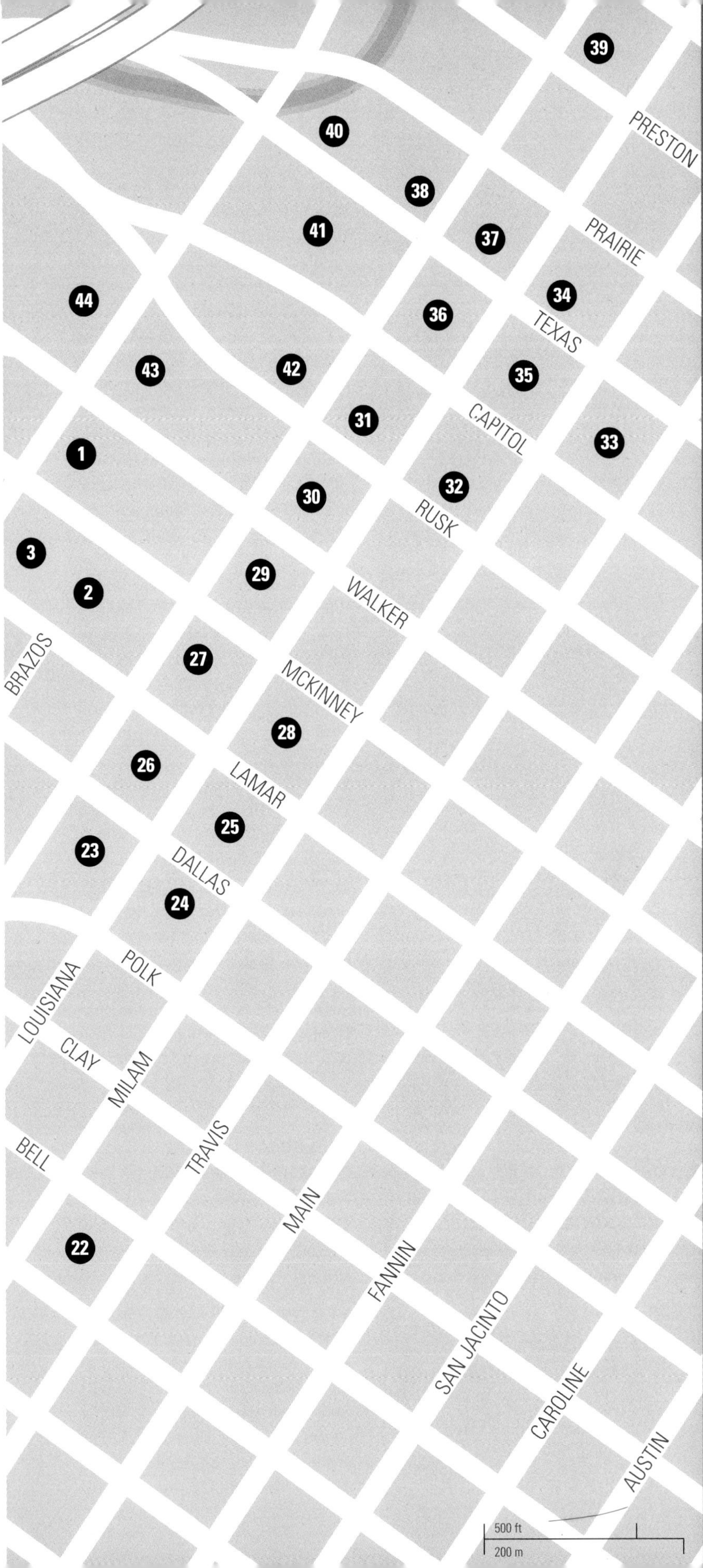

Downtown

Tour A-1

Streets shown: Preston, Prairie, Texas, Capitol, Rusk, Walker, McKinney, Lamar, Dallas, Polk, Clay, Bell, Brazos, Louisiana, Milam, Travis, Main, Fannin, San Jacinto, Caroline, Austin

Map markers: 1, 2, 3, 22, 23, 24, 25, 26, 27, 28, 29, 30, 31, 32, 33, 34, 35, 36, 37, 38, 39, 40, 41, 42, 43, 44

500 ft / 200 m

A-1 Houston City Hall

A-2 Julia Ideson Building-Houston Public Library

A-3 Central Library Building-Houston Public Library

A-4 Heritage Plaza

A-5 Sam Houston Park

A-1
Houston City Hall
901 Bagby Street
1939, Joseph Finger

More stolid than soaring, despite its skyscraper aspirations, Houston City Hall is resolutely official looking. Its solidly massed blocks are faced with Texas fossilized limestone, a favorite regional material for Texan public buildings in the 1930s and '40s. The allegorical sculpture is by Herring Coe and Raoul Josset; Finger's office detailed the aluminum screens above the principal entrances. The entrance lobby is colorfully finished with marble, nickel, and decorative plaster relief work. The main stair, on the west side of the building, and the Council Room, directly above the entrance lobby, are designed in a lighter, more streamlined manner. From the front of City Hall a series of paved terraces step down to Hermann Square, a block of ground bequeathed to the City of Houston in 1914 by the philanthropist George H. Hermann for use as a public park. In 1939 the Kansas City landscape architects Hare & Hare installed the reflecting basin that stretches out on axis with City Hall, as well as the broad grass terrace, hedgerows, and Live Oak trees that ring the pool. Simple in diagram Hare & Hare's design has proven to be an exemplary urban garden that is intensively used. City Hall was rehabilitated between 1992 and 2000 (Ray Bailey Architects).

A-2
Julia Ideson Building
Houston Public Library
500 McKinney Avenue
1926, Cram & Ferguson, William Ward Watkin, and Louis A. Glover
2010-11, Gensler

Set on a tree-shaded block, this low, masonry building with its arched windows, clay tile roofs, and sculptural decoration provides a welcome contrast to the tall, brittle towers that now surround it. The Boston architect Ralph Adams Cram detailed the building with Spanish plateresque ornament to insinuate a connection with Texas's Spanish past. The interiors, restored in 1979 by S. I. Morris Associates after a bad 1950s remodeling, contain a series of Public Works Art Project murals; the most ingenious of these is Ruth Pershing Uhler's *The First Subscription Committee*, 1854 (1935) at the first landing of the main stair. Named for the founding director of the public library system, the building houses the library's Houston Metropolitan Research Center, the principal repository for publications, maps, and documents (including architectural drawings) on the history of Houston. During the administration of Mayor Bill White the south wing and loggia, part of Cram, Watkin, and Glover's master plan, was finally built to house the Houston Metropolitan Research Center. Gensler was architect for this addition and rehabilitation of the original building.

A-3
Central Library Building
Houston Public Library
[now Jesse H. Jones Central Library]
400 McKinney Avenue
1975, S. I. Morris Associates

Eugene Aubry's Central Library Building is not contextual, yet it pulled its surroundings into a civic whole, due chiefly to the scale of its giant portico and the breadth of its original dark, bare, brick-paved plaza. Remodeling in 2008 (Prozign Architects) radically reconfigured the library's interior spaces and led to the destruction of Sally Walsh's subtle, stylish, and eminently usable interiors. Claes Oldenburg's steel sculpture, *Geometric Mouse, Scale X* (1968), the first work of modern public art installed downtown, was relocated to the corner of McKinney and Bagby, and Aubry's plaza was resurfaced with a "fun" and "exciting" (the library's description) color field pattern.

A-4
Heritage Plaza
1111 Bagby Street
1987, M. Nasr & Partners

The boom in office building construction that reshaped the downtown skyline in the late 1970s and early '80s ended with this display of postmodern exhibitionism. Heritage Plaza's granite, stepped pyramid cap was inspired by architect Mohammed Nasr's vacation in Yucatán. A final flourish occurs at the plaza entrance, where a concave peristyle is deployed to reconcile the tower with the back of the ex-Federal Land Bank Building (1929, Hedrick & Gottlieb), which the developer, R. W. Wortham III, preserved.

A-5
Sam Houston Park
1100 Bagby Street

After the giddiness of Heritage Plaza, it is refreshing to cross Bagby and step into Houston's oldest public park, acquired in 1899. The grounds slope down to Buffalo Bayou, just as it is crossed by an elevated segment of I-45, built through the park in the mid 1950s. Since 1956 Sam Houston Park has been administered by the Heritage Society, Houston's oldest preservation organization. The Heritage Society has brought eight historic buildings into the park to join one that has always stood in its grounds. Restored and furnished, they are maintained by the society as an open-air historical museum. Tour information is available in the Long Row building, which also contains a shop specializing in Houstoniana. The adjoining annex contains the Museum of Texas History, featuring changing exhibitions.

A-6 St. John Church

A-7 San Felipe Cottage

A-8 Yates Homestead

A-9 Staiti House

A-10 Pillot House

A-6
St. John Church
Sam Houston Park
1891

Built for a congregation of German-speaking Evangelical Lutherans and originally located amid the farms of northwest Harris County, St. John Church is an example of the 19th-century Southern church house type. It is a gable-roofed wood box, its identity as a church signaled architecturally by its pointed arched openings and broach spire. The church was moved to Sam Houston Park in 1968.

A-7
San Felipe Cottage
Sam Houston Park
1868

San Felipe Cottage is representative of one of the most common house types built in Houston through the 1870s, the Gulf Coast cottage, with its full-width veranda inserted beneath a side-gabled roof. It was moved from its original site on San Felipe, now West Dallas, just behind the Kellum-Noble House, in 1963 and restored by Harvin C. Moore.

A-8
Yates Homestead
Sam Houston Park
c 1870

The Reverend John Henry Yates, pastor of Antioch Baptist Church and a former slave, purchased the property in Fourth Ward on which he built this 2-story house in 1870. The Yates Homestead is a 3-bay Southern townhouse, typologically akin to the Nichols-Rice-Cherry House. In 1994 Yates's great-granddaughter presented the house to the Heritage Society, which moved the house from its original site at 1318 Andrews in Fourth Ward to Sam Houston Park. Gensler & Associates meticulously restored the Yates Homestead (1996).

A-9
Staiti House
Sam Houston Park
1905; 1915, Alfred C. Finn

This large, turn-of-the-20th-century house, described at the time of its completion as in the California bungalow style, was moved here from 421 Westmoreland in 1986. The identity of the original architect has not been determined, but it is the mirror image of a contemporary house designed by the Houston architects Jonas & Tabor. Alfred C. Finn extensively remodeled the house.

A-10
Pillot House
Sam Houston Park
1868

The Pillot House indicates how the Gulf Coast cottage was transformed by the taste for vertical emphasis, complex massing, and exuberant decoration that began to appear in Texas just before the Civil War and became firmly established during the 1870s. The interiors are furnished with high-style pieces of the 1860s, '70s, and '80s. The house was located at 1803 McKinney (now the site of the George R. Brown Convention Center) until it was moved to Sam Houston Park in 1965 and restored by Denney & Ray in 1966. Adjacent to the Pillot House stands Louis Amateis's *Spirit of the Confederacy* installed in the park in 1908. This bronze statue of a mournful winged youth figured as the talisman of Robert Altman's enigmatic film, *Brewster McCloud* (1970).

A-11
Old Place
Sam Houston Park
c 1825

Originally located on Clear Creek in southern Harris County, this cabin exemplifies the earliest type of house built in the Houston region after Anglo-American settlement began in the 1820s. It has a rough-hewn cedar frame surfaced with clapboards. A mudcat chimney stands to one side of the single-pen house, and a porch, a standard feature of Houston houses until the 1920s, is carried across the front.

A-12
Nichols-Rice-Cherry House
Sam Houston Park
c 1850

The Nichols-Rice-Cherry House, an elite townhouse of the pre-Civil War period, is compact in plan, but, without closets, kitchen, or bathrooms, it is quite spacious. The architrave and front door are embellished with Grecian detail that reappears inside along with fancy graining patterns. The house was built on Congress facing Courthouse Square. It was moved on its original site in 1886 and then moved from that site to a new location in 1897 to become the studio of Houston's first resident artist (and, by default, first historic preservationist), Emma Richardson Cherry. Following Mrs. Cherry's death, it was acquired by the Heritage Society and became the first building moved into the park. It was restored in 1960 by Harvin C. Moore.

A.11 Old Place

A-12 Nichols-Rice-Cherry House

A-13 Casatanié-Fromm House

A-14 Kellum-Noble House

A-15 One Allen Center

A-16 Antioch Baptist Church

A-13
Casatanié-Fromm House
Sam Houston Park
c 1850

According to Randy Pace's research this tiny, three-room, side-gabled cottage is associated with Justin Castanié, who in 1848 had the architect, F. J. Rothhaas, survey the Castanié Addition in what became, after the Civil War, the African-American sector of Fourth Ward. When given to the Heritage Society in 2002 by architect-developer Larry Davis, the Castanié-Fromm House stood at 809 Robin, where it had been moved on its original block to become part of a row of rental cottages. The front porch was once equipped with ladder-like steps ascending to a trap door in the ceiling, a detail common in the Acadian parishes of south central and southwestern Louisiana.

A-14
Kellum-Noble House
Sam Houston Park
1847, Francis McHugh, builder

The oldest surviving building in Houston, the Kellum-Noble House, was built on this site outside the original townsite in the "upper part" of Houston, adjacent to Nathaniel Kelly Kellum's brickyard. It is a double-pen house with a central dogtrot passage. The hipped roof, encircling galleries, and brick construction were all departures from conventional Houston house types. The house was included in the city's purchase of the park in 1899. A move to demolish it in 1954 led to the formation of the Harris County Heritage Society (now Heritage Society), which rescued the building and opened it to the public as a house museum in 1958, following restoration by Harvin C. Moore.

A-15
One Allen Center
500 Dallas Avenue
1972, Wilson, Morris, Crain & Anderson

Allen Center, named for the founders of Houston, A. C. and J. K. Allen, and begun by the Dallas developer Trammell Crow with Metropolitan Life Insurance Company, is the only downtown office complex where streets have been closed to create a superblock. The faceted brick planes of the base of the 34-story One Allen Center conceal two stories of pedestrian circulation and retail lease space. After Century Development Corporation of Houston acquired Crow's interests, the company retained Lloyd Jones Brewer & Associates to design the not-quite-matching, 36-story Two Allen Center (1977), the polygonal, aluminum-paneled, 50-story Three Allen Center (1980), and the 20-story Hotel Meridien (1980, now the Doubletree). The firm disregarded the original architects' urbanistic strategy. Instead they connected the office buildings with a network of air-conditioned pedestrian bridges that bypass the hotel and the suburbanized landscape installation at the center of the complex. The SWA Group was landscape architect.

A-16
Antioch Baptist Church
500 Clay Avenue
1879, Richard Allen
1895, Robert Jones

Antioch Baptist Church, organized in 1866 for emancipated slaves, houses the oldest African American Baptist congregation in Houston. The church building, designed by Richard Allen, an African-American architect, was significantly enlarged in 1895 by Robert Jones and has been expanded subsequently. It remains in what was once the heart of Fourth Ward, the city's oldest African-American community, despite attempts by real estate developers to acquire the property in the 1970s. Next door to the church is Antioch Park (1981, The SWA Group), an abstract composition of shaped landscape forms installed by Century Development Corporation.

A-17
Four Allen Center (Enron Building)
1400 Smith Street
1983, Lloyd Jones Brewer & Associates

Aligned on the Fourth Ward grid rather than the South Side Buffalo Bayou grid that prevails downtown, the 50-story, oval-planned Four Allen Center tower is always seen in perspective. The density and thickness of its steel framed-tube perimeter is suppressed beneath a sleek membrane composed of alternating bands of silver reflective glass and white aluminum spandrel. At night, a neon halo atop the tower's summit outlines and emphasizes the building's smooth curves. The elevator lobby, surfaced in polished light gray granite, is refreshingly calm. At the corner of Smith and Andrews rises *Frozen Laces-One* (1980) by Louise Nevelson, installed in 1987 by Century Development Corporation, Metropolitan Life Insurance Company, and American General Realty Company, the developers of Four Allen Center. Four Allen Center was the headquarters of Enron, the notorious energy-trading corporation, which went bankrupt in 2001.

A-17 Four Allen Center

A-18 Enron Center

A-18
Enron Center
[now 1500 Louisiana Street Building]
1500 Louisiana Street
2002, Cesar Pelli & Associates and Kendall/Heaton Associates

Pelli's office produced this 40-story tower for Enron, which pays architectural homage to Four Allen Center across Smith. Oval in plan the building externalizes its geometry at its summit, where two engaged cylindrical towers support a flat-lidded roof plate. On the tower's south side, facing Louisiana, the spandrels project beyond the curtain wall to offer minimal sunshading. A circular skybridge hovering above the Smith-Bell intersection connects 1500 Louisiana and 1400 Smith with Pelli's garage in the 1400 block of Smith. Since 2004 this has been Houston headquarters of California-based Chevron.

A-19 1600 Smith Building

A-19
1600 Smith Building
1600 Smith Street
1984, Morris*Aubry Architects

This pearl gray, 51-story tower is faceted in plan, projecting the collision of street grids upward in tiered setbacks that culminate in a polygonal cap, which, like its neighbor at 1400 Smith, is illuminated at night. Conceived as half of a two-building complex, 1600 Smith departs considerably from the planning and architectural standards that prevailed in earlier phases of Cullen Center, of which it is a part. The jokey rolled-up sidewalk and the plaza fountain (best appreciated from the wall slit on Pease) are the work of The SWA Group. What might at first appear to be the entrance to a subway station at Smith and Ruthven is an air-conditioned passage that links 1600 Smith to an extremity of the downtown tunnel system. From 1998 to 2010 this building was the headquarters of Continental Airlines.

A-20 500 Jefferson Building

A-20
500 Jefferson Building
500 Jefferson Avenue
1963, Welton Becket & Associates

This 20-story building and its 12-story companion, the Hotel America (now the Crowne Plaza-Cullen Center, 1963, also by Welton Becket & Associates of Los Angeles), were the initial buildings in Cullen Center, the first multi-block development in downtown Houston. The Becket office proposed a series of slab-shaped buildings, rotated to minimize obstruction of view and interconnected with air-conditioned pedestrian bridges across the intervening streets. Precast concrete panels provide the architectural order; slender columns and a marble faced terrace in front of the hotel offered ground-level amenity. The hotel was refaced in 2005 and the plaza reconfigured. Subsequent additions to the complex—the 20-story Cullen Center Bank & Trust Co. Building (1971) at 600 Jefferson and the 40-story Dresser Tower [now KBR Tower] (1973) at 601 Jefferson, both by Neuhaus & Taylor—ignored the Becket master plan. As in other group developments, the chance to create a unified and distinctive whole lost out to the Houston penchant for individualism.

A-21
Tellepsen Family Downtown YMCA Building
808 Pease Avenue
2011, Kirksey

Kenneth Franzheim's YMCA Building on Louisiana (demolished 2011) was replaced by this box-like, 107,000-SF, glass-faced building, which is packed with a complexly sectioned array of athletic and community spaces. The building is named for the family of Houston general contractor Tom Tellepsen, a Danish immigrant who took architectural drafting classes at the Houston YMCA's first purpose-designed building in 1910 and subsequently served on its board of trustees. This building was constructed by Tellepsen Construction under its fourth generation of family management.

A-21 Tellepsen Family Downtown YMCA Building

A-22 Humble Building

A-23 Hyatt Regency Houston

A-22
Humble Building
[now ExxonMobil Building]
800 Bell Avenue
1963, Welton Becket & Associates
with Golemon & Rolfe and George
Pierce-Abel B. Pierce

At 600 feet in height, the 44-story Humble Building, headquarters of the Humble Oil & Refining Company (now ExxonMobil Corp.), was briefly the tallest building west of the Mississippi River. Becket's designer, Louis Naidorf, sought to give the slender tower a pronounced regional identity—within the context of mid-20th-century corporate modern architecture—by emphasizing sun control. The tiers of horizontal aluminum sunshades encircling the building, together with the oversailing bands of aluminum fins at its summit, succeed in giving the tower a light, graceful appearance from a distance, although at close range the curtain wall is finicky in detail. The Humble Building gave Becket its first opportunity to exercise what it described as "total design." Another innovative feature was the architecturally coordinated 1,300-car Humble Garage at 1602 Milam. This carries the air-conditioning equipment for the tower, leaving the top of the Humble Building free for the 2-story Petroleum Club and an observation deck that has been closed since 1971, when One Shell Plaza out-topped Humble.

A-23
Hyatt Regency Houston
1200 Louisiana Street
1972, JV III (Koetter, Tharp & Cowell, Caudill Rowlett Scott, and Neuhaus & Taylor)

Charles E. Lawrence of Caudill Rowlett Scott was director of design for the first hotel that Hyatt built after it split with the Atlanta architect John Portman, whose hotels in Atlanta, Chicago, and San Francisco gave the corporation its distinctive architectural identity. Portman's signature devices reappear here: a 30-story, 350-foot high lobby surrounded by balcony corridors, glass-cased elevator cabs, and a revolving cocktail lounge atop the hotel, whose name, Spindletop, is a punning tribute to the 1901 oil gusher from which 20th-century Houston's growth and good fortune stemmed. The Hyatt lobby is the closest thing to an urban living room that downtown Houston possesses: tidy, air-conditioned, and access-controlled. Up the escalator and across the runway above the indoor sidewalk cafe, visitors will find glass doors that lead (during weekday business hours) to a steel box truss pedestrian bridge across the Louisiana-Dallas intersection. The bridge provides a stunning vista of the Louisiana office corridor. The Hyatt Regency, the 2,750-car Regency Southwest Garage, and 1100 Milam (now CenterPoint Energy Plaza) were jointly developed by Tenneco and the Prudential Insurance Company of America.

A-24
United Gas Building
[now Total Plaza]
1201 Louisiana Street
1972, Lloyd, Morgan & Jones
1996, Ziegler Cooper Architects

Built as a speculative office building by Century Development Corporation, the 35-story United Gas Building was the first Houston high-rise clad with mirror-finished glass. Reflecting the oscillations of Houston's real estate market in the 1980s and '90s, the building was recycled, rather than demolished and replaced, and updated with Ziegler Cooper's handsome lobby design. This opens the base of the building to the street, articulates the structural column grid as a rhythmic element, and marks points of entry with projecting stainless steel canopies.

A-24 United Gas Building

A-25 1100 Milam Building

A-26 First International Plaza

A-25
1100 Milam Building
[now CenterPoint Energy Plaza]
1111 Louisiana Street
1973, JV III (Koetter, Tharp & Cowell, Caudill Rowlett Scott and Neuhaus & Taylor)
1996, DMJM and Keating and Kendall/Heaton Associates

This building, jointly developed by Tenneco and the Prudential Insurance Company of America, was built at the same time as the Hyatt Regency and the Regency Southwest Garage. Despite its 47-story height, it was architecturally ho-hum until it received a stunning makeover by Los Angeles architect Richard Keating for Houston Industries, predecessor of CenterPoint. DMJM Keating reconstructed the base of the building with neo-modern granite panels, which appear to slide out of alignment with gravity-defying ease. To give the tower more presence on the skyline, DMJM Keating added a 6-story, illuminated top hat to the building's summit, a monumental restatement of the freestanding pavilion Keating earlier designed (while heading the Houston office of Skidmore, Owings & Merrill) across Louisiana for Allied Bank Plaza.

A-26
First International Plaza
[now 1100 Louisiana Building]
1100 Louisiana Street
1980, Skidmore, Owings & Merrill and 3D/International

This pink granite-and glass-clad 55-story tower, developed by Gerald D. Hines Interests and PIC Realty Corporation, pays homage to the Bank of America Building in San Francisco. Skidmore, Owings & Merrill-San Francisco's designers, Edward C. Bassett and Lawrence S. Doane, used a diagonal array of triangular window bays to establish a geometrical theme that jumps from plan to section in the banking hall, 106 feet high at its summit. In 2007 the building's new owner disposed of Jean Dubuffet's *Monument au Fantóme* (1977), installed under

Doane and Bassett's supervision in 1983, and replaced it with Enterprise Plaza, a fountain and planted landscape in the reconstructed plaza (2008, Gensler, WET Design, and Office of James Burnett). The Dubuffet was resited in Discovery Green across from the George R. Brown Convention Center. Scenes from Terrence Malick's film *Tree of Life* (2011) were shot in PSP's office in the ex-banking hall.

A-27
Allied Bank Plaza
[now Wells Fargo Bank Plaza]
1000 Louisiana Street
1983, Skidmore, Owings & Merrill and Lloyd Jones Brewer & Associates

The second tallest building in Houston (71 stories, 970 feet), Allied is an extension of Bassett and Doane's predilection for having it both ways: buildings that are urbanistically responsive and sculpturally arresting. The tower is a vertical extrusion of two quarter circles slipped off-center in plan, a fractured cylinder sheathed in green reflective glass that has given rise to numerous quips: everything from Emerald City to an inflated dollar sign. Its great curves charge the surrounding space with a sense of movement and expansiveness; this perceptual sensation becomes perilously literal when the breeze picks up and wind action at the base of the building commences. Bassett and Doane acknowledged life along the street with a pair of basement level courtyards facing Louisiana, the one place downtown where a direct visual connection is made between the street and the subterranean tunnel system. Mammoth-scaled balustrades of polished granite frame these courts, which are backed by thin sheets of water pouring hypnotically over dark, speckled granite walls. Inside two double-decked sky lobbies offer views from different heights during business hours. Exposed trusses that emphasize the massive steel, bundled-tube structure behind the tower's green glass skin are visible in the lower set of sky lobbies on the 34th and 35th floors.

A-27 Allied Bank Plaza

A-28 Tenneco Building

A-29 One Shell Plaza

A-28
Tenneco Building
[now El Paso Energy Building]
1001 Louisiana Street
1963, Skidmore, Owings & Merrill

The 33-story Tenneco Building is a classic, the standard against which all succeeding tall buildings in downtown Houston have been measured. It has yet to be surpassed. So much of what makes this building special derives from intangibles: proportion, light and shadow, surface and void. For instance by slightly recessing the plane of the beams behind the plane of the columns, Skidmore, Owings & Merrill's designer, Edward C. Bassett, created a sense of depth that one hardly notices. But the resulting play of shadows charges Tenneco's technologically conceived façades with the richness and animation ascribed in postmodern polemics to classical architecture. The 50-foot-high colonnade at the base of the tower achieves a degree of monumentality that no subsequent downtown building has been able to recapture. It provides a transition in scale from the street to the building that effortlessly lifts passersby to its heroic measure, without violating the logic of the building's constructional engineering. In 2011 Gensler rehabilitated the building, reconstructing the first three floors.

A-29
One Shell Plaza
910 Louisiana Street
1971, Skidmore, Owings & Merrill and Wilson, Morris, Crain & Anderson

Shell Oil Company's decision to move its headquarters to Houston from New York occasioned construction of One Shell Plaza and precipitated Houston's rise to the status of U.S. energy capital. The 50-story, 715-foot-high One Shell was the first downtown project of Gerald D. Hines Interests and the first for which Hines employed nationally known architects in order to attract top corporate tenants and expedite financing. Architecturally it is the result of a collaboration between Skidmore, Owings & Merrill Chicago's chief designer, Bruce J. Graham, and its engineer, Fazlur R. Khan. One Shell is the optimal highrise office building: economically determined, efficiently planned, and architecturally detailed to express its engineering and constructional innovations. A pioneering application of Khan's framed-tube concept, One Shell's structure is concentrated in its perimeter walls and central service core, leaving the floors free of interior columns and dramatically reducing the building material required. Graham treated the exterior wall surfaces of the cast-in-place concrete tower as a dense file of structural piers, thickening them near the corners of the building, where structural loads are most intense, to produce One Shell's distinctive rippling profiles. One Shell Plaza was the tallest concrete building in the world at the time of its completion. Despite its structural distinction, One Shell Plaza lacks the urbanistic and architectural presence of its immediate predecessors, Tenneco, Humble, and the First City National Bank Building. Drenched in polished travertine, it stands aloof from the surrounding city. Diagonally across Louisiana at 777 Walker is a 26-story companion, Two Shell Plaza (1972, Skidmore, Owings & Merrill and WMCA), also built by Hines Interests. The gradual deformation of the window grid into arch shapes on the lower floors expresses the distribution of gravity loads. The density of Skidmore, Owings & Merrill buildings in these blocks led Ann Holmes, fine arts editor of the *Houston Chronicle* from 1948 to 1988, to dub this stretch of Louisiana "Skid Row."

A-30
Electric Tower
[now Bob Lanier Public Works Building]
611 Walker Avenue
1968, Wilson, Morris, Crain & Anderson with Robert O. Biering
1998, Kirksey & Partners

The 27-story Electric Tower, built for the Houston Lighting & Power Company, was the first of the office towers that would transform Smith into the downtown avenue of skyscrapers by the 1980s. The slab-shaped office building, inspired by Eero Saarinen's CBS Building in New York, is prefaced along Walker by a dry moat detailed by landscape architect Fred Buxton & Associates as a Japanese rock garden (destroyed by the City of Houston in 1996 when it converted the Electric Tower into a city office building). The low block along Rusk was designed to contain HL & P's computer operations. To conserve energy, WMCA outfitted the Electric Tower with "sunglasses," panes of glass installed between the column lines that sit in front of the building's recessed curtain wall.

A-30 Electric Tower

A-31 RepublicBank Center

A-31
RepublicBank Center
[now Bank of America Center]
700 Louisiana Street
1983, Johnson/Burgee Architects
and Kendall/Heaton Associates

RepublicBank tried valiantly to redress the urbanistic shortcomings associated with tall buildings of the 1960s. In an effort to avoid being sterile and unresponsive, it fills its one-block site to the saturation point with elaborate details. Monumentality is the theme: from the rolled moldings at the base of the street walls to the vast Romantic Classical portals on the Louisiana and Smith sides of the building; from the awesome internal volumes of its lobby, concourses, and banking hall to the fantastically stepped skyline rising from the banking hall pavilion up the 56-story, 780-foot-high office tower. Yet RepublicBank presents a troubling paradox: the more one experiences, the less one is satisfied. Philip Johnson and John Burgee tried to create a neo-1920s skyscraper, with all the richness associated with such buildings. Their exaggerations of scale and disregard for the realities of constructing the building are not sufficient to reproduce that richness, however, and the building's efforts to entertain and amaze have little substance behind them. Encased at the Louisiana-Capitol corner of the skylit, 125-foot high banking hall is a pre-existing 2-story building. This accounts for the extremely high level of the second floor. Gensler & Associates are responsible for interior design of the bank's spaces. Gerald D. Hines Interests, which built RepublicBank, installed the 1913 Seth Thomas clock in the concourse between the banking hall and elevator lobby.

A-32
Pennzoil Place
711 Louisiana Street
1976, Johnson/Burgee Architects
and S. I. Morris Associates

In the annals of late 20th-century skyscraper architecture, Pennzoil Place is as historically significant as One Shell Plaza and much more appealing. It was built by Gerald D. Hines Interests for the Pennzoil Company, whose chairman, J. Hugh Liedtke, specifically wanted a building that did not look like One Shell Plaza. Philip Johnson and John Burgee, hastily brought in to replace Bruce Graham, responded to this directive by proposing two buildings instead of one, separated by a pedestrian path that crossed the square-block site diagonally from corner to corner. This diagonal (which Philip Johnson described as a "processional" route) imposed the 45-degree geometry, visible in the dramatically splayed inner walls of both towers, their counter-sloped roofs, and the tilted glass planes that enclose a pair of air-conditioned indoor plazas. The 36-story towers are held in tense equilibrium by the 10-foot-wide slot that separates them. Through this slot one can play peek-a-boo with the tempietto atop the Niels Esperson Building. Pennzoil became the harbinger of a new generation of American skyscrapers by flouting the engineering logic so perfectly expressed in One Shell Plaza. Its sharp angles, inflected planes, and tight bronze glass sheath appealed instead to a higher order of logic: profit. Pennzoil Place was so compelling that, despite the economic recession of 1973-75, Hines Interests added two floors to each tower during construction to meet the demand for lease space. Pennzoil decisively reoriented Johnson/Burgee toward developer architecture, and it catapulted Gerald Hines to national recognition as a patron of adventurous—and profitable—architecture. Since 1999 Pennzoil Place has been owned by German investor and architectural aficionado, Johannes Mann.

A-32 Pennzoil Place

A-33 Texas Commerce Tower in United Energy Plaza

A-33
Texas Commerce Tower in United Energy Plaza
[now J. P. Morgan Chase Tower]
600 Travis Street
1981, I. M. Pei & Partners and 3D/International

Constructed by Gerald D. Hines Interests for Texas Commerce Bancshares, this is the most recent in a series of Houston buildings to claim the distinction of being tallest west of the Mississippi (a distinction it lost when the Pei firm designed the First Interstate World Center in Los Angeles, which is 16 feet higher). It is 75 stories, 1,002 feet in height. The building is understated and precise in composition and detail but nonetheless aggressive, both in its height and in its site planning. In order to take advantage of its position on the skyline, New York architect Pei backed the tower up to the main thoroughfare, Texas, and faced it toward the intersection of two less important streets, Milam and Capitol. The huge plaza tries to be both imposing and inviting. A raised terrace to the side contains an Islamic-influenced water garden that is genuinely charming, although a bit incongruous next to the building's massive granite shaft. A stepped causeway leading diagonally to the main entrance fills out the block. The plaza also contains Joan Miró's, *Personage and Birds* (1970), a marvelous, giant-scaled, painted bronze sculpture that Pei persuaded Hines and Texas Commerce to install in 1982. From the plaza one can glimpse the setback top of the Gulf Building as well as Pennzoil Place at its bulkiest. And from the 60th-floor observation deck—accessible during business hours from the elevators that face the main entrance—one has a panoramic vista of southwest Houston. Texas Commerce is the quintessential skyscraper in the polished gray granite suit. Good grooming and the public amenities generously provided by Texas Commerce Bank compensate for a lackluster personality.

A-34
Auditorium Hotel
[now Lancaster Hotel]
701 Texas Avenue
1926, Joseph Finger

The 12-story Auditorium Hotel had never been one of the city's more notable hostelries until it was acquired by General Leisure Corporation and transformed into a boutique hotel called the Lancaster (1983, Hightower-Alexander). It represents an intelligent act of urban conservation that set an important example in downtown Houston in the 1990s. Sharing the block front on Texas with the hotel is the 34 story Calpine Center [now 717 Texas Building] (2003, Hellmuth, Obata + Kassabaum and Kendall/Heaton Associates).

A-34 Auditorium Hotel

A-35 Jesse H. Jones Hall for the Performing Arts

A-35
Jesse H. Jones Hall for the Performing Arts
615 Louisiana Street
1966, Caudill Rowlett Scott

Jones Hall, home of the Houston Symphony Orchestra, is in the culture center style of the 1960s, a mix of architectural metaphors that was supposed to look both modern and classical. Caudill Rowlett Scott conceived the building as a composite structure: a steel space-frame roof canopy, supported on reinforced concrete columns, that would enclose the stage, auditorium, and lobby, all sheltered between two freely curved shells. Due to budgetary constraints the structural concept was simplified, but the forms stuck. Bland and scaleless externally and wallpapered in travertine, Jones Hall comes off at first glance as a provincial reflection of New York's Lincoln Center. This is unfortunate for the building's formal image does not do justice to its ingenious planning or its technical innovations. Theatrical consultant, George C. Izenour, worked with Caudill Rowlett Scott and acoustical consultant, Robert Newman, to devise an intricate moveable ceiling that allowed the hall to be reconfigured for different types of performances. The teak-lined, 3,000-seat auditorium is serene and unpretentious, while the lobby, animated by Richard Lippold's suspended stainless steel sculpture, *Gemini II* (a tribute to Houston's identity in the 1960s as Space City), is exuberantly activated in section. Jones Hall was built by Houston Endowment, a charitable foundation established by Mr. and Mrs. Jesse H. Jones, and presented to the City of Houston upon completion. Like other American cultural centers of its period, it was constructed within a purpose-made, civic-cultural enclave intended to arrest the disintegration of downtown. Rehabilitation of Jones Hall, which entailed reconstruction of basement-level facilities damaged by flooding from Tropical Storm Allison in 2001 and repairing the travertine facing, was completed in

2004. Built simultaneously by the City of Houston were Caudill Rowlett Scott's Albert Thomas Convention and Exposition Center [now Bayou Place] (1967) and Jones Plaza, the raised plaza that lies between Albert Thomas and Jones Hall, and the 3-level, subterranean, 1,750-car Civic Center Garage.

A-36
Jones Plaza
600 block Louisiana Street
1966, Caudill Rowlett Scott
2001, Bricker + Cannady Architects

Caudill Rowlett Scott's full-block Jones Plaza was a stepped, flat-topped plateau set atop the underground Civic Center Garage. It was completely reshaped by Bricker + Cannady designer Mark Wamble to become an open-air performance space, complementing the performance halls that surround it. Taking advantage of the block's south-to-north down slope, Wamble opened the plaza toward the entrance of Jones Hall and organized perimeter platforms containing seating and a stage as an unwinding of Jones Hall's internal spiral to frame a central arena. Tubular steel Y-columns support translucent plastic canopies above the raised platforms. Restroom pods and screen walls are faced with Mexican glass tiles. Clark Condon Associates was the landscape architect, and Natalye Appel + Associates Architects designed the perforated stainless steel screens that face ventilation shafts at the four corners of the block (2005).

A-36 Jones Plaza

A-37 Alley Theatre

A-38 Gus S. Wortham Theater Center

A-37
Alley Theatre
615 Texas Avenue
1968, Ulrich Franzen & Associates
with MacKie & Kamrath

The Alley Theatre is one of the finest modern buildings in Houston. The New York architect Ulrich Franzen was striving for a design that would be the antithesis of Jones Hall, expressing externally the complexities of planning, circulation, and servicing rather than submerging them within a simplistic formal package. Franzen overstated his case: the Alley's battered walls of cast-in-place concrete and its towers capped with gunnery turrets (actually penthouses for the air-handling equipment) are a bit aggressive from the perspective of the sidewalk. But inside the Alley has a magical ambience. The stairs that lead from the entrance vestibule to the second-floor lobby introduce a directed spatial flow that spirals volumetrically upward through the building and expands outward to the generous open-air terraces visible from the street. Jim Love's standing metal sculpture, *Area Code* (1962), occupies the first landing of the main stairs. Although Franzen's detailing bears no resemblance to that of Frank Lloyd Wright, the Alley's spatial compression and diminutive scale are definitely Wrightian. The building contains two theaters: the 800-seat thrust stage Hubbard Theater, which fills the swelling bay at Texas and Smith, and the 300-seat Arena Theater in the basement, named in memory of architect Hugo V. Neuhaus, Jr., who chaired the Alley's building committee. The driveway through the building is a clever condensation of a typical Houston landscape feature and is a spatial pun on the company's name. Behind the Alley Theatre, at 600 Prairie, lies the 15-story Alley Theatre Center (1984, Morris*Aubry Architects with Peter D. Waldman), a 1,000-car parking garage built by Gerald D. Hines Interests to serve RepublicBank Center. The garage is faced with precast granite-aggregate concrete panels. Its top three floors contain the Alley's shop and storage space. Peter Waldman alludes to Franzen's building with a curved balcony that forms (as Waldman put it) a Jack-O'-Lantern face.

A-38
Gus S. Wortham Theater Center
550 Prairie Avenue
1987, Morris*Aubry Architects

The Wortham, built to house the Houston Grand Opera and the Houston Ballet, contains two side-by-side theaters: the 2,225-seat Brown Theater and the 1,102-seat Cullen Theater. The building occupies municipal property, but it was built entirely with private donations and, upon its completion, turned over to the City of Houston. The Wortham had a long and troubled planning history, occasioned chiefly by unrealistically low initial cost estimates, which led to difficulties with funding during the years of a particularly serious economic recession and, ultimately, to controversy over the design of the exterior. The two performance spaces, planned with acoustician Christopher Jaffee and theatrical consultants Nananne Porcher and Clyde Nordheimer, work quite well. However, public circulation is awkwardly handled, and the architectural detailing is garish and pretentious. The Wortham does contain one noble space: the Grand Foyer, a civic-scaled room that occupies the bridge span. The Grand Foyer and lobby offer marvelous framed views of the downtown skyline. A series of unfurling bronze banners by the sculptor, Albert Paley (who also modeled the door pulls), line the escalator from the main entrance to the foyer. The SWA Group designed the plaza at Texas and Smith that is punctuated with over-scaled globes on blocky pedestals.

A-39
Houston Ballet Center for Dance
601 Preston Avenue
2011, Gensler

Occupying a block front on Smith facing Sesquicentennial Park, the Houston Ballet Center for Dance is a 6-story, 115,000-SF complex containing nine dance studios, a 200-seat laboratory theater, student housing, the company's administrative offices, and the Ben Stevenson Academy. Gensler's Marshall Strabala stacked double-height dance studios in projecting wings faced with black granite. Window walls transform these rehearsal studios into public theater. A pedestrian bridge, funded by the Houston Redevelopment Authority, connects the Center for Dance to the backstage area of the Wortham Theater, the company's primary performance space.

A-39 Houston Ballet Center for Dance

A-41 Albert Thomas Convention and Exposition Center

A-42 Federal Office Building and U. S. Courthouse

A-40
Sesquicentennial Park
Buffalo Bayou between Texas and Washington
1989, TeamHou and 3D/International
1998, TeamHou and Ray + Hollington

Built to commemorate the 150th anniversary of Houston's founding in 1836, Sesquicentennial Park represents an architectural vision for treating the banks of Buffalo Bayou as a terraced landscape that dates to the beginning of the 20th century. In 1986 the Rice Design Alliance organized a national design competition for this site, which was won by a group of young Houston architects (Guy Hagstette, John Lemr, and John Liner) under the name TeamHou. The stepped fountain flowing around the base of the lookout pavilion next to the Wortham Theater Center, the ramped paths, and the hanging gardens take advantage of this rare bit of topographic variation, where the coastal plain descends steeply to the bayou channel. The suburban feel of the park's low-budget concrete facing materials does not diminish the exuberance of the design, which has withstood periodic floods to which Buffalo Bayou is subject. The second phase of the park design, built nearly ten years after the first, incorporates the most heroic work of public art in Houston, Mel Chin's 70-foot tall stainless steel towers, *Seven Wonders*. Each of the seven towers contains 150 cutouts based on drawings made by Houston children born in 1986. Complementing Chin's towers is artist Dean Ruck's, *Big Bubble* (press the red button in the tower on the Preston bridge to activate the art).

A-41
Albert Thomas Convention and Exposition Center
[now Bayou Place]
500 Texas Avenue
1967, Caudill Rowlett Scott
1998, Gensler & Associates
2005, Powers Brown Architecture

The notion of transforming the ex-convention center (made redundant by the opening of the George R. Brown Convention Center in 1987) into a downtown entertainment mall turned into a 10-year soap opera of extravagant proposals that routinely fizzled until a Baltimore developer, the Cordish Company, finally succeeded with Bayou Place, which contains a mixture of movie theaters, live theaters, restaurants, and clubs. By skillfully managing parking and by treating the once dreary arcades of the Albert Thomas as urban front porches, Gensler enabled Bayou Place to emerge as an unpretentious, yet immensely lively addition to downtown Houston. In 2005 Powers Brown Architecture completed phase two of Bayou Place's rehabilitation, which includes the Architecture Center Houston (ArCH) gallery and offices of the American Institute of Architects, Houston Chapter, at 315 Capitol.

A-42
Federal Office Building and U. S. Courthouse
[now Bob Casey Federal Building]
515 Rusk Avenue
1962, Staub, Rather & Howze, Rustay & Martin, and Harvin C. Moore

No building in downtown Houston better illustrates the unpredictability of history on questions of taste than the 13-story Federal Office Building. It was reviled and abominated from the time of its completion until its inadvertent rehabilitation as a precursor of postmodernism after the Princeton architect, Michael Graves, produced a similar—albeit more effusive—design for the Public Services Building in Portland, Oregon in 1980. Since then the Federal Building has come in for a bit more respect. Architect J. T. Rather, Jr. made the building's grid of four-foot square windows, set in fields of Texas fossilized limestone, the principal design element. The lobby features two pairs of murals, commissioned in 1941 from the foremost Regionalist painters in Texas, Alexandre Hogue and Jerry Bywaters of Dallas. They depict historic (Hogue) and contemporary (Bywaters) scenes on Buffalo Bayou.

A-40 Sesquicentennial Park

A-43 Tranquility Park

A-45 Buffalo Bayou Sabine to Bagby Promenade

A-43
Tranquility Park
800 block Smith Street
1979, Charles Tapley Associates

Tranquility Park was designed to tie together the architecturally unrelated, indifferently developed blocks that comprise the Civic Center. Covering three city blocks (beneath two of which lies an extension of the Civic Center Garage), the park is aptly characterized by its architect as a "roof garden." Charles Tapley and Jerry Lunow's thrusting diagonal walkways, smoothly shaped land formations, clustered cylindrical fountains (the stainless steel towers house the exhaust stacks for the underground garage), and frequent grade changes were intended to imbue the site with a lively, intense atmosphere, a choice that has always had its critics. The park's name is derived from the lunar Sea of Tranquility in commemoration of the fact that the first word spoken from the moon to earth was Houston: "Houston, the Eagle has landed." (A wall-mounted plaque at the Smith-Rusk intersection gives further details.) Tranquility Park offers a superlative prospect point, rare within downtown, from which to survey the skyline.

A-44
Hobby Center for the Performing Arts
800 Bagby Street
2002, Robert A. M. Stern and Morris Architects

The Hobby Center was built to accommodate traveling stage productions. It replaced the Sam Houston Coliseum and Music Hall (1938, Alfred C. Finn), the Public Works Administration-era performance hall and livestock arena. New York architect Robert Stern designed the 2,650-seat Sarofim Hall and the 500-seat Zilkha Hall to evoke early 20th-century Broadway theaters although public interiors and the exterior are retro-mod in style. The second-floor lobby serves both theaters and offers a superb prospect of Tranquility Park and the downtown skyline. Installed in the lobby is a Sol LeWitt wall drawing; at the Bagby-Walker intersection are the spiraling cast bronze components of *In Minds* by Scottish sculptor Tony Cragg.

A-45
Buffalo Bayou Sabine-to-Bagby Promenade
Sabine Street Bridge to Bagby Street Bridge
2006, The SWA Group, landscape architect

The Buffalo Bayou Partnership, a non-profit organization founded in 1986 to coordinate improvements along Buffalo Bayou, oversaw design and construction of this 23-acre, 1.25-mile linear park along both sides of the bayou channel between Sesquicentennial Park and the Sabine Street Bridge. Landscape architect Kevin Shanley of SWA designed the park to make the channel (which lies well below street level) both accessible and attractive to pedestrians, especially those portions beneath the elevated lanes of Interstate 45. SWA's sun and shade ground cover plantings, walkways, and steel truss pedestrian bridge (behind the Hobby Center Garage) imbue Buffalo Bayou with a welcome civic presence. Artist Stephen Korns and lighting designers L'Observatoire International are responsible for the stunning blue nocturnal illumination, which changes with the phases of the moon. Artist Stephen Runnels produced the upside down canoes marking street level points of access to the park. The Promenade is the first phase of a broader master plan prepared for the Buffalo Bayou Partnership in 2002 by the Thompson Design Group of Boston.

A-44 Hobby Center for the Performing Arts

Downtown

46. **Lee P. Brown METRO Administration Building and Downtown Transit Center,** 1900 Main Street
47. **Co-Cathedral of the Sacred Heart,** 1111 St. Joseph Parkway
48. **Sacred Heart Catholic Church,** 1111 Pierce Avenue
49. **St. Joseph Hospital, South Wing,** 1916 Crawford Street
50. **Beaconsfield,** 1700 Main Street
51. **Houston House,** 1617 Fannin Street
52. **Masonic Temple Building,** 1401 Fannin Street
53. **First United Methodist Church,** 1320 Main Street
54. **Houston Pavilions,** 1201 Main Street
55. **Humble Building,** 906–914 Dallas Avenue
56. **Foley's,** 1100 Main Street
57. **Main Street Square,** 1000 block Main Street
58. **Reliant Energy Plaza,** 1000 Main Street
59. **First City National Bank Building,** 1001 Main Street
60. **City National Bank Building,** 1001 McKinney Avenue
61. **Two Houston Center,** 909 Fannin Street
62. **Gulf Tower,** 1301 McKinney Avenue
63. **Hess Tower,** 1501 McKinney Avenue
64. **Discovery Green,** 1500 McKinney Avenue
65. **George R. Brown Convention Center,** 1001 Avenida de las Américas
66. **Hilton Americas Hotel,** 1600 Lamar Avenue
67. **The Park in Houston Center,** 1221 Lamar Avenue
68. **First City Tower,** 1001 Fannin Street
69. **1010 Lamar Building,** 1010 Lamar Avenue
70. **The Smart Shop,** 905 Main Street
71. **Bank of the Southwest Building,** 919 Milam Street
72. **Walker@Main Garage,** 820 Main Street
73. **BG Group Place,** 812 Main Street
74. **Battelstein's,** 811 Main Street
75. **Melrose Building,** 1121 Walker Avenue
76. **Gulf Building,** 712 Main Street
77. **Niels Esperson Building,** 808 Travis Street
78. **S. H. Kress & Company Building,** 705 Main Street
79. **Texas Commerce Center,** 601 Travis Street
80. **Rice Hotel,** 909 Texas Avenue
81. **Post-Dispatch Building,** 1100 Texas Avenue
82. **Christ Church Cathedral,** 1117 Texas Avenue
83. **Chancery of the Episcopal Diocese of Texas and the John R. Dunn Outreach Center at the Beacon,** 1225 Texas Avenue
84. **Federal Reserve Bank of Dallas Branch Building,** 1301 Texas Avenue
85. **Petroleum Building,** 1314 Texas Avenue
86. **Annunciation Catholic Church,** 1618 Texas Avenue
87. **Union Station and Minute Maid Park,** 501 Crawford Street
88. **Houston Cotton Exchange and Board of Trade,** 1310 Prairie Avenue
89. **Sam Houston Hotel,** 1119 Prairie Avenue
90. **Texas State Hotel,** 720 Fannin Street
91. **Texas Company Building,** 720 San Jacinto Street
92. **U.S. Post Office,** 701 San Jacinto Street

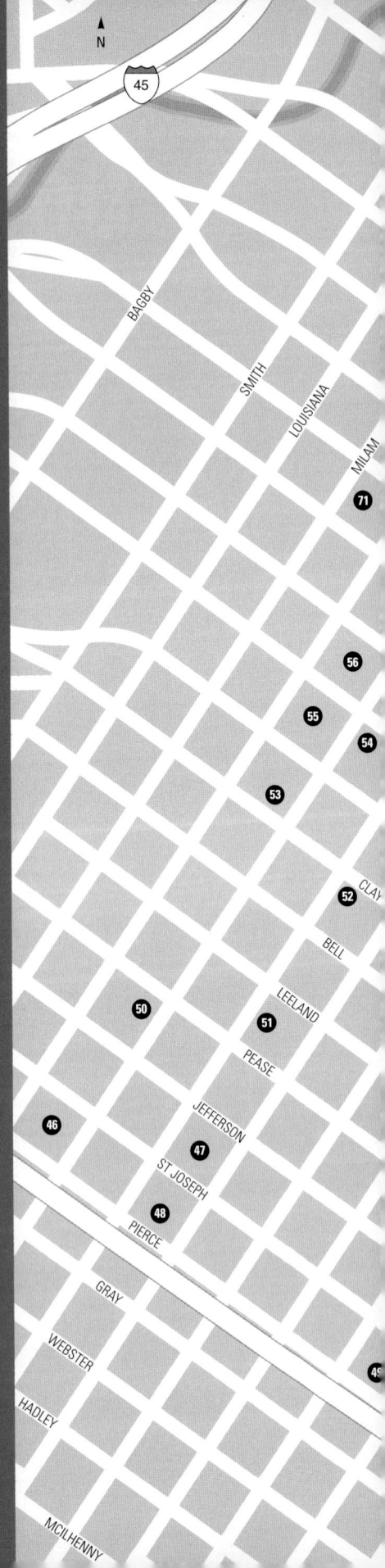

A-46 Lee P. Brown METRO Administration Building and Downtown Transit Center

A-47 Co-Cathedral of the Sacred Heart

A-48 Sacred Heart Catholic Church

A-46
Lee P. Brown METRO Administration Building and Downtown Transit Center
1900 Main Street
2005, PGAL

The Metropolitan Transit Authority of Harris County was constituted in 1978 to manage public transit in Houston, unincorporated portions of Harris County, and 14 adjacent participating communities. Between 2001-2003, Metro built the 7.5-mile Red Line, the first phase of a light rail transit system that complements Metro's extensive bus system. The Red Line links the Warehouse District, Downtown, Midtown, Museum District, Hermann Park, Rice University, Texas Medical Center, and the Astrodome-Reliant Park sports complex. Metro's headquarters on Main, built concurrently, is a 14-story slab of reinforced concrete construction faced with a neomodern, precast-concrete curtain wall, onto which sections of aluminum-and-glass curtain wall have been collaged. Behind the office slab are the three steel-framed vaulted bays of Metro's downtown transit center, where buses connect to the light rail. The complex was named for Lee P. Brown, mayor of Houston (1998-2003), during whose administration the light rail line was authorized and built. M2L Associates was the landscape architect.

A-47
Co-Cathedral of the Sacred Heart
1111 St. Joseph Parkway
2008, Ziegler Cooper

In 1847 Pope Pius IX authorized creation of the Catholic Diocese of Galveston, and in 1959 Pope John XXIII authorized renaming the diocese Galveston-Houston and transferring the diocesan see to Houston. Bypassing Houston's oldest parish, Annunciation, Sacred Heart, the other downtown parish, was designated co-cathedral of the diocese. In 2000 bishop Joseph Fiorenza determined to build a church better suited than Sacred Heart to serve as diocesan cathedral. Scott Ziegler, Kurt Hull, and their associates produced a dignified, conservative design built of cast-in-place concrete faced with Indiana limestone. Based on a Latin cross plan, the cathedral seats 1,820 worshippers. The vaulted nave is 72 feet high. The interior is exceptionally luminous, with natural light brought down from high set clerestory windows and indirectly through window slots in the side chapels that line the nave. The tonality of limestone facing inside is complemented by the baptistery, altar, and sanctuary screen, all of dark diaspro rosso marble. Rohn & Associates Design was liturgical consultant; Mellini Art Glass & Mosaics of Florence produced the stained glass; and The SWA Group was landscape architect. In 2004 Pope John Paul II elevated the diocese to the status of an archdiocese, making Sacred Heart the metropolitan cathedral of the new archdiocese of Galveston-Houston.

A-48
Sacred Heart Catholic Church
1111 Pierce Avenue
1912, O. J. Lorehn

Sacred Heart served the affluent suburban parish of the South End when its permanent church was built here adjacent to the Main Street residence district. Olle Lorehn's neo-Gothic detailing, executed in buff brick and limestone, was surprisingly academic for a Victorian architect. The church, co-cathedral of the Roman Catholic Diocese of Galveston-Houston 1959-2008, bears with stoic resignation its proximity to the Pierce Elevated Freeway (I-45).

A-49
South Wing, St. Joseph Hospital
[now St. Joseph Medical Center]
1916 Crawford Street
1941, I. E. Loveless

This streamlined, pink-stucco-faced building is one of four that Loveless, a Beverly Hills architect, designed at St. Joseph Hospital between the mid 1930s and late 1940s for the Sisters of Charity of the Incarnate Word. It was built as the south wing of the 1895 original hospital, designed by the Galveston architect N. J. Clayton, and was retained when the 1895 building was replaced by the present main building (1964, Golemon & Rolfe). Loveless also designed the sisters' sedate, 4- and 5-story, brick-faced convent at 1903 Crawford and Calhoun (1940). Founded in 1887 St. Joseph's is the oldest hospital in Houston. It was sold by the Sisters of Charity in 2006.

A-49 South Wing, St. Joseph Hospital

A-50 Beaconsfield

A-51 Houston House

A-52 Masonic Temple Building

A-53 First United Methodist Church

A-50
Beaconsfield
1700 Main Street
1911, A. C. Pigg

Alonzo Pigg was not a particularly brilliant interpreter of classical architecture. Nonetheless this 8.5-story, 16-unit domestic high-rise is a real apartment house typical of its era. Cleverly planned by developer and builder, E. C. Lamb, the apartment units (just two per floor originally) are arranged around open-air loggias (indicated by the wide central apertures on the front and side elevations) that ensured cross ventilation in all rooms. Rehabilitated in 1978 the Beaconsfield still functions as a luxury apartment building.

A-51
Houston House
1617 Fannin Street
1966, Charles M. Goodman with Irving R. Klein & Associates

The Washington, D.C. architect Charles Goodman's 33-story apartment slab, with 400 units stacked atop a parking garage and ground-level retail space, represents an effort to lure middle-income residents back downtown. Houston House was built by the Lumbermen's Investment Corporation of Austin, which also initiated the development of Greenway Plaza in Houston as well as building Edward Durell Stone's 26-story Westgate apartment tower (1965) in Austin.

A-52
Masonic Temple Building
1401 Fannin Street
1924, Alfred C. Finn

Finn's 3-story Masonic Temple embodies a degree of civility that in the 1920s was taken for granted, yet today seems almost unattainable. The wrought iron hardware at the main entrance contributes to its self-assured urbanity, which was reinforced with a 1981 rehabilitation. Trying very hard to do in the '80s what the Masonic Temple achieved so effortlessly in the '20s is M. Nasr

& Partners' 11-story Fannin Garage (1112 Clay, 1984), faced in granite aggregate precast concrete.

A-53
First United Methodist Church
1320 Main Street
1910, Sanguinet, Staats & Barnes

When First United Methodist Church moved to this site from Texas, across from the site of Texas Commerce Tower, its new church building went up amid large Victorian houses in shaded gardens, set two or three to a block behind cast iron fences. Now First Methodist sits on the edge of downtown Houston, the point where continuous building along Main stops, and a daunting new landscape of asphalt-surfaced parking lots begins. Sanguinet & Staats's design is not refined, but it is lively. The tall, stout corner tower with its attenuated detail, the big, flat-arched windows filled with murky stained glass, and the contrast of brown brick with green tiles, cream terra cotta, and dark marble decorative panels make the church a welcome presence. Urban change came swiftly: when the 6-story Educational Building at Travis and Clay (1929, James Ruskin Bailey) was erected, it was designed for possible future conversion into an office building. The church's architectural dominance was challenged by the 21-story Texas National Bank Building (now Travis Tower) at 1300 Main, built right up against its north edge in 1955 (Kenneth Franzheim).

A-54
Houston Pavilions
1201 Main Street
2008, Hellmuth, Obata + Kassabaum and Laguarda.Low

Spanning three city blocks between Polk and Dallas, the Houston Pavilions retail, entertainment, and office complex transposes the "lifestyle center" building type from the suburbs to downtown. Forsaking an air-conditioned mall, developers William Denton and Geoffrey Jones had Hellmuth, Obata + Kassabaum's Houston office and Dallas architects Laguarda.Low design a 2-and 3-story roofed, but open-air, central passageway that curves and angles through the block centers and bridges Fannin and San Jacinto with structural pyrotechnics. The neo-mod design theme is applied most stylishly on the 9-story Pavilions Tower at Fannin and Polk, with its randomly offset vertical panels. It gets spread a bit thin along the side streets, where cladding materials change with dizzying rapidity. The SWA Group was the landscape architect.

A-54 Houston Pavilions

A-55 Humble Building (Humble Tower)

A-56 Foley's

A-55
Humble Building
[now Marriott Courtyard and Residence Inn]
904-916 Dallas Avenue
1921, Clinton & Russell

The Humble Oil & Refining Company completed its first headquarters building at the foot of the Main Street Victorian residence district, demonstrating Houston's tendency to grow by leaps rather than by increments and hastening the old residential district's demise. When new, the 9-story office block at Main and Polk must have looked like a fragment of midtown Manhattan dropped onto the coastal plain. The New York architects Clinton & Russell detailed the building quite handsomely with a mixed blend of brown tapestry brick and unobtrusive classical ornament executed in limestone. The principal façade of the Humble Building faces Polk, to facilitate daylighting and ventilation. Such considerations ceased to be necessary after 1932, when the Humble Building became the first office building in Houston equipped with central air-conditioning. From the motor court at Main and Dallas one can survey an annex to the Humble Building, the 17-story Humble Tower (1936, John F. Staub and Kenneth Franzheim) with its elegant penthouse lantern in the style of the English architect E. L. Lutyens. It contains cooling towers for the building's central air-conditioning. In 2003 a certified rehabilitation of the Humble Building and Tower by investors Kimberly-Clark of Dallas and Leddy Ventures of San Antonio transformed the complex into a 191-room Courtyard by Marriott, a 171-room Marriott Residence Inn, and the 80-unit Humble Tower Apartments. HCI Design & Construction was the rehabilitation architect.

A-56
Foley's
[now Macy's]
1100 Main Street
1947, 1957, Kenneth Franzheim

When Federated Department Stores opened Foley's in 1947, it was the building of the hour—the model of the postwar, downtown American department store. Who would have guessed that it was to be the last of its kind? The store's major innovations were total environmental control (therefore, no windows except ground floor display windows), interiors by Raymond Loewy and William T. Snaith that stylishly rationalized the distribution of goods and customers, and the 5-story Foley's Garage at Lamar and Travis, connected to the store by an underground tunnel. Franzheim's office detailed the exteriors of the building (which it expanded from six to ten stories in 1957) with great assurance. The Main Street front, divided vertically into inset panels of orange Kasota stone studded with exposed aluminum bolts, appears neither blank nor busy. This is also true of the other street faces, surfaced with patterned brickwork broken by strategically placed grills. The canopy that shades the sidewalk on all four sides has the up-curved profile, back-lit with neon that was characteristic in Houston from the late '30s through the early '50s. In 2006 Federated converted Foley's into Macy's; it is the only department store left in downtown Houston. Across from Foley's at 1111 Main is Sakowitz Brothers (1951, Alfred C. Finn), built for Houston's foremost locally owned specialty store. Surfaced entirely in polished white Vermont marble, it projected an appropriately snob image until its interiors were demolished and ignominiously converted into a parking garage in 1997.

A-57
Main Street Square
1000 block Main Street
2004, Ekrenkrantz, Eckstut & Kuhn and PGAL; M2L Associates

Conceived as the downtown centerpiece of the Metrorail Red Line, Main Street Square is a fountain basin occupying almost all of the street right-of-way in the 1000 block of Main. At six-minute intervals on weekdays, trains traverse the pool, often framed by dramatic fountain sprays. The Main Street Coalition, a nonprofit civic group organized by architect (and subsequently City Councilman) Peter H. Brown, collaborated with Central Houston, Inc., a nonprofit civic corporation, to raise funds to construct the square in order to ensure that urban design was integrated with the Metrorail transit project. Houston artist Floyd Newsome's brightly colored standing sculptures, *Planter and Stems I and II*, are located adjacent to the stations. Architectural lighting consultants Fisher Marantz Stone of New York designed the ornamental lighting display using tall light towers with graceful ranks of curved reflectors.

A-57 Main Street Square

A-58 Reliant Energy Plaza

A-59 First City National Bank Building

A-58
Reliant Energy Plaza
1000 Main Street
2003, Gensler

Between 1926-1928, Houston's first urban real estate impresario, Jesse H. Jones, shifted the center of the downtown retail, entertainment, and hotel district to the south by filling this block with the 16-story Lamar Hotel, the opulent Metropolitan and Loew's State movie theaters, and an office building, the Democratic Building. In 1985 Hines imploded Jones's buildings but, because of the economic recession of the '80s, never replaced them. A sign that downtown's fortunes had rebounded was the decision of Hines's one-time rival, Century Development (headed by architect C. Richard Everett until he dissolved the company in 2006), to construct this 36-story office tower, which contains a 1,300-car garage. Like most 21st-century development downtown, Reliant Energy Plaza involved considerable financial participation by nonprofit and public entities: Central Houston, Inc., its affiliate the Houston Downtown Management District, the Downtown Redevelopment Authority, and Metro, the public transit authority. They subsidized the 2-story lobby facing Main, which opens to the basement-level pedestrian tunnel, a major interchange in the downtown tunnel system, in order to visually link the tunnel system to Main Street Square and its transit stops. Architecturally Reliant appears to be a bulkier version of the First City building across Main Street, with its tower on McKinney rising alongside the thick podium on Lamar. Ground-and-polished precast concrete panels are collaged onto the tower's glass curtain wall to form a supergrid. Fisher Stone Marantz's lighting installation for Main Street Square climbs up the Main-Lamar corner of the garage; LED lighting outlines the top of the tower.

A-59
First City National Bank Building
[now One City Centre]
1001 Main Street
1961, Skidmore, Owings & Merrill
with Wilson, Morris, Crain & Anderson

Gordon Bunshaft of the New York office of Skidmore, Owings & Merrill designed the First City National Bank Building, a 32-story tower originally paired with a freestanding steel and glass banking pavilion. First City was the first high modern office building erected in downtown Houston. Its crisp, clean, airy look set the style locally for image-conscious tall buildings of the 1960s. The tower consists of a steel frame "exo-skeleton" (to use Skidmore, Owings & Merrill's terminology), originally faced with polished white Vermont marble, behind which the gray glass and aluminum curtain wall is recessed for sun shading, the same strategy used at Humble and Tenneco. First City depended on contrast with the masonry buildings around it for maximum visual impact. As these have given way to taller glass-faced buildings, its clarity has come to seem much less startling. Contributing to this lessening of intensity was the demolition of the banking hall in 1998 by McCord Development, Inc., for replacement with a parking garage. To the end, the banking pavilion retained its impact: a lofty, free-spanned modernist space animated by a profusion of light and air, and the discreetly luxurious finishes for which Skidmore, Owings & Merrill was famous. In 1999 the tower's marble cladding was replaced with light gray granite.

A-60
City National Bank Building
[now 1001 McKinney Building]
1001 McKinney Avenue
1947, Alfred C. Finn

The 24-story City National Bank Building was the first tall office building constructed downtown after World War II. It looked back to the late 1920s with its stepped massing, vertically-channeled window bays, and odd L-shaped plan, which makes the most of very narrow Main Street frontage. As stodgy as it must have appeared at the time of its completion, the building exercises a strong positive influence on its surroundings today. Its determined profile, its piers of buff brick (a Southwestern standard from the 1920s through the '50s), and dark red-striped spandrels stand out against the slick, monochrome, reflective surfaces of the buildings that it is now seen against. The merger of City National Bank and First National Bank in 1956 set in motion plans for a new building that would overshadow Finn's building. The City National Bank Building underwent a certified rehabilitation in 1999.

A-60 City National Bank Building

A-61 Two Houston Center

A-62 Gulf Tower

A-61
Two Houston Center
909 Fannin Street
1974, William L. Pereira Associates
and Pierce Goodwin Flanagan

In 1970 Texas Eastern Transmission Corporation, a natural gas pipeline company, assembled 33 square blocks stretching from Fannin eastward along McKinney and Lamar to the Eastex Freeway. For this 75-acre site, spotted with remnant buildings and surface parking lots, William L. Pereira Associates of Los Angeles prepared a master plan for that perennial 20th-century American urban fantasy, the city-within-the-city. Pereira and his designer, Frank Dimster, proposed a 4-level, 40,000-car parking megastructure that would cover the entire site, leaving only street intersections open to the sky. The upper surface of this Texas-sized garage was to be the landscaped promenade deck for a futuristic city of towers. So vast were the dimensions of the complex that it required an elevated loop road, tied directly to the Eastex Freeway, and a people-mover tramline (The X-bracing visible on the Walker side of Two Houston Center marks what was to have been the people mover's terminus.) Two Houston Center, the only building that Pereira's office designed, took seriously its role as gateway to Houston Center. At the Fannin-McKinney intersection there is a complex entry and ascent sequence (accessible only during business hours): up staggered rows of escalators from circular pavilion to circular pavilion, to the fourth-level promenade, a multi-level concourse through the 44-story tower, and finally to an open-air terrace spanning San Jacinto. This is the only segment of deck built according to the Pereira plan. The smooth glazed surfaces and curved corners with which Dimster shaped Two Houston Center's curtain wall reflect the impact of César Pelli and Anthony Lumsden on the Los Angeles architecture scene of the early '70s. Further plans were halted by the recession of the mid-1970s and a public outcry against covering the streets, while Pennzoil Place architecturally upstaged Two Houston Center. The 46-story One Houston Center (1221 McKinney, 1978, S. I. Morris Associates, Caudill Rowlett Scott, and 3D/International) shows the transition from lavish showmanship to excessive caution.

A-62
Gulf Tower
[now Fulbright Tower]
1301 McKinney Avenue
1982, Caudill Rowlett Scott

The 52-story Gulf Tower, although square in plan, is treated sectionally as an exercise in geometric rotation. Its polished gray granite and silver reflective glass curtain wall is slickly detailed. Pedestrian through-traffic on the skybridge leading from One Houston Center (during business hours) is funneled through triangular scissor arches. Texas Eastern Corporation and its partner from 1978 to 1986, Cadillac Fairview Corporation, settled on the air-conditioned skybridges as a compromise between Pereira's vision and economic and political realities. At street level, however, this compromise has an obvious consequence: an urban environment devoid of human presence. One block to the east at 1401 McKinney, the 27-story Five Houston Center (2002, HKS of Dallas) displays the supergrid curtain wall pattern popular in the 1980s.

A-63
Hess Tower
1501 McKinney Avenue
2010, Gensler

For the Trammell Crow Company of Dallas, Gensler designed the 29-story Hess Tower as a dramatic exposition in transparency. The tower, regional headquarters of the Hess energy corporation, achieved LEED gold certification with a high performance clear glass curtain wall with low-E coating and 10 vertical access wind turbines stationed at attic level.

A-63 Hess Tower

A-64 Discovery Green

A-65 George R. Brown Convention Center

A-64
Discovery Green
1500 McKinney Avenue
2008, Hargreaves Associates, PageSoutherlandPage, and Lauren Griffith Associates

Among the projects of Mayor Bill White's administration (2002-09), construction of a 12-acre public green in what had been a sprawling field of parking lots in front of the George R. Brown Convention Center stands out dramatically. San Francisco landscape architects Mary Margaret Jones and Jacob Peterson of Hargreaves and Lawrence W. Speck of PSP collaborated on the design of a public space programmed by the New York-based Project for Public Spaces. Rather than having the green constructed and administered by the city's Parks and Recreation Department, White oversaw creation of two nonprofits, the Houston Downtown Park Corporation and the Discovery Green Conservancy, to superintend the design, construction, and long-term management of the green. The conservancy staff (initially headed by architect and urban designer Guy Hagstette) programs a wide array of public activities and coordinates use of spaces by different groups. Discovery Green has proved to be an immensely popular destination. Following the Project for Public Spaces program, Hargreaves transformed the flat site to provide areas for 25 activities, selectively using existing street alignments and avenues of Live Oak trees, remnants of the Third Ward's status at the turn of the 20th century as one of Houston's elite neighborhoods, to spatially restructure the new green. A 672-car garage is tucked beneath the northeast corner of the site, and the one-acre Kinder Lake stretches along McKinney. The Andrea and Bill White Promenade spans the park in a north-south direction along the right-of-way of Crawford while the Live Oaks that once lined Lamar separate intensively planted gardens to the south from the central green, Jones Lawn. PSP and Speck's linear, shed-roofed brick and glass-walled buildings—the Lake House and Alkek Building bordering the lake and The Grove restaurant alongside the Lamar allée—are unpretentious and incorporate generous shaded spaces and open decks. Artist Margo Jones is responsible for *Synchronicity of Color*, the intricate composition of interlocking colored squares and rectangles encrusting freestanding stairways to the garage. Doug Hollis produced *Mist Tree* on the Sarofim Picnic Lawn. Jean Dubuffet's *Monument au Fantôme* (1977), a whimsical, enigmatic allegory in painted fiberglass, was reinstalled in Discovery Green facing Avenida de las Américas after it was moved from its original site at 1100 Louisiana. Discovery Green is not legally a City of Houston park but a complexly constructed public-private operation that, to date, has borne out the Houstonian conviction that such a mixed organization can provide publicly accessible green space more reliably and with higher amenity standards than can be found in city parks. Framing the narrow west end of Discovery Green is the 37-story, 346-unit One Park Place apartment tower, built by the Finger Companies in 2009 (Jackson & Ryan Architects).

made architecture out of the programmatic, spatial, constructional, and servicing requirements for the 1.15 million-SF center. With admirable clarity he joined three huge, double-volume exhibition halls side-by-side, topped them with a third level of exhibition, meeting, and reception spaces, then prefaced the whole with a stacked set of public promenades that open out behind the west-facing walls of glass, providing convention visitors with panoramic vistas of Discovery Green and the downtown skyline. The exteriors express the big scale and straightforward organization of the center with effervescence and wit. Arrangements to tour the center can be made through the City of Houston Civic Center office. The site of the George R. Brown Convention Center was given to the City of Houston by Texas Eastern Corporation and Cadillac Fairview Corporation, then owners of Houston Center. The Houston infrastructure contractor George Brown, for whom the center was named, was a founder of Texas Eastern. In 2003 the convention center was expanded by 650,000 SF with Golemon & Bolullo as lead architects.

A-65
George R. Brown Convention Center
1001 Avenida de las Américas
1987, Houston Convention Center Architects & Engineers

Houston's downtown convention center is an extraordinary sight, whether viewed across Discovery Green or from the Eastex Freeway. It is big, bold, and articulately designed by a consortium of Houston architectural firms (Golemon & Rolfe Associates, John S. Chase, Molina & Associates, Haywood Jordan McCowan, and Moseley Associates with Bernard Johnson and 3D/International) under the guidance of Golemon's Mario Bolullo. Bolullo

A-66 Hilton Americas Hotel

A-67 The Park in Houston Center

A-68 First City Tower

A-66
Hilton Americas Hotel
1600 Lamar Avenue
2003, Arquitectonica and Gensler

The Miami architects Arquitectonica first made their mark on Houston in the early 1980s with a series of subversive townhouses and small retail buildings. Twenty years later Arquitectonica returned to Houston as a large corporate practice specializing in hospitality (hotel and convention center) design. The tartan grid of gray, green, and yellow spandrels comprising the curtain wall of the 24-story, 1,200-room hotel, sharp vertical incisions, disorienting diagonals, and precarious protrusions of the Hilton Americas—Houston's largest hotel—are signature devices of Arquitectonica's principals Bernardo Fort-Brescia and Laurinda Spear. The hotel frames the south side of Discovery Green and is connected to the Brown Convention Center by skybridges. The generously scaled lobby, accessible from Lamar and Avenida de las Américas, features work by contemporary Texan artists. The ballroom concourse above is hung with flamboyant lighting fixtures produced by the Venetian glass studio of Barovier & Toso of Murano. The 24th floor houses a spectacular swimming pool terrace and open-air viewing platform. Wilson & Associates of Dallas with John S. Chase Architects of Houston were interior designers. The hotel and an adjacent 1,600-car parking garage were built by the Houston Convention Center Hotel Corporation, a nonprofit corporation created by the City of Houston during the administration of mayor Lee P. Brown to plan, build, and oversee operation of a convention center hotel. Just south of the hotel at 1510 Polk is the 18,300-seat Toyota Center (2003, HOK Sport, Morris Architects, and John S. Chase) and its ancillary, the 2,500-car Toyota Tundra Garage (2003, Prozign Architects). Both were built by the Harris County-Houston Sports Authority, a nonprofit corporation created by Harris County and the City of Houston in 1997. Toyota is home to the National Basketball Association's Houston Rockets and the American Hockey League's Houston Aeros. Although Clark Condon Associates designed landscapes at the major entrances to the Toyota Center, the character of the public landscape in this precinct, which is totally dominated by public projects, is bleak, especially the two blocks of Leeland alongside the Tundra garage, evoking Alex S. MacLean's notorious aerial photo of the east side of downtown Houston of the late 1970s.

A-67
The Park in Houston Center
[now the Shops at Houston Center]
1221 Lamar Avenue
1983, Morris*Aubry Architects and RTKL Associates

The Houston Center skybridge loop comes full circle in the Shops at Houston Center. A two-block long, elevated shopping mall spanning Caroline, the Shops are bracketed by a 16-story office slab. The center's 400-foot interior spine, a double-level shopping arcade capped by a glazed half vault, was tracked by a playful screen of freestanding colored pipes, part fountain, designed by Kevin Shanley of The SWA Group, which was removed in a makeover of the mall by Morris Architects (2004). At the east end of the mall, where bridges connect to the Fulbright Tower and the 29-story, 430-room Four Seasons Hotel-Houston Center at 1300 Lamar (1981, Caudill Rowlett Scott), is the mall's anchor—a food court that opens onto a balcony above Austin. At the west end are escalators down to the street level entrance on San Jacinto. Like the Fulbright Tower, The Shops ignore the street. The original design called for a more open and variegated exterior, but as built it is an insulated fortress opening only at the postmodern entrance portal on San Jacinto.

A-68
First City Tower
1001 Fannin Street
1981, Morris*Aubry Architects

With this 49-story tower, built by First City Bancorporation of Texas and Urban Investment & Development Company, designer Eugene Aubry fused urbanity and sculptural presence to create a pair of triangular plazas that originally opened out and embraced the surrounding city. The building, a slab tautly deflected onto the diagonal in plan, features a series of vertical notches that rise in a stair-step pattern across its two angled faces and afford outside views from the upper-floor elevator lobbies. The flat plane of mottled gray soapstone, with which the plaza and the lobby floor surfaces were originally paved, the green tinted glass, and the white aluminum wall panels used externally and internally made the airy, light-filled lobby feel like a continuation of the plazas rather than a separate, conditioned space. Extensive alterations to the plaza and lobby in 2005 by Morris Architects made the base of the building more secure but at the price of eroding the sense of openness that was its most appealing characteristic.

A-69 1010 Lamar Building

A-69
1010 Lamar Building
1010 Lamar Avenue
1981, Nasr Penton & Associates and
The Falick/Klein Partnership

Mohammed Nasr's tutelage under Philadelphia architect Romaldo Giurgola is evident in this 20-story office building, ingeniously planned for a restricted site. Nasr manipulated the building's section to bring daylight in from above, as well as from slots inset in its blind party walls. In lieu of a plaza, he introduced a vertically staged sequence of interior public spaces, paneled in wood and treated as rooms rather than an internalized exterior. Intelligence and modesty pay off handsomely in this easily overlooked building. Tony Rosenthal's *Bronco* hovers tensely above the open, basement-level restaurant.

A-70 The Smart Shop

A-70
The Smart Shop
[now Holy Cross Chapel]
905 Main Street
1929, Alfred C. Finn
2003, Gensler

After it was slipcovered with a new façade in 1965, the Smart Shop lost the exuberant Art Déco elevation Finn had designed, an extension of the elevations of his adjoining (and still slipcovered) Krupp & Tuffly shoe store at 901 Main. Gensler's Paul Homeyer went to the Finn architectural archive at the Houston Metropolitan Research Center to retrieve documentation enabling him to reproduce the Smart Shop's damaged or lost architectural details. In 2006 Gensler completed an adaptive reuse of the former ground floor retail area as Holy Cross Chapel, the downtown chapel of the Roman Catholic Archdiocese of Galveston-Houston, which was also responsible for the exterior restoration.

A-71
Bank of the Southwest Building
[now 919 Milam Building]
919 Milam Street
1956, Kenneth Franzheim

This 24-story building was the largest office building constructed downtown during the 1950s. Its bulky massing, clunky granite-veneered base, and bland curtain wall (the first all-aluminum curtain wall in Houston) make it clear why the First City National Bank Building and its successors were received locally with such relief. Franzheim's office was trying to be modern, as the shallowly curved façade facing Travis attests. The building initiated the downtown tunnel system with its underground connections to the Ten-Ten Garage and the Commerce Building. Tragically the Bank of the Southwest Building lost its greatest asset as a result of the 1989 failure of the Bank of the Southwest's successor, MBank Houston. Rufino Tamayo's mural *America* (1956), the major work of public art installed in Houston in the 1950s, was sold when the original second-floor banking hall was subdivided as office space. Franzheim ardently championed the incorporation of works of art in his buildings. During the politically volatile 1950s this could be risky. The bank rejected a huge, already fabricated cast aluminum sculpture by William Zorach, *The New State of Texas*, which was to have been installed in the recess above the Travis entry, because it feared the piece's modernity would provoke public controversy. Repositioning the building in the chancy Houston real estate market of the '90s led to the closing of the upstairs banking hall, redesign of public interiors, particularly the tunnel concourse, rechristened Mid City Shops (1993, Gensler & Associates), and a tactful updating of the building's base (1994, Morris Architects). In another intervention made in 2007, the base was completely reconstructed internally by Hines to contain a 300-car parking garage (PageSoutherlandPage).

A-71 Bank of the Southwest Building

A-72 Walker@Main Garage

A-74 Battelstein's

A-72
Walker@Main Garage
820 Main Street
2007, PageSoutherlandPage

The German real estate investment corporation that owns Pennzoil Place built this 11-story, 975-car garage on the site of the San Jacinto Building (1952, Kenneth Franzheim). Were the design of Walker@Main comparable to the 13-story McKinney Place Garage a block away at 930 Main (2001, Morris Architects), one might well lament demolition of the Franzheim building. But reflecting the sensibilities of its clients, Walker@Main is a precisely proportioned frame of exposed cast-in-place concrete with open bays screened by railings of taut steel cables. The ground floor retail lease spaces are similarly straightforward yet refined. PSP's designer, Blair Satterfield, made urban architecture out of the basics—materials, construction, proportions—demonstrating that when these are taken seriously, the architecture doesn't have to be added on. The only complaints about Walker@Main have come from residents of the Commerce Towers condominiums at 914 Main and Walker: the headlights of cars in the garage shine into their apartment windows after dark. Commerce Towers began as Levy's, a 9-story department store and office building (1929, Joseph Finger), which Jesse H. Jones acquired and transformed into the Commerce Building by adding the top 13 floors (1939, Alfred C. Finn). In 2003 the Commerce Building was transformed into the 132-unit Commerce Towers (PageSoutherlandPage).

A-73
BG Group Place
811 Main Street
2011, Pickard Chilton and Kendall/Heaton Associates

In the early 1960s, downtown high-rise office construction migrated west of Main in search of lower priced real estate. The same factor attracted such development back to Main around the turn of the 21st century, especially after construction of the Metrorail Red Line promised to reverse the decline Main Street experienced during the 1980s and '90s. Hines's first major building downtown in more than 25 years, the 46-story, one million-SF, concrete-framed BG Group Place, is the work of Pickard Chilton of New Haven. They shaped the glass tower with shallow elliptical curves on its long sides, inserting vertical notches to give the glass skinned building a sense of depth. A 5-story indentation near the top of the Fannin elevation dramatizes long distance views of the building. Horizontal fins on the curved north and south elevations and vertical fins on the Main elevation moderate sun penetration. At Main and Walker, a 10-story base contains part of the 1,130-car garage. BG Group Place wraps around the 10-story Stowers Building (1913, Green & Finger) at 820 Fannin, rehabilitated in 2005 by the Spire Realty Group.

A-74
Battelstein's
812 Main Street
1950, Finger & Rustay

Vacancy and neglect have not entirely dimmed the sophistication of Joseph Finger and George Rustay's additions to and refacing of the former Battelstein's specialty store. The horizontal strip windows let into the planar limestone façade and the inset second-floor balcony (originally intensively planted) were elements of a high-fashion retail look that also appeared in Alfred C. Finn's elegant refacing of The Fashion (917 Main, 1947, subsequently Neiman-Marcus, now CVS Pharmacy—only the ground-floor storefront remains intact). Together with Foley's and Sakowitz Brothers, these projects date from the last episode of new construction along the Main Street retail and entertainment corridor, the traditional axis of downtown Houston.

A-73 BG Group Place

A-75 Melrose Building

A-76 Gulf Building

A-75
Melrose Building
1121 Walker Avenue
1952, Hermon Lloyd & W. B. Morgan

This was the first tall building in Houston to be designed with modern architectural attributes, although they were applied to a conventional U-plan, party wall building. The 21-story Melrose Building was built by Melvin A. Silverman. A news report of the period asserted that it looked to Rio de Janeiro, Mexico City, and Sweden for its modern architectural features. The original turquoise ceramic spandrel panels have been replaced with bronze anodized aluminum; otherwise the exteriors have suffered no major alterations.

A-76
Gulf Building
[now J. P. Morgan Chase Bank Building]
712 Main Street
1929, Alfred C. Finn, Kenneth Franzheim, and J. E. R. Carpenter

The Gulf Building, with its striking chamfered corner bay dominating the intersection at Main and Rusk, is an urbane skyscraper in the best tradition of 1920s American city buildings. Constructed by the real estate magnate, banker, newspaper publisher, and New Deal recovery czar, Jesse H. Jones, the 36-story, 450-foot-high Gulf Building was the tallest skyscraper in Houston from 1929-1963. The profile of the tower, which rises in setback stages to an attenuated vertical crown, and its prolific crypto-Gothic ornament were inspired by Eliel Saarinen's never-built, but much-copied, Chicago Tribune Building design of 1922. What makes the Gulf Building so remarkable is that Franzheim and Finn gave substance to their borrowed image by thoroughly integrating the building into downtown Houston. Its 6-story, limestone-clad base originally contained the Sakowitz Brothers store at Main and Rusk, several smaller shops, and a vaulted lobby that still extends from Main through the building to the majestic banking hall of Jones's National Bank of Commerce (now J. P. Morgan Chase Bank). The office tower above, faced with buff tapestry brick, was the first in Houston to be treated architecturally on all four sides. The Main Street lobby (accessible during business hours) is faced with polished Sienna travertine and floored in richly patterned terrazzo. It contains a series of murals by the New York painter Vincent Maragliotti depicting Texas historical scenes; the one entitled *Modern Houston* is especially entertaining. The Art Déco decorative detailing in polished Benedict nickel is the finest in Houston. When Franzheim remodeled the 3-story high banking hall in 1959, he replicated the Art Déco balcony rails for new openings that he cut into the north wall of the room. He was also responsible for the installation of the stained glass panel over the Travis entry. In 1987 Chase's predecessor, Texas Commerce Bank, signaled completion of a $50 million certified rehabilitation of the Gulf Building (Sikes Jennings Kelly and CRS Sirrine) by relighting the upper stages of the tower's crown.

A-77
Niels Esperson Building
808 Travis Street
1927, John Eberson

Mellie Keenan Esperson built the 32-story Niels Esperson Building as a memorial to her husband, a Danish-born real estate and minerals speculator. The architect, John Eberson of New York, had earlier designed for Niels Esperson the Majestic Theater (1923, demolished 1971) across the street at Rusk and Travis, the most opulent of Houston's three 1920s movie palaces and the one in which Eberson introduced his contribution to the genre, the "atmospheric" ceiling. The Italian Renaissance detail that Eberson liberally applied to the Majestic was also used to give the Esperson Building its architectural identity. Thus the monumental entrance portal on Travis, framed by a pair of fluted Corinthian columns, and the high arched windows set into rusticated limestone walls and crowned by keystones bearing bucrania—the Roman version of a Texas steer skull—were matched high above the sidewalk with balustraded terraces, urns, obelisks, and the cylindrical, terra cotta-faced tempietto, a classical architectural monument *par excellence*. Mrs. Esperson maintained her offices on the 25th floor, where she and her friends were photographed having a tea party on one of the expansive setback-level terraces. In 1939 Mrs. Esperson had Eberson and his son Drew add a 19-story annex to the Niels Esperson Building, which she named the Mellie Esperson Building (1941). Its Walker entrance portal and elevator lobby retain some Art Déco detail, although the interior has been altered. Unfortunately the same is true of the elevator lobby and banking hall of the Niels Esperson Building. Nonetheless the building's Westminster chimes still ring the hours, and Esperson's crowning temple-like memorial is lit nightly, just as it was when the Niels Esperson Building dominated the downtown skyline. In 2003 Gensler completed a phased rehabilitation of the Esperson buildings. The lucid and serene architecture studio of Lauren Rottet occupies the Guardian Trust Company's ground-floor banking hall.

A-77 Niels Esperson Building

A-78 S.H. Kress & Company Building

A-79 Texas Commerce Center

A-78
S. H. Kress & Company Building
[now St. Germain Lofts]
705 Main Street
1913, Seymour Burrell

The Kress Building, constructed by S. H. Kress & Company and occupied by it until 1980, is the only Houston building faced entirely with terra cotta. Burrell, Kress's corporate architect, dexterously used the material to produce a range of classical detail in a bright array of colors. The Kress Building has lost its cornice and its original storefront. The latter was replaced by a spirited postmodern storefront, part of a rehabilitation of the building carried out in 1983 by Ray Bailey Architects. In 1999 the Kress Building was rehabilitated as an apartment building by developer Randall Davis.

A-79
Texas Commerce Center
[now J. P. Morgan Chase Center]
601 Travis Street
1982, I. M. Pei & Partners and 3D/International

The Pei firm made a major urban contribution to Main Street with the 19-story Texas Commerce Center, companion to Pei's Texas Commerce Tower at 600 Travis. The center contains ground-floor shop spaces, an auditorium, a 2,000-car garage, five floors of offices, and, originally, a health club. Its Main Street sidewalk front is a shopping arcade, faced with a great piano-curved wall of butt-jointed glass inset behind bright red columns. Even the parking garage is urbanistically engaged; it affords great mid-level views of downtown to those spiraling up or down its ramps. During Hurricane Ike in September 2008, a wind funnel suctioned most of the glass from the Travis side of this building and the Chase Tower across the street.

A-80
Rice Hotel
[now Post Rice Lofts]
909 Texas Avenue
1913, Mauran, Russell & Crowell

The Rice was Houston's traditional downtown hotel. It occupies the site where in 1837 Houston's founders constructed a 2-story wooden building that served until 1839 as temporary capitol of the Republic of Texas. This building was demolished in 1883 and replaced by an ambitious Victorian hostelry, the 5-story Capitol Hotel. The Capitol gave way to the 17-story, 650-room Rice Hotel, a steel-framed, U-planned skyscraper built by Jesse H. Jones. The St. Louis architects, Mauran, Russell & Crowell, ornamented the red brick-faced building with ample cream-colored, terra cotta sculptural decoration. The classically detailed cast iron canopy with which they surrounded the ground floor of the hotel doubled as a terrace for public rooms on the second floor. Early photographs indicate that it was once fitted with rows of rocking chairs from which guests could survey the world at Main and Texas, traditionally considered the center of downtown Houston. The hotel also provided both a "cooled, washed air ventilating system" and an open-air, pergola-covered roof garden for dining and dancing. Jones added a matching third wing to the hotel at Texas and Travis (1926, Alfred C. Finn), and by 1924 had installed a proto-air-conditioning system in the basement level cafeteria. The hotel's original "French" style interiors were continually altered; notable successors were Kenneth Franzheim's modernistic Empire Room (1938) and Staub, Rather & Howze's 18th-floor addition for the Petroleum Club (1951). The scene of numerous events of local historical significance, the Rice was closed in 1977. In 1996 during the tenure of Mayor Bob Lanier (1992-97), the City of Houston, through the Houston Housing Finance Corporation, bought the Rice Hotel and went into partnership with developer Randall Davis to convert it into a 365-unit apartment building. The phased renewal of the Rice (1998, PageSoutherlandPage) entailed a certified rehabilitation of the building with reconstruction of long vanished exterior features and interior public spaces. The Downtown Redevelopment Authority, a tax increment reinvestment zone enacted by the city in 1995 in conjunction with the acquisition of the Rice, finally raised historic preservation and rehabilitation to the status of public policy, at least in the Main Street-Market Square Historic District. The commercial success of the Rice, which was acquired by Post Properties of Atlanta in 1997, stimulated additional historic rehabilitation and residential conversions downtown during the late 1990s and early 2000s.

A-80 Rice Hotel

A-81 Post-Dispatch Building

A-82 Christ Church Cathedral

A-83 Chancery of the Episcopal Diocese of Texas and the John R. Dunn Outreach Center at the Beacon

A-81
Post-Dispatch Building
[now Magnolia Hotel Houston]
1100 Texas Avenue
1926, Sanguinet, Staats, Hedrick & Gottlieb

The Post-Dispatch Building is an authoritative classical presence on Texas. At 22 stories it was the tallest reinforced concrete building constructed in Houston during the 1920s. It is faced entirely in limestone and features monumental screens of Corinthian pilasters at the third and fourth floors and in its attic zone. The building was constructed by Ross S. Sterling, publisher of the *Houston Post-Dispatch* newspaper, oilman, banker, future governor, and real estate developer, who in the 1920s challenged Jesse H. Jones for entrepreneurial supremacy. Since Jones had staked out Main Street, Sterling took on Texas Avenue. Across Fannin he and his son-in-law, architect Wyatt C. Hedrick, were responsible for the last of Houston's '20s-style skyscrapers, the 21-story, Art Déco Sterling Building (1931). Now called the 608 Texas Tower, the building has lost its modernistic storefronts and its crowning pinnacles. In 2003 the Denver-based Steven Holtze Corporation completed the conversion of the Post-Dispatch Building into the Magnolia, a 314-room boutique hotel. Guy Thornton Design of Denver and Mitchell Stone Carlson of Houston were rehabilitation architects. This entailed reconstruction of the base of the building, which had been sacrificed to "modernization" in the 1960s.

A-82
Christ Church Cathedral
1117 Texas Avenue
1893, Silas McBee with J. Arthur Tempest

Christ Church, the second oldest Episcopal parish in Texas and cathedral church of the Diocese of Texas, has occupied this site since 1839. McBee, a commissioner of endowments at the University of the South

(Sewanee), was an ecclesiologist and amateur architect. His molded brickwork, decorative arches, and heavy, stepped, sandstone-capped parapets pay homage to the early 18th-century "Gothic Survival" architecture of St. Luke's, Isle of Wight County, Virginia, the oldest Anglican church building in the United States, a salute to Christ Church's founding parishioners, who were from Virginia. The nave is quite broad; consequently, the wide-span, darkly stained timber trusses dominate the interior. The art glass windows are characteristic of the turn of the 20th century. The Jeanette I. Ennis memorial window (1898), on the Fannin side of the nave next to the transept bay, is the only authenticated installation by Tiffany Studios in Houston. A comprehensive restoration of the church's interior in 1994 revealed subtle tonal variations present in the nave and chancel that had been lost to decades of grime and dark staining (Volz & Associates and Clovis Heimsath Associates). The Guild Hall (1892, McBee with Tempest) and the austere, exquisitely finished Golding Memorial Chapel (1939, William Ward Watkin) are behind the arched cloister bays. At the corner of Texas and San Jacinto is Latham Memorial Hall (1952, Maurice J. Sullivan). Facing Prairie is an extensive set of contextually deferential additions (1990, Ray Bailey Architects). The cathedral close, which opens onto Texas behind a traditional iron fence and a fringe of palm trees (a landscape feature essential to English-inspired Victorian buildings in hot, humid climates), is one of the most enjoyable outdoor spaces downtown. The 3-story McGehee Hall at the San Jacinto-Prairie corner completed Christ Church's occupation of the block (2007, Leo A. Daly/LAN and PageSoutherlandPage).

A-83
Chancery of the Episcopal Diocese of Texas and the John R. Dunn Outreach Center
1225 Texas Avenue
and 1212 Prairie Avenue
2007, Leo A. Daly/LAN and PageSoutherlandPage

Christ Church Cathedral was responsible for the most provocative building constructed in downtown Houston in the early 21st century. It is a combination parking garage, social welfare center, urban garden, and office building. The social welfare center, the Beacon, at the Prairie-Caroline corner, offers services to the homeless on weekends. PSP's Lawrence W. Speck exposed the reinforced concrete construction of the 4-story garage, which spans the Prairie front of the block. He offset its visual toughness with panels of orange-red brick and translucent spandrels and screens of sandblasted glass. The glass introduces a contrasting perception of lightness, especially at night when panels are back-lit. The Texas front is outlined by a steel-framed, wood-slatted pergola that encircles the public garden at Texas and San Jacinto, and continues on as a 2-story structure shading the glass walls of the diocesan chancery at the Texas-Caroline corner. The architectural mixture of toughness and vulnerability visible at Christ Church's mixed-use complex materializes the parish's efforts to minister to very different communities: the homeless, parishioners, diocesan officials, and families waiting in the garden to visit prisoners in the federal detention center across Texas.

A-84 Federal Reserve Bank of Dallas Branch Building

A-84
Federal Reserve Bank of Dallas Branch Building
[now Houston Area Urban League]
1301 Texas Avenue
1922, Sanguinet, Staats, Hedrick & Gottlieb

A compact neo-Classical block decorated with Adamesque detail, the Federal Reserve Bank Branch Building was stunningly transformed into a small, but monumental, office building for the Crispin Company by Howard Barnstone (1973). Since 1997 it has been the headquarters of the Houston Area Urban League.

A-85
Petroleum Building
[now Great Southwest Building]
1314 Texas Avenue
1927, Alfred C. Bossom with Maurice J. Sullivan and Briscoe & Dixon

Bossom, a New York architect born and trained in England, proposed the Mayan stepped pyramids of Central America as an indigenous model for modern American skyscrapers. He gave form to this idea in one of the last buildings he completed before returning to England in 1926, the 22-story Petroleum Building. Built by the oilman J. S. Cullinan, the Petroleum Building has the limestone base and buff brick-faced shaft characteristic of 1920s Houston skyscrapers. But it also features Mayan relief figures protruding from the spandrel panels above the arched second-floor windows and more abstract pre-Columbian decoration in the spandrels of its three setback stages. Even the ceiling slab of the 2-story garage facing Austin, which Bossom was prescient enough to append to the Petroleum Building, was embossed with a Mayan glyph.

A-85 Petroleum Building

A-86
Annunciation Catholic Church
1618 Texas Avenue
1871; 1884-1895, N. J. Clayton

Annunciation Catholic Church, which houses the oldest Roman Catholic parish in Houston, is the distinguished product of a long building history. The nave and the two low towers flanking the tall central tower were completed in 1871. By 1883 sizeable cracks had opened up in the nave walls and the towers were pulling away from the body of the church. The noted 19th-century Galveston architect N. J. Clayton was called in. During the next 11 years Clayton completely reconstructed and expanded the church. All visible fabric, externally and internally, bears the evidence of his involvement. Clayton bolstered the nave walls with the arched buttresses visible from Texas. He re-roofed the church and braced the front towers with twin entrance pavilions and the intense, slender central tower that they bracket. This tower, which exhibits the robust modeling of masonry surfaces that was one of Clayton's hallmarks, is 175 feet high. It was the tallest structure in Houston from its completion in 1889 until 1912. The interior of the church (open only during scheduled services) is quite lyrical. Clayton developed the figure of the arch into full volumetric expression in the apsidal sanctuary that he added to the nave in 1895. This receives the directional thrust of the vaulted nave ceiling and appears to expand to accommodate it. The spatial complexity of the sanctuary and the sense of upward movement that Clayton imparted to its symmetrically composed rear wall animate the interior of the church. Numerous minor alterations have been made to the church. The fine exterior brickwork was stuccoed in the early 20th century. On the south side of the nave near the narthex is a tiny added bay that contains the jewel-like Burkett Memorial Chapel of Our Lady of Perpetual Help (1925, Maurice J. Sullivan) with windows by Charles J. Connick of Boston. South of the church, at 1611 Capitol, is Incarnate Word Academy (1905, N. J. Clayton). This is one of three buildings Clayton designed for this girls' school. Unfortunately the finest of these, the Auditorium (1899) at Jackson and Capitol, was pulled down in 1978. From Capitol, one has an especially good view of the downtown skyline.

A-86 Annunciation Catholic Church interior

A-86 Annunciation Catholic Church

A-87 Union Station

A-87 Minute Maid Park

A-88 Houston Cotton Exchange and Board of Trade Building

A-89 Sam Houston Hotel

A-87
Union Station
[now Minute Maid Park]
501 Crawford Street
1911, Warren & Wetmore
2000, HOK Sports Facilities Group

The construction of a new union passenger station and freight yard by the Houston Belt & Terminal Railway Company between 1906 and 1911 drastically altered this section of Houston's Third Ward and precipitated its absorption into the central business district. Warren & Wetmore, the New York architects best known for Manhattan's Grand Central Terminal, produced a block-long station building with a high limestone base surmounted originally by a red brick-faced attic story and a wide, flat, bracketed cornice. Because the need for office space was greater than had been anticipated, two extra floors were added to the building in 1912. Capped by a heavy cornice and balustraded parapet, this addition subverts the original compositional scheme and gives the building a blander appearance than it initially possessed. Finishes and details, however, are superlative. Windows sunk into 2-story vertical channels are separated by steel spandrel panels decorated with exposed bolts in a sort of Beaux-Arts version of high tech. The three-bay Doric portico centered on the Crawford front of the station is a noble porte cochère, vaulted with a ceiling of acoustically resounding Guastavino tile. The double-volume waiting rooms inside, also vaulted, were lit by the thermal windows visible above the porticos. Passenger service was discontinued in 1974.

In 1996 during the administration of Mayor Bob Lanier, Houston voters authorized a $180 million bond issue enabling the newly constituted Harris County-Houston Sports Authority to proceed with real estate acquisition and construction of a 40,950-seat baseball stadium with a retractable roof on the Union Station track site. HOK Sport of Kansas City designed what was, until 2002, called Enron Field. Their design entailed the certified rehabilitation of Union Station as the principal entrance to the stadium. Neo-traditional façade bays of brick and cast stone, scaled to the side elevation of Union Station, line the Texas side of the ballpark, perhaps in expiation for all the genuinely old buildings demolished in this part of Houston during the second half of the 20th century. Above the brick and concrete base looms the immensely scaled steel superstructure of the stadium's retractable roof. Enormous, superimposed trusses bridge the playing field and stadium. The upper trusses support the retractable portion of the roof, enabling the park to have it both ways: open air or air-conditioned. Following the pattern HOK Sport set with its design of Oriole Park at Camden Yards in Baltimore (1992), Minute Maid Park is much more intimate spatially than the Astro's previous home, the Astrodome.

A-88
Houston Cotton Exchange and Board of Trade
[now Harris County Anderson Clayton Building]
1310 Prairie Avenue
1924, Sanguinet, Staats, Hedrick & Gottlieb

Despite the Cotton Exchange's importance in the economy of 19th- and early 20th-century Houston, it erected a very unpretentious 16-story office building when it outgrew its Victorian exchange. The limestone-faced base, with its paired Adamesque pilasters and double-height arched entrance portals on Prairie and Caroline, imbues the building with a decorous presence. Metal-framed casement windows in the central bays of the Prairie façade provided clear north light for grading cotton. The attic zone, elaborately ornamented with cast concrete classical detail, originally contained the vaulted trading room of the Cotton Exchange. Wedged into the crook of the L-plan building is a 2-story parking garage, one of the first to be structurally integrated into a Houston office building. Since 1992 the Cotton Exchange Building has been owned by Harris County, which named it in honor of Anderson, Clayton & Company, the most famous of Houston's cotton exporting firms. From the Prairie-Caroline intersection one can see skylights atop the Westheimer Building at 1217 Prairie (1913, G. W. Collignon), skewed to capture the north light, an indication that cotton exporters occupied the upper floor. Behind the Cotton Exchange, at 515 Caroline, is the charming, 2-story, Italian-Mediterranean style showroom built for the National Cash Register Company (1929, Joseph Finger).

A-89
Sam Houston Hotel
[now Alden Houston Hotel]
1119 Prairie Avenue
1924, Sanguinet, Staats, Hedrick & Gottlieb

The 10-story Sam Houston, midway between Houston's two major train stations when it opened, was a businessmen's hotel with no pretensions to glamour. This is no longer the case since the Spire Group's reinvention of the long-closed hotel as a 97-room boutique hotel, which opened in 2002 (Mitchell Carlson Stone). Under the direction of Alden's Tim Miller, Houston interior architects Whitney & Whitney, making a virtue out of such problematic conditions as a windowless lobby, produced public spaces that are serene, subtle, and sophisticated. New York lighting designer David Lander is responsible for installation of the light work, *Invitation*, in the lobby.

A-90 Texas State Hotel

A-91 Texas Company Building

A-90
Texas State Hotel
[now Club Quarters Hotel]
720 Fannin Street
1929, Joseph Finger

Finger emerged as a specialist in the design of multi-story downtown hotels during the boom years of the 1920s. The 16-story Texas State Hotel was one of his biggest commissions. It featured historically derived decoration (in this case of Spanish plateresque origin) at the base level and the summit. Sandwiched between these layers of terra cotta were sheer walls of tawny tapestry brick. In 2005 the hotel was rehabilitated and reopened as the 250-room Club Quarters (PageSoutherlandPage).

A-91
Texas Company Building
720 San Jacinto Street
1915, Warren & Wetmore

The most princely of Houston's early 20th-century skyscrapers, the 13-story Texas Company Building, is an exceptionally fine example of classical architectural detail applied to a multi-story office block. It was constructed to house the regional offices of Texaco, the first major oil company to establish its headquarters in Houston. The building makes its most notable contribution at ground level, where sidewalks are sheltered beneath grand limestone arcades supported on paired limestone columns armored with bronze bumper guards bearing the Texaco star. The arcades are vaulted with Guastavino tiles. At the top of the building, another screen of paired columns is wrapped around its street faces. The Texas Company Building was extended by three bays along San Jacinto by Warren & Wetmore in 1936. Kenneth Franzheim and Charles S. Chase III added the stylistically respectful annex at 1111 Rusk in 1960. Except for the reglazing of windows in 1975 and transfer of the main entry to the annex, the Texas Company Building was maintained externally without major alteration. Since Texaco moved out in 1989 the building has been vacant.

A-92
U.S. Post Office Building
701 San Jacinto Street
1911, James Knox Taylor, Supervising Architect of the Treasury

The U.S. Post Office and the Texas Company Building mark this block of San Jacinto as a small but triumphant outpost of classical architecture and a testament to the power of the City Beautiful movement at the turn of the 20th century. The office of the Supervising Architect of the Treasury in Washington, D.C., headed by the Minneapolis architect James Knox Taylor, produced designs that adhered to consistently high architectural and construction standards for hundreds of federal government buildings throughout the nation. Other American cities have near duplicates of Houston's elegant, granite-faced, 18th-century-French-style post office. At the time of the building's construction, Rusk had just begun to relinquish its 60-year role as one of Houston's most elite residential avenues, where pillared Greek revival houses and turreted Victorian mansions sat securely in a landscape of mature domestic gardens. The lone street trees on the block just east of the post office, marking the site of the Houston Academy, the town's first public school, are the only natural features in what has become a barren asphalt prairie.

A-92 U.S. Post Office Building

Downtown

93. **Armor Building,** 401 Louisiana Street
94. **Texas Commerce Bank Motor Bank,** 212 Louisiana Street
95. **Market Square Park,** 300 block Travis Street
96. **Kennedy Bakery Building,** 813 Congress Avenue
97. **Kennedy Corner Building,** 218 Travis Street
98. **W. L. Foley Dry Goods Company Building,** 214–216 Travis Street
99. **Houston Cotton Exchange and Board of Trade Building,** 202 Travis Street
100. **Southern Pacific Building,** 915 Franklin Avenue
101. **Commercial National Bank Building,** 917 Franklin Avenue
102. **First National Bank Building,** 201 Main Street
103. **Houston National Bank Building,** 201 Travis Street
104. **Union National Bank Building,** 220 Main Street
105. **Sweeney, Coombs & Fredericks Building,** 301 Main Street
106. **Harris County Courthouse,** Courthouse Square
107. **Harris County Family Law Center,** 1115 Congress Avenue
108. **Harris County Criminal Justice Center,** 1201 Franklin Avenue
109. **Palace Hotel,** 1417 Congress Avenue
110. **Metrorail Red Line Preston Station,** 300 block Main Street
111. **Kiam Building,** 320 Main Street
112. **Cotswold 2000,** 900 block Preston Avenue
113. **Ritz Theater,** 911 Preston Avenue
114. **Scanlan Building,** 405 Main Street
115. **Public National Bank Building,** 402 Main Street
116. **State National Bank Building,** 412 Main Street
117. **Byrd's Department Store,** 420 Main Street
118. **Henry Brashear Building,** 910 Prairie Avenue

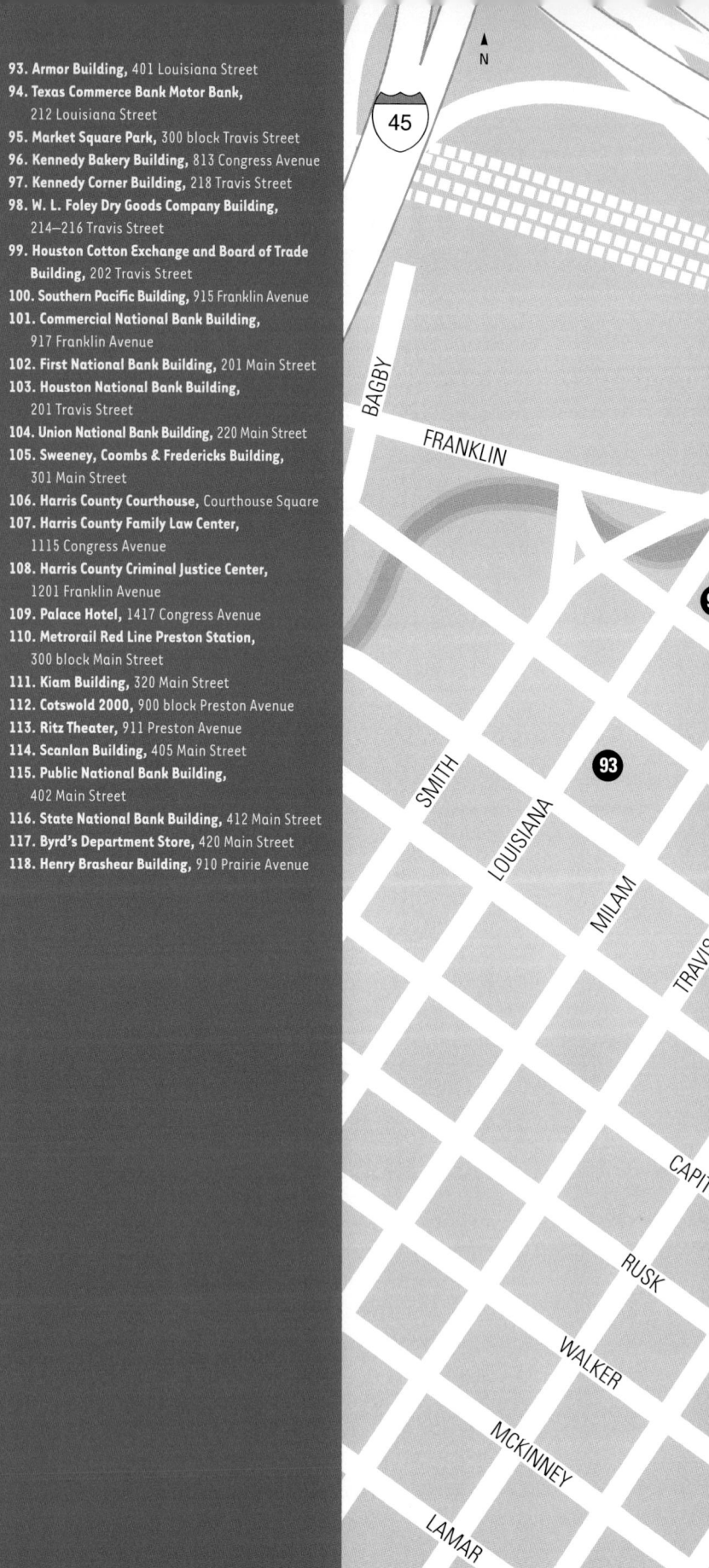

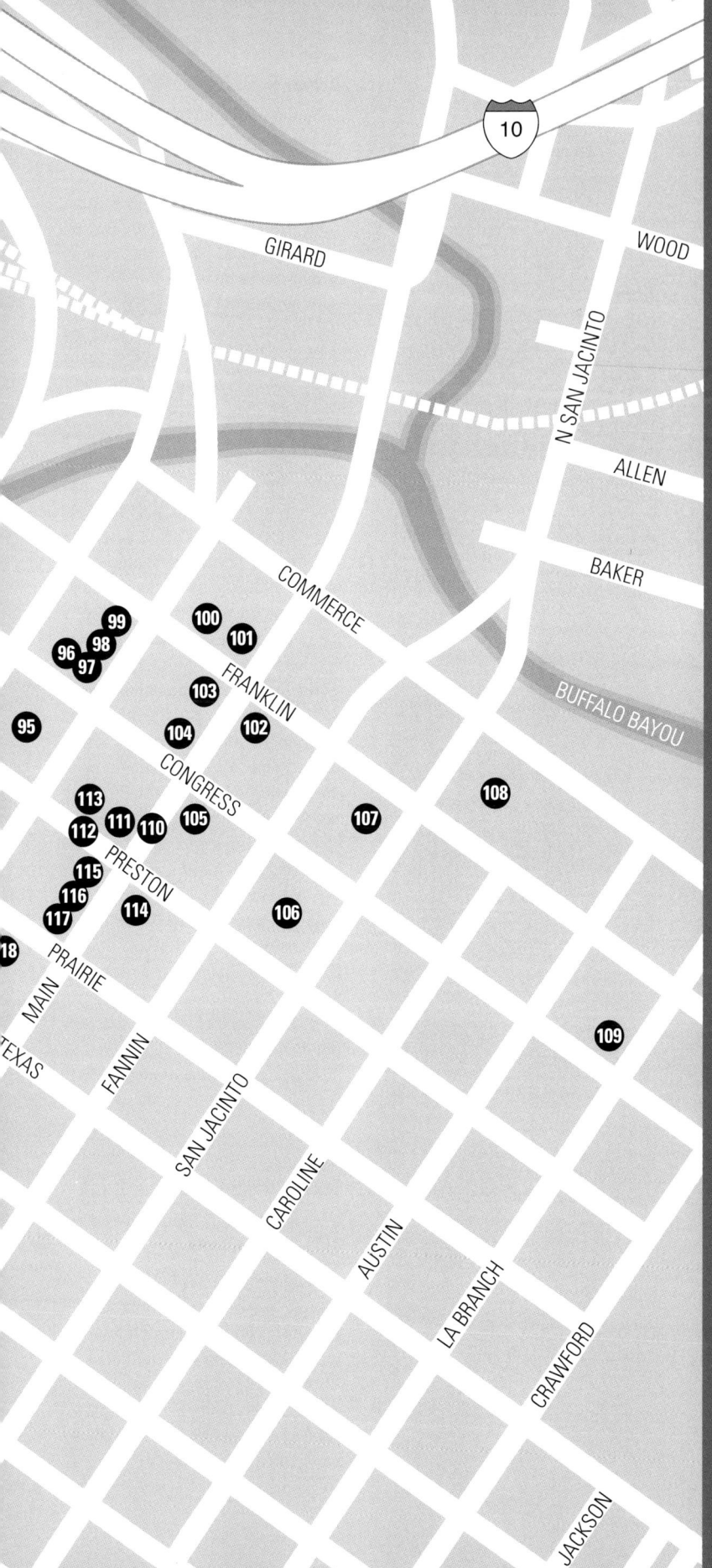

A-93 Armor Building

A-94 Texas Commerce Motor Bank

A-96 Kennedy Bakery Building

A-93
Armor Building
[now Hogg Palace Lofts]
401 Louisiana Street
1921, Barglebaugh & Whitson

Will C. Hogg and his brother, Mike, soon to develop the garden suburb of River Oaks, built the 8-story Armor Building as a combination auto showroom and office building. The street faces of the building acknowledge its reinforced concrete frame with a simple grid of vertical piers and horizontal spandrels infilled with steel-sash industrial windows. The architect, Charles Erwin Barglebaugh of Dallas, had worked for both Frank Lloyd Wright and Walter Burley Griffin just after the turn of the 20th century. The ornamental panels set into the building's piers are in the style of Wright's mentor, the progressive Chicago architect Louis H. Sullivan. On top of the building is a penthouse originally occupied by Hogg brothers and described at the time of the building's completion as a "bungalow in the clouds." Here Will Hogg hung his Frederic Remington paintings above his collection of 17th- and 18th-century American furniture. In 1978 the exterior of the Hogg Building was restored to its original appearance by Harvin Moore-Barry Moore Architects. In 1995 the Randall Davis Company carried out a certified rehabilitation, converting it into the Hogg Palace Lofts, an 80-unit apartment building (Kirksey & Partners).

A-94
Texas Commerce Motor Bank
[now J. P. Morgan Chase Motor Bank]
212 Louisiana Street
1983, I. M. Pei & Partners and 3D/International

A sleekly finished array of drive-in banking stations configured in a pinwheel arrangement. This is where Harry Dean Stanton spotted Nastassja Kinski in Wim Wenders's movie, *Paris, Texas* (1984).

A-95
Market Square Park
300 block Travis Street
2010, Lauren Griffith Associates and Ray + Hollington

Market Square is one of two public squares that the brothers Augustus C. Allen and John K. Allen set aside in their 1836 survey of the City of Houston. From 1840-1929 it was the site of the city's public market and from 1841-1939 site of the city hall. Three ornate Victorian City Hall and Market House structures occupied the square between 1873-1960; all were destroyed by fire. Throughout the 19th century and into the first decades of the 20th, Market Square was the hub for retail grocers, bakers, and butchers in Houston. The square was surrounded by 2- and 3-story brick buildings, most constructed in the decade following the Civil War. The east side of Travis still gives an indication of the scale and architectural detail once characteristic of this neighborhood. In 1986 DiverseWorks and the Downtown Houston Association joined in an effort to transform the square. Two California sculptors, Doug Hollis and Richard Turner, were commissioned to work with three Texas artists—painter Malou Flato, photographer Paul Hester, and sculptor James Surls—to effect the transformation, completed in 1992. But because Market Square failed to attract users, the Houston Parks and Recreation Department, the Houston Downtown Management District, and the Downtown Redevelopment Authority had the Turner-Hollis design demolished in 2010 for a replacement based on a program by the Project for Public Spaces. The redesigned square includes a dog run, a memorial to a Houstonian killed in the attacks of September 11, 2001, and a food kiosk. The 1992 art works remain in the square.

At 301 Travis is the Louis and Anne Friedman Clock Tower (1996, The Mathes Group with Barry Moore) built to contain the market clock from the 1904 City Hall and Market House, the last to occupy Market Square.

A-96
Kennedy Bakery Building
[now La Carafe]
813 Congress Avenue
1861

The narrow, 2-story Kennedy Bakery, the oldest downtown building that has not undergone significant alteration, retains such notable details as the rudimentary classical architrave that crowns its front door and the decorative brickwork visible in its cornice. The interior of what is now a pub is dark, intimate, and full of character. Its ground-floor window looks out toward the towers of downtown, offering a contrast of old and new. Architect Harvin C. Moore first rehabilitated the building in 1960 for the great-grandson of the original owner, Irish immigrant merchant John Kennedy.

A-95 Market Square Park

A-97 Kennedy Corner Building (left)

A-98 W. L. Foley Dry Goods Company Building (center)

A-99 Houston Cotton Exchange

A-100 Southern Pacific Building

A-97
Kennedy Corner Building
[now Hearsay]
218 Travis Street
1889, Eugene T. Heiner

Between 1994-2001 artist Lee Benner, with partners Larry Wilsford and Peter García, personally shored, stabilized, and externally restored what remained of the south half of the Kennedy Corner, built as part of a 4-bay range of 3-story brick buildings about 1860. Seriously damaged by fire in 1888 and reconstructed by Heiner, then turned into a roofless shell by another fire in 1988, Kennedy Corner seemed fated to go the way of the fourth bay of the complex at 220, demolished in 1992. Benner and his associates persevered, re-roofing and re-opening it as the Twelve Spot Bar in 2001. The 1988 fire revealed the ground-floor cast iron columns that separate the structural columns from the frame for the street doors, which Brenner handsomely restored. He also executed the railing that encloses the sidewalk seating area. In 2009 it became the Hearsay bar.

A-98
W. L. Foley Dry Goods Company Building
214-216 Travis Street
1889, Eugene T. Heiner

The *Houston Daily-Post* described the Foley dry goods store, the northern two bays of the original 4-bay range, as "magnificent" and "palatial" at the time of its construction. Heiner detailed the store with High Victorian constructive ornament, including vertical incisions, sunk panels, frieze bands, and arched window heads of brick. The building is of brick bearing wall construction with timber floor structures and interior cast iron columns. It was seriously damaged by fires in 1976 and 1988. In 1995 a group of Market Square loyalists, including preservationist Minnette Boesel, restaurateurs Jamie Mize and Dan Tidwell, art dealer Doug Lawing, and architect Guy Hagstette rehabilitated the Foley Building for mixed commercial and residential use. They preserved such features as the storefronts, sidewalk canopies, and high-set curbs that were once typical of downtown Houston. These tie the Foley Building seamlessly into the adjoining Hermann Estate Building (1917, F. S. Glover & Son) at 204-212 Travis, rehabilitated as a 32-unit apartment building after a 20-year vacancy (1998, Gensler & Associates).

A-99
Houston Cotton Exchange
202 Travis Street
1884, Eugene T. Heiner

This is Houston's outstanding High Victorian building. Erected by the Houston Cotton Exchange to house its quarters, the building sits, Chicago-like, on a high, raised basement. Heiner, one of Houston's foremost 19th-century architects, designed the Cotton Exchange as a vibrant High Victorian version of a Renaissance palazzo. But as American architects of the 1870s and '80s were wont to do, he expressively distorted conventional classical details to elicit contrasts of shape, color, texture, and depth. Hard, red Philadelphia pressed brick, much of it molded and all of it laid with the thin mortar joints typical of the late 19th century, is interspersed with sunk panels of buff brick and incised, carved, or molded blocks of limestone. Originally only three stories high, the building was enlarged with the addition of a fourth story in 1907. At that time the exchange floor was moved to the first floor of the building; it occupied the room at the corner of Travis and Franklin whose painted ceiling is visible through the big plate glass windows. The Cotton Exchange was rehabilitated in 1971 by Graham B. Luhn for preservationists David Hannah and Jesse Edmundson. It is now an office building.

A-100
Southern Pacific Building
[now Bayou Lofts]
915 Franklin Avenue
1911, Jarvis Hunt

The Renaissance palazzo was also the model used by the Chicago architect Jarvis Hunt for this 9-story regional headquarters of the Southern Pacific Railway Company. Hunt's progressive interpretation is so abstract that few overtly classical details are visible: the arabesques that frame the entrance portals and the horizontal bands of moldings at intervals between the second-floor window sills and cornice. Patterned brick pendants and ornamental panels of brick and tile in the building's attic zone take the place of sculptural ornament. The Southern Pacific Building and the Texas Company Building on San Jacinto illustrate the era's contrasting attitudes toward the use of conventional historical detail in tall buildings: progressive Chicago versus eclectic New York. This L-plan building has a reinforced concrete frame. Like several other contemporary tall buildings in Houston, it was originally equipped with a refrigerated air ventilation system. The building was occupied by the Southern Pacific Transportation Company until its merger with the Union Pacific Railroad Company. It was then transformed into the 100-unit Bayou Lofts (1999, Gabriel Architects) for the Spire Realty Group.

A-101 Commercial National Bank Building

A-102 First National Bank Building

A-101
Commercial National Bank Building
917 Franklin Avenue
1904, Green & Svarz

This 6-story buff brick building, with its rounded corner bay, was one of the first in Houston to display the return to classical architecture that succeeded the picturesque eclecticism of the Victorian era. Especially notable are the trio of colossal arched openings centered on the Franklin and Main façades. This was the first skyscraper built in the financial district on lower Main Street. The building is of cage construction: load-bearing masonry perimeter walls envelop an interior steel frame. It was rehabilitated in 2001 by Kaldis Development Interests and 917 Franklin Land Ltd. (PageSoutherlandPage).

A-102
First National Bank Building
[now The Corinthian and Franklin Lofts]
201 Main Street
1905, 1909, Sanguinet & Staats;
1925, Sanguinet, Staats, Hedrick & Gottlieb

From 1866-1956 the First National Bank, the first chartered bank in Houston, occupied this corner. In 1904 the bank replaced its small, 2-story building with the first steel-framed skyscraper in Houston. This 8-story building was a long, narrow sliver. Its Main frontage included only the 25-foot-wide corner bay at Main and Franklin; the additional two bays along Main were not added until 1909. In 1925 a third major addition carried the building through the block to Fannin. A double-height banking hall, installed in 1925, runs the entire depth of the building. Its detailing is rather coarse in comparison to the opulently classical, rusticated exterior, where the building's limestone base and buff brick, stone-trimmed shaft hold the Main- Franklin corner with authority. All three phases of the building program were carried out by the Houston branch office of the Fort Worth architects, Sanguinet & Staats. Marshall R. Sanguinet and Carl G. Staats were the skyscraper kings of early 20th-century Texas. In 2002 a certified rehabilitation of the building by Frank Garvey and caterer Jackson Hicks transformed the majestic banking hall into The Corinthian, a special events space, and the upper floors into 62 condominium apartments (Kurt Aichler).

A-103
Houston National Bank Building
[now Islamic Da'wah Center]
201 Travis Street
1928, Hedrick & Gottlieb

The last of the bank buildings constructed in the Main Street financial district was this formidable neo-Classical block. Wyatt C. Hedrick, the Fort Worth architect who succeeded to Sanguinet & Staats' practice in 1926, and his Houston partner, R. D. Gottlieb, made up in massiveness and scale what they gave up in potential height. Rusticated limestone walls bracket screens of fluted Doric columns on the building's street façades. High steel sash windows behind these screens are shielded by tall bronze railings. The frieze and cornice atop the building are ornamented with sculptural decoration. The interior is as awesome as the exterior: the ceiling of the 56-foot-high banking hall is a single vault finished with mosaic tile murals. Visible from the rear, on Travis, is a miniature temple on the building's roof, which framed the bank's original proto-air-conditioning equipment. Hedrick clearly gave his father-in-law, Ross S. Sterling, the bank's chairman, the most that money could buy. The vacant building was bought by Nigerian-American basketball star, Hakeem Olajuwon, and under his direction transformed into the Islamic Da'wah Center. The banking hall is now a mosque.

A-103 Houston National Bank Building

A-104 Union National Bank Building

A-105 Sweeney, Coombs & Fredericks Building

A-104
Union National Bank Building
[now Hotel Icon]
220 Main Street
1912, Mauran, Russell & Crowell

The Main Street base of this 12-story, reinforced concrete framed building is detailed like a Roman commemorative arch with freestanding Corinthian columns of Bedford limestone supporting ressauted architraves. The keystones above the arched ground-floor openings are carved with the likeness of Mercury, Roman god of commerce (and trickery). The office floors above the 2-story base are faced with buff brick and topped with screens of alternating piers and pilasters. On the Congress face of the building, the detail is flatter and more compressed. Mauran, Russell & Crowell were St. Louis architects with an extensive Texas practice. Most of their Houston work was done for Jesse H. Jones, a director of the Union National Bank. In 2004 the Randall Davis Companies opened the 135-room Hotel Icon in the former bank building. Mitchell Carlson Stone were restoration architects, J. K. Wagner & Company was preservation consultant, and Candra Scott & Associates of San Francisco were responsible for the theatrical interiors that take maximum advantage of the grand ground-floor banking hall.

A-105
Sweeney, Coombs & Fredericks Building
301 Main Street
1889, George E. Dickey

This narrow, 3-story building is one of the two surviving Houston works of George Dickey, the city's most spirited Victorian architect. The Main Street façade features a corner turret, arched upper-floor windows, molded brickwork, and thick, flat, constructive ornament. Its intensity contrasts so jarringly with the plain Congress flank that preservationists speculate Dickey reused parts of the W. A. Van Alstyne

Building (constructed on this site in 1861) in the Sweeney Building. Rehabilitated by Welton Becket & Associates in 1968, it was almost demolished in 1974 by the Harris County Commissioners to provide a site for the adjacent, 9-story Harris County Administration Building (1978, Kenneth Bentsen Associates and Brodnax Phenix Associates). The court was persuaded to spare the building, and it has been rehabilitated. Behind it, at 1016 Congress, is the Pillot Building (c. 1860), once a 3-story brick business block. All that remains of the original is the ground-floor cast iron storefront. The rest is a reconstruction (1990, Morris*Architects with Barry Moore Architects).

A-106
Harris County Courthouse
Courthouse Square
1910, Lang & Witchell

The county courthouse, either domed or turreted and set in a centrally located, tree-shaded square, is a recurring feature of the Texas landscape. The Allen brothers reserved this block, two blocks east of Market Square, as the site for a county courthouse, and it has been occupied by the Harris County government since 1837, when the congress of the Republic of Texas designated Houston as the county seat. This domed, classical courthouse is the fifth to stand in the square. Although superseded by a newer courthouse in 1952, it remains the focal symbol of county government. Lang & Witchell, Dallas's most prolific architects at the turn of the 20th century, won out over local competitors for the job in 1907. A dome and columns were specified by the commissioners court. Lang & Witchell's progressive, Chicago-trained designer, Charles Erwin Barglebaugh, revealed his preference for something less conventional in the Wrightian detailing of the piers between windows in the attic story. In 2011 the Harris County Courthouse was restored under the auspices of the Texas Historical Commission's Texas Historic Courthouse Preservation Program. Alterations from the 1950s carried out to convert the courthouse into the civil courts building were demolished, and Lang & Witchell's interiors were reconstructed. PGAL and preservation specialists ArchiTexas of Dallas were restoration architects.

A-106 Harris County Courthouse

A-107 Harris County Family Law Center

A-107
Harris County Family Law Center
1115 Congress Avenue
1969, Wilson, Morris, Crain & Anderson

This 7-story office and courtroom building is the architect's homage to Skidmore, Owings & Merrill's American Republic Insurance Company Building in Des Moines. The upper floors are constructed of widely cantilevered, prestressed, precast tees, neatly balanced on pyramidally shaped steel hinges atop the ground-floor columns. Window glass is inset deeply within the concrete frame. This is the finest modern addition to the complex of county government buildings that cluster around Courthouse Square. Walter A. Quebedeaux Plaza at Congress and San Jacinto, in front of the Family Law Center, was the original site of the Nichols-Rice-Cherry House now in Sam Houston Park. In 2007 the Harris County Commissioners Court proposed demolishing the Family Law Center once a new and larger replacement was completed because the commissioners consider it an architectural eye sore.

A-108 Harris County Criminal Justice Center

A-108
Harris County Criminal Justice Center
1201 Franklin Avenue
1999, PGAL

The neo-Art Déco style of the Justice Center was perhaps intended to mitigate the building's purpose, while giving it an "official" look. From North San Jacinto, its shaped tower figures as an urban landmark. Far more problematic architecturally is the 17-story Harris County Civil Courthouse at 201 Caroline (2005, PGAL). Its distortion of the conventions of classical architecture constitutes cruel and unusual aesthetic punishment. The city block bounded by Caroline, Congress, San Jacinto, and Franklin is now Transportation Plaza, a park built above the subterranean Harris County Jury Assembly Center (2011, PageSoutherlandPage).

A-108 Harris County Civil Courthouse

A-110 Metrorail Red Line Preston Station

A-109
Palace Hotel
1417 Congress Avenue
1903

This 3-story brick building with rock-faced cast concrete trim and a chamfered corner entrance bay stands in for the shredded fabric of early 20th-century downtown Houston. Perhaps as a reward for just surviving, it was preserved and rehabilitated by Harris County and developers Jerry Patchen and Avi Ron in 2005 in conjunction with construction of the Civil Courthouse and its adjoining garage (Urban Architecture). Bruce Fehr was preservation architect, and Anna Mod was preservation consultant.

A-110
Metrorail Red Line Preston Station
300 block Main Street
2004, PGAL and M2L Associates

Although it took the public transit authority nearly 20 years to secure consensus on the value of rail-based public transit, the initial 7.5-mile Red Line has exceeded ridership estimates since going into operation in 2004, and Metro will have four cross-town lines in operation by 2013. In addition to providing an alternative mode of transit, the Red Line revolutionized urban design in downtown Houston. The handsome stations by PGAL, each incorporating works of public art (artist Tim Glover is represented at the Preston Station), the planted medians, expanded sidewalks, narrowed streets, and brick paving by landscape architect Michael P. Mauer of M2L Associates—all coordinated with the Houston Downtown Management District—give Main Street a room-like quality it did not have prior to the light rail line.

A-109 Palace Hotel

A-111 Kiam Building

A-112 Cotswold 2000

A-113 Ritz Theater

A-111
Kiam Building
320 Main Street
1893, H. C. Holland

Ed Kiam's clothing store set a new standard in Houston. Its 5-story red brick building, featuring a bull-nose corner bay and a concave entrance alcove, ushered in the era of downtown urbanity on Main that would prevail through the middle of the next century. Holland was an obscure English-born architect who practiced only briefly in Houston. He carefully differentiated the end bay on Preston to mark the access point to the upper office floors. He also battered the thick brick piers along this side of the building, highlighting their structural role. The Kiam Building was restored in 1981 by Barry Moore Architects. Next door, at 314-16 Main, behind the neon rays of the Home of Easy Credit, lies the Kiam Annex (1893), which has been preserved internally—rather than reconstructed—by performance artist Jim Pirtle as his "anti-scrape" protest against the commercialization of historic restoration. In the middle of the block, attorney Scott Arnold uncovered and rehabilitated what was left of the façade of the Sweeney & Coombs Building at 310 Main (1880, Eugene T. Heiner) in 1998. The trio of buildings at 308, 306, and 304 Main are the Stuart Buildings (1880). Each originally exhibited slight variations in their Victorian neo-Grec ornament. Such distinctions were not emphatic enough for the Guaranty National Bank, which refaced the middle building at 306 in a restrained classical style (1924, Alfred C. Finn). Anchoring the end of the block is the Sterne Building at 302 Main Street (1916, Green & Finger).

A-112
Cotswold 2000
900 block Preston Avenue
2005, 2006, The SWA Group and
RdlR Architects

In 1996 construction corporation official Leo F. Linbeck III commissioned San Francisco landscape architects Peter Walker & Partners to produce a plan for transforming 79 downtown blocks between Buffalo Bayou and Texas with expanded sidewalks, tree-lined streets, a canal along Congress, and a centralized parking authority that would generate the revenue to maintain this ambitious public landscape. In 1998 the project was turned over to the Houston Downtown Management District, which coordinated public infrastructure improvements with the City of Houston. The SWA Group and Rey de la Reza Architects expanded sidewalks along east-west avenues and incorporated angled parking to radically change the experience of walking along downtown streets. At Main and Preston and at Main and Congress, Dallas artist Brad Goldberg installed *Houston Waters* (2006), combining grooved stone stele with serpentine water channels. Cotswold has not magically transformed Houston; its wide, tree-lined sidewalks still pass entire block fronts of surface parking. But it has accomplished what intelligently designed infrastructure ought to do: it provides a frame of generously scaled public space, in conjunction with Metro's redesign of Main Street, that new development can fill in and flesh out.

A-113
Ritz Theater
[now Majestic Metro]
911 Preston Avenue
1926, William Ward Watkin

Houston's three great movie palaces of the 1920s—the Majestic, Metropolitan, and Loew's State—were demolished in the 1970s. From that era this side-street theater alone remains. Watkin's office gave it a delicately ornamented classical façade finished in stucco. In 1991 entrepreneur Gary Warwick rehabilitated the exterior and transformed its interior, *sans* theater seats, into the Majestic Metro, a special events space.

A-114
Scanlan Building
405 Main Street
1909, D. H. Burnham & Co.

The 11-story Scanlan Building was the tallest in Houston at the time of its completion. It was built by Kate Scanlan and her sisters as a memorial to their father, T. H. Scanlan, an Irish-born real estate and utilities investor who had been Houston's Reconstruction-era mayor. Miss Scanlan retained Daniel H. Burnham of Chicago to design the building, which exhibits finely crafted classical ornament at its base, "Chicago" windows (a fixed pane of plate glass between two operable sash windows) on the second floor, and a series of terra cotta wreaths stationed between attic windows. Its broadly projecting rooftop cornice is now gone. On this site Sam Houston's official residence, grandly called the President's House, was completed in 1838. After the national capital was transferred to Austin in 1839, the President's House became a retail store. In 2002 the Scanlan Building was rehabilitated by Kaldis Development Interests and 405 Main Land Ltd. (Stinson Design Group).

A-114 Scanlan Building

A-115 Public National Bank Building

A-116 State National Bank Building

A-117 Byrd's Department Store

A-115
Public National Bank Building
[now 402 Main Building]
402 Main Street
1925, James Ruskin Bailey

During the 1920s the financial district began to slide southward up Main as several new bank buildings, among them the Public National Bank, were constructed outside the confines of the old Victorian banking corridor. This is a restrained, classically detailed office block. Arched windows mark the ground floor and what was originally the topmost floor, which is ringed by a cantilevered balcony. Bailey added the setback ninth floor to the building in 1928.

A-116
State National Bank Building
412 Main Street
1924, Alfred C. Finn

This 12-story building is a slender infill tower with a rooftop penthouse capped by a tile-roofed lantern and flanked front and back by broad terraces. The rusticated pink granite base was reconstructed when the building was rehabilitated in 1982 (Stuart L. Rothman).

A-117
Byrd's Department Store
[now Byrd's Lofts]
420 Main Street
1934, Joseph Finger

Simon and Tobias Sakowitz, founders of Sakowitz Brothers, built this 3-story retail building as an investment. Finger reproduced the chamfered-corner retail building type but designed the austere Main and Prairie elevations with modernistic planes of Texas cream limestone recessed to accept thin steel sash glazing. Seventy years after its completion, the building was rehabilitated as a mixed-use residential and retail complex by Ray + Hollington for Houston general contractor Robert Fretz, whose grandfather built Byrd's. Diagonally across Main from

Byrd's is the Isis Theater Building at 510 Main (1912, C. D. Hill & Co.), rehabilitated by Gabriel Architects for the Spire Group in 1999.

A-118
Henry Brashear Building
910 Prairie Avenue
1882, Eugene T. Heiner

Tucked in behind the Rice Hotel is another Victorian survivor, a narrow, but exuberant, 3-story commercial building. The fine stucco-surfaced façade and cast iron cornice again reveal Heiner's predilection for a constructive deconstruction of Renaissance classicism. The Brashear Building was restored in 1992 by Guy Hagstette and Randle Pace. Next door are the Scholibo Building (912 Prairie, 1880) and the Stegeman Building (502 Main, c. 1879). Across the street the exterior of the defaced Roco Building (c. 1870) at 419 Travis was extensively reconstructed in 1998 by Goulas & Associates. As part of the Cotswold urban design program, artist Elena Cusi Wortham installed *Movement* at Prairie and Travis, which courses off the back of the Post Rice Lofts garage

A-118 Henry Brashear Building

Downtown

119. **Siewerssen and Hogan-Allnoch Buildings,** 800–806 Commerce Avenue
120. **Magnolia Cafe Building,** 715 Franklin Avenue
121. **U.S. Post Office,** 401 Franklin Avenue
122. **Merchants and Manufacturers Building,** 1 North Main Street
123. **Allen's Landing Park,** 1001 Commerce Avenue
124. **Texas Packing Company Building,** 1119 Commerce Avenue
125. **Peden Company Building,** 610 North San Jacinto Street
126. **City of Houston Willow Street Pump Station,** 811 North San Jacinto Street
127. **Henry Henke's Fifth Ward Store,** 1200 Rothwell Street
128. **Erie City Iron Works,** 1302 Nance Street and 1311 Sterrett Street
129. **James Bute Paint Company Warehouse,** 711 William Street
130. **McKee Street Bridge,** McKee Street and Buffalo Bayou
131. **National Biscuit Company Building,** 15 Chenevert Street
132. **Grocer's Supply Company Building,** 101 North Jackson Street
133. **Western Electric Company Building,** 1610 Commerce Avenue
134. **New Hope Housing,** 320 Hamilton Street

Downtown

Tour A-4

A-119 Siewerssen and Hogan-Allnoch Buildings

A-120 Magnolia Café Building

A-121 U. S. Post Office

A-119
Siewerssen and Hogan-Allnoch Buildings
800-806 Commerce Avenue
1894 and 1906

The little Siewerssen Building and the Hogan-Allnoch Building, with its wide-spanning arches, were conjoined in a rehabilitation (1975, Wilson/Crain/Anderson/Reynolds) that transformed them into law offices.

A-120
Magnolia Cafe Building
[now Magnolia Ballroom]
715 Franklin Avenue
1911, Cooke & Company

A rhythmically bracketed cornice and upswept corner parapet mark the Magnolia Cafe Building, originally part of an extensive brewery complex that spanned Buffalo Bayou. The cafe was located on the second floor; its handsome decor is still intact. The building was rehabilitated in 1968 by owner-architect Bart Truxillo. Next door to the cafe building, at 110 Milam, is the company's 3-story cold storage and packing building (1906, Cooke & Company). Its rear section was washed away in the flood of 1935, and it stood in this condition until 1999, when the building was dramatically transformed into a private residence, and the jagged bayou elevation was encapsulated with a rippling glass curtain wall.

A-121
U.S. Post Office
401 Franklin Avenue
1962, Wilson, Morris, Crain & Anderson

Nominally part of the Civic Center, the main post office lies on the north side of Buffalo Bayou, isolated from its environs by street intersections, freeways, parking lots, and railroad tracks. It was built on the site of what had been, since 1886, the Southern Pacific Railway's Grand Central Station (Amtrak passenger trains still serve a bus-stop-like station behind the post office). The 5-story administration building, a slab set on columns and faced with white, precast concrete fins, projects the clean, detached look of 1960s modern American architecture. In 2009 the United States Postal Service began the process of soliciting proposals for replacement of this complex, which would entail sale of the 16-acre site and demolition of the post office building.

A-122
Merchants & Manufacturers Building
[now University of Houston-Downtown]
1 North Main Street
1930, Giesecke & Harris

This enormous 11-story building, designed by a firm of Austin architects in the modernistic Perpendicular style, was constructed to serve as the Merchandise Mart of Houston. Before it was completed, its fate was sealed economically by the great flood of May 1929 and the stock market crash five months later. Since 1974 the M & M Building has been the campus of the University of Houston-Downtown. Charles Tapley Associates contributed the jazzy exterior repainting and also converted the south parking deck into a terrace, with pedestrian access to Buffalo Bayou down below. In 1997 the 8-story Academic/Student Life Building was added to the west side of the building by Rey de la Reza Architects. The university's Shea Street Building (PGAL and Natex Corporation), a 4-story classroom building, was completed on North Main between Shea and Naylor in 2007.

A-122 Merchants & Manufacturers Building

A-123 Allen's Landing Park

A-124 Texas Packing Company Building

A-125 Peden Company Building

A-123
Allen's Landing Park
1001 Commerce Avenue
2001, The SWA Group

Through the early 1900s, this was Houston's public wharf area at the foot of Main Street, which expanded westward into the 900 block of Commerce (today a surface parking lot). Across Buffalo Bayou, beneath the Houston & Texas Central Railway trestle, White Oak Bayou empties into Buffalo. Houston's founders, A. C. and J. K. Allen, claimed this confluence of waterways as the head of navigation on Buffalo Bayou and staked the future of their town site on this claim. At Buffalo Bayou, Main Street is deflected off-axis to cross the bayou on the high, arched Main Street Viaduct (1913, F. L. Dormant, City Engineer), the largest single-arch, concrete span (150 feet) in Texas at the time of its construction. The Houston Chamber of Commerce reclaimed half the wharf east of Main for a park, called Allen's Landing, in 1967 (W. H. Linnstaedter, architect). After part of the 1967 car turn-around on the bank fell into the bayou, the Buffalo Bayou Partnership took on the task of rescuing the area. Kevin Shanley and The SWA Group restructured the sloping site with a long flight of stairs (replacing the 1967 auto driveway) that descend to a paved bulkhead lined with steel mooring bollards. A concrete retaining wall is inscribed with selected passages from the text of an 1836 advertisement with which the Allen brothers sought to attract settlers to their new town of Houston. The retaining wall secures a raised shelf of land occupied by the International Coffee Company Building (1910). Across Commerce from the park at 1 Main Street is the University of Houston-Downtown Commerce Street Building, a 4-story academic building (2005, Gensler).

A-124
Texas Packing Company Building
[now Open 24/7/365 Store]
1119 Commerce Avenue
1924, Joseph Finger

This concrete-framed, brick-faced, 1- and 2-story building is not as impressive at street level as it is when seen from the Fannin or San Jacinto bridges over Buffalo Bayou. There are three additional floors beneath street level; the lowest contains a water-gate dock for bayou barge traffic. This pattern is repeated at the Central Warehouse and Forwarding Company Building at 1201 Commerce (1927) with three of its nine floors below street level. Now owned by Harris County, the Central Warehouse is slated to be demolished as is the county-owned Gordon, Sewall & Company Building—aka the Coffee Pot Building—at 102 San Jacinto (1913, Sanguinet, Staats & Barnes). Demolition of these historic buildings by Harris County will destroy the last increment of the commercial waterfront along Buffalo Bayou and Produce Row, where wholesale grocers and other food-related businesses clustered after the International & Great Northern Railroad freight line was built along Commerce in 1902. The San Jacinto Street Bridge (1914, F. L. Dormant, City Engineer) over Buffalo Bayou is a condensed version of the Main Street Viaduct.

A-125
Peden Company Building
[now Harris County Peden Community Correction Facility]
610 North San Jacinto Street
1930, James Ruskin Bailey

One of the last major buildings constructed in the Fifth Ward "factory district" was this 4-story retail store and administration building for the Peden Iron & Steel Company, whose extensive wholesale hardware operations were located across Baker in the 1-story Peden Wholesale Building with arched openings (700 North San Jacinto, 1906, C. H. Page & Company, demolished by Harris County 2011). Bailey designed the Peden Building in the modernistic Perpendicular style. Like other buildings along the bayou, it was constructed with levels below the street that could be served by commercial barges. In the 1990s Harris County moved aggressively into the Factory District to expand its correctional empire. Across North San Jacinto, the 9-story, red brick and white-trimmed warehouse is a radical reconstruction of the 5-story Houston Terminal Warehouse and Cold Storage Building (1927) into a second Harris County Jail (1991, Morris Architects) housing 4,000 inmates. To placate public indignation about the damage to prospects for urbanizing the confluence of White Oak and Buffalo bayous this inflicted, the county and the Harris County Flood Control District had Tapley/Lunow landscape the downward slopes of White Oak Bayou and install stepped concrete quays along its banks, making the edge of the water easily accessible. Just below the jail, the arch of the Main Street Viaduct frames a spectacular prospect of Buffalo Bayou.

A-126 City of Houston Willow Street Pump Station

A-127 Henry Henke's Fifth Ward Store

A-128 Erie City Iron Works Warehouse

A-129 James Bute Company Warehouse

A-126
City of Houston Willow Street Pump Station
[now University of Houston-Downtown Willow Street Pump Station]
811 North San Jacinto Street
1902, Alexander Potter, consulting engineer

Marking an important infrastructural milestone, this was Houston's first sewage lift pump station, part of a system designed by Potter, a New York engineer, to improve water pollution conditions on Buffalo Bayou, which were imperiling efforts to secure aid from the U.S. government for navigational improvements to Buffalo Bayou. The pump house was subsequently joined by a crematory (trash incinerator—therefore the smokestack). The complex's two original buildings, the Storage Building and the Pump House, are built of red pressed brick with thin mortar joints. The molded brick arches are especially impressive. In 2003 UH-Downtown completed rehabilitation of these buildings for art exhibitions and gatherings, adding the metal-roofed building to the south (Gensler).

A-127
Henry Henke's Fifth Ward Store
[now North San Jacinto Cafe]
1200 Rothwell Street
1883

A rare Victorian survivor in this section of Fifth Ward, this branch of Henry Henke's Market Square grocery store predated development of the Factory District. Next door at 1206 Nance is the Fifth Ward Hotel (1883), the ground floor of what was once a 3-story building. It was rehabilitated in 2002 and since 2003 has been the studio of mArchitects.

A-128
Erie City Iron Works Warehouse
1302 Nance Street and
1311 Sterrett Street
1909

This showroom and warehouse for a wholesale machinery agent is of arcuated brick bearing-wall construction, which shows to special advantage at the chamfered entrance bay at Nance and Richey and in the array of full-arched openings on the Sterrett side of the building. In the 2000s it was converted into live-work studios.

A-129
James Bute Company Warehouse
[now Dakota Lofts]
711 William Street
1910, O. J. Lorehn

Occupied until 1990 by the paint manufacturing and sales company for which it was built, this 4-story brick building was the largest warehouse in Houston at the time of its completion. In 1993 real estate developer Randall Davis converted the Bute warehouse into apartments, sparking the conversion of loft buildings to residential use that became one of the major phenomena of downtown Houston real estate in the 1990s.

A-130
McKee Street Bridge
McKee Street and Buffalo Bayou
1932, James Gordon McKenzie,
City Bridge Engineer

During his tenure as bridge engineer for the City of Houston, McKenzie put ingenuity back into engineering. The undulating concrete girders bracketing the roadway expressively reveal the distribution of structural forces in their shapes, moment curves that rise above the piers beneath the roadway. Artist Kirk Farris coordinated the colorizing of the bridge and extensive landscape improvements to both the north and south banks of the bayou in 1985.

A-130 McKee Street Bridge

A-132 Grocer's Supply Company Building

A-133 Western Electric Company Building

A-134 New Hope Housing

A-131
National Biscuit Company Building
[now CityView Lofts]
15 Chenevert Street
1910, A. G. Zimmerman

This 5- and 6-story brick and terra cotta-faced, concrete-framed building is the most monumental in the Second Ward wholesale district, made more so by its corner stair tower. Zimmerman, Nabisco's corporate architect, produced similar structures for the firm in Kansas City and New York. The Chenevert facility served as the company's southwest headquarters for baking, packaging, and shipping cookies until 1949, when Nabisco sold the property to Purse and Co., a wholesale furniture dealer. The building was designated a City of Houston Landmark in 1998. Cisneros Design Studio converted the building into the 57-unit CityView Lofts in 2008.

A-132
Grocer's Supply Company Building
101 North Jackson Street
1941, Joseph Finger

Finger's streamlined modernistic Grocer's Supply Company headquarters, occupying a full block front on North Jackson, was the last major wholesale company building constructed in the Wholesale District.

A-133
Western Electric Company Building
1610 Commerce Avenue
c 1915

This 3-story warehouse retains its original high-set sidewalk and canopy. The architectural offices of Stern and Bucek, occupying the ground floor, reveal the building's historic fabric. At the west end of the block is the 3-story Eller Wagon Works Building at 1606 Commerce (1909), which subsequently became part of the Pittsburgh Plate Glass Company complex, including the 3-story building at 101 Crawford that PPG built in 1920 (Alfred C. Finn).

A-134
New Hope Housing
320 Hamilton Street
1995, 1998, Jackson & Ryan Architects

New Hope Housing, a nonprofit organization founded in 1993, constructed this single-room-occupancy, affordable-housing complex, which contains 129 fully-furnished units. This was the first purpose-built SRO in Houston.

A-131 National Biscuit Company Building

Fourth Ward / Midtown / Montrose

Fourth Ward / Midtown / Montrose

Tour B

Houston is a city of boundless optimism. Yet this very expansiveness can have paradoxical spatial repercussions. Since everything seems possible and there are no public planning mechanisms to encourage the concentration of efforts toward any particular purpose or in any particular locale, activity is diffused. Where it ultimately will collect is unpredictable, and land-use patterns are so volatile that long-term stability cannot be taken for granted even when concentrations do occur. Main Street in Midtown illustrates this predicament. It was once Houston's most fashionable residential street, then its most fashionable suburban retail corridor. Now so few vestiges of either of these episodes survive that it is difficult to envision South Main in either role. It remains a street of great potential, but there are many such streets in Houston. Montrose Boulevard, to the west, has undergone a similar evolution. The Montrose Addition and surrounding neighborhoods succeeded Main Street as the city's elite residential area in the early 20th century. Most of these subdivisions were protected by restrictive covenants intended to guard against commercial encroachment and its destabilizing consequences. However, the inability

of Montrose to resist these economic forces meant that the boulevard has relived the history of Main Street.

Whether in a city where change is the constant urban assets can be consolidated and expanded is questionable. North of the Montrose neighborhoods lies the community now called Fourth Ward, the oldest African-American settlement in Houston. Fourth Ward was until the mid 1990s the antithesis of the popular image of Houston. It embodied everything the city is supposed to lack: tradition, history, stability, and a rooted community culture. But because it was African American and poor, Fourth Ward endured official neglect for most of its history, yet it was, as the novelist, Olive Hershey, observed, "the soul of Houston."

1. **San Felipe Courts,** 1400 Allen Parkway
2. **Federal Reserve Bank of Dallas Houston Branch Building,** 1801 Allen Parkway
3. **American General Building,** 2727 Allen Parkway
4. **Star Engraving Company Building,** 3201 Allen Parkway
5. **Rein Company Building,** 3401 Allen Parkway
6. **Adams Architects Studio and House,** 717 Rochow Street
7. **Clarke & Courts Building,** 1210 West Clay Avenue
8. **One-Two Townhouses,** 608 Stanford Street
9. **Houses,** 1501–19 Victor Street
10. **Gregory Elementary School,** 1300 Victor Street
11. **Buckley Lofts,** 1316 Cleveland Street
12. **Yates House,** 1314 Andrews Street
13. **Temple of Rest, Beth Israel Cemetery,** 1207 West Dallas Avenue
14. **House,** 1105 West Webster Avenue
15. **House,** 2802 Albany Street
16. **DePelchin Faith Home,** 2710 Albany Street
17. **Post Midtown Lofts,** 302 Gray Avenue
18. **Kirby House,** 2000 Smith Street
19. **First City Motor Bank Building,** 2111 Fannin Street
20. **Houston Typewriter Exchange Building,** 2201 Caroline Street
21. **Waggaman House,** 2218 Caroline Street
22. **Gallery Sonja Roesch,** 2309 Caroline Street
23. **Gibraltar Building,** 2302 Fannin Street
24. **Knoll Building Houston,** 2301 Main Street
25. **Fire Station No. 7,** 2325 Milam Street
26. **Duff House,** 2421 Milam Street
27. **Lovett Square,** 401 Anita Avenue
28. **Swenson Studio,** 3106 Brazos Street
29. **Transcontinental Gas Pipeline Corporation Building,** 3100 Travis Street
30. **Pacific Mutual Life Insurance Company Building,** 2701 Fannin Street
31. **Jennings Cleaning and Dyeing Building,** 3000 Caroline Street
32. **Cohen Building,** 2935–2925 Main Street
33. **Southwestern Bell Telephone Company Building,** 3100 Main Street
34. **Houston Telephone Employees Federal Credit Union Building,** 3303 Main Street
35. **Trinity Episcopal Church,** 3415 Main Street
36. **Holy Rosary Catholic Church,** 3601 Milam Street
37. **LaMont Apartments,** 3704 Travis Street
38. **South End Junior High School,** 1300 Holman Avenue
39. **First Evangelical Lutheran Church,** 1311 Holman Avenue
40. **Temple Beth Israel,** 3517 Austin Street
41. **Richardson House,** 3307 Austin Street
42. **Magnificat House Children's Chapel and Retreat,** 3300 Caroline Street
43. **Southwestern Bell Telephone Company Building,** 3333 Fannin Street
44. **Houston Light Guard Armory,** 3816 Caroline Street
45. **Isabella Court,** 1003–1005 Isabella Avenue
46. **South Main Baptist Church,** 4000 Main Street
47. **Monotech Gallery,** 4411 Montrose Boulevard
48. **Sterling House,** 4515 Yoakum Boulevard
49. **Phillips Studio and Townhouses,** 4204 Yoakum and 1105–07 Colquitt
50. **Central Church of Christ,** 4100 Montrose Boulevard
51. **The Court at Museum's Gate,** 4004 Montrose Boulevard

◀ Map continues on next spread

Fourth Ward / Midtown / Montrose

52. **Link House,** 3800 Montrose Boulevard
53. **Par IV and Parc V,**
    3614 and 3600 Montrose Boulevard
54. **Fondren House,** 3410 Montrose Boulevard
55. **Annunciation Hellenic Eastern Orthodox Church,**
    3520 Yoakum Boulevard
56. **Hille House,** 804 Hawthorne Avenue
57. **Hamman House,** 802 Lovett Boulevard
58. **Courtlandt Place Wall,**
    Brazos Street and Courtlandt Place
59. **Autry House,** 5 Courtlandt Place
60. **Cleveland House,** 8 Courtlandt Place
61. **Dorrance House,** 9 Courtlandt Place
62. **Neville House,** 11 Courtlandt Place
63. **Carroll House,** 16 Courtlandt Place
64. **Donoghue House,** 17 Courtlandt Place
65. **Garrow House,** 19 Courtlandt Place
66. **Taylor House,** 20 Courtlandt Place
67. **Jones House,** 24 Courtlandt Place
68. **Nazro House,** 25 Courtlandt Place
69. **Westfall House,** 303 Hawthorne Avenue
70. **Nash House,** 215 Westmoreland Avenue
71. **Waldo House,** 201 Westmoreland Avenue
72. **Lightfoot House,** 3702 Audubon Place
73. **Cohen House,** 607 Kipling Street
74. **Holland House,** 3820 Roseland Avenue
75. **The 505,** 505 West Alabama Avenue
76. **High School for the Performing and Visual Arts,**
    4001 Stanford Avenue
77. **University of St. Thomas,**
    3812–3910 Yoakum Boulevard
78. **Rothko Chapel,** 1409 Sul Ross Avenue
79. **Byzantine Fresco Chapel Museum,**
    4011 Yupon Street
80. **Menil Foundation Business Office,**
    1427 Branard Avenue
81. **Cy Twombly Gallery,** 1501 Branard Avenue
82. **The Menil Collection,** 1515 Sul Ross Avenue
83. **Zemanek House,** 1723 Colquitt Street
84. **Forty-eight Foot House,** 1851 Lexington Avenue
85. **De Santos Gallery,** 1724 Richmond Avenue
86. **House,** 4409 Mt. Vernon Street
87. **House,** 1418 Kipling Street
88. **House,** 1625 Harold Street
89. **Conn House,** 1802 Missouri Avenue
90. **Parra House,** 2323 Yupon Street
91. **Handmade House,** 1608 Indiana Street
92. **Hyde Park Double,**
    1212–1216 Hyde Park Boulevard
93. **Mirabeau B. at Hyde Park,** 2410 Waugh Drive
94. **Tower Theater,** 1201 Westheimer Road
95. **Montrose Townhouse Lofts,**
    2602–2608 Montrose Boulevard
96. **L'Encore,** 415 Hyde Park Boulevard
97. **Houston Lighting & Power Hyde Park Substation,** 100 block Tuam Avenue
98. **House,** 1225 Jackson Boulevard
99. **Jiménez Studio,** 1116 Willard Street
100. **Jiménez House,** 1115 Willard Street
101. **Zemanek House,** 1117 Peden Street
102. **House,** 1306 Eberhard Street
103. **Art League of Houston Building,**
     1953 Montrose Boulevard
104. **Montrose Veterinary Clinic,**
     1701 Montrose Boulevard
105. **Welch City Residences,** 2107 Converse,
     805–07 Welch, and 2106–08 Crocker

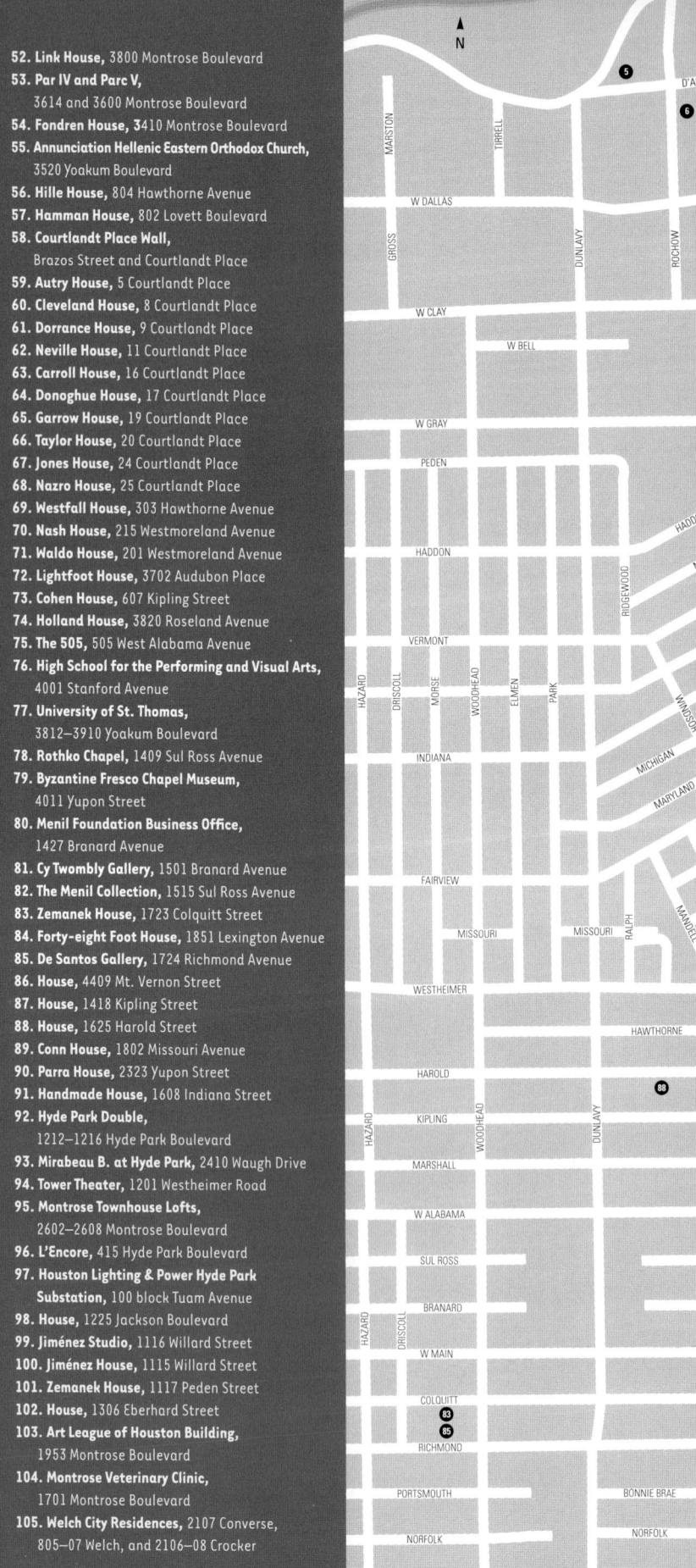

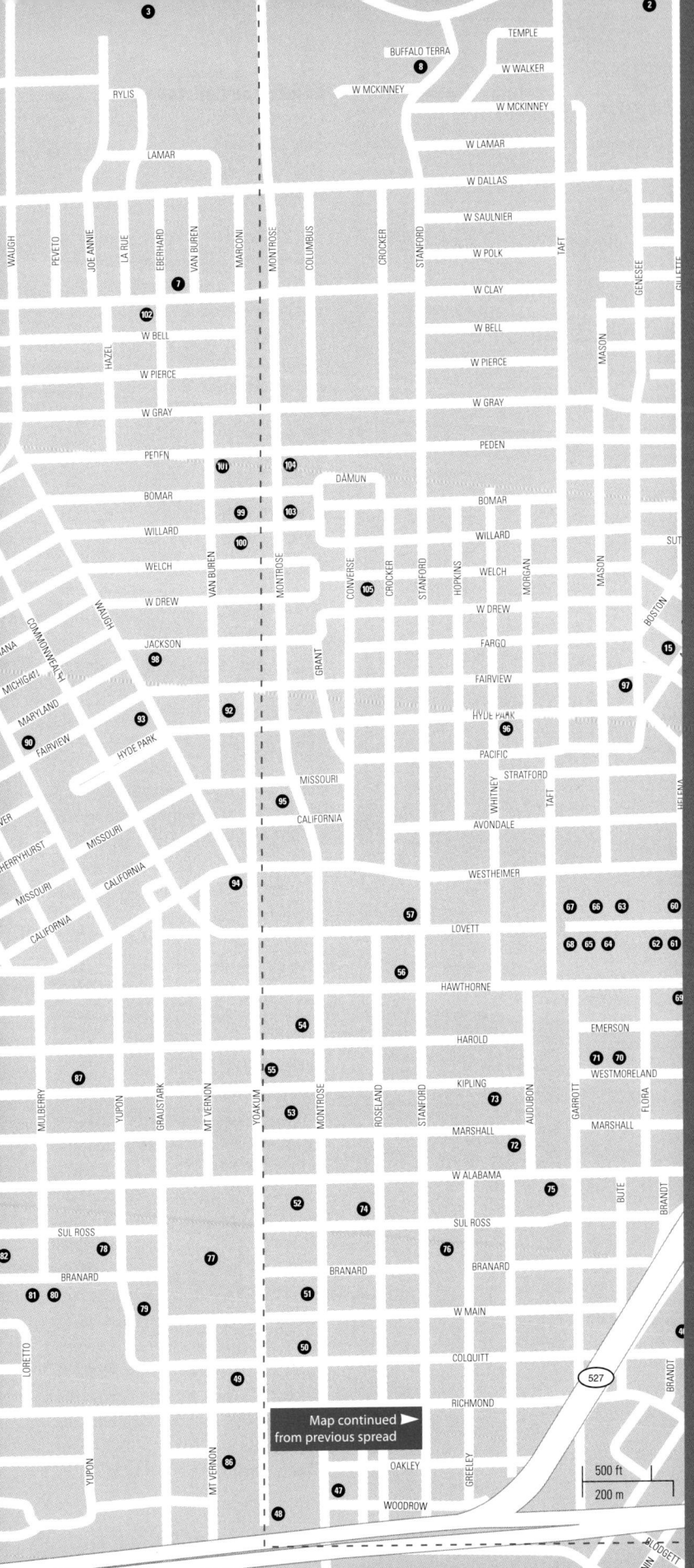

B-1 San Felipe Courts

B-1
San Felipe Courts
[now Allen Parkway Village]
1400 Allen Parkway
1942, 1944, Associated Housing
Architects of Houston

Buffalo Bayou Parkway, a "pleasure drive" now called Allen Parkway, was built between 1925-1926 to the designs of Kansas City landscape architects, Hare & Hare. It ran from Sam Houston Park westward along Buffalo Bayou to the newly planned garden suburb of River Oaks, skirting Fourth Ward, Houston's oldest African-American neighborhood. Once Fourth Ward was exposed to the view of the elite, its continuing existence became a civic problem. This was solved in 1940 by clearing the historic houses on 37-acres adjoining the parkway and replacing them with San Felipe Courts, the largest United States Housing Authority (USHA) financed, low-income public housing project constructed in the South during the 1940s. It was also one of the most outstanding architecturally, due to the participation of MacKie & Kamrath as designers for Associated Housing Architects, a consortium of 12 Houston firms. San Felipe Courts' precisely defined contours, cantilevered concrete canopies, and artful brick and tile banding represented a much higher standard of design and detailing than was customary for USHA housing. The landscape architect, J. Allen Myers, Jr., laid out an avenue of Live Oaks to define the center spine and densely planted gardens between the apartment blocks on either side of the oak allée. From 1942-1964, San Felipe Courts was restricted to Caucasian occupancy. Not until the 1970s was the complex (which had a high vacancy rate in the 1950s and early '60s) fully occupied for the first time since the 1940s, principally by African-American families. This coincided with the decision by city officials to depopulate the complex and sell the property for redevelopment. From 1978-1996 public housing residents resisted. In

1987 residents, led by tenant council president, Lenwood Johnson, had the complex listed in the National Register of Historic Places as a historic district of exceptional national significance. Nonetheless, with the acquiescence of the Texas Historical Commission and the Advisory Council on Historic Preservation, 70% of the complex was demolished in 1996, and the remaining 30% was gutted. Replacement construction took the form of wood-stud apartments and townhouses in mawkish styles (1999-2000, Rey de la Reza Architects). The ratio of paved space to green space in the formerly park-like setting was reversed. What remained of San Felipe Courts became a security-gated enclave named the Historic Oaks of Allen Parkway Village.

B-2
Federal Reserve Bank of Dallas Houston Branch Building
1801 Allen Parkway
2005, Michael Graves & Associates and PGAL

The sprawling complex of the Federal Reserve Branch Bank of Dallas replaced Jefferson Davis Hospital, the Public Works Administration-financed public health hospital (1937; demolished 1999). The postmodern architect Michael Graves secured this commission by indicating his willingness to design the complex in a "southwestern" style. The gable fronted, 4-story main building evokes a classical temple front. Thin cylindrical concrete piers and striation of the red brick facing with bands of blue brick, suggesting mortar joints between blocks of stone, advance Graves's effort to devise a personal analogue to classical architecture. Alongside the main building, facing Allen Parkway, the Currency Vault is surfaced with tile the color of money. The ceremonial front entrance is marked by Kent Ullberg's bronze eagle, *The Guardian*. Visitors park in a 300-car on-site garage and enter the main building from the rear. Graves's firm designed the interiors. The playfulness of Graves's style does not cohere with the solemnity to which his crypto classicism aspires. Clark Condon Associates was the landscape architect. Across Allen Parkway from the hospital, on the crest of a low hill, sits Henry Moore's bronze, *Large Spindle Piece*, (1968, 1974) installed in 1979.

B-2 Federal Reserve Bank of Dallas Houston Branch Building

B-3 American General Building

B-4 Star Engraving Company Building

B-5 Rein Company Building

B-3
American General Building
[now Wortham Tower]
2727 Allen Parkway
1965, Lloyd, Morgan & Jones

The 25-story American General Building was the first in a complex of office buildings developed by the American General Life Insurance Company during the 1960s, '70s, and '80s. Arthur Jones designed the tower to stand on a terrace plinth concealing the parking garage, above the rolling terrain alongside the bayou. The glass curtain wall is recessed behind a precast concrete grid, giving the tower its light, clean, '60s modern look. Other buildings in the complex are the 6-story American General Life Building (1979, Lloyd Jones Brewer & Associates) behind the Wortham Tower, the 15-story LNG-Liberty Tower at 2711 (1977, Lloyd Jones Associates), the 15-story Riviana Building at 2731 (1974, Lloyd Jones Associates), and the 42-story America Tower at 2929 (1983, Lloyd Jones Brewer & Associates). The American General Building remains the best.

B-4
Star Engraving Company Building
[now 3201 Allen Parkway Building]
3201 Allen Parkway
1930, R. D. Steele

Perched atop a bluff overlooking the parkway, this Spanish-style printing plant looks far better today than it must have when new. The snappy color combinations are particularly effective. Mainland Building and Development Group was responsible for the building's recycling as offices, temporary quarters for the Children's Museum, and the repertory theater, Stages (1985, W. O. Neuhaus Associates). In 1992 the City of Houston acquired the Star Engraving Company Building to prevent its demolition and ensure its continued use as an art center. Will Hogg, the developer of River

Oaks, had assisted the city with land acquisition for the parkway in the 1920s, and he was determined that no inappropriate land use occur along its length. Hogg had no legal jurisdiction, but his influence must have been considerable, for the three printing plants built along the parkway in the late 1920s each adapted Spanish-Mediterranean attributes to conceal their industrial status. The area itself was euphemistically described as the "crafts district."

B-5
Rein Company Building
[now Clocktower Building]
3401 Allen Parkway
1928, Howell & Thomas

The Rein Company, designed by a firm of Cleveland architects that specialized in printing plants, clearly distinguished the 2-story office and advertising studio wing from the single-story plant wing. The clock tower is the pivot point about which both the building and the parkway drive rotate. Charles Tapley Associates was responsible for the building's conversion into a savings and loan institution in 1976. Threatened with demolition in the early 2000s (the fate of the Rein Co.'s architectural companion, the Gulf Publishing Company Building, replaced by the 33-story Royalton at River Oaks; 2003, Steinberg Design Collaborative), the Rein Building was acquired and preserved by Maloney, Martin & Mitchell, WLS Interests, and Southcorp Realty Advisors, which had the Cisneros Design Group rehabilitate the building (2004). Across D'Amico, to the rear, is the round-towered Stedman Studio (3327 D'Amico, 1927), built by a commercial artist as his studio and residence.

B-6
Adams Architects Studio and House
717 Rochow Street
1991, Adams Architects

Built on a small corner lot, the house and architectural studio Gail and Joe Adams designed for themselves is a suggestive model for how inner-city neighborhoods might be urbanized with hybrid live-work buildings that respect the scale and character of their surroundings. That Houston developers in the 1990s chose a different path is oppressively evident just across Rochow.

B-6 Adams Architects Studio and House

B-7 Clarke & Courts Building

B-8 One-Two Townhouses

B-9 Shotgun Houses

B-11 Buckley Lofts

B-7
Clarke & Courts Building
[now Tribeca Lofts]
1210 West Clay Avenue
1936, Joseph Finger

The continuous horizontal bands of steel sash windows, bulbous horizontal speed lines, curved corners, and, above all, the stepped-back pylon tower with architecturally integrated graphics make this one of the modernistic highlights of Finger's career. The building, a commercial printing plant, is built entirely of reinforced concrete. In 1993 it was rehabilitated by developer Randall Davis as an apartment building.

B-8
One-Two Townhouses
608 A-B Stanford Street
2007, FdM: Arch

Developer Carol Isaak Barden had the New York architect François de Menil design a pair of intensely white tower houses for this peninsular site in the Temple Terrace neighborhood. Stacking the thin 3-story-plus-rooftop-terrace houses above street-level garages, Menil produced a tense relationship of interlocking volumes, accentuated with narrow horizontal strip windows and expansive projecting window bays with views of the downtown skyline.

B-9
Shotgun Houses
1501-1519 Victor Street
1914, 1920-22

This row of cottages lies in Fourth Ward, the neighborhood on the west edge of Houston where emancipated slaves settled in the late 1860s. Of the housing types associated with African-American urban settlement in the South, the shotgun cottage is the best known. It is usually a long, narrow, 1-story house prefaced by a porch. Its rooms are lined up in single file with all doorways aligned. The traditional explanation of the term "shotgun" is that if one fired a shotgun through the front door, the pellets would pass straight through the house and out the back door. This row of ten identical shotgun cottages, which seems to have been built in phases, is an illustration of the remarkable urban impact that such simple vernacular houses can have when grouped in series. Comprising about 90 blocks, the Fourth Ward once extended as far north as Buffalo Bayou (San Felipe Courts sits on what was the original site of Freedmantown, as it was originally spelled) and as far east as Smith, where an institutional center existed around Antioch Baptist Church. West Dallas (the original San Felipe) was the main business corridor. Neighborhood residents under the leadership of Gladys House succeeded in having half of Fourth Ward listed in the National Register of Historic Places as the Freedmen's Town Historic District in 1985. This retarded, but ultimately did not stop, the destruction of the district and displacement of its low-income residents during the administration of Mayor Bob Lanier in the mid-1990s. By the turn of the 21st century, the Freedmen's Town National Register Historic District had largely been rebuilt with townhouse complexes and clusters of single-family houses constructed by community development corporations. The narrow width of Fourth Ward's streets preserves its spatial distinctiveness.

B-10
Gregory Elementary School
[now African-American Library at the Gregory School]
1300 Victor Street
1926, Hedrick & Gottlieb
2010, Smith & Company Architects

The City of Houston bought Gregory Elementary School, successor to the first Gregory Institute building constructed by the Freedmen's Bureau in 1870 at a different location, and had Terry Smith rehabilitate it as the Houston Public Library's African-American research library and interpretive center. Smith filled the shallow rear courtyard of the 2-story, U-plan brick building with a double-height, glass-walled lobby accessible from the parking court on Cleveland. Exhibitions on Houston's African-American history are installed in the former first-floor classrooms.

B-11
Buckley Lofts
1316 Cleveland Street
2009, Studio 333

Slotted side-by-side onto a single lot, these four row houses by architect Charles Toomey stand out by virtue of their planar economy, decisive proportions, and dark green exterior rainscreens.

B-10 Gregory Elementary School

B-12 Yates House

B-13 Beth Israel Cemetery, Temple of Rest

B-14 House

B-16 Depelchin Faith Home

B-12
Yates House
[now Rutherford B. H. Yates Museum]
1314 Andrews Street
c. 1912

Built by Houston's first African-American commercial printer, Rutherford Yates, this late Victorian cottage was restored by community activist Catherine Roberts in 1997-98 to demonstrate the feasibility of rehabilitating Fourth Ward's historic housing stock rather than obliterating it. Curtis & Windham were restoration architects. Across the street at 1319 Andrews is the substantial raised cottage of the Rev. Ned P. Pullum, pastor of Bethel Baptist Church and owner of a brickyard. At 1218 Wilson at Andrews is Van Court, home of the lawyer J. Vance Lewis (1908). Andrews contained some of the most substantial houses remaining in Fourth Ward until wholesale demolition began in the mid 1990s. They contrasted markedly with the towers of downtown Houston, which at this point loom dramatically over the neighborhood.

B-13
Beth Israel Cemetery Temple of Rest
1207 West Dallas Avenue
1935, Joseph Finger

Finger's modernistic classicism takes on an appropriately funereal note in this limestone-faced mausoleum. It is situated in Beth Israel Cemetery (originally Hebrew Cemetery), the oldest Jewish institution in Texas. The cemetery was founded in 1844, 10 years before the organization of Congregation Beth Israel, the oldest Jewish congregation in Texas. Next to Beth Israel is Founders Memorial Park (originally City Cemetery), where John K. Allen, one of the founders of Houston, is buried. Like other early cemeteries, Beth Israel and Founders were located on the outskirts of the Houston townsite, in this case along the main highway to San Felipe de Austin, another pioneer Anglo-American settlement, on the Brazos River.

B-14
House
1105 West Webster Avenue
2007, Rodrigo Tovar

In the midst of the depressing construction that replaced the vernacular landscape of Fourth Ward, this tower house stands out by virtue of the contrast between its white stucco facing and a wall plane of brilliant orange.

B-15
House
280? Albany Street
2005, Metropolitan Design Group

Of steel frame construction faced with concrete block, this courtyard house by architect-developer Su Nguyen opens dramatically to its walled enclosure through folding walls of glass.

B-16
DePelchin Faith Home
[now Villa Serena]
2710 Albany Street
1913, Mauran & Russell

The Italianate imagery of this graceful building perhaps owed something to the new buildings of the Rice Institute. It was built as an orphanage. Above the arcaded loggia across the ground floor were two floors of sleeping porches—originally screened—and wide, bracketed eaves. After DePelchin Faith Home vacated the building in 1938, it went through many uses. In 2002 it was rehabilitated by HHN Homes to become a 15-unit apartment building. Kaldis Development Interests were historical consultants and the Spencer Partnership was architect.

B-15 House

B-17 Post Midtown Square Lofts

B-19 First City Motor Bank Building

B-20 Houston Typewriter Exchange Building

B-17
Post Midtown Square Lofts
302 Gray Avenue
2000, RTKL

In 1994 the City of Houston authorized the Midtown Redevelopment Authority/Tax Increment Reinvestment Zone No. 2 to promote new development in what was previously called the South End—neighborhoods flanking Main between downtown to the north and the Museum District to the south. At the turn of the 20th century, the South End was Houston's most elite residential neighborhood. But lack of deed restrictions mandating single-family occupancy meant that, as the city's economy and population expanded in the 1910s and '20s, the South End became a magnet for apartment development and the extension of the downtown retail district. Of new development after the mid-1990s, the most interesting is Post Properties' 4-block Midtown Square. The buildings, mostly 4-story, are organized around communal courtyards, housing is stacked above ground floor retail, parking is integrated with residential, and the redevelopment authority's expanded, brick-paved sidewalks, planted with cypress trees, add up to a home-grown version of a New Urbanist, livable, walkable city. In Houston, however, this charming illusion persists for only two blocks in any direction.

B-18
Kirby House
[now Philip Azar Law Office]
2000 Smith Street
1926, James Ruskin Bailey

Houston is a city of surprises. Here, next to the Pierce Elevated Freeway (I-45), at the edge of downtown, is a picturesquely massed, opulently decorated, neo-Jacobean country house in excellent condition. The house was built for John Henry Kirby, a lawyer, lumberman, and entrepreneur from East Texas, who emerged at the turn of the 20th century as Houston's first tycoon. He and his family had lived on this site since 1897, but in 1925 they replaced their florid Victorian house with this rambling, 36-room, English manor house, retaining part of the old building's fabric because, it was said, Kirby was superstitious about living in a totally new house. Since 1948 the Kirby House has been used as an office building, but its major reception rooms have been preserved. The house was rehabilitated in 1978 by oilman Thomas C. Thompson. Unfortunately the once-famous gardens have been converted to surface parking lots.

B-19
First City Motor Bank Building
[TJK Investments Building]
2111 Fannin Street
1983, Sikes Jennings Kelly

As is apparent from the Gray or Webster sides of this building, Frank Kelly organized it in section, then extruded it laterally across the block to provide a double-fronted, but offset arrangement of drive-in stations served by tellers inside the central spine. Curved corners, a glossy white aluminum panel wall system, and green glass gave this building a refreshingly cool look. After the failure of First City National Bank, the motor bank sat vacant and deteriorating until it was turned into a sleek convenience store, car wash, gas station, and fast food restaurant in 1998. This illustrates the process of urbanization, as high style corporate architecture is colonized by homely but useful small business ventures.

B-20
Houston Typewriter Exchange Building
2201 Caroline Street
1956, Joseph Krakower

As the nutty plaster soffit indicates, something is awry with what, at first glance, seems to be a prosaic commercial building. Herb Greene, Krakower's designer, was responsible for injecting this touch of whimsy into the building type—brick-faced, windowless, and flat-roofed—with which Houston was relentlessly suburbanized in the 1950s. At 1218 Webster is the former Benjamin Apartments (1920, Alfred C. Finn), rehabilitated as an office building in 2000 by preservationist Patrick Van Pelt.

B-18 Kirby House

B-21 Waggaman House

B-22 Gallery Sonja Roesch

B-23 Gibraltar Building

B-24 Knoll Building Houston

B-21
Waggaman House
2218 Caroline Street
c. 1904

Rehabilitated in 1997 this house exemplifies the type of 2-story, clapboard-surfaced house that once filled the expansive, middle income, South End neighborhoods. The rock-faced plaster cement work at the base of the porch was very popular in Houston in the 1905 period. Across the street at 2222 Austin is a small housing complex that has been carefully inserted into its fractured setting (1997, Courtney Harper & Partners). In its architectural modesty and responsive site planning, it contrasts markedly with the bulk of new developer housing built in the South End in the late 1990s.

B-22
Gallery Sonja Roesch
2309 Caroline Street
2002, Bluebox Architekten Rösch Schubert Hanisch

The Würzburg-based firm of Bluebox Architects designed this combination live-work building for art dealer Sonja Roesch. The gallery is located on the ground floor, parallel to Caroline. The building's "live" component is a 2-story bar balanced atop the gallery component.

B-23
Gibraltar Building
[now University of Houston Small Business Development Center Network]
2302 Fannin Street
1959, Greacen & Brogniez
with J. Victor Neuhaus III

The 5-story Gibraltar Building is a minor modern landmark; it was the first building in Houston to have walls faced entirely in heat absorbing, solar gray glass. Raymond H. Brogniez incorporated drive-in windows beneath the building; the double-volume banking hall occurred on the second floor. The building was originally lit at night to reveal its internal sectional organization. The Fannin front and the south-facing side walls have been refaced in silver reflective glass, and both the double-height banking hall and the interiors by Knoll Associates have vanished.

B-24
Knoll Building Houston
2301 Main Street
1984, Tigerman Fugman McCurry with Ray Bailey Architects

Stanley Tigerman's transformation of an old auto showroom into a showplace of corporate design included the application of a snappy red grid to the exterior and a superimposed "negative" pediment to mark the main entrance. The parking lot is a *cour d'honneur,* studded with trees and more axially-aligned virtual pediments. The interior is much less exceptional, despite a skylight that parallels the central runway, changes in floor level, and wavy cross walls. Knoll left its building in 1995; it housed a charter school until 2010.

B-25
Fire Station No. 7
[now Houston Fire Museum]
2325 Milam Street
1899, Olle J. Lorehn

The oldest fire station remaining in city ownership, Fire Station No. 7 was built to serve the South End neighborhoods that flanked upper Main Street. Rough-faced cast stone trim contrasted with smooth pressed brickwork and the decorative roundels above the square-headed stall openings were characteristic of Lorehn. Since 1982 the building has contained a museum documenting the history of the Houston Fire Department. The Fire Museum was rehabilitated by Austin architects Volz & Associates in 1997.

B-25 Fire Station No. 7

B-26 Duff House

B-27 Lovett Square

B-28 Swenson Studio

B-29 Transcontinental Gas Pipeline Corporation Building

B-26
Duff House
[now Hoang Vu CPA]
2421 Milam Street
1911, George Freuhling

The house that Freuhling designed and built for Mr. and Mrs. R. C. Duff was once a South End showplace, famous for the international musical celebrities whom Mrs. Duff entertained and the terraced formal gardens, which extended to the corner of McGowen and Travis. The Colonial revival house originally faced McGowen; it was turned to face Milam and moved to one corner of its site in 1937, when the property was subdivided. Duff built the 3-story Sheridan Apartments across McGowen at 2603 Milam in 1922. They are typical of the many apartment buildings constructed in the South End suburbs along the trolley lines that tied the area to the downtown core. Across Milam from the Duff House was another grandiose neighborhood landmark, St. Paul's Methodist Church (1909, R. D. Steele and E. J. Fountain). The domed classical building later became Second Baptist Church; it was demolished in 1969. In 1995 the Duff House was remodeled for use as a professional office building. In 1998 it was surrounded by The Park at Midtown, a 3-block, 335-unit apartment complex (Wallace/Garcia & Associates), a painful example of inner-city residential construction lacking the urban consciousness its site demands, but which appears restrained when contrasted with developer-built housing of the 2000s.

B-27
Lovett Square
401 Anita Avenue
1978, William T. Cannady & Associates

Architect Cannady envisioned Lovett Square as a low-rise, high-density prototype for the devastated neighborhoods of the South End. Thirty-six condominium units are organized around six courtyards, which are stepped in section to give access to units entered at the second level; all units open to a landscaped common that traverses the center of the block. Parking is confined to grade level with direct access to all units. The stucco-surfaced buildings were constructed without architectural supervision and show it. An unenthusiastic market response, coupled with escalation of real estate values in the area, discouraged replication of Lovett Square. When new housing began to be built in the tax reinvestment zone after 1994, it followed less urbanistically conceived models.

B-28
Swenson Studio
3106 Brazos Street
1958, Swenson & Linnstaedter

Bailey A. Swenson's own house was a tower, 20 feet square in plan that sandwiched two levels of living space between a ground-floor patio and a fourth-floor roof garden. The house was tacked on in a very spontaneous way to an old garage-apartment building that contained Swenson's studio. At various times, the building was the studio of Donald Barthelme, the André Emmerich Gallery, and, from the late 1950s to the mid-1960s, Houston's most vanguard gallery, New Arts, operated by Swenson's wife, Kathryn. Like Lovett Square, the Swenson studio-townhouse remains the single example of a potential prototype.

B-29
Transcontinental Gas Pipeline Corporation Building
[now High Fashion Building]
3100 Travis Street
1951, Zimmerman & Bible

Transco's former home is a windowless 3-story box (the top floor is a later addition) that relied upon central air-conditioning and fluorescent lighting for total environmental control. The patterned façades, horizontally banded brick framed with panels of limestone, suggest a measure of design desperation over how to cope with windowlessness, an anxiety perhaps shared by the occupants. The highlight of the building is Edward Z. Galea's relief panel above what was the Travis entrance. In 2005 George Levan had Gensler perform a sympathetic rehabilitation of the building as a fabric and design emporium, High Fashion.

B-30
Pacific Mutual Life Insurance Company Building
2701 Fannin Street
1960, Neuhaus & Taylor

This was the first in a series of 1-story office buildings straddling their own parking lots that Neuhaus & Taylor produced—a distinctly Houston building type. Here the glass walls are screened by cantilevered fascia panels.

B-30 Pacific Mutual Life Insurance Company Building

B-31 Jennings Cleaning and Dyeing Shop

B-33 Southwestern Bell Telephone Company Building

B-34 Houston Telephone Employees Federal Credit Union Building

B-35 Trinity Episcopal Church

B-31
Jennings Cleaning and Dyeing Shop
[now 13 Celsius]
3000 Caroline Street
1926

Entrepreneurs Ian Rosenberg and Doug Sammons rescued a defunct dry cleaners and had Infill Planning and Development transform it into a neighborhood wine bar in 2005.

B-32
Cohen Building
2935-2925 Main Street
1929, Joseph Finger

The upper end of the Main Street residence district was redeveloped in the 1920s with 1-story commercial buildings, "taxpayers" in the jargon of the time. Finger's building for Ben Cohen was both more elaborate than others and considerably more exotic. Contemporary newspaper reports described it as detailed in the Chinese style.

B-33
Southwestern Bell Telephone Company Building
[now Houston Community College Administration Building]
3100 Main Street
1965, George Pierce-Abel B. Pierce and Wilson, Morris, Crain & Anderson

This 12-story office building seems to float above the Main-Elgin intersection by virtue of its projecting horizontal trays, which shade recessed glass curtain walls. It exemplifies what historian Michelangelo Sabatino describes as the "heat-and-light" approach of 1960s architecture in Houston, using sunlight and shadow to regionalize modern design without, of course, sacrificing the comfort of air-conditioning.

B-34
Houston Telephone Employees Federal Credit Union Building
[now Communications Federal Credit Union Building]
3303 Main Street
1979, Urban Architecture and Sanders & Sanders

This is an intelligently conceived modern building that acknowledges its responsibilities to both function and site. Architects Hossein Oskouie and Paul Martin carefully adjusted the cast-in-place concrete frame, infilled with recessed walls of dark solar glass, to respond to particularities of solar orientation and internal spatial organization. The grand stairway and the raised terrace facing Main pay tribute to the importance of the street and simultaneously shield at-grade parking. Unfortunately the later replacement of an adjoining building with the motor bank has left the raised terrace awkwardly stranded in midair.

B-35
Trinity Episcopal Church
3415 Main Street
1919, Cram & Ferguson and William Ward Watkin

The Boston architect Ralph Adams Cram first made his mark on American architecture in the 1890s with suburban parish churches rendered in a suave neo-Gothic style. Trinity, his Houston example of the type, was designed in collaboration with his former employee, William Ward Watkin. Trinity demonstrates that Texas Anglicans commanded more limited resources than their coreligionists in the northern United States. Nonetheless its limestone facing, pinnacled Ralston Memorial Tower (1921), and lofty, simply finished interior give it the reassuringly churchly look that Cram championed. The sculptor Oswald J. Lassig executed the altar and reredos (1920). Cram and Watkin's parish house at Fannin and Holman burned down. Its replacement (1949), as well as additions grouped around the courtyard to the north (1951), are by Cameron D. Fairchild. The Visitors Center is by Environment Associates and Hall/Merriman (1993). The interior of the church was restored by Hall/Barnum Architects in 1997.

B-32 Cohen Building

B-36 Holy Rosary Catholic Church

B-37 La Mont Apartments

B-38 South End Junior High School

B-39 First Evangelical Lutheran Church

B-36
Holy Rosary Catholic Church
3601 Milam Street
1933, Maurice J. Sullivan

Holy Rosary is one of Sullivan's finest churches, a disciplined neo-Gothic parish church finished externally with Texas limestone and crowned by a slender copper flèche. Holy Rosary's prismatic massing and substantial, but carefully proportioned, planar composition show the impact of Ralph Adams Cram's former partner, the New York architect Bertram G. Goodhue, whose "modern" interpretation of traditional styles powerfully affected American architecture during the 1920s. Sullivan was also responsible for the rectory, facing Travis behind the church. Oswald J. Lassig executed the sculpture in the tympanum above the front door and the altar.

B-37
La Mont Apartments
[now Berg & Androphy Building]
3704 Travis Street
1919

The 3-story, 6-unit La Mont Apartments feature stacked solarium front porches, oriented to the morning light and the prevailing breeze. The top two floors have been imaginatively remodeled to serve as law offices (1988, William F. Stern & Associates).

B-38
South End Junior High School
[now San Jacinto Memorial Building, Houston Community College Learning Resources Center]
1300 Holman Avenue
1914, Layton & Smith

One of Houston's most imposing City Beautiful landmarks, South End Junior High School (subsequently San Jacinto Senior High School), is a monumental 3-story classical block. A screen of limestone Doric columns is framed by pedimented end bays in the style of the 18th-century Parisian architect Ange-Jacques

Gabriel. Alongside these end pavilions are modernistic setback towers with sculptural figures sprouting from the tops of piers, parts of two symmetrical additions made in 1928 (Hedrick & Gottlieb) and 1936 (Joseph Finger). Subsequent additions fail to do the complex justice. The *cour d'honneur,* which terminates Caroline, has been turned into a parking lot. The Oklahoma City architects Layton & Smith won this commission in competition; they would go on to design the Oklahoma State Capitol. Kirksey designed the 4-story, glass-faced Learning Hub and Science Building bounding the east side of the central court in 2007.

B-39
First Evangelical Lutheran Church
1311 Holman Avenue
1927, Joseph W. Northrop, Jr.

Despite his apprenticeship with Ralph Adams Cram, Northrop tended toward a rather mechanical treatment of the Lombard Romanesque, as the adaptation of the medieval brick architecture of northern Italy was known during the 1920s. A neat touch is the setback upper stage of the campanile; it evokes the skyscraper profiling that traditionalists used in the 1920s to connote modernity. The First Evangelical Church, which moved to the South End from downtown, was founded in 1851. It is the oldest Lutheran congregation in Houston and the second oldest in Texas.

B-40
Temple Beth Israel
[now Erwin R. Heinen Theater, Fine Arts Department, Houston Community College]
3517 Austin Street
1925, Joseph Finger

Finger applied what he described as Egyptian decorative motifs to the faceted, block-like masses of the temple building. Its hermetic look was reinforced when most of the exterior windows were sealed in 1950 at the time the building was air-conditioned. Behind the temple at Holman and LaBranch is the Abe M. Levy Community House, part of Finger's original design. To the south is the Freed Memorial Tower (1950, Irving R. Klein and Theo G. Keller), a spirited exercise in the modernistic Regency style; the stair hall is a delight.

B-40 Temple Beth Israel

B-41 Richardson House

B-42 Magnificat House Children's Chapel & Retreat

B-43 Southwestern Bell Telephone Company Building

B-44 Houston Light Guard Armory

B-41
Richardson House
[now Magnificat House St. Joseph Clubhouse]
3307 Austin Street
1903, J. Perkins Richardson

Built for the cotton factor E. R. Richardson, this large columned house was one of the first Colonial revival houses constructed in Houston. Architectural historian Steph McDougal identified the architect, Perkins Richardson, as the client's father; he was also the father of Houston artist Emma Richardson Cherry. The house was unusual among Colonial revival houses locally because of the extent to which it replicated 18th-century architectural features, such as the pedimented ground floor windows and the corner pilasters. The Richardson House was moved to this site in 1926 from its original location on the block now occupied by the First Evangelical Church. Across the street is the Colonial revival Sallie Sewall Horton House at 3208 Austin (1913).

B-42
Magnificat House Children's Chapel and Retreat
3300 Caroline Street
1996, Leslie Elkins Architecture

This simple wood building near the corner of Francis and San Jacinto is both a children's playhouse and a backyard chapel. It is serene and unobtrusive.

B-43
Southwestern Bell Telephone Company Building
[now Indochinese Cultural Center]
3333 Fannin Street
1958, Joseph Krakower

The organic expressionist architect Herb Greene was Krakower's designer 1954-1957. He detailed this 2-story office building with concrete masonry units, deployed as relief ornament. During the building's occupation by a subsequent tenant, Uniroyal, the upper floor was painted black so that the decoration might read as tire treads.

B-44
Houston Light Guard Armory
[now Buffalo Soldiers National Museum]
3816 Caroline Street
1925, Alfred C. Finn

By the time this National Guard Armory was built, the Houston Light Guard had ceased to be an elite social institution, yet the use of the streamlined traditionalism associated with Bertram G. Goodhue gives the building an air of clubbyness. Finn's office detailed it to suggest 16th- and 17th-century English masonry buildings without incorporating Elizabethan or Jacobean features. Tapestry brick and limestone banding are combined in a composition of taut, faceted wall planes relieved by sculptural detail, notably relief panels exhibiting bellicose iconography. In 2012 the armory was rehabilitated to become the Buffalo Soldiers National Museum.

B-45
Isabella Court
1003-1005 Isabella Avenue
1929, W. D. Bordeaux

The centerpiece of Main Street's Spanish Village shopping district was Isabella Court. Two floors of apartments, organized around a roofed, open-air courtyard, are stacked on ground floor shop spaces. Bordeaux introduced picturesque internal variations by inserting a 1.5-story photography studio at 3911 Main (where the belt course between the first and second floors is arced) and carrying this sectional shift upward into second- and third-floor apartments. The central courtyard is not accessible, but one can walk into the vestibule on Isabella; the original finishes are all preserved in a glorious state of seediness. Pierre D. Michael, who built Isabella Court, also constructed the Ironcraft Studio Building next door (3901-07 Main, 1927, Hiram A. Salisbury), a 2-story Spanish precursor that featured apartments above shops and a Mediterranean courtyard, now filled in. In 1990 Trudy Hutchings Herolz and architect Robert A. Herolz, Jr. bought Isabella Court, and eventually the Ironcraft Studio, sensitively rehabilitating both.

B-45 Isabella Court

B-46 South Main Baptist Church

B-47 Monotech Gallery

B-49 Phillips Studio and Townhouses

B-50 Central Church of Christ

B-46
South Main Baptist Church
4000 Main Street
1930, Hedrick & Gottlieb

This high and mighty example of the Lombard Romanesque was executed in the buff tapestry brick characteristic of Houston in the 1920s. The interior of the church, featuring painted plasterwork, is as festive as a 1920s movie palace. Multiple additions are by Wirtz & Calhoun (1940s-1980s) and Hall/Merriman (1992). Its name notwithstanding, South Main did not gain access to frontage on Main Street until the 1960s, a consummation it celebrated with an expansive grass forecourt and fountain.

B-47
Monotech Gallery
4411 Montrose Boulevard
2005, Peter Jay Zweig

This 2-story, steel-framed, stucco-faced building was designed to house art galleries. All interior circulation space is open air, opening off the central ground-floor passage that architect Zweig calls the "runway."

B-48
Sterling House
[now Howard L. Nations Law Office]
4515 Yoakum Boulevard
1916, Russell Brown Company
1919, Alfred C. Finn

Ross S. Sterling built this house speculatively in Rossmoyne, a private place-type subdivision that he began to develop in 1914. Two years after its completion, he and his family moved in. It was then that Finn's designer, H. Jordan MacKenzie, produced the spectacular front porch: a wide-span, reinforced concrete structure bracketed by a cantilevered canopy on the north end and an inglenook on the south, framed by a bulbous concrete column. Centered above the front step is MacKenzie's signature device, an elongated cartouche. The Sterling

House was rehabilitated by William F. Stern and Associates in 1981.

B-49
Phillips Studio and Townhouses
4204 Yoakum Boulevard and
1105-1107 Colquitt Street
1977-1981, W. Irving Phillips, Jr.

This startling complex of buildings includes a 1920s Montrose house that sprouts both a vaulted extension and a 4-story protrusion, a 2-story garden house, a 3-story row house whose rotated stucco mass is prefaced by a wooden façade screen, and a 2-story row house set far back from the street. The existing house, its additions, and the 3-story house, were originally occupied by the architect. Phillips, a student of Colin Rowe, incorporated into this group an array of rhetorical-analytical devices that range from the phenomenological to the contextual to the outrageous (the ostensibly modest 2-story house has a swimming pool in the living room). The house at 1107 Colquitt was reconstructed in 2010.

B-50
Central Church of Christ
[now The Campanile]
4100 Montrose Boulevard
1941, 1947, William Ward Watkin

Built in two stages this Lombard Romanesque style complex was the last church designed by Watkin, who published two books on the subject of church architecture. It was also the first non-residential building to be constructed on the boulevard, following the expiration of Montrose deed restrictions in 1936. After acquiring the property in 1981, the developer, John Hansen, had the educational wing transformed into shops and a restaurant and made the church available to the Houston Public Library for conversion into its Eleanor Freed Montrose Branch Library (1986, 1988, Ray Bailey Architects). The Campanile represents an urbanistically responsible reuse of existing buildings that renews the city and its fabric instead of ripping it to shreds. Hansen also had Bailey rehabilitate the house across the street at 4203 Montrose (1923, William Ward Watkin) as office space.

B-48 Sterling House

B-51 The Court at Museum's Gate

B-52 Link House

B-54 Fondren House

B-55 Annunciation Hellenic Eastern Orthodox Church

B-51
The Court at Museum's Gate
4004 Montrose Boulevard
1985, Compendium

Stepped, banded, and bichromatic, this 47-unit low-rise, high-density condominium designed by Jay Baker is in the effusive postmodern style of the '80s. The complex sits on a plinth, beneath which cars are parked, so that the only green spaces are along the street fronts.

B-52
Link House
[now Administration Building, University of St. Thomas]
3800 Montrose Boulevard
1912, Sanguinet, Staats & Barnes

J. W. Link, who developed the Montrose addition in 1911, built this flamboyant, quasi-progressive style house on a square block site in the very middle of his subdivision. Its severe, set-back massing contrasts with the opulence of its surfaces, faced with vitrified buff brick, enameled terra cotta, glazed tile, and limestone. Since 1947 the house has been the administration building of the University of St. Thomas, which conscientiously maintains it, the garage-apartment building, and the pergola that connects them. In 1988 the university caved in to the temptation of a corporate identity package and permitted installation of the gratuitous brick and metal screen walls that disfigure the terraced lawn (The SWA Group). In 2007 the university built the Edward P. White Memorial Plaza at the Montrose-West Alabama intersection. The freestanding plane of polished black granite, bearing a tilted cross, is the posthumous work of Philip Johnson.

B-53
Parc IV and Parc V
3614 and 3600 Montrose Boulevard
1963, 1965, Jenkins Hoff Oberg Saxe

William R. Jenkins and Roy Gee designed this handsome pair of 12-story apartment slabs. Their concrete frame construction, infilled with brick and sliding window and door sash, is expressed without reservation. The careful proportioning of the framed divisions gives the towers an urbane, rather than an industrial, aspect. Their relationship to the street is well considered, too, for while one edges the sidewalk, the other steps back to preserve a vestige of tree-shaded lawn.

B-54
Fondren House
[now La Colombe d'Or]
3410 Montrose Boulevard
1923, Alfred C. Finn

Walter W. Fondren, an oil driller and cofounder of the Humble Oil & Refining Company, built one of the last large houses on Montrose. Its big scale, unsubtle frontality, and lack of specific historical derivation were traits more typical of the 1910s than the 1920s. Despite conversion into a restaurant, it retains a strong sense of its historic identity, including specimens of the palm trees that Link planted in 1911 to give his flat, treeless Montrose addition that Pasadena look, an arboreal analogy that would signify its aspirations to the status of a millionaires' community. Several of the boulevard lots were improved with houses by Finn, of which only the Westheimer House at 3700 Montrose (1919) remains.

B-55
Annunciation Hellenic Eastern Orthodox Church
[now Annunciation Greek Orthodox Cathedral]
3520 Yoakum Boulevard
1952, Peter E. Camburas

Camburas, a Chicago architect, designed this church for Houston's oldest Greek Orthodox parish in a stripped-down version of the Romanesque style. He faced it with limestone, however, rather than brick. The interior features a stone ikonostasis and a vaulted apse surfaced with mural work by the New York painter Stelios Maris. In the 1990s the parish and its school commenced expansion into the neighborhood, resulting in the destruction of the historic residential fabric of Montrose for replacement by bulky buildings and surface parking lots.

B-53 Parc IV and Parc V

B-56 Hille House

B-57 Hamman House

B-58 Courtlandt Place

B-59 Autry House

B-60 Cleveland House

B-56
Hille House
804 Hawthorne Avenue
1913, Teich & Gideon

Off the major boulevards—Montrose, Yoakum, and Lovett—the Montrose subdivision consisted primarily of 2-story, four-square houses and 1-story bungalows. This house, with its wide-span front porch and big-scaled urns, is one of the more notable Montrose bungalows. Research by Montrose preservationist Gary Coover revealed that the original owner of the house, Karl Hille, was a decorative painter. This perhaps explains its vaulted living room, replete with musicians' gallery and extensive scenographic decoration.

B-57
Hamman House
802 Lovett Boulevard
1925, R. D. Steele

Harrie T. Lindeberg of New York, one of the most outstanding country house architects of the 1910s and 1920s, designed five houses in Houston; this was the only one located outside the Shadyside neighborhood. The client, John Hamman, an independent oil man, had Lindeberg's specifications and drawings modified by R. D. Steele, a veteran Houston architect, as the shutters and roof tiles (neither characteristic of Lindeberg) make clearly evident. Thus the house is not a consistent expression of Lindeberg's predilections. From 1951-1997 it was occupied by a succession of architectural firms—Kenneth Franzheim, the Houston branch of Welton Becket & Associates, and Lloyd Jones Fillpot Associates—which ensured its survival. The 1-story drafting room addition is by the Becket office.

B-58
Courtlandt Place
Brazos Street and Courtlandt Place
1988, Eubanks/Bohnn Associates

Courtlandt Place, platted in 1907, is a small neighborhood modeled quite literally on the private streets of

St. Louis. It consists of a boulevard divided by a landscaped median and bracketed at either end by colossal gate piers. The east end lost its concave screen of piers and spur walls to the construction of the Southwest Freeway in 1969. This wall of textured concrete block and cast concrete moldings belatedly replaced it. (Drive up to it and it will open automatically.) *Houston's Courtlandt Place* in the Images of America series (2009) by Sallie Gordon and Penny Jones offers a concise historical account of the families who built the houses of Courtlandt Place.

B-59
Autry House
5 Courtlandt Place
1913, Sanguinet & Staats

The Colonial revival portico appears here at big scale, but with a homelike charm that is carried inside this house. Across the street at 2 Courtlandt Place is the J. W. Parker House, a discreet English manorial style house by John F. Staub in 1926.

B-60
Cleveland House
8 Courtlandt Place
1911, Sanguinet, Staats & Barnes

Sanguinet & Staats had established themselves as architects of choice to Houston's elite by 1910, not only as designers of skyscrapers, but also of pretentious suburban houses as well. These included the half-timbered Sterling Meyer House at 4 Courtlandt Place and the New England Federal style C. L. House House at 6 Courtlandt Place (both 1910). This house for A. Sessums Cleveland is more ingratiating than the other two, although it shares with its neighbors the attributes of frontality, symmetry, big scale, and widely projecting eaves. The lattice fence is by Eubanks/Bohnn Associates (1987).

B-61
Dorrance House
9 Courtlandt Place
1914, Sanguinet & Staats

An Italian villa style was adopted for this grand house. The 1-story porch wing on the east, balanced by a porte-cochère on the west, occurs on most of the houses of Courtlandt Place. The preference given to the south and east exposures in order to catch the prevailing southeast breezes, and the corollary tendency to place serving spaces on the north or west, indicate the impact of climate on domestic planning in Houston. The balustraded terrace in front of the main entrance is a vestige of the front porch, a feature that would disappear altogether from stylish Houston houses in the 1920s.

B-61 Dorrance House

B-62 Neville House

B-63 Carroll House

B.65 Garrow House

B.66 Taylor House

B.67 Jones House

B-62
Neville House
11 Courtlandt Place
1914, Birdsall P. Briscoe

Briscoe, in the Neville House, one of his earliest houses, gave evidence of the suave eclecticism that would mark his long career. The image is English picturesque, but the loggias, French doors, and low terrace that he introduced reconcile it to Houston's climate. The house was built for Daphne Palmer and Edwin L. Neville.

B-63
Carroll House
16 Courtlandt Place
1912

J. J. Carroll, who built this house, was managing partner of a lumber business begun by his father-in-law, W. T. Carter. According to family tradition, Carroll was responsible for designing this house, with its big classical portico infilled with subsidiary classical porches. Birdsall P. Briscoe carried out later interior alterations. The Carroll House was part of a family enclave: Mrs. Carroll's mother, Mrs. W. T. Carter, Sr., lived at 14 Courtlandt Place (1920, Birdsall P. Briscoe); her brother, W. T. Carter, Jr., lived at 18 Courtlandt Place (1912, Olle J. Lorehn).

B-64
Donoghue House
17 Courtlandt Place
1916, Warren & Wetmore

At the same time that Warren & Wetmore designed the Texas Company Building downtown, they produced this exquisite neo-Georgian house for the family of Thomas J. Donoghue, executive vice-president of Texaco. Like earlier Courtlandt Place houses, it is frontal and symmetrical. But the consistency and precision of its 18th-century English Adamesque detail, the ornamental enrichment of exterior surfaces, and the lack of bulkiness and pretension demonstrate by contrast how provincial Houston's prevailing domestic architectural standards were. The bowed profile of the sun porch screening is a delightful touch.

B-65
Garrow House
19 Courtlandt Place
1914, Birdsall P. Briscoe

Another early Briscoe house, designed for Etta Brady and J. W. Garrow, is a suburban pavilion with a Baroque front portal. The 1-story east wing is a later addition.

B-66
Taylor House
20 Courtlandt Place
1916, Birdsall P. Briscoe

This is a Georgianized version of Briscoe's house at 19 across the street. It was built for a fourth member of the W. T. Carter family, Jessie Carter and her husband, Dr. Judson Taylor. The striped awnings still in use here were once standard equipment in the South End.

B-67
Jones House
24 Courtlandt Place
1921, Alfred C. Finn

The stepped plan of this house, which exhibits nominal Tudor detail, enables the principal reception rooms to have access to the prevailing southeast breeze. Finn incorporated parts of the interior of Sarah Brashear Jones's Victorian house on Main into her new home. Her son, Murray B. Jones, lived next door at 22 Courtlandt Place (1917, Birdsall P. Briscoe).

B.64 Donoghue House

B-68 Nazro House

B-69 Westfall House

B-70 Nash House

B-71 Waldo House

B-73 Cohen House

B-74 Holland House

B-68
Nazro House
25 Courtlandt Place
1916, Sanguinet, Staats & Gottlieb

The impact of Warren & Wetmore is evident in Sanguinet & Staats's last house in Courtlandt Place at the west end of the boulevard. Proportion, scale, detail, and plan configuration all defer to the authority of 17 Courtlandt Place and set this house apart from Sanguinet & Staats' earlier work.

B-69
Westfall House
303 Hawthorne Avenue
1905

A flamboyant airplane bungalow (so-called because the ridge of the second-floor roof runs perpendicular to that of the first floor), this was one of the earliest examples of this progressive middle class house type built in Houston. The rock-faced concrete work and the billowing roofs give this house a lilting character. The design is Design 775 from *Art and Architecture* (1902), one of the many catalogues of house designs published by the Knoxville architect George F. Barber, as Houston architectural historian Margaret Culbertson determined. The late Victorian cottage next door at 219 Hawthorne is also one of Barber's designs.

B-70
Nash House
215 Westmoreland Avenue
1907, Cooke & Company

Colonial revival at its most grandiose, this is one of the two most imposing houses remaining in Westmoreland, the first of the South End enclaves to challenge the primacy of Main Street. As the name itself implies, Westmoreland was laid out in 1902 by the St. Louis engineer Julius Pitzman, whose master works are the most opulent of St. Louis's private streets, Westmoreland and Portland Places. This house was rehabilitated in 2009.

B-71
Waldo House
201 Westmoreland Avenue
1905, Wilmer Waldo

Between 1902-1905 the civil engineer, Wilmer Waldo, dismantled his mother's elaborate Victorian house at Rusk and Caroline (1886, George E. Dickey) and reconstructed it, with modifications, here in Westmoreland, where the open prairie spread out just beyond Garrott to the west. The Waldo House's Victorian proportions are evident, although Waldo modernized it by removing Dickey's tall tower and replacing the wooden porches with an arcaded brick loggia. Occupied by the Waldo family until the late 1960s, the house was subsequently owned by architect Clovis Heimsath and his family. Heimsath used the stable at the rear as his studio. He designed the dark, brick-faced row houses with the eyebrow windows at 3524 and 3526 Garrott (1973).

B-72
Lightfoot House
3702 Audubon Place
1924, E. H. Lightfoot

The impact of Pasadena as a trendsetter in American architecture during the 1910s and '20s is evident not only in the palm trees of Montrose and Yoakum Boulevards but in the house types built in Montrose and other contemporary Houston subdivisions as well. This chalet style bungalow, with its bracketed eaves, stucco walls, and shingled second-story studio, appears to have been translated directly from southern California. Ewart H. Lightfoot, who built this house for his family, was an architect-builder.

B-73
Cohen House
607 Kipling Street
1919; 1938, William Ward Watkin

This house, purchased in 1922 by George Cohen, president of Foley Brothers department store, began modestly enough. But in the late '30s Cohen and his wife embarked on a series of alterations and additions, carried out by Watkin and his associate, Nolan Barrick, which transformed it into a mini-mansion replete with an Art Déco room that simulates a ship's interior.

B-74
Holland House
3820 Roseland Avenue
1914

Mission type details—stucco wall surfaces and tile copings—are yet another echo of Pasadena. They give this rather severe house its distinctive image.

B-72 Lightfoot House

B-75 The 505

B-76 High School for the Performing and Visual Arts

B-75
The 505
505 West Alabama Avenue
2006, Collaborative Designworks

Architect James M. Evans packed four 3-story townhouses onto a single lot, organizing them around a central motor court. The right-angled "5" figure in white stucco, visible on the street elevations, expresses the ingenious sectional organization of the living units.

B-76
High School for the Performing and Visual Arts
4001 Stanford Street
1981, Cavitt McKnight Weymouth and Barry Moore Architects

Occupying the former site of Montrose Elementary School (1916, John McLelland), a Spanish-style patio school, HSPVA presents an image of urban toughness to the neighborhood with its walls of rough textured concrete masonry units, mitigated by sprightly red trim.

B-77
University of St. Thomas
Welder Hall, Jones Hall, and Strake Hall
3812-3910 Yoakum Boulevard
1958, 1959, Philip Johnson Associates with Bolton & Barnstone

The University of St. Thomas is significant in Philip Johnson's career as his first realized multiple-building project and one of the last occasions on which he worked in the style of his mentor, Ludwig Mies van der Rohe. Johnson, who was commissioned to plan the university's campus in 1956 at the behest of Dominique and John de Menil, combined the idea of a monastic community with the model of Thomas Jefferson's academic village for the University of Virginia. He devised a double-level, steel-framed walkway that circumscribes a rectangular green lawn at the center of the 3-block site. Two-story rectilinear buildings attach to the walkway, whose steel columns describe the 10-foot, 4-inch planning grid with which Johnson organized the entire site. The careful composition of steel framing members and window units, infilled with panels of pink St. Joe brick, gives the campus buildings a strong sense of proportioned grace. Johnson modulated the intervals between his three initial buildings with brick screen walls. This lends a modest degree of spatial complexity to the ordered simplicity of the campus. M. D. Anderson Hall (1966, Howard Barnstone & Eugene Aubry) and the Doherty Library (1971, Eugene Aubry and Wilson, Morris, Crain & Anderson) upheld the precepts and maintained the subtleties of Johnson's buildings. Cullen Hall (1978, S. I. Morris Associates) does not. Robertson Hall (1997, Merriman Holt) is a virtual replica of Anderson Hall, although it is a steel-trimmed, concrete-framed building. During the 1960s St. Thomas was the center of vanguard culture in Houston, due largely to the connection of Mr. and Mrs. de Menil with its art department, run by Jermayne MacAgy from 1959-1964, and then by Dominique de Menil until 1969. The second-floor gallery at Jones Hall was the setting for MacAgy's legendary exhibitions; the double-volume common room in Welder Hall (floored-over in 1977) was where local nabobs, students, priests, and artists rubbed shoulders with the luminaries of international culture. With his Miesian architecture, Philip Johnson provided a frame that was authoritative yet accessible; it was through this frame that the spirit of the new entered Houston. From the upper deck of the walkway one can glimpse Philip Johnson's Transco Tower to the west. Across Yoakum from Strake Hall is the Modern Languages Building, originally the childhood home of the reclusive Howard R. Hughes (3921 Yoakum, 1918, William Ward Watkin).

In 1997 the Chapel of St. Basil at the north end of the academic mall was dedicated. The work of Philip Johnson, Ritchie & Fiore with John Manley, and Merriman Holt Architects, it is more complicated formally than Johnson's earlier buildings and much more aggressive in its scale, mixture of materials, and decoration. The 55-foot high, top-lit interior gives some sense of how Johnson wanted to illuminate the nearby Rothko Chapel. Liturgical furnishings, the Stations of the Cross, and the bronze figure of *Our Lady Seat of Wisdom* are the work of Beaumont sculptor David Cargill.

West of the university's academic mall lies the 21st-century sector of the campus, built along the right-of-way of Mount Vernon. The Student Life Plaza (2003, TBG Partners of Austin, landscape architects), framed by the Moran Center (2004, Kirksey), a mixed-use parking garage, fit into the complacent suburban landscape that has been constructed here. The Student Life mall possesses none of the ambition, rigor, or austerity that make Johnson's academic mall so memorable.

B-77 University of St. Thomas

B-78 Rothko Chapel

B-80 Menil Foundation Business Office

B-78
Rothko Chapel
1409 Sul Ross Avenue
1971, Howard Barnstone
& Eugene Aubry

The Rothko Chapel, an ecumenical center built by Dominique and John de Menil to contain 14 paintings executed especially for it by the abstract expressionist painter Mark Rothko, is a provocative building. Although built for the display of paintings, it is not a picture gallery. Although conceived as a chapel, it is not a church. Externally it is apt to appear contrived in its centrality and bland because it lacks constructive detail. Internally it profoundly embodies a sense of tragedy, reconciliation, and silence. The Rothko Chapel is a paradox—the building is mute, there is nothing to see in the paintings—yet this is an intensely moving place.

The reflecting pool in front of the chapel contains Barnett Newman's Cor-ten piece, *Broken Obelisk* (1967), installed by Mr. and Mrs. de Menil as a memorial to the Rev. Martin Luther King, Jr. Philip Johnson was originally the chapel's architect. It was planned as part of the University of St. Thomas to be constructed on the site where the Doherty Library eventually was built. Rothko so strongly disapproved of Johnson's designs that Johnson withdrew from the project in 1967. Two years later Mr. and Mrs. de Menil parted company with the University of St. Thomas and chose a new site, adjacent to, but not on, the campus. Barnstone & Aubry adapted Johnson's ground plan and Johnson consulted with Eugene Aubry on the resolution of certain details, such as the location of the reflecting pool. The baffles that distribute skylight inside the chapel are later modifications (1978, S. I. Morris Associates; 2001, James McReynolds and Arup). Available at the chapel are publications documenting the wide array of religious, political, and cultural activities that have transpired here, including Susan J. Barnes's history, *The*

Rothko Chapel, An Act of Faith, and Sheldon Nodelman's *The Rothko Chapel Paintings: Origin, Structure, Meanings*. The Rothko Chapel is open daily.

B-79
Byzantine Fresco Chapel Museum
4011 Yupon Street
1997, François de Menil

The exterior proportions of this precast concrete box are neither as felicitous nor as austere as those of the Japanese architect Tadao Ando, whose work seems to have been the general model for the Byzantine Fresco Chapel. But the interior chamber, in which two 13th-century Cypriot Byzantine frescoes are displayed, is a tour-de-force. Sandblasted laminated glass panels, lit from below, evoke the configuration of the rural Cypriot chapel in which the frescoes were originally installed. A complex structural design (for which Ove Arup & Associates were consultants) of tensioned steel rods, suspended from the ceiling, uphold the glass vaults, central cylinder, and frescoes. To protect the light sensitive paintings, this structure is encased in a plate steel box hung from the roof. Yet paradoxically light washes the outer walls of the chapel, admitted through perimeter skylights between the outside walls of the box and the walls of the chapel. Consequently natural light never penetrates the zone within the steel box. The Byzantine Fresco Chapel was the last work built by Dominique de Menil. It is a moving tribute to her quest to ensure that art and architecture cohere in a spiritual realm. In 2012 the chapel was closed after the frescos were repatriated by the Church of Cyprus.

B-80
Menil Foundation Business Office
[now DaCamera of Houston]
1427 Branard Avenue
c 1925
1974, Howard Barnstone

A spirited conversion of a 1920s bungalow provided offices for one of the departments of the Menil Foundation. Anthony E. Frederick modified the building somewhat when it was transferred to this site from across the street in 1984; he also was responsible for the subtle, but exhilarating, transformation of three other bungalows for use as Menil outposts. During the late 1960s Dominique and John de Menil began to amass property in this neighborhood for construction of a museum and study center to contain their collection. In 1974, under the direction of Howard Barnstone, all the buildings in this precinct were painted gray with white trim, giving the area a distinctly Surreal aspect.

B-79 Byzantine Fresco Chapel Museum

B-82 The Menil Collection

B-83 Zemanek House

B-81
Cy Twombly Gallery
1501 Branard Avenue
1995, Renzo Piano Building Workshop and Richard Fitzgerald & Associates

The Menil Collection built this gallery to contain a permanent exhibition of the art of the American painter Cy Twombly. Piano worked with Twombly, as well as Collection director, Paul Winkler, and Dominique de Menil, on the design of the gallery. Spatially it is organized as a nine-square grid, oriented east toward the rising sun rather than toward the street. A centered entrance and windowless walls of cast stone block give the gallery a remote, hieratic aspect. The internal ambiance is voluptuous because the building is suffused with filtered skylight. Plastered walls and naturally finished American oak floors reflect the static, even light, which in its precious quality responds to the character of Twombly's art. This virtuoso ambiance is achieved through layering four types of light screening devices, integrated in a complex (and hard to see from the street) roof system, which Piano designed with Ove Arup & Associates.

B-82
The Menil Collection
1515 Sul Ross Avenue
1987, Renzo Piano and Richard Fitzgerald & Associates

Dominique Schlumberger de Menil built this extraordinary building to contain the extensive collection of modern, Byzantine, classical, and indigenous art and artifacts that she and her husband John assembled. The Italian architect Renzo Piano, working with the English engineers Ove Arup & Associates, was commissioned in 1981 to design the museum building. (Louis I. Kahn and Howard Barnstone each had done preliminary schemes between 1973-1979.) Piano produced a building that is noble in scale, generous in dimension, and devoid of pretension. The broad terrace that circumscribes the museum frames views of—and imposes a sense of measure on—the flat Texas landscape. The Menil's crisp, rectilinear masses, framed with white-painted steel structural members and surfaced with gray painted cypress clapboards, provide a subtly proportioned backdrop for the intricate roof assembly, which consolidates skylighting, supporting structure, the graceful S-curve light baffles, which Piano calls "leaves" lighting, and air-conditioning. The amplitude and luminosity of interior spaces make one realize that designing the "feel" of the place took priority over considerations of image. Nonetheless Piano fused the rigorous, yet delicate, modernism of St. Thomas with the austerity of the Rothko Chapel and the distilled homeyness of the neighborhood's bungalows to construct an understated summation of Mr. and Mrs. de Menils' architectural patronage. The working spaces of the museum (not open to the public) are as interesting as the galleries and the promenade that joins them. Staff spaces and conservation and preparation areas are on the ground floor, behind the Branard elevation. Above is what Piano calls the "Treasure House," the isolated third-floor area that contains a series of spacious rooms where scholars can study pieces in the collection. Mrs. de Menil's insistence on the importance of technical, curatorial, and scholarly activities meant that these parts of the museum were as attentively designed as the public galleries. Sunk into the turf in front of the museum are three pieces by Michael Heizer: *Isolated Mass/Circumflex (#2)* (1968-78), *Dissipate* (1970), and *Rift* (1968-72); across the street at Sul Ross and Mulberry is Mark di Suvero's *Bygones* (1976). Richmond Hall, an ex-Weingarten's grocery market (1930, Joseph Finger) at 1416 Richmond, has been transformed by Anthony E. Frederick into the Menil's own alternative gallery, which now permanently houses the artist Dan Flavin's last installation (1998).

B-83
Zemanek House
1723 Colquitt Street
1968, John Zemanek

The house that the architect Zemanek built for himself demonstrates the possibility of intensifying the attributes of place (which, in Houston, can often seem non-existent) through architecture. The modest, 2-story house and gardens are, as Zemanek's student, Carlos Jiménez, has written, "a genuine encounter between detail and memory, recalling the ingenuity of the Texas rural vernacular on one wall, the nuance of a Japanese detail on the other."

B-81 Cy Twombly Gallery

B-84 Forty-eight Foot House

B-85 De Santos Gallery

B-87 House

B-88 House

B-89 Conn House

B-84
Forty-eight Foot House
1851 Lexington Street
2006, Interloop A/D

Architects Dawn Finley and Mark Wamble designed this 2-story, 48x24-foot, live/work house on a lot backing up to a freeway sound barrier in a 1920s subdivision. Containing a ground-floor design studio, a carport, and second-story residential space, the metal-faced house aimed for maximum volume and maximum economy of construction. In setting the house at the back of the lot they also maximized outdoor space. Because of its siting and impeccable proportions, the Forty-eight Foot House complements its neighborhood setting although it is unlike the surrounding 1920s and '30s houses.

B-85
De Santos Gallery
1724 Richmond Avenue
2003, Brave/Architecture

Fernando L. Brave designed this 3-story art gallery and studio on a narrow lot facing a busy street, where available space was at a premium. Low-set windows bring daylight into the gallery, control external views to minimize awareness of narrow setbacks, and preserve wall hanging space. The building's volumetric organization is emphasized by alternating bays of white stucco and corrugated steel siding.

B-86
House
4409 Mt. Vernon Street
1995, I. Phillips/Wild Design

Architect W. Irving Phillips, Jr. and interior designer Kathleen S. Wild collaborated on this tower house, added atop a row house designed by Jim Powers (1973). Stacking garage, living room, office, and rooftop deck and swimming pool one above the other, they concentrated an extraordinary array of uses in this amazing sliver.

B-87
House
1418 Kipling Street
1997, Val Glitsch

A spirited example of a combined living and working environment, this complex consists of a house and professional studio. Nearby at 1425 Kipling is the Kipling Academy by Brave/Architecture (2010) and at 1634 Marshall a house of ascending shed roofs (1999, Natalye Appel).

B-88
House
1625 Harold Street
2007, Allen Bianchi

Bianchi deftly slotted this 2-story house into a confined site in a 1920s neighborhood. A receding 2-story plane of black brick, a projecting white stucco volume, and a wood fence that spans the lot's front setback line spatially animate the street front of the house while also setting it firmly in line with its neighbors. The east side yard doubles as both courtyard and driveway.

B-89
Conn House
1802 Missouri Avenue
1922, Crain Ready-Cut Building Company

The "Alamo" parapet was a popular device for brick-faced bungalows.

B-86 House

B-90 House

B-91 Handmade House

B-92 Hyde Park Double

B-93 Mirabeau B. at Hyde Park

B-95 Montrose Townhouse Lofts

B-90
House
2323 Yupon Street
2002, Parra Design Group

This is a model urban house. Low key and unassuming, it uses windows to frame interior views but protect privacy. Shallow screened enclosures guard against the west sun but make the inside feel very open. The back yard is borrowed from the property of a pair of row houses facing Fairview, also by Camilo Parra.

B-91
Handmade House
1608 Indiana Street
2010, Strasser Ragni

Another essay in urban domesticity, this single-family city house, built by developer Carol Isaak Barden, spatially frames the good, edits out the iffy, and produces serene interior spaces.

B-92
Hyde Park Double
1212-1216 Hyde Park Boulevard
2010, Collaborative Designworks

Architect-developer James Evans demolished a neighborhood landmark, the Charles E. Richardson House of 1927, to build this pair of houses. With typical sleight of hand, Evans made one house the inside-out version of the other. Next door is a surviving landmark, the James L. Du Ross House of 1927 at 1206 Hyde Park.

B-93
Mirabeau B. at Hyde Park
2410 Waugh Drive
2011, Rohde Partners

Mark Oberholzer of Austin's Rohde Partners worked with developer Joey Romano to produce an exemplar of sustainable architecture, a 4-story, 14-unit apartment building, the first LEED-certified condominium in Houston. It takes its name from Mirabeau B. Lamar, second president of the Republic of Texas. Although no friend of Houston (he moved the national capital from Houston to Austin in 1839), Lamar did occupy a country house on the property that, 70 years later, became the Cherryhurst addition.

B-94
Tower Theater
[now El Real Tex-Mex Café]
1201 Westheimer Road
1936, W. Scott Dunne

In the mid 1930s Interstate Circuit, Inc. of Dallas, the major film distributor in Texas, moved out into the suburbs to develop neighborhood theater-shopping center complexes. The Tower was its first such venture in Houston. Although the adjacent Tower Community Center, between Montrose and Yoakum (1937, Joseph Finger), has had its flamboyant modernistic frontispieces embalmed in sprayed-on stucco, the theater itself, by the Dallas architect, Scott Dunne, who specialized in this building type, retains its splendid pylon and illuminated front. The Tower underwent exterior restoration by Barry Moore Architects in 1988. In 1995 the theater was gutted and refitted as a video store, bookstore, and cafe. Behind the theater at 1201-B Westheimer is Mo Mong, an elegant lean-to designed by David Guthrie (1997). In 2011 the Tower became El Real's restaurant that celebrates Tex-Mex cuisine.

B-95
Montrose Townhouse Lofts
2602-2608 Montrose Boulevard
1997, I. Phillips/Wild Design

Phillips produced a series of neo-lofts, the hot Houston real estate phenomenon of the late '90s, on prominent Montrose sites (other examples are the Tower Lofts at Waugh and Missouri and the Gateway Lofts at 101 Westheimer, both built in 1998). All are insouciant stucco boxes to which big scaled ornament is appended, in this case streamlining and a pylon that pay homage to the nearby Tower Theater.

B-94 Tower Theater

B-97 Houston Lighting & Power Company Hyde Park Substation

B-98 House

B-99 Jiménez Studio

B-100 House

B-101 Zemanek House

B-96
L'Encore
415 Hyde Park Boulevard
1927, Frederick Leon Webster

This 3-story Mediterranean tower house was designed, built, and occupied by Frederick Leon Webster, director of the Little Theater of Houston. It is a prime example of the fascination with the quaint, the diminutive, and the exotic that typified American architectural eclecticism in the 1920s. Occupying a 20x22-foot pad, it sits at one corner of a half-lot site to make room for the dense, intimate gardens that Webster planted. The other half of the lot, at 411 Hyde Park, is occupied by a shingled double house that Webster built in 1921 as his original studio, then expanded in 1927 with the addition of a small apartment.

B-97
Houston Lighting & Power Company Hyde Park Substation
100 block Tuam Avenue
1986, Denny*Ray*Wines Associates

Neighborhood protest against the unsightliness of an electrical substation installation paid off when the light company retained Denny*Ray*Wines to screen it with this lively brick, textured block, glass block, and chain link wall, incorporating a bus stop pavilion and ample planting.

B-98
House
1225 Jackson Boulevard
1998, Cameron Armstrong

This is a compact but volumetrically expansive house. Styrofoam blocks were assembled to form molds for monolithic reinforced concrete walls cased with masonry inside and out.

B-99
Jiménez Studio
1116 Willard Street
1983, 1984, 1986, 1998, Carlos Jiménez

The three stucco-surfaced buildings that comprise this group radiate an intensity that belies their apparent simplicity. Built in stages to contain Jiménez's architectural studio, they absorbed the original component, the Red House, which in 1998 became a story-and-a-half, blue-painted extension of Jiménez's studio.

B-100
House
1115 Willard Street
1994, Carlos Jiménez

Complementing the studio cluster across the street is this austere, planar walled component: a 2-story house.

B-101
Zemanek House
1117 Peden Street
2001, John Zemanek

Walls of exposed concrete masonry units and steeply pitched roofs mark this courtyard house, which evokes the domestic architecture of China with poetic rigor.

B-96 L'Encore

B.102 House

B-104 Montrose Veterinary Clinic

B-105 Welch City Residences

B-102
House
1306 Eberhard Street
2004, William Price

This vertically organized 4-level house possesses an air of tranquility because of the decisive proportioning of the openings penetrating its big-scaled corrugated steel siding.

B-103
Art League of Houston Building
1953 Montrose Boulevard
2006, W. Irving Phillips, Jr.

Phillips's building combines studio and workshop spaces, a gallery, and a coffee shop. The corrugated steel siding identifies it as a "tin house," coding it in Houston as artist space.

B-104
Montrose Veterinary Clinic
1701 Montrose Boulevard
1989, L. Barry Davidson Architects

Leslie Davidson picturesquely extrapolated elements of the early 20th-century house types common in this neighborhood for a veterinary clinic building.

B-105
Welch City Residences
2107 Converse Street, 805-807 Welch Street, 2106- 2108 Crocker Street
2009-2010, M. L. Reid

The Alquimia development group had Marshall Reid design a series of 3-story courtyard houses occupying a half-block site in the Weston Addition. Boundary walls of concrete block and projecting and receding planes of corrugated steel siding and stucco imbue this housing group with crisply proportioned distinction.

B-103 Art League of Houston Building

Museum District / Hermann Park / Boulevard Oaks / Southampton

Museum District / Hermann Park / Boulevard Oaks / Southampton

Tour C

Despite Houston's reputation as an unplanned city, there are precincts where civic planning has produced memorable public landscapes. The most impressive of these lies along Main Boulevard in its passage between the Museum of Fine Arts, and the Texas Medical Center, near Hermann Park and the Rice University campus. The park and boulevard improvement scheme, carried out in 1916 and 1917 under the direction of the St. Louis landscape architect George E. Kessler, responded wholeheartedly to the initial impetus for large-scale planning in the neighborhood: the new Rice Institute campus laid out by the Boston architects Cram, Goodhue & Ferguson and opened in 1912. The staged rows of Live Oak trees that flank this segment of Main, the lanes of the Rice campus, and streets in many nearby neighborhoods developed in the 1920s give the public way here a strong sense of spatial definition. Streets are positive spaces that have been transformed through use into distinctive public places. The voluntary cooperation of various institutions and individuals in shaping this civic landscape has resulted in a collective realm that provides a coherent spatial frame for buildings and sites connected to it. On the doorstep of this

exemplary district, the Texas Medical Center comes as a shock. The lesson in civic decorum that Main offers has gone unheeded here. In this district devoted to human well-being, contempt for the environment prevails, reducing this dense cluster of hospital, teaching and research, office, hotel, and parking buildings to a competitive, hostile, and—to outsiders—incoherent agglomeration, garnished around the edges with inconsequential bits of suburban shrubbery. The act of vandalism that the Medical Center's administrative agency, the Texas Medical Center, Inc., committed in 1987 when it demolished one of Houston's most popular landmarks, the Shamrock Hotel, bespeaks the elementary failure of this public institution to accept the responsibility of citizenship, of being part of the city. As Richard Ingersoll noted in 1989, "unless the Texas Medical Center instills in its members a sense of greater public responsibility, the confusion will continue. . . ." At what seems like, but isn't, the end of Main lies the ultimate popular Houston landmark, the Astrodome, now overshadowed by its successor, Reliant Park. Here the Texas condition of vast space can be powerfully experienced in an exaggerated contrast between emptiness and the plentitude of the spatial tunnels of Main.

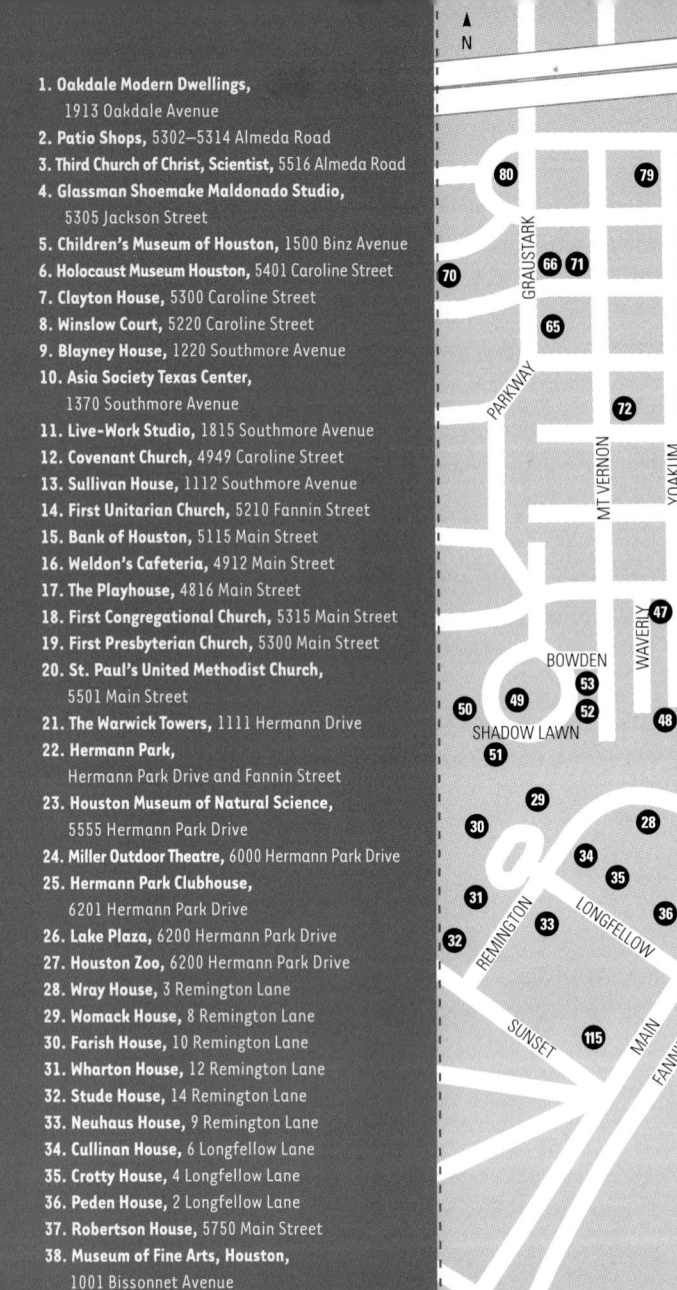

1. **Oakdale Modern Dwellings,** 1913 Oakdale Avenue
2. **Patio Shops,** 5302–5314 Almeda Road
3. **Third Church of Christ, Scientist,** 5516 Almeda Road
4. **Glassman Shoemake Maldonado Studio,** 5305 Jackson Street
5. **Children's Museum of Houston,** 1500 Binz Avenue
6. **Holocaust Museum Houston,** 5401 Caroline Street
7. **Clayton House,** 5300 Caroline Street
8. **Winslow Court,** 5220 Caroline Street
9. **Blayney House,** 1220 Southmore Avenue
10. **Asia Society Texas Center,** 1370 Southmore Avenue
11. **Live-Work Studio,** 1815 Southmore Avenue
12. **Covenant Church,** 4949 Caroline Street
13. **Sullivan House,** 1112 Southmore Avenue
14. **First Unitarian Church,** 5210 Fannin Street
15. **Bank of Houston,** 5115 Main Street
16. **Weldon's Cafeteria,** 4912 Main Street
17. **The Playhouse,** 4816 Main Street
18. **First Congregational Church,** 5315 Main Street
19. **First Presbyterian Church,** 5300 Main Street
20. **St. Paul's United Methodist Church,** 5501 Main Street
21. **The Warwick Towers,** 1111 Hermann Drive
22. **Hermann Park,** Hermann Park Drive and Fannin Street
23. **Houston Museum of Natural Science,** 5555 Hermann Park Drive
24. **Miller Outdoor Theatre,** 6000 Hermann Park Drive
25. **Hermann Park Clubhouse,** 6201 Hermann Park Drive
26. **Lake Plaza,** 6200 Hermann Park Drive
27. **Houston Zoo,** 6200 Hermann Park Drive
28. **Wray House,** 3 Remington Lane
29. **Womack House,** 8 Remington Lane
30. **Farish House,** 10 Remington Lane
31. **Wharton House,** 12 Remington Lane
32. **Stude House,** 14 Remington Lane
33. **Neuhaus House,** 9 Remington Lane
34. **Cullinan House,** 6 Longfellow Lane
35. **Crotty House,** 4 Longfellow Lane
36. **Peden House,** 2 Longfellow Lane
37. **Robertson House,** 5750 Main Street
38. **Museum of Fine Arts, Houston,** 1001 Bissonnet Avenue
39. **Audrey Jones Beck Building, Museum of Fine Arts, Houston,** 5601 Main Street
40. **Lillie and Hugh Roy Cullen Sculpture Garden,** 1000 block Bissonnet Avenue
41. **Glassell School of Art,** 5101 Montrose Boulevard
42. **Museum of Fine Arts Administration and Glassell Junior School,** 5100 Montrose Boulevard
43. **Contemporary Arts Museum,** 5216 Montrose Boulevard
44. **Cannady House,** 5301 Bayard Lane
45. **Hail House,** 1 West 11th Place
46. **Helmet House,** 5215 Yoakum Boulevard
47. **Morris House,** 2 Waverly Court
48. **House,** 10 Waverly Court
49. **Copley House,** 17 Shadowlawn Circle
50. **Graves House,** 11 Shadowlawn Circle
51. **House,** 9 Shadowlawn Circle
52. **Coleman House,** 6 Shadowlawn Circle
53. **Monteith House,** 5 Shadowlawn Circle

◀ Map continues on next spread

500 ft
200 m

Museum District / Hermann Park / Boulevard Oaks / Southampton

54. **Cochran House,** 1324 South Boulevard
55. **Kuldell House,** 1400 South Boulevard
56. **Walne House,** 1405 South Boulevard
57. **Anderson House,** 1515 South Boulevard
58. **Tennant House,** 1505 North Boulevard
59. **Wier House,** 1411 North Boulevard
60. **Hutcheson House,** 1405 North Boulevard
61. **Pincoffs House,** 1323 North Boulevard
62. **Lester House,** 1324 North Boulevard
63. **Gilmer House,** 1318 North Boulevard
64. **Dargan House,** 1317 North Boulevard
65. **Graustark Family Townhouses,**
    4923–4927 Graustark Street
66. **Milford Townhomes,** 1220 Milford Street
67. **House,** 1414 Milford Street
68. **Down and Up House,** 1514 Banks Street
69. **House,** 1425 Banks Street
70. **Act II House,** 1319 Banks Street
71. **Stern House,** 1202 Milford Street
72. **House,** 1118 Bartlett Street
73. **Keating House,** 4949 Yoakum Boulevard
74. **Lindsey House,** 1110 Milford Street
75. **Streetman House,** 1117 Banks Street
76. **Chelsea Market,** 4611–4621 Montrose Boulevard
77. **Cotswold Manor,** 242 Portland Avenue
78. **Holland Lodge No. 1,** 4911 Montrose Boulevard
79. **Townhouses,** 4706–4710 Yoakum Boulevard
80. **Vassar Place Apartments,** 1303 Vassar Place
81. **Mandell Residences,** 4901–4903 Mandell Street
82. **Anderson House,** 1638 Banks Street
83. **Vassar Place Townhouses,** 1731–1733 Vassar Place
84. **Finnell House,** 1908 Vassar Place
85. **House X2,** 4904–4906 S. Shepherd Drive
86. **Milford Live/Work,** 2207 Milford Street
87. **Howell House,** 1601 Milford Street
88. **Bonner House,** 1705 North Boulevard
89. **Anderson House,** 1660 South Boulevard
90. **Howard House,** 1707 South Boulevard
91. **Morgan House,** 1818 South Boulevard
92. **House,** 1928 South Boulevard
93. **Edgar Allan Poe Elementary School,**
    5100 Hazard Street
94. **Anderson House,** 2003 Bissonnet Avenue
95. **David House,** 1807 Wroxton Road
96. **House,** 1825 Albans Road
97. **House,** 1809 Dunstan Road
98. **Suit House,** 1828 Dunstan Road
99. **House,** 1930 Bolsover Road
100. **Smith House,** 2007 Dunstan Road
101. **House,** 2032 Bolsover Road
102. **Aubry House,** 2217 Bolsover Road
103. **Sunnystones,** 2230 Rice Boulevard
104. **Cannady House,** 2246 Quenby Road
105. **Bachelors Club,** 2229 Quenby Road
106. **Townhouse,** 2238 Albans Road
107. **House,** 2231 Wroxton Road
108. **House,** 2115 Wroxton Road
109. **Wagner House,** 2110 Albans Road
110. **House,** 2129 Quenby Road
111. **House,** 5331 Cherokee
112. **Morris House,** 5326 Mandell Street
113. **First Christian Church,** 1601 Sunset Boulevard
114. **Congregation Emanu El Temple,**
    1500 Sunset Boulevard
115. **Wiess House,** 2 Sunset Boulevard

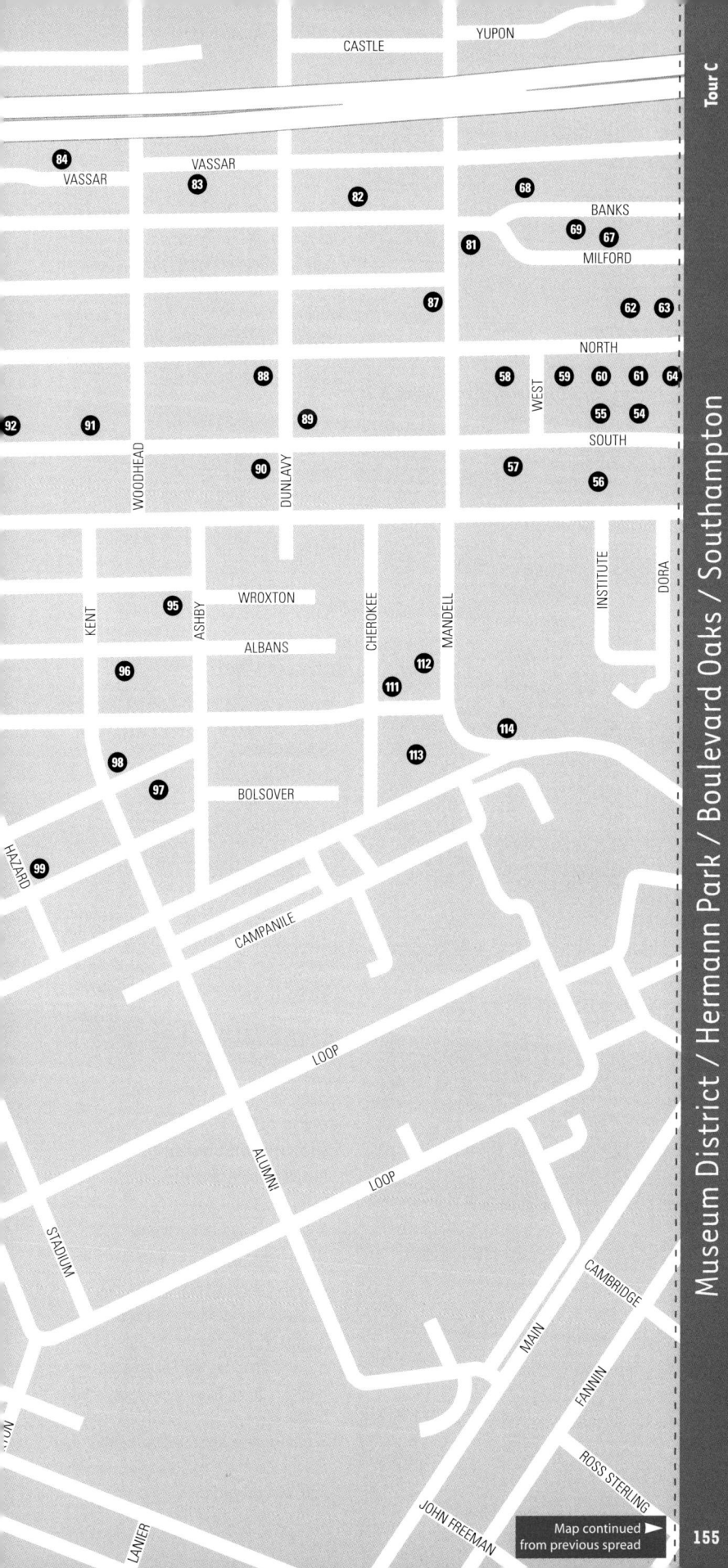

C-1 Oakdale Modern Dwelling

C-2 Patio Shops

C-3 Third Church of Christ Scientist

C-4 Glassman Shoemake Maldonado Studio

C-5 Children's Museum of Houston

C-1
Oakdale Modern Dwellings
1319 Oakdale Avenue
2009, Brett Zamore

Zamore lined up three freestanding, 3-story houses on a single lot. By proportionally offsetting window and balcony openings beneath reverse gabled roofs, he created visual rhythms that lend the houses distinction within the tight economy of speculative housing.

C-2
Patio Shops
5302-5314 Almeda Road
1931, B. W. Holtz and H. M. Sanford

The Patio Shops are a vintage strip shopping center liberally decorated with Spanish detail and organized to take advantage of a wedge-shaped site.

C-3
Third Church of Christ, Scientist
[now The Parador]
5516 Almeda Road
1928, Jonas & Tabor

J. Rodney Tabor's Mediterranean-style church pays homage to the First Church of Christ, Scientist in Palo Alto, California by the architect Elmer Gray. With its octagonal lantern, tile roofs, and pink stucco walls, it is a distinctly Californian amalgamation of north Italian and Byzantine detail.

C-4
Glassman Shoemake Maldonado Studio
5305 Jackson Street
2007, Glassman Shoemake Maldonado

Carrie Glassman Shoemake and Ernesto Maldonado designed their architectural studio as a pair of narrow, shed-roofed, clapboard-sided bays set at right angles to each other at the back of a residential lot in the Southmore Addition. Contrasting and complementary colors are used to animate the simple sheds.

C-5
Children's Museum of Houston
1500 Binz Avenue
1992, Venturi, Scott-Brown & Associates and Jackson & Ryan Architects
2009, Jackson & Ryan Architects

The Philadelphia architects Robert Venturi and Denise Scott-Brown invented the concept of the "decorated shed" in the 1970s, deriving inspiration from the ordinary, often expedient architecture of late 20th-century American suburban landscapes. They gave expression to this concept in this pair of pre-engineered metal buildings. The freestanding yellow propylaeum at the corner, with its cartoon-like rendition of classical architectural detail, is meant to symbolize "museum." The application of scored synthetic stucco panels to the Binz façade identifies this as the building's ceremonial front, while other elevations candidly reveal the museum's economical corrugated metal surfacing. The architecture is most intense where the glass slot (indicating the location of an interior spine, along which internal spaces are organized) is rotated outward just behind the propylaeum, evoking the fractured geometries of the Finnish master, Alvar Aalto. Overshadowing this architectural crescendo, however, are the Caryakids (a classical architectural pun), who uphold the school bus drop-off canopy along Crawford. In 2008 Venturi & Scott Brown's rear building was demolished; the front building was expanded, and the original exterior color scheme was changed. Jackson & Ryan designed the museum's 3-story, metal-faced E. Rudge Allen, Jr., Educational Annex at 1615 Binz. The Children's Museum was the first of several small cultural institutions that have transformed this neighborhood into an extension of the Museum District to the west.

C-6
Houston Holocaust Museum, Education Center, and Memorial
[now Holocaust Museum Houston]
5401 Caroline Street
1996, Ralph Appelbaum Associates and Mark S. Mucasey

The New York exhibition designer Ralph Appelbaum designed a dramatic wedge-shaped concrete addition, pierced by a sinister funnel, to a former orthopedic clinic (1970, Wilson, Morris, Crain & Anderson). Although some of the decorative detail added to the clinic is heavy handed, Appelbaum's museum and exhibition design are powerful and moving. At the peak of the wedge, facing a rear garden, is a tall Memorial Room designed by Murphy Mears of Houston to contain installations by the Philadelphia artists Patricia and Robert Moss-Vreeland. The Alexander Memorial Garden at the rear of the property is by Carlos Jiménez (1998), and the World War II Holocaust Railcar installation is by the Rice Building Workshop (2006).

C-6 Houston Holocaust Museum, Education Center, and Memorial

C-7 Clayton House

C-8 Winslow Court

C-9 Blayney House

C-11 Live-Work Studio

C-12 Covenant Church

C-7
Clayton House
[now Clayton Library Center for Genealogical Research]
5300 Caroline Street
1917, Birdsall P. Briscoe

Briscoe designed this well-proportioned, neo-Georgian house for Susan Vaughan and William L. Clayton. Clayton was cofounder of the cotton-exporting firm of Anderson, Clayton & Co. and Under-Secretary of State for Economic Affairs during the Truman administration. Briscoe altered and expanded the house on several occasions, converting the original garage at Oakdale and San Jacinto into a delightful guesthouse, and transforming a sun porch into a paneled library, replete with wood carving by the Austin craftsman Peter Mansbendel that celebrates iconographically the source of Clayton's wealth (1932, 1936). Since 1966 the house has been open to the public as the Houston Public Library's genealogical research center. In 2010 a comprehensive rehabilitation was completed by Glassman Shoemake Maldonado, which included discrete additions to the two outbuildings; Asakura Robinson was the landscape architect for the heritage garden restoration.

C-8
Winslow Court
5220 Caroline Street
1929, Russell Brown Company

At first sight the Winslow Court appears to be a slightly eccentric mansion. One presumes that the intention was for it to blend with its context because it was the first apartment building constructed along what had been a boulevard of single-family houses.

C-9
Blayney House
1220 Southmore Avenue
1914, Green & Finger

This stucco-surfaced, tile-roofed house, one of the earliest built in the Southmore Addition, appears to have been a sympathetic reaction to the Mediterranean style residential halls on the nearby campus of the Rice Institute. Like them it has a 3-story belvedere tower. L. S. Green and Joseph Finger's client was T. Lindsey Blayney, professor of German at Rice, one of a number of first generation Rice faculty members to live in Southmore.

C-10
Asia Society Texas Center
1370 Southmore Avenue
2011, Yoshio Tanaguchi & Associates and Kendall/Heaton Associates

The Tokyo architect Yoshio Tanaguchi designed the 38,000-SF headquarters of the Asia Society as a serene 1- and 2-story pavilion of Jura limestone wall planes scored with rectangular window openings and thin planar roof overhangs. The Office of James Burnett was the landscape architect.

C-11
Live-Work Studio
1815 Southmore Avenue
2006, Intexure

Architects Rame and Russell Hruska designed this combination studio and house for their own practice and family. Projecting and receding bays gathered beneath an inverted gable roof contain different program spaces. Offsetting the building is a simple gridded gravel terrace. Adjacent to the Live-Work Studio is Southmore Terrace, 3- and 4-story townhouses designed and developed by Intexure (2008).

C-12
Covenant Church
4949 Caroline Street
2001, Natalye Appel + Associates Architects and Rogers + Labarthe

Appel and Rogers + Labarthe collaborated on this 1-story complex for a liberal, ecumenical Baptist congregation. The wood-framed church and classroom wing are house-like in scale. Large windows illuminate the church's simply finished worship space with crisp northern light.

C-10 Asia Society Texas Center

C-13 Sullivan House

C-14 First Unitarian Church

C-15 Bank of Houston Building

C-16 Weldon's Cafeteria

C-17 The Playhouse

C-13
Sullivan House
[now The Chateau]
1112 Southmore Avenue
1923, Maurice J. Sullivan

Sullivan designed this house for his family. It represents a combination of attributes often seen in the 1920s: the English-influenced picturesque manor house prominently displaying an Italian loggia, a cultural conjunction especially welcome in sultry Houston. Conversions to a fraternity and then to a music club have taken their toll.

C-14
First Unitarian Church
[now First Unitarian Universalist Church]
5210 Fannin Street
1952, Thomas E. Greacen II

Greacen configured the church and its educational building around a central courtyard. The influence of Eliel Saarinen's mid-Western churches of the 1940s is evident in this understated complex. Val Glitsch was responsible for the 3-story rear addition (1996). Layered massing and a stepped skyline cleverly mitigate the addition's impact on the original components of the complex.

C-15
Bank of Houston Building
[now Whitney Bank Main Street]
5115 Main Street
1967, Wilson, Morris, Crain & Anderson

John Bertini, who designed this steel framed, glass-walled pavilion, paid tribute to Ludwig Mies van der Rohe's National Gallery in Berlin. However, as one of Bertini's partners observed, the homage was completed before the original.

C-16
Weldon's Cafeteria
4912 Main Street
1949, MacKie & Kamrath

The taut horizontals, precise stone copings, and cantilevered balcony display the Kamrath touch, which transformed what might otherwise have been a nondescript storefront into a spirited exposition of modern design. In 2005 Weldon's was splendidly rehabilitated by Ray + Hollington for their architecture studio which no longer occupies the space. Next door at 4910 Main is Joseph Finger's Art Deco Barker Brothers Studio of 1930, housing the handsomely rehabilitated Lawndale Art and Performance Center since 1993.

C-17
The Playhouse
4816 Main Street
1951, Dixon & Greenwood

The Playhouse was one of the first theaters in the U.S. designed specifically for theater-in-the-round performances. Contributing to this end of the Museum District is the Houston Center for Contemporary Craft, next door at 4848 Main, housed in a warehouse recycled into galleries and workshops in 2001.

C-18
First Congregational Church
[now St. Matthew Lutheran Church]
5315 Main Street
1927, Joseph W. Northrop, Jr.

Northrop employed both a Lombard Romanesque stylistic formula and materials quite similar to those of his First Evangelical Church, which was designed and built at the same time. Their effect has proved compelling. Extensive additions to St. Matthew by Bailey A. Swenson (1942, Parish Hall) and Harry A. Turner & Charles E. Geyer (1955, chapel and cloister extension on Prospect and school wing on Oakdale) are almost indistinguishable from the original structure.

C-18 First Congregational Church

C-19 First Presbyterian Church

C-19
First Presbyterian Church
5300 Main Street
1949, Hobart Upjohn and Maurice J. Sullivan

In its isolated setting the big scale of First Presbyterian is not as monumental as it ought to be, although the austere classical detail framing the Main entrance portal is quite grand. Herring Coe executed the sculptural work. Upjohn, a New York architect, was the last in a dynasty of American church architects, each member of which designed a Texas church. The grandfather, Richard Upjohn, was responsible for St. Mark's, San Antonio; the father, Richard M. Upjohn, for St. James, La Grange; the grandson for First Presbyterian, which could easily hold the other two. Extensive additions to the rear are by Ray Bailey Architects (1987) and Merriman Holt (2000).

C-21 The Warwick Towers

C-20
St. Paul's United Methodist Church
5501 Main Street
1930, Alfred C. Finn

Pious competition asserted itself along Main in the late 1920s. St. Paul's, a sleek, neo-Gothic, cathedral-style church, was clearly the winner. Like so many in that decade, the church owes much to the influence of the Boston architect Ralph Adams Cram. The lofty interior of the steel-framed church is as impressive as the limestone-clad exterior, although the insertion of a Protestant preaching box surmounted by a choir, in place of the expected high altar, is a bit disconcerting.

C-22 Sam Houston Statue

C-21
The Warwick Towers
1111 Hermann Drive
1983, Golemon & Rolfe and Werlin, Deane & Associates

Golemon & Rolfe's designer, Allen Rice, was responsible for this handsome pair of 30-story condominium apartment towers built of precast concrete. The bridge levels spanning between the towers contain living rooms in the most deluxe apartment units.

C-22
Sam Houston Statue
Hermann Park
1925, Enrico F. Cerracchio, sculptor, Joseph W. Northrop, Jr., architect

Cerracchio's bronze equestrian statue of Sam Houston, the frequently outrageous adventurer, statesman, and soldier for whom the city is named, faces east. His outstretched arm, intended to point toward the San Jacinto battlefield 19 miles away, where Houston's victory over the army of Mexico in 1836 ensured Texas' independence from Mexico, now seems to direct incoming traffic toward the park's central parking lot. This was the major work of public art erected in Houston during the heyday of the City Beautiful movement. The monument terminates the view up Montrose, or at least it did until the Mecom Fountain (1964, Eugene Werlin) was installed in what had been the Sunken Garden at Montrose and Main. The Sam Houston Statue's location is pivotal since it deflects traffic off-axis onto the curving loop roads that originally subdivided the 410-acre park. This was all part of the master plan devised by the St. Louis landscape architect George E. Kessler in 1916, two years after the property was donated to the city by George H. Hermann. Kessler's master plan included the conversion of Main Street, from McGowen all the way south to Bellaire, into Main Boulevard. It was under Kessler's direction that the magnificent allée of Live Oaks was planted along Main between Bissonnet and University. After Kessler's death in 1923, the master plan was carried out into the 1950s by Kansas City landscape architects, Hare & Hare. In the 1970s, however, Kessler's and Hare & Hare's improvements began to be whittled away in an effort to accommodate increasing use, increasing traffic, and the growth of various cultural institutions located in the park. To combat the gradual erosion of the park, a group of concerned citizens organized the Friends of Hermann Park (now the Hermann Park Conservancy) in 1992, and in 1995 commissioned the Philadelphia landscape architects Hanna/Olin Associates to prepare a comprehensive plan to renew Hermann Park. Under the auspices of Laurie Olin's plan, the Conservancy has coordinated phased improvement projects with the Houston Parks and Recreation Department.

C-20 St. Paul's United Methodist Church

C-23 Houston Museum of Natural Science

C-24 Miller Outdoor Theater

C-25 Hermann Park Clubhouse

C-23
Houston Museum of Natural Science
5555 Hermann Park Drive
1964, George Pierce-Abel B. Pierce and Staub, Rather & Howze

The original Museum of Natural Science complex, including the domed Burke Baker Planetarium, was expanded to include the Wortham IMAX (1989), the Memorial Sundial, Fountain and Garden (1990), and, most spectacular of all, the conical, 70-foot tall Cockrell Butterfly Center and Donor Wing (1994, Hoover & Furr). The 4-story Duncan Family Wing (2011, Gensler) along San Jacinto fills out the museum's last available piece of real estate.

C-24
Miller Outdoor Theatre
6000 Hermann Park Drive
1968, Eugene Werlin & Associates

The dramatic canopy shielding fixed seating is composed of three triangular folded plates of Cor-ten steel that span 95 feet between support points. Extensive support facilities were added to the back of the complex by Ray Bailey Architects (1998).

C-25
Hermann Park Clubhouse
6201 Golf Course Drive
1933, Arthur E. Nutter

Nutter's clubhouse is a picturesque Mediterranean style building organized around a flagstone-paved common room. Broad *portales* face the golf course, which was redesigned in 1999. The clubhouse contains the offices of the Hermann Park Conservancy.

C-26
Lake Plaza
6200 Hermann Park Drive
2004, Olin Partnership
and The SWA Group
2009, Laurie Olin, Overland Partners,
and White Oak Studio

Laurie Olin's efforts to restore Hermann Park are most impressively evident along the axis that spans from the Sam Houston Statue to the entrance of the Houston Zoo. Working with Overland Partners of San Antonio and Houston landscape architects, White Oak Studio, Olin dealt with the problematic terminus of the axis in front of the Zoo by installing a braided landscape of grass mounds and stepped terraces that visually camouflages an immense parking lot and distributes visitors across the site in ways that emphasize long views to the north across McGovern Lake. Overland's timber and brick concession buildings frame the east side of the plaza.

Olin and The SWA Group reshaped and expanded the lake, stabilizing its banks and making it accessible to park visitors. The more formal sequence of spaces that commence with the Molly Ann Smith Plaza on the north shore of the lake and continue with the long, axial reflecting basin are generously scaled and handsomely detailed. These spaces, which are pedestrian zones and not visible from cars, contribute to the most inspiring public landscape built in Houston at the turn of the 21st century.

Midway along the Jones Reflection Pool, a grove of trees to the east of the main axis contains a memorial garden dedicated to Rice architecture professor and urban designer O. Jack Mitchell. After Mitchell's death in 1992, the Rice Design Alliance organized the Heart of the Park design competition with the Hermann Park Conservancy and the Houston Parks and Recreation Department to restore the reflecting basin axis as a memorial to Mitchell. The winning design by Melton Henry/Maurice Robison, Peter H. Brown, Scott Slaney, and Steve Harding was adapted by Olin and SWA.

C-26 Lake Plaza

C-27 Houston Zoo

C-28 Wray House

C-27
Houston Zoo
6200 Hermann Park Drive
1950, Hare & Hare, landscape architects, Irving R. Klein & Associates, architects

The concourse of the Houston Zoo is one of the most beautiful public open spaces in Houston. Hare & Hare demonstrated how compelling Houston can be when plantings, water, and architectural structures are coordinated to give form to a place in what is too often a flat, monotonous landscape. The central water channel is flanked by rows of Live Oak trees and low, stepped terraces faced with benches. Defining the outer edges of the concourse is a pair of freestanding concrete canopies that run the entire length of the water channel. At the right of the head of the channel lies Klein's elegant Concession Building, which forms an open-air circle adjacent to a shallow lagoon containing two mature cypress trees. Regrettably the exceptional quality of this space has not been respected and preserved by the city's Parks and Recreation Department. The original gates were demolished to build the intrusive Kipp Aquarium and Entrance Building (1982, Pierce Goodwin Alexander) and the viewing stand for the Seal Pool at the foot of the concourse (1988) departs considerably from Hare & Hare's and Klein's architectural standards. The Primate House (1950, Irving R. Klein & Associates), the concourse's architectural terminus, was demolished rather than reconfigured to install the Wortham World of Primates. Other additions to the zoo grounds do adhere to original design standards, especially the Large Cat Facility (1984, Caudill Rowlett Scott), an ambitious piece of landscape architecture, and the George R. Brown Education Center (1988, Ray Bailey Architects), which incorporates Herring Coe's cast stone plaques (1952), salvaged from the demolished entry gate piers.

[The listings C-28 through C-36 in Shadyside are no longer accessible from a public street.]

C-28
Wray House
3 Remington Lane
1939, John F. Staub

Staub's particular gifts as an architect are admirably demonstrated in this house. Its splayed plan responds to the curvature of the street, its shallow depth allows through ventilation, and its assured composition gracefully disguises the fact that major rooms are oriented toward the private rear garden rather than the street. The house is a condensation of early 19th-century English Regency architectural themes, regionalized in a Louisiana-Creole interpretation. The house was designed for Andrew Jackson Wray and his wife, Margaret, the daughter of J. S. Cullinan, founder of the Texas Company (Texaco). Cullinan developed this small enclave neighborhood, Shadyside, in 1916. He retained George E. Kessler to lay out the subdivision, and then invited his friends and business associates to build their houses here. Across the street lies the site of Cullinan's own house, a huge brick pile demolished in 1972. It was replaced in the 1990s by a pair of houses designed by Eubanks/Bohnn Associates.

C-29
Womack House
8 Remington Lane
1923, Harrie T. Lindeberg

Lindeberg was one of New York's foremost "country house" architects when he was commissioned to design four houses in Shadyside in the early 1920s. He displayed his considerable versatility by designing each in a different style. This pink stucco-surfaced, tile-roofed Spanish farmhouse, designed for Kenneth E. Womack, turns its arcaded loggia toward the prevailing breeze. Consequently, the front door ends up in the backyard, an environmentally-sanctioned breach of convention frequently employed by John F. Staub, who came to Houston in 1921 to supervise construction of the four houses for Lindeberg and remained to start his own practice.

C-29 Womack House

C-30 Farish House

C-31 Wharton House

C-32 Stude House

C-33 Neuhaus House

C-34 Cullinan House

C-30
Farish House
10 Remington Lane
1925, Harrie T. Lindeberg

Designed for Libbie Rice and William Stamps Farish, this very restrained English Regency style house is a work of considerable architectural stature: quite grand, but extremely understated in the best country house tradition. One of Lindeberg's trademarks, the spider-in-the-web iron grille, is visible at the front entrance. Delicate wrought iron pergolas create a complex play of shadows on the lower half of the textured stucco walls. Extensive additions are by Jay Baker Architects (1999).

C-31
Wharton House
12 Remington Lane
1920, Alfred C. Finn

When Lindeberg arrived in Shadyside, this is what local architects were producing: big-scaled, unsubtle versions of the country house look, here of remote English Jacobean derivation. The original owners were Mr. and Mrs. Earl Wharton.

C-32
Stude House
14 Remington Lane
1924, Briscoe & Dixon

Not all of J. S. Cullinan's friends were rich; those who weren't demonstrated that it was possible to live with propriety and grace in such modest houses as this French manorial style dwelling. Briscoe cleverly pulled the garage into the architectural composition to make the building mass seem larger.

C-33
Neuhaus House
9 Remington Lane
1923, Harrie T. Lindeberg

Considered Lindeberg's outstanding work in Houston, this spectacular house is in the picturesque cottage style with which Lindeberg made his reputation. The roof of closely-lapped shingles that imitate the texture of thatch is called a "Lindeberg roof." As was customary of American country house architects, Lindeberg took careful note of climate and planning, organizing the L-plan house so that major rooms open toward a rear garden and the prevailing southeast breeze. The client, investment banker Hugo V. Neuhaus, was so enthusiastic that he secured for Lindeberg his other Shadyside commissions. Neuhaus's eldest son, the modern architect, Hugo V. Neuhaus, Jr., grew up in this house.

C-34
Cullinan House
6 Longfellow Lane
1926, Birdsall P. Briscoe

Briscoe seems to have learned from Lindeberg's Shadyside houses by the time he designed this Jacobean style house for J. S. Cullinan's son, Craig Cullinan. It is a richly, but subtly, ornamented house, as a close look at its decorative brick bonding, stained glass windows, and wood carving by Peter Mansbendel reveal.

C-35
Crotty House
4 Longfellow Lane
1923, Briscoe & Dixon

A formal neo-Georgian production; like all good country house architects, Briscoe was a master of many styles.

C-36
Peden House
2 Longfellow Lane
1924, Harrie T. Lindeberg

This is a clever mannerist version of an English Georgian style house. It is symmetrical on its garden elevation, but asymmetrical on its motor court side. There Lindeberg juggled divergent axes of approach and composition to compensate for the fact that the house faces the side property lines to facilitate ventilation, rather than facing the street. Architect Charles W. Ligon carried out a restoration of the house (2010), removing intrusive alterations and additions.

C-37
Robertson House
5750 Main Street
2007, Robertson Design

Christopher Robertson designed this expansive modern house as a forum for entertaining that enthusiastically embraces the city. Next door at 5330 Montrose Boulevard is an austere neo-Classical house by Miller Dahlstrand (2007).

C-35 Crotty House

C-36 Peden House

C-37 Robertson House

C-38 Museum of Fine Arts, Houston

C-38 Museum of Fine Arts, Houston

C-40 Lillie and Hugh Roy Cullen Sculpture Garden

C-38
Museum of Fine Arts, Houston
[now Caroline Wiess Law Building]
1001 Bissonnet Avenue
1924, 1926, William Ward Watkin; Ralph Adams Cram, consulting architect
1958, Ludwig Mies van der Rohe with Staub, Rather & Howze
1974, Office of Ludwig Mies van der Rohe

The Museum of Fine Arts, the first public art museum built in Texas, was designed to sit opposite Shadyside and the entrance to Hermann Park in order to comprise (along with the campus of Rice University) a new precinct on the edge of the city in the 1920s, planned with the precepts of the City Beautiful movement and exemplifying the best of Houston. Watkin's limestone-faced museum—a screen of Ionic columns framed by slightly angled wings—is a paradigmatic City Beautiful temple of high culture, taking its place alongside the large Gothic and Romanesque churches of Main in a kind of textbook presentation of great moments in architectural history.

When additions were needed, they were made by encasing the rear of the Watkin building; as has become the case elsewhere, what was once the front door no longer admits visitors to the museum. The magisterial Brown Pavilion and Cullinan Hall, by the great German-American architect Ludwig Mies van der Rohe, form the new front. Mies, once director of the Bauhaus and a founder of the Modern Movement in 20th-century architecture, was commissioned in 1954 to prepare a plan for the expansion of the Watkin building. He proposed filling in a rear courtyard with Cullinan Hall, an awesome double-volume space a half-level above the main entrance on Bissonnet, and, wrapping around its north face, the 2-story Brown Pavilion. This plan was carried out in two stages, the second completed five years after Mies died in 1969. The Mies building is one of those great moments in architectural history for which the 1920s buildings surrounding it are stand-ins. It is a classic: precise, subtle, serene, and charged with spatial grandeur, full of the "nothing" to which Mies paradoxically aspired to reduce architecture. It is the finest modern building in Houston.

C-39
Audrey Jones Beck Building, Museum of Fine Arts, Houston
5601 Main Street
2000, Rafael Moneo and Kendall/Heaton Associates

To accommodate the growth of its collection, the museum built the 3-story, 185,000-SF Beck Building across Main from the original museum. The Madrid architect, Rafael Moneo, designed the Beck Building as a sober limestone-faced box that deferred to Mies externally, while hinting at the complexity of its interior spatial organization with its village of rooftop light monitors. The 3-story atrium is awesome in scale and dazzlingly white; top-floor galleries were designed for the museum's permanent collection of European and Impressionist paintings. In good Houston fashion, Moneo and Kendall/Heaton also designed a block-square visitors center and parking garage to complete the expansion. An underground tunnel connecting Moneo and Mies features *The Light Within*, a shallow-space light sculpture by the artist James Turrell.

C-40
Lillie and Hugh Roy Cullen Sculpture Garden
1000 block Bissonnet Avenue
1986, Isamu Noguchi with Fuller & Sadao

The Japanese-American sculptor, Isamu Noguchi, produced a solemn place in which to contemplate the Museum of Fine Arts's sculpture collection, a walled garden that does not so much shut out Houston as it edits, condenses, and intensifies it. The broad granite causeways replicate the essential flatness of Houston. Walls, hillocks, and freestanding granite planes modulate this horizontally extensive, slow-moving space. In the Cullen Sculpture Garden, Noguchi came to terms with Houston. His interpretation is utterly unlike Hare & Hare's at the Houston Zoo. But its subtlety (the way an angled gravel bed along the Montrose wall seems to have been thrust into the garden by the Contemporary Arts Museum across the street) and intensity are profound and powerfully affecting.

C-39 Audrey Jones Beck Building, Museum of Fine Arts, Houston

C-41 Glassell School of Art

C-42 Museum of Fine Arts Administration and Glassell Junior School Building

C-44 Cannady House

C-41
Glassell School of Art
5101 Montrose Boulevard
1978, S. I. Morris Associates

Eugene Aubry, Guy Jackson, and Carl Aeschbacher, who designed the museum's art school building, exposed its cast-in-place concrete frame externally and internally, filling it with a gridded, reflective membrane of insulated, reflective glass block. The central gallery, where changing exhibitions are mounted, is a double-volume, skylit spine that slices the building in two. Illuminated at night the Glassell School becomes an inhabited cut-away section, revealing its contents and occupants.

C-42
Museum of Fine Arts Administration and Glassell Junior School Building
5100 Montrose Boulevard
1994, Carlos Jiménez and
Kendall/Heaton Associates

This is a quiet but remarkable building. With very little fanfare, it accomplishes what so few new Houston buildings seem inclined to do: it restores urban spatial unity and heals the jarring fragmentation typical of Houston. Next door at 5020 Montrose is the Plaza Apartment Hotel [now Tradition Bank Plaza] (1926, Joseph Finger), which was rehabilitated by Cisneros Design Studio as a medical office building (2007).

C-43
Contemporary Arts Museum
5216 Montrose Boulevard
1972, Gunnar Birkerts & Associates
with Charles Tapley Associates

The pointy, knife-edged corners and reflective stainless steel sheathing of the Contemporary Arts Museum represent the attempt of the Ann Arbor architect, Gunnar Birkerts, to deflect the building away from Mies's museum across the street. The parallelogram-shaped exhibition space inside never quite came off as the warehouse loft it was intended to resemble; however, it was considerably improved with a remodeling carried out by Morris*Architects (1987). Down below are a smaller gallery, the museum shop, and a coffee shop, restructured by William F. Stern & Associates (1997). Stern collaborated with Philadelphia landscape architect, Laurie Olin, to reshape the entrance to the museum, which includes the Ballard Fountain. Mel Chin's *Manila Palm* (1978) is installed behind the museum.

C-44
Cannady House
5301 Bayard Lane
1991, William T. Cannady & Associates

This imposing house occupies a lot in Shadyside that had never been built on because of its exposed corner location. Cannady took advantage of this condition to shape the house as a postmodern urban villa.

C-43 Contemporary Arts Museum

C-45 Hail House

C-47 Morris House

C-48 House

C-49 Copley House

C-50 Graves House

C-45
Hail House
1 West 11th Place
1925, William Ward Watkin

A compact French provincial style house that sits at the foot of a small private street laid out by architect Joseph W. Northrop, Jr. in 1920. Northrop was responsible for the houses at 4 and 6 West 11th Place. Dillion Kyle designed the compound-like house at 5 West 11th (2012).

C-46
Helmet House
5215 Yoakum Boulevard
1985, Alan Hirschfield

Hirschfield described this aggressively composed infill house as a Teutonic knight.

C-47
Morris House
2 Waverly Court
1952, Wilson, Morris & Crain

This small-scaled contemporary house, closed off from the traffic along Bissonnet, is focused on a series of internal garden courts.

C-48
House
10 Waverly Court
1997, Eubanks/Bohnn Associates
with Peter H. Brown

Proportions and details evoke a small Parisian *hôtel particulier*.

C-49
Copley House
17 Shadowlawn Circle
1926, John F. Staub

Shadowlawn, like Waverly Court and West 11th Place, took advantage of its proximity to Shadyside to offer itself to discriminating home builders on what, in the 1920s, was the edge of Houston. Staub's marvelous French Breton style manor house seems slightly incongruous with its steep shingled roofs and almost windowless walls. But like so many Staub houses, it opens at the rear through French doors and arched loggias to a private garden and the prevailing breeze. Additions in 1990 by Cannady, Jackson & Ryan precipitated demolition of Staub's freestanding garage apartment.

C-50
Graves House
11 Shadowlawn Circle
1926, William Ward Watkin

A formidably-scaled neo-Georgian house offset with palm trees.

C-51
House
9 Shadowlawn Circle
1961, Anderson Todd

Holding its own among the 1920s eclectic country houses is this unobtrusive, but generously proportioned, courtyard house of steel, brick, and glass, a rigorously conceived, disciplined development of the precepts of Mies van der Rohe.

C-51 House

C-46 Helmet House

C-52 Coleman House

C-53 Monteith House, 5 Shadowlawn Circles

C-54 Cochran House

C-55 Kuldell House

C-52
Coleman House
6 Shadowlawn Circle
1933, Hiram A. Salisbury

Salisbury exploited the curve of the street to extend this manorial-style house laterally on its shallow site.

C-53
Monteith House
5 Shadowlawn Circle
1934, Hiram A. Salisbury and
T. George McHale

The pastoral allusions of this house take on urbanistic overtones as it continues the siting and stylistic strategies of the Salisbury-designed house next door.

C-54
Cochran House
1324 North Boulevard
1926, John F. Staub

One of six houses that Staub designed in Broadacres, a small private place neighborhood rendered extraordinary by the staggered rows of Live Oak trees that William Ward Watkin planted when he laid out the neighborhood in 1922. This austere manorial-style house recedes in plan so that all the major rooms have access to the prevailing breeze. The front door is on the west side of the house, beneath a corbelled brick archway inspired by the work of the English architect, E. L. Lutyens.

C-55
Kuldell House
1400 South Boulevard
1929, John F. Staub

Sumptuously detailed with molded brick and terra cotta shingle tiles, this manorial-style house was acclimatized with oversized window bays equipped with leaded casements; stylistic consistency was maintained without choking off the breeze. To the left of the protruding gabled bay, the ornamental brickwork patterns vary from panel to panel between the second-floor windows.

C-56
Walne House
1405 South Boulevard
1925, Briscoe & Dixon

Briscoe's version of the English manorial genre complements the Staub houses across the street. C. C. "Pat" Fleming designed the gardens (1946). Curtis & Windham sensitively and discreetly expanded the angled service wing (1998).

C-57
Anderson House
1515 South Boulevard
1928, Birdsall P. Briscoe

Briscoe considered this Tuscan villa style house one of his most accomplished works. It was restored by Ray Bailey Architects (1989); The SWA Group was responsible for landscape improvements. Across the street at 1505 South Boulevard is another Briscoe-designed house (1927), now almost invisible behind the densely planted gardens installed by New York landscape architect Ellen B. Shipman (1936).

C-58
Tennant House
1505 North Boulevard
1927, John F. Staub

Staub essayed considerable virtuosity in this neo-Georgian house by asymmetrically arranging windows in a symmetrically composed front façade. The big arched window lights the front stair; reception rooms all look out to a rear garden, where the topiary arches, planted to the designs of the landscape architect, J. Allen Myers, Jr., still bracket a central grass terrace.

C-59
Wier House
1411 North Boulevard
1928, Birdsall P. Briscoe

Briscoe reduced the front elevation of this restrained house to a manipulation of oversized window openings framing an inset central loggia. Ruth London designed the gardens.

C-56 Walne House

C-57 Anderson House

C-58 Tennant House

C-59 Wier House

C-60 Hutcheson House

C-61 Pincoffs House

C-62 Lester House

C-63 Gilmer House

C-65 Graustark Family Townhouses

C-60
Hutcheson House
1405 North Boulevard
1924, John F. Staub

This Connecticut Valley Colonial style house was the first that Staub designed in Houston. Its stylistic provenance was rationalized by arranging the rooms one deep in a long, thin file so that all were permeated by the prevailing breeze. Anthony E. Frederick restored the house (1984).

C-61
Pincoffs House
1323 North Boulevard
1927, Birdsall P. Briscoe

Of 17th-century French manorial derivation, this symmetrically composed house is set in formal gardens designed by Fleming & Sheppard.

C-62
Lester House
1324 North Boulevard
1927, Birdsall P. Briscoe

Briscoe abstracted the manorial genre to its geometric essence in this taut, planar house faced with inset triangular gables.

C-63
Gilmer House
1318 North Boulevard
1926, William Ward Watkin

Despite having planned the subdivision and its landscaping, Watkin designed only one house in Broadacres. It was, however, one of the most assured that he produced—a planar, white stucco-surfaced Spanish house, framed by almost identical end bays. The arched second-floor windows are a later alteration.

C-64
Dargan House
1318 North Boulevard
1930, John F. Staub

Staub's version of the formal French manorial style was imposing but, characteristically, he integrated major rooms with a rear garden through oversized, triple-hung windows.

F-65
Graustark Family Townhouses
4923-4927 Graustark Street
1972, Howard Barnstone

Barnstone designed this trio of row houses as an exercise in doing the most with the least. Each is 16 feet wide, but so cleverly organized in section that the interiors seem quite spacious. Externally his low-key urban vernacular incorporates such witty touches as glass garage doors that permit the car to be admired even when indoors. The house at 4927 was altered in 2012.

C-66
Milford Townhomes
1220 Milford Street
1984, Arquitectonica

Packed tightly together on a single lot, these row houses are ingeniously planned to ensure internal spaciousness. The gabled turquoise monitor admits light into a 3-story-high stairwell at the center of each house; the grid of glass block visible outside continues into the interior to filter skylight from the stairwells into adjoining rooms. The brash colors are a trademark of the Miami architects.

C-67
House
1414 Milford Street
1998, Michael Landrum

West Ranch Estates, a subdivision developed in 1948 with low-brow ranch style houses, was aggressively redeveloped in the 1990s with stylistically souped-up, hyper houses. In contrast to the surrounding hulks, Landrum's domed house exhibits his transplanted San Antonian sensibility in its defined shapes, textures, and coloration. The grounds were designed by the San Antonio landscape architect, Sarah Lake. Across the street at 1425 Milford is a house by Glassman Shoemake Maldonado (1998). Natalye Appel paid tribute to the neighborhood's original architecture in the house at 1535 Milford (1994).

C-68
Down and Up House
1514 Banks Street
2012, Enter Architecture

Architect Karen Lantz designed this modest, 2-story shed-roofed house as a model of sustainable practices, beginning with the deconstruction and recycling of the original Ranch Estates house this house replaced.

C-64 Dargan House

C-66 Milford Townhouses

C-67 House

C-68 Down and Up House

C-69 House

C-70 Act II House

C-71 Stern House

C-72 House

C-69
House
1425 Banks Street
2007, Strasser Ragni

With their customary subtlety, Strasser Ragni overlap and bend shallowly layered planes of black brick and stucco to frame interpenetrating indoor-outdoor spaces in a house that is closed from the street but quite open internally.

C-70
Act II House
1319 Banks Street
2001, FdM: Arch

New York architect François de Menil specializes in sublime assemblies of serene planes animated by daylight.

C-71
Stern House
1202 Milford Street
1992, William F. Stern & Associates

This lofty house is a virtual anthology of Houston architecture. Its stepped plan derives from John Staub's environmentally responsive houses. Its vertically stacked interior spaces pay tribute to the Howard Barnstone-designed townhouses on Graustark. Its louvered sunscreens and gray-painted cypress clapboards salute the Menil Collection. Its low-pitched roof reflects the characteristic shapes of surrounding neighborhood bungalows.

C-72
House
1118 Barlett Street
1993, Carlos Jiménez

Jiménez retained the shell of an existing 1920s hipped-roof, clapboard-surfaced house, but radically reconfigured its door and window openings and interiors. From Mount Vernon on the west, note the projecting V-plan stair window on the rear of the house and the ethereal carport.

C-73
Keating House
4949 Yoakum Boulevard
1983, Skidmore, Owings & Merrill

Skidmore, Owings & Merrill's one house in Houston was designed by, and for, the partner-in-charge of its local office from 1976-1986, Richard Keating. In the best tradition of Keating's native California, the house is very self-effacing from the street.

C-74
Lindsey House
1110 Milford Street
1926, J. T. Rather, Jr.

Rather worked for, and eventually became the partner of, John F. Staub. Here he produced the quintessential suburban dream house of the 1920s—a compact, Regency-style brick house with a latticed loggia to the side. Carlos B. Schoeppl designed the picturesquely composed house next door, at 1112 Milford (1926). Its expansive bay window was an addition by Stayton Nunn & Milton McGinty (1959).

C-75
Streetman House
1117 Banks Street
1931, J. T. Rather, Jr.

The last-to-be-built in this trio of houses (for the families of two brothers and a sister) was one of Rather's finest, a superb example of disciplined composition and exquisite detail in the Staub manner. Rather executed the classical ornament of this little French manorial style house in molded brick. Cameron Armstrong rehabilitated the house (1993).

C-76
Chelsea Market
4611-4621 Montrose Boulevard
1985, Kirksey-Meyers Architects

Notable for its urban design, this specialty retail center emphasizes pedestrian amenity rather than the parked car. It was developed in part by the architect, John H. Kirksey.

C-73 Keating House

C-74 Lindsey Townhouses

C-75 Streetman House

C-76 Chelsea Market

C-77 Cotswold Manor

C-78 Holland Lodge No. 1

C-79 Townhouses

C-80 Vassar Place Apartments

C-81 Mandell Residences

C-77
Cotswold Manor
242 Portland Avenue
1928, F. Stanley Piper

The homebuilder, C. C. Bell, Jr., had his brother-in-law, architect Stanley Piper of Bellingrath, Washington, design a complex of manorial-style apartment buildings that Bell expanded between 1945-1948 with 238, 220-222, and 216-218 Portland. Missing are the 2- and 3-story Gramercy Gables, which faced Montrose, and most of the 2-story Cotswold Manor at the head of Portland. These were demolished in 2000 by the Finger Companies, which replaced them with the 18-story, 187-unit Museum Tower (2002, Jackson & Ryan) at 4899 Montrose. Portland is a would-be private place boulevard that exemplifies the 1920s preference for diminutive scale. It traverses the Cotswold Court subdivision, developed by the architect-builder Arthur D. Boice in 1924. Boice's Hearthstone Company designed and built the manorial-style residential buildings at 239 (1929), 235 (1928), and 229-231 Portland (1924). At the opposite end of the street, the architect Joseph Finger built the brick-faced, tile-roofed duplex at 120 Portland (1926), where he and his family lived. Next to it is MacKie & Kamrath's clinic and house for Dr. W. A. Coole at 102 Portland (1941). Both the Finger and Coole houses have been allowed to fall into deplorable condition.

C-78
Holland Lodge No. 1
4911 Montrose Boulevard
1954, Milton McGinty

The centerpiece of this windowless box (from the heroic age of air-conditioning) is William M. McVey's inset mural sculpture. Executed *in situ* in Texas cream limestone, it depicts the founding of Masonry and its transmission to Texas.

C-79
Townhouses
4706-4710 Yoakum Boulevard
2003, Wittenberg Oberholzer

Gordon Wittenberg and Mark Oberholzer produced their 21st-century version of a Case Study House: a pair of 3-story houses set at right angles to each other, one facing the street, the other facing a side garden and motor court. The houses are of steel-frame construction, exposed inside, and are surfaced externally with steel panels.

C-80
Vassar Place Apartments
1303 Vassar Place
1965, Howard Barnstone

Barnstone's gift for working spatial miracles in confined circumstances is exemplified by this set of apartments, which radiates around the foot of Vassar Place. Intricately planned units are configured around private gardens and terraces that open, in a staged sequence, to a common green space at the back of the site. The artist, Gertrude Barnstone, fabricated the art gates visible from Vassar and Graustark.

C-81
Mandell Residences
4901-4903 Mandell Street
1985, Arquitectonica

Brown brick, white tile, and giant-scaled geometric incisions are used to induce a sense of spatial depth and individual identity in this row of four houses. Arquitectonica's shapes are a tongue-in-cheek salute to the metaphysical geometries of the Philadelphia architect, Louis I. Kahn, just the sort of insider's irreverence that sets their critics steaming. The backs of the houses (visible from Banks) zigzag in plan—something buildings aren't supposed to do.

C-82
Anderson House
1638 Banks Street
1960, Wilson, Morris, Crain & Anderson

Ralph A. Anderson, Jr., designed this modern, flat-roofed courtyard house as his own residence, confidently, but unobtrusively, inserting it onto a street of conventional suburban houses.

C-82 Anderson House

C-83 Vassar Place Townhouses

C-83
Vassar Place Townhouses
1731-1733 Vassar Place
1983, William F. Stern & Associates

This group of four brick-faced row houses defers to the neighborhood by maintaining the existing front setback line and preserving mature trees already on the site. Stern's elevations are urbane. Inside generous living lofts occupy the second floor, with bedrooms clustered on the ground floor behind the garages—a recurring pattern among Houston infill row houses.

C-84 Finnell House

C-84
Finnell House
1908 Vassar Place
1989, Wittenberg Partnership Architects

In a tribute to the unorthodox Los Angeles architect, Frank O. Gehry, Susan and Gordon Wittenberg adroitly managed the collision of shapes and mixture of despised materials in this lively house. Its big windows overlook the Southwest Freeway.

C-85 House X2

C-85
House X2
4904-4906 S. Shepherd Drive
2008, Collaborative Designworks

James M. Evans designed a pair of tall, sectionally activated rowhouses that fit together back-to-back rather than side-by-side. Deep spatial incisions give the pair sculptural dynamism.

C-86 Milford Live/Work

C-86
Milford Live/Work
2207 Milford Street
2009, StudioMET

Su Nguyen combined studio and residential spaces for an interior designer in this metal, wood, and stone-faced compound.

C-87 Howell House

C-87
Howell House
1601 Milford Street
1937, Campbell & Keller

This is a determinedly functionalist modern villa, flat-topped, stucco-surfaced, with pipe rail lined roof decks and glass block corner windows. Next door at 1609 Milford is its ideological opposite, a graceful neo-Georgian house by J. T. Rather, Jr. (1935).

C-88
Bonner House
1705 North Boulevard
1938, Hiram A. Salisbury and T. George McHale

Salisbury and McHale mixed Regency and regionalist metaphors in this graceful house, faced with symmetrical chimney stacks and cast iron galleries.

C-89
Anderson House
1660 South Boulevard
1929, Burns & James

Katharine Mott, a house builder from Indianapolis, settled in Houston in 1927. For the next four years she and her husband, Harry, built speculative houses in Houston's newest subdivisions, most of which she designed in association with the Indianapolis architects, Burns & James. The Mott houses were in the picturesque manorial style and exhibited skillful decorative detail in brick and stone, executed by a crew of craftsmen who built all the houses. Additions along Dunlavy are by Miller Dahlstrand (2011). Across the street at 1659 South is an earlier house by Mrs. Mott (1928).

C-90
Howard House
1707 South Boulevard
1927, Joseph W. Northrop, Jr.

Built for the banker and suburban real estate developer, George F. Howard, this house was in the neo-Georgian genre at which Northrop excelled. Note how Northrop preserved the symmetry of the front façade by varying the sill heights of the first-floor windows; such legerdemain was especially admired in the 1920s. Northrop carried this penchant for architectural gamesmanship up the street by designing a series of houses in which the composition of the Howard House is varied, but never beyond recognition: 1715 and 1749 South (1928), 1813 South (1929), and 1817 South (1931).

C-88 Bonner House

C-89 Anderson House

C-90 Howard House

C-91 Morgan House

C-93 Edgar Allan Poe Elementary School

C-94 Anderson House

C-95 David House

C-96 House

C-91
Morgan House
1818 South Boulevard
1999, Jay Baker Architects

A trimly proportioned gable-ended house front, surfaced with clapboards, enabled this house to take its place confidently alongside older neighbors.

C-92
House
1928 South Boulevard
1994, Carlos Jiménez

This house replaced a duplex in the Texas regional modern style (1954, William Tamminga). Its proportions, composition, and material pay homage to the earlier house as a way to preserve community continuity. Note the companion guesthouse at the rear of the property. Will Fleming was the landscape architect. In contrast to the aggressive neo-traditionals built on South and North in the 1990s, this and other modern houses have adapted a much more neighborhood-friendly approach, evident at 1820 South (2000, Carlos Jiménez), 1752 North (1993, Charles Tapley Associates), and the jaunty high-tech carport visible up the side driveway at 1912 North (1992, William F. Stern & Associates).

C-93
Edgar Allan Poe Elementary School
5100 Hazard Street
1929, Harry D. Payne

Payne came to Houston in 1925 from the office of the St. Louis architect, William B. Ittner, the foremost school design expert in the Midwest, as a consultant to the Houston school district. Poe is one of a series of neighborhood schools that Payne designed, all based on the same plan, but varied in their stylistic details. Spirited additions to the rear are by Kendall/Heaton Associates (1986). In-filling an interior courtyard to the south of the main entrance is the Mechanical Shade Tree (1996, Graduate Design/Build Studio, University of Houston College of Architecture and Patrick Peters), a multi-purpose steel canopy structure that provides shelter and anchors exercise and recreation equipment. Visible from the South-Wilton intersection is the Covered Walkway (1998, Rice Building Workshop, Rice University School of Architecture and Keith Krumwiede), another design-build project produced as a community service by architecture students and their instructors.

C-94
Anderson House
2003 Bissonnet Avenue
1968, William J. Anderson

The first in a series of modern houses with which Anderson and his partner Tom Wilson architecturally reinvigorated the 1920s neighborhood of Southampton Place. This inwardly-focused house, built for the architect's family, faces a busy intersection. Yet, despite its closed aspect, it has a strong figural presence due to its shingled wall surfaces and shapely profiles.

C-95
David House
1807 Wroxton Road
1970, Charles Tapley Associates

The modernist strategy for inserting new houses in Southampton in the 1960s and '70s generally entailed construction of a privacy wall insulating new from old. Behind this brick wall is a fascinating collection of little buildings strung together along a central causeway. All that is visible from the street, however, are the thrusting hoods and skylights of this architectural conclave.

C-96
House
1825 Albans Road
2007, HarrisonKornberg Architects

Maintaining the scale and front setback of older Southampton houses, this 2-story, U-plan, courtyard house sits comfortably in the neighborhood, even though its exterior materials (exposed clay tile, vertically ribbed steel wall panels, and a raised seam metal roof) are unconventional. The landscape design is notable.

C-92 House

C-97 House

C-98 Suit House

C-99 House

C-100 Smith House

C-101 House

C-102 Aubry House

C-97
House
1809 Dunstan Road
1993, Scott Ballard

Ballard deftly inserted this modern house amid older neighbors by pushing it to the back of the site. Living spaces on the second floor take advantage of tall ceiling heights and views out.

C-98
Suit House
1828 Dunstan Road
1970, Anderson Todd

The chocolate-colored paint on this very restrained brick and steel courtyard house is not original. Todd played the rectilinear architecture against the curvature of Kent with assurance.

C-99
House
1930 Bolsover Road
1994, Anderson Todd and Iris G. Todd

Nearly 25 years after designing the house at 1828 Dunstan, Todd and his partner (and wife), Iris Todd, produced another steel-framed, brick-walled pavilion that, within very tight confines, creates an extraordinary sense of spaciousness. Across the street at 2002 Bolsover (1932) is an unusual raised bungalow, one of several built in Southampton in the early 1930s. Even more unusual, the architect was Joseph W. Northrop, Jr., who also designed the more characteristic neo-Georgian house at 2006 Bolsover (1933).

C-100
Smith House
2007 Dunstan Road
1970, Anderson/Wilson

Behind the angled wooden plane is a house built of concrete tilt wall, with ceilings of exposed steel bar joists inside. It is set into the midst of suburban conventionality without too much ado, in contrast to the overscaled Georgian-burgers that began to go up in Southampton in the mid 1980s. Next door at 2003 Dunstan is a large house by Tom Wilson (1993).

C-101
House
2032 Bolsover Road
1989, Thomas Redyard Wilson

This sculpturally massed house of stucco-surfaced concrete block, a late, but confident assertion of faith in modern design, aggressively confronts the neighborhood context.

C-102
Aubry House
2217 Bolsover Road
1985, Morris*Aubry Architects and Charles Keith Associates

Multiple gables, a recurring theme in Eugene Aubry's residential designs, are used to domesticate this modern house.

C-103
Sunnystones
2230 Rice Boulevard
1935, Harvin C. Moore & Hermon Lloyd

Limestone veneer and steel casement windows precisely date this picturesque manorial house to the mid-1930s. It was designed for attorney Ira Allen and his family. L. Barry Davidson Architects remodeled and added to the house. McDugald Steele was the landscape architect.

C-104
Cannady House
2246 Quenby Road
1972, 1982, William T. Cannady & Associates

The initial house, barely visible on the east, is a 3-story, flat-roofed, wooden cube (now stucco-surfaced) that sits far back on what was originally a wooded greensward. Ten years after its completion, the architect-owner built a second version near the front property line that stylistically registered the changed spirit of the age.

C-105
The Bachelors Club
2229 Quenby Road
1926

Although Southampton was restricted to single-family houses from its inception in 1923, the Bachelors Club existed for 10 years before the house became a single family residence. It is a delightful English cottage configured around a miniature great hall.

C-103 Sunnystones

C-104 Cannady House

C-105 The Bachelors Club

C-106 House

C-107 House

C-108 House

C-109 Wagner House

C-110 House

C-106
House
2238 Albans Road
1987, Ziegler Cooper Architects

Ziegler Cooper concluded 20 years of modern residential architecture in Southampton with a new house that attempts to reconcile modernity with suburban convention.

C-107
House
2231 Wroxton Road
2008, Nonya Grenader

A shed-roofed, 2-story house that slides into the long dimension of the site, this residence was designed to open to its east sideyard and preserve existing trees, which are carefully framed by views from inside. One block to the west at 2303 Wroxton is a walled 2-story house by Strasser Ragni (2008).

C-108
House
2115 Wroxton Road
2009, Stern and Bucek Architects

Wall planes of dark gray brick screen the interiors of this cruciform-plan house from the street, while making it possible to open ground floor spaces to exterior courtyards. Wood rainscreens case the cross wing.

C-109
Wagner House
2110 Albans Road
1936, Fellheimer & Wagner

A subtle blend of rose-colored brick and gracefully proportioned windows mark this house, designed by New York architects, Fellheimer & Wagner, for the family of architect Stewart Wagner's brother.

C-110
House
2129 Quenby Road
2003, Leslie Elkins Architecture

A 1-story house that is architecturally unassuming yet spontaneous. At 2125 Quenby is a 2-story house by Glassman Shoemake Maldonado (2002).

C-111
House
5331 Cherokee
2005, Allen Bianchi

Wall planes of white stucco make this 2-story house, configured in an L plan around a walled courtyard, a distinct presence at this corner. Bianchi repeated this performance at the other end of the Cherokee subdivision at 5302 Mandell (2006).

C-112
Morris House
5326 Mandell Street
1927, Drink Milner

Architectural attributes of old Virginia were consolidated into this suburban cottage.

C-113
First Christian Church
1601 Sunset Boulevard
1958, Brown & McKim

Although the shape of the church's roof is most prominent externally, what one experiences inside are walled gardens flanking the church, visible through the nave's entirely glazed perimeter. Donald Barthelme, who was originally associated with Hamilton Brown on this project, conceived this building as a "church without walls," a notion that Brown carried through after Barthelme withdrew from the project. The landscape architect, Ralph Ellis Gunn, installed the plantings; Seymour Fogel was responsible for the glazed brick and stained glass mural on the front of the church. When the congregation sold its parking lot across Cherokee for the egregious Medical Clinic of Houston Building (2009, FKP Architects) and its 600-car garage, Merriman Holt designed a replacement Educational Building along the church's frontage on Cherokee that expands imaginatively on the themes of Brown's complex (2005).

C-111 House

C-112 Morris House

C-113 First Christian Church

C-114 Congregation Emanu-El Temple

C-115 Wiess House

C-114
Congregation Emanu El Temple
1500 Sunset Boulevard
1949, MacKie & Kamrath and Lenard Gabert

Temple Emanu El marks one of the high points of MacKie & Kamrath's career. Shunning historical imagery, they architecturally embodied the idea of a house of worship. The building's dominant horizontals are rhythmically countered by the gentle rise of the tent-like, steel-framed roof structure. The use of thin Roman brick with horizontally raked joints and stone coping and the detailing of the entrance show the influence of Kamrath's mentor, Frank Lloyd Wright. Wright bestowed official approval on the newly completed temple when he came to Houston in 1949 to accept the Gold Medal of the American Institute of Architects. Attached to the northeast side of the temple is a freestanding chapel by Clovis Heimsath Associates (1975). Ray Bailey Architects designed the extensive rear wing (1990) and the congregation's 4-story, 400-car garage (2009).

C-115
Wiess House
[now Rice University President's House]
2 Sunset Boulevard
1920, William Ward Watkin

Facing Main behind a stucco-faced wall (installed by John F. Staub in 1936), this tile-roofed Mediterranean villa-style house for Harry C. Wiess, co-founder of the Humble Oil & Refining Company, was designed by Watkin to harmonize stylistically with the Rice Institute campus buildings next door. The house was altered and expanded by Harrie T. Lindeberg (1926). Owned by Rice University since the mid 1970s, it was allowed to fall into an alarming state of disrepair. The house was rehabilitated by W. O Neuhaus Associates (2004) as the President's House of Rice University, which entailed destruction of much of the Lindeberg interior fabric.

Museum District / Hermann Park / Boulevard Oaks / Southampton

Rice University / Texas Medical Center

1. **Rice University Administration Building,** 6100 Main Street
2. **Physics Building,** Rice University
3. **Martel College,** Rice University
4. **McMurtry and Duncan Colleges,** Rice University
5. **Anne and Charles Duncan Hall,** Rice University
6. **Mechanical Laboratory and Power House Campanile,** Rice University
7. **Abercrombie Laboratory,** Rice University
8. **Chemistry Building,** Rice University
9. **M.D. Anderson Hall,** Rice University
10. **George R. Brown Hall,** Rice University
11. **M.D. Anderson Biological Laboratories, Keith-Wiess Geological Laboratories, Space Science and Technology Building, Hamman Hall,** Rice University
12. **Dell Butcher Hall,** Rice University
13. **Brockman Hall for Physics,** Rice University
14. **Oshman Engineering Design Kitchen,** Rice University
15. **Gibbs Wellness Center,** Rice University
16. **Rice Stadium,** Rice University
17. **Alice Pratt Brown Hall,** Rice University
18. **Media Center,** Rice University
19. **Reckling Park,** Rice University
20. **Tudor Fieldhouse and Youngkin Center,** Rice University
21. **James A. Baker III Institute for Public Policy,** Rice University
22. **McNair Hall,** Rice University
23. **Herring Hall,** Rice University
24. **Wiess College,** Rice University
25. **Brochstein Pavilion,** Rice University
26. **Humanities Building,** Rice University
27. **Baker College and Will Rice College,** Rice University
28. **Cleveland Sewall Hall,** Rice University
29. **Cohen House,** Rice University
30. **South Plant,** Rice University
31. **Rice University BioScience Research Collaborative Building,** 6500 Main Street
32. **Palmer Memorial Chapel,** 6221 Main Street
33. **Memorial Hermann Hospital,** 6411 Fannin Street
34. **Hermann Professional Building,** 6410 Fannin Street
35. **Prairie View A&M University School of Nursing Building,** 6436 Fannin Street
36. **Smith Tower,** 6550 Fannin Street
37. **Medical Towers Building,** 1709 Dryden Road
38. **Texas Children's Hospital,** 6621 Fannin Street
39. **St. Luke's Medical Tower,** 6624 Fannin Street
40. **Texas Woman's University Institute of Health Sciences Building,** 6700 Fannin Street
41. **Wortham Fountain,** Holcombe Boulevard and Main Street
42. **Fayez S. Sarofim Building, University of Texas at Houston Health Science Center,** 1825 Pressler Drive
43. **METRO Texas Medical Center Transit Facility,** 6910 Fannin Street
44. **University of Texas at Houston Health Science Center School of Nursing and Community Center,** 6901 Bertner Avenue
45. **Lowry and Peggy Mays Clinic Building, University of Texas M. D. Anderson Cancer Center Ambulatory Care Center,** 1212 Holcombe Boulevard

46. **Prudential Building,** 1100 Holcombe Boulevard
47. **Children's Nutrition Research Center,** 1100 Bates Avenue
48. **Texas Children's Hospital Clinical Care Building,** 6701 Fannin Street
49. **University of Texas M. D. Anderson Hospital and Tumor Institute,** 1515 Holcombe Boulevard
50. **Denton A. Cooley Building, St. Luke's Hospital and the Texas Heart Institute,** 6718 Bertner Avenue
51. **Methodist Hospital Research Institute Building,** 6670 Bertner Avenue
52. **John P. McGovern Texas Medical Center Commons,** 6550 Bertner Avenue
53. **Garden Club of Houston Park,** 6500 block Bertner Avenue
54. **Mary Gibbs Jones Building,** 1130 John Freeman Boulevard
55. **Baylor College of Medicine Cullen Building,** 1200 Moursund Avenue
56. **Baylor College of Medicine Margaret M. Alkek Building for Biomedical Research,** 1325 Moursund Avenue
57. **City of Houston Dept of Public Health Building,** 1115 South Braeswood Boulevard
58. **Ben Taub General Hospital,** 1502 Taub Loop
59. **Veterans Administration Medical Center,** 2002 Holcombe Boulevard
60. **National Biscuit Company Building,** 2450 Holcombe Boulevard
61. **Baylor College of Medicine Alkek Eye Center Building,** 7200 Cambridge Street
62. **Shell Information Center,** 1500 Old Spanish Trail
63. **The Astrodome,** Loop 610 and Kirby Drive
64. **Reliant Stadium,** 8400 Kirby Drive

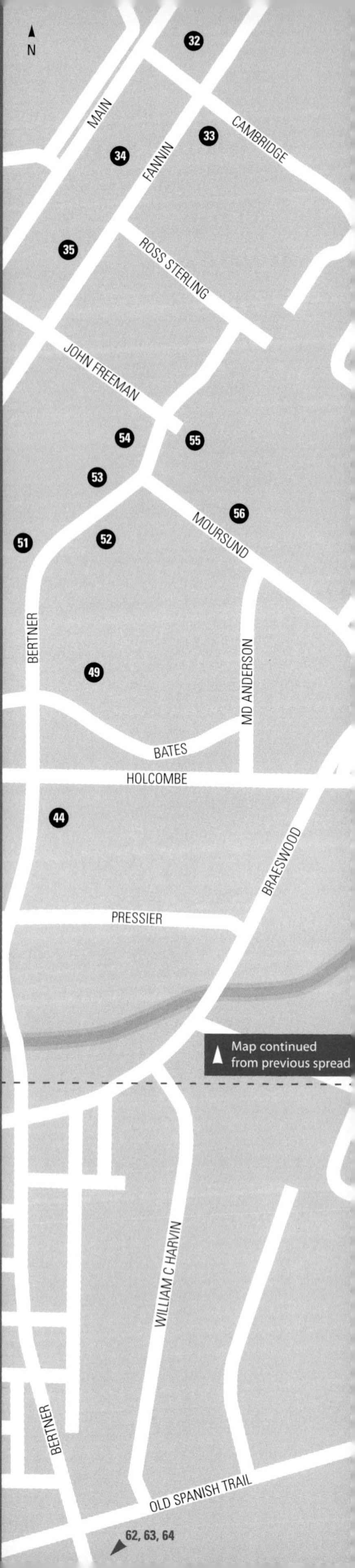

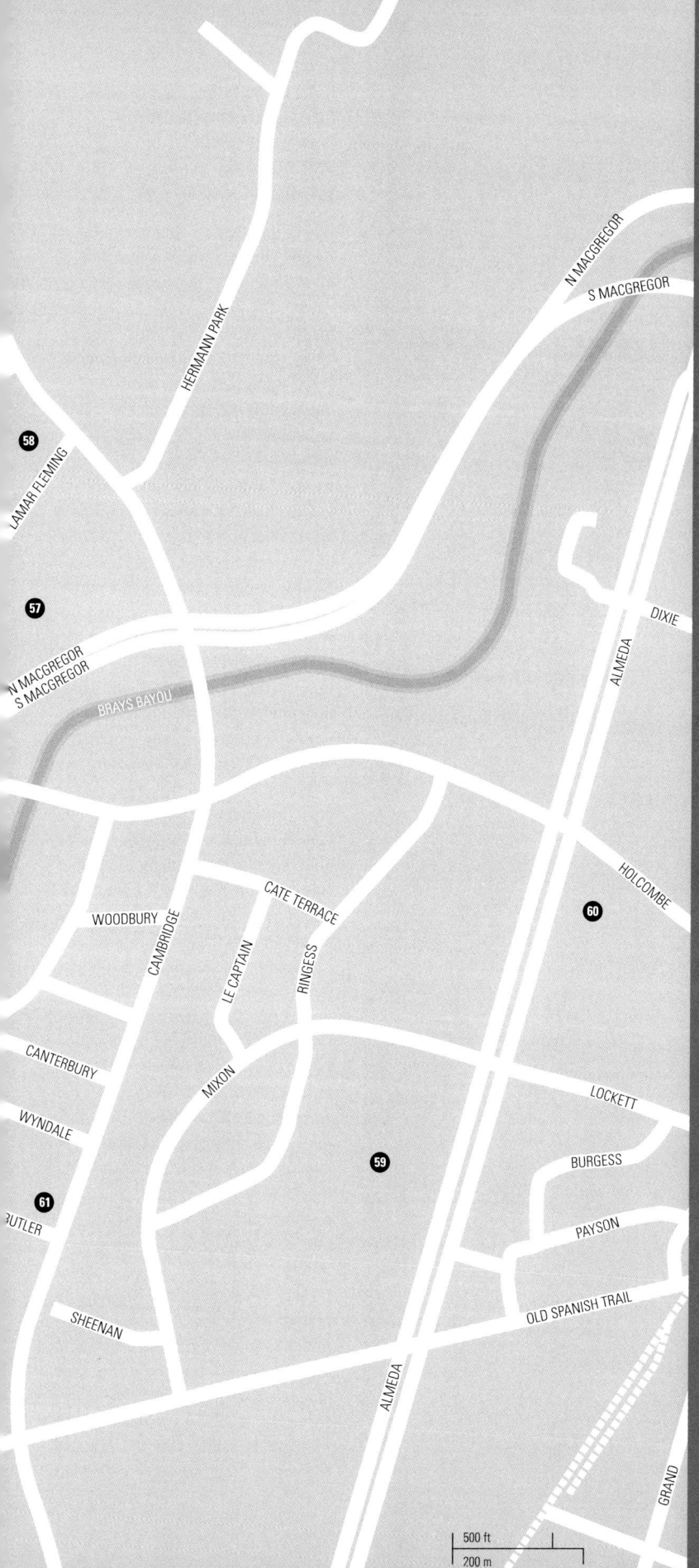

D-2 Physics Building

D-3 Marian Fox and Speros P. Martel College

D-1
Rice University Administration Building
[now Lovett Hall]
6100 Main Street
1912, Cram, Goodhue & Ferguson

When the Boston architect, Ralph Adams Cram, was commissioned in 1909 to plan the campus of the newly organized William M. Rice Institute (Rice University since 1960), he devised an architectural style appropriate to an institution of high culture set on an immense plain in a hot, humid, Southern locale. Although Cram was best known as a champion of Gothic-revival architecture, he deemed this utterly unsuitable for Houston. So, in one of the most inspired episodes in the history of 20th-century American eclecticism, Cram formulated a southern Gothic analog for Rice. He shaped long, thin, screen-like buildings to defer to the prevailing breeze, undercut them with arched, cloistered passageways, and encrusted them with Byzantine, Venetian, and northern Italian detail. Faced with brick, limestone, and colored marble, these buildings outlined sequences of quadrangular and axially elongated courts defined spatially by massed ranks of trees. The Administration Building (now Lovett Hall after the university's first president, Edgar Odell Lovett, a professor of astronomy from Princeton who retained Cram) was the first and most elaborately finished of Cram's buildings. It sits astride the main axis of the campus, which penetrates the building's arched portal, the Sallyport, and proceeds into the Academic Court. Because it initially contained not only the administrative offices, but classrooms, faculty offices, a library, and the double-volume Faculty Chamber, Cram varied the pattern of window openings within the building's symmetrically composed ranges to indicate differences in internal arrangements. The cloister on the Academic Court side of the building is ceiled with Guastavino tile vaults. Note the jokey collegiate iconography on column capitals and at the bases of the Sallyport arch. Oswald Lassig, an Austrian stonecutter, executed the figural sculpture on the Administration Building. Decorative tilework was executed by the Moravian Pottery and Tile Works of Doylestown, Pennsylvania.

D-2
Physics Building
[now Herzstein Hall]
Rice University
1914, Cram, Goodhue & Ferguson

Next to the Administration Building and connected to it by a freestanding extension of the cloistered walkway is the Physics Building. Cram varied the degree and character of architectural decoration on the exteriors of this 3-part building to relate its faces to different sectors of the campus: an elaborately detailed south façade facing the Academic Court, a stripped-down north elevation facing the Court of Engineering across the street, and transitional decoration for the Physics Amphitheater, a semidetached block containing a large lecture hall. Mary Chase Perry and the Pewabic Pottery Company of Detroit were responsible for the decorative tile work above the main entrance from the cloister. Inside this entrance is a vaulted vestibule ceiled with exposed Guastavino tiles bearing scientific insignia.

D-3
Marian Fox and Speros P. Martel College
Rice University
2002, Michael Graves and PGAL

Princeton architect, Michael Graves, planned this 4-story student residential complex around a broad central quadrangle, which he framed with a monumental gateway. Liberal use of column-like cylinders and big-scale brick banding patterns are a postmodern riff on Cram's architecture. Graves and PGAL were responsible for extensive additions to the adjoining Mary Gibbs Jones College and Margarett Root Brown College.

D-1 Rice University Administration Building

D-4 Deedee and Burton McMurtry College and Anne and Charles Duncan College

D-5 Anne and Charles Duncan Hall

D-7 Abercrombie Laboratory

D-8 Chemistry Building

D-4
Deedee and Burton McMurtry College and Anne and Charles Duncan College
Rice University
2009, Hopkins Architects and Hanbury Evans Wright Vlattas

The London architect, Michael Hopkins, designed two almost identical residential college complexes side-by-side. Each 5-story building houses 324 students and is organized around a square interior quadrangle focused on a glass-walled dining pavilion linked to a central kitchen and servery. In contrast to the adjoining Graves colleges, the Hopkins colleges are architecturally self-effacing. Exterior walls are structural brick-bearing walls erected on top of ground-floor concrete platforms. The top floors contain ample terrace space. Cypress sheathing is used extensively to offset the concrete and brick. The Office of James Burnett was the landscape architect.

D-5
Anne and Charles Duncan Hall
Rice University
1996, John Outram and Kendall/Heaton Associates

It should come as no surprise that the dedication booklet for this building by Keith D. Cooper, associate professor of computer science, took the form of an iconographic explication. The London architect, John Outram, fully indulged his penchant for mythologizing in the design of Duncan Hall, which contains computational engineering disciplines. Outram's narrative bravura is not matched by his spatial skills. Consequently Duncan Hall appears ponderous and overbearing externally. Internally it is (to use Outram's term) "operatic," especially the Main Hall with its dizzying programmatic mural, *The Birth of Consciousness*, a computerized magnification of the architect's drawing imprinted onto vinyl sheets. The bombastic spatiality of the main hall feels even less amusing when compared to the claustrophobic dimensions of interior halls throughout the building.

D-6
Mechanical Laboratory and Power House Campanile
Rice University
1912, Cram, Goodhue & Ferguson

Situated at the head of one of the cross axes that intersects the main axis is the Campanile, the symbolic theme structure Cram's office provided for the university. It was a smokestack for the university's power plant, not a bell tower, but it possessed the typological-historical-vertical associations that Cram felt a college campus required. The Mechanical Laboratory, to which the Campanile is attached, represents the pared-down version of Cram's Rice style that he considered appropriate to the lesser status of the Court of Engineering. Redressing this cultural estimation are three slabs of pink Texas granite installed by the New York sculptor, Michael Heizer, in 1984, *45°, 90°, 180°*.

D-7
Abercrombie Laboratory
Rice University
1948, Staub & Rather; William Ward Watkin, consulting architect

J. T. Rather, Jr., attempted to modernize Cram's Rice style with exaggerated horizontality. The relief sculpture next to the entrance portal is *Man Drawing Power From the Sun and Transforming It into Energy* by William M. McVey, an instructor of sculpture at the Cranbrook Academy of Art and a graduate of Rice's architecture department in the 1920s.

D-8
Chemistry Building
[now W. M. Keck Hall]
Rice University
1925, Cram & Ferguson and William Ward Watkin

Watkin, a draftsman in Cram's office, was sent to Houston in 1910 to supervise construction of Rice's initial buildings. President Lovett invited him to remain and begin a school of architecture, which Watkin headed from the Institute's opening in 1912 until his death in 1952. Watkin collaborated with his former employers on the design of the Chemistry Building, a more conventional rendition of the Lombard Romanesque than Cram had ventured in the 1910s. In 2000 the building was completely reconstructed internally by FKP Architects to provide state-of-the-art laboratory space; the exterior was conscientiously restored.

D-6 Mechanical Laboratory and Power House Campanile

D-9 M. D. Anderson Hall

D-10 George R. Brown Hall

D-12 Dell Butcher Hall

D-9
M.D. Anderson Hall
Rice University
1947, Staub & Rather; William Ward Watkin, consulting architect;
1981, James Stirling, Michael Wilford & Associates with Ambrose/McEnany

Rather designed this inoffensive classroom building just after the end of Rice's heroic age of architectural patronage (Cram died in 1942; Lovett retired in 1945). Thirty-two years later, with the addition of the Brochstein Wing to Anderson Hall (which had become the architecture building), Rice embarked on a second age of patronage by commissioning Stirling and Wilford of London as architects. Their addition to Anderson Hall causes it to conform to Cram's General Plan of 1910. Internally they opened a concourse through both the existing building and its added wing (the segment of the building closest to the street), marked at either end by conical skylights that salute Cram's Venetian Gothic tabernacles atop the Physics Building. Midway along the concourse, they made two double-volume spaces, the top-lit Jury Room (part of the new addition) and the Farish Gallery (a reclaimed space). Internal porthole windows and clerestories give the interiors a light, open feeling. Externally Stirling & Wilford playfully inverted the compositional codes of Rather's building, sometimes subtly, other times boldly, always with wit. The off-center bull's eye window on the west elevation of the Brochstein Wing is a clue to the sectional organization of the interior.

D-10
George R. Brown Hall
Rice University
1992, Cambridge Seven Associates and RWS Architects

Cambridge Seven's Charles Redmon followed the lead of Stirling & Wilford and César Pelli in turning to Cram's General Plan for direction in siting Brown Hall, the university's bioscience and bio-engineering research building. It frames the cross axis terminating at Hamman Hall, as proposed in the General Plan. Redmon's decision to treat the architectural languages articulated by Stirling & Wilford and Pelli as ready-mades available for re-combination means that Brown Hall lacks the sense of discovery and achievement that animated the earlier buildings. Rooftop silos house the building's vent stacks.

D-11
M.D. Anderson Biological Laboratories, Keith-Wiess Geological Laboratories, Hamman Hall
Rice University
1958, George Pierce-Abel B. Pierce
Space Science and Technology Building
1966, George Pierce-Abel B. Pierce

This row of three laboratory buildings and the 500-seat Hamman Hall auditorium (barely visible through the Sallyport of Brown Hall) represent a conscientious attempt by Pierce-Pierce's designer, Edwin J. Goodwin, Jr., to distill a modernist version of Cram's Rice architecture. What they lack is the scale and depth of Cram's originals and their defining presence in the landscape. David G. Parsons modeled the special bricks that appear in shiner courses, stamped with insignia appropriate to the various disciplines. The galleries of all three lab buildings have been enclosed.

D-12
Dell Butcher Hall
Rice University
1997, Antoine Predock Architects and Brooks/Collier

Like Stirling & Wilford and César Pelli, the Albuquerque architect, Antoine Predock, understood that the essence of Rice's architecture involves shaping space, not loading exterior surfaces with fulsome decoration. Rather than treat this building for nanoscience and technology, chemistry, physics, and electrical engineering as a big box, Predock configured it around an interior court with an upper-level, open-air amphitheater—a clever internalization of Rice Stadium. This courtyard spatially integrates Butcher Hall with the Pierce-Pierce buildings of the 1950s and provides views through to the playing fields to the west. Butcher Hall connects with what is around it and makes a new whole, where before there were only unpromising fragments.

D-11 M. D. Anderson Biological Laboratories, Keith-Wiess Geological Laboratories, Hamman Hall

D-13 Brockmann Hall for Physics

D-14 Oshman Engineering Design Kitchen

D-16 Rice Stadium

D-17 Alice Pratt Brown Hall

D-18 Media Center

D-13
Brockmann Hall for Physics
Rice University
2011, Kieran Timberlake Associates, Perkins + Will, and Jackson & Ryan Architects

The Philadelphia architect, James Timberlake, designed this 3-story-plus-basement, 110,000-SF lab building for a site that was not supposed to be built upon: a figural open space in front of Hamman Hall. Parallel bars contain labs (in the thicker, south bar, which almost touches Brown Hall) and faculty offices (the thinner bar on the north in front of Hamman Hall). Upper floors are elevated on concrete columns. Exterior finishes are keyed to internal use and solar orientation: a layered ceramic solar screen and glass block on the south and a north-facing glass curtain wall on which Penrose tiling patterns are silk screened. The Office of James Burnett was the landscape architect.

D-14
Oshman Engineering Design Kitchen
Rice University
1965, Wilson, Morris, Crain & Anderson
2008, Stern and Bucek Architects

Rice's move to satellite kitchens tied to new student housing rendered the former central kitchen redundant. Instead of being demolished, it was cleverly recycled by Stern and Bucek as an interdisciplinary "design kitchen" for undergraduate study in design and fabrication.

D-15
Barbara and David Gibbs Recreation and Wellness Center
Rice University
2009, Lake/Flato Architects and FS Partners

Lake/Flato of San Antonio and FS Partners of Dallas collaborated on the design of an athletic complex for students, staff, and faculty. Finishes are simple, but the scale is imposing. The Office of James Burnett was the landscape architect.

D-16
Rice Stadium
Rice University
1950, Hermon Lloyd & W. B. Morgan and Milton McGinty

Dominating the asphalt prairie at the western end of the campus are the upper decks of the 70,000-seat Rice Stadium. Built in only nine months, the stadium is an undisguised exposition of reinforced concrete construction technology made graceful by the lithe, 30-inch diameter columns supporting the upper decks. In Cram's General Plan this entire portion of the campus was designated as the site of a Persian garden.

D-17
Alice Pratt Brown Hall
Rice University
1991, Ricardo Bofill and the Taller de Arquitectura with Kendall/Heaton Associates

Just across the parking lot from Rice Stadium is Alice Pratt Brown Hall, home of the school of music. Designed by the Barcelona architect known for his boldness, the building is genuinely Texan in its magnitude. The southern tower contains the limestone-lined Edythe Bates Old Recital Hall, home to a 49-foot high Fisk/Rosales tracker organ (1997, Manuel Rosales and C. B. Fisk).

D-18
Media Center
Rice University
1970, Howard Barnstone & Eugene Aubry

Dominique and John de Menil built the Media Center and adjacent ex-Rice Museum to contain the Institute for the Arts, which they moved from the University of St. Thomas to Rice in 1969. Aubry's low-tech shed, finished off with galvanized sheet iron siding, was intended to symbolize the provisional status of this delightful building.

D-15 Barbara and David Gibbs Recreation and Wellness Center

D-19 Reckling Park

D-19
Reckling Park
Rice University
2000, Jackson & Ryan Architects

Rice's baseball stadium seats 3,021 spectators in two wings of bleachers framing the playing field. Jackson & Ryan's brick and stone screen wall with a sallyport-like entrance arch plays off the university's architectural and material identity. The Audrey Moody Ley Plaza (2009) connects the entrance to Reckling Park with the nearest campus street.

D-20 Tudor Field House and Youngkin Center

D-20
Tudor Field House and Youngkin Center
Rice University
1951, Jessen Jessen Millhouse & Greeven
2008, HOK Sport

HOK Sport redeemed what was perhaps the least architecturally inspired building on campus with their reconstruction, which opened the Autry Court arena to the street and substantially improved spectator amenities.

D-22 Janice Suber and Robert McNair Hall

D-21
James A. Baker III Institute for Public Policy
Rice University
1997, Hammond Beeby Babka and Morris Architects

Chicago architect Tom Beeby ostentatiously deferred to the authority of Cram by designing a building that conceivably could have been produced by Cram's office in the 1930s. Interior finishes have an eerie 1920s feel. The building's interior court carries out the exotic Middle Eastern theme of the architecture in a listless way; the only moment of levity is provided by a Texas-sized chandelier. The Kent Bloomer Studio of New Haven produced exterior architectural sculpture. Sasaki & Associates of Boston designed the Lee and Joe Jamail Plaza (1998) in front of Baker Hall.

D-23 Herring Hall

D-24 Wiess College

D-22
Janice Suber and Robert McNair Hall
Rice University
2002, Robert A. M. Stern and Morris Architects

New York architect Robert Stern produced this sprawling 167,000-SF complex for the Jesse H. Jones Graduate School of Management, Rice's business school, after it outgrew Herring Hall. Compulsive replication of Rice styling on the exterior is stultifying, while the interior is merely prosaic. Bloomer Studio is responsible for decorative bronze and stone architectural sculpture. Beneath this immense building lies the 2-story Central Campus Garage, Rice's first parking garage.

D-23
Herring Hall
Rice University
1984, César Pelli & Associates

Pelli, the New Haven architect, essayed a rigorous, disciplined, and very provocative postmodern interpretation of Rice's architectural heritage at Herring Hall, acknowledging both Cram and his successors. The 3-story, gable-roofed classroom block and offset reading room wing, with its odd truncated vault, are typologically derived from Rice's earliest buildings. The masonry curtain walls are treated as elaborately coded surfaces articulating the building's spatial organization and supporting structure. Herring Hall was built in a grove of mature Live Oaks, a building site reserved in Cram's General Plan. Across the central greensward from Herring Hall is the Rice Memorial Center, with the Ley Student Center addition by Pelli (1986), less satisfying than Herring Hall. Built for the Jones Graduate School of Administration, Herring Hall was remodeled internally in 2004 by Ray+Hollington to accommodate the English, Art History, and Linguistics departments.

D-24
Wiess College
Rice University
2002, Machado & Silvetti Associates and Kirksey

Rodolfo Machado and Jorge Silvetti of Boston designed this 4-story residential college as an austere exterior brick shell surrounding a large internal quadrangle, into which the dining commons projects. Horizontal metal fins screen the glass walls of the commons pavilion, paying homage to the work of Spanish architect, Rafael Moneo. On the west side of the complex, facing the student playing fields, a monumental flight of steps leads to a roof terrace on top of the college's kitchen. The Wiess College Master's House was designed by Stern and Bucek Architects (2010).

D-21 James A. Baker III Institute for Public Policy

D-25 South Plant

D-27 Humanities Building

D-28 Institute Commons and South Hall

D-25
South Plant
Rice University
2009, Antoine Predock and
Morris Architects

Built to supplement the service plant in Cram's Mechanical Laboratory and Power House of 1912, the South Plant is meant to supply Rice in the 21st century. Planar brick walls and an 85-foot-high tubular steel tower for cooling and recycling steam, faced with triangular sheets of dichronic glass, give this complex a mysterious presence when seen from Main. Sited at one edge of the campus, the South Plant is adjacent to Harris Gully, a buried tributary of Brays Bayou.

D-26
Raymond and Susan Brochstein Pavilion
Rice University
2008, Thomas Phifer & Partners

The most stunning 21st-century building in Houston is this small, white, steel and glass pavilion by New York architect, Thomas Phifer. Containing a coffee house and student lounge, the Brochstein Pavilion brilliantly addresses the paradox of building a glass-walled building in Houston's hot, humid, sunny climate with its delicate, lattice-like shade structure, which spreads out to encompass generous amounts of outdoor space surrounding the pavilion. The design of adjacent landscapes, by the Office of James Burnett, is as impressive as the design of the pavilion. Together they not only demonstrate the feasibility and attractiveness of living outside in Houston, they revolutionize perceptions of how Houston's landscapes can be transformed to construct sensations of spatial power and beauty.

D-27
Humanities Building
Rice University
2000, Allan Greenberg

Greenberg, a South African-born Washington, D.C. architect, designed this 3-story, 47,000-SF classroom and office building on a difficult site, framed by avenues of mature Live Oak trees and the Fondren Library. He carefully adjusted the building to respect (and take advantage of) the trees, as well as accommodate an existing circulation path that cut through the middle of the building site. Of the neo-traditional buildings constructed at Rice in the late 1990s and 2000s, the Humanities Building is the only one to treat architecture as more than a matter of style. One component of the complex is the 94-foot-tall Russ Pittman Tower.

D-28
Institute Commons and South Hall
[now Baker College and Will Rice College]
Rice University
1912, Cram, Goodhue & Ferguson
2010, Hopkins Architects and Hanbury Evans Wright Vlattas

Cram reserved the south side of the campus for the residential group for men and accorded it a distinct sub-style, based on the urban vernacular building traditions of Genoa. These buildings (originally a unit, now two separate residential colleges) were faced with stucco; the cloister arches are brick with only limited stonework. The towers were provided so students might have cool places to study on warm, humid evenings. East Hall (also part of Baker College) and West Hall (now part of Hanszen College) were added in 1914 and 1916. The London architect, Michael Hopkins, designed the 4-story brick wing of Baker that now obscures part of the north elevation of the Institute Commons and precipitated demolition of the 1912 kitchen wing of the Commons in 2009.

D-26 Raymond and Susan Brochstein Pavilion

D-29 Cleveland Sewall Hall

D-30 Cohen House

D-32 Edward Albert Palmer Memorial Chapel

D-29
Cleveland Sewall Hall
Rice University
1971, Lloyd, Morgan & Jones

Facing the Physics Building, across the Academic Court, and Lovett Hall to the east, Sewall Hall is a near-copy of Physics by instruction of the donor, Blanche Harding Sewall, an ardent admirer of Cram's architecture. Lloyd, Morgan & Jones brought this bit of literal contextualism off without anxiety, even where they had to improvise. Ross Coryell executed the decorative sculpture work. At the center of the Academic Court is a bronze statue of the founder, William M. Rice, modeled by the English sculptor John Angel and mounted on a pink Texas granite base designed by Cram & Ferguson (1930). Behind the Founder's Memorial is the ponderous Fondren Library (1949, Staub & Rather; William Ward Watkin, consulting architect), which, to satisfy university politics at the time of its planning, broke with Cram's General Plan and was built astride the main axis, prematurely terminating it. It has constituted a monumental obstruction in the center of the campus ever since.

D-30
Cohen House
Rice University
1927, William Ward Watkin

Watkin copiously employed Greek Byzantine ornament in the small-sized, big-scaled "house" for the Institute's faculty club.

D-31
BioScience Research Collaborative Building
6500 Main Street, Rice University
2009, Skidmore, Owings & Merrill, Perkins + Will, and FKP Architects

Rice University constructed this 10-story, 477,000-SF building on the threshold between its campus and the Texas Medical Center for advanced, interdisciplinary research and teaching. Craig Hartmann of Skidmore, Owings & Merrill's San Francisco office designed the concrete-framed building as a long, thin slab. The brick-clad elevations are lit by staggered, offset vertical windows. Facing west toward the Rice campus is an aluminum and glass curtain wall, from which emerges an elliptical bay containing stacked, double-height social spaces. A courtyard and 2-story rear wing are angled in plan toward the Rice campus; the 2-story wing is engineered to support a second 8-story research and teaching slab. Hartmann sought to make the BioScience Research Collaborative a city-positive building with retail and social spaces oriented to Main in hopes that other Medical Center institutions might follow this lead.

D-32
Edward Albert Palmer Memorial Chapel
[now Palmer Memorial Episcopal Church]
6221 Main Street
1927, William Ward Watkin

This Lombard Romanesque style church adds to what architecture critic Peter Papademetriou called the "Main Boulevard Mediterranean" lineup of 1920s buildings adjacent to Rice that sought to extend its Mediterranean architecture into the city. The church is decorated with exuberant Venetian Renaissance ornament in the style of Pietro Lombardo; his Church of Santa Maria dei Miracoli in Venice inspired the arrangement of the chapel's interior, with its high set chancel and sanctuary. Watkin was also responsible for the campanile. John F. Staub designed the Parish House of 1930, which occasioned another exuberantly decorated portal, to the north of the church. Next door at 6265 Main, Autry House (1921, Cram & Ferguson and William Ward Watkin) was built as a community house where Rice students could study and socialize. The 2-story, arch-windowed building that links Palmer Church and Autry House was designed by Bailey Architects (2006).

D-31 BioScience Research Collaborative Building

D-33 Hermann Hospital

D-34 Hermann Professional Building

D-35 Prairie View A&M University School of Nursing Building

D-33
Hermann Hospital
[now Cullen Pavilion, Memorial Hermann Hospital]
6411 Fannin Street
1925, Berlin & Swern and Alfred C. Finn

George H. Hermann, who donated property that became Hermann Park to the City of Houston, left the bulk of his estate to a foundation charged with building, equipping, and operating a charity hospital. The lavishly detailed Spanish Mediterranean-style hospital opened 11 years after Hermann's death in 1914, alongside his park at the very edge of Houston. The first floor lobby and corridors retain the brilliantly colored decorative tilework installed by Berlin & Swern, a firm of Chicago architects. These were restored along with the exterior of the building in 1990 by Austin architects, David Hoffman and Wayne Bell. In the mid 2000s construction of the flashy postmodern Memorial Hermann Heart and Vascular Institute (2008, Odell Associates of Charlotte and PhiloWilke Partnership) completely obscured the street fronts of the 1925 building. Towering over its backside is the postmodern Hermann Hospital Pavilion (1999, WHR Architects). To the south of the original building lies a newer Hermann Hospital (now the Robertson Pavilion), built in the first phase of the development of the Texas Medical Center (1949, Kenneth Franzheim and Wyatt C. Hedrick). The 9-story extension, the Jones Pavilion, is an addition to Hermann Hospital that turns into The University of Texas Health Science Center at Houston (1977, Brooks, Barr, Graeber & White of Austin).

D-34
Hermann Professional Building
[now UT Professional Building]
6410 Fannin Street
1949, Kenneth Franzheim and Wyatt C. Hedrick

Now overshadowed by the 2,500-car garage of the 31-story Memorial Hermann Medical Plaza at 6400 Fannin (2007, Kirksey), the 15-story Hermann Professional Building was the first high-rise building constructed in Houston outside downtown. It was built to entice doctors to relocate to the Texas Medical Center, which was conceived in the early 1940s by a group of Houston lawyers and bankers as an economic development venture financed by the M.D. Anderson Foundation. The Foundation acquired 133 acres of Hermann Park from the City in 1943, chartered the Texas Medical Center, Inc., and awarded grants that enabled several local hospitals, one out-of-town medical school (Baylor), and the state legislature to set up new facilities on the heavily wooded tract. In 1945 the independent oilman, Hugh Roy Cullen, made substantial donations to most of these institutions; by the late 1940s a building boom was underway that still continues, as the exponential expansion of the Medical Center in the 2000s demonstrates. The Hermann Professional Building represented the last gasp of the Main Boulevard Mediterranean attempt to design in a unifying civic style. Its bull-nosed corners, wrap-around windows, and stepped profile indicate that red tile roofs and scrolled windows alone were insufficient. The relief sculpture depicting medical emergencies that flanks the Fannin entrance is by Edward Z. Galea. In 1958 the building was doubled in size with a westward extension toward Main (Kenneth Franzheim with John H. Freeman, Jr.). The Finnish sculptor Mauno Oittenen was responsible for the amusing abstract relief sculpture around the Main Street entrance portal. It lost its original windows to a rehabilitation in 1998 (Willis, Bricker & Cannady) that allowed the building to become an up-to-date professional building.

D-35
Prairie View A&M University School of Nursing Building
6436 Fannin Street
2005, WHR Architects

WHR (Watkins Hamilton Ross) with FKP (Falick/Klein Partnership) and Kirksey dominated new building design in the Medical Center in the 2000s. As was true for most of the buildings constructed along the west side of Fannin during the 2000s, the 12-story Prairie View A&M Nursing Building replaced a substantial mid-rise building of the 1960s. Containing an 8-level garage, the 110,000-SF building is faced with an aluminum and glass curtain wall framed by end bays of precast concrete panels. The building's transition to the Fannin sidewalk is handled gracefully. WHR's much larger Methodist Hospital Outpatient Center next door at 6448 Fannin (2010), a 23-story, 1 million-SF building with a 1,450-car garage, does not fare so well. The building's collage of precast spandrels and curving reflective glass curtain walls and its prow-shaped profile try too hard to attract attention.

D-36 Smith Tower

D-37 Medical Towers Building

D-36
Smith Tower
6550 Fannin Street
1989, Lloyd Jones Fillpot & Associates

The 25-story Smith Tower is a sleekly detailed, precast concrete-faced tower backed by an even sleeker aluminum-clad parking garage. It was built as a for-profit venture by the non-profit Methodist Hospital in association with Century Development Corporation. Institutions in the Texas Medical Center must be non-profit. But Fannin is the Medical Center's west boundary, so Smith Tower lies across the street from the Medical Center proper. Air conditioned pedestrian bridges connect Methodist Hospital (on the non-profit side) to the 22-story Scurlock Tower at 6560 Fannin (1980, S. I. Morris Associates) and the 25-story Houston Marriott Medical Center at 6580 Fannin (1984, Sikes Jennings Kelly), both part of the Methodist real estate empire on the for-profit side of Fannin. Note the quadruple bypass pedestrian bridge across University connecting Smith and Scurlock towers.

D-37
Medical Towers Building
1709 Dryden Road
1956, Golemon & Rolfe;
Skidmore, Owings & Merrill, consulting architects

The 18-story Medical Towers was Skidmore, Owings & Merrill's first Houston building. It is an example of the Lever House modern building type Houstonized by converting the floating horizontal base at the bottom of the building into a parking garage. The building has been respectfully treated, and it retains its original turquoise porcelain-enameled curtain wall. It lies diagonally across Main from Rice's Skidmore, Owings & Merrill-designed BioScience Research Collaborative.

D-38
Texas Children's Hospital
6621 Fannin Street
2001, FKP Architects

The original Texas Children's Hospital (1954, Milton Foy Martin & Associates), the lower of the two buildings split by a driveway roofed with a glass vault, won a national design award from the American Institute of Architects the year it was completed. In 1970 the 3-story building was nearly tripled in height with an addition by Caudill Rowlett Scott. In 2001 it was resurfaced with a curtain wall of pink granite and rose-colored reflective glass to correspond to FKP's 20-story West Tower, the taller of this pair of Texas Children's buildings. The alphabet landscape installation along Fannin is by Charles Tapley.

D-39
St. Luke's Medical Tower
[now O'Quinn Medical Tower]
6624 Fannin Street
1991, César Pelli & Associates and Kendall/Heaton Associates

St. Luke's Episcopal Hospital had Gerald D. Hines Interests construct this 25-story, 483,000-SF office building, which straddles a boxy, 9-story, 1,350-car garage. Pelli made the best of the situation, integrating cars with the building's lobby by producing a decoratively walled motor entrance alongside pedestrian entrances. Handsome interior detail enables the lobby to accommodate large numbers of people with comfort and dignity. By shaping the big block of office space into twin octagonal towers, capped with white aluminum spires, Pelli gave St. Luke's something no other building in the Medical Center had sought to achieve since the Hermann Professional Building—a distinctive skyline presence. This building demonstrates that even a bloated building with too much parking can exert a civic presence when it is intelligently and imaginatively designed.

D-38 Texas Children's Hospital

D-39 St. Luke's Medical Tower

D-40 Texas Woman's University Institute of Health Sciences Building

D-41 Wortham Fountain

D-43 METRO Texas Medical Center Transit Center

D-40
Texas Woman's University Institute of Health Sciences Building
6700 Fannin Street
2006, Kirksey

Kirksey designed this building as a pair of slabs—a 10-story slab facing Fannin and a 7-story slab facing Old Main—encasing a 1,000-car garage that backs up to Main. An aluminum-and-glass curtain wall clads the Fannin front, while the Old Main side elevation is lit with horizontal strip windows that recall Medical Center buildings of the 1950s. Where the two slabs meet, a glass-walled corner bay reveals vertical interior circulation. The impact on Main is less happy. Super-sized parking garage construction since the 1980s has turned these blocks of Main into a service alley. Between the Texas Woman's University building and St. Luke's Medical Tower is the 16-story Texas Children's Hospital Maternity Center at 6701 Main by FKP Architects (2011).

D-41
Wortham Fountain
Holcombe Boulevard and Main Street
1993, John Burgee Architects with Richard Fitzgerald & Associates, Martha Schwarz, Ken Smith, and David Meyer

In expiation for demolishing the Shamrock Hotel, which occupied this site, the Texas Medical Center, Inc. built the Wortham Fountain, a curious mixture of events and spaces that combines columns of water that seem to anticipate a freeway overpass with a walled water court leading on axis to what was once the Shamrock's front door (now a parking lot). Still surviving is the former Shamrock Hotel Parking Garage and Exhibition Center at 2151 Holcombe (1949, Wyatt C. Hedrick). At 6977 Main and Pressler is the Shriners Hospital for Children (1996, Odell Associates). Kirksey was architect for the super-stretched, 12-story Life Science Plaza medical office building and garage at 2130 W. Holcombe (2008).

D-42
Fayez S. Sarofim Building, University of Texas at Houston Health Science Center
1825 Pressler Drive
2006, BNIM and Burt Hill Kossar Rittlemann Associates

Located on a vulnerable site backing up to Brays Bayou, Berkebile Nelson Immenschuh McDowell's building contains research labs housed in a pair of 6-story bars, the one facing Pressler deflected in plan to absorb the curve of the street. In between the bars is a multi-story light court. Faced with a rain screen of red clay tile, the Sarofim Building incorporates state-of-the-art sustainable practices.

D-43
METRO Texas Medical Center Transit Center
6910 Fannin Street
2004, Rey de la Reza Architects

Metro's Texas Medical Center Transit Center handles the interface between Metro's light rail Red Line and 14 bus lines. Two parallel rows of shelters are roofed with steel-framed fabric canopies anchored in concrete girders and piers. An elevated, steel-truss pedestrian bridge conveys transit riders from the Metrorail line across Fannin to the bus bays. Clark Condon Associates was the landscape architect, and CORE Design Studio installed the inset history of medicine in the Metrorail platform.

D-42 Fayez S. Sarofim Building, University of Texas at Houston Health Science Center

D-44 University of Texas at Houston Health Science Center School of Nursing and Student Community Center

D-45 Lowry and Peggy Mays Clinic, University of Texas M. D. Anderson Cancer Center

D-44
University of Texas at Houston Health Science Center School of Nursing and Student Community Center
6901 Bertner Avenue
2004, BNIM and Lake/Flato

The University of Texas School of Nursing Building was the first 21st-century public building in Houston to incorporate a wide range of environmentally sustainable practices. The relatively thin width of the 8-story building facilitates daylighting. Screening devices on the long west (Bertner) and east elevations deflect sun and heat build-up, and plantings on the roof terrace and recycled building materials contribute to its design economy.

D-45
Lowry and Peggy Mays Clinic, University of Texas M. D. Anderson Cancer Center
1212 Holcombe Boulevard
2004, Kaplan McLaughlin Díaz and FKP Architects

Across Bertner from the School of Nursing, M. D. Anderson's immense 8-story, glass and granite-faced Ambulatory Care Center is the architectural antithesis of the School of Nursing. Its sprawl, spatial bulk, imperious scale, and corporate facing materials bespeak power and pride rather than ingenuity and sustainability.

D-46
Prudential Building
[now The University of Texas M.D. Anderson Cancer Center Houston Building]
1100 Holcombe Boulevard
1952, Kenneth Franzheim

Like the lamented Shamrock Hotel, the 18-story Prudential Building represents an architectural paradox: it is extremely stodgy in composition yet, extraordinarily impressive in detail. The first corporate high-rise office building constructed outside downtown, it was one of a series of regional headquarters buildings erected by the Prudential Insurance Company in the late 1940s and early '50s that introduced new levels of amenity for office workers. In Houston these included convenient parking, generous landscaped grounds, tennis courts, and a beautifully detailed swimming pool and terrace located in the southeast corner of the building. The entrance sequence from Holcombe through the lobby is a marvel of spatial orchestration. It begins at the Azalea Forecourt, where Wheeler Williams' *The Family* is installed in a fountain, proceeds beneath a splendid, skylit porte cochère outfitted with sinuous benches and planting troughs, then through the double volume, cylindrical entrance vestibule, where Peter Hurd's American Scene genre piece, *The Future Belongs To Those Who Prepare For It*, occupies a curved panel and ends at the lobby, where those awaiting elevators could once look into the tropically planted swimming pool court. Since acquiring the building in 1975, M.D. Anderson Hospital has maintained it with the consideration that it deserves. Only the pair of illuminated signs stationed in the blank panels atop the tallest slab that depicted the Rock of Gibraltar have been removed. Public spaces of the Prudential show the Franzheim office at its best. From 1955-1969 the Contemporary Arts Museum occupied a small, but ingeniously designed, building by MacKie & Kamrath–a triangle in section–which stood on the grounds of the Prudential Building facing Fannin. It no longer exists. Nor will the Prudential Building. Despite preservationists' pleas and protests, M.D. Anderson will demolish it once a newer office building of equal size is completed, replacing the Prudential Building with phase two of the Ambulatory Care Center. Demolished in 2012.

D-46 Prudential Building

D-47 Children's Nutrition Research Center

D-48 Texas Children's Hospital Clinical Care Building

D-49 University of Texas M. D. Anderson Hospital and Tumor Institute

D-47
Children's Nutrition Research Center
1100 Bates Avenue
1989, 3/D International and Bernard Johnson, Inc.

It is the detailing of the curtain wall, thin panels of pink Texas granite alternately flame-finished and polished, that gave this ungainly building its strong visual presence. At night the stars atop the building's parapet light up. During the building boom of the 2000s, it was overshadowed by Texas Children's 20-story Feigin Center Building (2008, FKP Architects) on one side and its Clinical Care Building on the other.

D-48
Texas Children's Hospital Clinical Care Building
6701 Fannin Street
2002, FKP Architects

A sleekly curving, dark glass curtain wall, bracketed by horizontally aligned windows that slice through granite planes, architecturally turns the corner from Holcombe to Fannin at the southwest edge of the Medical Center.

D-49
University of Texas M. D. Anderson Hospital and Tumor Institute
[now University of Texas M.D. Anderson Cancer Center]
1515 Holcombe Boulevard
1954, MacKie & Kamrath; Schmidt, Garden & Erickson, consulting architects

M. D. Anderson, the University of Texas' cancer research hospital, was the Medical Center's resplendent champion of modern architecture when it opened. MacKie & Kamrath, reacting against modernistic compositional formulas, shaped the building as a series of offset slabs extended horizontally into the landscape in response to programmatic requirements. Windows were keyed to solar orientation and internal use. Wide bands of windows, undergirded by corrugated aluminum spandrels, faced north and south to light patient rooms. MacKie & Kamrath revetted the exteriors with flamboyant gray-veined Georgia Etowa pink marble. The Knoll Planning Unit planned and furnished the interiors. Like so much of the Texas Medical Center, M. D. Anderson's architecture has suffered from overexpansion. MacKie & Kamrath enlarged the building through the 1960s in accord with the original design. Then came the huge, polygonal towers of the Lutheran Pavilion and the Dunn Memorial Chapel (1976, MacKie & Kamrath and Koetter, Tharp & Cowell), built in front of the Holcombe face of the patient wing, followed by the anarchitectural R. Lee Clark Clinic (1987, Pierce Goodwin Alexander), which finished off the east side of the building. The Bertner Avenue rear wing was all that remained visible of the original until it, too, was obscured by the huge Alkek Patient Tower and Clinical Research Facility (1998; doubled in height 2011, HKS Architects/LAN) and the even bigger 19-story George and Cynthia Mitchell Basic Sciences Research Building (2004, Zimmer Gunsul Frasca and FKP Architects).

D-50
Denton A. Cooley Building, St. Luke's Episcopal Hospital and Texas Heart Institute
6718 Bertner Avenue
2002, Morris Architects and RTKL Associates

The 10-story Denton A. Cooley Building (named in honor of the first surgeon in the U.S. to perform a heart transplant—at St. Luke's Texas Heart Institute) is a slow curve of silver reflective glass elevated high above the street to protect the interior from flooding, which caused severe damage to the Texas Medical Center during tropical storm Allison in 2001. It is integrated with the 26-story Texas Heart Institute Building (1970, Caudill Rowlett Scott, Rustay, Martin & Vale, and Staub, Rather & Howze) and the original St. Luke's Hospital (1954, Staub & Rather and Hiram A. Salisbury).

D-50 Denton A. Cooley Building, St. Luke's Episcopal Hospital and Texas Heart Institute

D-52 John P. McGovern Texas Medical Center Commons Building

D-53 Garden Club of Houston Park

D-54 Mary Gibbs Jones Hall, Texas Women's University

D-51
Methodist Hospital Research Institute
6670 Bertner Avenue
2010, Kohn Pederson Fox and WHR Architects

An exuberant neo-Modern design, this 13-story, 300,000-SF building consists of a indented dark glass screen that accedes to the curve of Bertner and a planar back-up slab faced with precast concrete. The research institute was built in what had been Methodist Hospital's front yard. Its construction entailed the removal of many 50-year-old Live Oak trees. The research institute also consigned the first Methodist Hospital (a late modernistic design of 1951, Watkin, Nunn, McGinty and Phenix) to the status of rear annex. Methodist Hospital has doubled in size every decade; the pink, postmodern granite aggregate-faced Dunn Tower (1989, Morris Architects) was built in what had been space between buildings. This sort of architectural history—where design is completely subsumed in the programming, servicing, and management of space—explains why the Texas Medical Center is such a harried and bewildering place. It is a landscape of expanding or shrinking factories competing for advantage in the health industry, rather than a campus occupied by institutions dedicated to high-minded endeavors. At 6565 Fannin, Methodist's west wing (1959, Milton McGinty) is faced with the tile mural, *The Extending Arms of Christ* by Bruce Hayes, now obscured by the porte-cochère canopy.

D-52
John P. McGovern Texas Medical Center Commons Building
6550 Bertner Avenue
2002, Jackson & Ryan Architects

The McGovern Medical Center Commons epitomizes ebullient post-modern confusion in its jarring, but not uninteresting, mixture of uses: a mall-type food court on the ground floor, a fancy restaurant and meeting rooms at penthouse level, and two spectacular 55-foot high water walls—all sandwiching a 500-car garage.

D-53
Garden Club of Houston Park
6500 block Bertner Avenue
1982, Charles Tapley Associates

This exquisitely detailed garden court seeks valiantly to compensate for the mean, chaotic, indifferent treatment of public spaces within the Texas Medical Center. The fountain is a rewarding demonstration of what can be accomplished with thoughtfulness and ingenuity. Unfortunately the garden is an isolated retreat rather than the model for a more amenable public environment within the Medical Center.

D-54
Mary Gibbs Jones Hall, Texas Women's University
[now Methodist Hospital]
1130 John Freeman Boulevard
1969, Van Ness & Mower

This precisely detailed and trimly proportioned essay in the aesthetics of cast-in-place concrete frame construction was compromised by the subsequent addition of a bulbous penthouse story.

D-51 Methodist Hospital Research Institute

D-55 Baylor College of Medicine Cullen Building

D-56 Margaret M. Alkek Building for Biomedical Research, Baylor College of Medicine

D-57 City of Houston Department of Public Health Building

D-59 Veterans Administration Medical Center

D-55
Baylor College of Medicine Cullen Building
1200 Moursund Avenue
1948, Hedrick & Lindsley

The first building to open in the Texas Medical Center was this symmetrical, 4-story, late modernistic building sheathed in Texas cream limestone. It terminates the axis at the head of John Freeman Boulevard with its convex entrance bay. Edward Z. Galea executed the panels of relief sculpture. Ray Bailey Architects designed the porte cochère, motor court, and Alkek Fountain (1982), which take some of the edge off Hedrick & Lindsley's original.

D-56
Margaret M. Alkek Building for Biomedical Research, Baylor College of Medicine
1325 Moursund Avenue
2007, Lord, Aeck & Sargent

Atlanta architects, Lord, Aeck & Sargent, designed this 8-story, 200,00-SF, steel-framed research building to achieve maximum structural lightness and maximum diffusion of daylight deep into the building's thick floor plates. The Alkek Building indicates the extent to which advanced scientific research was the program of the 2000s decade in the Medical Center. The SWA Group was the landscape architect.

D-57
City of Houston Department of Public Health Building
1115 South Braeswood Boulevard
1963, MacKie & Kamrath

Horizontality is the compositional motif of this handsome building complex. In 1995 the brick facing was removed and replaced with orange synthetic stucco. Next door at 1441 Moursund is the rather contrived University of Houston Pharmacy Building, also by MacKie & Kamrath (1978).

D-58
Ben Taub General Hospital
1502 Taub Loop
1989, CRS Sirrine
and Llewelyn Davies Sahni

Close attention was paid to César Pelli's Herring Hall at Rice University when it came to designing and detailing the curtain wall of this monster building for Harris County's public health hospital. At 1510 Outer Belt Drive, in front of the earlier Ben Taub Hospital, is the Daughters of the Republic of Texas' Pioneer Memorial Log House, constructed to celebrate the centennial of Texas independence (1936, Harry Weaver). At the intersection of Cambridge and North MacGregor is the statue of Houston's Confederate hero, Lieutenant Dick Dowling, an Irish-born saloonkeeper who held off the U.S. at the Battle of Sabine Pass (1905, Frank W. Teich, sculptor). The Dowling Statue and Log House are both sited on Hermann Park land.

D-59
Veterans Administration Medical Center
[now Michael E. DeBakey Veterans Affairs Medical Center]
2002 Holcombe Boulevard
1991, 3/D International and Stone, Marracini & Patterson

Alfred C. Finn's original 1944 Veterans Administration Hospital was superseded by an even more overwhelming example of bureaucratic organizational design, a vast complex of interlocking rotated square bays that step up in section to a central spine. A system of interstitial floors devoted entirely to servicing this 1,047-bed hospital is hidden behind the building's horizontally banded face of precast concrete panels. Following completion the 1944 VA was demolished and much of the frontage of its formerly park-lined grounds has been privatized.

D-58 Ben Taub General Hospital

D-61 Alkek Eye Center Building, Baylor College of Medicine

D-62 Shell Information Center

D-60
National Biscuit Company Building
[now John P. McGovern Campus, TExas Medical Center]
2450 Holcombe Boulevard
1949, Robert M. Cummins, civil engineer
2001, W. O. Neuhaus Associates

Frank Zumwalt, Cummins's in-house architect, designed the late modernistic Nabisco baking and distribution plant. Neuhaus came up with a strategy for recycling (rather than replacing) the 660,000-SF building by preserving much of the existing interior and using it as flexibly serviced lease space for Texas Medical Center institutions requiring large volumes of clerical or lab space, but not necessarily on a permanent basis. The Office of James Burnett was the landscape architect.

D-61
Alkek Eye Center Building, Baylor College of Medicine
7200 Cambridge Street
2008, Kirksey

Although this 6-story building is a simple glass box, the startling transparency of the exterior curtain wall of low-iron, ultra-clear glass with a low-emissivity coating gives the whole building its compelling luminous quality. The Office of James Burnett was the landscape architect. The Alkek Eye Center was built on what had been the 35-acre site occupied by the 300-unit Parkwood Apartments (1949, William G. Farrington Company), a graceful garden apartment community demolished in 2006 by Baylor College of Medicine. Renamed the McNair Campus, it was here that Baylor began construction of its own 250-bed Baylor Clinic and Hospital in 2007 (Hellmuth, Obata + Kassabaum) on which it suspended construction in 2009 for financial reorganization.

D-62
Shell Information Center
1500 Old Spanish Trail
1972, Welton Becket & Associates

This pristine, white 6-story office building was built to anchor Plaza del Oro, a 525-acre mixed-use real estate development of the Shell Oil Company. By the time the center was completed, South Main's status as Houston's prime suburban development axis had passed decisively to Post Oak.

D-60 National Biscuit Company Building

D-63 The Astrodome

D-63 The Astrodome

D-63
The Astrodome
[now Reliant Astrodome]
Loop 610 and Kirby Drive
1965, Lloyd, Morgan & Jones and
Wilson, Morris, Crain & Anderson

With typical Texan bravado, Judge Roy Hofheinz, the expansive promoter who built the Astrodome (largely with public monies), called it the Eighth Wonder of the World. It was the first permanently enclosed, air-conditioned sports arena built to accommodate both baseball and football. The 642-foot clear span of the steel lamella-trussed roof, 218 feet high at the dome's summit, was the second longest in the world at the time of completion. The Astrodome originally had a maximum seating capacity of 66,000, including 53 skyboxes ringing the summit of the stadium with entertainment suites outrageously decorated in both Old World and Space Age themes. The scoreboard, 474 feet long and 4 stories high, blazed into action every time one of Judge Hofheinz's Astros hit a home run. In 1966 AstroTurf, developed especially for the dome, was installed on the playing field to replace mere natural grass. The Astrodome sat in the center of a flat, paved, 260-acre tract, where 30,000 cars could park. Adjacent to the dome is the Astrohall, an exhibition and livestock arena. Hofheinz developed both Astrovillage, a complex of four motels, including the flagship Astroworld Motor Hotel with its fabled, top-floor Celestial Suite, continuing the Skybox decorating aesthetic (1969, Brodnax, Phenix & Associates; extensively altered), and Astroworld, a 57-acre amusement park (1968, Randall Duell & Associates, designers, Linesch & Reynolds, landscape architects; demolished 2005-06), all connected by a bridge constructed across Loop 610. In 1968 the Hofheinz interests asserted that the Astrodomain's 13,600 tons of air-conditioning not only exceeded the total tonnage of many northern U.S. cities, but that of entire nations!

Astrodomain has always evoked strong responses. The Italian critic Vicky Alliata wrote in 1974: "the whole thing far surpasses all current definitions of kitsch, obscenity, and bad taste." Robert Altman transformed it into a theater of sinister obsession in his film, *Brewster McCloud* (1970). Guru Maharaj Ji and his devotees attempted to levitate the dome in 1973. In 1970 Peter Papademetriou wrote that the Astrodomain enshrined late 20th-century American values, just as the Vatican complex celebrated those of the Counter-Reformation for Renaissance Rome. In observance of the Astrodome's 21st anniversary in 1986, journalist, David Kaplan, had the last word: "Let it rain." Since completion of the adjoining Reliant Stadium in 2002, the Astrodome has been shuttered, and its future is in doubt, although the Harris County Commissioners Court has repeatedly said it will not be torn down.

D-64
Reliant Stadium
8400 Kirby Drive
2002, Hellmuth, Obata + Kassabaum Sport+Venue+Event and Houston Stadium Consultants

For the last third of the 20th century, the shallow dome of the Astrodome rose in awesome isolation above the center of its immense parking lot. By the beginning of the 21st century, it was joined by a structure that managed to make it look small by comparison, the 69,500-seat Reliant Stadium, home of the National Football League's Houston Texans and the Houston Livestock Show and Rodeo. Dominated visually by the gigantically scaled structural track for its retractable roof, Reliant Stadium, more so than the Astrodome, presents itself as a work of civic architecture rather than of colossal infrastructure, especially in its spatial relation to the Kirby-Murworth intersection. A glistening white steel panel wall system and extensive glazing contribute to Reliant Stadium's architectural substance.

D-64 Reliant Stadium

The Village / West University / Braeswood

The Village / West University / Braeswood

Tour E

The urbanization of the southwest sector of inner Houston dates to the beginning of the 20th century. As patterns of real estate development demonstrate, urbanization was tied to development of transportation infrastructure. The construction of the Houston Electric Company's South End streetcar line in 1910, which ran south from downtown Houston along the line of Fannin Street then turned

at what is now Holcombe Boulevard to proceed westward along the right-of-way of Bellaire Boulevard to serve the new town of Bellaire, marked the opening chapter. Development of the first, isolated sections of West University Place, adjacent to the streetcar tracks on Bellaire, began just after World War I. This process of growth by distension—"leap-frogging"—was not capricious. It reflected the crucial importance of access. During the 1920s Houston began to be transformed by the impact of automobiles. The broad plain north of Brays Bayou came to be filled with middle-income subdivisions that gravitated toward the campus of the Rice Institute. By the late 1930s the emergence of suburban shopping districts, such as the Village, relaxed dependence on the merchants of Main Street. Easy off-street parking was provided in these shopping centers without abandoning the linear, street-related building typology characteristic of downtown. Parking places were just pushed farther back from the curb line and stretched out laterally. The subdivisions of West University Place eventually opted for incorporation as a city in 1924, as did their tiny neighbor, Southside Place, in 1931. Today they are autonomous cities within Houston. Beginning in the 1970s, their ethnic and economic homogeneity, zoning codes, and low taxes enticed affluent families to settle there. In the 1980s this incited speculative residential building on a scale not seen since the communities' initial development. Although carried out under existing planning controls, this building boom has had a profound impact upon the two towns. By the early 21st century, Southside Place had been transformed into a "new" neighborhood. The post-World War II infilling of the numerous gaps between the subdivisions of the 1920s accounts for the string of subdivisions along Holcombe-Bellaire (its dual designation a result of differing municipal jurisdictions) that stretches south to Brays Bayou. The model that postwar subdivisions tried to emulate was Braeswood, a 1920s garden suburb with a curvilinear street network and substantial houses on large lots. But Braeswood's initially successful development fell victim to the Great Depression, and it ended up emulating the imitators. Its northwest quadrant, bordering Kirby Drive, was developed in the early 1950s with the long, low, one-story ranch houses that dominated Houston residential construction during the late 1940s and '50s. These, in turn, are rapidly being replaced by bulky 2- and 3-story houses of the 1990s and 2000s, especially in response to the chronic problem of flooding along Brays Bayou.

1. **Wroxton Townhouses,** 2427–33 Wroxton Road
2. **Albans Townhouses,** 2311–2315 Albans Road
3. **Southampton Court Townhomes,** 2347 Albans Road
4. **Wroxton Road Residences,** 2621–2629 Wroxton Road
5. **Kelvin Design Group Studio,** 4916 Kelvin Drive
6. **House,** 2401 Nottingham Road
7. **University Savings Association Building,** 2500 Dunstan Road
8. **Christ The King Lutheran Church,** 2353 Rice Boulevard
9. **Rice Children's Campus,** 5504 Chaucer Drive
10. **House,** 2239 University Boulevard
11. **Shorthand House,** 2233 University Boulevard
12. **House 2045,** 2045 University Boulevard
13. **West House,** 2245 Dryden Road
14. **Thompsen House,** 2004 Southgate Boulevard
15. **Brave House,** 2206 Sheridan Road
16. **Southgate House,** 2429 Southgate Boulevard
17. **Peterson's Pharmacy Building,** 2439 University Boulevard
18. **House,** 6136 Kirby Drive
19. **Cohen House,** 2812 Amherst Street
20. **House,** 6001 Charlotte Street
21. **House,** 6501 Brompton Avenue
22. **House,** 6438 Belmont Avenue
23. **House,** 6512 Vanderbilt Street
24. **Leibrock House,** 6435 Vanderbilt Avenue
25. **Mixon House,** 3211 Pittsburgh Street
26. **Burgan House,** 6533 Mercer Avenue
27. **Wilson House,** 6416 Sewanee Avenue
28. **Ake House,** 3124 Amherst Street
29. **House,** 3114 Tangley Road
30. **Casita,** 3122 Sunset Boulevard
31. **HEB Buffalo Market,** 5225 Buffalo Speedway
32. **KTRK Channel 13 TV Studio,** 3310 Bissonnet Avenue
33. **House,** 3502 Sunset Boulevard
34. **House,** 3901 Arnold Street
35. **House,** 4124 Case Street
36. **House,** 3833 Oberlin Street
37. **House,** 3708 Ingold Street
38. **House,** 3728 Garnet Street
39. **Southside Place Bath House,** 3730 Farbar Street
40. **House,** 3735 Gramercy
41. **Robertson House,** 3718 Gramercy
42. **House,** 3526 Bellefontaine
43. **House,** 3515 Aberdeen Way
44. **John P. McGovern Branch, Houston Public Library,** 7405 Stella Link Road
45. **House,** 4154 Bellefontaine
46. **House,** 4131 Turnberry Circle
47. **Benedit House,** 4111 Drummond
48. **House,** 3615 North Braeswood Boulevard
49. **Style-in-Steel Townhouses,** 4156–4160 Meyerwood Drive
50. **Holmes Shopping Center,** 4115–4117 Willowbend Boulevard
51. **Brochsteins, Inc. Building,** 11530 Main Street
52. **Rice University Library Service Center and Primary Data Center,** 11620 Main Street
53. **Houston Cardiac Association Clinic,** 10480 Main Street
54. **Bethany United Methodist Church,** 3511 Linkwood Drive
55. **Linkwood Community Center,** 3699 Norris Drive

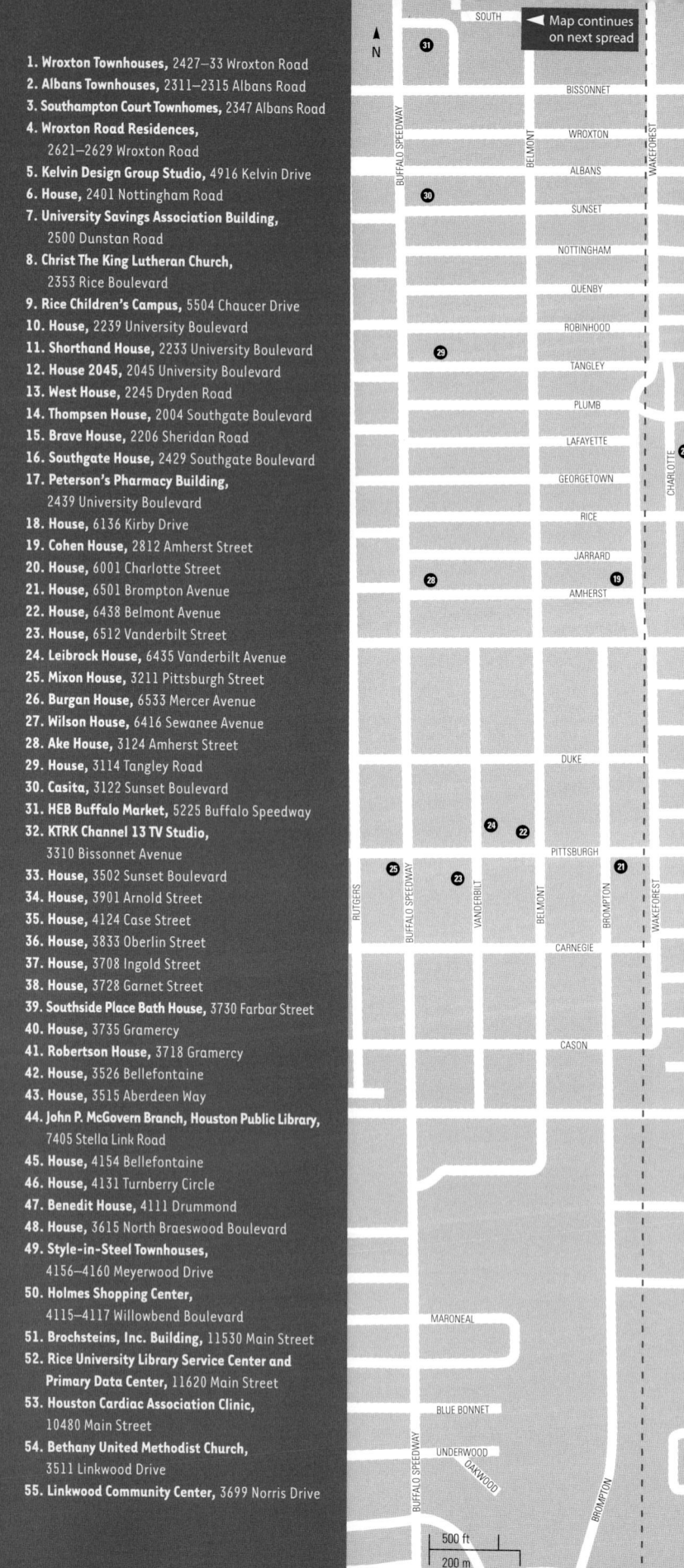

56. **Solomon House,** 3615 South Braeswood Boulevard
57. **Hurwitz House,** 3007 South Braeswood Boulevard
58. **Rice School-La Escuela Rice,** 7500 Seuss Drive
59. **Allen House,** 2337 Bluebonnet Boulevard
60. **Braeswood Corporation House,**
    2329 Bluebonnet Boulevard
61. **Braeswood Corporation House,**
    2309 Bluebonnet Boulevard
62. **Gordon House,** 2307 Bluebonnet Boulevard
63. **House,** 2308 Glenn Haven Boulevard
64. **Herzog House,** 2523 Maroneal Boulevard
65. **Glesby House,** 2405 Bellefontaine

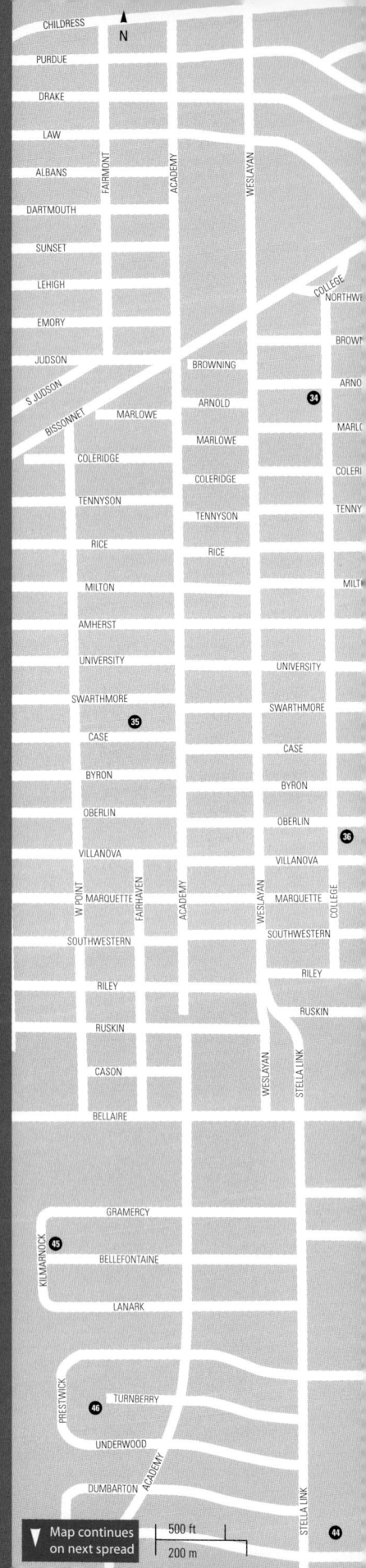

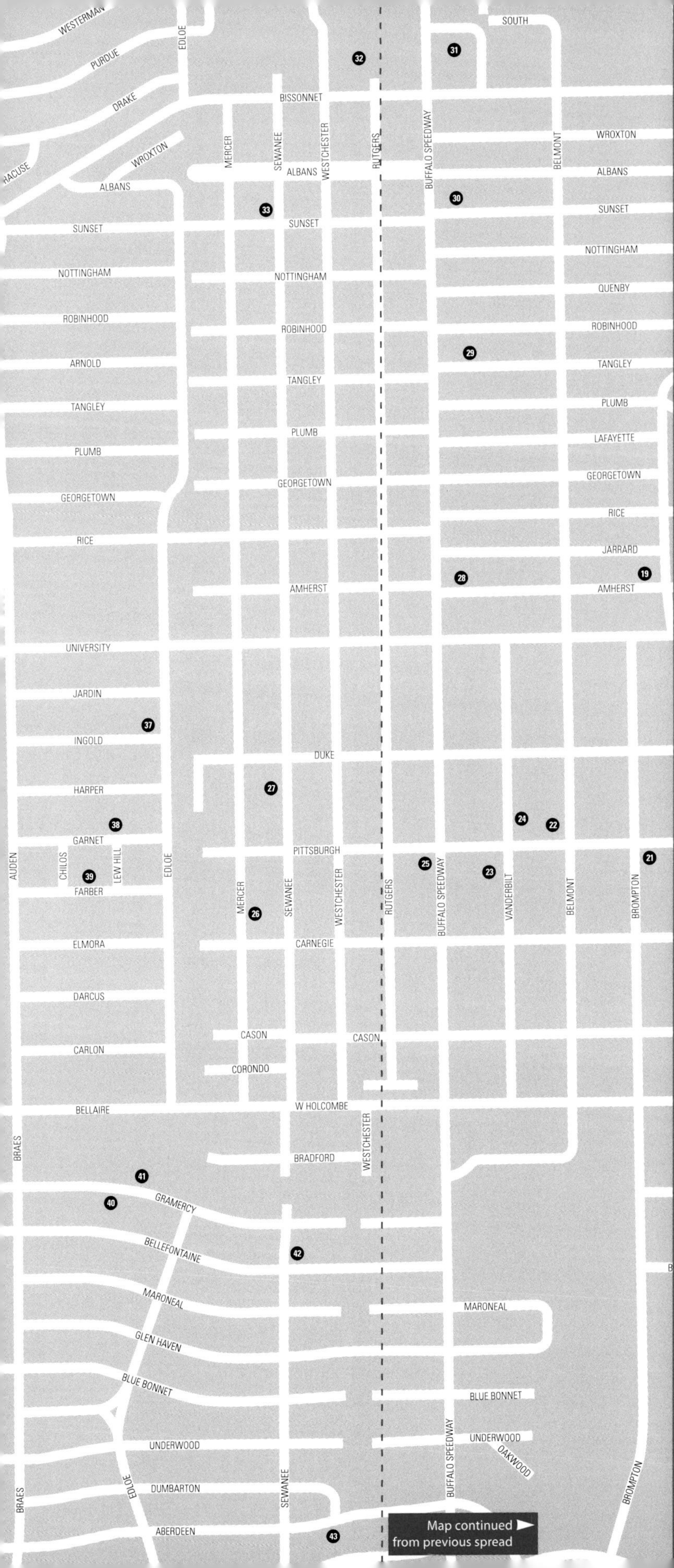

The Village / West University / Braeswood

Tour E

239

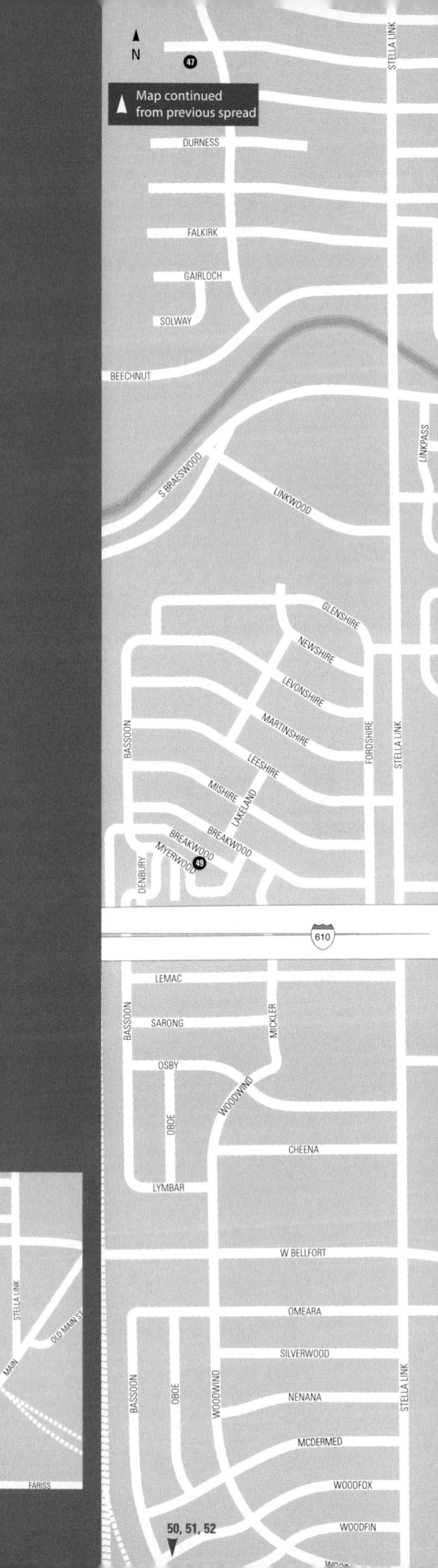

E-1 Wroxton Townhouses

E-2 Albans Townhouses

E-3 Southampton Court Townhomes

E-4 Wroxton Road Residences

E-6 House

E-1
Wroxton Townhouses
2427-2433 Wroxton Road
1992, Pope + Sherman

A brick plane set forward of a gray-colored stucco backup wall imbues this low-key, but rigorously conceived, row of houses with a sense of spatial depth. Albert Pope and William Sherman incorporated many different kinds of spaces behind the self-effacing frontal plane, including a compelling exterior courtyard designs—virtually an open air room.

E-2
Albans Townhouses
2311-2315 Albans Road
1982, William F. Stern & Associates

Tubular oriel windows capped by gabled bays mark this pair of stucco-surfaced row houses. Across the street at 2330 Albans are a pair of townhouses by Ziegler Cooper (1980) combined into a single-family house by architect Lenya Gould, who also designed the mysterious side garden.

E-3
Southampton Court Townhomes
2347 Albans Road
1980, Ziegler Cooper

Ziegler Cooper arranged these brick-faced row houses in a mews, hanging the fireboxes and cylindrical flues of the prefabricated fireplace units off the upper floor as a sign of domestic habitation. Diagonally across the street at 4614 Morningside are the peach-colored Morningside Townhomes (1986), also by Ziegler Cooper. One block to the south at 2401-2403 Sunset and Morningside are the white stucco, round-cornered Sunset Terrace Houses (1979, William T. Cannady & Anderson Todd), now extensively altered.

E-4
Wroxton Road Residences
2621-2629 Wroxton Road
1982, William F. Stern & Associates

Here, in the independent municipality of West University Place, Stern paired row houses to conform to the city's zoning code. The use of brick and wood clapboard siding, gabled roofs, and front porches are intended to connote "home."

E-6
House
2401 Nottingham Road
1997, Willis, Bricker & Cannady

What is especially captivating about this house is its walled gardens and motor court, landscaped by William Cannady.

E-5
Kelvin Design Group Studio
4916 Kelvin Drive
1960, David D. Red

For an advertising and graphics studio, Red provided a 2-story office building bracketed by a 1-story wing, the interior of which is lit by sloped panes of north-facing glass.

E-5 Kelvin Design Group Studio

E-7 University Savings Association Building

E-8 Christ The King Lutheran Church

E-9 Rice Children's Campus

E-11 Shorthand House

E-7
University Savings Association Building
[now 24-Hour Fitness]
2500 Dunstan Road
1964, Bank Building and Equipment Corporation of America

Wenceslao A. Sarmiento, the Peruvian-born designer for the St. Louis-based Bank Building Corp., let himself go with this delightfully wacky 6-story building in the Village. Its interiors were completely reconstructed following its conversion into a health spa in 1988. Across the street in the ex-Village State Bank Building (1955, Don D. Rupe and Fred L. Lewis) at 2424 Dunstan is Benjy's Restaurant, with interiors by Austin architect, Dick Clark, (1996) supplemented by David Guthrie (1998).

E-8
Christ The King Lutheran Church
2353 Rice Boulevard
1982, Charles Tapley Associates

Alongside Hiram A. Salisbury's existing limestone-faced education building (1949), Gerald Moorhead designed the long-delayed second phase, a church and freestanding belfry. Externally this is a postmodern interpretation of Salisbury's cozy suburban Cotswold style. Internally it is spacious, yet intimate, and bracingly austere. The 3-story education building bridging the Salisbury and Tapley buildings is by Merriman Holt (2002). Nearby are several other examples of interpretive contextualism: Village Square, a 2-story retail and office building faced with steel panels at 2365 Rice (1995, William T. Cannady & Associates), a second Village Square at 2370 Rice, a rehabilitated 1955 office and retail building (1983, William T. Cannady & Associates), and Morningside Square around the corner at 5555 Morningside (1984, Barry Moore Architects), which also combines retail with office uses.

E-9
Rice Children's Campus
5504 Chaucer Drive
2008, Taft Architects

Rice architecture professors John J. Casbarian and Danny Samuels designed this small institutional building to contain a Montessori school for the children of Rice University faculty and staff. The repeating profile of shed-roofed skylights and the collage of different facing materials—some recycled from the duplexes that previously occupied the site—give the school its distinctive image.

E-10
House
2239 University Boulevard
2009, Strasser Ragni
with Emily Sing

Like many of Erick Ragni and Scott Strasser's houses, this planar house seems closed on the outside, yet it is amazingly open inside. The house was built in the subdivision of Southgate, which began to be developed in 1930. Despite a slow start Southgate filled up with moderate-sized houses, many designed by architects, in the second half of the 1930s.

E-11
Shorthand House
2233 University Boulevard
1997, Francois de Menil

Assured proportions and ingenious interior planning animate this simply organized courtyard house. Note the louvered shutters on second-story windows. William Hartman was the landscape architect. This house launched Houston architecture's "white house" movement in the 2000s. Evidence of this trend is visible at 2233 University (2002, Allen Bianchi) and 2169 University (2004, Metropolitan Design Group).

E-10 House

E-12
House 2045
2045 University Boulevard
2005, Collaborative Designworks

Another example of the "white house" trend, this house—begun when architect James M. Evans was affiliated with the New York firm Openshop Studio—embraces the street with its expansive picture window.

E-13 West House

E-13
West House
2245 Dryden Road
1937, Claude E. Hooton

During the 1930s Southgate passed through three changes of ownership. The second owner, R. W. Gillette, had Claude Hooton, a Rice graduate who had worked in Europe in the early 1930s, design a number of speculative houses. Hooton also worked for individual clients, as in this miniature French house, built for interior designer Virginia West and her husband, contractor R. C. West. Hooton designed the quite similar house at 2207 Dryden for his own parents.

E-14 House

E-14
House
2004 Southgate Boulevard
2010, Allen Bianchi

Bianchi made the most of one of Southgate's angled street intersections, outlining the site with a perimeter wall that emphasizes the triangular shape of the lot, then sculpturally countering this implied volume with projecting horizontal fascias. At 2145 Southgate is the 1-story, modern courtyard house that architect Charles B. Thomsen designed for his family (1965). At 2201 Southgate is a dramatically configured house by architect Dillon Kyle (2006).

E-15 Brave House

E-16 Southgate House

E-17 Peterson's Pharmacy Building

E-15
Brave House
2206 Sheridan Road
2004, Brave/Architecture

Buenos Aires architect Alejandro Brave, while associated with his brother, Houston architect Fernando Brave, designed this planar house faced with pale green stucco.

E-16
Southgate House
2429 Southgate Boulevard
2009, Robertson Design

Floating planes of brick are offset with incised and recessed planes faced with glass or wood in this big-scaled, courtyard-centered house.

E-17
Peterson's Pharmacy Building
2439 University Boulevard
1940, Bailey Swenson

Peterson's retains Swenson's modernistic graphics and fenestration. It was one of the first buildings constructed in the Village, a suburban, auto-oriented shopping district begun in 1938.

E-18
House
6136 Kirby Drive
1996, Wittenberg Architects

This 3-story house in West University Place engages the street with stacked verandas that double as outdoor rooms. Across the street at 6111 Kirby is another vintage Village storefront, Wagner Hardware Building—now New Living Green Building + Home Store (1948, Bailey A. Swenson).

E-18 House

E-12 House 2045

E-19 Cohen House

E-21 House

E-22 House

E-23 House

E-24 Leibrock House

E-19
Cohen House
2812 Amherst Street
1937

A cubic modernistic box rehabilitated and expanded by Carlos Jiménez (1989). Next door, at 2808 Amherst, is a suburban cottage tactfully expanded by Alfonso Varela (1985).

E-20
House
6001 Charlotte Street
2005, Price Harrison & Associates with Anthony E. Frederick

In a West University neighborhood of exceptionally modest houses, this 2-story house by Nashville architect, Price Harrison, although not large, stands out as dramatically white and modern.

E-21
House
6501 Brompton Avenue
1993, L. Barry Davidson Architects

Leslie Davidson based this house on the Italianate villa house type. The angled corner entrance is a detail one might find in the East End of Galveston.

E-22
House
6438 Belmont Avenue
1992, L. Barry Davidson Architects

Stepping the gables and decorating the blank front wall plane with diagonal brick bonding patterns disguises the priority given to the garage on this narrow site. Next door at 6428 Belmont Carlos Jiménez had the opportunity to expand this pink stucco house across a 2-lot site (1991).

E-23
House
6512 Vanderbilt Avenue
1996, L. Barry Davidson Architects

At the behest of her client, Davidson paid tribute to the Creole house types of south Louisiana in the design and detailing of this 2-story house.

E-24
Leibrock House
6435 Vanderbilt Avenue
1984, L. Barry Davidson Architects

To cope with the demand for houses much larger than those initially built in West University (1930s-1950s), Davidson ingeniously retrieved traditional Southern house types. This house is derived from the suburban raised cottages of New Orleans and Galveston. Its high, arched porch, which wraps around the principal reception room, is a neighborly feature. Stringcourses on the south side of the pink stucco-faced house describe its stepped-sectional organization. Davidson demonstrates the relevance of traditional typologies for urbanizing suburban neighborhoods, an intelligent alternative to the conspicuous overbuilding, the consequences of which are omnipresent in West University Place.

E-25
Mixon House
3211 Pittsburgh Street
1984, Taft Architects
2004, Glassman Shoemake Maldonado

Built on a mid-block sliver site, this vertically organized house wittily deconstructs conventional images of "traditional" domesticity. When new owners needed to expand the house, architects Carrie Shoemake and Ernesto Maldonado duplicated the Taft original design. Now there are two.

E-25 Mixon House

E-20 House

E-26 Burgan House

E-27 Wilson House

E-28 Ake House

E-30 Casita

E-31 HEB Buffalo Market

E-26
Burgan House
6533 Mercer Avenue
1985, L. Barry Davidson Architects

The Gulf Coast Cottage, Houston's fundamental house type, is here neatly transformed into a suburban house, a much more civil and gracious addition to the neighborhood than the hulking Georgian-burgers that have proliferated in West University since the mid 1980s.

E-27
Wilson House
6416 Sewanee Avenue
1977, Anderson/Wilson

Tom Wilson also followed Southern precedent in the siting, if not the architectural design, of this low-key, medium-tech house. The Charleston single house, with rooms aligned behind a narrow street front and facing south toward a long side garden, appears here as a pre-engineered steel structure, surfaced with metal and wood panels. In place of a side gallery, Wilson substituted a wooden deck and lap pool, screened from the street by a latticed privacy wall that doubles as a front porch.

E-28
Ake House
3124 Amherst Street
1986, Anthony E. Frederick

The undemonstrative exterior conceals a cool, generously proportioned interior, hinted at by the casement-filled kitchen window bay projecting from the east side.

E-29
House
3114 Tangley Road
2009, Dean Strombom and Intexure

By dividing this loft-like house into a front garage wing and taller rear block, architects Strombom and Intexure inserted it among its lower neighbors, acknowledging their architectural differences without demeaning the surroundings.

E-30
Casita
3122 Sunset Boulevard
2009, W. Jude Le Blanc

Atlanta-based architect, Jude Le Blanc, describes the white stucco-faced backyard tower, visible up the driveway, as a "casita." It incorporates a garage, living room, and guest accommodations. Le Blanc designed the little building to be an architectural analog of the Live Oak tree with which it shares the backyard.

E-31
HEB Buffalo Market
5225 Buffalo Speedway
2009, Selser Schaefer and Lake/Flato

The San Antonio-based HEB grocery chain made architectural design central to its West University neighborhood market. Selser Schaefer of Tulsa and Lake/Flato of San Antonio designed the market as an architecturally literate, steel-framed shed infilled with extensive glazing to naturally illuminate the store's interior. Colored panels face the west (Buffalo Speedway) elevation. This straightforward retail building demonstrates the extraordinary improvements that can be achieved in even the most ordinary building types by thoughtful and deliberate architectural design.

E-29 House

E-32 KTRK Channel 13 TV Studio

E-33 House

E-34 House

E-35 House

E-36 House

E-32
KTRK Channel 13 TV Studio
3310 Bissonnet Avenue
1963, Lloyd, Morgan & Jones
1995, OA+D/Office for Architecture+Design

Lloyd, Morgan & Jones' original station anticipated their design of the Astrodome. OA+D's additions complement the existing complex.

E-33
House
3502 Sunset Boulevard
2005, David Heymann

Austin architect David Heymann organized interior spaces beneath a projecting roof plate, staggering the gridded, street-facing curtain wall in plan to produce the house's lively syncopated south elevation. A screened porch on the east end is juxtaposed with a stone-lined bay on the west. The exuberant landscape is the work of Houston landscape gardener Will Fleming.

E-34
House
3901 Arnold Street
1996, L. Barry Davidson Architects

This cottage-like house expands upward around an amazing central stair well.

E-35
House
4124 Case Street
1996, Thomas Redyard Wilson

The versatile Tom Wilson, here produced an unpretentious modern house.

E-36
House
3833 Oberlin Street
1996, Curtis & Windham

William Curtis and Russell Windham demonstrated skill and tact in discreetly inserting this manorial style house into a block in West University Place originally built out with smaller, less architecturally ambitious houses.

E-37
House
3708 Ingold Street
1988, Carlos Jiménez

Receding planar surfaces of metal, peach-colored stucco, and exposed concrete block subtly establish the presence of this courtyard house in Southside Place, while minimizing the impact of its front-facing garages. The metal canopy above the garden gate imparts a jaunty touch.

E-38
House
3728 Garnet Street
2006, Jay Baker Architects

Baker's evocation of an English Cotswolds house is precise, economical, and so confidently proportioned that it easily absorbs three street-facing garage doors. The architectural virtues of this house identify what its neighbors are missing when they substitute gratuitous stylistic detail for architectural design. Located nearby at the east end of Garnet is another Cotswolds house at 6447 Edloe by Hill Swift (1999).

E-39
Southside Place Bath House
3730 Farbar Street
1983, Taft Architects

Southside Place, the smallest incorporated municipality in Harris County, is one block wide and 10 blocks long. The public swimming pool is its civic center, a fact that Taft Architects acknowledged with the mock-heroic wall of polychrome concrete block, which provides backing for two changing rooms. Sharing the block-square park with the swimming pool is the Southside Place Club House at 3743 Garnet by Val Glitsch (2004).

E-37 House

E-38 House

E-39 Southside Place Bath House

E-41 Robertson House

E-42 House

E-43 House

E-44 John P. McGovern Branch Library

E-45 House

E-40
House
3735 Gramercy
1998, Marshall Reid

Reid designed the street front of this house as two windowless planes faced with horizontally corrugated steel panels. The landscape design by the Office of James Burnett perfectly complements the architecture's proportioned planarity. The house is located in the subdivision of Braes Heights, developed in 1945 according to a master plan by the landscape architects Hare & Hare.

E-41
Robertson House
3718 Gramercy
2007, Robertson Design

In a nimble reversal of the "Not-in-My-Backyard" prejudice, Christopher Robertson deployed shifting horizontal planes of limestone, stucco, and mahogany to minimize the impact of the Shell Oil Company's Bellaire Technology Center on the backyard of this dramatically massed house. Interior views are oriented to the east side of the property and away from the research center. At 3521 Gramercy is a quiet 2-story house by Murphy Mears (2000).

E-42
House
3526 Bellefontaine
1994, Thomas Redyard Wilson

Although changed in appearance, this Braes Heights house adopts the typological characteristics of Wilson's own house in West University Place to demonstrate the intelligence of the side-courtyard house plan.

E-43
House
3515 Aberdeen Way
2002, Rob Civitello Local Architect

In designing this 1- and 2-story house in the Braes Oaks subdivision, Civitello emphasized profile, planarity, and shallow recession and advance.

E-44
John P. McGovern Branch Library
7405 Stella Link Road
2005, Bailey Architects

A sweeping roof that peaks at both ends and dips in the center lends a sense of exuberant dynamism to what is actually a box-like building. The library is part of a complex of civic buildings and green space that includes Pershing Middle School at 3838 Bluebonnet (2007, PGAL). The library replaced apartment buildings that a neighborhood-based nonprofit, the Stella Link Redevelopment Association, acquired and demolished in the 1990s after their tenancy shifted from middle- to lower-income. The Weekley Family YMCA Building (2002, Curry Boudreaux) at 7101 Stella Link is part of the complex.

E-45
House
4154 Bellefontaine
2005, Rob Civitello Local Architect

Built along the railroad embankment and power transmission easement that separates Houston from Bellaire, this refined, articulately constructed house takes advantage of a large Live Oak tree, which shelters its long side street elevation from the west sun. Ordinary materials are used purposefully and with precision

E-46
House
4131 Turnberry Circle
1999, Morris Gutiérrez

Deborah Morris and Gabriella Gutiérrez oriented this house in the postwar subdivision of Ayrshire Place to a generous, south-facing side yard and used architectural screening to shade exterior walls.

E-46 House

E-40 House

E-47 Benedit House

E-48 House

E-49 Style-in-Steel House

E-50 Holmes Shopping Center

E-51 Brochsteins Inc. Building

E-47
Benedit House
4111 Drummond
1952, Lars Bang

Dating from the first generation of houses built in Ayrshire, which came on the market in 1946, this flat-roofed house, 2,200-SF in size, is the perfect Houston house. Lars Bang extended the flat roof plate outward to shade walls of brick, wood, and glass. Skylights and interior garden courts bring daylight and nature into the house. And a backyard swimming pool was how occupants were expected to beat the summer heat. Surrounded by 1-story ranch houses and aggressive replacement housing of the 1990s and 2000s, this house is a forcible reminder of how beautiful and rewarding simplicity and good sense can be. Architect Steven Curry rehabilitated the house. Bang also designed the 1-story house at 4135 Durness (1955).

E-48
House
3615 North Braeswood Boulevard
1957, Joseph Krakower

Herb Greene's hand is evident in this low-slung Braes Heights house, especially in the vertical slot windows that take the place of corners and the tense profile of the hipped roof. Next door at 3611 North Braeswood, it is the attenuated Japanese-like eaves that point to Greene's involvement (1957, Joseph Krakower). Facing Brays Bayou at 3506 Glen Arbor is another Krakower contemporary (1955).

E-49
Style-in-Steel Townhouses
4156-4160 Meyerwood Drive
1968, Wilson, Morris, Crain & Anderson

The American Iron & Steel Institute, Houston Lighting & Power, and General Electric built these three demonstration houses, designed by Talbott Wilson and Hal Weatherford. They are courtyard pavilions, simply detailed and quite spacious. The central 2-story house has been modified with the addition of a pitched roof. The house at 4156 was restored by Michael John Smith, FAIA, and Malcolm M. Perry (1997).

E-50
Holmes Shopping Center
4115-4117 Willowbend Boulevard
1962, Burdette Keeland

Upon returning to Houston from graduate school at Yale, Keeland produced a number of small buildings that attested to then-current trends. This strip shopping center, faced with white glazed brick, registers the influence of the Philadelphia architect, Louis I. Kahn, in its arched lunette windows, which illuminate the upper reaches of the ends of the center.

E-51
Brochsteins Inc. Building
11530 Main Street
1940, 1947, I. S. Brochstein with Lenard Gabert

When Brochstein designed this building for his custom woodworking plant, South Main was the undisputed axis of Houston. Retaining its civic attributes—the streamlined central pylon and ceremonial reflecting basin—Brochsteins still defers to Main's honorific status.

E-52
Rice University Primary Data Center and Library Service Center
11620 Main Street
2004, Carlos Jiménez Design Studio with Kendall/Heaton Associates
2007, Carlos Jiménez Design Studio with PGAL

Occupying a flat, open site bounded by a highway overpass, a railroad line, and electrical transmission lines, these buildings were designed to be works of infrastructure. Built to contain back-up services that do not need to be on Rice University's main campus, the two warehouses are constructed of concrete-tilt walls. Jiménez profiled the concrete walls with canted fascias and painted them in intense tones of green to give these otherwise ordinary buildings an electrifying presence on their highly visible site. The Office of James Burnett was the landscape architect.

E-52 Rice University Primary Data Center and Library Service Center

E-53 Houston Cardiac Association Clinic

E-54 Bethany United Methodist Church

E-55 Linkwood Community Center

E-56 Solomon House

E-57 Hurwitz House

E-53
Houston Cardiac Association Clinic
10480 Main Street
2007, Wittenberg Oberholzer Architects

Gordon Wittenberg and Mark Oberholzer treated this highway-side building as a long container faced with concrete masonry units sheltered beneath a billowing, asymmetrical steel-framed roof vault.

E-54
Bethany United Methodist Church
3511 Linkwood Drive
1952, 1958, Gehring & Reichert

The modern style of Eliel Saarinen, with its emphasis on crafted decoration rather than engineering, influenced the design of this church complex. The pierced block screens and the cast stone detailing, especially the Saarinen-like bell tower pylon, make Bethany a strong presence in the neighborhood.

E-55
Linkwood Community Center
3699 Norris Street
2002, Bricker + Cannady and Ray Bailey Architects

William Cannady and Mark Wamble designed this small community building in Linkwood Park as a pair of steel-framed, counterthrust shed-roofed rectangles faced with a curtain wall of glazed tile block, brilliantly striped with slashes of blue, dark blue, and green. A simple interior program became the occasion for developing internal spatial "knots."

E-56
Solomon House
3615 South Braeswood Boulevard
1956, Brooks & Brooks

During the 1950s Houston's director of city planning, Ralph S. Ellifrit, cajoled subdivision developers into donating the rights-of-way for

North and South Braeswood, parkway boulevards that follow the course of Brays Bayou upstream to South Gessner. Few buildings along the 6.5-mile parkway architecturally acknowledge the parkway's civic stature. One small exception is this 1-story modern house in the Braes Manor subdivision. Its porte cochère (the modern replacement for the front porch), walled courtyards, flat roof, skylights, and clerestory-lit living room facing a rear garden were associated with architects David G. and E. B. Brooks.

E-57
Hurwitz House
3007 South Braeswood Boulevard
1958, Lenard Gabert & W. Jackson Wisdom

An indication of the extent to which the flat-roofed courtyard house constituted the cutting edge of Houston modernism by the mid-1950s is this example by Gabert and Wisdom, who theretofore had been identified with the Usonian modern trend.

E-58
Rice School-La Escuela Rice
7500 Seuss Drive
1994, Taft Architects

The Rice School, a public elementary and middle school, was one of Houston's major public buildings of the 1990s. Taft confidently demonstrated the relevance of ambitious architecture to public-school design in their spirited departure from the boxy schools that the Houston Independent School District has built since the 1960s.

E-58 Rice School-La Escuela Rice

E-59 Allen House

E-60 Braeswood Corporation House

E-61 Braeswood Corporation House

E-62 Gordon House

E-63 House

E-59
Allen House
2337 Bluebonnet Boulevard
1936, Wirtz & Calhoun

This was the most famous modern house built in Houston in the 1930s. White stucco walls, flat roofs, terrace decks, glass block panels, and tubular metal railing brought the spirit of the new to Braeswood, planned in 1928 by Hare & Hare. The steel-framed house retains some of its original furnishings, designed especially for it by J. Herbert Douglas. The architects, L. M. Wirtz and Harold Calhoun, were as adroit with traditional styles as they were with advanced ones. For the business partner of L. D. Allen, who built this house, they produced a very carefully detailed American Georgian house around the corner at 2356 Underwood (1936). Glassman Shoemake Maldonado rehabilitated and tactfully expanded the Allen House (2002).

E-60
Braeswood Corporation House
2329 Bluebonnet Boulevard
1929, Carl A. Mulvey

This picturesque Manorial style house, one of four that Mulvey designed for the Braeswood Corporation, demonstrates his attentive study of contemporary houses by John F. Staub. The molded brick chimney and the brick nogging in the timber-faced front porch are notable details.

E-61
Braeswood Corporation House
2309 Bluebonnet Boulevard
1929, Carl A. Mulvey

Mulvey worked for Birdsall P. Briscoe before starting his own practice, which is evident in the composition and proportions of this graceful house. The Braeswood Corporation described the house as being in the French Colonial style.

E-62
Gordon House
2307 Bluebonnet Boulevard
1955, Bolton & Barnstone

Howard Barnstone achieved critical recognition in the mid-1950s with this 2-story, steel-framed modern house. Closed off from the street by a garage and a walled entrance court, the house is opened at the back with walls of glass two-stories high. Original interiors were by Florence Knoll, and the landscape design was by Thomas D. Church. In 2003 the house was restored by new owners in consultation with Preston Bolton.

E-63
House
2308 Glenn Haven Boulevard
1987, Michael Underhill

This is the most prepossessing of a number of adventurous houses designed by young Houston architects and built in Braeswood in the 1980s. Its brick terrace gives the tripartite, stucco-faced house a monumental aspect. The denticulated-ventilated cornice is a postmodern paraphrase of a traditional architectural detail.

E-64
Herzog House
2523 Maroneal Boulevard
1952, Paul László with Howard Barnstone

In its contrast of house types, Braeswood distinctly exhibits the two periods of its development, the 1920s and 1950s. This low, remarkably long house, on a block of low, long houses, was designed by the Hungarian-born, Beverly Hills architect, Paul László. Its cantilevered entrance canopy, north-facing brise-soleil, and vertical redwood siding are organized beneath a continuous fascia. László incorporated a front-facing garage, and, in the best California manner, made it seem like a civilized amenity rather than a necessary evil.

E-65
Glesby House
2405 Bellefontaine
1953; 1995, Gerald Moorhead

This 1-story ranch-type house was expanded upward with what the architect calls a "camelback" addition. By repeating the configuration and proportions of the original house, the new second-story reads as an integral part of the house.

E-64 Herzog House

E-65 Glesby House

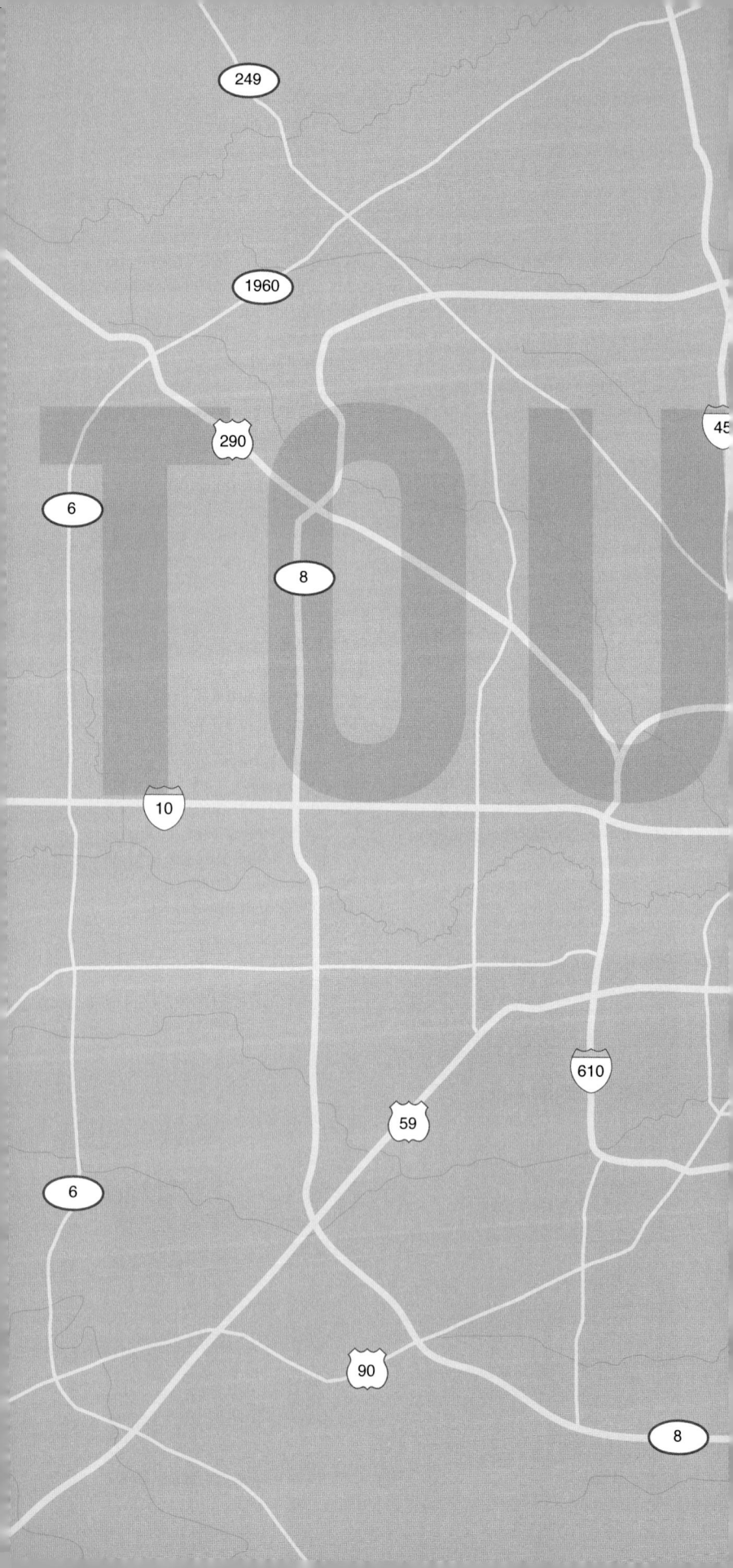

Third Ward / Riverside / Universities

Third Ward / Riverside / Universities

Tour F

Houston is a Southern city. Whatever connotations of graciousness and civility this characterization may evoke, it also raises the issue of race. Houston's ex-Third Ward, as it expands southward into Riverside Terrace, is a landscape that spatially depicts the development of Houston's African-American community from a culture formed under the impact of legal segregation to one that has

won nominal equality, but persists as a distinct subculture, not just as a matter of ethnic pride, but because of continuing social and economic disparities that sharply divide black from white. Dowling Street, the main street of the old Third Ward, is in ruins. The end of segregation in the 1960s meant that the external political and economic forces that gave the street cohesion dissipated. With these have gone the portion of the community that could afford to leave, moving southward over the old color barriers into neighborhoods developed in the 1920s and 1930s as white middle- to upper-middle-income subdivisions. Texas Southern University, the central institution of black Houston in the second half of the 20th century, sits on this old color line. To the north are Third Ward and Cuney Homes, the first low-income public housing complex in Houston; to the west and south are the middle-class cottage neighborhoods of Washington Terrace. Stretching along the Brays Bayou corridor park that connects Hermann and MacGregor parks are the elite neighborhoods of black Houston in the late 20th century, Riverside Terrace and its ancillaries. From the 1930s through the early 1960s these were where Houston's most established Jewish families were concentrated. The decision of almost all of these and other white households to abandon Riverside Terrace in the 1960s, documented in Jon Schwartz's film, *This Is Our Home, It Is Not For Sale* (1987), marks almost the only occasion in Houston's history when insulated middle-class whites had to come to terms with the negative consequences of a system of racial privilege in which they were supposed to be beneficiaries. Jewish families settled in Riverside Terrace in the 1930s because they were not welcome in River Oaks. This is one of the few instances of real estate transition that has not merely been absorbed into the collective amnesia of a city where real estate volatility is the norm. The University of Houston has encapsulated itself from urban demographic changes. Through purchase and exercise of its power of eminent domain, it has surrounded itself with a swath of territory that buffers the campus on all four sides. Displaced neighborhoods and apartment complexes have been replaced with suburban institutional landscaping, a noncommittal approach to urban design typical of Houston's largest university.

Just to the north of the university's campus the Gulf Freeway, the first inter-city freeway in Texas, was built along the right-of-way of the Galveston-Houston Electric Company's Interurban railroad, a poetic symbol of the triumph of the private car over rapid mass transportation. Completion of the Gulf Freeway in 1952 sparked Houston's first episode of freeway-related development. It was along this corridor that the first suburban corporate office complex and regional shopping mall were built, forecasting a future that has now bypassed many of these pioneer installations.

In Third Ward and Riverside Terrace, as in other inner city Houston neighborhoods, new real estate patterns emerged in the mid 1990s. Market housing (that is, middle-income housing) began to be built here sporadically (the only way things happen in Houston) but marking a transition in attitude as middle-income buyers, of whatever racial or ethnic background, became willing to live in what was still a low-income neighborhood because it was affordable. Since property, especially in the Third Ward area, was rarely owner-occupied, developers' perennial search for low-cost real estate introduced new insecurities into these neighborhoods, where residents cannot afford to compete with much more affluent newcomers.

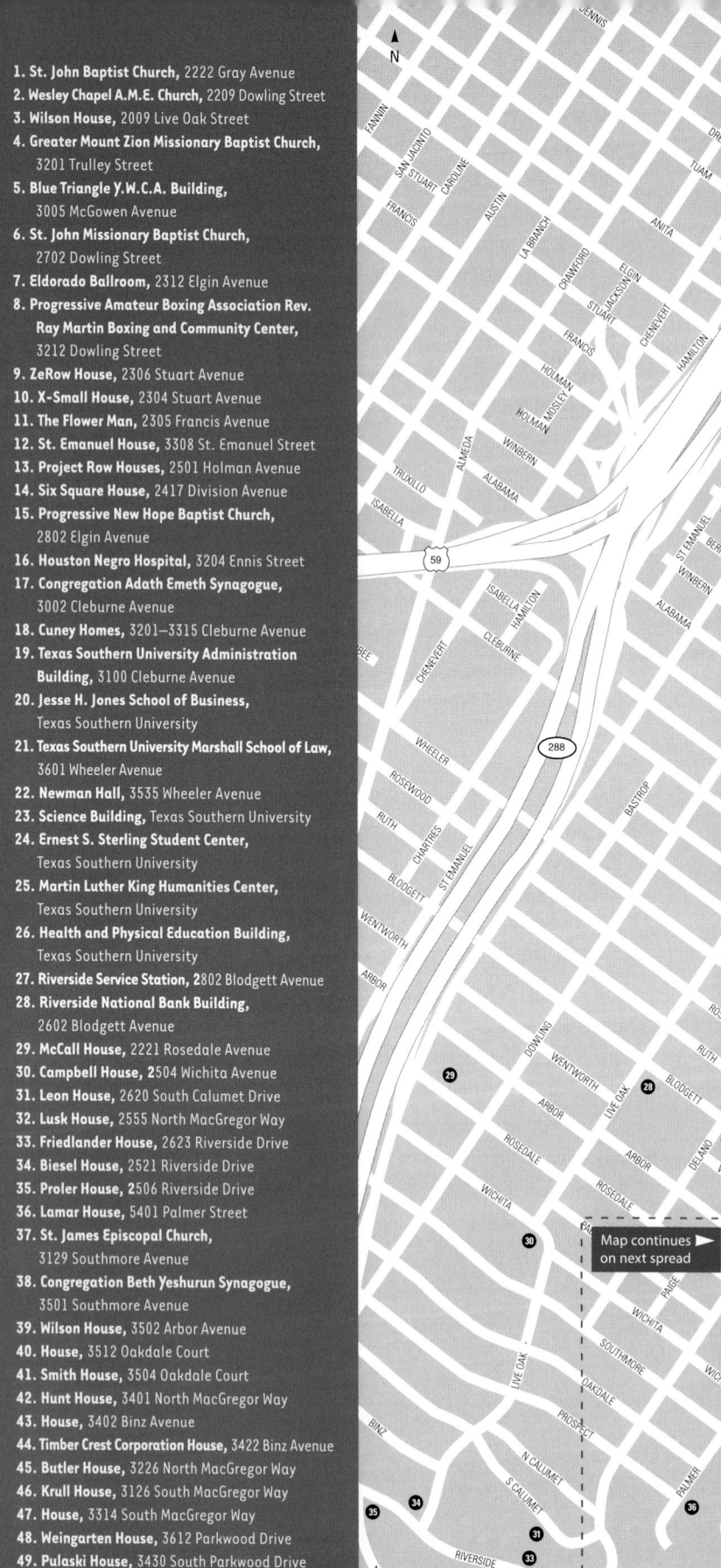

1. **St. John Baptist Church,** 2222 Gray Avenue
2. **Wesley Chapel A.M.E. Church,** 2209 Dowling Street
3. **Wilson House,** 2009 Live Oak Street
4. **Greater Mount Zion Missionary Baptist Church,** 3201 Trulley Street
5. **Blue Triangle Y.W.C.A. Building,** 3005 McGowen Avenue
6. **St. John Missionary Baptist Church,** 2702 Dowling Street
7. **Eldorado Ballroom,** 2312 Elgin Avenue
8. **Progressive Amateur Boxing Association Rev. Ray Martin Boxing and Community Center,** 3212 Dowling Street
9. **ZeRow House,** 2306 Stuart Avenue
10. **X-Small House,** 2304 Stuart Avenue
11. **The Flower Man,** 2305 Francis Avenue
12. **St. Emanuel House,** 3308 St. Emanuel Street
13. **Project Row Houses,** 2501 Holman Avenue
14. **Six Square House,** 2417 Division Avenue
15. **Progressive New Hope Baptist Church,** 2802 Elgin Avenue
16. **Houston Negro Hospital,** 3204 Ennis Street
17. **Congregation Adath Emeth Synagogue,** 3002 Cleburne Avenue
18. **Cuney Homes,** 3201–3315 Cleburne Avenue
19. **Texas Southern University Administration Building,** 3100 Cleburne Avenue
20. **Jesse H. Jones School of Business,** Texas Southern University
21. **Texas Southern University Marshall School of Law,** 3601 Wheeler Avenue
22. **Newman Hall,** 3535 Wheeler Avenue
23. **Science Building,** Texas Southern University
24. **Ernest S. Sterling Student Center,** Texas Southern University
25. **Martin Luther King Humanities Center,** Texas Southern University
26. **Health and Physical Education Building,** Texas Southern University
27. **Riverside Service Station,** 2802 Blodgett Avenue
28. **Riverside National Bank Building,** 2602 Blodgett Avenue
29. **McCall House,** 2221 Rosedale Avenue
30. **Campbell House,** 2504 Wichita Avenue
31. **Leon House,** 2620 South Calumet Drive
32. **Lusk House,** 2555 North MacGregor Way
33. **Friedlander House,** 2623 Riverside Drive
34. **Biesel House,** 2521 Riverside Drive
35. **Proler House,** 2506 Riverside Drive
36. **Lamar House,** 5401 Palmer Street
37. **St. James Episcopal Church,** 3129 Southmore Avenue
38. **Congregation Beth Yeshurun Synagogue,** 3501 Southmore Avenue
39. **Wilson House,** 3502 Arbor Avenue
40. **House,** 3512 Oakdale Court
41. **Smith House,** 3504 Oakdale Court
42. **Hunt House,** 3401 North MacGregor Way
43. **House,** 3402 Binz Avenue
44. **Timber Crest Corporation House,** 3422 Binz Avenue
45. **Butler House,** 3226 North MacGregor Way
46. **Krull House,** 3126 South MacGregor Way
47. **House,** 3314 South MacGregor Way
48. **Weingarten House,** 3612 Parkwood Drive
49. **Pulaski House,** 3430 South Parkwood Drive
50. **Kurth House,** 3418 South Parkwood Drive

51. **Bishkin House,** 3402 South Parkwood Drive
52. **Finger House,** 3403 North Parkwood Drive
53. **Proler House,** 3403 Charleston Street
54. **Pasternak House,** 3417 Charleston Street
55. **Hutsell House,** 3711 Charleston Street
56. **Kuhlman House,** 3716 Charleston Street
57. **Flatow House,** 3807 South MacGregor Way
58. **Weingarten House,** 4000 South MacGregor Way
59. **Gregory House,** 3939 Roseneath Drive
60. **Proler House,** 4216 Fernwood Drive
61. **Rabinowitz House,** 4511 North Roseneath Drive
62. **Rosenthal House,** 4506 North Roseneath Drive
63. **Alamo Plaza Motel,** 4343 Old Spanish Trail
64. **MacGregor Park Clubhouse,** South MacGregor Way and MacGregor Loop Drive
65. **University of Houston Ezekiel W. Cullen Building,** 4800 Calhoun Road
66. **Cullen Family Plaza,** University of Houston
67. **Student Life Plaza,** University of Houston
68. **University Center,** University of Houston
69. **Michael J. Cemo Lecture Hall, Bauer College of Business,** University of Houston
70. **Philip Guthrie Hoffman Hall,** University of Houston
71. **Agnes Arnold Hall,** University of Houston
72. **Science & Research Center,** University of Houston
73. **Science and Engineering Classroom Building,** University of Houston
74. **Architecture Building,** University of Houston
75. **Burdette Keeland, Jr. Design Exploration Center,** University of Houston
76. **Cynthia Woods Mitchell Center for the Arts,** University of Houston
77. **Moores Opera House,** University of Houston
78. **100 Chairs,** University of Houston
79. **Rother's Bookstore,** 3503 Elgin Avenue
80. **Bates College of Law,** University of Houston
81. **Schlumberger Well Services Headquarters,** 5000 Gulf Freeway
82. **Small House and Small House 2,** 5910 Grace Lane
83. **Houston Texans YMCA Building,** 5202 Griggs Road

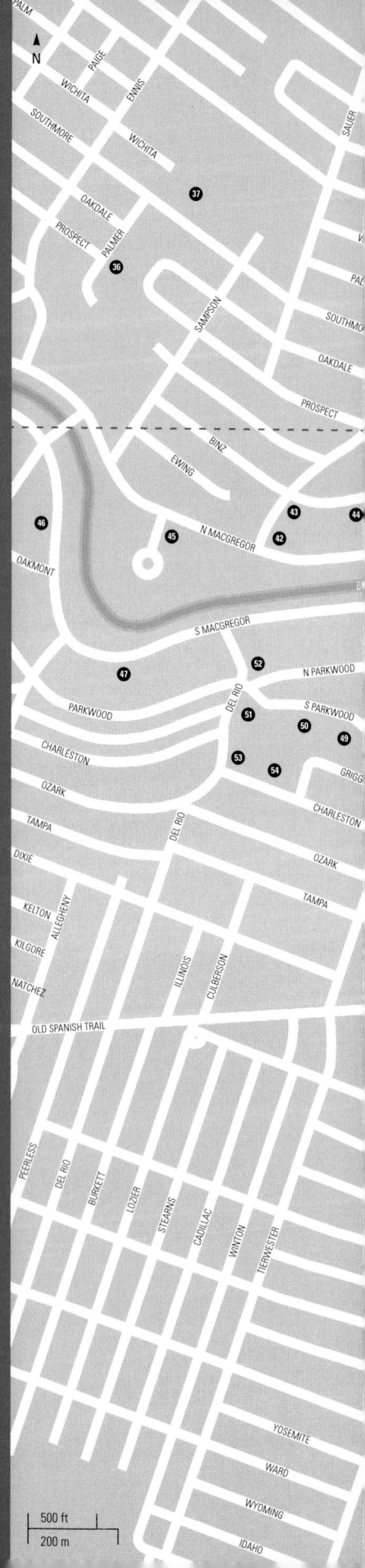

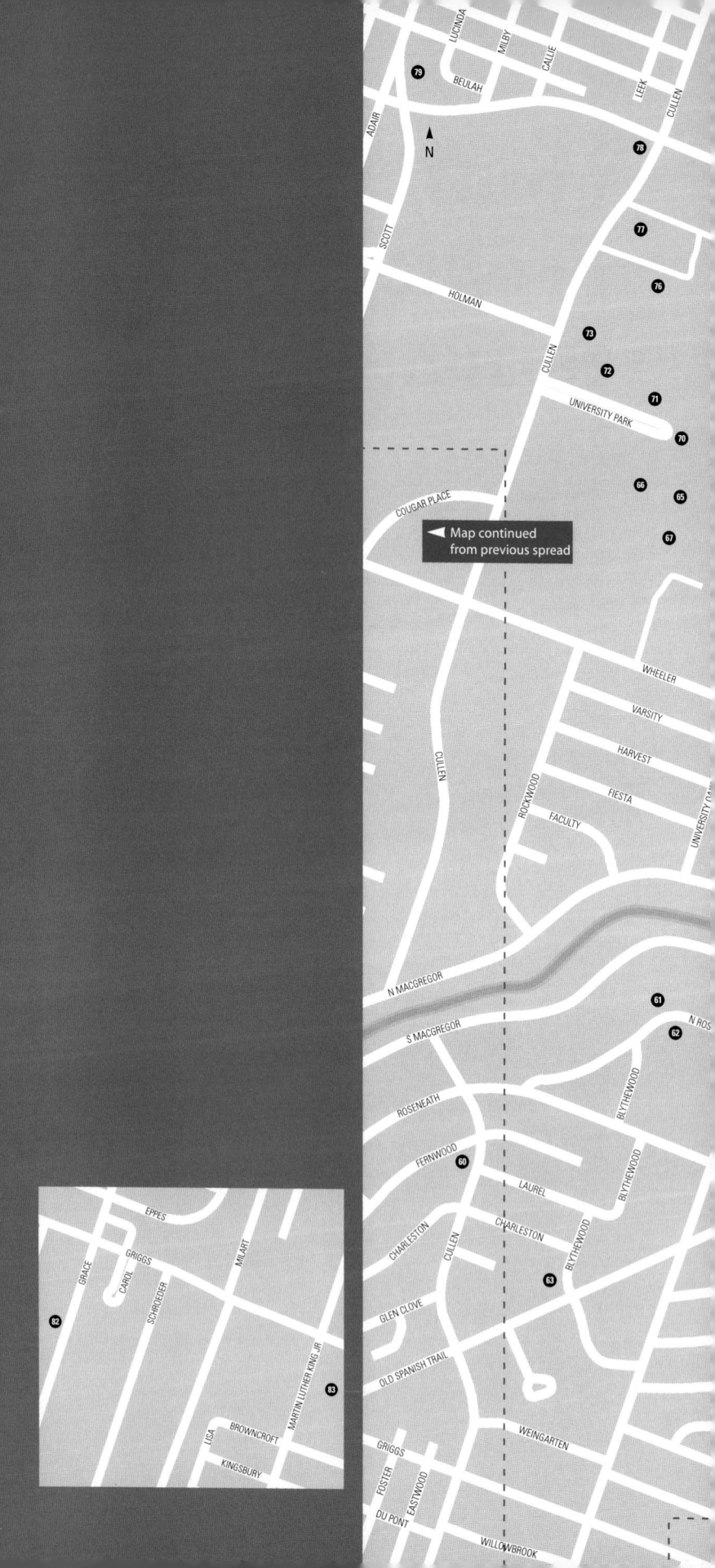

F-1 St. John Baptist Church

F-2 Wesley Chapel African Methodist Episcopal Church

F-3 Wilson House

F-4 Greater Zion Missionary Baptist Church

F-1
St. John Baptist Church
2222 Gray Avenue
1946, James M. Thomas

St. John's nave, elevated above a raised basement, and its twin towers exemplify a church building type favored by local African-American congregations in the 1930s, '40s, and '50s. Vertical strips of glass block are used here as architectural decoration. The builder, James M. Thomas, specialized in church construction and design.

F-2
Wesley Chapel African Methodist Episcopal Church
2209 Dowling Street
1926, W. Sidney Pittman

This high-set, vertically attenuated, brown brick-faced church is the only extant work in Houston of W. Sidney Pittman. A son-in-law of Booker T. Washington, Pittman was the first professional black architect to practice in Texas. Pittman's use of a towered church front and an elevated nave seems to have established the prototype for such churches as St. John Baptist. Located just a few blocks apart, these two churches still preside with authority over the deteriorating center of what was once a thriving community in Third Ward. H. D. Frankfurt was responsible for additions to Wesley Chapel in 1946. Next door a companion building, Pittman's bungalow-style pastor's house, was demolished by the congregation and replaced with a temporary building.

F-3
Wilson House
2009 Live Oak Street
c. 1907

Occupied by the family of a porter employed by the Pullman Company, this turreted cottage was one of the more pretentious houses built in this section of Third Ward. (Demolished)

F-4
Greater Zion Missionary Baptist Church
3201 Trulley Street
1955, John S. Chase with David C. Baer

The neo-Romanesque was a favored style for Houston churches in the 1920s and '30s. Chase's application represents a late, and very flat, interpretation of this ecclesiastical genre. This was one of the architect's first major projects.

F-5
Blue Triangle Branch Y. W. C. A. Building
[now Blue Triangle Multicultural Association]
3005 McGowen Avenue
1951, Hiram A. Salisbury and Birdsall P. Briscoe

The semicircular entrance portico, faced with limestone and decorated with a running fret pattern, is a device that Briscoe frequently employed on his public building projects of the 1930s and '40s. The contrast between high style (stone facing) and low style (steel sash casement windows) was a favorite theme of the '40s, as was the raised brick banding used to decorate the walls of the rear gymnasium wing. John Biggers' mural, *The Negro Woman in American Life and Education*, (1953) is inside.

F-6
St. John Missionary Baptist Church
2702 Dowling Street
1948, Beckmann, Williams & Williams

A firm of San Antonio architects produced the grandest of the Dowling Street churches. St. John, with its Ionic temple front, is curiously anachronistic, more typical of the 1920s than the late '40s. Even so, it ennobles its surroundings.

F-5 Blue Triangle Branch Y. W. C. A. Building

F-6 St. John Missionary Baptist Church

F-7 Eldorado Ballroom

F-8 Progressive Amateur Boxing Association Rev. Ray Martin Boxing and Community Center

F-9 ZeRow House

F-10 X-Small House

F-11 The Flower Man

F-7
Eldorado Ballroom
2312 Elgin Avenue
1939, Lenard Gabert

Gabert's streamlined modernistic nightclub and commercial building for the jazz impresario C. W. Dupree is another Third Ward landmark, although rather different in character than the magisterial churches of Dowling. Roger Wood celebrates the role the Eldorado played in Houston's mid-century black music scene in his book, *Down in Houston: Bayou City Blues* (2003). The bull-nosed corner at Dowling and Elgin and the second-floor windows, framed by horizontal speed lines, still distinguish the Eldorado. In 1998 the property was given to Project Row Houses, which has rehabilitated it as a performance space. Behind the Eldorado, at Elgin and Bastrop, Project Row Houses has installed artist Bert L. Long, Jr.'s sculptural ensemble, *Field of Vision* (1999). Across Elgin at 3018 Dowling is Emancipation Park, 10 acres acquired as a public gathering place by Houston's African-American community in 1872 and transferred to the City of Houston in 1916 as the first public park in Houston accessible to African Americans. The annual celebration of Juneteenth, the anniversary of the enactment of the Emancipation Proclamation in Texas on June 19, 1865, began in Emancipation Park. William Ward Watkin designed its modernistic recreation center, amphitheater, and bathhouse (1939).

F-8
Progressive Amateur Boxing Association Rev. Ray Martin Boxing and Community Center
3212 Dowling Street
1988, Padilla Associates

John Padilla ingeniously used glazing to describe the sectional organization of this prefabricated metal building. Its upbeat image attempts to ward off the gloominess of the depressed surroundings.

F-9
ZeRow House
2306 Stuart Avenue
2009, Rice Building Workshop

This 520-SF demonstration house was conceived by Rice University electrical engineering student, Roque Sánchez, designed by a team of Rice architecture students led by David Dewane, and constructed by students as Rice's entry in the 2009 Solar Decathlon in Washington, D.C., a biennial competition between teams of students from 20 universities for the design of a sustainable house. The competition was sponsored by the U.S. Department of Energy and the National Renewable Energy Laboratory. The ZeRow House was designed as a contemporary interpretation of a shotgun cottage (row house) that maximizes energy conservation practices.

F-10
X-Small House
2304 Stuart Avenue
2003, Rice Building Workshop

The Rice University School of Architecture's Building Workshop, in partnership with Project Row Houses, involved students led by Christian Sheridan in the design and construction of this 500-SF, one-person house. Based on the historic shotgun cottage prototype, the X-Small House was conceived as a prototype for new, affordable housing in Houston.

F-11
The Flower Man
2305 Francis Avenue
1999, Cleveland Turner

Cleveland Turner is the Flower Man. This is the third cottage in Third Ward that he has transformed into a riotous display of color with found objects and profuse floral vegetation.

F-12
St. Emanuel House
3308 St. Emanuel Street
2009, Ronnie Self and Robert Burrow

On the west edge of Third Ward, overlooking the U.S. Highway 59 freeway, Ronnie Self designed this 1,850-SF house elevated a full story above grade on a concrete substructure. A marvel of spatial compactness, the house functions as an observatory, offering spectacular vistas of the downtown skyline from inside as well as from a roof deck.

F-12 St. Emanuel House

F-13 Project Row Houses

F-15 Progressive New Hope Baptist Church (Demolished)

F-16 Houston Negro Hospital

F-13
Project Row Houses
2501 Holman Avenue
1939, 1994

One of the most extraordinary phenomena of the 1990s in Houston was Project Row Houses, a public art project through which Houston artists, led by founder and artist Rick Lowe with Michael Peranteau and Deborah Grotfeldt, addressed the relationship of art making and exhibition to community involvement, social service provision, historic preservation, and neighborhood revitalization. With initial guidance from University of Houston architecture professor Sheryl Tucker, two blocks of 22 back-to-back cottages, built in the late 1930s as rental housing for African-American families, were rehabilitated in stages, mostly by teams of corporate volunteers from throughout Houston. The repetition of gabled house fronts echoes a series of paintings made by John Biggers in the 1980s based on the theme of the shotgun cottage. Ten cottages are used for changing installations by local and out-of-town artists. Another 10 provide transitional housing for young mothers. Others are used for a community, literacy, and music programs. Project Row Houses in an inspiring demonstration of how artistic vision engages community life and discharges civic responsibility. Although it operates on a small scale, it has become a model for other community-based artists' initiatives. At 2600 Holman is Trinity United Methodist Church (1951, George Pierce-Abel B. Pierce), the oldest African-American congregation in Houston, founded in 1848 as the slave congregation of First Methodist Church. The congregation's history is movingly evoked in stained glass windows by the Dallas artist, Jean Lacy, installed in 1995.

F-14
Six Square House
2417 Division Avenue
1998, Rice Building Workshop

The first new construction at Project Row Houses was this 800-SF house designed by Rice University architecture students Kathy Dy and Kim Neuscheler and built by student volunteers under the direction of Rice architecture professors, Danny Samuels and Nonya Grenader. Between 2004-08, 24 new duplex units, based on the Six Square House, were built alongside and behind the prototype. To address the problem of gentrification in a neighborhood occupied primarily by low-income renters, Project Row Houses in 2003 formed the Row House Community Development Corporation, which is housed in the ex-Delia's Lounge at 3409 Dowling (rehabilitated by Rice Building Workshop, 2005). The wall separating Division from the back of Delia's is faced with murals by South African artist Esther Mahlangu (2003). Adjacent to the back of Delia's is the Rice Building Workshop's Workyard Shelter, distinguished by its serrated roof (2006). The book, *Live Work: Architecture at Rice 42* documents Rice's collaboration with Project Row Houses.

F-15
Progressive New Hope Baptist Church
2802 Elgin Avenue
1942

Yet another example of the twin-towered church type, surfaced in red tapestry brick. The double volume arched loggia of the adjoining educational building gives the complex an unexpectedly monumental scale. (Demolished)

F-16
Houston Negro Hospital
[now Riverside General Hospital]
3204 Ennis Street
1926, Maurice J. Sullivan

J. S. Cullinan, founder of the Texas Company, built both the 3-story hospital, facing Elgin, and the 2-story School of Nursing Building (Maurice J. Sullivan, 1931), facing Holman. Both are pared-down examples of Mediterranean architecture. The School of Nursing, the more engaging of the two, was rescued from near-ruin in the 1990s.

F-14 Six Square House

F-17 Congregation Adath Emeth Synagogue

F-18 Cuney Homes

F-19 Texas Southern University Administration, Classroom, and Auditorium Building

F-17
Congregation Adath Emeth Synagogue
[now Charles P. Rhinehart Music Center Auditorium, Texas Southern University]
3002 Cleburne Avenue
1948, Irving R. Klein & Associates

The tautly inflected brick planes of Klein's synagogue show the influence of Eliel Saarinen on modern architecture in Houston in the late 1940s and early '50s. The stepped section and telescoped plan are coordinated to produce a delightful rounded bay at the east end of the building. From the 1920s to the early 1950s, Alabama Avenue was the dividing line between the African-American neighborhoods of Third Ward and what developed as a middle-income neighborhood with a pronounced Jewish presence to the south, a historic distinction preserved in the contrast between the wood frame rent houses of the one and the brick veneer suburban cottages and duplexes of the other. As the congregation's sale of its synagogue to Texas Southern University in 1958 attests, this color line dissolved, presaging the end of legal racial segregation in Houston.

F-18
Cuney Homes
3201-3315 Cleburne Avenue
1940, Stayton Nunn-Milton McGinty with John F. Staub
1942, Associated Housing Architects of Houston

This project, the first U.S. Housing Authority-financed, low-income housing complex constructed in Houston, was built in two stages. Nunn and McGinty's original section is spartan, although site planning by the Kansas City landscape architects, Hare & Hare, downplayed the repetitiveness of the apartment blocks by skillful use of curved and angled streets and by preserving existing trees. The second phase, for which MacKie & Kamrath were responsible, employed brick banding, thin concrete canopies, and horizontal slot windows to give the housing blocks a distinctly modern look. The gratuitous addition of pitched roofs by the Housing Authority (1993-96, Bradfield, Richards & Associates) has compromised the architectural and historic integrity of the complex, while in no way affecting living conditions for residents. During this episode of "revitalization" the original community center was demolished and replaced by a larger structure.

F-19
Texas Southern University Administration, Classroom, and Auditorium Building
[now Mack H. Hannah Hall]
3100 Cleburne Avenue
1950, Lamar Q. Cato

Cato's three-part main building recalls Italian state architecture of the 1930s, especially its crypto-classical porticos with their flat roof slabs and thin, square piers. Replacement of steel sash windows with bronze solar glass has taken some of the edge off the contrast between industrial glazing and the requisite material of regional monumentality, Texas fossilized limestone. This was one of the first buildings to open on TSU's new campus. The university began in 1927 as Houston Colored Junior College, a racially segregated institution whose establishment and development paralleled that of the University of Houston. In 1947 it was elevated to the status of a state university in an unsuccessful effort by the Texas Legislature to forestall the racial desegregation of state universities.

F-20
Jesse H. Jones School of Business
Texas Southern University
3400 block Cleburne Avenue
1998, PGAL

Taut brick surfaces and horizontally aligned windows relate this building to the campus's contemporary style buildings of the 1950s. Adjacent to the Jones School in the 3800 block of Tierwester is the 4-story Barbara Jordan-Mickcy Leland School of Public Affairs Building (2008, Kirksey).

F-20 Jesse H. Jones School of Business

F-22 Newman Hall (1968)

F-23 Science Building

F-24 Ernest S. Sterling Student Center

F-25 Martin Luther King Humanities Center

F-27 Riverside Service Station

F-26 Health and Physical Education Building

F-21
Thurgood Marshall School of Law Building
Texas Southern University
3601 Wheeler Avenue
1976, John S. Chase

The combination of white precast concrete panels, bronze solar glass, and bronze anodized aluminum produces a high contrast color scheme that is simple, yet forceful. The protruding second-story bay curves outward to interact with the curve of Wheeler, making the building's presence felt despite its confined site.

F-22
Newman Hall
3535 Wheeler Avenue
1968, Clovis Heimsath Associates

Heimsath and his designer, W. Irving Phillips, Jr., used an extensive array of wall and roof shapes to indicate the interior spatial composition of this chapel and student center. Across the street at 3530 Wheeler is St. Luke the Evangelist Church (1967, John S. Chase), as ebullient on its terms as Newman Hall.

F-23
Science Building
[now Samuel M. Nabrit Science Center]
Texas Southern University
Corner Wheeler and Tierwester
1958, Wyatt C. Hedrick

Hedrick's no-nonsense '50s contemporary look (orange brick and horizontally aligned windows) was reinterpreted with considerable panache in Cavitt McKnight Weymouth's addition of 1984. The relief panel, next to the principal entrance is, *Man and the Universe* by sculptor Carroll Simms, who, with John Biggers, started TSU's art department in the early 1950s.

F-24
Ernest S. Sterling Student Center
Texas Southern University
1976, John S. Chase

In the mid 1970s Chase gave the center of the TSU campus a new architectural identity. The most distinctive of the several buildings for which his office was responsible is the Sterling Student Center. Like the law school, the long, low student center is faced with vertically striated white precast concrete panels and bronze solar glass. It is crowned by a glazed penthouse, which hovers dramatically between four vertical towers. The architecture is not refined, but the building's bold shapes and sharp chromatic contrasts compel attention. Also by Chase is the adjacent School of Education Building (1981).

F-25
Martin Luther King Humanities Center
Texas Southern University
1969, John S. Chase

With its oversailing cylindrical pavilion serving as pivot point for two symmetrically extended wings, this forceful building marked the first departure from TSU's previously unambitious architectural work. Stationed in front of the building is Carroll Simms' *African Queen Mother* (1968).

F-26
Health and Physical Education Building
Texas Southern University
1989, Haywood Jordan McCowan

TSU's aggressive move into surrounding residential neighborhoods in the early 1980s made Ennis the campus's new western boundary. The campus presence is announced by this sports arena, which is handsomely surfaced in earth-toned concrete tiles. At Ennis and Eagle is the university's Science Building (2008, 3D/International).

F-27
Riverside Service Station
2802 Blodgett Avenue
c. 1940

This neighborhood convenience is detailed with suburban Mediterranean attributes.

F-21 Thurgood Marshall School of Law Building

F-28 Riverside National Bank Building

F-29 McCall House

F-30 Campbell House

F-31 Leon House

F-32 Lusk House

F-28
Riverside National Bank Building
[now Unity National Bank Building]
2602 Blodgett Avenue
1963, John S. Chase

This glass, brick, and marble-faced bank is notable for its jaunty, folded-plate roof structure. The first African-American-owned bank in Texas, it became a symbol of community pride and achievement in Third Ward.

F-29
McCall House
2221 Rosedale Avenue
1929, Joseph Finger

This house is not subtle, but it stands out by virtue of its scale, massing, and arcaded loggia. It is located in the first section of Riverside Terrace, a middle-income neighborhood that was opened in 1924 and developed along both sides of Brays Bayou.

F-30
Campbell House
2504 Wichita Avenue
1930, W. D. Bordeaux

Bordeaux worked in Los Angeles before coming to Houston in the late 1920s. Here he produced one of the first local examples of an American regional style, based on the mid-19th-century buildings of Monterey, California, that was to become quite popular in the 1930s—the Monterey style.

F-31
Leon House
2620 South Calumet Drive
1936, Burns & James with Lenard Gabert

North and South Calumet and Riverside were the elite streets in the 1920s sections of Riverside Terrace. After the deed restrictions lapsed in the early 1960s, the large lots invited redevelopment. This French manorial-style house survives, although no longer as a single-family dwelling. Designed by a firm of Indianapolis architects, its asymmetrical massing is a typical '30s touch. Across Riverside Park, the colonnaded house at 2619 North Calumet (1930) is by J. M. Glover.

F-32
Lusk House
2555 North MacGregor Way
1929, Burns & James

The prevailing eclectic genre in this section of Riverside Terrace was the picturesque manorial style. This example, constructed by Katharine and Harry Mott, occupies a pivotal site at the confluence of North MacGregor and Riverside. The Motts were especially active in Riverside Terrace in the late 1920s, building speculative houses in which a characteristic mixture of ornamental brickwork and stone was always evident. The Motts, with their architects, Burns & James, produced 2620, 2612, and 2417 Riverside, as well as 2519 North MacGregor, in 1928-1929.

F-33
Friedlander House
2623 Riverside Drive
1936, Birdsall P. Briscoe

Briscoe's only house in Riverside Terrace conformed to the manorial mode. It was, in fact, his last foray into that particular genre. The graceful Regency-style porch is a charming anachronism, just the sort of historical "mistake" that eclectic architects of the 1920s and '30s committed with delight.

F-34
Biesel House
2521 Riverside Drive
1929, Charles Dieman

The corner turret and 3-story tower make this house a local landmark.

F-33 Friedlander House

F-34 Biesel House

F-35 Proler House

F-36 Lamar House

F-37 St. James Episcopal Church

F-38 Congregation Beth Yeshurun Synagogue

F-35
Proler House
2506 Riverside Drive
1936, Bailey A. Swenson

Horizontal speed lines framing second-floor windows and an inset bull-nosed corner send this white stucco-surfaced, flat-roofed modern house around the sharply curved Riverside-North MacGregor intersection. This was the first of a series of modern houses that Swenson designed for Mr. and Mrs. Ben Proler and their children.

F-36
Lamar House
5401 Palmer Street
1941, MacKie & Kamrath

Taut planar façades, a flat roof, and slot windows still mark this house as modern, despite unsympathetic alterations.

F-37
St. James Episcopal Church
3129 Southmore Avenue
2007, Ray+Hollington

In 2003 a tornado destroyed the parish's 1940 church building. Richard Hollington's replacement church is much more substantial with its blocky central tower and striking red roof. Haywood Jordan McCowan designed other components of the parish complex (1983-84).

F-38
Congregation Beth Yeshurun Synagogue
[now Lucian L. Lockhart Elementary School]
3501 Southmore Avenue
1949, Finger & Rustay

Only the education wing of Finger & Rustay's formidable modernistic Regency-style complex for Houston's oldest Conservative congregation was built. Its limestone-banded, tapestry brick-faced walls and bronze accoutrements are impressive.

F-39
Wilson House
3502 Arbor Avenue
1959, John S. Chase

With its flared eaves, solar screens, and orange Roman brick, this house summarizes the 1950s contemporary look in Houston.

F-40
Chase House
3512 Oakdale Court
1959, John S. Chase

The architect's own house is bisected by a 2-story glass wall lighting a cantilevered stair that dramatically spans a fountain trough.

F-41
Smith House
3504 Oakdale Court
1948, Wilson, Morris & Crain

WMC's designer, Ralph A. Anderson, Jr., set the horizontally aligned windows of this flat-roofed contemporary house into recessed panels above lengths of corrugated industrial siding.

F-40 Chase House

F-41 Smith House

F-39 Wilson House

F-42 Hunt House

F-43 House

F-44 Timber Crest Corporation House

F-45 Butler House

F-46 Krull House

F-42
Hunt House
3401 North MacGregor Way
1956, Lenard Gabert & W. Jackson Wisdom

This flat-roofed house, with its stone base and vertically boarded upper story, steps down in section as it fans out in plan. Closed to the street, it opens to a rear garden replete with period landscape fixtures, including a kidney-shaped pool spanned by an arched bridge. Note the Loblolly Pine tree that grows through a hole in the soffit above the front porch, a classic '50s organic touch.

F-43
House
3402 Binz Avenue
1963, John S. Chase

Chase was extremely deferential to the architectural context of the Timber Crest enclave when he designed this large house, with its stone base, boarded upper story, and widely projecting eaves with curved stucco soffits.

F-44
Timber Crest Corporation House
3422 Binz Avenue
1941, Harvin C. Moore

This is one of two houses Moore designed for Carl M. Knapp and Payson W. Moreland, developers of the Timber Crest subdivision. An example of the California Monterey type, it suggests the upper-middle-income clientele Knapp and Moreland hoped to attract. At 3303 North MacGregor is the 2-story contemporary-style house of Cynthia Woods and George P. Mitchell (1950) by Milton Foy Martin.

F-45
Butler House
3226 North MacGregor Way
1949, MacKie & Kamrath

This austere, hard-edged house with its glazed corner bay exhibits neither the pronounced horizontality nor the Wrightian ornament one expects of MacKie & Kamrath. Around the corner at 5808 Bayou Bend Court is the 1-story Gose House by MacKie & Kamrath (1950).

F-46
Krull House
3126 South MacGregor Way
1952, Bailey A. Swenson

Riverside Terrace is known especially for its uninhibited contemporary houses of the 1950s. This trim house contained beneath a monopitch roof plane is a subdued example.

F-47
House
3314 South MacGregor Way
1984, Haywood Jordan McCowan

Despite its 3-story height and geometrically configured projections, this house recedes visually into its site, due in part to its dark-stained wood surfaces.

F-48
Weingarten House
3612 Parkwood Drive
1938, Joseph Finger

This handsomely composed and proportioned house is detailed in a suburban rendition of the traditional architecture of Charleston, South Carolina. In siting the house, Finger's office made the most of the low promontory it occupies. Across the street at 3615 Parkwood is another house by Finger (1940), a stylistic companion to 3612.

F-49
Pulaski House
3430 South Parkwood Drive
1942, Lenard Gabert

This attenuated Regency-style house was the biggest that Gabert designed in Riverside Terrace. Its long front elevation conceals the shallow depth of the house. Large Houston houses of the 1920s, '30s, and '40s were frequently extended in plan in order to open them to the prevailing southeast breezes.

F-47 House

F-48 Weingarten House

F-49 Pulaski House

F-50 Kurth House

F-51 Bishkin House

F-52 Finger House

F-53 Proler House

F-54 Pasternak House

F-55 Hutsell Speculative House

F-50
Kurth House
3418 South Parkwood Drive
1938, Henry A. Stubee

The "southern colonial" plantation image struck a very responsive chord in affluent new Houston neighborhoods of the 1930s. This was the first house built in the Parkwood section of Riverside Terrace.

F-51
Bishkin House
3402 South Parkwood Drive
1951, Philip G. Willard

The counterthrust roof plane of the glazed second-story bay gives this low-slung contemporary house, set on a broad undulating site, the dynamic look so prized in the early '50s.

F-52
Finger House
3403 North Parkwood Drive
1953, Philip G. Willard &
Lucian T. Hood, Jr.

This concrete-framed, '50s-modern house, one of the most exuberant in Riverside Terrace, looks as though it is about to take flight. The protruding second-story bay, a concession to the restrictive covenants requiring 2 stories, is a typical neighborhood feature that was jokingly called the "mother-in-law room." Alan Hess and Noah Sheldon profiled the Finger House in their book, *The Ranch House* (2005).

F-53
Proler House
3403 Charleston Street
1952, Bailey A. Swenson

Another of the Proler family houses, this appears to have been Swenson's belated tribute to the Prairie School work of Frank Lloyd Wright.

F-54
Pasternak House
3417 Charleston Street
1953, Philip G. Willard &
Lucian T. Hood, Jr.

The tubular steel struts upholding the porch canopy add a bravura touch to this Riverside contemporary.

F-55
Hutsell Speculative House
3711 Charleston Street
1940, C. D. Hutsell

Hutsell was a Dallas architect and builder who specialized in a quirky, Texanized versions of the Mediterranean style. He and his brother, A. E. Hutsell, built this house and the one next door at 3707 Charleston on speculation. Both have been altered, but the Hutsells' distinctive touch is still visible.

F-56
Kuhlman House
3716 Charleston Street
1907

This turn-of-the-20th-century cottage was the home of the carpenter, Theo H. Kuhlman, whose family's dairy farms covered much of what became Riverside Terrace. Kuhlman's house originally sat on South MacGregor near Scott. He had it moved here in 1937, after development of that section of the subdivision began.

F-57
Flatow House
3807 South MacGregor Way
1953, Flatow, Moore, Bryan & Fairburn

The Albuquerque architect, Max Flatow, designed this house for his brother's family. A cantilevered entrance canopy and paneled walls exude the optimistic spirit of '50s modernism. Flatow engineered the flat roof so that it would retain rainwater to provide evaporative cooling.

F-58
Weingarten House
4000 South MacGregor Way
1939, Joseph Finger

Finger designed the biggest house in Riverside Terrace, a French manorial-style suburban chateau, for the family of grocery chain magnate Joe Weingarten.

F-56 Kuhlman House

F-57 Flatow House

F-58 Weingarten House

F-59 Gregory House

F-60 Proler House

F-61 Rabinowitz House

F-62 Rosenthal House

F-63 Alamo Plaza Motel

F-59
Gregory House
3939 Roseneath Drive
1978, O'Neil Gregory, Jr.

A discreet cluster of box-like shapes that turn in on each other, this wood-sheathed house was built for the architect's family. Across the street discretion clearly was not a priority with the aggressively bow-windowed house at 3934 Roseneath (1949, Bailey A. Swenson).

F-60
Proler House
4216 Fernwood Drive
1949, Bailey A. Swenson

Yet another Proler house, this one is drawn out in an extremely long wing facing Fernwood that is deftly pivoted in plan and activated in section to respond to the Cullen intersection. This is a remarkable demonstration of the Swenson office's facility with contemporary design.

F-61
Rabinowitz House
4511 North Roseneath Drive
1952, Philip G. Willard &
Lucian T. Hood, Jr.

The glazed void of the staircase, executed in curved corrugated glass, is superlative, as is the crisp precision of the eaves lines. This house echoes the formula visible next door at 4505 North Roseneath (1950, Bailey A. Swenson), with the mother-in-law room thrust above the long ground-floor wing.

F-62
Rosenthal House
4506 North Roseneath Drive
1954, Bolton & Barnstone

Howard Barnstone's rebuke to the excesses of contemporary styling took form with this brick, stucco, and wood-surfaced house. The street face is closed, while the south-facing rear garden elevation is extensively glazed. The maid's room was stacked on top of the garage to beat the 2-story deed restriction caveat against single-story houses.

F-63
Alamo Plaza Motel
4343 Old Spanish Trail
1948

It is a tribute to its quintessentially Texan image that this motel, located along what was once the main east-west highway through Houston, is still in operation. Architecturally the scalloped gable (actually the product of a mid-19th-century repair to the famous mission church in San Antonio) has been used to screen a multitude of sins in chauvinistic Texas.

F-64
MacGregor Park Clubhouse
South MacGregor Way and
MacGregor Loop Drive
1931, A. E. Nutter

The first of three delightful Mediterranean-style park clubhouses that Nutter designed in the early 1930s was built in the park that Peggy Stevens MacGregor donated to the City of Houston in 1926 as a memorial to her husband, the real estate developer, Henry F. MacGregor (commemorated in a cenotaph across from the clubhouse by William Ward Watkin in 1937). She also provided funds for the city to acquire the rights-of-way along Brays Bayou for the linear park between MacGregor and Hermann parks and its flanking drives, which became North and South MacGregor. All were laid out by the landscape architects, Hare & Hare.

F-64 MacGregor Park Clubhouse

F-65 Ezekiel W. Cullen Building

F-66 Cullen Family Plaza

F-67 Student Life Plaza

F-68 University Center

F-65
Ezekiel W. Cullen Building
University of Houston
4800 Calhoun Road
1950, Alfred C. Finn

A tall, frontal central block flanked symmetrically by low wings was the established formula for modernistic public buildings. Finn did not deviate from convention when his office produced the architectural set piece of the university's campus. A fan-shaped auditorium (restored in 1987 by Barry Moore Architects) projects off the east front of the building, on axis with University at the campus entrance from Spur 5. Fossilized limestone facing, allegorical relief sculpture, and decorative cast aluminum work completed the package. The Cullen Building fit into Hare & Hare's 1937 campus master plan, joining the pair of fossilized limestone-faced, tile-roofed buildings to either side, Science and Roy Gustav Cullen (both 1939, Lamar Q. Cato). Reglazing has robbed the Cullen Building of the aluminum screens that once filled the central register above the west entrance doors.

F-66
Cullen Family Plaza
University of Houston
1972, Fred Buxton & Associates and Cornell, Bridges & Troller

Replacing an oval reflecting basin installed in 1939, this sculpturally activated fountain pool is bridged by a series of concrete plateaus with which Lee Kelly's stainless steel piece, *Waterfall, Stele, and River* (1972), has been integrated. Conceived as a people place rather than an architectural focus, Cullen Family Plaza establishes itself as an autonomous activity zone rather than a ceremonial, representative place. Hare & Hare's master plan used architecturally defined quadrangular spaces to form a coherent whole. A new approach was initiated in Caudill Rowlett Scott's replanning of the campus in 1966 in hopes of achieving informal, natural, and spontaneous arrangements.

The suburban residential plantings installed along the sides of the fountain court further detach the plaza from its surroundings.

F-67
Student Life Plaza
University of Houston
1971, John Zemanek and Fred Buxton

A small, charming garden incorporating water, paving, and trees that evokes the contrasting colors and textures of each, the Student Life Plaza is a precious interlude in an otherwise oppressively banal landscape that denies the campus a sense of definition and identity. Adjacent to the plaza is the Student Life Building (1968, Richard S. Colley and Ford, Powell & Carson), where the Texas modern regional look associated with Colley and O'Neil Ford has been turned into a routine formula.

F-68
University Center
University of Houston
1967, George Pierce-Abel B. Pierce

Sectionally activated public buildings organized around collective spaces were an innovation in Houston in the 1960s. The University Center's engineering aesthetic—long spans infilled with repetitive wall systems and the use of concrete as a finish material—lacks the fine-grained detail needed to enliven such spaces. The University Center and the adjoining Conrad N. Hilton College of Hotel and Restaurant Management and Continuing Education Center (1974, Pierce Goodwin Flanagan) seem scaleless and anonymous, despite the visible evidence of architectural design they present.

F-69
Michael J. Cemo Lecture Hall, C. T. Bauer College of Business
University of Houston
2010, BNIM

A freestanding annex to the business college's triangular home, Melcher Hall (1986, White Budd Van Ness Partnership), the linear, 2-story Cemo Hall contains a circular auditorium to which a long file of large lecture rooms is attached. It is the university's first building to incorpoate sustainable practices.

F-69 Michael J. Cemo Lecture Hall, C. T. Bauer College of Business

F-70 Philip Guthrie Hoffman Hall

F-71 Agnes Arnold Hall

F-72 Science and Research Center

F-74 Architecture Building

F-70
Philip Guthrie Hoffman Hall
University of Houston
1974, Kenneth Bentsen Associates

An homage to I. M. Pei's cast-in-place concrete buildings of the 1960s and '70s, the 6-story Hoffman Hall is the one building at UH that masters the spatial concepts inherent in the replanning of the campus after 1966. Its height, breadth, and solid, well-proportioned, well-detailed frame enable it to architecturally control the laterally expansive space of Anne Garrett Butler Plaza, an immense, inclined lawn free of the busy plantings that disfigure other campus spaces. Hoffman Hall sits on a raised terrace that counters the topographical variation of the lawn. It also frames an important pedestrian connection, architecturally creating a sense of having arrived at a significant place. In the center of Butler Plaza is Peter Forakis's tall Corten piece, *Tower of the Cheyenne* (1972).

F-71
Agnes Arnold Hall
University of Houston
1966, Kenneth Bentsen Associates

This 6-story concrete frame and brick infill classroom building was the first on the campus to engage in sectional manipulation and the integration of outdoor with interior space. The estimation of Houston's potential to sustain open-air balcony corridors proved overly optimistic and retrofitting was necessary to control wind turbulence through the building. Yet despite these experiential shortcomings, Arnold Hall is one of the liveliest gathering places on campus.

F-72
Science and Research Center
University of Houston
1969, MacKie & Kamrath

The architects' inflation of Wrightian details to huge scale may seem bizarre at first sight. But their effort to control the elevations of this overwhelmingly big building by introducing staged levels of horizontal banding, contrasting window alignments, and articulation of vertical shafts can only be appreciated when the building is compared to its listless neighbors. A second-generation annex to the Science and Research Center, the Houston Science Center Addition (1991, Houston Science Center Architects), is an intelligently conceived and articulately detailed building designed by Gilbert Hoffman of White Budd Van Ness Partnership and Mario Bolullo of Harry Golemon Architects.

F-73
Science and Engineering Classroom Building
University of Houston
2006, Pelli Clarke Pelli and Kendall/Heaton Associates

The architects divided the program for this complex between a rectangular 5-story block of research laboratories faced with a glass curtain wall and a 2-story auditorium and lecture hall "tail" that curves away from the bigger block to frame a broad courtyard on the west side of MacKie & Kamrath's Science and Research Center. Although details are engaging, the complex does not quite cohere architecturally. Artist, Jackie Ferrara, is responsible for the long granite fountain and a stained maple plywood mural in the lobby of the auditorium, *Wall of Towers* (2007).

F-74
Architecture Building
University of Houston
1986, Johnson/Burgee Architects and Morris*Aubry Architects

Philip Johnson's *jeu d'esprit* at UH was to expropriate the 18th-century French architect C.-N. Ledoux's never-built design for a House of Education in the ideal town of Chaux, inflate it to Texan proportions, and then drop it on axis with the campus's major parking lot entrance from Elgin to become the university's new architectural set piece, home to the Gerald D. Hines College of Architecture. The frontality, figuration, and symmetry of the building are a relief compared to its trivial or merely anonymous neighbors. But in its perfunctory detailing and concern with superficial image, it is more like its neighbors than it would have us believe. Stacked trays of studio space are organized around an interior court, centered beneath the roofless stone temple atop the building. The arched windows on the third floor afford fine views of both the university and the downtown skyline. Installed to either side of the south entrance are hieratic granite benches by the sculptor Scott Burton (1985).

F-73 Science Engineering Research and Classroom Building

F-75 Burdette Keeland, Jr. Design Exploration Center

F-77 Rebecca and John J. Moores School of Music Building

F-78 *100 Chairs*

F-79 Rother's Bookstore

F-80 Bates College of Law

F-75
Burdette Keeland, Jr., Design Exploration Center
University of Houston
2007, GBA Architects with Charles Tapley and Chula Ross Sánchez

The Hines College of Architecture recycled an adjoining steel shed, which had been acquired by the university in 1947 from a World War II training camp in Galveston County, as the college's model-making and fabrication workshop. Architect Geoffrey Brune took advantage of big interior spaces and natural light in the two assembly sections. Charles Tapley and Chula Ross Sánchez were responsible for the green roof above the south entrance bay.

F-76
Cynthia Woods Mitchell Center for the Arts
University of Houston
2006, Lake/Flato

Honoring preservationist and philanthropist Cynthia Woods Mitchell, this center fosters interdisciplinary exchange between the university's visual, performing, and literary arts programs. Lake/Flato reconfigured portions of the Wortham Theater Building (1977, Lloyd, Jones & Associates), expanding the lobby, performance, and rehearsal spaces and installing a new front elevation with a more welcoming public countenance than the 1977 building possessed.

F-77
Rebecca and John J. Moores School of Music Building
University of Houston
1997, The Mathes Group

The lobby of the performance hall is the setting for a heroic mural by Frank Stella. A smaller installation by Stella is suspended above the interior of the hall. The San Antonio architect, Isaac Maxwell, designed and fabricated the lighting fixtures in the lobby and the performance hall.

F-78
100 Chairs
University of Houston
1998, Mary Miss, artist

Given a strip of left-over real estate wrapped around two sides of the Athletic/Alumni Facility Building's baseball field, artist Mary Miss distributed 100 stainless steel chairs of varying sizes and in various arrangements in a meadow sown with wild flowers. Suggesting an informal symposium, the Chairs also evoke the front porch sociality of the neighboring Third Ward, a rare instance of UH acknowledging the neighborhood in which it is set.

F-79
Rother's Bookstore
3503 Elgin Avenue
1997, Gordon Bohmfalk & Troy Kennedy, QMET Architects

A post-postmodern collage of shapes, colors, textures, and materials, this is a strip center that doesn't aim to look like a strip center. The architects' Austin provenance shows. However it will take more than limestone, corrugated metal, and pergolas to transform Elgin into a Houston version of Austin's Guadalupe Street drag.

F-80
Bates College of Law
[now Law Center]
University of Houston
1969, Freeman, Van Ness & Mower

Clarity, proportion, and restraint characterize this assembly of exposed, poured-in-place concrete components that make up the Law Center's several buildings. These are arranged around a paved agora, beneath which the library is located. The northern-most classroom building is an addition by Pitts, Phelps & Mebane (1975). Situated at the approach to the college is Gerhard Marcks' seated bronze figure, *Albertus Magnus* (1955).

F-76 Cynthia Woods Mitchell Center for the Arts

F-81 Schlumberger Well Services Headquarters

F-82 Small House and Small House 2

F-81
Schlumberger Well Services Headquarters
[now UH Energy Research Park]
5000 Gulf Freeway
1953, MacKie & Kamrath

The Gulf Freeway was completed in 1952 along the right-of-way of the Interurban trolley line between Houston and Galveston. Schlumberger was the first corporation to construct a suburban headquarters complex along the new freeway. In designing the 2- and 3-story front office building, the architects adopted the modern industrial vernacular that the Walter Kidde Company had used for the research and testing buildings in the complex: low, flat-roofed buildings with alternating horizontal bands of brick spandrel, window glass, and corrugated aluminum spandrel and header panels. The entrance is marked by a slender brick pylon, which visually counters the building's horizontality and a dramatic cantilevered porte-cochère canopy. These features indicate Karl Kamrath's indebtedness to Frank Lloyd Wright and also to the Dutch architect, W. M. Dudok. After Schlumberger moved to Sugar Land in the 1990s, this 70-acre site became a business park. The University of Houston acquired the entire complex in 2009.

F-82
Small House and Small House 2
5910 Grace Lane
2002 and 2006, m+a architecture studio

Mark Schatz and Anne Eamon made their first real estate purchase in the Griggs Terrace subdivision off Griggs in 1994 when they were architecture students at the University of Houston. In this lower-income neighborhood, which backs up to the grounds of a company specializing in hazardous waste management, Schatz and Eamon designed and personally constructed their 2-story, 1-bedroom, 700-SF house. Four years after completing it, they designed and built a second, slightly larger house, incorporating a garage, which they use as their studio. Karrie Jacobs acclaimed their achievements in *The Perfect $100,000 House* (2006).

F-83
Houston Texans YMCA
5202 Griggs Road
2011, Brave/Architecture

Adjacent to the much-altered Palms Center (1955, Irving R. Klein & Associates), the first shopping mall in Houston, this is an expansive 1- and 2-story building. Overlapping volumes, clad in different materials, highlight the spatial organization of program components.

F-83 Houston Texans YMCA

North Side / East End

North Side / East End

Tour G

Railroad lines largely bypassed downtown Houston and the South End, which accounted in part for their historic identification as high-status districts. The construction of some of the earliest railroad lines in Texas gave quite a different character to the parts of Houston they traversed, north of Buffalo Bayou and east of downtown. The North Side, which lay largely in Houston's Fifth Ward, was the site of the Southern Pacific Company's railroad shops and yard, which were completed in 1886. This employment center attracted subsidiary industries and a large working-class population occupying residential neighborhoods between White Oak Bayou, Quitman Street, and Elysian Street. Today these neighborhoods are home to a large Mexican-American community. The portion of Third Ward due east of what is now downtown was also a working-class residential neighborhood, bounded on the east by the diagonally aligned rail yards of the Galveston, Houston & Henderson Railroad. This sector was redeveloped between the 1920s and the 1950s as a warehouse district tied to the San Antonio & Aransas Pass rail line on Bastrop Street. Since the early 1950s Asian-owned retail businesses have been operated here. The East End, on the east side of the G. H. & H. yards, was developed for moderate income housing beginning in the early 20th century. This is also where industrial manufacturing and oil field equipment and servicing operations began locate in the 1930s and '40s, infilling between residential areas along the major east-west streets: Leeland, Polk, McKinney, Harrisburg, Canal, and Navigation. These replaced the last bits of open countryside that, in the 19th century, separated Houston from the town of Harrisburg, 5.5 miles away. There dairy farms, fruit orchards, and the country houses of the Lockart and Brady families had been located. Modernization of the waterfront along Buffalo Bayou commenced with the completion of Navigation Boulevard and Clinton Drive in the late 1920s, along which new, planned industrial districts in the 1930s and '40s were developed. Farther east still is Magnolia Park, a large, working-class neighborhood laid out in 1909 near the site of the Turning Basin of the Houston Ship Channel. When Mexican Americans began to settle in large numbers in Houston during the 1910s, it was in *barrios* on the North Side and the East End, especially in Magnolia Park. Just south of Magnolia Park, on South Wayside Drive, lie the original grounds of the Houston Country Club (now Gus S. Wortham Park). The club's opening here in 1909, along the banks of Brays Bayou, sparked development of several adjacent suburban neighborhoods. These treated the bayou as a scenic amenity rather than a commercial thoroughfare, the role it shared with railroads throughout the 19th century. The North Side and the East End were the industrial workshops of 20th-century Houston with a gritty texture that has survived. The presence in these areas of working-class Hispanic Houstonians results in a degree of popular street life that is missing from the city's more affluent precincts. The presence of cleared sites and unused buildings attracted new speculative residential construction in the late 1990s and 2000s, bringing a startling change in the socioeconomic status of what had never been middle class residential areas. This change attests to the fluidity and unpredictability of real estate in Houston, as well as a broader phenomenon in many U.S. cities during this period as middle-income housing began to gentrify declining industrial real estate.

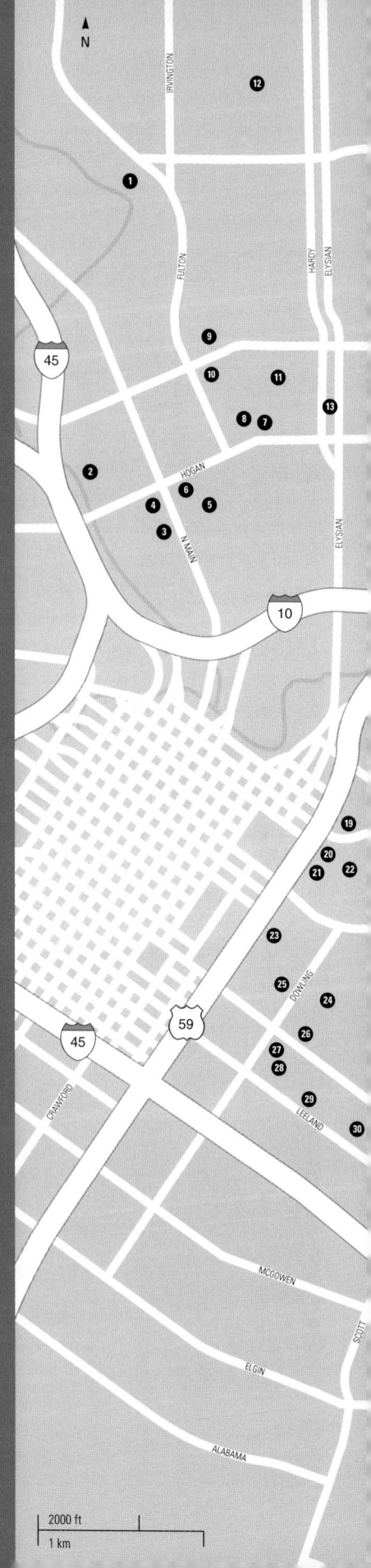

1. *Vaquero,* 3725 Fulton Street
2. **Sunset Hospital,** 2015 Thomas Street
3. **Casa de Amigos Community Health Center,** 1615 North Main Street
4. **La Nueva Casa de Amigos,** 1809 North Main Street
5. **Mission German Methodist Episcopal Church South,** 1703 Chestnut Street
6. **City of Houston Fire Station No. 9,** 702 Hogan Street
7. **Casa de Amigos,** 1906 Cochran Street
8. **Holy Name Catholic Church,** 1920 Marion Street
9. **Jefferson Davis Senior High School,** 1200 Quitman Street
10. **Carnegie Branch, Houston Public Library,** 1050 Quitman Street
11. **Cade House,** 1317 Lee Street
12. **Casa de la Amistad,** 4017 Gano Street
13. **Morris Zax Grocery Store Building,** 2020 Hardy Street
14. **Habitat for Humanity Demonstration Houses,** 2901 A and B Gillespie Street
15. **Merkel House,** 416 North Hutcheson Street
16. **Canal Street Apartments,** 2821 Canal Street
17. **Our Lady of Guadalupe Catholic Church,** 2405 Navigation Boulevard
18. **Guadalupe Plaza,** Runnels Street and Jensen Drive
19. **Gribble Stamp and Stencil Company Building,** 121 St. Emanuel Street
20. **Standard Brass & Manufacturing Company Building,** 2018 Franklin Avenue
21. **Cheek-Neal Coffee Company Building,** 2017 Preston Avenue
22. **Commercial Buildings,** 2209, 2213, 2219 Congress Avenue
23. **On Leong Chinese Merchants Association Building,** 801–811 Chartres Street
24. **908 Live Oak Street—Wald Transfer & Storage Company Building**
25. **Standard Sanitary Manufacturing Company Building,** 2300–2310 McKinney Avenue
26. **Houston Lighting & Power Company Substation,** 2501 Polk Avenue
27. **Houston Post Building,** 2410 Polk Avenue
28. **St. Nicholas Catholic Church,** 2508 Clay Avenue
29. **Tien Hou Temple,** 1507 Delano Street
30. **House,** 3113 Bell Avenue
31. **Straus-Frank Company Building,** 4000 Leeland Avenue
32. **City of Houston Water Customer Service Building,** 4200 Leeland Avenue
33. **City of Houston E. B. Cape Center for Public Works,** 4501 Leeland Avenue
34. **Lard Investment Company Community Center,** 702–10 Telephone Road
35. **Stephen F. Austin Senior High School,** 1700 Dumble Street
36. **Rufus Cage School,** 1417 Telephone Road

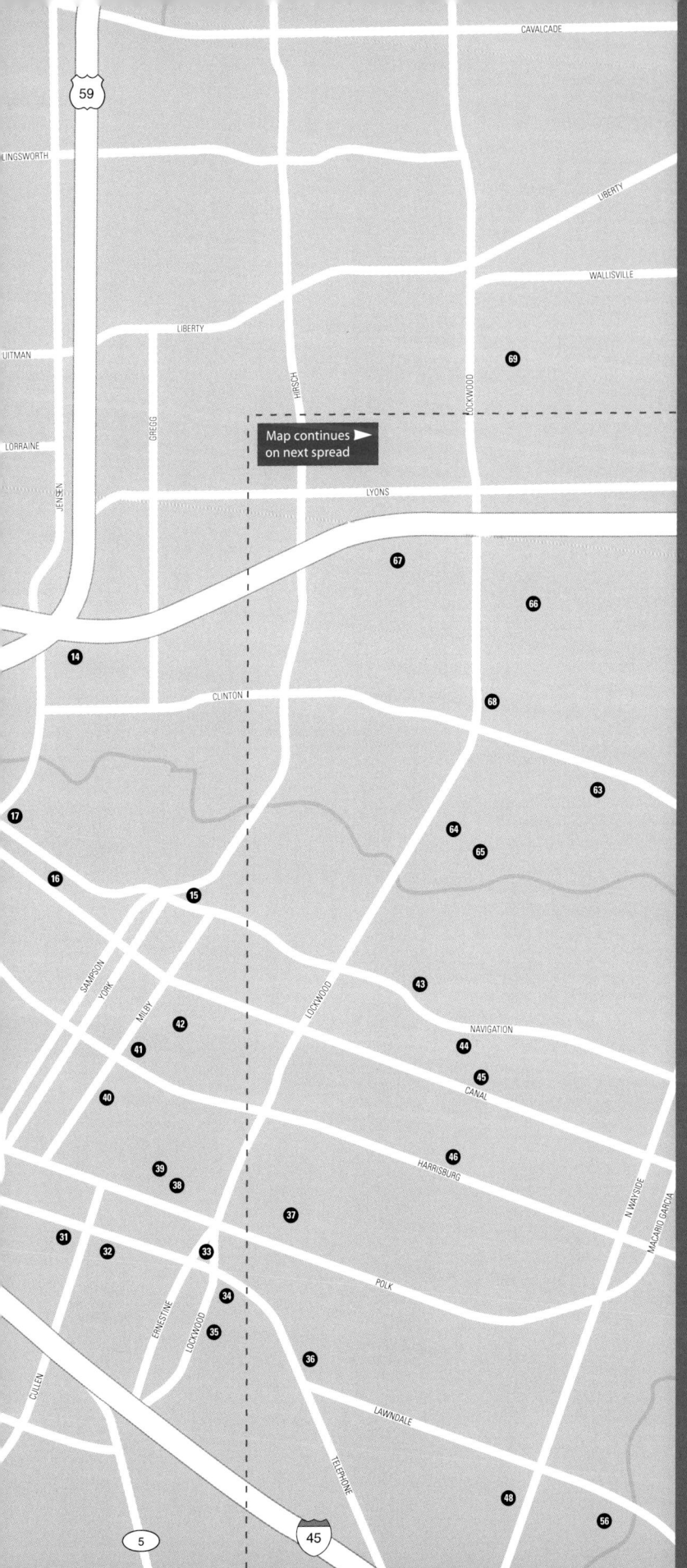

37. **Shot-Trot House,** 4914 Curtin Street
38. **Church of the Redeemer, Episcopal,** 4411 Dallas Avenue
39. **Eastwood Elementary School,** 100 Telephone Road
40. **Cameron Iron Works Building,** 711 Milby Street
41. **Brady House,** 3805 Wilmer Street
42. **Blessed Sacrament Catholic Church,** 4015 Sherman Street
43. **Parker Brothers & Company Building,** 5303 Navigation Boulevard
44. **J. A. Folger Coffee Company Building,** 235 North Norwood Street
45. ***The Rebirth of our Nationality,*** 5801 Canal Street
46. **Fullerton School,** 5803 Harrisburg Road
47. **Hidalgo Park Kiosk,** J.W. Peavy Drive and North 70th Street
48. **Conventual Chapel of the Villa de Matel,** 6510 Lawndale Avenue
49. **Association for the Advancement of Mexican Americans Learning Center,** 6001 Gulf Freeway
50. **Brays Crossing,** 6311 Gulf Freeway
51. **Brookline School,** 3901 Telephone Road
52. **Farnsworth & Chambers Building,** 2999 South Wayside Drive
53. **Freeway Baptist Church,** 144 Winkler Drive
54. **The Orange Show,** 2401 Munger Street
55. **House,** 2279 Jean Street
56. **Mc Neal House,** 6740 Meadow Lawn Drive
57. **Cooke House,** 1724 Alta Vista Avenue
58. **Radetzki House,** 1766 Pasadena Avenue
59. **Mason Park Shelter House,** 541 South 75th Street
60. **Habitat for Humanity Jimmy Carter Work Project Houses,** 7800–7900 blocks Avenue B and 7700–7800 blocks Avenue C
61. **Sidney Sherman Bridge,** East Loop 610 and Houston Ship Channel
62. **Houston Public Elevator,** 8400 block Clinton Drive
63. **Ford Motor Company Building,** 5800 Clinton Drive
64. **National Steel Products Company Building,** 750 Lockwood Drive
65. **Pittsburgh Plate Glass Company Building,** 5520 Armour Drive
66. **John L. McReynolds Junior High School,** 5910 Market Street
67. **Phillis Wheatley Senior High School,** 4910 Market Street
68. **Howard Flint Ink Company Building,** 1024 Lockwood Drive
69. **2424 Sakowitz Housing,** 2424 Sakowitz

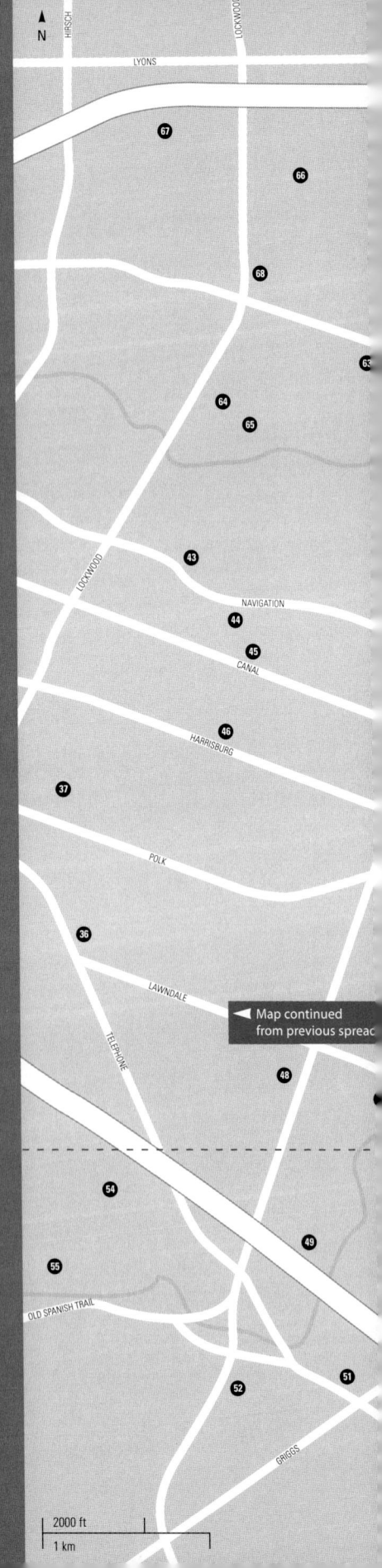

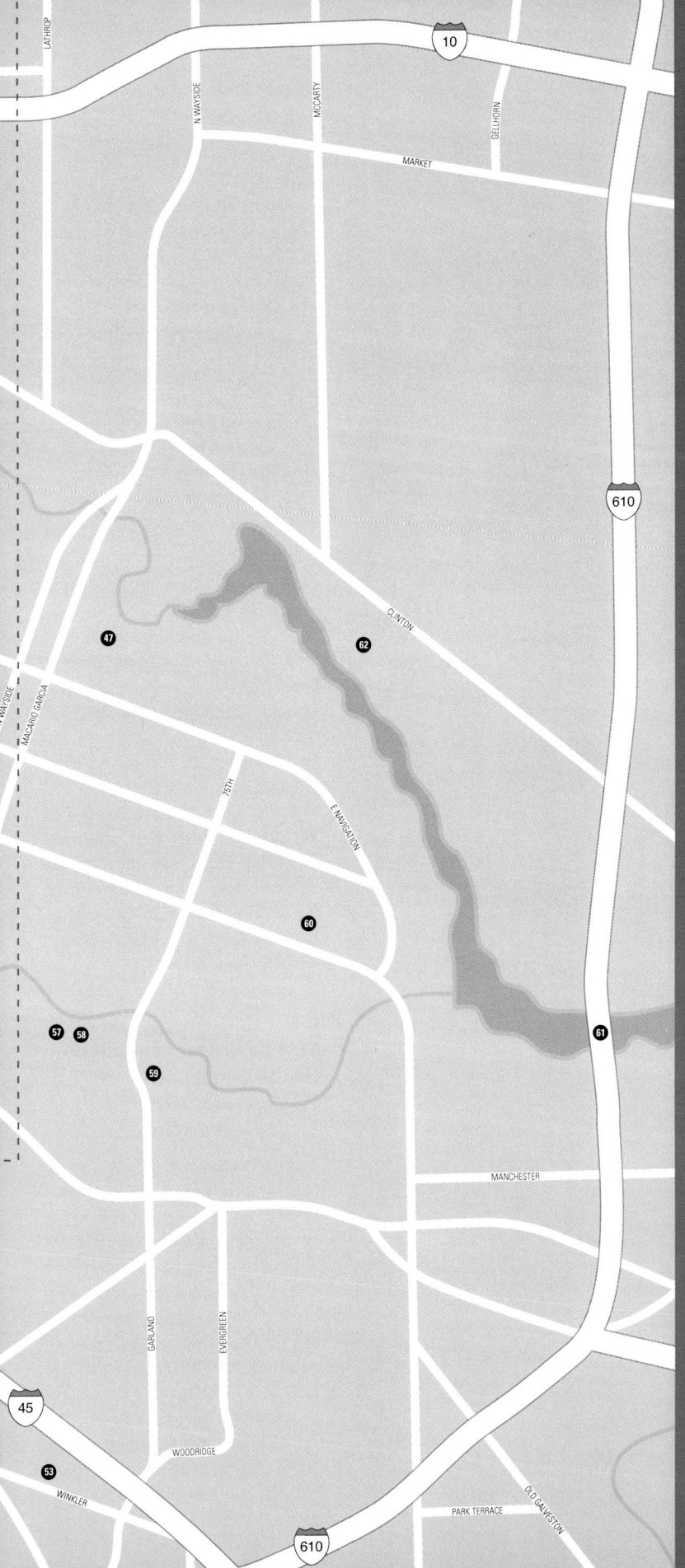

G-1 Moody Park, Vaquero

G-1
Moody Park, *Vaquero*
3725 Fulton Street
1978, Luis Jiménez, sculptor

Jiménez's brilliantly colored, action-packed molded fiberglass cowboy is one of the liveliest and most popular public art installations in Houston. Moody Park also provides a marvelous vantage point from which to survey the downtown skyline.

G-2 Sunset Hospital

G-2
Sunset Hospital
[now Thomas Street Center]
2015 Thomas Street
1911, Department of Buildings and Bridges, Galveston, Houston & San Antonio Railway

Built by a subsidiary of the Southern Pacific Railway as a staff hospital (shops of Southern Pacific, Houston's major industrial employer at the turn of the 20th century, were nearby), the Sunset Hospital has been remarkably well preserved. The combination of three colors of brick, molded brick decoration, and red roof tiles gives the building a rich but subdued aspect. The palm trees, the street fence, and the pergola-covered entry gate remain intact. Sunset Hospital underwent a certified rehabilitation in 1993 (Lo/Kester and Bouchard Architects).

G-3 Casa de Amigos Community Health Center

G-3
Casa de Amigos Community Health Center
1615 North Main Street
1983, Urban Architecture

This neighborhood health center, built by the Harris County Hospital District, is a lively building that pays special attention to its down (but not out) surroundings. In giving shape to the streamlined brick and glass block faced building, Paul Martin and Hossein Oskouie took note of both nearby modernistic warehouse and industrial buildings and the incomparable (no longer extant) Pan América Ballroom next door at 1705 North Main. Martin and Oskouie ensured that this building functions

G-6 City of Houston Fire Station No. 9

as the gateway to the North Side by positioning it diagonally on its site. They demonstrated how sympathetic concern for context can lead to a building that draws its environs into a greater whole, a message that their clients seem not to have understood, judging by the additions that have been crudely grafted onto the building's street front.

G-4
La Nueva Casa de Amigos
1809 North Main Street
1997, Bay Architects

The third purpose-built building for the Hospital District's Casa de Amigos follows its predecessors in displaying an urban flair keyed to its setting.

G-5
Mission German Methodist Episcopal Church, South
[now Templo Jerusalén]
1703 Chestnut Street
1892

This Victorian cottage church is characteristic of the North Side neighborhood in the city's Fifth Ward, a working-class district dependent on the Southern Pacific yards just south of Burnett Street. The building's occupants chart demographic transitions within the area. After serving its original German congregation, from 1938-1961 it was the parish seat of St. George Syrian Orthodox Church and the cultural center of Houston's Arab community. Since 1961 it has been the home of a Spanish-language Protestant congregation. Just across Harrington, at 1626 Chestnut, is an unexceptional house that has begun to petrify, reflecting the popularity of decorative concrete work in the 1930s and '40s.

G-6
City of Houston Fire Station No. 9
702 Hogan Street
1971, W. Irving Phillips, Jr. & Robert W. Peterson

Phillips used brick and precast concrete to shape this box-like fire station. Incisions of various depths and widths imbue the building with a sense of tension and spatial complexity.

G-5 Mission German Methodist Episcopal Church, South

G-4 La Nueva Casa de Amigos

G-7 Casa de Amigos Health Center

G-8 Holy Name Catholic Church

G-9 Jefferson Davis Senior High School

G-10 Carnegie Branch, Houston Public Library

G-11 Cade House

G-7
Casa de Amigos Health Center
[now SER Jobs for Progress]
1906 Cochran Street
1974, Dennis Kilper and
Harry Ransom

Kilper differentiated the brick end walls of this city health clinic from the stucco-surfaced cross panels, exhibiting the building's steel-bar, joist-roof structure along the latter. The building is not well maintained. The North Side Methodist Church (1923, 1928, Alfred C. Finn), to which Kilper and Ransom's building was attached, has been demolished.

G-8
Holy Name Catholic Church
1920 Marion Street
1926, Frederick B. Gaenslen

Gaenslen, a San Antonio architect, detailed his twin-towered church with French Romanesque motifs finished with dark red tapestry brick. It exerts a strong presence in this neighborhood of modest houses.

G-9
Jefferson Davis Senior High School
1200 Quitman Street
1927, Briscoe & Dixon and Maurice J. Sullivan, William Ward Watkin, consulting architect

Cast stone detail of Georgian provenance imparts a strong semblance of classical order and civic decorum to this high school. Together with John Marshall Junior High School, across Quitman at 1115 Noble Street (1925, Hedrick & Gottlieb), it forms an enclave of public buildings near the center of the neighborhood.

G-10
Carnegie Branch, Houston Public Library
1050 Quitman Street
1982, Ray Bailey Architects

Although a part of the civic arena formed by the two school buildings, this branch library was designed in response to other factors. The building's east elevation faces a small park behind a gridded surface of bronze solar glass, where the classical colonnade set up in the park is all that remains of the original Carnegie Branch Library of 1925. The west elevation is a stucco screen, painted in bright pastel colors. The library succeeds at being an unintimidating public building, but its lack of a clearly distinguishable façade makes it seem rather equivocal in a setting where other public buildings are unambiguously frontal. The interior is light, airy, and enjoyable.

G-11
Cade House
1317 Lee Street
c 1888

This portion of Houston's former Fifth Ward, better known today as the Near North Side, possesses one of Houston's rare surviving 19th-century neighborhoods. The most imposing house in the A. C. Allen Addition was occupied by James R. Cade, general foreman of the Southern Pacific Shops.

G-12
Casa de la Amistad
4017 Gano Street
1963

Hidden in an obscure working class neighborhood, this delightful little house seems to have been transported from one of the back streets of Santa Fe's Barrio de Guadalupe.

G-13
Morris Zax Grocery Building
2020 Hardy Street
c 1905

Complementing the now altered Borgstrom Grocery Co. Building at 2104 Hardy (c 1905) is this 2-story brick corner store, ornamented with a finial-capped pediment. Zax operated another grocery store on this block before constructing this building, in which he also lived.

G-13 Morris Zax Grocery Building

G-12 Casa de la Amistad

G-15 Merkel House

G-16 Canal Street Apartments

G-17 Our Lady of Guadalupe Catholic Church

G-14
Habitat for Humanity Demonstration Houses
2901 A and B Gillespie Street
1999, Venturi, Scott-Brown & Associates with Anthony E. Frederick and Scott Waugh

An unusual confluence of agencies (Fifth Ward Community Redevelopment Corporation, Menil Collection, UH Hines College of Architecture, and Habitat for Humanity) were brought together by Drexel Turner to construct a pair of demonstration houses built by volunteers, mostly UH architecture students. The houses show persuasively that low-cost, inner-city housing need not be meanly scaled versions of suburban builders' houses. Spacious interiors and such amenities as usable front porches make these 2-story houses important models for future neighborhood developments.

G-15
Merkel House
416 North Hutcheson Street
c 1880

Houston historian and preservationist Thomas McWhorter traced the history of this little Gulf Coast cottage to 1880, when it was first occupied by Joseph Merkel. Merkel operated Merkel's Grove, a rural pleasure ground, and the Houston Schützen Verein, a shooting club, on the property that his widow and sons subsequently developed as the Merkel Addition.

G-16
Canal Street Apartments
2821 Canal Street
2005, Val Glitsch

The non-profit New Hope Housing built this 2- and 3-story complex of 133 single-room-occupancy apartments. Glitsch configured housing around an interior courtyard and in a tail that shoots off to the north. Two tones of green stucco complement the landscaping by Asakura Robinson.

G-17
Our Lady of Guadalupe Catholic Church
2405 Navigation Boulevard
1923, Leo M. J. Dielmann

During his long career, San Antonio architect Dielmann produced an extraordinary number of Roman Catholic churches across Texas. After designing Our Lady of Guadalupe in San Antonio for a Spanish-speaking parish, he was commissioned to design churches for parishes of the same dedication in Laredo and Houston. The Houston church is an enlarged version of the San Antonio prototype. It is detailed with Lombard Romanesque features and finished in light red brick. Subsequent additions, such as the front porch, detract from the church's integrity. Dielmann's building replaced a wood frame structure dating from the founding of the parish in 1912. Our Lady of Guadalupe, located in Second Ward, has been an important community center for Mexican immigrants since that time.

G-14 Habitat for Humanity Demonstration Houses

G-18 Guadalupe Plaza

G-19 Gribble Stamp & Stencil Company Building

G-21 Cheek-Neal Coffee Company Building

G-22 Commercial Buildings

G-23 On Leong Chinese Merchants Association Building

G-18
Guadalupe Plaza
Runnels Street and Jensen Drive
1988, Hispanic Consortium

The City of Houston installed this generously scaled, Mexican-themed plaza across from Our Lady of Guadalupe in the parking lot of the ill-fated Mercado del Sol, a twice-failed festival marketplace occupying the former Lottman Manufacturing Company mattress plant (1904, 1910, 1926). The simple, but effective, spatial organization, substantial construction, bright colors, and such details as tropical plantings, the encircling pergola, and the large fountain make the plaza as urbane a space as could be hoped for in the middle of what had been a parking lot. On the north side, across the railroad track, is a *placita* that steps down the bank of Buffalo Bayou to become a water gate. Luis Bodmer and the landscape architect, George S. Porcher, were the park's designers. In 1997 a Houston developer began the conversion of the Lottman complex into condominium lofts, selling the project to Trammell Crow Residential in 2001. Crow converted it into the 250-unit Alexan Lofts (2003) and sold the 3-acre parking lot to Perry Homes, which developed a subdivision of 72 townhouses on the site (2003).

G-19
Gribble Stamp & Stencil Company Building
121 St. Emanuel Street
1948, C. R. Berry & Company

The 2-story glass block cylinder functions as the pivot point for this building's diverging wall planes, which are finished with red and tan brick banding.

G-20
Standard Brass & Manufacturing Company Building
2018 Franklin Avenue
1937, Staub & Rather

Architect J. T. Rather, Jr. emphasized the planar walls of this industrial building with horizontally banded steel sash windows. Deep and shallow volumetric incursions provide for vehicular and pedestrian access.

G-21
Cheek-Neal Coffee Company Building
2017 Preston Avenue
1917, Finger & Bailey

Joseph Finger and James Ruskin Bailey were responsible for this now ill-maintained, 5-story building, which forthrightly expresses its reinforced concrete frame construction. The Cheek-Neal Coffee Company manufactured Maxwell House Coffee here.

G-22
Commercial Buildings
2209, 2213, 2219 Congress Avenue
1896-1907

These three buildings exhibit details characteristic of local commercial construction of the time. The partially collapsed red brick building at 2209 had window openings handsomely framed by round arches. The central building at 2213 shows remnants of a brick cornice. And the corner building, at 2219, retains its ground-floor cast iron front. The upper stories of these buildings were rented to boarders. At the turn of the 20th century, this section of Second Ward was almost entirely residential. Its conversion into a warehouse and industrial district did not begin until after the opening of Union Station in 1911.

G-23
On Leong Chinese Merchants Association Building
801-811 Chartres Street
1951, Irvine & Hoyt

This 3-story retail, office, and apartment building was the first architectural expression of Houston's Chinese community. Designed in a self-conscious Sino-modernistic style, it became the nucleus of a small Asian business center that expanded dramatically in the 1980s with the opening of Indochinese establishments nearby. Farther south, at the corner of Chartres and Dallas, the Chinese American Citizens Alliance Hall asserted its presence in the late 1950s by grafting Chinese style detailing onto an existing Four Square house.

G-20 Standard Brass & Manufacturing Company Building

G-24 Wald Transfer & Storage Company Building

G-25 Standard Sanitary Manufacturing Company Building

G-26 Houston Lighting & Power Company Substation

G-27 Houston Post Building

G-28 St. Nicholas Catholic Church

G-24
Wald Transfer & Storage Company Building
908 Live Oak Street
1949, Irving R. Klein & Associates

This block-long building is one of the highlights of the East End warehouse district. The contrast of horizontal strip windows with the vertical pylon, two-toned masonry finishes, and use of concrete framing strips and canopies are handled with great flair.

G-25
Standard Sanitary Manufacturing Company Building
2300-2310 McKinney Avenue
1924, Alfred C. Finn

Finn's use of dark brick makes this 4-story warehouse—quite large by Houston standards of the time—a brooding presence. Close by, at 2205 McKinney, is Finn's stylistically similar Crane Company Building (1926). These warehouses attest to the former presence of the San Antonio & Aransas Pass rail line along the right-of-way on Bastrop.

G-26
Houston Lighting & Power Company Substation
2501 Polk Avenue
c 1948

Minimally detailed with louvered openings, identifying graphics, and a centered doorway, this 2-story planar building is a very spirited example of modernistic design.

G-27
Houston Post Building
2410 Polk Avenue
1955, Herbert Voelcker & Associates

Voelcker made his reputation as an architect of modernistic county courthouses in north and west Texas. This building, headquarters of one of Houston's three daily newspapers during the 1950s and '60s, is in a late, heavy rendition of the style. Its street fronts have been sealed.

G-28
St. Nicholas Catholic Church
2508 Clay Avenue
1923, Leo M. J. Dielmann

Dielmann produced a vaguely Spanish mission image for St. Nicholas, an African-American Roman Catholic parish. Its quirkiness is representative of his work.

G-29
Tien Hou Temple, Sino-Indochinese Association of Texas
1507 Delano Street
1987, 1992

Although this Taiwanese Confucian and Daoist temple complex would appear exotic anywhere in Houston, here, in this depressed neighborhood, it seems almost like a mirage. Construction materials were imported from Taiwan, although some of the carving was executed in Houston by Chinese artisans.

G-30
House
3113 Bell Avenue
2009

Horizontal slots that erode corners are the hallmark of this 2-story, flat-roofed, stucco-faced house, linked to its garage by screen walls. Construction of such a house in this East End neighborhood would have been unthinkable before the 2000s. As the surrounding townhouse complexes attest, what was previously unthinkable has now become commonplace. It is design distinction that causes this house to stand out on its isolated site.

G-30 House

G-29 Tien Hou Temple, Sino-Indochinese Association of Texas

G-31 Straus-Frank Corporation Building

G-32 City of Houston Water Customer Service Building

G-33 City of Houston E. B. Cape Center for Public Works

G-35 Stephen F. Austin Senior High School

G-37 Shot-Trot House

G-31
Straus-Frank Corporation Building
[now CarQuest Distribution Center]
4000 Leeland Avenue
1949, Lloyd & Morgan

The streamlined curvature of the street front of this substantial industrial production is the more impressive for being faced with fossilized limestone. Robert D. Straus, the client, became one of Houston's air-conditioning pioneers when his business became the local distributor for Carrier in 1933, just as such technology was becoming available.

G-32
City of Houston Water Customer Service Building
4200 Leeland Avenue
1984, Kendall/Heaton Associates

Kendall/Heaton sleekly retrofitted the ex-East End State Bank Building to become a service and operations center for the city's water department.

G-33
City of Houston E. B. Cape Center for Public Works
4501 Leeland Avenue
1997, Willis, Bricker & Cannady

Assertive scale and gestural appendages give this training center for City of Houston employees in the Public Works Department high visibility.

G-34
S. S. Lard Investment Company Community Center
702-710 Telephone Road
1930, B. W. Holtz

This is one of the oldest architecturally designed strip shopping centers in Houston. Its French provincial theme is complemented by the fanciful wrought iron weather vane that crowns its corner turret. B. W. Holtz was an architect-builder who was associated with another innovative suburban shopping complex of the same period, the Patio Shops on Almeda.

G-35
Stephen F. Austin Senior High School
1700 Dumble Street
1937, Birdsall P. Briscoe, Maurice J. Sullivan, Sam H. Dixon, Jr., and Joseph Finger

The Public Works Administration financed the construction of two public high schools in Houston that were virtually identical in plan, but strikingly different in outward appearance: Austin and Lamar (on Westheimer). Austin's conservative architectural imagery is enlivened with imaginative ornamental brick detailing.

G-36
Rufus Cage School
1417 Telephone Road
1910, Jones & Tabor

The high-set, 2-story brick building was constructed as a county school outside the limits of Houston's public school system in 1910 then reopened under the auspices of HISD until 1983. It continues as an HISD storage facility in 2012 with some hope of preservation and rehabilitation.

G-37
Shot-Trot House
4914 Curtin Street
2004, Brett Zamore

Fusing two historic regional house types—the shotgun cottage and the dogtrot cabin—Zamore produced a long, thin, gable-roofed house that can be opened up at its center with sliding louvered panels. Karrie Jacobs expressed enthusiastic admiration for the Shot-Trot House in her book, *The Perfect $100,000 House* (2006).

G-34 S. S. Lard Investment Company Community Center

G-36 Rufus Cage School

G-38 Church of the Redeemer, Episcopal

G-38
Church of the Redeemer, Episcopal
4411 Dallas Avenue
1952, Tellepsen Construction Company

Tom Tellepsen, a general contractor who was a parishioner of Redeemer, built a new church based on a vision he had in a dream. At the time of its completion, the concrete building was described as the first windowless church in Houston. It was centrally air-conditioned, and the nave was illuminated with concealed fluorescent lighting. Behind the altar is William Orth's mural, *Christ of the Workingman*. In 2011 the congregation abandoned this complex.

G-39
Eastwood Elementary School
[now Dora Lantrip Elementary School]
100 Telephone Road
1916, Maurice J. Sullivan

This school and the Church of the Redeemer are located in Eastwood, developed in 1911 by the William A. Wilson Company, developers of Woodland Heights. The company donated this site near the center of the subdivision for a school, planned by Maurice Sullivan, then City Architect of Houston. Designed in the Spanish mission style, with arcaded loggias and patios, it was described at the time of its construction as being the first school in Houston arranged on the "cottage plan," with classrooms occupying a series of freestanding pavilions. In 1927 sympathetic additions by Harry D. Payne and James Ruskin Bailey were made at the rear of the complex (demolished). A new school building (2006, Sustaita Architects) now obscures the original school, which the Houston Independent School District would have demolished had it not been for neighborhood protest.

G-40
Cameron Iron Works Building
711 Milby Street
1935

This elaborately detailed modernistic office building was nonchalantly plugged onto an existing industrial installation. Cameron Iron Works began in 1920 as a partnership between steel fabricator Harry Cameron and oil driller J. S. Abercrombie. In 1922 Abercrombie and Cameron developed the device that established the company's reputation: the oil well blowout preventer. Cameron became one of Houston's major producers of oilfield tools and, after the 1940s, an important defense contractor.

G-41
Brady House
3805 Wilmer Street
1906

This raised Victorian cottage was once part of a compound of family houses built by relatives of John Thomas Brady, who owned 2,000 acres east of Houston that he sought to develop in the early 1890s. One of his sons, Sherman Brady, constructed this house of brick to advertise the products of the Sherman Brady Brick Company, which produced the salmon colored brick for the original buildings of Rice University at its brickyard on Buffalo Bayou. After J. T. Brady's death, his heirs subdivided the family enclave along Milby Street into the Brady Addition, naming streets after family members.

G-40 Cameron Iron Works Building

G-41 Brady House

G-39 Eastwood Elementary School

G-42 Blessed Sacrament Catholic Church

G-43 Parker Brothers & Company Building

G-44 J. A. Folger Coffee Company Building

G-46 Fullerton School

G-42
Blessed Sacrament Catholic Church
4015 Sherman Street
1924, Frederick B. Gaenslen

This is the best of Gaenslen's Houston churches and one of the finest of his career. Its distinguishing feature is its ornamental brickwork, a conspicuous attribute of San Antonio architecture of the 1920s. The church was constructed on a site that the Brady family donated in the Brady Addition. In 2004 the Diocese of Galveston-Houston demolished the substantial, 2-story parish hall (1910, Green & Briscoe), one of Birdsall Briscoe's earliest buildings. In 2001 Briscoe's other major East End building, Ripley House, a social services center at 4401 Lovejoy (1940, with Maurice J. Sullivan), was also demolished. Briscoe's great-grandfather, John R. Harris, was the founder of Harrisburg, platted in 1826, the oldest town on Buffalo Bayou, which was annexed by Houston in 1926.

G-43
Parker Brothers & Company Building
5303 Navigation Boulevard
1939, Joseph Finger

Mellie Esperson developed the Esperson Industrial District along the south shore of Buffalo Bayou just upstream from the turning basin of the Houston Ship Channel. Navigation curves sinuously through the slightly rolling terrain of this district, its entrance marked by this small, but prepossessing, modernistic office building for a construction products supply company.

G-44
J. A. Folger Coffee Company Building
[now Farmer Brothers Coffee]
235 North Norwood Street
1938, 1947, Robert J. Cummins, engineer

Set at the highest point in the Esperson Industrial District is the 5-story manufacturing plant for Folger's coffee, designed by Cummins's staff architect, Frank Zumwalt. The horizontally banded brick elevations feature two kinds of glass block interspersed with operable steel sash windows.

G-45
The Rebirth of Our Nationality
5801 Canal Street
1972-1973, Leo Tanguma, painter

Tanguma directed dozens of local Chicano artists in creating a work of community art on the side of the Continental Can Company Building and purposefully deployed the rhetorical style of the great Mexican muralists for this long reflection on the condition of poor Mexican Americans in Houston in the 1970s. Unfortunately the surface is deteriorating.

G-46
Fullerton School
[now Open Door Mission]
5803 Harrisburg Road
1910

The scale of the public county schools erected in the East End before they were absorbed into HISD attests to the area's rapid population growth in the first two decades of the 20th century. Fullerton is a substantial 2-story building raised a full story above grade. Scalloped Mission style gables mark major and minor points of entry.

G-45 *The Rebirth of Our Nationality*

G-47 Hidalgo Park Kiosk

G-48 Conventual Chapel of the Villa de Matel

G-49 Association for the Advancement of Mexican Americans Learning Center

G-51 Brookline School

G-47
Hidalgo Park Kiosk
J.W. Peavy Drive and North 70th Street
1935, Vidal Lozano

This high-set kiosk is built entirely of molded concrete: its stone base, its writhing tree trunk and branch vertical supports, and its conical thatched roof. Mexican-American residents raised the money to purchase this small piece of property facing Buffalo Bayou within sight of the turning basin of the Ship Channel, turning it over to the City of Houston as a public park, and sponsoring the construction of Lozano's kiosk. Sharing the park with the kiosk is Parque Amistad, an action-adventure playground built by the community (1987, Leathers & Associates).

G-48
Conventual Chapel of the Villa de Matel
6510 Lawndale Avenue
1928, Maurice J. Sullivan

Villa de Matel, the motherhouse and novitiate of the Sisters of Charity of the Incarnate Word, a nursing order, was Sullivan's first major commission after he began his own practice in 1919. The complex, designed in the Lombard Romanesque style, is set on a 72-acre site. The Conventual Chapel, which lies south of the motherhouse, is the grandest church built in Houston during the 1920s. It is detailed with neo-Byzantine decor. Sullivan employed exposed aggregate concrete mosaic for the wall surfaces and Guastavino tile vaults for the chapel's ceiling. Numerous varieties of polished, colored marbles are used. Sullivan designed the stained glass windows, which were fabricated in Munich. Seating in the chapel is in collegiate choir arrangement. North of the Sisters' tract, across Lawndale, was the 210-acre estate of the oilman E. F. Simms, which began to be subdivided in the 1940s. Villa de Matel, the Simms property, and the Houston Country Club (now Gus Wortham Park) were an island of green in the East End.

G-49
Association for the Advancement of Mexican Americans Learning Center
6001 Gulf Freeway
2009, RdlR Architects

The Association for the Advancement of Mexican Americans is a non-profit community organization formed in 1970 in the East End. In 1990 it acquired Houston Office City, built as an office park at the time of the construction of the Johnson Space Center at Clear Lake City. Rey de la Reza's 3-story building is as formally bold as the original Office City buildings are self-effacing.

G-50
Brays Crossing
6311 Gulf Freeway
2010, Glassman Shoemake Maldonado

The non-profit New Hope Housing had Glassman Shoemake Madonado recycle the 1960s-era Gulfway Apartments as 149 single-room-occupancy apartments. Vivid colors and laser cut steel panels that screen courtyards between the original seven buildings make the complex stand out, even along the Gulf Freeway. Artist Carmen Lomas Garza is responsible for the steel panels (*Las Mañanitas*, *El Jardín*, *Papel Picado*, and *Baile*), the laser cur perforations being the high tech version of the traditional Mexican *papel picado* handicraft. Artist Kim Clark Rentería designed interior stained glass panels.

G-51
Brookline School
3901 Telephone Road
1914, F. S. Glover & Son

Built to serve the rural Brookline community, this 1-story, raised county school building is identified by its Spanish mission style gable.

G-50 Brays Crossing

G-52 Farnsworth & Chambers Building

G-53 Freeway Baptist Church

G-54 The Orange Show

G-55 House

G-56 McNeal House

G-52
Farnsworth & Chambers Building
[now City of Houston Department of Parks and Recreation Gragg Building]
2999 South Wayside Drive
1957, MacKie & Kamrath

In this suburban corporate office building, the battered walls of randomly coursed green Arizona quartzite, contained by insistent horizontals, are a Kamrath trademark. Indicative of the status of the automobile, the front entrance is identified by a weighty porte-cochère. Given its setting in Gragg Park, lush interior garden courts (Eckbo, Dean & Williams of Los Angeles was the original landscape architect), and the building's green color, it is fitting that it has served as headquarters for the city parks department since 1976. Built as the headquarters of a construction company, the building also functioned as temporary headquarters for NASA while the Manned Spacecraft Center at Clear Lake City was under construction. The Farnsworth & Chambers Building was rehabilitated in 2009 by HarrisonKornberg Architects.

G-53
Freeway Baptist Church
144 Winkler Drive
1972, Edward Koerber

Proclamation of the word is what this little church is all about.

G-54
The Orange Show
2401 Munger Street
1979, Jeff D. McKissack

McKissack, a retired postal worker, began the Orange Show in 1968 and worked on it until just before his death in 1980. He dedicated this open-air compound to his belief that the orange functioned as a privileged transmitter of energy from the sun to humankind. Its museum, maze-like passages, arenas, and viewing pavilions were all intended to focus on didactic spectacles about orange power. McKissack built the compound himself, using concrete block and scavenged materials for decoration. His colorful metal work, both stationary and mobile, animates the Orange Show. Following acquisition in 1981 by the Orange Show Foundation, it was restored by Barry Moore Architects. The Orange Show was recognized for its stature as an outstanding work of outsider art in John Beardsley's international survey, *Gardens of Revelation* (1995). It is open to the public for events and on a varying schedule; check orangeshow.org for hours.

G-55
House
2279 Jean Street
2006, Stern and Bucek Architects

Monopitch roof planes mark this 1- and 2-story house, which wraps around an interior courtyard in a U-plan configuration.

G-56
McNeal House
6740 Meadow Lawn Drive
1941

Indicative of the high standards of domestic design that prevailed in Houston in the 1930s and early '40s is this modest 1-story, brick-faced house. It is located in the subdivision of Idylwood, developed in 1928 along an extension of the Brays Bayou Parkway. Next door at 6748 Meadow Lawn is the modernistic L'Roy House (1940, Harry A. Turner), somewhat the worse for coarse alterations. Nearby at 1402 North MacGregor, facing the bayou park, is a Spanish Mediterranean house (1935, S. R. Slaughter).

G-57
Cooke House
1724 Alta Vista Avenue
1912, Cooke & Company

The architect, W. A. Cooke, designed this expansive Mission style bungalow, faced with stucco and red roof tiles, for his family. It is located in Forest Hill, planned in 1910 by the Kansas City landscape architect Sid J. Hare as the first subdivision in Houston with a curvilinear street plan. Forest Hill was laid out across Brays Bayou from what was then the Houston Country Club (now Gus S. Wortham Park). The Cooke House was one of three large houses built there. These did not presage Forest Hill's future, however, as during the 1920s they were surrounded by much smaller houses.

G-58
Radetzki House
1766 Pasadena Avenue
1911, Lang & Witchell

This Colonial revival house was the largest built in Forest Hill. Designed in the Houston branch office of Dallas's most prolific architects, it sits on a small hillock looking out to Brays Bayou.

G-57 Cooke House

G-58 Radetzki House

G-59 Mason Park Shelter House

G-60 Habitat for Humanity, Jimmy Carter Work Project Houses

G-61 Sidney Sherman Bridge

G-62 Houston Public Elevator

G-63 Ford Motor Company Building I

G-65 Pittsburgh Plate Glass Company Building

G-59
Mason Park Shelter House
541 South 75th Street
1932, A. E. Nutter

Nutter designed the simpler of these two stucco-surfaced, tile-roofed Mediterranean buildings. It is similar to his shelter houses in Hermann and MacGregor parks. The second, by Hiram A. Salisbury & T. George McHale (1950), is joined to Nutter's original by a tile-roofed Doric colonnade.

G-60
Habitat for Humanity, Jimmy Carter Work Project Houses
7800-7900 blocks Avenue B and 7700-7800 blocks Avenue C
1998, Gerald Moorhead

This was one of two communities of new housing built by Habitat for Humanity volunteers as part of the 1998 Jimmy Carter Work Project. Former President and Mrs. Carter participated in the construction of these houses.

G-61
Sidney Sherman Bridge
East Loop 610 and Houston Ship Channel
1972, A. C. Kyser, Texas Highway Department, designer

This bridge, carrying Loop 610 across Buffalo Bayou, was the longest strut-girder bridge in the U.S. at the time of its completion. Two steel strut girder structures, one on each bank, carry ten lanes of traffic across the Ship Channel. The bridge is 1,230 feet long and rises 135 feet above the water. Visible from the bridge on a clear day is one of the most exhilarating prospects of Houston. The downtown skyline falls into alignment with the Greenway Plaza and Post Oak skylines, giving the impression of a single file of tall structures expanding Manhattan-like across the coastal prairie.

G-62
Houston Public Elevator
[now Public Grain Elevator]
8200 block Clinton Drive
1926

The immense network of clustered grain storage bins, conveyor houses, and loading chutes makes the Public Elevator the dominating presence on the Long Reach of the Houston Ship Channel. The cluster of bins behind the tallest cluster and the entire row perpendicular to it are additions to the original. The complex can also seen across the water from the east end of Harbor Drive, east of 75th.

G-63
Ford Motor Company Building
5800 Clinton Drive
1947, Giffels & Vallet

The Detroit architects shaped this late modernistic style building for Ford Motor Company's service and parts operation with curved corners, streamlined ribbon windows, and a high, glazed central bay. The building is set on a spacious lawn, an indication of the post-war suburbanizing trend that was beginning to affect design standards even in industrial districts.

G-64
National Steel Products Company Building
[now Electric Wire & Cable Company]
750 Lockwood Drive
1950

Both the production plant and head office advertised this corporation's foremost product with a semicircular, corrugated steel structural shell—a Quonset hut in all but name.

G-65
Pittsburgh Plate Glass Company Building
5520 Armour Drive
1955, Milton McGinty

As was often the case with Houston industrial buildings of the 1940s and '50s, masonry of contrasting types, textures, and colors was skillfully combined here to elicit an appearance that was economical, but not merely utilitarian. McGinty's building programmatically differentiates between office and production space. It also incorporates that favorite modernistic device, the pylon.

G-64 National Steel Products Company Building

G-66 John L. McReynolds Junior High School

G-67 Phillis Wheatley Senior High School

G-68 Howard Flint Ink Company Building

G-69 2424 Sakowitz Housing

G-66
John L. McReynolds Junior High School
5910 Market Street
1956, Stayton Nunn

Nunn ventured a bright array of colors, as well as decorative grillwork, on this large complex of buildings. The stairwells are marked by projecting V-shaped bay windows, which, in combination with the polychrome brick, anticipate César Pelli's work at Rice University of the 1980s.

G-67
Phillis Wheatley Senior High School
4910 Market Street
1949, MacKie & Kamrath

Construction of a replacement school for Wheatley High School (2006, ESPA Group) at 4901 Providence led to the demolition of all but a sliver of the MacKie & Kamrath building. Behind Wheatley, in the 5100 block of Sonora, is MacKie & Kamrath's Finnegan Park Recreation Building (1949).

G-68
Howard Flint Ink Company Building
1024 Lockwood Drive
1940, Harley & Ellington

A small modernistic office building, designed by a firm of Detroit architects. Across the street, at 1111 Lockwood, is MacKie & Kamrath's Thornhill-Craver Company Building (1949).

G-69
2424 Sakowitz Housing
2424 Sakowitz Street
2010, Val Glitsch

New Hope Housing built this 166-unit single-room-occupancy apartment complex in the heart of Fifth Ward. Asakura Robinson was the landscape architect.

Tour G

North Side / East End

The Heights

The Heights

Tour H-1

Like the North Side and East End, the Heights was historically a working-class area of Houston, its fortunes historically tied to railroad lines. The route of the Houston & Texas Central, the pioneer Houston railroad, parallels Washington Avenue, one route leading out of Houston. It was along such roads that cemeteries were established in the 19th century. Washington provides access to the opulent Glenwood Cemetery and, next-door, the solemn Washington Cemetery, originally called Deutsche Gesellschaft. Germans comprised the largest bloc of resident immigrants in 19th-century Texas, and their presence in Houston is still evident in the Baker Addition of what had been the Sixth Ward, now the city's oldest intact residential neighborhood. Electrification of streetcar lines in 1891 allowed real estate developers to expand much farther out from the compact centers in cities across America. Houston Heights, a new community developed by Midwestern investors in the early 1890s, took advantage of this technical advance. The chief investor went so far as to purchase Houston's streetcar company to ensure its extension to Houston Heights, 2.5 miles from Market Square. He then used the profits to keep the Heights development afloat economically during the Panic of 1893.

Houston Heights was no mere "addition" to the city of Houston. It was the first large, planned community undertaken locally, and its central thoroughfare, Heights Boulevard, was the first divided boulevard laid out in the Houston area. Although it was never a high-status neighborhood, the Heights introduced a much more comprehensive and rational approach to community planning than had been tried before in Houston. It also demonstrated that suburban communities could exist in proximity to, but without being a part of, the central city, at least until its eventual annexation by Houston in 1918. The extension of streetcar lines from downtown also accounted for development between the Heights and Houston proper of the Brooke-Smith Addition and Woodland Heights. To better compete for moderate-income buyers, Woodland Heights, opened in 1907, adopted the symbols and strategies of more elite neighborhoods: landscape amenities, gate piers (no-longer extant), and restrictive covenants (which are still enforced). North of Houston Heights, also tied to the streetcar line, is Independence Heights, developed in 1910 as a subdivision where African-American families could buy home sites. The Heights, as this whole area is now collectively known, has become a mixture of old-time, working-class families, both Anglo- and Mexican-American, young families seeking relatively inexpensive housing, and specialized groups—most visibly artists. The Heights has a slightly ragged look, appealing to some as homey, while appearing to others as merely run-down. With this aspect goes a small-town ambiance typical of many Houston neighborhoods, which could easily be located in East Texas or at some crossroads on the coastal plain, far removed from skyscrapers and freeways.

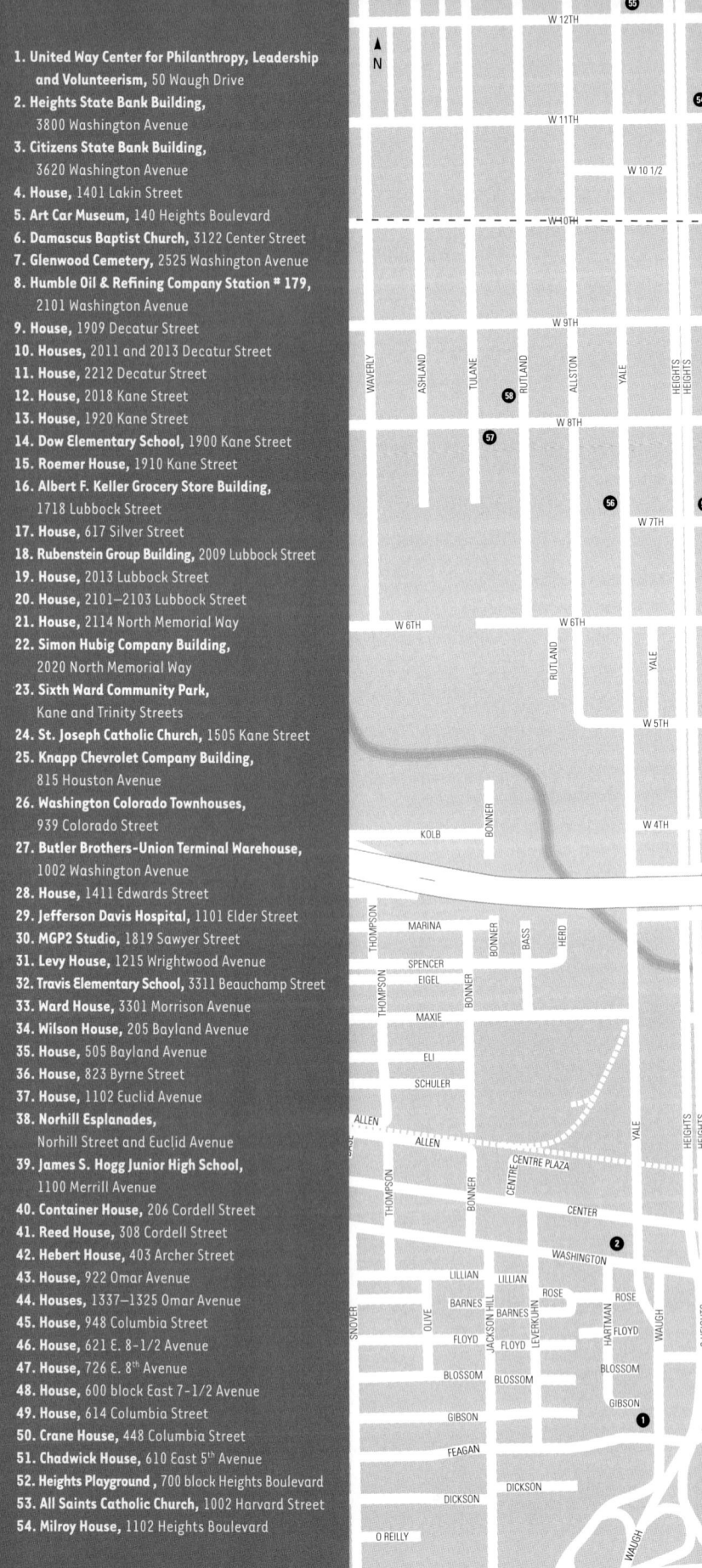

1. **United Way Center for Philanthropy, Leadership and Volunteerism,** 50 Waugh Drive
2. **Heights State Bank Building,** 3800 Washington Avenue
3. **Citizens State Bank Building,** 3620 Washington Avenue
4. **House,** 1401 Lakin Street
5. **Art Car Museum,** 140 Heights Boulevard
6. **Damascus Baptist Church,** 3122 Center Street
7. **Glenwood Cemetery,** 2525 Washington Avenue
8. **Humble Oil & Refining Company Station # 179,** 2101 Washington Avenue
9. **House,** 1909 Decatur Street
10. **Houses,** 2011 and 2013 Decatur Street
11. **House,** 2212 Decatur Street
12. **House,** 2018 Kane Street
13. **House,** 1920 Kane Street
14. **Dow Elementary School,** 1900 Kane Street
15. **Roemer House,** 1910 Kane Street
16. **Albert F. Keller Grocery Store Building,** 1718 Lubbock Street
17. **House,** 617 Silver Street
18. **Rubenstein Group Building,** 2009 Lubbock Street
19. **House,** 2013 Lubbock Street
20. **House,** 2101–2103 Lubbock Street
21. **House,** 2114 North Memorial Way
22. **Simon Hubig Company Building,** 2020 North Memorial Way
23. **Sixth Ward Community Park,** Kane and Trinity Streets
24. **St. Joseph Catholic Church,** 1505 Kane Street
25. **Knapp Chevrolet Company Building,** 815 Houston Avenue
26. **Washington Colorado Townhouses,** 939 Colorado Street
27. **Butler Brothers–Union Terminal Warehouse,** 1002 Washington Avenue
28. **House,** 1411 Edwards Street
29. **Jefferson Davis Hospital,** 1101 Elder Street
30. **MGP2 Studio,** 1819 Sawyer Street
31. **Levy House,** 1215 Wrightwood Avenue
32. **Travis Elementary School,** 3311 Beauchamp Street
33. **Ward House,** 3301 Morrison Avenue
34. **Wilson House,** 205 Bayland Avenue
35. **House,** 505 Bayland Avenue
36. **House,** 823 Byrne Street
37. **House,** 1102 Euclid Avenue
38. **Norhill Esplanades,** Norhill Street and Euclid Avenue
39. **James S. Hogg Junior High School,** 1100 Merrill Avenue
40. **Container House,** 206 Cordell Street
41. **Reed House,** 308 Cordell Street
42. **Hebert House,** 403 Archer Street
43. **House,** 922 Omar Avenue
44. **Houses,** 1337–1325 Omar Avenue
45. **House,** 948 Columbia Street
46. **House,** 621 E. 8-1/2 Avenue
47. **House,** 726 E. 8th Avenue
48. **House,** 600 block East 7-1/2 Avenue
49. **House,** 614 Columbia Street
50. **Crane House,** 448 Columbia Street
51. **Chadwick House,** 610 East 5th Avenue
52. **Heights Playground,** 700 block Heights Boulevard
53. **All Saints Catholic Church,** 1002 Harvard Street
54. **Milroy House,** 1102 Heights Boulevard

55. **Houston Heights City Hall and Fire Station,** 107 West 12th Avenue
56. **Koelsch Gallery,** 703 Yale Street
57. **Townhouses,** 416–418 W. 8th Avenue
58. **House,** 807 Rutland Street
59. **Heights Branch, Houston Public Library,** 1302 Heights Boulevard
60. **Woodward House,** 1605 Heights Boulevard
61. **Heights Christian Church,** 1703 Heights Boulevard
62. **Heights High School,** 139 East 20th Avenue
63. **Banta House,** 119 East 20th Avenue
64. **Heights Transit Center,** East 20th Avenue and North Main Street
65. **Mansfield House,** 1802 Harvard Street
66. **Heights Church of Christ,** 120 East 16th Avenue
67. **Second Church of Christ, Scientist,** 1400 Harvard Street
68. **Schleseer House,** 1123 Harvard Street
69. **John H. Reagan Senior High School,** 401 East 13th Avenue
70. **Columbia House,** 1436 Columbia Street
71. **Arlington Court,** 300 East 14th Avenue
72. **Immanuel Lutheran Church,** 306 East 15th Avenue
73. **Drumheller House,** 1525 Cortland Street
74. **House,** 1233 Allston Street
75. **Studio-Shed Building,** 1236 Waverly Street
76. **House,** 1435 Rutland Street
77. **House,** 1512 Rutland Street
78. **House,** 1528 Tulane Street
79. **House,** 1536 Tulane Street
80. **House,** 1501 Allston Street
81. **House,** 1515 Ashland Street
82. **Heights Theater,** 341 West 19th Avenue
83. **Harold's,** 350 West 19th Avenue
84. **Zagst House,** 347 West 20th Avenue
85. **Oriental Textile Mill,** 611 West 22nd Avenue
86. **House,** 921 East 25th Avenue
87. **House,** 1013 East 26th Avenue
88. **House,** 7415 North Main Street
89. **House,** 914 West 23rd Avenue
90. **Shady Acres Village,** 1301–11 West 25th Avenue
91. **Live Oak Friends Meeting House,** 1318 West 26th Avenue
92. **Houses,** 1506 West 26th Avenue
93. **House,** 2021 West 14-1/2 Avenue

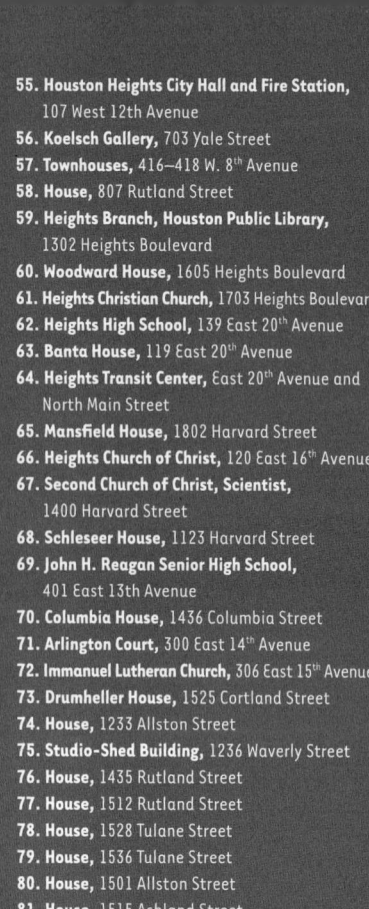
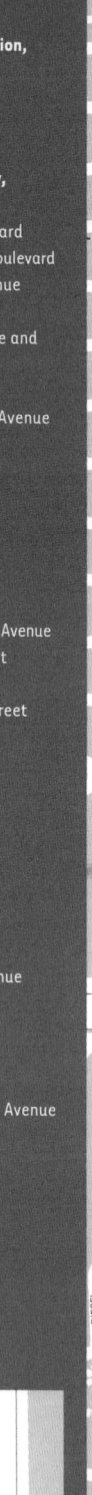
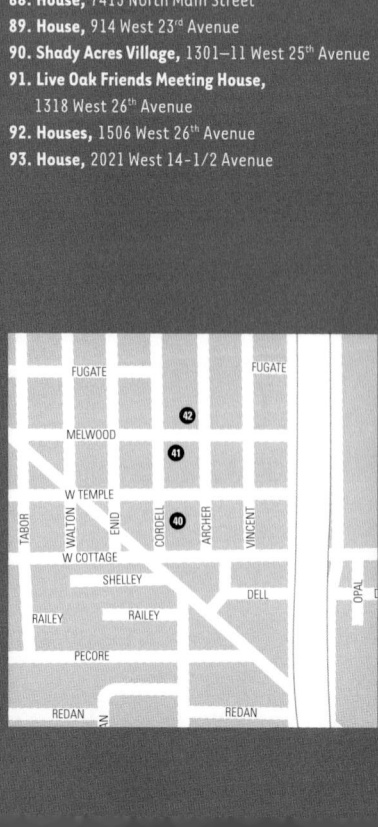

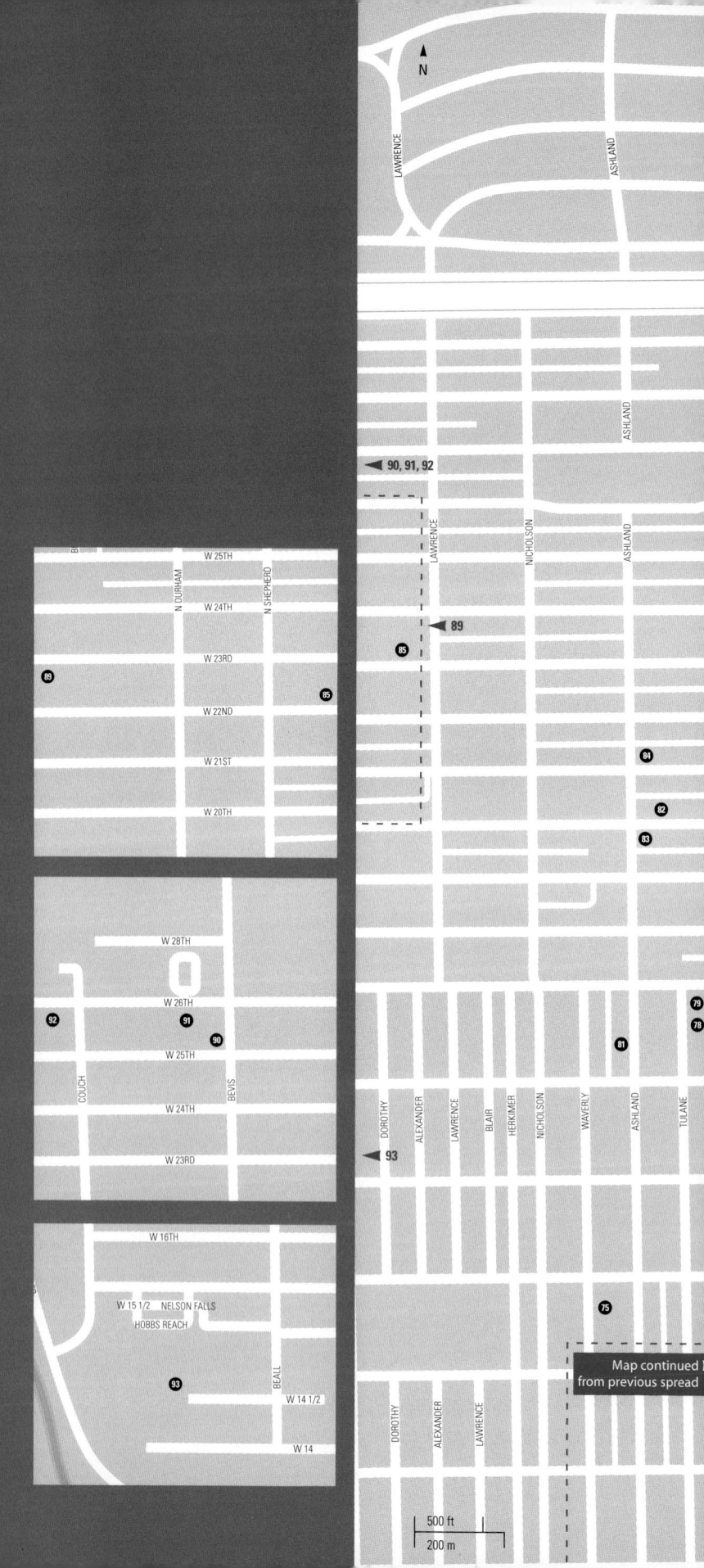

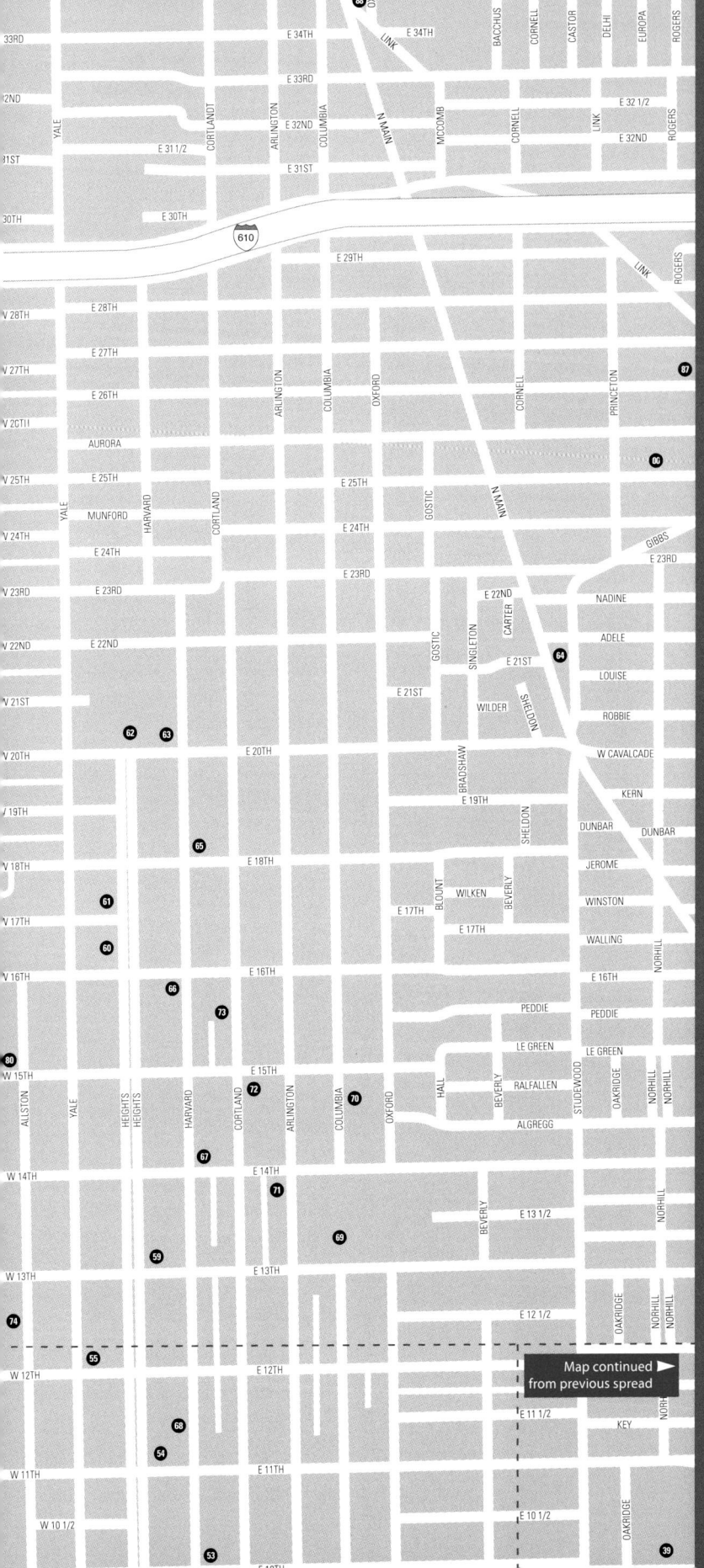

H-1 United Way Center for Philanthropy, Leadership and Volunteerism

H-2 Heights State Bank Building

H-3 Citizens State Bank Building

H-4 House

H-1
United Way Center for Philanthropy, Leadership and Volunteerism
50 Waugh Drive
2004, Gensler, Office of James Burnett, landscape architects

This rectangular building, parallel to Waugh, has 2.5-story shed-roofed bays that break forward of its street front. The sleek, reflective glass surfaces of the projecting bays play off the brick and concrete facing of the recessed block.

H-2
Heights State Bank Building
[now Primeway Federal Credit Union]
3800 Washington Avenue
1962, Wilson, Morris,
  Crain & Anderson

This concrete and glass pavilion lost some of its precision when two bays were added along its Washington frontage—and then regained it after they were demolished. Ralph A. Anderson, Jr. stacked radial precast concrete "trees" above a grid of cast-in-place concrete columns, topping the whole thing off with a cast-in-place roof slab. This was the one locally designed Houston building that Arthur Drexler included in his, "Transformations in Modern Architecture" exhibition at The Museum of Modern Art in 1979.

H-3
Citizens State Bank Building
[now Rockefeller Hall]
3620 Washington Avenue
1925, Joseph Finger

The previous home of Heights State Bank illustrates how drastically attitudes about appropriate architectural imagery changed between the 1920s and 1960s. Finger's classically detailed façade stands out from, yet is still a part of, the strip of commercial buildings along Washington. It is closed and secure looking, but it doesn't try to distance itself from the street. The handsome façade was rehabilitated in 1978 by Taft Architects, who cleverly transformed the interior into a nightclub for Sanford Criner and J. B. Cirincione, respecting the old without attempting to conceal their own interventions.

H-4
House
1401 Lakin Street
2004, Michael Landrum

Yale Street Acres, as this subdivision is known, is a classic, paradoxical bit of Houston obscurity, isolated by the Houston & Texas Central Railroad line to the south, Heights Boulevard (to which it has no connection) to the west, and White Oak Bayou to the north. Although the rail corridor provides a spectacular vista of the downtown skyline, if you turned your back on it you could believe you were in a semi-rural neighborhood at the edge of the city. Landrum and his clients respected the mysterious character of the landscape with the design of this 2-story courtyard house, isolated behind white stucco walls and accessible through a wood gate portal salvaged from India. Unfortunately other new buildings don't respect this character, overpowering the neighborhood and dispossessing its traditional low-income, African-American residents. At the north end of Court Street is the historic African-American Olivewood Cemetery.

H-5
Art Car Museum
140 Heights Boulevard
1998, David Best

The Art Car Museum celebrates the art of the found as practiced locally, with a special reverence for the automobile. Cars were raised to the stature of art for the Art Car Parade, initiated by artists and the Orange Show Foundation in 1988 as a free-spirited contribution to the annual, very official Houston Festival. The Art Car Museum, a pre-engineered steel shed with some fancy add-ons, treats this genre with the respect it deserves. The museum was the first of several alternative art institutions established by art provocateurs and human rights advocates, Ann O'Connor and James Harithas.

H-5 Art Car Museum

H-6 Damascus Baptist Church

H-7 Glenwood Cemetery, Solitude

H-8 Humble Oil & Refining Company Station #179

H-9 House

H-10 House

H-6
Damascus Baptist Church
3122 Center Street
1937, James M. Thomas

This was the first independent work of Thomas, a contractor who specialized in building churches. It is an example of the twin-towered church type, especially popular in Houston from the 1920s–1950s. At 1015 Court, just in front of the church, is an extravagantly roofed 1927 bungalow. Damascus Baptist Church is located in a small African-American neighborhood in Chaneyville, a settlement along the westward extension of Washington that follows the ridge between Buffalo Bayou to the south and White Oak Bayou to the north. Chaneyville was the point at which the Galveston, Harrisburg & San Antonio Railway line crossed Buffalo Bayou to intersect the Houston & Texas Central Railroad line. Around this juncture a small industrial enclave developed in the late 19th century. In the 1990s and 2000s aggressive residential development—first apartments, then townhouses in gated enclaves, then high-rises—and retail development replaced industrial installations and working class neighborhoods on the south side of Washington. (Demolished)

H-7
Glenwood Cemetery, *Solitude*
2525 Washington Avenue
1926, Marcel Bouraine, sculptor

Dr. Ethel Lyon Heard acquired this Bouraine figure in Paris, when it was exhibited there in 1927, and brought it to Houston for her husband's grave. The Heard monument is one of many in Glenwood Cemetery, laid out in 1871 by the English horticulturalist, Alfred Whitaker, on what was then the western edge of Houston. Glenwood is Houston's Victorian landscape cemetery. It was one of the earliest professionally designed and landscaped public spaces in the city. Because of its proximity to Buffalo Bayou, the 65-acre site is topographically varied and heavily wooded. Along its curving drives lies everyone who was anyone in Houston, including the architects Eugene T. Heiner, Henry C. Cooke, Kenneth Franzheim, John F. Staub, and Hugo V. Neuhaus, Jr. *Houston's Silent Garden: Glenwood Cemetery, 1871-2009*, by Suzanne Turner and Joanne Seale Wilson, documents the history of the first picturesque garden cemetery in Texas.

H-8
Humble Oil & Refining Company Station #179
[now Liberty Station]
2101 Washington Avenue
1930, John F. Staub

Staub designed a series of gas station prototypes for the Humble Oil & Refining Company in 1929. This station represents one of the larger models. Beneath layers of paint it retains its decorative tile cornice.

H-9
House
1909 Decatur Street
c 1875

As the twin front doors imply, this is a double house, a type built for the rental market. Its solemn front elevation, with a veranda incorporated beneath the side-gabled roof, identifies it as a Gulf Coast cottage. Across the street at 1910 Decatur is another example of the Gulf Coast cottage (1866, 1885). Both were rescued and restored between 1994-1996. These houses lie in the W. R. Baker Addition in what had been Houston's Sixth Ward. This is Houston's oldest intact neighborhood, a working-class district developed in the late 1850s near the shops of the Houston & Texas Central Railroad Company, which lay north of Washington. In 1978 it became the Sixth Ward Historic District, the first historic district in Houston listed in the National Register of Historic Places. In 2007 the Houston City Council, on the recommendation of Mayor Bill White, made it the city's first Protected Historic District.

H-10
Houses
2011 and 2013 Decatur Street
c 1890

This pair of ornamented shotgun cottages was donated by owner Fred V. Cannata to the Greater Houston Preservation Alliance, which rehabilitated both in 1995 (Barry Moore, architect) and sold them as affordable housing.

H-11
House
2212 Decatur Street
c 1890

The wooden gingerbread brackets beneath the porch lintel are profiled to look like birds on the wing. Such distinctive bits of decoration recur on the modest wooden houses of the Sixth Ward.

H-12
Lighthouse House
2020 Kane Street
1906

Henry R. Lighthouse, a brick manufacturer, built this Colonial revival house, the most pretentious in the Sixth Ward, on the site of his wife's childhood home. The combination of tan brick and red mortar is a detail visible on other Houston buildings of the 1910 period.

H-11 House

H-12 Lighthouse House

H-13 House

H-14 Dow Elementary School

H-15 Roemer House

H-16 Albert F. Keller Grocery Store Building

H-17 House

H-13
House
1920 Kane Street
c 1875

This is a classic 2-story, I-house, so-named because of its rectangular plan configuration and narrow width. Sitting in a fenced garden, the house strongly conveys a sense of what the Sixth Ward must have been like at the end of the 19th century.

H-14
Dow Elementary School
[now Multicultural Education and Counseling through the Arts Center]
1900 Kane Street
1912, C. H. Page & Brother

When new Dow exemplified the modern neighborhood school, occupying a full-block site rather than the smaller lots typical of Victorian-era schools. Austin architect, Charles Page, specialized in school design, and versions of Dow can be found throughout Texas, reflecting the extent of the Page brothers' practice. Neighborhood activist, Alice M. Valdez of MECA, rescued Dow School after the Houston Independent School District closed it, rehabilitating it as a community center. Patrick Peters led the University of Houston Graduate Design/Build Studio responsible for the outdoor amphitheater at the Kane-Silver corner (2005). Galveston architects Michael Gaertner & Associates are responsible for Dow School's phased rehabilitation.

H-15
Roemer House
1910 Kane Street
c 1889

The largest Victorian house in the Sixth Ward, this features a gable surfaced with fish-scale shingles, a favorite ornamental finish in the 1890s. It was the home of Frederick Roemer, a carpenter for the Houston & Texas Central Railway.

H-16
Albert F. Keller Grocery Store Building
[now Richard Roeder Associates]
1718 Lubbock Street
c 1913

The corner store, with apartment above, is executed here in brick. This building was rehabilitated and expanded by Roeder to house his interior design studio.

H-17
House
617 Silver Street
1875

This simple wood cottage, raised high on brick piers, is redolent of Galveston. Like so much of the Sixth Ward, it bespeaks a way of life at variance with the image of Houston that its downtown skyline projects, which can be appreciated in its full splendor from the generous front porch of this house. Rehabilitated by architect Herbert Linnstaedter.

H-18
Rubenstein Group Building
[now the Crispin Company]
2009 Lubbock Street
1984, Rubenstein Group

Built by the architect Larry Rubenstein to house his studio, this 2-story building of wood post-and-beam construction is surfaced with corrugated metal. Roger Detherage, the art cabinetmaker, oversaw construction, which is evident in its meticulous, but simple, finishes and carefully worked out joinery. The saw-tooth skylights admit north light into the second-floor production space.

H-19
House
2013 Lubbock Street
1999, Cameron Armstrong

Armstrong was accused of driving a knife through the heart of the Sixth Ward when he designed this Galvalume-faced house and a companion next door at 2017 (1999). Architecturally speaking, assailant and victim have been reconciled; Armstrong's houses blend imperceptibly into the fabric of the district.

H-19 House

H-18 Rubenstein Group Building

H-20 House

H-21 House

H-22 Simon Hubig Company Building

H-23 Sixth Ward Community Park

H-24 St. Joseph Catholic Church

H-20
House
2101 Lubbock Street
2001, George G. McMillin

This is a neo-shotgun cottage designed and built by architect George McMillin and his wife, Elizabeth, as a model of compatible new construction in the Sixth Ward Historic District. The McMillins were also responsible for the adjoining pair of brick bearing-wall row houses at 609-611 Henderson (1996), which are based on the corner store type.

H-21
House
2114 North Memorial Way
1997

This house and the cottage next door at 504 Hemphill, built by Harlan Smith, are economical houses designed to be compatible with the historic fabric of the Sixth Ward.

H-22
Simon Hubig Company Building
[now Upstream Insurance Brokers]
2020 North Memorial Way
1927, Frank T. Singleton

Dark red brick was especially identified with production buildings in Houston in the 1910s and '20s. In this case the Dallas-based Simon Hubig Company manufactured pies. The Hubig Building has been handsomely recycled as an insurance company headquarters (1995, Cameron Armstrong).

H-23
Sixth Ward Community Park
Kane Street and Trinity Street
1989, Slaney Santana Group, landscape architects

The design of this small park grew out of collaboration between MECA (the St. Joseph Multi- Ethnic Cultural Arts Committee before it became a free-standing non-profit) and a landscape architecture studio from

Texas A&M University, translated into reality under the guidance of landscape architect Scott Slaney. The park's most remarkable feature is the walled courtyard at Kane and Trinity, which contains painted tiles and facemasks made by residents working with the artists Paul Kittleson and Carter Ernst. Another notable feature is the splendid cactus water fountain by Tim Glover. The mural, *A United Community*, on the side of the parish school building is the work of Sylvia Orozco and Pio Pulido (1985).

H-24
St. Joseph Catholic Church
1505 Kane Street
1902, Patrick S. Rabitt
with George E. Dickey

Rabitt was a Galveston architect trained by N. J. Clayton, whose influence is apparent in the exceptional ornamental brickwork with which this church is profusely detailed. St. Joseph's was the German parish in Houston. Across the street, at 800 Houston, is Trinity Lutheran Church (1954, Travis Broesche), built for one of the oldest German Evangelical congregations in the city. And at 1018 Houston, just north of Washington, is the ex-Congregation Adath Emeth Synagogue (1912). These three houses of worship testify to the strength of the German and central European presence in the Sixth Ward during the late 19th and early 20th centuries. Following a fire in 1995, St. Joseph's underwent reconstruction and a much-needed restoration (L. Barry Davidson Architects).

H-25
Knapp Chevrolet Company Building
815 Houston Avenue
1941, R. Newell Waters with
E. Kelly Gaffney

Waters, who practiced in Weslaco in the Lower Rio Grande Valley, differentiated the showroom bay from the low, unadorned service bay with bull-nosed corners framing plate glass display windows. The two bays are divided by a glass block-filled modernistic pylon that identifies the building on top and admits the public below. The Greater Houston Preservation Alliance, which featured the Knapp showroom in Jim Parsons and David Bush's, *Houston Deco: Modernistic Architecture of the Gulf Coast* (2008), participated in the successful effort to keep General Motors from disenfranchising the dealership in 2009.

H-25 Knapp Chevrolet Company Building

H-26 Washington Colorado Townhouses

H-27 Butler Brothers-Union Terminal Warehouse

H-28 House

H-29 Jefferson Davis Hospital

H-26
Washington Colorado Townhouses
939 Colorado Street
2000, Murphy Mears

This 22-unit complex is deftly fit into the fabric of the Sixth Ward. Although the townhouses are larger than typical Sixth Ward cottages, they reinforce, rather than disrupt, the historic neighborhood's northeast corner.

H-27
Butler Brothers-Union Terminal Warehouse
[now City of Houston Central Permitting Center]
1002 Washington Avenue
1920; 1941, Henry F. Jonas & Tabor
2011, Studio Red

This 4-story, concrete-frame warehouse (the first two floors and basement built in 1920, the top two floors added in 1941) was rehabilitated by Studio Red to become the City of Houston's Central Permitting Center and a demonstration of sustainable building practices. Studio Red used recycled materials, installed a raised-floor air-conditioning system, and constructed a rainwater-harvesting network to irrigate the vegetated roof above the first-story east face extension.

H-28
House
1411 Edwards Street
2002, MC² Architects

Lying just east of Houston Avenue in the former First Ward, this 2-story, shed-roofed house with a side garden was inserted into a very mixed setting so deftly that it seemed like it had always been there. Now, in typical Houston style, it is the setting that has changed around it.

H-29
Jefferson Davis Hospital
[now Elder Street Artists Lofts]
1101 Elder Street
1924, W. A. Dowdy
2005, W. O. Neuhaus Associates

Constructed as Houston and Harris County's public health hospital, Jefferson Davis experienced such rapid expansion in use that a replacement was planned in 1930 and completed in 1937. Thereafter this stolid, 2- and 3-story classical block, built partially on a Confederate cemetery (therefore the dedication to Jefferson Davis), was used for various purposes before being abandoned. In 2002 the Avenue Community Development Corporation and Minneapolis-based Artspace USA bought the building from the county. Architect Bill Neuhaus carried out a certified rehabilitation, transforming the hospital into 34 live-work spaces for artists. Although quite visible from Interstate 45 as it circles the west side of downtown, Jefferson Davis Hospital feels quite insulated in the First Ward, perched on the crest of a ridge that descends toward White Oak Bayou.

H-30
MGP2 Studio
1819 Sawyer Street
2005, Natalye Appel + Associates Architects

Because the Shearn and Baker Additions in the First-Sixth Ward neighborhood were bisected by the Houston & Texas Central Railroad and the Missouri, Kansas & Texas Railway tracks, they attracted businesses wanting both railroad access and housing. Sawyer, the neighborhood's historic west edge, was re-engineered to curve through an offset intersection, leaving the residual triangular lot on which Appel designed this production studio for photographer Mark Green. Stepped in plan and section, the studio is alternately closed or open as interior uses require. Galvalume panels and exposed concrete block pick up on the neighborhood's industrial identity.

H-30 MGP2 Studio

H-31 Levy House

H-32 Travis Elementary School

H-33 Ward House

H-34 House

H-35 House

H-31
Levy House
1215 Wrightwood Avenue
c 1920

This Mission style bungalow, with its scalloped "Alamo" gable, is finished with stucco and faced with an arcaded porch.

H-32
Travis Elementary School
3311 Beauchamp Street
1926, Joseph Finger
2006, Taft Architects

Neighborhood pressure in Woodland Heights kept the Houston Independent School District from demolishing this school, complicating Taft Architects' charge to more than double its square footage with an architecturally compatible addition on a rock-bottom budget. By using contrasting shades of brick and proportioning window openings to correspond to those in Finger's building, Taft made its extension contribute to a greater whole.

H-33
Ward House
3301 Morrison Avenue
1910

The William A. Wilson Company, developers of this neighborhood, Woodland Heights, built many of the houses here speculatively and publicized them in *Homes*, a monthly magazine it issued in 1911-1912. This fine Craftsman bungalow was one such house. It retains its porch piers of concrete, cast to look like stone, and the division of its external wall surfaces into contrasting zones of shingles and clapboard. The ganged windows in the broad roof dormer and the exposed rafter ends beneath the porch roofline are other identifying traits. This house was flanked by the equally notable 3305 Morrison (1911) to the north, and 3215 Morrison (1910) to the south. The latter, however, was demolished for replacement by a never-built townhouse complex in the 2000s.

H-34
Wilson House
205 Bayland Avenue
1911

William Wilson's own house was the largest on Woodland Heights's main thoroughfare, Bayland, which Wilson lined with Live Oaks. His propensity for planting street trees, unusual for the developer of a lower middle-income subdivision, led to his appointment to the City of Houston's first Board of Park Commissioners in 1910. The Wilson House is "progressive" in style. Lack of historically derived detail and pronounced horizontality ally it with the Progressive School of Chicago. The house suffered decades of inappropriate alterations, but in 2005 it was rescued by Bill Baldwin and José González, who undertook a restoration by Creole Design (2006) that has returned the Wilson House to its former glory.

H-35
House
505 Bayland Avenue
1992, Thompson-Frater Associates

This is a new house that revives the Craftsman bungalow type. 503 Bayland (1992) is by the same architect.

H-36
House
823 Byrne Street
1992, Peter D. Waldman

Endeavoring to build a house free of chemically treated components, Waldman used masonry, tile, and metal to configure this small house on its site. The result is a sequence of outdoor and indoor spaces that perceptually expands the size of the house.

H-37
House
1102 Euclid Avenue
1994, Joan Callis and Pia Wortham

Reflecting the influence of their mentor, Enric Miralles, the Houston-born architect Pia Wortham and her husband Joan Callis, who practice in Barcelona, shaped this house and studio as a series of spatial facets. Its interiors open to a walled garden and protected views of the neighborhood.

H-38
Norhill Esplanades
Norhill Street and Euclid Avenue
1920

One of Will C. Hogg's earliest ventures in suburban real estate development was this neighborhood, Norhill. It was laid out in several sections on the former dairy farm of Hogg's partner, Henry W. Stude, beginning in 1920. Like Woodland Heights to the east, Norhill was a lower middle-income subdivision. Nonetheless it was planned with civic amenities: 2-block-long esplanades landscaped as small parks that bring a measure of garden city charm to this modest neighborhood.

H-37 House

H-36 House

H-38 Norhill Esplanades

H-39 James S. Hogg Junior High School

H-40 Container House

H-41 Reed House

H-42 Herbert House

H-39
James S. Hogg Junior High School
[now James S. Hogg Middle School]
1100 Merrill Avenue
1926, Briscoe & Dixon and Maurice J. Sullivan, William Ward Watkin, consulting architect

In place of an esplanade park at Norhill and Merrill, Hogg and Stude's Varner Realty Company donated property for the construction of a public school, which was named in honor of Hogg's father, Texas governor J. S. Hogg. The school building, as was customary, was functionally planned. But it also served as a neighborhood civic monument, lined up on the axis of Norhill and decorated with Jacobean architectural detail.

H-40
Container House
206 Cordell Street
2008, Numen Development with Robertson Design

Katie Nichols and John Walker of Numen Development worked with architect Christopher Robertson to design a prototype speculative house incorporating steel cargo shipping containers and sustainable and recycled materials. They grouped three containers around a central open space, then roofed over the open space to provide a room wider and higher than the containers. A wood slat sunscreen provides exterior insulation.

H-41
Reed House
308 Cordell Street
1910

Frank R. Reed, a plasterer, built this bungalow in the Brooke-Smith Addition. Reed clearly saw the advertising potential that his own house offered for business and took full advantage of it.

H-42
Hebert House
403 Archer Street
c 1917

The grandest house in the Brooke Smith Addition is this temple-fronted Colonial revival, which lords it over more modest surrounding houses.

H-43
House
922 Omar Street
2000, Dillon Kyle

Controversial when new because it did not replicate a 19th- or early 20th-century house type, this 1-story house respects the scale of the Woodson Place Addition. It is a quirky neo-modern design that is both distinctive and self-deprecating.

H-44
Houses
1337-1325 Omar Avenue
1998, Creole Design

It is surreal to encounter the Garden District of New Orleans here on the east edge of Houston Heights. Such abrupt transpositions to somewhere else are very Houston. The houses produced by Sam Gianukos's Creole Design do a credible job of updating mid-19th-century New Orleanian town house prototypes. They make a much more civil urban residential streetscape than the front-end-loaded, garage-door faced "town houses" that are their authentic, turn-of-the-21st-century Houston counterparts.

H-45
House
948 Columbia Street
2000, Val Glitsch

With its offset garage, recessed, shed-roofed rear wing, and generous side garden, this modern house respects the scale and spatiality of the Heights.

H-46
House
621 E. 81/2 Avenue
2007, McIntyre/Robinowitz

Constructed to one side of a double lot, this expansive, 2-story, gable-roofed house opens out to its site rather than maximizing lot coverage as surrounding new houses do. Low pitched, raised seam metal roofs and a shed-roofed front porch give the house a relaxed feeling redolent of the "old" Heights.

H-43 House

H-44 Houses

H-45 House

H-46 House

H-47 House

H-48 Sterling Heights

H-49 House

H-50 Crane House

H-52 Heights Playground

H-47
House
726 E. 8th Avenue
2009, Natalye Appel + Associates Architects

Inserting a 3-story house on what had been a street of 1-story bungalows required considerable spatial and material tact. Gabled roofs with overhanging eaves and diagonal struts, a stepped section, lapped wood siding, and even a front porch acknowledge what the neighborhood used to be. The carport-pass through introduces a new type of indoor-outdoor transitional space. Next door at 730 E. 8th is a steel-framed and paneled house by Cameron Armstrong (2010).

H-48
Sterling Heights
600 block E. 7½ Avenue
1994

After the Garden District, why not? Anything does go in Houston, including the neo-Heights, with a selection of late 19th- and early 20th-century American house prototypes conveniently clustered on a cul-de-sac developed by Steve Waters for his Sterling Victorian Homes company.

H-49
House
614 Columbia Street
2001, Carlos Jiménez

Vivid green-painted stucco walls give this otherwise subdued 2-story house a bold presence. The street-facing garage wing is offset in plan, shielding the rear side garden from the street.

H-50
Crane House
448 Columbia Street
2001, Rogers + Labarthe

John Rogers and Suzanne Labarthe cite the corner store as a precedent for this cubic, 2-story, steel-framed house faced externally with structural clay tile block. There is even a dedicatory plaque centered on the front elevation commemorating the owners' dog.

H-51
Chadwick House
610 E. 5th Avenue
1992, Carlos Jiménez

This economical tower house is a condensation of the Heights's wood cottage vernacular, projected vertically to take advantage of stunning views of the downtown skyline that existed before adjacent townhouse development obliterated them.

H-52
Heights Playground
700 block Heights Boulevard
1996, Leathers & Associates

Shapes, materials, and colors identify this action-adventure playground as the work of the Ithaca, New York, architect Robert Leathers. It was built in Donovan Park in customary Leathers fashion by community volunteers in an intensive, week-long construction session.

H-53
All Saints Catholic Church
1002 Harvard Street
1927, Frederick B. Gaenslen

Gaenslen, a San Antonio architect, designed a number of Roman Catholic churches in Houston during the 1920s. All Saints was the largest of these. Its French Romanesque detail is very attenuated.

H-51 Chadwick House

H-53 All Saints Catholic Church

H-54 Milroy House

H-55 Houston Heights City Hall and Fire Station

H-56 Koelsch Gallery

H-57 Townhouses

H-58 House

H-54
Milroy House
1102 Heights Boulevard
c 1896

The suburban town of Houston Heights was laid out in 1891 by the Omaha & South Texas Land Company, a syndicate of investors from Omaha, Nebraska. Its street grid was bisected by a grand avenue, Heights Boulevard. Although the Heights was envisioned as an industrial, working-class suburb, a number of large houses were built along Boulevard (as the street was called in its early years) by individuals connected with the development company. This is the only one of those houses that survives. It was built speculatively by Henry F. MacGregor and sold to John A. Milroy, a company official who served as mayor of Houston Heights. (The Heights was an independent municipality from 1896 until 1918, when it allowed itself to be annexed by Houston.) Margaret Culbertson's research indicates that the design is adapted from Design No. 30 in the *Cottage Souvenir No. 2* of 1891, a pattern book by the Knoxville architect George F. Barber.

H-55
Houston Heights City Hall and Fire Station
[now Houston Heights Association]
107 West 12th Avenue
1915, A. C. Pigg

The consolidation of municipal offices with a fire station gave rise to a distinctive public building type that became widespread in small Texas towns during the 1920s. This is a very early example of this type. The Houston Heights Association, the neighborhood community organization, begun in 1973, leased and rehabilitated the City Hall and Fire Station (1997), then bought it from the City of Houston in 2009.

H-56
Koelsch Gallery
703 Yale Street
2006, Dillon Kyle

Kyle built what appears to be only half of a pre-engineered steel warehouse for this art gallery. Interior wood systems are maximally economical, but there is no limit on the wit and sense of style.

H-57
Townhouses
416-418 W. 8th Avenue
2004, Strasser Ragni

A pair of 3-story row houses designed for their occupants, these vertically organized dwellings play red-painted fin walls against the light colored rainscreen that gives the upper part of the houses their diaphanous appearance. Architect-developer Rodolfo Fabre had Strasser Ragni filled the west quadrant of this block with four additional units (2009).

H-58
House
807 Rutland Street
2006, Palmer Brook Schooley Design

An existing wood cottage was expanded with much larger additions that enhance the qualities of spontaneity and idiosyncrasy associated with the Heights.

H-59
Heights Branch, Houston Public Library
1302 Heights Boulevard
1925, J. M. Glover

Glover used big scale to give a sense of presence to this, one of the first two branch libraries constructed in Houston. Italian Renaissance detail, executed in cast stone, marks the entrance bay, which projects slightly forward of the tile-roofed library building. Ray Bailey Architects rehabilitated the building and added a large extension that complements, but does not mimic, the original (1979).

H-59 Heights Branch, Houston Public Library

H-60 Woodward House

H-61 Heights Christian Church

H-62 Heights High School

H-63 Banta House

H-64 Heights Transit Center

H-60
Woodward House
[now Houston Zen Center]
1605 Heights Boulevard
1919, Alfred C. Finn

Because the Heights was not an upper-income neighborhood, this spacious, Montrose Boulevard-like Spanish Mission style house, built by the independent oilman, Emerson F. Woodward, still stands out as exceptional. Until the 1950s its site encompassed the entire block front between W. 16th and 17th. The house is now crowded by incompatible construction.

H-61
Heights Christian Church
1703 Heights Boulevard
1927, C. N. Nelson

To judge by the number and prominence of its churches, the Heights seems to have been an exceptionally pious community. The Christian Church is the most outstanding of these religious buildings by virtue of its elevated situation, over-scaled, slightly chunky proportions, and the stone Doric column screen with which Nelson decorated the exterior.

H-62
Heights High School
[now Alexander Hamilton Middle School]
139 East 20th Avenue
1920, Maurice J. Sullivan

Sullivan was serving as official architect for the Houston city government when he designed this school, the quintessential suburban public building type of the 1920s. It terminates the vista at the north end of Heights Boulevard and is decorated with Tudor detail.

H-63
Banta House
119 East 20th Avenue
1918

A 2-story concrete porch, consisting of a stepped roof parapet, thick, tapered columns, and cut out balusters, gives this 2-story brick house an archaic appearance. This was not an uncommon trait for Texas buildings of the 1900-1920 period, when historically derived stylistic images were deliberately rejected in favor of various kinds of progressive experimentation. The house was built for the candy manufacturer, Jonathan E. Banta.

H-64
Heights Transit Center
East 20th Avenue
and North Main Street
1992, Rey de la Reza

The steel shed canopy of this Metro bus transit center evokes 19th-century train platform canopies to acknowledge the historic architectural identity of the Heights.

H-65
Mansfield House
1802 Harvard Street
1899

This Victorian towered villa is a variation on the house at 1102 Heights Boulevard. One of the remaining grand houses in the Heights, it has been restored by the architect Bart Truxillo. Here, however, the Heights's real Victorian architecture is at risk of being overwhelmed by *faux* Victorians, exemplified by 1648 Harvard (1992, Sterling Victorian Homes). At the north end of the 1800 block, reaffirming the characteristic modesty of the Heights, is the bungalow of the Heights Women's Club (1912) at 1846 Harvard.

H-65 Mansfield House

H-66 Heights Church of Christ

H-67 Second Church of Christ, Scientist

H-68 Schleser House

H-69 John H. Reagan Senior High School

H-70 Columbia House

H-66
Heights Church of Christ
120 East 16th Avenue
1925, Alfred C. Finn

Rejecting conventional religious imagery, Finn detailed this small, but imposing, box-like church with an extremely reduced neo-Georgian vocabulary. The location of the nave atop a raised basement was characteristic of Protestant churches in the 1910s and '20s, as can be seen time and again in the Heights.

H-67
Second Church of Christ, Scientist
1400 Harvard Street
1920

In a part of town where the bungalow was the predominant house type of the 1910s and '20s, it seems only suitable that there should be a bungalow church. When the congregation found it was unable to maintain the church, it sold the property to developer Steve Waters. He detached the church's educational wing and rehabilitated it as a house. He built a florid neo-Victorian house in what had been the church's parking lot and transformed the church into another a house (1996). The Second Church of Christ, Scientist, has lost some of its earlier architectural innocence, but the building does survive.

H-68
Schleser House
1123 Harvard Street
1912

Harvard contains the largest concentration of rehabilitated houses of any street in the Heights. This "Alamo" bungalow, the most substantial and elaborate of its kind in Houston, is one of the most notable of these houses. It was built by Joseph Schleser, a brick contractor, for his own family.

H-69
John H. Reagan Senior High School
401 East 13th Avenue
1927, John F. Staub and Louis A. Glover, William Ward Watkin, consulting architect

The Tudor style of 16th-century England was a favorite for educational buildings from the 1890s-1920s. As is to be expected, Staub applied it to this rationally planned school building with great aplomb. The original building has been outflanked with numerous additions, none of which is comparable in quality to the original.

H-70
Columbia House
1436 Columbia Street
2007, Dillon Kyle

By subdividing the house into thin wings offset in both section and plan around an interior courtyard, Kyle deftly inserted it into a block front of older, smaller houses. Asymmetrical roof gables sustain the neighborhood rhythms, while giving the house its distinguishing point of difference.

H-71
Arlington Court
300 East 14th Avenue
1985, William F. Stern & Associates

Taut, rounded bays, high-pitched roofs, and pale lavender-colored stucco walls distinguish this complex of 18 row houses, aligned along a central greensward. Houses turn their backs to the street, and the complex is secured from within. But Stern handled these attributes with such delicacy that the complex does not project a paranoid or forbidding aspect. The gatehouse, facing East 14th, is a tribute to the Scottish Arts and Crafts architect, Charles Rennie Mackintosh. Next door to Arlington Court, at 1317 Arlington, is the brightly painted and profusely landscaped studio of the artist Sharon Kopriva. Visible from the 14th and Arlington intersection is the Schauer Filling Station at 1400 Oxford, a classic vernacular shed gas station (1929).

H-71 Arlington Court

H-72 Immanuel Lutheran Church

H-73 Drumheller House

H-74 House

H-75 Studio-Shed Building

H-76 House

H-72
Immanuel Lutheran Church
306 East 15th Avenue
1926, 1932

This small church, raised on a high basement, exhibits the hard-edged planar interpretation of Gothic architecture characteristic of the 1920s and '30s. It is handsomely finished and detailed. Long unused, but still owned by the congregation, the church was on the verge of being demolished in 2010 when the pleas of preservationists persuaded the congregation to reconsider, a reprieve rare in Houston.

H-73
Drumheller House
1525 Cortlandt Street
c 1911

This is one of the most intact Craftsman bungalows in the Heights.

H-74
House
1233 Allston Street
2006, Anthony E. Frederick

A contemporary interpretation of the Louisiana Creole cottage.

H-75
Studio-Shed Building
1226 Waverly Street
2007, Stern and Bucek Architects

This narrow, shed-roofed, 2-story building is a storage shed, an artist's studio, and a residential unit—a mixed-use program set serenely among small cottages.

H-76
House
1435 Rutland Street
1996, Gary Eades

Eades's postmodern rendition of a turreted Victorian house is intensely vertical. Note the tin-clad back building.

H-77
House
1512 Rutland Street
2009, Parra Design Group

To take its place among neighboring cottages without drawing attention to itself, this linear house, its narrow end facing the street, employs a monopitch roof. Architect Camilo Parra included a screened porch overlooking the generous side garden.

H-78
Moeller House
1528 Tulane Street
c 1899

This diminutive wooden house was built by Frederick Moeller, a carpenter who worked for the Houston & Texas Central Railroad. It was imaginatively rehabilitated by Val Glitsch.

H-79
House
1536 Tulane Street
2003, Robert Burrow

Counterposed shed roofs shelter a complex house that is part existing and part new.

H-78 Moeller House

H-79 House

H-77 House

H-80 House

H-81 House

H-82 Heights Theater

H-83 Harold's

H-84 Zagst House

H-80
House
1501 Allston Street
2005, Murphy Mears Architects

Using a combination of cementitious planks and panels, Murphy Mears and their associate, Larry Albert, produced a house that is open inside but, from the outside, holds its corner location with confident rectangular solids.

H-81
House
1515 Ashland Street
2002, Rob Civitello, Local Architect

This metal-faced house is composed with eccentric shapes that suggest its unusual and varied interior spaces.

H-82
Heights Theater
341 West 19th Avenue
1934; 1988, Robert Morris

West 19th is the Heights's retail district, and its architectural centerpiece is this neighborhood movie theater, rescued from dereliction and rehabilitated by architect Robert Morris, artist Sharon Kopriva, and her husband Gus. Its neo-Modernistic exuberance animates the street. In 1988 West 19th became one of the first two urban demonstration projects of the Texas Historical Commission's Main Street program, leading to its economic revitalization through the conservation and reuse of its historic buildings. At 250 W. 19th, occupying an existing storefront, is Claire Smith and Russell Murrell's restaurant, Shade (2003), featuring spare, elegant modern interiors.

H-83
Harold's
350 West 19th Avenue
1960, Brooks & Brooks

This pert 1- and 2-story commercial building is W. 19th's outstanding modern landmark. The sales area, treated as a glass pavilion, is differentiated from the closed service block. Note the fountain and planter on the Ashland side of the building.

H-84
Zagst House
347 West 20th Avenue
1904

The 2-story curved veranda of this wooden house, set back in an enclosed yard, communicates the homey, old-fashioned ambience of the Heights. The property was originally owned by Stephen R. Zagst, a carpenter and builder.

H-85
Oriental Textile Mill
[now Clocktower Lofts]
611-631 West 22nd Avenue
c 1892
2003-08, Nonya Grenader

Built by the developers of the Heights and originally housing a mattress factory, this brick industrial building was located in the Heights's factory district in the town's northwest corner. It bespeaks the Omaha & South Texas Land Company's conception of the Heights as an industrial suburb. The original building core has had numerous additions, of which the most visible is the 6-story clock tower facing Lawrence Street. During the 2000s, the complex was incrementally rehabilitated by architect Grenader, who transformed it into a mixed-use residential and commercial complex. Among the occupants is Scott Tycer's restaurant, Textile, at 611 W. 22nd with interiors by Ferenc Dreef of Kollectiv (2008).

H-86
House
921 East 25th Avenue
2009, Rogers + Labarthe

In the subdivision of Sunset Heights, an existing workshop building was rehabilitated as a secondary residence, complementing it with a new, freestanding 1-story house faced with structural clay tile, metal paneling, and a cementitious plank rainscreen.

H-86 House

H-85 Oriental Textile Mill

H-87 Dvořák House

H-88 General Mercantile Store Building

H-89 House

H-90 Shady Acres Village

H-91 Live Oak Friends Meeting House

H-87
Dvořák House
1013 East 26th Avenue
c 1912

Václav Dvořák, the first occupant, was a brick mason and the presumed builder of this cottage, which is constructed entirely of cast-in-place concrete. It lies in Sunset Heights, one of a number of "heights" subdivisions developed around the edges of Houston Heights.

H-88
General Mercantile Store Building
7402 North Main Street
c 1920

This decaying wood commercial building lies in Independence Heights, another of the "heights" subdivisions. It was developed in 1910 by the Wright Land Company, a real estate firm that developed and marketed real estate to African-American Houstonians through the 1940s. According to the National Register nomination for this property, the mercantile company was initially operated by two residents of Independence Heights, W. R. Knox and H. S. Dotson. Between 1915-1929, Independence Heights was a separately incorporated town, with elected African-American officials and its own public school district. As with Houston Heights and other working-class municipalities, Independence Heights' citizens voluntarily surrendered the town's charter of incorporation to be annexed by Houston when the town could no longer afford to comply with state requirements for mandatory municipal services. In 1997 the townsite was listed in the National Register of Historic Places through the efforts of local residents.

H-89
House
914 West 23rd Avenue
2004, Carl Brunsting

Shady Acres, just west of the northwest corner of Houston Heights, is rustic in feeling with a mixture of small houses, commercial properties, and apartments. This began to change drastically in the 2000s as new residential construction surged in this and other historically working class Houston neighborhoods. This 2-story, shed roofed house, which presents its short end to the street, is more considerate of the neighborhood fabric than most of the new construction. Brunsting preserved a sense of the neighborhood's spatial openness and existing shade trees by holding the house to one side of its lot.

H-90
Shady Acres Village
1301-1311 West 25th Avenue
2007, Cisneros Design Studio

Working with an existing plat that called for row houses to be aligned to either side of a central driveway spanning between W. 25th and W. 26th, Tim Cisneros organized these wood houses to face and spatially frame the open space of the Quaker meeting house next door.

H-91
Live Oak Friends Meeting House
1318 West 26th Avenue
2001, Leslie K. Elkins;
James Turrell, artist

Art dealer Hiram Butler was instrumental in bringing Houston's Quaker meeting together with artist James Turrell and architect Leslie Elkins to produce a meeting house incorporating one of Turrell's *Skyspaces*—a 12-foot-long aperture in the ceiling of the meeting room that is completely open to the sky. Elkins's meeting house makes Quaker plainness and simplicity architecturally transcendent. The meeting house is open to the public on Fridays, half an hour before sunset (if it's not raining) to experience Turrell's skyspace.

H-92
Houses
1506 West 26th Avenue
2004, MC²

Brothers Chung and Choung Nguyen, principals of MC², designed a 2-house complex in Shady Acres for a multigenerational family of Vietnamese immigrants. The houses are focused on a glass pavilion, centered in a shallow reflecting pool and roofed with a creased and curved roof plate. With imagination, the Nguyen brothers translated Vietnamese domestic practice to a Houston vernacular setting, making architecture out of this cultural intersection.

H-93
House
2021 West 14-1/2 Avenue
1999, Rob Civitello, Local Architect

Located at the end of a dead-end street that runs into the White Oak Bayou linear park, this is a 1-story, shed-like house. Its respectful, rustic tendencies were lost on subsequent residential construction, which chokes off and privatizes distant views of the bayou landscape.

H-92 Houses

H-93 House

West End

West End

Tour H-2

The West End represents a familiar pattern of 19th-century American urban growth. It comprises a chain of working class neighborhoods that pushed westward from Houston's core along the line of the Houston & Texas Central Railroad, which lies just north of, and parallel to, Washington Avenue and the old streetcar lines. This pattern of incremental extension was encouraged (in classic 20th-

century Houston fashion) by suburban distension, exemplified by the platting in 1888 of the A. Brunner Addition considerably beyond the western reach of Houston's horse-and-mule-drawn streetcar system. Electrification and extension of the streetcar system in connection with the development of Houston Heights in 1891 were necessary to facilitate the settlement of Brunner. But it became the anchor in this surge of western growth, which undergoes a highly visible transformation at Wescott Drive. There, occupation by a higher income population is apparent in the modern, deed-restricted subdivisions developed on the east edge of Memorial Park in the 1930s, when the west side of Houston began to replace the South End as the new zone of affluent residential development thanks to the success of River Oaks.

94. **Taggart Park Townhouses,** 6402 Taggart Avenue
95. **House,** 6522 Haskell Street
96. **House,** 6420 Haskell Street
97. **Townhouses,** 6322–6320 Haskell Street
98. **House,** 202 Crestwood Drive
199. **House,** 6024 Memorial Drive
100. **House,** 17-A Crestwood Drive
101. **House,** 103 Glenwood Drive
102. **Lora Jean Kilroy Visitor and Education Center,** 1 Westcott Street
103. **House,** 5715 Logan Lane
104. **Beer Can House,** 222 Malone Avenue
105. **House,** 256 Malone Avenue
106. **House,** 604 Malone Avenue
107. **Houses,** 702–704 Malone Avenue
108. **Houses,** 5815–5811 Rose Street
109. **House,** 802 Knox Street
110. **House,** 1211 Malone Avenue
111. **House,** 1302 Knox Street
112. **House,** 6013 Clyde Street
113. **New World Museum,** 5230 Center Street
114. **Washington Plaza,** 5555 Washington Avenue
115. **House,** 619 Asbury Street
116. **House,** 615 Asbury Street
117. **House,** 311 Asbury Street
118. **House,** 5402 Crooms Street
119. **Townhouses,** 119–131 Detering Street
120. **House,** 237 Reinicke Street
121. **Townhouses,** 245–301 Reinicke Street
122. **House,** 5421 Dickson Street
123. **National Art Services Company Building,** 5411 Feagan Street
124. **House,** 5423 Gibson Street
125. **House,** 5419 Blossom Street
126. **House,** 5420 Floyd Street
127. **House,** 5303 Floyd Street
128. **House,** 5228 Blossom Street
129. **Shadow Design Studio,** 5218 Gibson Street
130. **House,** 5201 Gibson Street
131. **House,** 414 Reinerman Street
132. **House,** 5201 Blossom Street
133. **Love House,** 5019 Blossom Street
134. **Houses,** 5011–5015 Blossom Street
135. **Tin Houses,** 5001–5003 Blossom Street
136. **Urban Meridian Group Building,** 4808 Gibson Street
137. **House,** 4522 Gibson Street
138. **House,** 4509 Feagan Street
139. **House,** 4401 Gibson Street
140. **Butler Gallery,** 4520 Blossom Street
141. **House and Workshop,** 4706 Lillian Street
142. **Townhouses,** 712–716 Parker Street
143. **Lauricella Grocery Store Building,** 701 Patterson Avenue
144. **Grove Court Townhouses,** 4318–4326 Floyd Street
145. **Avalon Place Projects Houses,** 4307–4311 Center Street

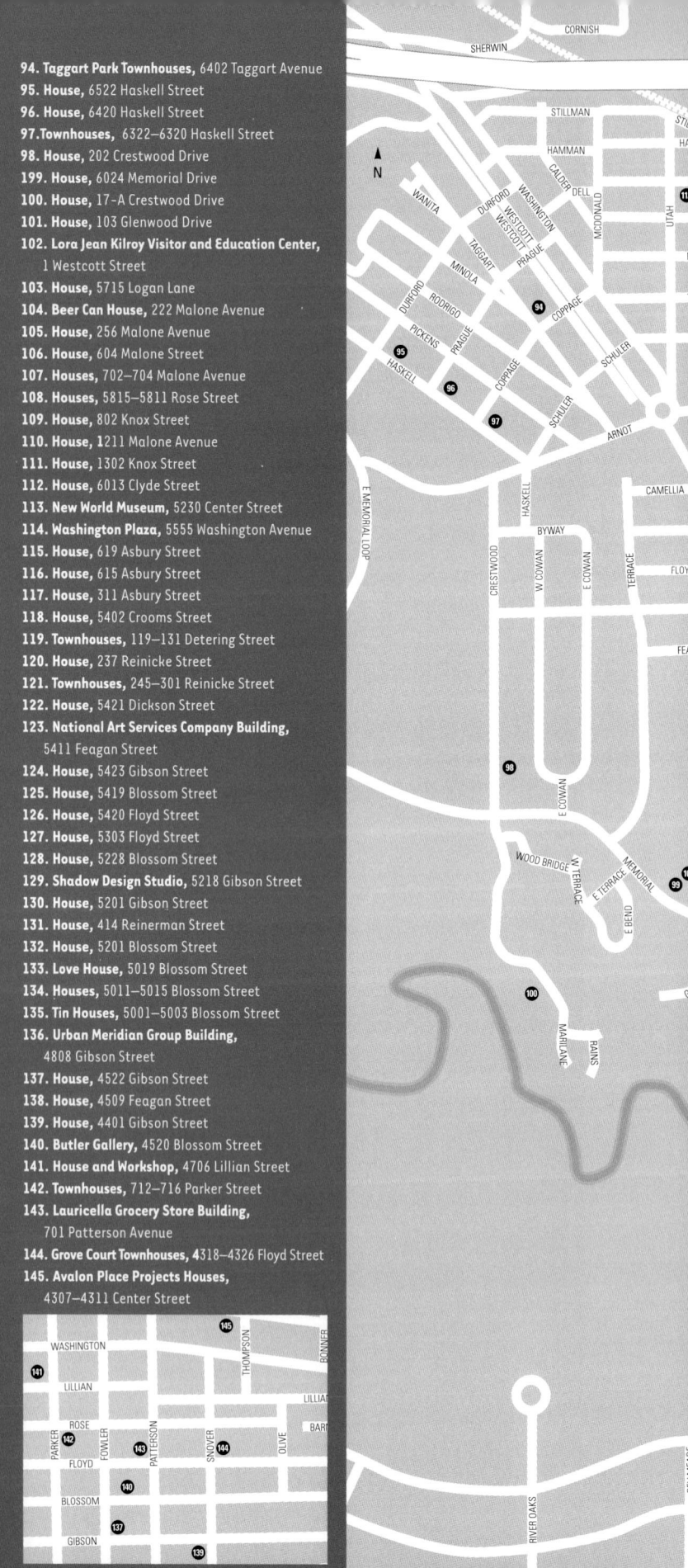

H-94 Taggart Park Townhouses

H-95 House

H-96 House

H-97 Townhouses

H-98 House

H-94
Taggart Park Townhouses
6402 Taggart Avenue
1984, Arquitectonica

Taking advantage of a square corner site, Arquitectonica grouped these four houses in an unorthodox arrangement: the blue house is L-shaped in plan and wraps around the pink house at the corner. Perforated screen walls and pastel colors allow these houses to exert a big presence on the street.

H-95
House
6522 Haskell Street
1994, Natalye Appel

Facing Memorial Park in the Camp Logan Addition (named for the World War I Army training camp that occupied the east portion of Memorial Park), this is a compact house of varying shapes.

H-96
House
6420 Haskell Street
2006, MC^2

Diagonally inclined steel columns enable this tall, thin house to lean out over a fault line beneath this lot in the Camp Logan Addition.

H-97
Townhouses
6322-6320 Haskell Street
1995, Natalye Appel

Appel staged this row house complex as a series of stepped and turned planes. From the street the houses read as a unified structure, but within each townhouse varied spaces are illuminated with generous side lighting. The Office of James Burnett was the landscape architect.

H-98
House
202 Crestwood Drive
2003, MC²

Chung and Choung Nguyen designed this dramatically white, 3-story house to take advantage of views of the thick tree canopy of Memorial Park across the street, themes they repeated at 302 Crestwood (2005). The Office of James Burnett was the landscape architect.

H-99
House
6024 Memorial Drive
2010, Ike Kligerman Barkley

Slotted onto a residual site facing busy Memorial Drive, this tall, graceful, neo-Classical design is the second house New York architects Ike Kligerman Barkley produced for their Houston clients.

H-100
House
17-A Crestwood Drive
1997, Ken Tate

Louisiana architect Tate built his reputation with traditional architectural designs that reprise Southern historical themes. This hipped roofed house is turned, Charleston style, on its long lot, with a veranda running along the south side elevation. Garden parterres step down toward Buffalo Bayou. Most of the once bucolic Crestwood Drive has been wrecked with grotesque new residential construction.

H-101
House
103 Glenwood Drive
2007, Robert Burrow

Faced with green stucco and dark wood, this linear house slides sinuously between the tall pine trees characteristic of Memorial Park and the Memorial area.

H-100 House

H-101 House

H-99 House

H-103 House

H-104 Beer Can House

H-105 House

H-106 House

H-107 House

H-102
Lora Jean Kilroy Visitor and Education Center
Bayou Bend Collection and Gardens of the Museum of Fine Arts, Houston
1 Westcott Street
2010, Leslie Elkins Architecture and Kendall/Heaton Associates

Bayou Bend, the Hogg family's country house in River Oaks, is entered by the public from the Hogg Bird Sanctuary, which lies on the north bank of Buffalo Bayou, across from the gardens of Bayou Bend. Forty-five years after the house and gardens were opened to the public, the administrative offices and visitor center in the Bayou Bend garage were outgrown. The Museum of Fine Arts built this 2-story, 18,000-SF building at the Westcott-Memorial intersection to give Bayou Bend a degree of public visibility it had not previously possessed. Rather than referencing the architecture of Bayou Bend, Elkins designed a modern, steel-framed building faced with corrugated steel siding and generous expanses of glass. McDugald-Steele was the landscape architect.

H-103
House
5715 Logan Lane
1995, Taft Architects

A tall, box-like house, its upper reaches are open to the thick tree canopy blanketing the edge of Buffalo Bayou.

H-104
Beer Can House
222 Malone Avenue
1974, John Milkovisch

Milkovisch, a retired upholsterer who had worked for the Southern Pacific Railway, proudly claimed to have drunk the beer from every can he used to festoon his modest house. The grounds also came in for considerable improvement. The result is an enthusiastic paean to the virtues of recycling. Milkovisch's extensive use of aluminum qualifies the Beer

Can House as the mother of all tin houses, the Houston architectural phenomenon that brought the West End to architectural prominence in the 1990s. After Milkovisch's death in 1988, his widow lived in the house until the year before her death in 2002. The Milkovisch estate sold the property to the Orange Show Center for Visionary Art, which completed a restoration of the site in 2008 and now opens the house and grounds to the public. The Beer Can House lies in the West End, a blue-collar neighborhood that predates the Memorial Drive neighborhoods alongside the park and the bayou.

H-105
House
256 Malone Avenue
2001, Rob Civitello, Local Architect

The diagonally inclined walls of this steel-faced house were designed to defer to trees on the site.

H-106
House
604 Malone Street
1997, Cameron Armstrong

On a tight corner site Armstrong designed this house to be very closed at street level while spiraling spatially upward toward the light.

H-107
Houses
702-704 Malone Avenue
1999, Cochran & Cochran

Architects Catherine and Stephen Cochran designed and developed a pair of steel-paneled houses inserted onto a single lot in the Rice Military Addition.

H-108
Houses
5815-5811 Rose Street
1997, Donna Kacmar, Christopher Craig, and Mary Ann Young

Three architects pooled their resources and talent to build this row of extremely affordable houses. The ground floor and party walls are of exposed concrete block construction; the upper floors are surfaced with cementitious panels.

H-108 Houses

H-102 Lora Jean Kilroy Visitor and Education Center

H-109 House

H-110 House

H-111 House

H-112 Monotech House

H-113 New World Museum

H-109
House
802 Knox Street
1992, Val Glitsch

Roof shapes and window alignments distinguish between the residential and studio portions of this artist's house, which became the model for subsequent houses Glitsch designed that opened to side gardens.

H-110
House
1211 Malone Avenue
1999, Cameron Armstrong

Armstrong pulled the components of this Galvalume-surfaced house and studio complex apart to shape a sequence of outdoor spaces.

H-111
House
1302 Knox Street
2002, Savino Architecture

Monica Savino rehabilitated an existing cottage as a professional work space, then added a back building facing Schuler to contain the site's primary dwelling, as well as parked cars and a home workshop—a mixture of uses that is not out of character with the rest of the Woodcrest Addition.

H-112
Monotech House
6013 Clyde Street
2005, Peter Jay Zweig with Philip Johnson

Zweig enlisted the elderly Johnson as design consultant for this introverted courtyard house, which Zweig describes as a 21st-century version of Johnson's mid-20th-century Glass House. Zweig built the house with the Monotech Building System he developed—wall panels of expanded polystyrene that are transformed into a rigid, load-bearing monocoque structure when sprayed on both sides with a half-inch of Zweig's concrete blend material, Monocrete.

H-113
New World Museum
5230 Center Street
2009, Armando Palacios and Cinda Ward

Architect Ward and restaurateur Palacios transformed a former door factory into an art and performance space with orange paint and an instinct for spare, serene landscape spaces. Palacios initiated this minimal approach in his earlier transformation of one of the working-class bungalows of the Moy Studer Addition at 5229 Nett, which he painted *all* white.

H-114
Washington Plaza
5555 Washington Avenue
2005, Rogers + Labarthe

Although a conventional Houston strip shopping center with front loaded parking, the block-long Washington Plaza achieves dignity with its coherent center-and-ends spatial organization, its soberly colorful facing of dark red clay tile block, and projecting rooftop pergolas. Rogers + Labarthe also designed the Durham Center retail complex at 1711 Durham (2004) and Cyclone Anaya's Mexican Kitchen at 1710 Durham (2004).

H-115
House
619 Asbury Street
1996, Rob Civitello, Local Architect

Civitello shaped this L-plan house with sculptural subtlety. It originally wrapped around a huge tree on its double-lot site; the living room wing was floated on steel beams to ride above the tree's root system. Just up Asbury at 5600-5606 Rose are three townhouses by MC² Architects (2002).

H-116
House
615 Asbury Street
1999, Rob Civitello, Local Architect

Subtle changes in wall plane give this boxy, 2-story house its taut spatiality. Civitello played the house's corrugated steel siding off against the clay tile block parking enclosure.

H-117
House
311 Asbury Street
1996, 2002, 2011,
Cameron Armstrong

This is the tin house version of one of Frank Lloyd Wright's Usonian houses: a very small family dwelling that feels quite expansive by virtue of spatial ingenuity. Armstrong has added onto the house twice, transforming it from one to two stories.

H-114 Washington Plaza

H-115 House

H-116 House

H-117 House

H-118 House

H-119 Townhouses

H-120 House

H-121 Townhouses

H-122 House

H-118
House
5402 Crooms Street
1996, Brave/Architecture

This is a very economical tin house that is quite open to its site, maximizing use of limited lot space while preserving privacy from the street.

H-119
Townhouses
119-131 Detering Street
1997, Larry S. Davis & Associates

These townhouses represent a deftly proportioned prototype for a row house scheme that Davis, who is both architect and developer, repeated elsewhere in the West End before exporting it to Houston's South End-Midtown district.

H-120
House
237 Reinicke Street
1997, Frank Zeni

The colonnade on the south side of this house is a Zeni signature. Next door at 239 is a sculptural house by MC^2 Architects (2005); next door to that is a 2-building residential compound at 5502 Lacy by Natalye Appel + Associates Architects (2002).

H-121
Townhouses
245-301 Reinicke Street
1997, Linda Steffy and
Mohammed Nasr

This pair of freestanding tin houses combine zinc and aluminum-coated steel with wood facing.

H-122
House
5421 Dickson Street
1992, Natalye Appel

This free-spirited house is spatially spontaneous. It respected the unpretentious scale and demeanor of neighboring houses, almost all of which have since been demolished and replaced by new construction that does not appreciate the virtue of modesty.

H-123
National Art Services Company Building
5411 Feagan Street
1996, Palmer Brook Schooley Design

Schooley made the most of a small addition to a warehouse, giving prominence to the office wing with an expressively profiled roof. The West End is a neighborhood of mixed uses, with warehouses and light-manufacturing enterprises, such as this, scattered among the neighborhood's wood cottages.

H-124
House
5423 Gibson Street
1993, Cameron Armstrong

Taut geometries and the play of plane and void energize this tin house. Artist Terrell James was responsible for its architecturally integral, acid-treated steel panel "paintings." Alice Y. Liddell and Timothy Patout planted the luxuriant garden with indigenous vegetation.

H-125
House
5419 Blossom Street
1995, Cameron Armstrong

Set as close to the street as possible, this coated steel and shingle-surfaced house has the luxury of expansive side and rear gardens.

H-126
Tempietto Zeni
5420 Floyd Street
1990, Frank Zeni

Italian-born artist and architect Zeni built his house and studio inside this outrageous 3½-story shed, decorated with colossal Ionic columns and acroteria.

H-126 Tempietto Zeni

H-124 House

H-125 House

H-123 National Art Services Company Building

H-127 House

H-129 Shadow Design Studio

H-130 House

H-131 House

H-132 House

H-127
House
5303 Floyd Street
1996, Cameron Armstrong

The tin houses made the West End so visible as desirable and economical real estate that, in the mid-1990s, the Soho syndrome ensued. Land values skyrocketed and developers moved in. The results (both architectural and demographic) are horrifying, as the mass of row houses on this large block site attests. This tin house seeks to preserve the élan of what is rapidly becoming a vanishing vernacular landscape. Lack of zoning and restrictive covenants made the West End the mixed neighborhood that it was. However absence of controls also meant there was no way to avert the rude transformations that began in the mid-1990s.

H-128
House
5228 Blossom Street
1993, Terry Milam and Paul E. Martin

Milam, a carpenter, built this house; its façades were designed by Martin. Next door at 5218 Blossom the West End Lofts (1998, Larry S. Davis & Associates) consume their site with building and concrete, portending the end of the vernacular landscape that Milam's house celebrates.

H-129
Shadow Design Studio
5218 Gibson Street
1998, Frank Zeni

An art production studio built for James Groff, this steel-framed building confirms the working ethos of the West End.

H-130
House
5201 Gibson Street
1994, Natalye Appel

A tin palace with a vivid yellow tree-like sculpture by Houston artist Lee Littlefield.

H-131
House
414 Reinerman
1994, Murphy Mears Architects

This small house, surfaced with cementitious board, was built to accommodate musical performances.

H-132
House
5201 Blossom Street
2000, Robert Morris

Morris describes this steel-framed, steel-sheathed house as a "living machine" because it was designed to perform sustainable practices. The house's most visually striking elements are its self-supporting steel Quonset roof vaults. The site was landscaped by gardener Camille Waters, who extended the sustainable theme to the landscape. Artist Gertrude Barnstone is responsible for the painted steel sculpture intertwined with the garden gate.

H-128 House

H-133 Love House

H-134 Houses

H-135 Tin Houses

H-136 Urban Meridian Group Building

H-137 House

H-133
Love House
5019 Blossom Street
2004, Nonya Grenader

This meticulously detailed but simple house was designed for the artist Jim Love, whose tubular steel sculpture, *Giant Bird House*, is installed in the back yard. The shed roof and high-set windows hint at the sectional organization of interior space.

H-134
Houses
5011-5015 Blossom Street
2008, Nonya Grenader

Next door to the Love House, Grenader had the opportunity to design a pair of houses that engage her earlier house in a rhythmic juxtaposition of roof slopes, aligned windows, and Galvalume siding. The two newer houses—one with its narrow end to the street, the other with its broad dimension to the street—frame an expansive rear courtyard. Grenader demonstrates the potential for neighborhood spatial continuity that can be attained even with freestanding, single-family houses.

H-135
Tin Houses
5001-5003 Blossom Street
1984, Ian Glennie and
Urban Architecture

Glennie designed this pair of corrugated metal-surfaced townhouses for his associate, Fredericka Hunter, as a tribute to the Roy Avenue Townhouses a block away. His vertically elongated proportions, studio windows, and dramatic exposed stair on the west side make them more visible, and exceptional, within the context of this neighborhood. Hunter coined the name "tin house." In 1974 she and Simone Swan built the first pair of tin houses a block to the west at 507 Roy and Blossom. These were designed by Hunter's brother-in-law, architect Eugene Aubry. Progenitors of the Tin House movement in West

End architecture, they were demolished in 2011. Across Sandman from the Tin Houses at 4916 Gibson is the studio built by artist Karin Broker (1990).

H-136
Urban Meridian Group Building
4808 Gibson Street
2005, Wittenberg Oberholzer

Gordon Wittenberg and Mark Oberholzer produced a live-work building, constructed in two phases and capped by an asymmetrical steel roof vault.

H-137
House
4522 Gibson Street
2001, Steven Paul Dumas

Low, stucco-faced bays and an exuberant porch supported on diagonally inclined pipe columns give this house a retro-modern look.

H-138
House
4401 Gibson Street
c 1895

The Magnolia Grove Addition, on Brunner's east edge, was platted in 1895. Its grandest house was, and remains, this one built by carriage manufacturer Conrad Schwarz.

H-139
House
4509 Feagan Street
2008, Strasser Ragni

Strasser Ragni converted a 1-story warehouse, built of clay tile block and steel bar joists, into an unusual single-family house and gallery. They carved a courtyard out of one corner of the original interior and hoisted a subsidiary box, painted purple, through the roof to accommodate upstairs bedrooms.

H-139 House

H-138 House

H-140 Butler Gallery

H-141 House and Workshop

H-142 Townhouses

H-143 Lauricella Grocery Store Building

H-144 Grove Court Townhouses

H-140
Hiram Butler Gallery
4520 Blossom Street
1989, Phillips/Ryburn

Dallas architect Robert Van Buren designed this precisely detailed wood shed building to fit as unobtrusively as possible into the Brunner neighborhood. Most of the block-front site is used to display sculpture. 601 Patterson is an 1880s-era house restored in 1989 by William H. McDugald, Jr.

H-141
House and Workshop
4706 Lillian Street
2002, ArchitectWorks

Architect Donna Kacmar countered one shed roof with another in this steel-faced house and workshop complex.

H-142
Townhouses
712-716 Parker Street
2003, Strasser Ragni

Three 3-story row houses form a rectangular plane of stucco modulated with rectangular window openings and a recessed first floor bays. With minimal architectural effort Strasser Ragni produced a powerful sensation of proportioned composure.

H-143
Lauricella Grocery Store Building
701 Patterson Avenue
1921

A traditional corner grocery store with the proprietor's living quarters above, once common in Southern towns and suburbs of Southern cities.

H-144
Grove Court Townhouses
4318-4326 Floyd Street
1980, Taft Architects

The staggered siting of these six houses permitted the inclusion of both private walled gardens and a central common green, differentiated by undulating walls. The tile detailing retrieves a type of architectural graphics common in Houston in the 1910s and '20s. Interiors at Grove Court consist of open lofts, where daylight and internal vistas create a sense of spaciousness, anticipating interior spatial arrangements that would not become common in Houston for another 15 years.

H-145
Avalon Place Projects Houses
4307-4309 Center Street
2008, Brett Zamore Design

Mark Johnson's Avalon Place Projects commissioned Zamore to produce this pair of 1,250-SF houses based on Zamore's KIT02 standardized design. Behind the cottage at 4311 is Zamore's 400-SF KIT100 version.

H-145 Avalon Place Projects Houses

River Oaks

River Oaks

Tour I-1

Because Houston has grown at ever accelerating rates of diffusion, sites that began on or beyond the edge of town often find themselves migrating closer and closer toward the center. River Oaks, Houston's highest status residential neighborhood, is a case in point. It began not only beyond the edge of Houston in 1924, but on the wrong side of downtown for an ambitious, upper-income garden suburb. The provision of a direct connection to downtown in the form of what is now Allen Parkway, the first in a series of Olmsted-like bayou parkway corridors planned by the landscape architects Hare & Hare for the City of Houston, overcame River Oaks's isolation. By the late 1930s its pre-eminence had become so firmly established that it began to influence development patterns downtown: the first office buildings to be constructed west of the Main Street corridor went up on the cross street that connected Main to Allen Parkway. River Oaks now lies at the geographic center of Houston, with downtown to the east and Post Oak to the west. Privately instituted and administered planning controls, conspicuous amenities, and access were key to River Oaks's success and long-term durability—lessons that over time have been absorbed by developers of nonresidential properties.

1. **Harris County Center for the Retarded,** 3550 West Dallas Avenue
2. **River Oaks Gate Piers,** Kirby Drive and South Shepherd Drive
3. **House,** 901 Kirby Drive
4. **House,** 2 Tiel Way
5. **Kamrath House,** 8 Tiel Way
6. **González House,** 48 Tiel Way
7. **Stude House,** 56 Tiel Way
8. **House,** 1407 Kirby Drive
9. **House,** 2345 Pine Valley Drive
10. **House,** 2127 Troon Road
11. **Rienzi,** 1406 Kirby Drive
12. **Neuhaus House,** 2910 Lazy Lane
13. **House,** 2920 Lazy Lane
14. **Bayou Bend,** 2940 Lazy Lane
15. **House,** 2950 Lazy Lane
16. **Neal House,** 2960 Lazy Lane
17. **Green House,** 2970 Lazy Lane
18. **House,** 2975 Lazy Lane
19. **Ravenna,** 2995 Lazy Lane
20. **Bruton House,** 2929 Inwood Drive
21. **Heyer House,** 2909 Inwood Drive
22. **Young House,** 2126 Pine Valley Drive
23. **Burke House,** 2158 Brentwood Drive
24. **Lamb House,** 2421 Brentwood Drive
25. **Sauer House,** 2229 Inwood Drive
26. **Loy House,** 2105 Inwood Drive
27. **River Oaks Community Center,** 2017–2047 West Gray Avenue
28. **Haddon Street Townhouses,** 2013–2029 Haddon Street
29. **River Oaks Courts,** 2517–2529 Stanmore Drive
30. **Oliver House,** 2508 Pelham Drive
31. **Hubbard House,** 2523 Del Monte Drive
32. **Underwood House,** 2923 Del Monte Drive
33. **Bullington House,** 3023 Del Monte Drive
34. **Redbird House,** 3237 Inwood Drive
35. **House,** 1807 River Oaks Boulevard
36. **Paddock House,** 3229 Groveland Lane
37. **Michael House,** 1903 Bellmeade Road
38. **Dean House,** 1912 Bellmeade Road
39. **Hobby House,** 3202 Huntingdon Place
40. **House,** 3105 Ella Lee Lane
41. **Letzerich House,** 3256 Locke Lane
42. **Childress House,** 3239 Locke Lane
43. **House,** 2526 Bellmeade Road
44. **Lamar-River Oaks Community Center,** 3256–3272 Westheimer Road
45. **Mirabeau B. Lamar Senior High School,** 3325 Westheimer Road
46. **St. John The Divine Church,** 2450 River Oaks Boulevard
47. **Bryan House,** 3315 Ella Lee Lane
48. **Menil House,** 3363 San Felipe Road
49. **Cullen House,** 1620 River Oaks Boulevard
50. **Mott House,** 3325 Inwood Drive
51. **Chew House,** 3335 Inwood Drive
52. **Christie House,** 3358 Inwood Drive
53. **Brown House,** 3363 Inwood Drive
54. **Clayton Summer House,** 3376 Inwood Drive
55. **House,** 3390 Inwood Drive
56. **Sewall House,** 3456 Inwood Drive
57. **Staub House,** 3511 Del Monte Drive
58. **Mellinger House,** 3452 Del Monte Drive
59. **Belt House,** 3451 Del Monte Drive

◀ Map continues on next spread

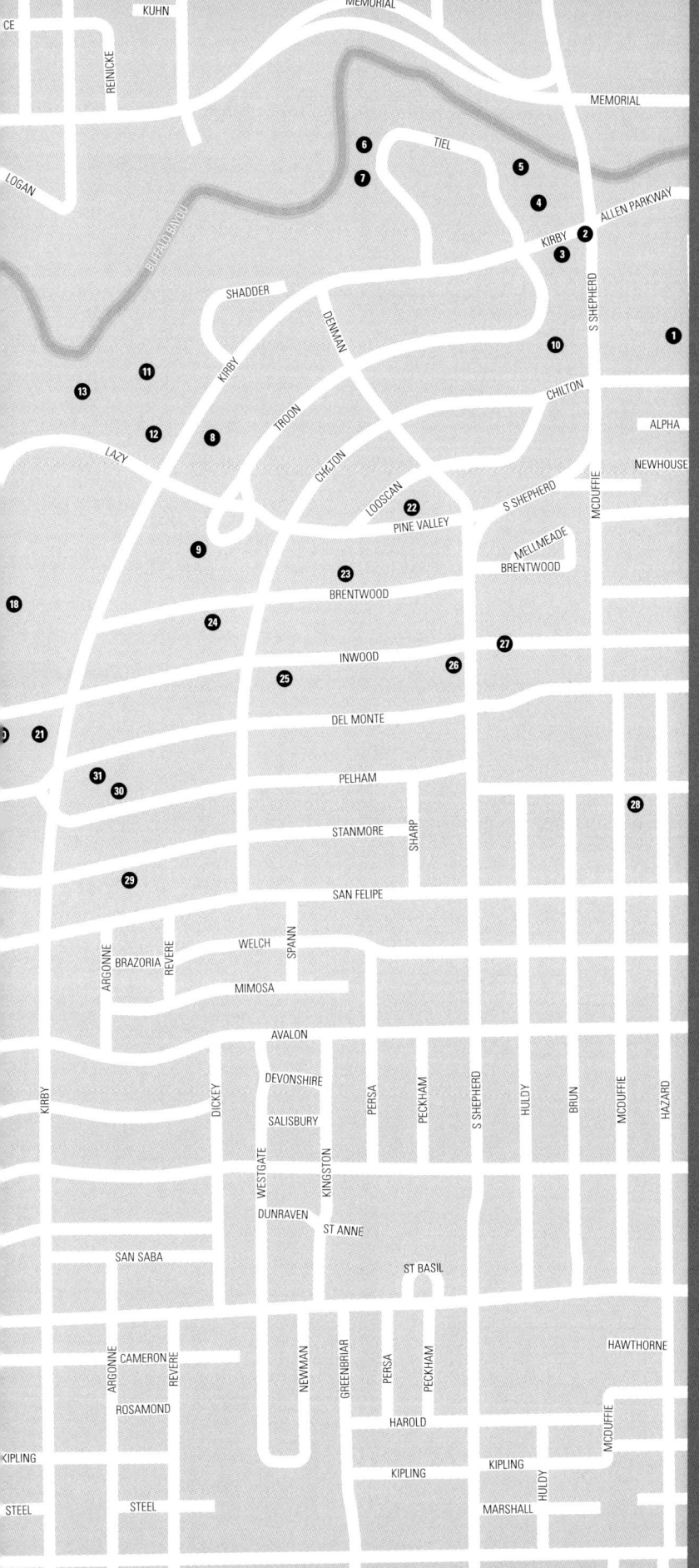

60. **Pinckney House,** 3439 Del Monte Drive
61. **Anderson House,** 3414 Del Monte Drive
62. **House,** 3404 Chevy Chase Drive
63. **Nelms House,** 3391 Sleepyhollow Court
64. **House,** 4401 Sleepyhollow Court
65. **Scurry House,** 1912 Larchmont Road
66. **Austin House,** 3606 Chevy Chase Drive
67. **House,** 3811 Del Monte Drive
68. **Vaughan House,** 3701 Del Monte Drive
69. **House,** 3707 Inwood Drive
70. **House,** 3606 Knollwood Drive
71. **House,** 9 Pine Hill Lane
72. **Anderson House,** 3740 Willowick Road
73. **Turner House,** 3744 Willowick Road
74. **White House,** 3780 Willowick Drive
75. **House,** 3707 Knollwood Drive
76. **House,** 3632 Inverness Drive
77. **House,** 3737 Inverness Drive
78. **House,** 3808 Inverness Drive
79. **Cizik House,** 3971 Inverness Drive
80. **House,** 4007 Inverness Drive
81. **Farfel House,** 18 Westlane Place
82. **House,** 3736 Chevy Chase Drive
83. **Inwood Manor,** 3711 San Felipe Road
84. **House,** 2113 Maconda Lane
85. **House,** 3710 Overbrook Lane
86. **House,** 3702 Ella Lee Lane
87. **House,** 2405 Maconda Lane
88. **House,** 3451 Piping Rock Lane
89. **House,** 3436 Piping Rock Lane
90. **House,** 3459 Overbrook Lane
91. **House,** 3635 Overbrook Lane
92. **House,** 3603 Wickersham Lane
93. **House, 3448 Locke Lane**
94. **Burke House,** 3402 Wickersham Lane
95. **Tatham Art Center, St. John's School,** Westheimer Road and Buffalo Speedway
96. **The Willowick,** 2200 Willowick Road
97. **House,** 4002 Meadow Lake Lane
98. **House,** 4002 Piping Rock Lane
99. **House,** 2019 Drexel Drive
100. **Crate & Barrel Building,** 4000 Westheimer Road
101. **House,** 4002 Chatham Lane
102. **House,** 4029 Chatham Lane
103. **4311 Bettis Apartments,** 4311 Bettis Drive

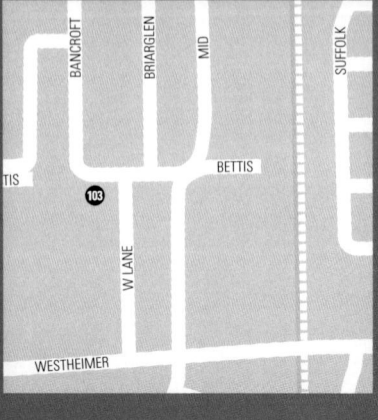

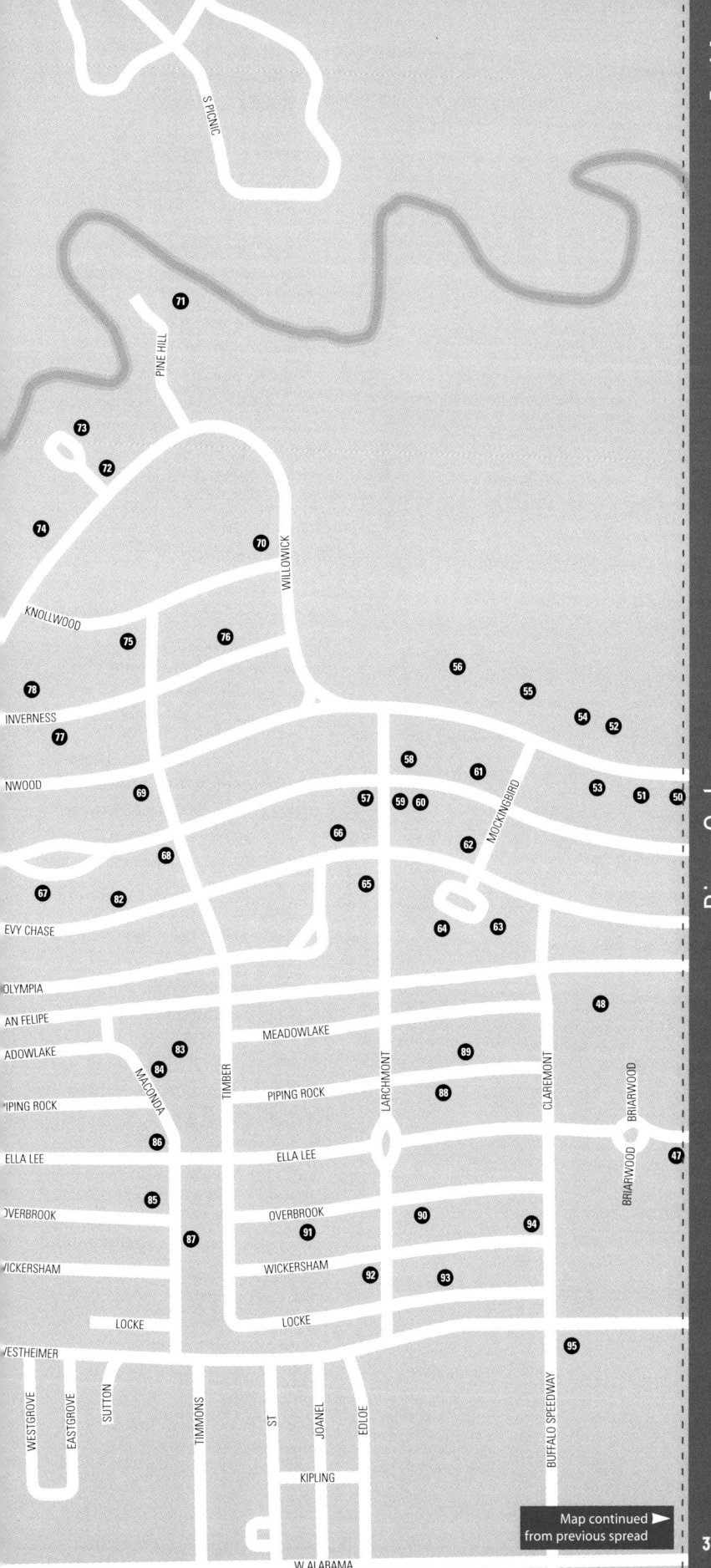

I-1 Harris County Center for the Retarded

I-2 River Oaks Gate Piers

I-3 House

I-4 House

I-1
Harris County Center for the Retarded
[now The Center]
3550 West Dallas Avenue
1966, Howard Barnstone &
Eugene Aubry

This complex of buildings is constructed of overscaled, articulated concrete structural members infilled with brick and glass. The Center backs up to Allen Parkway, where it appears austere and intimidating. A closer look shows that it is actually a village-like campus of elemental buildings linked by covered passageways on a sloping site. Adjoining the center is the 6-story Cullen Residence Hall (1978, S. I. Morris Associates).

I-2
River Oaks Gate Piers
Kirby Drive and South Shepherd Drive
1926, Charles W. Oliver and
John F. Staub

When Staub's biographer, Howard Barnstone, called these pink stucco-faced piers the "gates of Paradise," he succinctly characterized the status of River Oaks, Houston's most elite residential neighborhood. This pair was built to mark the entrance to River Oaks from the Buffalo Bayou parkway drive now called Allen Parkway, which links the neighborhood directly to downtown Houston. River Oaks was begun in 1924 by lawyer Will C. Hogg, his brother Mike, and their friend Hugh Potter. Hogg envisioned River Oaks as an exemplary planned residential community that would provide a model for the rest of Houston to follow. In Hugh Potter he found the perfect executive to carry this vision into reality. Potter, who bought the Hogg family's interest in the development in 1936, ran the River Oaks Corporation until its dissolution in 1955. He and Herbert A. Kipp, the engineer who laid out the community, oversaw the initial development of its entire 1,100 acres. Despite Hogg's advocacy of civic planning, River Oaks did not set a Houston pattern. Instead it became the exception to Houston's reputation for unplanned expansion and a much-coveted reward for those who profited from that expansion.

I-3
House
901 Kirby Drive
2003, Ike Kligerman Barkley

New York architect Joel Barkley adapted the neo-Classical townhouse type associated with early 19th-century Boston or Manhattan for a 3-story house constructed on a small site with a restricted building area. Ike Kligerman Barkley also designed the 3-story house next door at 903 Kirby (1998). Behind its unassuming exterior are interiors that evoke the Winter Palace in St. Petersburg.

I-4
House
2 Tiel Way
1961, MacKie & Kamrath

A concrete block house with Japanese overtones, very closed and secure in appearance. The extraordinary plantings in the rainforest-like ravine are the work of A. J. Ballantyne.

I-5
Kamrath House
8 Tiel Way
1951, MacKie & Kamrath

Karl Kamrath's multi-level house for his own family nestles securely into its sloping site between a deep ravine and Buffalo Bayou. Kamrath internalized this landscape in the spatial organization of the house. Eckbo, Dean, Austin & Williams of Los Angeles was the landscape architect.

I-5 Kamrath House

I-6 González House

I-7 Stude House

I-8 House

I-9 House

I-12 Neuhaus House

I-6
González House
48 Tiel Way
1957, MacKie & Kamrath

Planned on a 30°-60° reflexive geometric grid, this angled house is wedged into a small hillock on its street side, while the rear is opened to a view of Buffalo Bayou. Typical of Kamrath's work, organic decorative detail contributes substantially to the character of the building. Also by MacKie & Kamrath are 59 Tiel Way (1951) and 67 Tiel Way (1951).

I-7
Stude House
56 Tiel Way
1952, Cowell & Neuhaus

This early work of Hugo V. Neuhaus, Jr. bespeaks his training at the Harvard Graduate School of Design in the early 1940s. The small wood house turns into a glass-walled pavilion at the rear, overlooking Buffalo Bayou. Restored by Leslie Elkins in 1992 and expanded by the landscape architects McDugald-Steele (2009).

I-8
House
1407 Kirby Drive
1930, Charles W. Oliver

Oliver, staff architect for the River Oaks Corporation from 1926-1931, designed numerous houses in a wide variety of styles. This picturesque manorial style house, located on an undulating site along the parkway drive that leads downtown, was one of his best. Complementing it next door at 1419 Kirby Drive is a turreted manorial style house built by Katharine B. Mott (1930, Burns & James).

I-9
House
2435 Pine Valley Drive
1993, Taft Architects

The geometries that characterize this exceptional house relate to its oddly configured site, which is much larger at the rear than on the street front. The house's most contained space is the cylindrical motor court, visible from the street. At 2454 Pine Valley Drive, a conventional manorial style house (1929, Charles W. Oliver) is of steel frame construction. The trimly detailed, flat-roofed, glass-walled pavilion at 2252 Troon is by Neuhaus & Taylor (1961).

I-10
House
2127 Troon Road
2000, Jay Baker Architects

Troon Road descends into the remnant of an old ravine in what the River Oaks Corporation called the River Oaks Rock Garden, the elevated landform around which the street divides. This grade change leaves lots on either side of the street raised high above curb level. Baker took advantage of this condition in designing this stucco-faced, tile-roofed house, which brings a trace of the Berkeley Hills to the otherwise insistently flat landscape of Houston. The house at 2125 Troon is also by Jay Baker (2009).

I-10 House

I-11
Rienzi
[now Rienzi Center for European Decorative Arts, Museum of Fine Arts, Houston]
1406 Kirby Drive
1954, Staub, Rather & Howze

Staub's mastery of scale and composition is apparent in this inventive and witty house, a combination Palladian villa and 1950s ranch house set in terrraced gardens by the landscape architect, Ralph Ellis Gunn. The house's owners, Carroll Sterling and Harris Masterson III, bequeathed Rienzi and its collection of European decorative arts to the Museum of Fine Arts, which opened it to the public in 1999. A bulky wing, added in 1972, is not as refined as Staub's original.

I-12
Neuhaus House
2910 Lazy Lane
1950, Cowell & Neuhaus

Hugo V. Neuhaus, Jr. designed this stunning modern house for his own family on half a lot that he split with Harris Masterson. A U-shaped pavilion configured around a garden court, it brought high-style Miesian modernism into the Homewoods section of River Oaks, a stronghold of eclectic design. C. C. "Pat" Fleming was the landscape architect.

I-11 Rienzi

I-13 House

I-16 Neal House

I-13
House
2920 Lazy Lane
1992, Robert A. M. Stern Architects
and Richard Fitzgerald & Partners

A very large reaffirmation of Homewoods's allegiance to the eclectic country house tradition. Not visible from the street.

I-14
Bayou Bend
[now Bayou Bend Collection and Gardens, Museum of Fine Arts, Houston]
2940 Lazy Lane
1928, John F. Staub
with Birdsall P. Briscoe

Will and Mike Hogg built Bayou Bend, which is not visible from the street, for their sister, Ima. Miss Hogg loved the Creole architecture of New Orleans, which led Staub to design this house in a style she called "Latin Colonial," a mixture of early 19th-century American Federal, early 19th-century English Regency, and New Orleanian Spanish Creole. Surfaced with pale pink stucco, green louvered blinds, and a copper roof, it is a tripartite Classical country house that sits with assurance—and warmth—at the end of the entrance drive. Parts of the 14-acre site have been left in their natural condition. The East Terrace Garden was designed by the landscape architect Ruth London; the Diana Garden, a series of terraces that step down from the north side of the house toward Buffalo Bayou, is the work of Fleming & Sheppard. Since 1966 the house has contained the American decorative arts collection of the Museum of Fine Arts, acquired and installed under Miss Hogg's guidance. This comprises an important collection of 17th-, 18th-, and 19th-century American furniture, paintings, silver, and ceramics. Bayou Bend is open to the public with access from 1 Westcott at its intersection with Memorial.

I-15
House
2950 Lazy Lane
2011, Alexander Gorlin

Replacing Dogwoods (1928), a French manorial style house designed for Frederick C. Proctor by Birdsall P. Briscoe with John F. Staub, this immense T-plan house by New York architect Gorlin features lantern-like projecting windows set in wood bays that advance forward of the house's white planar walls. Not visible from the street.
* Not pictured.

I-16
Neal House
2960 Lazy Lane
1933, John F. Staub

J. Robert Neal and his father sold the family business, Maxwell House Coffee, to General Foods in the late 1920s. With his share of the proceeds Neal built this opulent, limestone-faced chateau style house, detailed with Louis XV ornament. It is distended in plan to take advantage of the prevailing breeze. Staub incorporated steel casement windows, which give the house a distinctive '30s edge. Olmsted Brothers designed the gardens.

I-17
Green House
2970 Lazy Lane
1934, James C. Mackenzie with Charles W. Oliver; Birdsall P. Briscoe, consulting architect

Mackenzie, a New York architect, planned this attenuated neo-Georgian house around a landscaped motor court, framing the opposite side of the court with a long garage and service building that mirrors the configuration of the house. The gardens were designed by Louis Frothingham; Ellen B. Shipman designed the camellia garden. Not visible from the street.

I-14 Bayou Bend

I-18 House

I-19 Ravenna

I-20 Bruton House

I-21 Heyer House

I-22 Young House

I-23 Burke House

I-18
House
2975 Lazy Lane
1939, John F. Staub

Staub's version of a Natchez plantation house, blown up to Texan scale. The gardens were designed by Fleming & Sheppard.

I-19
Ravenna
2995 Lazy Lane
1935, John F. Staub

This large but exquisite house is English Georgian on the front and Deep South on the back, where a double-height Tuscan portico overlooks an expansive lawn.

I-20
Bruton House
2929 Inwood Drive
1934, John F. Staub

Staub excelled at austere design, as is evident in this disciplined house, with its elliptical-arched openings and slender chimneys.

I-21
Heyer House
2909 Inwood Drive
1936, John F. Staub

Staub virtually repeated the plan diagram of the house next door in this somewhat more expansive neo-Georgian house, faced with cast aluminum balconies. The allée of Live Oaks on the garden side of the house was laid out by C. C. "Pat" Fleming. Curtis & Windham replaced the original garage with a freestanding Orangerie (2006).

I-22
Young House
2126 Pine Valley Drive
1936, Claude E. Hooton

Hooton, a member of the first generation of Houston architects to be trained locally at Rice, worked in Finland in the late 1920s and was conversant with Nordic modern architecture. This is one of the best of a series of modernized traditional houses that he produced in the mid 1930s. It still impresses, despite subsequent alterations.

I-23
Burke House
2158 Brentwood Drive
1933, F. M. Sawyer

Sawyer was an obscure architect who designed two quirky Spanish style houses in Houston built of reinforced concrete blocks. Interior fixtures, including the frames for window screens that retract into side pockets, are also of concrete.

I-24
Lamb House
2158 Brentwood Drive
1929, Burns & James

This charming house, with its arched loggia entrance way, was the first of 10 houses Katharine Mott built in River Oaks.

I-25
Sauer House
2229 Inwood Drive
1935, H. A. Salisbury & T. G. McHale

The crisp detail and assured proportions of this compact house show Salisbury & McHale at their best. The clapboard-faced house front framed by brick chimney end walls derives from New England.

I-26
Loy House
2105 Inwood Drive
1966, P. M. Bolton Associates

With this house, located at the intersection of two busy streets, Preston Bolton gave form to the preferred River Oaks house type of the '70s: the inwardly-focused dwelling walled off from its surroundings. The oversized paneled doors were an attempt to compensate with monumental urban scale for the house's anti-suburban introversion.

I-24 Lamb House

I-25 Sauer House

I-26 Loy House

I-27 River Oaks Community Center

I-28 Haddon Townhouses

I-29 River Oaks Court

I-30 Oliver House

I-31 Hubbard House

I-27
River Oaks Community Center
2017-2047 West Gray Avenue
1937, Stayton Nunn-Milton McGinty with Oliver C. Winston, consulting architect

Hugh Potter, president of the River Oaks Corporation, developed the community center with two crescent-shaped retail buildings symmetrically framing the western terminus of West Gray. A model of suburban convenience, the shopping center was designed to enhance, rather than threaten, River Oaks. Winston, a Washington, D.C. architect, introduced the backlit, upcurved canopy detail to Houston. Architectural historian Richard Longstreth describes the center as "the most publicized and praised example of its kind until the post-World War II era." The River Oaks Corporation added to the center through the 1950s. Consequently it stretches along West Gray as far as Driscoll Street. In 1979 Weingarten Realty Investors, which acquired the center in 1972, had its various components painted white and installed the Washingtonia Palm trees along West Gray (S. I. Morris Associates). Yet in 2007 Weingarten defied public outrage and demolished the north quadrant at 2018-2048 West Gray, replacing it with a bulky, flashy Barnes & Noble and a 4-story parking garage (2009, Heights Venture Architects).

I-28
Haddon Townhouses
2013-2029 Haddon Street
1983, Arquitectonica

Arquitectonica's first Houston project consisted of this terrace front of ten row houses symmetrically flanking modest little McDuffie Street. All stops were pulled out to advertise externally the internal spatial organization of the narrow 3-story houses and the two expansive studio houses that bracket the terrace at either end. A restrictive covenant protects the color scheme.

I-29
River Oaks Court
2517-2529 Stanmore Drive
1936, Cameron D. Fairchild

In 1935 Herbert A. Kipp, vice president of the River Oaks Corporation, platted a series of greenway courts along the south side of Stanmore and the east side of Sharp Place. This was a remedial effort aimed at salvaging the lots that otherwise would face directly onto San Felipe and South Shepherd. Houses now back up to those busy streets and face common greens instead. Cameron Fairchild was commissioned by the corporation to design all the houses on the first of the Stanmore courts. In 2002 architect Jay Baker replaced the Fairchild-designed house at 2517 Stanmore with a shingle-clad successor that respects the scale and rhythms of the ensemble.

I-30
Oliver House
2508 Pelham Drive
1927, Charles W. Oliver

Oliver, River Oaks Corporation's architect, designed in all styles. But his favorite was the Mediterranean, as evidenced by the house he designed for his own family. It shows the influence of one of the most persuasive interpreters of the Mediterranean genre, the Pasadena architect Wallace Neff. Today Oliver's house is nearly upstaged by the fantastic Live Oak tree in front of it.

I-31
Hubbard House
2523 Del Monte Drive
1936, Armon E. Mabry

The formal French manorial style seems to have been Mabry's preferred genre. This relatively small house represents his most engaging rendition of the type.

I-32
Underwood House
2923 Del Monte Drive
1934, Birdsall P. Briscoe

Here Briscoe essayed a Southern version of the Georgian style, incorporating oversized windows to admit light and breezes.

I-33
Bullington House
3023 Del Monte Drive
1938, Birdsall P. Briscoe

With this design Briscoe paid tribute to the early 19th-century Le Carpentier-Beauregard House in the French Quarter of New Orleans. He suburbanized the original without sacrificing its neo-Classical dignity.

I-33 Bullington House

I-32 Underwood House

I-34 Redbird House

I-35 House

I-36 Paddock House

I-37 Michael House

I-38 Dean House

I-40 House

I-34
Redbird House
3237 Inwood Drive
1925, Briscoe & Dixon

Of the nine houses built by the River Oaks Corporation in 1925-26 to promote the development of Country Club Estates, its first section, this is the only one that remains intact. It preserves Will Hogg's vision of River Oaks as a community of well-designed, not necessarily expensive, houses. Briscoe transcribed details from the architecture of 18th-century Charleston onto this suburban neo-Regency house. The combination of Southern detail and English domestic type appealed to Ima Hogg, under whose tutelage the nine original houses were built. On account of the centerpiece in the window grilles, this house is known as the Redbird House. It was rehabilitated and expanded by Patton W. Brooks (1997).

I-35
House
1807 River Oaks Boulevard
1991, Anthony E. Frederick

The boulevard is where architectural competition is unashamedly pursued.

I-36
Paddock House
3229 Groveland Lane
1936, Birdsall P. Briscoe

Another neo-Georgian production by Briscoe, deftly proportioned with classical architectural detail executed in molded brick. The tripartite Wyatt windows effectively counter the closed aspect of the central register.

I-37
Michael House
1903 Bellmeade Road
1926, Charles W. Oliver

The advertising man Pierre L. Michael, who built the Isabella Court on Main Street, had Oliver design this diminutively scaled, intricately planned Mediterranean house for his family. It was sensitively rehabilitated by William F. Stern & Associates in 1987.

I-38
Dean House
1912 Bellmeade Road
1926, John F. Staub

A New England Colonial style house set in a lush Houston garden. The house was tactfully expanded in 1987 by Larry S. Davis. Across the street, at 1915 Bellmeade, is a contextual salute by Charles W. Oliver (1928).

I-39
Hobby House
3202 Huntingdon Place
1972, Ford, Powell & Carson

The San Antonio architect Chris Carson shaped this high-set brick house around internal courtyards so that it presents a closed aspect from all directions. The client, Oveta Culp Hobby, was publisher of the *Houston Post*, commanding officer of the Women's Army Corps during World War II, and the first secretary of the Department of Health, Education and Welfare.

I-40
House
3105 Ella Lee Lane
1994, Jay Baker Architects

Paying homage with its sweeping roof to one of Harrie T. Lindeberg's houses in Shadyside, this very large house adapts to its setting with flair. At 3209 Avalon Place is another traditional style house that copes skillfully in fitting a 1990s program onto a 1920s site (1999, Scott Ballard).

I-41
Letzerich House
3256 Locke Lane
1966, Neuhaus-Wingfield Associates

Behind the low street wall is an exceptional small house, a crisply detailed pavilion that also manages to be an urbane town house. Hugo Neuhaus provided privacy here without transforming the house into a fortress.

I-41 Letzerich House

I-39 Hobby House

I-42 Childress House

I-43 House

I-44 Lamar-River Oaks Community Center

I-45 Mirabeau B. Lamar Senior High School

I-47 Bryan House

I-42
Childress House
3239 Locke Lane
1937, Harvin Moore & Hermon Lloyd

A delightful modernistic house that preserves its jaunty original features. This was the first modern house in River Oaks.

I-43
House
2526 Bellmeade Road
2006, Glassman Shoemake Maldonado

Carrie Shoemake and Ernesto Maldonado built a new, multi-generational family house on the site of the client's prior house on one of River Oaks' most problematic sites, facing busy Westheimer Road. Treating this liability as a challenge, they collaborated with landscape architects McDugald-Steele to shape a series of garden courts around which the house is adroitly configured.

I-44
Lamar-River Oaks Community Center
3256-3272 Westheimer Road
1948, William G. Farrington Company

Raymond H. Brogniez, Farrington's designer, made the most of masonry detailing and the bow-front pavilion and pylon tower when designing this strip center for the River Oaks Corporation.

I-45
Mirabeau B. Lamar Senior High School
3325 Westheimer Road
1937, John F. Staub and Kenneth Franzheim with Louis A. Glover, Lamar Q. Cato, and Harry D. Payne

Terminating the south end of River Oaks Boulevard is this PWA-built public school building, notable for its streamlined modernistic detail. The auditorium bay is fronted with a screen of fossilized Texas limestone bearing a relief map of the State of Texas executed by Nino Lenarduzzi.

Franzheim expanded the complex in 1950. Sympathetic additions and a rehabilitation of the existing buildings are by Ray Bailey Architects (1991). It was once said, in reference to Lamar, that River Oaks Boulevard was the only street with a country club at either end.

I-46
St. John The Divine Church
2450 River Oaks Boulevard
1954, MacKie & Kamrath with
H. A. Salisbury & T. G. McHale

MacKie & Kamrath repackaged traditional liturgical arrangements in this finely crafted modern building. The architects ultimately succeeded in the dubious task of modernizing, without really changing, accepted conventions. The freestanding Chapel facing River Oaks Boulevard is by H. A. Salisbury & T. G. McHale with MacKie & Kamrath and Birdsall P. Briscoe (1941). To the west of the church is the large, but self-effacing, Parish House (1979, Ray Bailey Architects). In 2004-05 the interior of the church was completely gutted and reconstructed to accommodate a new organ (Jackson & Ryan Architects).

I-47
Bryan House
3315 Ella Lee Lane
1938, J. T. Rather, Jr.

This small house features the shallow layering of wall planes that Rather used frequently. It was rehabilitated by Eubanks, Bohnn & Associates (1997).

I-46 St. John The Divine Church

I-49 Cullen House

I-50 Mott House

I-51 Chew House

I-52 Christie House

I-53 Brown House

I-48
Menil House
3363 San Felipe Road
1951, Philip C. Johnson Associates and Cowell & Neuhaus

Architecturally and culturally, this large, flat-roofed house, built for Dominique Schlumberger and John de Menil, is the modernist equivalent of Bayou Bend. It was Philip Johnson's first work in Houston, and with it he established the architecture of his mentor, Ludwig Mies van der Rohe, as the high style of Houston modernism. The house turns a nearly blank brick wall, capped by a white-painted Miesian fascia, toward the street. The principal reception rooms are arranged around an internal garden court, roofed over with an intersecting barrel-vaulted canopy, installed by Howard Barnstone (1961). This is where Mr. and Mrs. de Menil brought Houston face to face with 20th-century modernism in all its cultural aspects: art, architecture, music, theology, and human rights. Dominique de Menil bequeathed the house to the Menil Foundation upon her death in 1997. The foundation carried out a comprehensive restoration of the house (2004, Stern and Bucek Architects). It is used by the Menil Collection for special events and is not presently open to the public.

I-49
Cullen House
1620 River Oaks Boulevard
1935, John F. Staub

This limestone-faced Regency villa was the most expensive house built in Houston during the Great Depression. According to his biographers, the independent oilman, Hugh Roy Cullen, was motivated to build it partly to provide much-needed jobs. Staub turned the garden face of the house south, toward Inwood, from which it can best be seen. As in many Staub houses, the front door is in the back yard and faces a very grand motor court. Staub laid out the gardens, transplanting specimen trees from Louisiana to give the landscape instant maturity. In 2002 the house was rehabilitated and expanded by architects Martha B. Bute-Robert L. King; a new landscape plan was installed by McDugald-Steele. Next to the entrance gate, at the head of River Oaks Boulevard, is the overbearing clubhouse of the River Oaks Country Club (1966, Golemon & Rolfe), which replaced Staub's too-modest, too-understated original.

I-50
Mott House
3325 Inwood Drive
1930, Burns & James

Katharine Mott built this whitewashed brick and timbered house to be her family's home.

I-51
Chew House
3335 Inwood Drive
1926, John F. Staub

A setting of Live Oaks draped with Spanish moss has always made this picturesque English manorial style house, with its angled service wing, especially beguiling.

I-52
Christie House
3358 Inwood Drive
1930, Charles W. Oliver

This was the first of many plantation style houses built in River Oaks. It was intended to celebrate the provenance of its owner, Theodosia Campbell Christie, who was from Natchitoches, Louisiana.

I-53
Brown House
3363 Inwood Drive
1933, J. T. Rather, Jr.

Rather designed this shingled and gabled house as an outsized version of John F. Staub's own house at 3511 Del Monte. It was built for the geologist and contractor George R. Brown, for whom Houston's convention center is named, and his wife, cultural philanthropist Alice Pratt.

I-48 Menil House

I-55 House

I-56 Sewall House

I-57 Staub House

I-58 Mellinger House

I-59 Belt House

I-60 Pinckney House

I-54
Clayton Summer House
3376 Inwood Drive
1924, Briscoe & Dixon

This was the first house in River Oaks, built by the cotton exporter Will Clayton and his wife, Susan Vaughan, as a summerhouse for their family. Briscoe used Mount Vernon as the organizing image; amusingly, the kitchen is "correctly" placed in one of the twin dependencies connected to the main house by curved hyphens. In addition Briscoe installed a swimming pool and tennis courts. Since 1930 the house has been occupied year round by Clayton's descendants. Alterations and additions are by Glassman Shoemake Maldonado (2004).

I-55
House
3390 Inwood Drive
2004, Curtis & Windham

An astounding English manorial country house modeled on the Edwardian "butterfly plan."

I-56
Sewall House
3456 Inwood Drive
1926, Cram & Ferguson with Stayton Nunn

Blanche Harding Sewall was so enamored of Ralph Adams Cram's buildings at the Rice Institute that she commissioned him to design this house. Cram worked from Mrs. Sewall's sketches in designing the stucco-faced, tile-roofed Spanish style house. Interior detail is based on the House of El Greco museum in Toledo. Mrs. Sewall travelled to Spain with Mildred Stapley and Arthur Byne to acquire artifacts and furniture. Ellen Shipman designed gardens for the small estate in the mid 1930s, but they no longer survive. The house was rescued from dereliction and superlatively restored in 1979 by Charles Tapley Associates. Additions are by W. O. Neuhaus Associates (1991).

I-57
Staub House
3511 Del Monte Drive
1926, John F. Staub

Staub designed this much-copied New England Colonial style house for his own family; he chose the style to remind his wife of her native Massachusetts. At the time it was completed the house stood on the western edge of Houston. Still occupied by the architect's descendants, it was extended in 1984 by Charles Keith Associates.

I-58
Mellinger House
3452 Del Monte Drive
1931, John F. Staub

Here Staub wittily produced an American Colonial style house with two fronts that don't match; one formal facing the street, the other picturesque facing a rear motor court. The projecting wing to the right is a carefully detailed addition by Anthony E. Frederick (1982).

I-59
Belt House
3451 Del Monte Drive
1930, J. W. Northrop, Jr.

Completing the neo-Colonial lineup at the Del Monte-Larchmont intersection is this large American Georgian style house.

I-60
Pinckney House
3439 Del Monte Drive
1937, Birdsall P. Briscoe

Briscoe demonstrated his gift for discreet mannerism in this asymmetrically composed neo-Regency house. Next door at 3427 Del Monte is a symmetrical house with a graceful wrought iron balcony (1936, Eugene Werlin).

I-61
Anderson House
3414 Del Monte Drive
1938, Birdsall P. Briscoe

A somewhat more archeological approach to the Regency genre, this house is faced with a bowed portico and framed by recessed polygonal wings. Rehabilitated and expanded by Rudolph Colby (1992).

I-61 Anderson House

I-54 Clayton Summer House

I-62 House

I-63 Nelms House

I-64 House

I-65 Scurry House

I-68 House

I-62
House
3404 Chevy Chase Drive
1978, S. I. Morris Associates

Eugene Aubry compressed this large house into a hard-edged, gable-roofed village.

I-63
Nelms House
3391 Sleepyhollow Court
1929, Frank J. Forster

The New York architect Forster specialized in extravagantly picturesque recreations of French Norman farmhouses, often incorporating salvaged materials he acquired on periodic trips to Europe to give them authentic ambiance. This house, built for Mr. and Mrs. Haywood Nelms, was one of his largest. It is very long and quite thin, organized around a neo-Medieval great hall decorated with a mural by the Santa Fe artist, Gerald Cassidy, depicting characters from the Robin Hood legends. Forster also designed a garage, stable, kennel, and playhouse, as well as the dovecote at the rear gate, facing San Felipe. The house was rehabilitated in 1979 by Langwith Wilson King & Associates, who designed the wall along San Felipe. The most recent alterations and additions are by Curtis & Windham (2009), who are also architects of the house at 3394 Chevy Chase Drive (2012).

I-64
House
3401 Sleepyhollow Court
2012, Allan Greenberg

Although its construction entailed the demolition of Birdsall Briscoe's J. M. Johnson House of 1937, this grand country house responds ambitiously to its axial site, centered on Sleepyhollow Court.

I-65
Scurry House
1912 Larchmont Road
1936, John F. Staub

Staub adapted the design of this house from the Kellum-Noble House in Sam Houston Park, the oldest house in Houston. He emphasized the Kellum-Noble's vernacular origins by basing this house on an L-plan rear elevation rather than its symmetrical front elevation. This enabled him to orient the principal rooms to a south-facing side garden. Additions are by Harvin C. Moore (1957) and Val Glitsch (1991).

I-66
Austin House
3606 Chevy Chase Drive
1951, Birdsall P. Briscoe

Briscoe came to favor this planar compositional type, prefaced by a flat-roofed iron porch, in the houses he designed near the end of his long career.

I-67
House
3811 Del Monte Drive
1969, Howard Barnstone & Eugene Aubry

Behind the self-effacing, cypress-sheathed exterior of this flat-roofed house lies one of Barnstone & Aubry's master works. Alterations and additions are by Eugene E. Aubry (1970s) and William F. Stern (1994, 1998).

I-68
House
3701 Del Monte Drive
2008, Curtis & Windham

This Mediterranean style stucco-faced, tile-roofed courtyard house is a masterpiece of deferential design in a mature neighborhood setting. The scale, spatial organization, materials, and detail are exquisitely calibrated to work with the rhythms and texture of the street. Curtis & Windham was the landscape architect as well as architect. Across the intersection at 3690 Del Monte is a house with substantial, but discreet, alterations and additions (2008, L. Barry Davidson Architects).

I-66 Austin House

I-67 House

I-69 Vaughan House

I-70 House

I-71 House

I-72 Anderson House

I-73 Turner House

I-69
Vaughan House
3707 Inwood Drive
1950, Birdsall P. Briscoe

A delicately scaled Charleston house transplanted to River Oaks. Val Glitsch performed tactful additions (2002).

I-70
House
3606 Knollwood Drive
2003, Curtis & Windham

Built on the site of a Birdsall Briscoe house demolished by a previous owner of the property, this graceful house pays tribute to the early 20th-century country houses of the New York architect, Charles A. Platt. The acid-washed, sand-surfaced stucco walls are especially compelling. The gardens were also designed by Curtis & Windham.

I-71
House
9 Pine Hill Lane
1989, Carlos Jiménez

This brilliantly colored complex represents a total reconstruction of a small house by the San Antonio architect, O'Neil Ford, (1957). Its multi-hued component parts and square windows presage a beautifully modulated and lit interior. The house is tucked back on Pine Hill, a private lane, like Tiel Way, reminiscent of Los Angeles, with houses set close to the narrow, winding street, yet buffered by luxuriant vegetation and motor courts. Also on this street are houses by Anthony E. Frederick at 10 Pine Hill (1995) and Frank Welch & Associates at 2 Pine Hill (1976).

I-72
Anderson House
3740 Willowick Road
1958, Staub, Rather & Howze

Into the 1950s Staub continued to adapt historic Southern prototypes to contemporary domestic programs. Here a Greek revival cottage is merged with a classic 1950s ranch house.

I-73
Turner House
3744 Willowick Road
1955

This is a 1950s condensation of the early 19th-century Baltimore country house, Homewoods. Next door, at 3760 Willowick, is a trim, contemporary style house by Hermon Lloyd & W. B. Morgan (1953). At 3734 Willowick is a limestone-faced *maison de plaisance* (1964, Robert W. Maurice & Richard M. Wilkins).

I-74
House
3780 Willowick Drive
2005, Curtis & Windham

In the 1930s white-painted brick and dark green trim materialized patrician identity in River Oaks, whether a house was grand or small. Curtis & Windham revived this color combination to impress this new house with similar associations.

I-75
White House
3707 Knollwood Drive
1940, Birdsall P. Briscoe and George W. Rustay

This large house is set behind a monumental portico supported by fluted Doric columns.

I-76
House
3632 Inverness Drive
2008, Strasser Ragni

This planar, flat-roofed, white stucco-faced house pushed the limits of neighborhood tolerance. Although built in conformance with the neighborhood's design standards, it nonetheless started a move in 2009-10 to have the River Oaks Property Owners Association (the neighborhood association, which approves new construction and enforces the deed restrictions) ban modern design as incompatible with River Oaks. Cooler heads prevailed. The incident reflects the tensions that replacement of older houses with much larger new houses introduced not only in River Oaks, but in many other Houston neighborhoods as well.

I-74 House

I-76 House

I-75 White House

I-77 House

I-78 House

I-79 Cizik House

I-80 House

I-81 Farfel House

I-77
House
3737 Inverness Drive
1993, Taft Architects

This is Tafts' deconstruction of a "traditional" style River Oaks house.

I-78
House
3808 Inverness Drive
2001, Curtis & Windham

This exceptionally grand house is a limestone-faced homage to the late 18th-century Pavillon de La Lanterne at Versailles. It is a one-room-deep house that internally possesses the spatial intimacy associated with 18th-century French domestic architecture. Paris architect, Laurent Bourgois, collaborated with Curtis & Windham on the interior architecture. The gardens were designed by the New York landscape architects, Deborah Nevins & Associates.

I-79
Cizik House
3971 Inverness Drive
1984, Ray Bailey Architects

Constructed on a sliver site excerpted from a larger lot, this house is a graceful postmodern interpretation of a New England house. Across the street is the rolling site that was the Hogg brothers' weekend camp, Tall Timbers, from which this section of River Oaks takes its name.

I-80
House
4007 Inverness Drive
2007, Curtis & Windham

Amid the uncertain, often expedient, interpretations of "tradition" epidemic in high-end Houston houses of the 2000s, Curtis & Windham's work stands out for their discipline, rigor, and refinement.

I-81
Farfel House
18 Westlane Place
1957, Bolton & Barnstone

A testament to the persuasive example of Philip Johnson's Menil House on San Felipe, this flat-roofed, steel-trimmed, but wood-framed, modern house is very much in the Miesian-Johnson mode. Thomas D. Church, the San Francisco landscape architect, designed the axial brick causeway that visually penetrates the house and organizes open space adjoining it in a subtle, but powerfully architectonic way. Rehabilitated by Curtis & Windham (2010). At 23 Westlane is another flat-roofed modern house (1970) by Dallas architect Scott Lyons.

I-82
House
3736 Chevy Chase Drive
2009, Jay Baker Architects

With this 2-story modern house, Jay Baker introduced a new house type to River Oaks: the free-spanned loft. The house even incorporates exterior wall panels of steel siding, but not facing the street.

I-83
Inwood Manor
3711 San Felipe Road
1965, Neuhaus & Taylor

During the first half of the 1960s, high-rise apartment buildings clustered around the edges of River Oaks. The most imaginative was Harwood Taylor's 16-story Inwood Manor. Its cast-in-place concrete frame pays homage to Philip Johnson's contemporary work.

I-83 Inwood Manor

I-82 House

I-84 House

I-85 House

I-86 House

I-87 House

I-88 House

I-84
House
2113 Maconda Lane
1996, W. O. Neuhaus Associates

Layered shapes imbue this house with a sense of spatial complexity. It is located in Royden Oaks, a postwar subdivision that sought to capitalize upon its proximity to River Oaks. Lawson Carter Epstein of Washington, D.C. was the landscape architect.

I-85
House
3710 Overbrook Lane
1994, Jay Baker Architects

Corner windows accentuate the house's taut planes.

I-86
House
3702 Ella Lee Lane
1991, Ziegler Cooper

Scott Ziegler diverged from his firm's corporate work to design this handsomely composed and detailed manorial style house.

I-87
House
2405 Maconda Lane
2004, Dillon Kyle

Kyle's skill in designing settings keyed to his clients is apparent in the subtle rustic qualities of this 1- and 2-story house.

I-88
House
3451 Piping Rock Lane
2005, Dillon Kyle

Fieldstone and shingles are collaged in this 2-story house.

I-89
House
3436 Piping Rock Lane
1994, Jay Baker Architects

Like the best neo-traditional houses built in River Oaks in the 1990s, this yellow stucco-faced manorial style house is carefully scaled so as not to overwhelm its more compact neighbors.

I-90
House
3459 Overbrook Lane
1995, L. Barry Davidson Architects

An echo of the south of France.

I-91
House
3635 Overbrook Lane
2004, HarrisonKornberg Architects

The brick and copper exteriors of this 2-story, L-plan house stand out amid its more conventional neighbors.

I-92
House
3603 Wickersham Lane
2004, Cameron Armstrong

Armstrong finished this steel-framed, Galvalume-sheathed house with stucco to assuage River Oaks sensibilities.

I-90 House

I-91 House

I-92 House

I-89 House

I-93 House

I-94 Burke House

I-95 Virginia Stuller Tatham Fine Arts Center

I-97 House

I-93
House
3448 Locke Lane
2009, Jay Baker Architects

Baker had the unenviable task of replacing not one, but two MacKie & Kamrath houses from the 1930s with this horizontally extensive house, unified beneath a steeply pitched shingled roof. The interior contains an expansive open-air room and the front yard is partially walled off from the street so interior spaces have a protected southern exposure.

I-94
Burke House
3402 Wickersham Lane
1938, F. Talbott Wilson & S. I. Morris, Jr.

This Monterey style house is offset in plan so that all rooms have access to the prevailing breeze. Privacy was insured by the low garden wall. The house exemplifies the high standard of domestic planning in Houston at the end of the eclectic era, just before central air-conditioning abolished the need for climatic responsiveness. In 2002 the house was discreetly expanded by new owners in an effort to demonstrate the value of preserving rather than replacing River Oaks's historic housing stock.

I-95
Virginia Stuller Tatham Fine Arts Center
St. John's School
Westheimer Road and
Buffalo Speedway
2000, Graham Gund Associates
and Morris Architects

Founded in 1946 St. John's is a day school occupying 28 acres on both sides of Westheimer adjacent to the parish complex of St. John The Divine Church. The school's first building, the quadrangle-centered Farish Hall (1947–1948, H. A. Salisbury & T. G. McHale), set the tone for future additions with its limestone walls, steep shingled roofs, and romantic English Cotswolds architectural imagery.

MacKie & Kamrath's lower school on the south campus (1953) has been replaced by bigger buildings, including the Tatham Center. Neuhaus Associates designed Winston Hall (1971) on the north campus. Caudill Rowlett Scott designed the Stude-Sarofim Learning Resources Center on the north campus and the Libbie Rice Farish Building on the south campus (both 1980). Ziegler Cooper completed a master plan for expansion in 2006 and was architect of Mewbourne Hall on the north campus at Westheimer and Claremont.

I-96
The Willowick
2200 Willowick Road
1962, Neuhaus & Taylor

The 15-story Willowick was the first high-rise built to Neuhaus & Taylor's designs and by developer Gerald D. Hines. Its oversailing concrete floor slabs, shading the all-glass curtain wall, give the apartment building its now classic look of mid-century modern grace.

I-97
House
4002 Meadow Lake Lane
2011, m+a architecture studio

This 2-story concrete block house turns its back on busy San Felipe. Projecting window bays reach out to the light and view.

I-96 The Willowick

I-98 House

I-99 House

I-100 Crate & Barrel Building

I-101 House

I-98
House
4002 Piping Rock Lane
1999, Jay Baker Architects

Baker exhibits his modern design approach in this austere Oak Forest house.

I-99
House
2019 Drexel Drive
2006, Intexure

Highland Village's transformation portended redevelopment of Frank W. Sharp's mid-market, postwar Oak Estates subdivision just north of Highland Village. This is the most imposing architect-designed replacement house constructed in Oak Estates, a juxtaposition of boldly angled wall and roof planes that contrast degrees of transparency and opacity. The Office of James Burnett was the landscape architect.

I-100
Crate & Barrel Building
4000 Westheimer Road
2001, Jacques Verlinder
and Good, Fulton & Farrell

Highland Village shopping center was begun by S. N. Adams in 1949 in tandem with his development of the Highland Village subdivision (1949-50). In the 1980s Highland Village began to be transformed from an aging neighborhood shopping center into an upscale lifestyle center, at first by remodeling existing buildings and then by demolishing and replacing them. The Crate & Barrel store is not only the most architecturally ambitious work of retail architecture in Highland Village, it is also the most ambitious in Houston of the 2000s. Crate & Barrel's in-house design team, headed by Chicago architect, Jacques Verlinder, with Dallas architects Good, Fulton & Farrell, paid homage to New York architect Richard Meier in the building's crisp lines, floating planes, and porcelain enameled panel wall system.

I-101
House
4002 Chatham Lane
2008, MC²

The redevelopment process visible in Oak Estates has also transformed the Highland Village subdivision south of Westheimer. Brothers Chung and Choung Nguyen emphasized modern luxury in this spectacularly white, speculatively built courtyard house of stucco and glass.

I-102
House
4029 Chatham Lane
2005, Val Glitsch

Emphasizing the sectional organization of this 2-story house on its narrow street front, Glitsch aligned its long dimension parallel to a side garden, screened from the street by translucent panels set in a steel frames. Asakura Robinson was the landscape architect.

I-103
4311 Bettis Apartments
4311 Bettis Drive
1955, Robert Wilson

In the 1950s the Mid Lane neighborhood was built out with small apartment complexes, giving the area its reputation as a hotbed of swinging singles social life. Among the survivors from what now seems like an innocent era is the duplex apartment building designed and occupied by architect-interior designer Robert Wilson. Its walled street front and spacious interior garden court made it a harbinger of the townhouse types introduced to Houston in the 1960s.

I-102 House

I-103 4311 Bettis Apartments

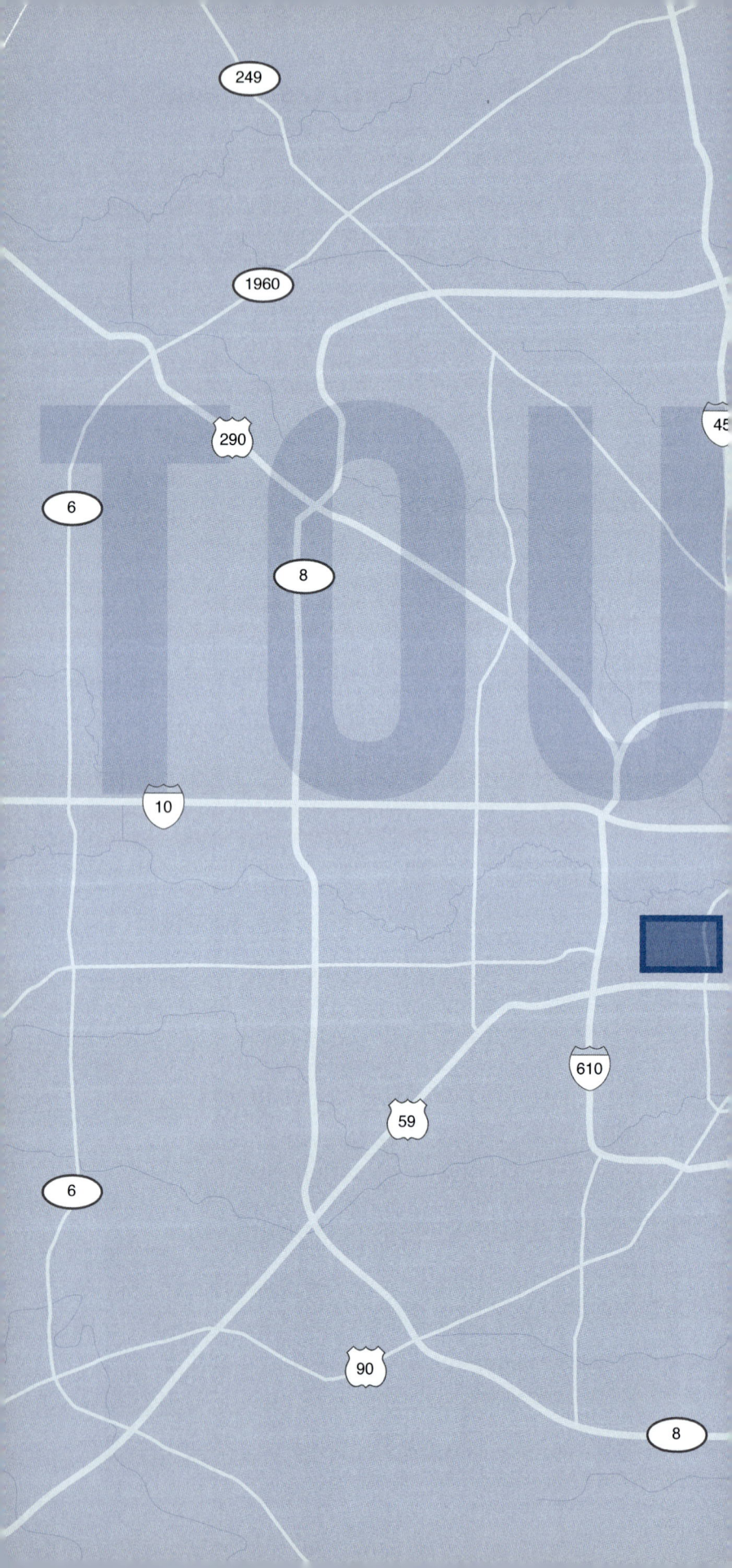

Kirby / Greenway

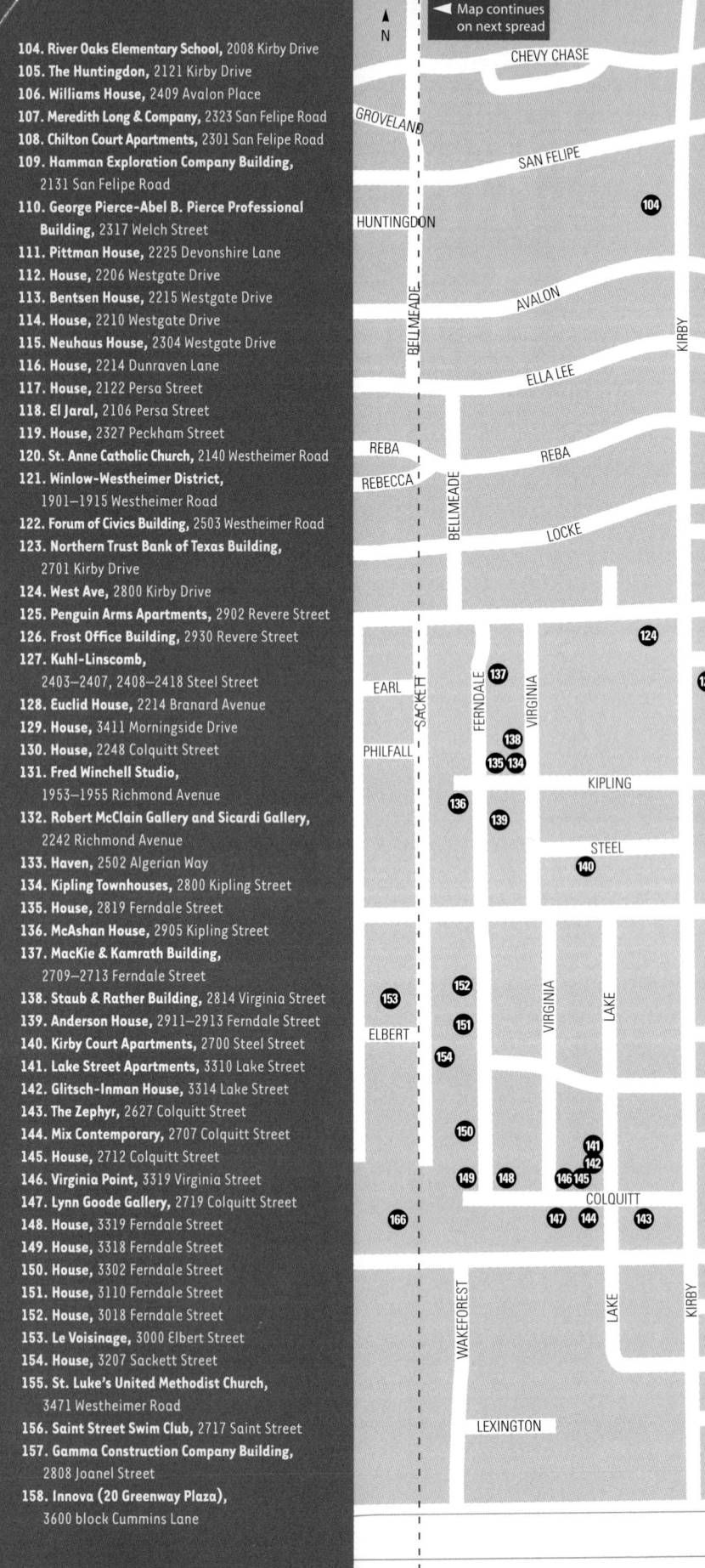

104. River Oaks Elementary School, 2008 Kirby Drive
105. The Huntingdon, 2121 Kirby Drive
106. Williams House, 2409 Avalon Place
107. Meredith Long & Company, 2323 San Felipe Road
108. Chilton Court Apartments, 2301 San Felipe Road
109. Hamman Exploration Company Building, 2131 San Felipe Road
110. George Pierce-Abel B. Pierce Professional Building, 2317 Welch Street
111. Pittman House, 2225 Devonshire Lane
112. House, 2206 Westgate Drive
113. Bentsen House, 2215 Westgate Drive
114. House, 2210 Westgate Drive
115. Neuhaus House, 2304 Westgate Drive
116. House, 2214 Dunraven Lane
117. House, 2122 Persa Street
118. El Jaral, 2106 Persa Street
119. House, 2327 Peckham Street
120. St. Anne Catholic Church, 2140 Westheimer Road
121. Winlow-Westheimer District, 1901–1915 Westheimer Road
122. Forum of Civics Building, 2503 Westheimer Road
123. Northern Trust Bank of Texas Building, 2701 Kirby Drive
124. West Ave, 2800 Kirby Drive
125. Penguin Arms Apartments, 2902 Revere Street
126. Frost Office Building, 2930 Revere Street
127. Kuhl-Linscomb, 2403–2407, 2408–2418 Steel Street
128. Euclid House, 2214 Branard Avenue
129. House, 3411 Morningside Drive
130. House, 2248 Colquitt Street
131. Fred Winchell Studio, 1953–1955 Richmond Avenue
132. Robert McClain Gallery and Sicardi Gallery, 2242 Richmond Avenue
133. Haven, 2502 Algerian Way
134. Kipling Townhouses, 2800 Kipling Street
135. House, 2819 Ferndale Street
136. McAshan House, 2905 Kipling Street
137. MacKie & Kamrath Building, 2709–2713 Ferndale Street
138. Staub & Rather Building, 2814 Virginia Street
139. Anderson House, 2911–2913 Ferndale Street
140. Kirby Court Apartments, 2700 Steel Street
141. Lake Street Apartments, 3310 Lake Street
142. Glitsch-Inman House, 3314 Lake Street
143. The Zephyr, 2627 Colquitt Street
144. Mix Contemporary, 2707 Colquitt Street
145. House, 2712 Colquitt Street
146. Virginia Point, 3319 Virginia Street
147. Lynn Goode Gallery, 2719 Colquitt Street
148. House, 3319 Ferndale Street
149. House, 3318 Ferndale Street
150. House, 3302 Ferndale Street
151. House, 3110 Ferndale Street
152. House, 3018 Ferndale Street
153. Le Voisinage, 3000 Elbert Street
154. House, 3207 Sackett Street
155. St. Luke's United Methodist Church, 3471 Westheimer Road
156. Saint Street Swim Club, 2717 Saint Street
157. Gamma Construction Company Building, 2808 Joanel Street
158. Innova (20 Greenway Plaza), 3600 block Cummins Lane

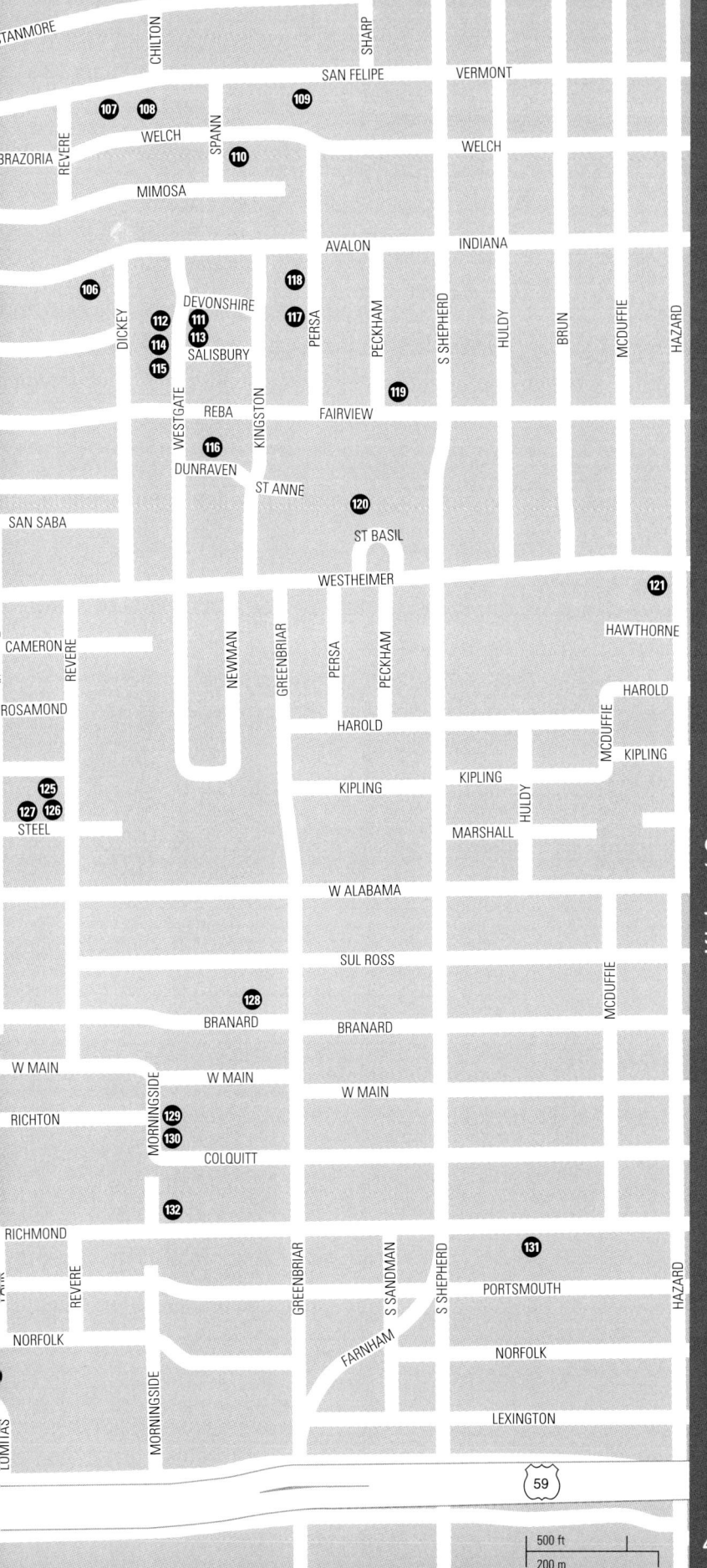

159. **Central Presbyterian Church,**
    3788 Richmond Avenue
160. **8–12 and 9–11 Greenway Plaza,**
    3700 block Richmond Avenue
161. **1, 2, 3, and 5 Greenway Plaza,**
    3500 block Richmond Avenue
162. **Jefferson Chemical Company Building,**
    3336 Richmond Avenue
163. **Humble Research Center,** 3102 Buffalo Speedway
164. **Macham Building,** 3230 Sul Ross Avenue
165. **Phoenix Insurance Company of Hartford Building,** 3323 Richmond Avenue
166. **2990 Richmond Building,** 2990 Richmond Avenue

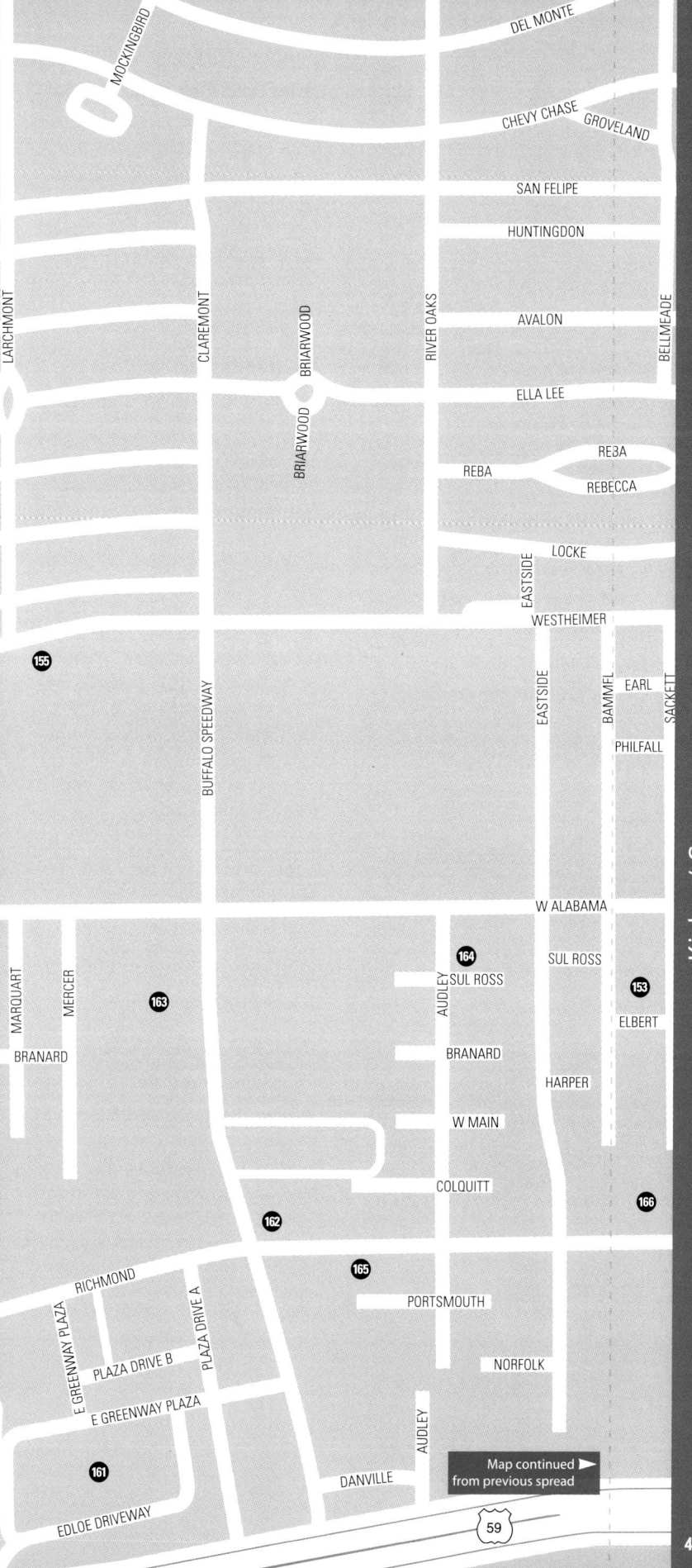

I-104 River Oaks Elementary School

I-105 The Huntingdon

I-106 Williams House

I-107 Meredith Long & Company Carport

I-108 Chilton Court Apartments

I-104
River Oaks Elementary School
2008 Kirby Drive
1929, Harry D. Payne

Another state-of-the-art elementary school that Payne produced in the late 1920s. Additions along Avalon Place fail to maintain Payne's architectural standards.

I-105
The Huntingdon
2121 Kirby Drive
1983, Talbott Wilson

The 34-story Huntingdon condominium tower, despite its height and slender profile, does not quite live up to expectations aroused by its pretentious baroque gate piers. Nonetheless in the 1990s it became Houston's power tower, where the top drawer moved when they decided to give up their big houses. Next door at 2001 Kirby is the 13-story River Oaks Bank & Trust Co. Building (1970, Wilson, Morris, Crain & Anderson), which, up close, suffers from the same finicky detailing as The Huntingdon.

I-106
Williams House
2409 Avalon Place
1956, Wilson, Morris, Crain & Anderson
2009, Interloop Architecture

Interloop's Mark Wamble and Dawn Finley reconstituted a 1950s Contemporary style house in the Avalon Place subdivision with an addition angled to conform to a 9-degree skewing of the site's boundaries. A perforated rain screen replaces what had been shingle cladding. The steel tripod supporting a new stair bay at the northwest corner marks the transition from old to new.

I-107
Meredith Long & Company Carport
2323 San Felipe Road
2008, Dillon Kyle

On the site of a demolished apartment building, a twin of the one now housing the Meredith Long art gallery, Kyle and landscape architect, Cedar Baldridge, designed a walled parking court and the witty, steel-framed carport, faced with a digitally composed photomural of green leaves.

I-108
Chilton Court Apartments
2301 San Felipe Road
1939, F. Talbott Wilson & S. I. Morris

This was an ingeniously conceived apartment complex. Units are offset in plan so that each seems like a detached 2-story house, with light and air entering from all four sides. Originally eight units flanked a central green space. In 1997 the west row at 2307 was demolished to clear the site for a prosaic swimming academy, pushed back behind a street-front parking lot. A duplex designed to look like a River Oaks house survives at 2247 San Felipe (1941, F. Talbott Wilson and S. I. Morris).

I-109
Hamman Exploration Company Building
2131 San Felipe Road
1940, Harvin Moore & Hermon Lloyd

Here 1930s Regency is streamlined with a stainless steel portico and glass block strip windows. The building is now occupied by the Hobby Family Foundation.

I-109 Hamman Exploration Company Building

I-110 George Pierce-Abel B. Pierce Professional Building

I-111 Pittman House

I-112 House

I-113 Bentsen House

I-114 House

I-110
George Pierce-Abel B. Pierce Professional Building
[now Brown Foundation Building]
2317 Welch Street
1963, George Pierce-Abel B. Pierce

George and Abel Pierce and their partner, E. J. Goodwin, designed a 1-story, steel-framed, courtyard-centered brick pavilion to house their architectural practice. Since 1990 the building has been occupied by one of Houston's principal cultural philanthropies, the Brown Foundation. William F. Stern carried out a rehabilitation for the foundation. A block away at 2201 Welch is a handsome, L-plan apartment building with a New Orleans-like courtyard (1938, Cameron Fairchild) that should have been the model for others like it. Across the street at 2200 and 2134 Welch are a 2-story building and a 1-story U-plan building, both by George Pierce-Abel B. Pierce (1952).

I-111
Pittman House
2225 Devonshire Lane
1982, Frank Welch & Associates

This row house is composed with planes of rose-colored brick. Its aloofness is tempered by balcony railings designed in a sort of Texas version of Chinese Chippendale. It lies in Glendower Court, one of a pair of 1920s-era subdivisions intensively redeveloped since the late 1980s to accommodate spillover from River Oaks.

I-112
House
2206 Westgate Drive
1992, Rudolph Colby with
John F. Houchins

An extremely refined design, this house civilly incorporates a front garage and allows for daylight to enter the house from either side.

I-113
Bentsen House
2215 Westgate Drive
1988, Kenneth Bentsen Associates

This self-effacing house is centered around a tranquil courtyard, separated from the street by a high wall.

I-114
House
2210 Westgate Drive
1994, Curtis & Windham

Although filling the street front of its site, this house takes neighborliness seriously by providing openings on its north lot line side and by aligning with the house to the south.

I-115
Neuhaus House
2304 Westgate Drive
1994, Carlos Jiménez

Working with a double lot, Jiménez expanded this courtyard house to generous dimensions. From the street its cast-stone-block facing and distinctive profiles are most evident.

I-116
House
2214 Dunraven Lane
1997, Anthony E. Frederick

The Tuscan villa as a Houston townhouse.

I-117
House
2122 Persa Street
1996, Taft Architects

The shed roofs and coated metal facing mark this as an artist's house.

I-118
El Jaral
2106 Persa Street
1993, Taft Architects

A triple lot enabled the architects to stretch this house of exposed concrete block in a long, one-room-deep configuration. The sculptor, Dorman David, executed the pivoting front door; Laura R. Hamman and Will Fleming are responsible for the profuse plantings, which evoke the ecologies of east and south Texas.

I-115 Neuhaus House

I-116 House

I-117 House

I-118 El Jaral

I-119 House

I-120 St. Anne Catholic Church

I-122 Forum of Civics Building

I-123 Northern Trust Bank of Texas Building

I-124 West Ave

I-119
House
2327 Peckham Street
1997, Wittenberg Associates

This 3-story tower house was built speculatively to demonstrate that there is a market for alternatives to the inept historicism that dominates new residential construction in Houston.

I-120
St. Anne Catholic Church
2140 Westheimer Road
1940, Maurice J. Sullivan

The staged bell tower of St. Anne's and its gabled planar façade, punctuated with restrained Renaissance classical detail, are the elements that make this church such a distinctive landmark. In contrast to its Spanish exterior, the vaulted basilican interior is decorated in the neo-Byzantine style that Sullivan had earlier used at the Conventual Chapel of the Villa de Matel. Pink exposed aggregate concrete mosaic on the interior contrasts with rows of dark green, polished plaster-faced columns dividing the nave from the side aisles. Sullivan designed the adjacent school, built in stages between 1930-1953, and the freestanding parish house facing South Shepherd, the first increment of the complex completed (1929). The interior of St. Anne's was rehabilitated by Ray Bailey Architects (1991).

I-121
Winlow-Westheimer District
1901-1915 Westheimer Road
1997, Mirador

In Shepherd Square (1989, Watkins Carter Hamilton) at Westheimer and South Shepherd, Friendswood Development adapted the suburban shopping center type to an older neighborhood with 2-story construction and pattern brick facing. In contrast Mirador's Kevin Batchelor adaptively reused the ex-Stewart Service Station (c 1936) and a 1-story brick building at 1915, and added the 1-story link, clock tower, and landscaped terraces (McDugald-Steele, landscape architect) facing Westheimer. Parking was subordinated to the edges of the premises away from the streets. This street-friendly approach was pioneered by architect Daniel Fergus at his nearby coffee house, Brasil, 2604 Dunlavy in the former Westheimer Bicycle and Lawnmower Shop (1936). Fergus expanded his backyard empire with the graphics-oriented Domy Books in the bungalow at 1709 Westheimer. And the trend has been continued by antique dealer Kay O'Toole in the garden pavilion that Murphy Mears designed behind her shop at 1921 Westheimer (2009).

I-122
Forum of Civics Building
[now River Oaks
Garden Club Building]
2503 Westheimer Road
1910, E. Lane
1927, John F. Staub, Birdsall P. Briscoe, and J. W. Northrop, Jr.

For Will C. Hogg, Staub remodeled the old John Smith County School into a "New England Town Hall"—a community center from which Hogg's Forum of Civics could promote the benefits of planned urban development. Hogg's ideals for Houston were not generally shared, and, after his death in 1930, the organization lapsed. Since 1942 the building has been the headquarters of the River Oaks Garden Club, which installed a series of handsome gardens behind the Forum of Civics (1955, J. Allen Myers, Jr. and Herbert Skogland). The building was restored in 1986 by Graham B. Luhn.

I-123
Northern Trust Bank of Texas Building
2701 Kirby Drive
1992, William T. Cannady & Associates

Tectonic refinement gives this bank building, with its echo of the Italianate architecture of Rice University, a dignified presence along the Kirby strip. Next door at 2727 Kirby, is a 30-story, 96-unit condo tower by Ziegler Cooper (2009). The tower's forward-tilting profile and vertically accentuated curtain wall of glass and stainless steel dramatize its height. Next door Tigerman Fugman McCurry's Hard Rock Café (1986) at 2801 Kirby was demolished in 2006.

I-124
West Ave
2800 Kirby Drive
2010, Looney Ricks Kiss

West Ave is a 5-acre, 7-story, mixed-use retail, residential, and parking complex occupying four blocks. Developed by Urban Partners of Dallas and the Gables Residential real estate investment trust of Atlanta, it introduces intensive urbanism to the Kirby retail corridor, a bastion of Houston-style suburbanism since the 1950s. The architecture, described by the developers as classic Art Deco with southern Mediterranean accents, does not do the project justice. Substituting styling clichés for architecture deprives West Ave of the urban dignity and authority it might otherwise have exerted.

I-121 Winlow-Westheimer District

I-125 Penguin Arms Apartments

I-126 Frost Office Building

I-127 Kuhl-Linscomb

I-128 Euclid House

I-129 House

I-125
Penguin Arms Apartments
2902 Revere Street
1950, Arthur Moss

Moss's zany Penguin Arms, a Houston version of a much-publicized California house by Harwell Hamilton Harris, was one of the original examples of "Googie" architecture decried by Douglas Haskell in a famous satirical diatribe published in 1952. John Kaliski aptly described this building: "It seems either poised for take-off or imploding even as one views it."

I-126
Frost Office Building
2930 Revere Street
1985, Ray Bailey Architects

This compact office and apartment building with structured parking tucked below is a colorful homage to the work of Taft Architects. Indicative of the turn-of-the-millennium real estate cycle in the Kirby corridor was the replacement of the Plaza Lincoln-Mercury dealership, one of the many auto dealerships built along Kirby in the 1950s, with Whole Foods Market (2000) at 2955 Kirby by the Austin architects Hatch Partnership.

I-127
Kuhl-Linscomb
2403, 2407, 2408, 2410, 2416, 2418 Steel Street
2004

Interior designer Pam Kuhl-Linscomb was inspired to take six very uninspiring duplex apartment buildings constructed in the 1950s and reimagine them as settings for her "lifestyle" store, a marketing and style sensation in Houston, where retail presentation otherwise remains firmly fixed in the conventions of the 1970s.

I-128
Euclid House
2214 Branard Avenue
1999, Dillon Kyle and Grace Pierce

Investor Christopher Knapp built this as an experiment to test the market for compact, architect-designed houses.

I-129
House
3411 Morningside Drive
1998, Wulf Focke and Geoffrey Brune

This house is a concatenation of lively shapes.

I-130
House
2248 Colquitt Street
2004, Wittenberg Oberholzer Partnership

Faced with corrugated steel panels, this house focuses on an east-side garden court. The Colquitt Court subdivision, where this house is located, became the site of new, architect-designed housing in the 2000s. Joining this house are one at 2223 Colquitt by Metropolitan Design Group (2005) and a pair by architect Scott Ballard at 2228 (2000) and 2217 (2000).

I-131
Fred Winchell Studio
1953-1955 Richmond Avenue
1954, Harwood Taylor and Burdette Keeland

Built in front of a 1-story, steel-framed studio for photographer Fred Winchell, a pair of apartments raised on steel columns above parking stalls were the model for Taylor's subsequent Richmond office buildings. In the early 1960s Keeland remodeled the high-ceilinged, sky-lit Winchell Studio to turn it into the elegantly unconventional house of Houston's great modern interior designer, Sally Sherwin Walsh. Kathy Heard Design occupies the studio and is responsible for conservation of this modernist gem.

I-130 House

I-131 Fred Winchell Studio

I-132 Robert McClain Gallery and Sicardi Gallery

I-133 Haven

I-134 Kipling Townhouses

I-135 House

I-136 McAshan House

I-132
Robert McClain Gallery and Sicardi Gallery
2242-2246 Richmond Avenue
2001, Marshall Reid

Architect Reid designed this restrained building for art dealer Robert McClain. It is faced with calmly proportioned planes of brick and steel panels that step back around outdoor spaces for art exhibition and a parking lot. The Office of James Burnett was the landscape architect.

I-133
Haven
2502 Algerian Way
2009, Collaborative Projects

For a restaurant based on the theme of modern, sustainable cuisine, Jim Herd, Geoffrey Brune, and Melanie Pereira fitted out a basic steel shed with sleek, understated design.

I-134
Kipling Townhouses
2800 Kipling Street
1974, Burdette Keeland & Associates with Donald C. Reese

By manipulating shallowly layered planes and degrees of transparency within openings, Keeland created a complex set of elevations for this row of four houses, which directs attention upward and away from the double-car garage doors at street level. Diagonally across the intersection at 2900 Virginia are the Virginia Townhouses (1983, Burdette Keeland & Associates with Donald C. Reese), triangular in section with iron gates detailed after the interlocking geometric figures of Josef Albers. The ski-slope profiling does attract one's attention, but the houses don't hold their own at street level with the assurance of the Kipling Townhouses.

I-135
House
2819 Ferndale Street
1976, I. W. Coburn & Associates

Coburn, a Chicago architect, walled off the street sides of this freestanding house and organized rooms around two patio gardens. Details are hard edged, but the atmosphere is Mexican. The circles that penetrate the chimney stacks are a signature Coburn detail.

I-136
McAshan House
2905 Kipling Street
1981, Val Glitsch

To cope with a sliver site at the end of a cul-de-sac, Glitsch designed this tall, thin, gable-roofed house as a clapboard-faced superstructure set atop an exposed concrete block substructure. The Ferndale Addition neighborhood, with its eclectic mix of modern and florid neo-Georgian row houses, is what Laura Furman described in her novel, *The Shadow Line*, as "shallow River Oaks"—not in the mother community but near enough to absorb some of its less conventional spill-over population.

I-137
MacKie & Kamrath Building
2709-2713 Ferndale Street
1947, MacKie & Kamrath

Fred MacKie and Karl Kamrath developed this office building complex, which included their studio at 2713. The small scale, the lovingly crafted organic materials, and the dynamic shaping of roof and wall planes, cut into with glass, still radiate their enthusiasm for the new. Since Kamrath's death in 1988, his family has maintained the complex in exemplary condition.

I-138
Staub & Rather Building
2814 Virginia Street
1948, Staub & Rather

Staub and Rather's associate, William C. Caldwell, designed this Contemporary style building to house their architecture studio. The angled, canopy-covered breezeway that leads from Virginia to the front door, with its big-scaled concrete *brise-soleil*, has more architectural presence than the building itself.

I-139
Anderson House and Shop
2911-2913 Ferndale Street
1976, Anderson/Wilson

Beginning with this free-standing, urban courtyard house that incorporates a retail shop at ground level, Bill Anderson staked out Ferndale as his territory, designing 2912-14 (1992), 2915 (1986), 2917 (1985), and 2923 (1992).

I-137 MacKie & Kamrath Building

I-138 Staub & Rather Building

I-139 Anderson House and Shop

I-140 Kirby Court Apartments

I-141 Lake Street Apartments

I-142 Glitsch-Inman House

I-143 The Zephyr

I-144 Mix Contemporary

I-140
Kirby Court Apartments
2700 Steel Street
1949, Robert W. Clemens & Associates

Dr. William T. Dickey, his son William M. Dickey, and grandson W. T. Dickey have owned, developed, leased, and managed property along Kirby since the 1890s. William M. Dickey built this 64-unit apartment complex in 14 2-story buildings that line Steel and are framed by a majestic avenue of Live Oak trees. Dr. Dickey platted the West Park Addition in the 1890s and replatted a portion of it, including the Kirby Court site, as the College Park Addition in 1910. William M. Dickey developed the Avalon Place subdivision along Kirby between San Felipe and Westheimer between 1935 and 1941, and, after World War II, he negotiated long-term leases for much of the commercial property along Kirby between Westheimer and West Alabama. He also built the 12-story Regency House at 2701 Westheimer (1963, Harry A. Turner & Charles Geyer).

I-141
Lake Street Apartments
3310 Lake Street
1952, William N. Floyd with Harwood Taylor and William R. Jenkins

This is set of modern courtyard apartments bespeaks the influence of Los Angeles on Houston in the 1950s.

I-142
Glitsch-Inman House
3314 Lake Street
1998, Val Glitsch

Architect Glitsch and her husband, contractor Gary Inman, built this compact, vertically organized, steel panel-faced courtyard house on a site that seems tight on the outside but is spatially expansive from within. Next door at 2709 Colquitt is a more sculpturally assertive house by architect Sharon Tyler Hoover (1996).

I-143
The Zephyr
2627 Colquitt Street
1985, Arquitectonica

Ever ready with a new slant on design, Arquitectonica refaced this existing commercial building with parallelogram-shaped windows framed with gold-spray-painted aluminum, and writhing, flexible red drain pipes. Tenant spaces are occupied principally by art galleries. The 2600-2800 blocks of Colquitt contain one of Houston's most intensive cluster of art galleries.

I-144
Mix Contemporary
2707 Colquitt Street
2006, Albert Marichal

New York architect Marichal designed this 3-story, concrete-framed townhouse as a high fashion women's clothes store, incorporating an exhilarating roof terrace and code-required, ground-level parking.

I-145
Studio-House
2712 Colquitt Street
2000, 2007, Val Glitsch

Glitsch designed this very thin, steel-faced, 2-story building as flexible space that could be used for work or dwelling. Initially the house served as her architectural studio, but in 2007 she remodeled and expanded it into a single-family house.

I-146
Virginia Point
3319 Virginia Street
2008, Adams Architects

Gail and Joe Adams designed this 2-story, single-family, steel-framed and -faced house as a demonstration of environmentally sustainable practices and technologies. Asakura Robinson was the landscape architect. Facing it at 3318 Virginia is a walled house by Allen Bianchi (2007). On the same block, at 3207 Virginia, is a dramatic 2-story house by Metropolitan Design Group (2008).

I-147
Lynn Goode Gallery
2719 Colquitt Street
1991, Carlos Jiménez

Jiménez designed this former art gallery as an homage to the square. It engages the surrounding Live Oaks outside and from within. But bereft of the bright orange mango color with which it was originally painted, the building no longer exerts its presence in the landscape.

I-146 Virginia Point

I-145 Studio-House

I-147 Lynn Goode Gallery

I-148 House

I-148
House
3319 Ferndale Street
2002, Dillon Kyle

The David Crockett Addition, a 32-acre subdivision developed in 1949 by Frank W. Sharp, was built out with small, 1-story ranch houses. During the 1990s these began to be replaced by much larger houses, many of them designed by architects. This 2-story, brick-faced house incorporates an old-fashioned screened porch.

I-149 House

I-149
House
3318 Ferndale Street
2009, Strasser Ragni

Scott Strasser and Erick Ragni specialized in houses that are outwardly simple, but inwardly complex. The cubic proportions of this green-painted, stucco-faced house are mirrored in a square-shaped window that from inside frames the neighborhood's oak trees. Note the "stepped" driveway leading up to the garage.

I-150 House

I-150
House
3302 Ferndale Street
2007, Wittenberg Oberholzer Partnership

Evoking the adobe-walled houses of Santa Fe, this 1- and 2-story house is very closed from the street, which makes its internal amplitude and expansiveness all the more surprising.

I-151 House

I-151
House
3110 Ferndale Street
1997, William F. Stern & Associates

This modern house subtly evokes early 20th-century Houston houses in its four-square proportions and openness to the out doors. Stern and Bucek Architects designed the gray-painted wood house next door at 3114 (2001).

I-152 House

I-152
House
3018 Ferndale Street
1995, Carlos Jiménez

Because they share rose-colored St. Joe brick facing, this planar-fronted house engages in a dialogue with the Stern-designed house at 3110. Jiménez also alluded to the 1950s contemporary buildings flanking the gallery he designed on Colquitt to preserve a sense of continuity in the David Crockett Addition.

I-153
Le Voisinage
3000 Elbert Street
1993, Adams Architects

Gail and Joe Adams approached the design of this 15-house complex as a problem in community design. They spatially shaped houses so that they frame a hierarchical sequence of community green spaces within the center of the site. Across Elbert Street, at 3202 Bammel, is a sculpturally aggressive tin house, also by Adams Architects (1993).

I-154
House
3207 Sackett Street
1997, Michael Landrum

Landrum's houses never lack bravado. This bracketed, neo-Italianate production is finished in dark red stucco. Landrum also designed the Mexican-flavored house next door at 3203 Sackett (1996). Sarah Lake of San Antonio was the landscape architect for both.

I-155
St. Luke's United Methodist Church
3471 Westheimer Road
1951, 1954, 1957, Mark Lemmon

Dallas architect Lemmon specialized in Texan-sized, Georgian style churches for affluent Protestant congregations. St. Luke's is splendidly big. Next door at 3435 Westheimer is the 16-story River Oaks Apartments by Cameron Fairchild & Associates, a glass-walled slab shaded by its expanded floor slabs.

I-153 Le Voisinage

I-154 House

I-155 St. Luke's United Methodist Church

I-156 Saint Street Swim Club

I-157 Gamma Construction Company Building

I-158 Innova (20 Greenway Plaza)

I-159 Central Presbyterian Church

I-156
Saint Street Swim Club
2717 Saint Street
1995, Kendall Hamman

Hamman neatly encapsulated an indoor pool for this swimming school in a utilitarian building designed with economy and style. North-facing garage doors can be retracted to open the pool to the outdoors. The Swim Club was built in Luvin' Canada (its legal name is Audubon Place), which had been an African-American neighborhood stretching from Westheimer south past West Alabama. Former residents, who began to be displaced in the late 1960s, and almost all of the community's modest houses are gone. Saint, Joanel, and Alabama Court still retain a trace of difference that sets Luvin' Canada apart from surrounding development.

I-157
Gamma Construction Company Building
2808 Joanel Street
1993, Kirksey-Meyers

A base course of textured concrete block, an elongated eave sheltering east-facing second-floor windows, and a projecting vault-roofed entrance bay give this professional building strong architectural presence. At 3600 West Alabama (but entered from Joanel) is the Thompson + Hanson landscape architects compound (1999), a rare effort in Houston to design an outdoor garden setting for retail and social events. Allen Bianchi designed the buildings. The compound also contains the Tiny Boxwoods restaurant at 3614 West Alabama (2008).

I-158
Innova (20 Greenway Plaza)
[now Koch Building]
3600 block Cummins Lane
1984, Cambridge Seven Associates
and Lloyd Jones Brewer & Associates

Innova, a 10-story box sheathed in polished black Impala granite, was built to contain contract furniture manufacturers' showrooms. The stair-stepped openings on its north and south sides externalize the ingenious organizational scheme that Cambridge Seven's Charles Redmon devised for the building. Innova is fissured in two by a stepped-section escalator core that rises diagonally in 2-story increments to a sky-lit exhibition and restaurant court at the top of the building. This provides for the admission of daylight into and views out from what otherwise was a windowless box. The architectural detailing, inside and out, was superlative. Innova is located in Greenway's third tier, in what had been the Lamar-Weslayan subdivision. Century Development, which developed Greenway Plaza, bought out the entire restricted subdivision in 1968 and an adjoining subdivision in 1969 in order to facilitate the westward expansion of Greenway Plaza. Houston's real estate depression of the 1980s wiped out the office furniture market, for which Innova was built. Consequently much of its floor space remained unleased. In 1997-98 Innova was radically altered through transformation into an office building for Koch Industries. This entailed the insertion of windows in its previously solid walls.

I-159
Central Presbyterian Church
3788 Richmond Avenue
1962, Wilson, Morris, Crain & Anderson

Architect Talbott Wilson designed this church complex for the congregation of which he was a member. Beautifully detailed and richly ornamented, the Saarinen-inspired church faces inward to a cloistered courtyard surrounded by classroom and community buildings and a freestanding chapel that is a smaller version of the church. In 2010 the site was put up for sale by the congregation after it determined it could no longer afford to operate. (Demolished in 2012)

I-160 8-12 and 9-11 Greenway Plaza

I-161 1, 2, 3, 5 Greenway Plaza

I-162 Jefferson Chemical Company Building

I-163 Humble Research Center

I-160
8-12 and 9-11 Greenway Plaza
3700 block Richmond Avenue
1982, 1978, 1979, Lloyd Jones Brewer & Associates

Four reflective glass office buildings straddling Richmond—two rounded 15-story (8 and 12) and two slab-shaped 31-story (9 and 11)—were built as part of Greenway Plaza's third phase of development. The uninflected, gridded surfaces of 9 (Coastal Tower) and 11 (Summit Tower) gleam like a pair of turquoise ice cubes; they are especially dramatic just before sunset. Poised between 9 and 11 is *Archway* by Ben Woitena. The elegant skyways spanning Richmond are also by Lloyd Jones Brewer & Associates, as are the twin towers of the 30-story Greenway Condominiums (1980, 1981) in the 3600 block of Timmons. Century had a propensity for constructing buildings in pairs.

I-161
1, 2, 3, 5 Greenway Plaza
3500 block Richmond Avenue
1969, 1971, 1972, 1973. Lloyd, Morgan & Jones

Century's initial phase of development, after it acquired the 4-year-old, 41-acre Greenway office park in 1967, was this complex of buildings: the twin 11-story Eastern Airlines and Union Carbide buildings, followed by the 21-story Kellogg Building and the 31-story Conoco Tower. This entire phase incorporated a massive 3,500-car underground garage, the largest continuous concrete pour in Houston's construction history at the time of its construction. The garage encompasses The Underground, a subterranean retail concourse modeled, like 3 and 5, on the work of I. M. Pei. The Underground is connected to the second phase of Greenway's development, which included the Stouffer's Hotel (now Renaissance Houston, 1976, Lloyd

Jones Associates) and the city-owned sports and entertainment arena, The Summit (1976, Kenneth Bentsen Associates, Lloyd Jones Associates, consulting architects), one of Kenneth Bentsen's finest works. It was extensively altered by Morris Architects, Clarence Shaw Architects, and Studio Red in 2005 when it was transformed into Lakewood Church. Because of the expense involved with below ground construction, Century developed the later phases of Greenway with conventional, above-grade parking structures. This actually makes for a more coherently organized site plan, given that Greenway Plaza is car-oriented and not a pedestrian environment. Across Richmond were two Century projects that predate its involvement with Greenway: the 2-story Dow Center at 3636, an early Houston work of Caudill Rowlett Scott (1960; demolished in 2005), and the 9-story 3616 Richmond Building (1966, Caudill Rowlett Scott), extensively altered when it was transformed into an apartment building in 2006.

I-162
Jefferson Chemical Company Building
3336 Richmond Avenue
1965, Neuhaus & Taylor

Prior to the development of Greenway Plaza, this was one of Century Development's largest office buildings, a 4-story, glass-surfaced box set atop a depressed parking garage and organized around two open-air courtyards. The building's formal image is indebted to Minoru Yamasaki's Northwestern Life Insurance Company Building in Minneapolis; the veranda of stick-like columns supporting plaster vaults was intended to evoke historic colonnades while still remaining modern.

I-163
Humble Research Center
[now ExxonMobil Research Center]
3102 Buffalo Speedway
1954, MacKie & Kamrath

The Humble Oil & Refining Company pioneered the transfer of technical support operations from the industrial East End and Ship Channel, where such operations had been concentrated, to the west side of Houston, where its white-collar staff lived. As a result Buffalo Speedway was transformed into one of the earliest suburban office corridors in Houston. MacKie & Kamrath's authorship is obvious in the horizontal organization of the elevations and the detailing of its brick and limestone facing. A third floor and a pair of wings were added to the building by MacKie & Kamrath in 1959. In 2004 the 100,000-SF Upstream Technical Training Center by PageSoutherlandPage, a sleek, retro-mod salute to the MacKie & Kamrath building, was completed next to the Research Center.

I-164 Macham Building

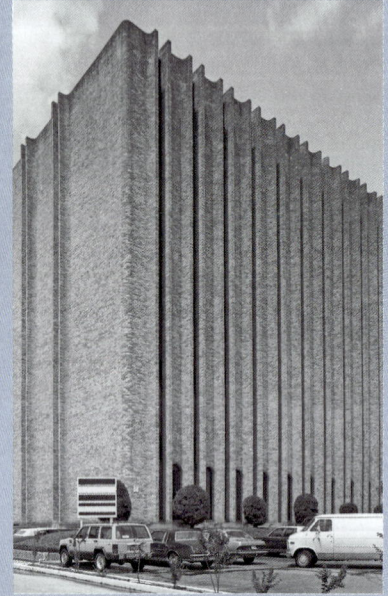

I-166 2990 Richmond Building

I-164
Macham Building
3230 Sul Ross Avenue
1959, Thompson McCleary and Hamilton Brown

During the late 1950s the back streets off West Alabama were developed in a spontaneous (not to say haphazard) manner with small professional buildings, some built to house architects' studios. McCleary and Brown produced one of the best of these, a pair of flat-roofed, courtyard offices, detailed with exposed glue-laminated wooden beams, and connected, in the best Los Angeles style, by a roofed central drive-through. Studio Red completed a remodeling of the building in 2009.

I-165
Phoenix Insurance Company of Hartford Building
3323 Richmond Avenue
1961, Neuhaus & Taylor

Gerald D. Hines and Century Development's Kenneth Schnitzer, between them, were chiefly responsible for Office Park, as the blocks of Richmond between Wakeforest and Buffalo Speedway were called. In reaction to the confused patterns of development in the Alabama corridor, they neatly lined up office buildings along Richmond. En route typologies shifted from this classic Neuhaus & Taylor box-on-stilts-above-parking, built by Hines (the eyebrow overhangs are quintessential period pieces), to conventional multi-story office blocks. Style was displayed exuberantly; every design mannerism from the first half of the 1960s is visible in these three blocks. A more sedate version of the Phoenix type, also by Neuhaus & Taylor for Hines, is the Pontiac Motor Division Building at 3121 Richmond (1961).

I-166
2990 Richmond Building
2990 Richmond Avenue
1966, Neuhaus & Taylor

This 5-story speculative office building, faced with curved masonry fins that peel back to reveal vertically aligned strip windows, was Hines's biggest office building prior to One Shell Plaza downtown. Harwood Taylor purposefully played off the adjoining 2900 Richmond Building (1964) and the 3000 Richmond Building (1964, Wilson, Morris, Crain & Anderson) in order to achieve a unified streetscape. The district south of River Oaks between Kirby Drive and Weslayan Avenue spatially illustrates the sequence from roadside strip developments along secondary streets to corporate installations along major thoroughfares to comprehensively managed office parks tied to the regional freeway network. Where Buffalo Speedway (an evocative name dating from the 1920s) and Richmond Avenue intersect, these three stages are juxtaposed. In 2002 preservation students at the University of Houston surveyed Office Park. Their documentation was published in Barry Moore and Anna Mod's, *City Houston/Style Modern: The Richmond Corridor* (2002).

I-165 *Phoenix Insurance Company of Hartford Building*

Post Oak

Post Oak

Tour J-1

Post Oak was not transformed from countryside into the second city center of Houston overnight. But it gives the impression that change occurred with just such abruptness. Post Oak Boulevard exudes newness. Gleaming buildings, deflected into provocative shapes, are widely spaced on the flat prairie west of River Oaks, a plain artificially bounded on the east by Loop 610 and crisscrossed by major westbound thoroughfares: Richmond, Westheimer, San Felipe, and Woodway. Post Oak Boulevard is now what Main Street used to be, the prime retail corridor of the city. It is anchored by the Galleria, an introverted, air-conditioned, pedestrian-scaled mixed-use complex. What one sees in Post Oak is downtown with all the big buildings pushed far apart in order to leave plenty of room for cars, both moving and parked. Success, though, has brought to this area a recurrence of the very problem that occasioned the gradual disintegration of the downtown retail district – levels of traffic congestion that Houston motorists consider unacceptable. A far smaller percentage of the real estate in Post Oak is devoted to streets than is the case downtown, so that congestion here constitutes an even more serious problem. One suggestion for alleviation, not altogether facetious, has been to impose a grid of streets and

blocks on the area. Concern has even emerged over the lack of pedestrian amenities and connections within the area, which force people to drive from place to place. Post Oak now finds, paradoxically, that it has experienced that shift from periphery to center that River Oaks underwent. Houstonians who live within the confines of Loop 610 are apt to think of it as the suburban usurper of downtown Houston. But from the perspective of far Houston, downtown and Post Oak are the high-density edges of the center city.

1. **Five Post Oak Park Building,** 5 Post Oak Park Drive
2. **Owsley House,** 65 Briar Hollow Lane
3. **Post Oak Park Townhouses,** 1317 Post Oak Park Drive
4. **U.S. Home Building,** 1177 West Loop South
5. **Caudill Rowlett Scott Building,** 1111 West Loop South
6. **Four Seasons Inn on the Park,** 4 Riverway
7. **IBM Building,** 2 Riverway
8. **Allied Chemical Building,** 1 Riverway
9. **5000 Longmont,** 5000 Longmont Drive
10. **Four-Leaf Towers,** 5100 San Felipe Road
11. **Cosmopolitan Condominiums Houston,** 1600 Post Oak Boulevard
12. **Four Oaks Place,** 1300–1400 Post Oak Boulevard
13. **Southern National Bank Uptown Banking Center,** 1101 Post Oak Boulevard
14. **Uptown Park,** 1101 Uptown Park Boulevard
15. **Post Oak Arches,** Post Oak Boulevard
16. **Blvd Place,** 800 Post Oak Boulevard
17. **Post Oak Row,** 1801 Post Oak Boulevard
18. **Warwick Post Oak,** 2001 Post Oak Boulevard
19. **Post Oak Central,** 1980–2000 Post Oak Boulevard
20. **Dominion Post Oak,** 2323 McCue Road
21. **One West Loop Plaza,** 2425 West Loop South
22. **3D/International Tower,** 1900 West Loop South
23. **Control Data Corporation Building,** 2000 West Loop South
24. **Stewart Title Building,** 2200 West Loop South
25. **Galleria,** 5015 Westheimer Road
26. **Transco Tower,** 2800 Post Oak Boulevard
27. **The Lake on Post Oak Park,** 3000–3050 Post Oak Boulevard
28. **Mercer West Tower,** 3388 Sage Road
29. **Ranger Insurance Company Building,** 5333 Westheimer Road
30. **Guest Quarters Galleria West,** 5353 Westheimer Road
31. **One Westheimer Plaza,** 5718 Westheimer Road
32. **Memorial Lutheran Church,** 5800 Westheimer Road
33. **J. Frank Jungman Branch, Houston Public Library,** 5830 Westheimer Road
34. **Augusta Green Building,** 2603 Augusta Drive
35. **San Felipe Plaza,** 5847 San Felipe Road
36. **Emerson Unitarian Church,** 1900 Bering Drive
37. **The Park Regency Terrace Residences,** 2333 Bering Drive
38. **Marathon Oil Tower,** 5555 San Felipe Road
39. **St. Michael The Archangel Catholic Church,** 1801 Sage Road
40. **Kaim House,** 5203 Stamper Way

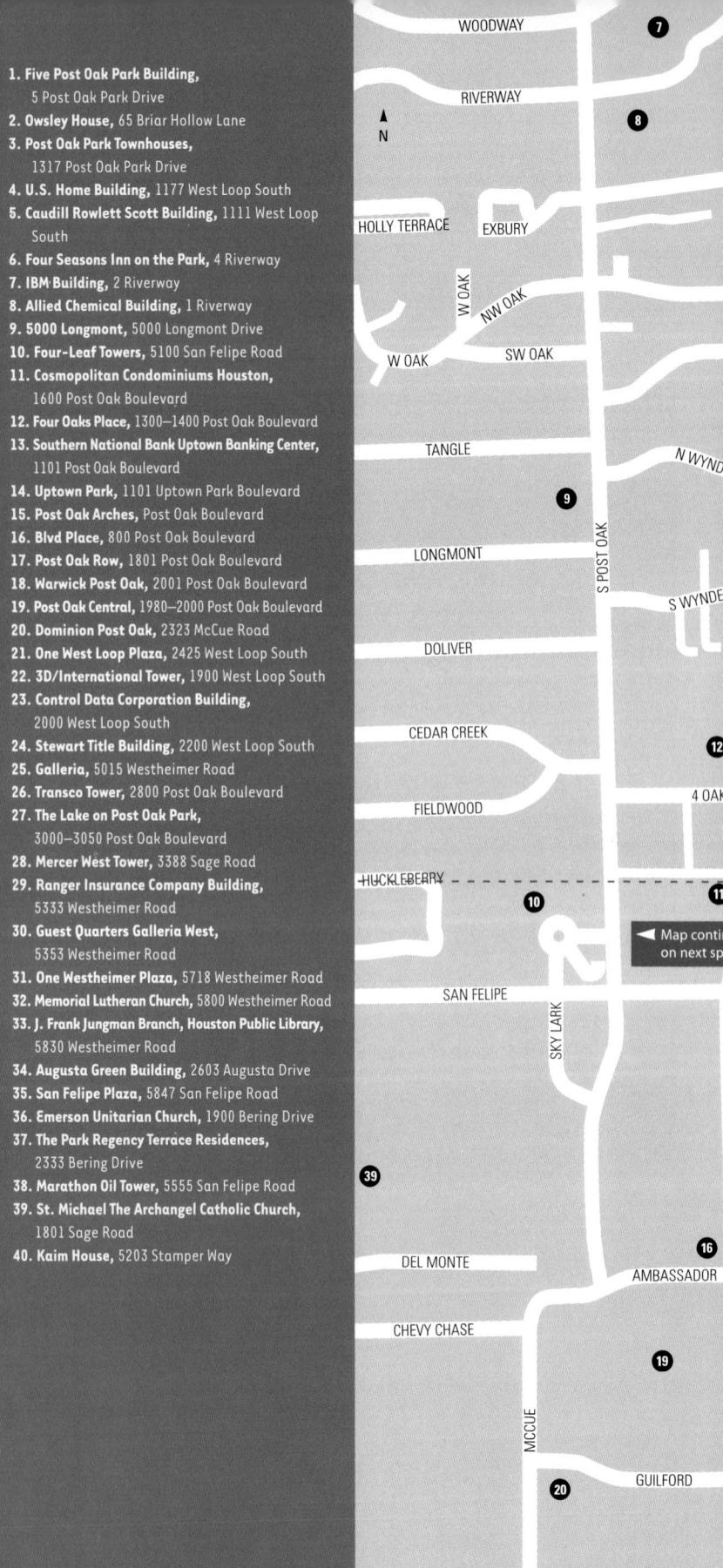

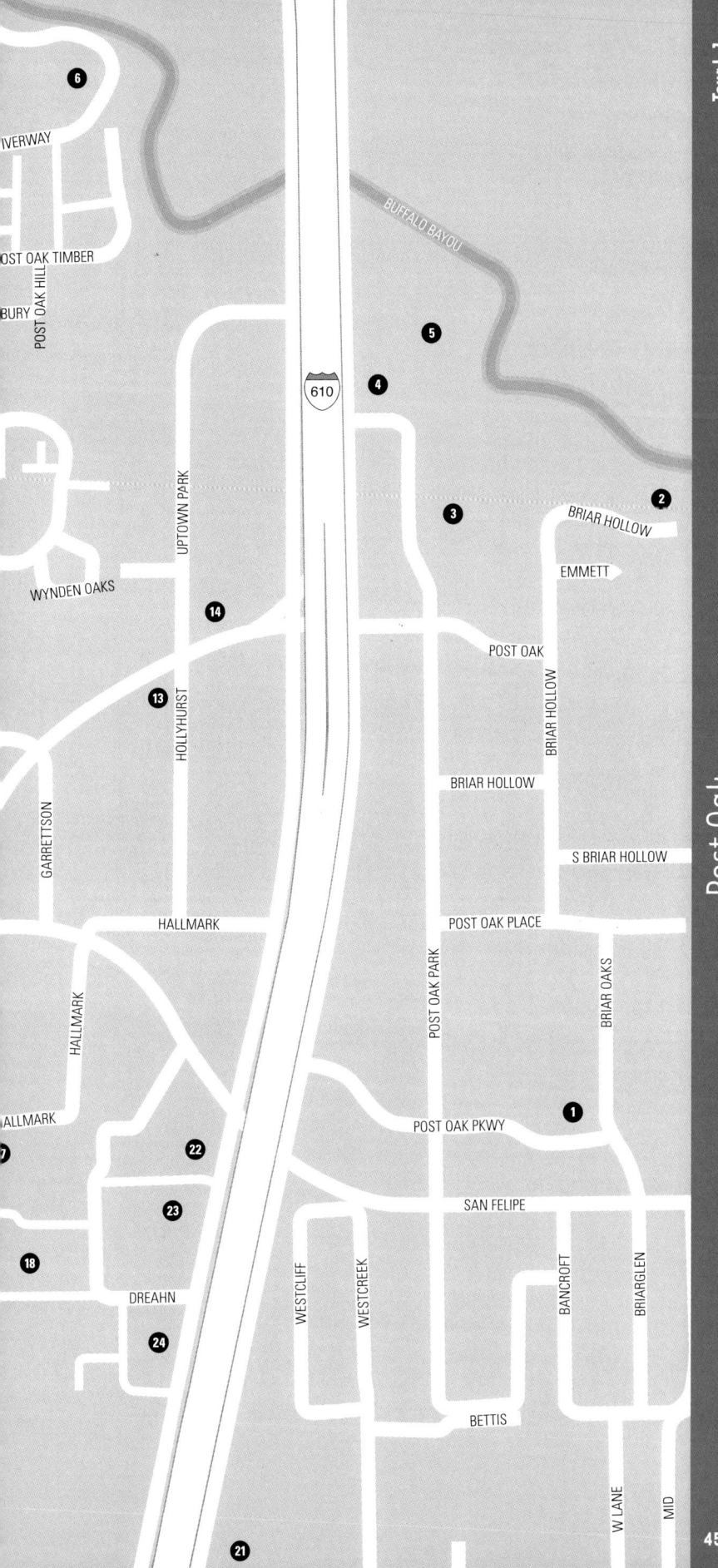

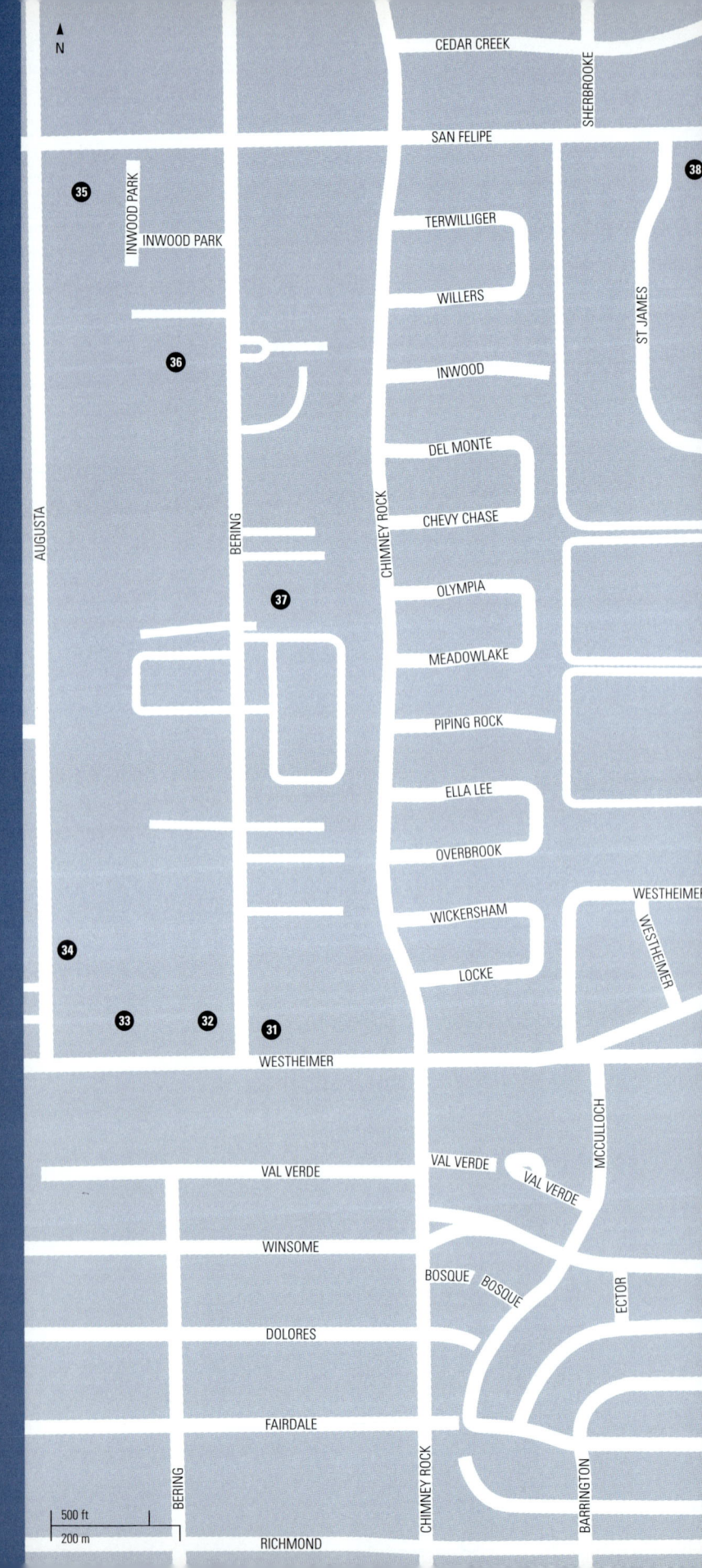

Post Oak

Tour J-1

461

J-1 Five Post Oak Park Building

J-2 Owsley House

J-3 Post Oak Townhouses

J-1
Five Post Oak Park Building
5 Post Oak Park Drive
1983, Morris*Aubry Architects

This sculpturally shaped office tower is clad in travertine and bronze solar glass. Its flared base, stepped windows, and curved top betrayed the first stirrings of corporate postmodernism in Houston. Across the street at 1919 Briar Oaks is the deluxe 12-story, 248-room Remington Hotel (now the St. Regis Houston Hotel, 1982, Shepherd+Boyd), notable for its chic motor courts and upscale mod-trad decor. Next to the Remington, at 1811 Briar Oaks, is the Junior League of Houston Building (1985, Morris*Aubry Architects), which does nothing to dispel the ethnic stereotype implied in the descriptive term Junior League Georgian.

J-2
Owsley House
65 Briar Hollow Lane
1960, Bolton & Barnstone

This is one of Howard Barnstone's most sensational houses, a 3-story pavilion framed in steel with walls that are entirely of glass set far back on a site that falls away to Buffalo Bayou. Steel galleries entirely surround the house. The crisp lines, sure proportions, and stunning transparency of the house remain quite captivating. Fred Buxton was the landscape architect. It was rehabilitated in 2011. Around it the Briar Hollow neighborhood imploded in the 1990s and 2000s as single-family houses were demolished and each lot converted into a gated subdivision. Still surviving are the modern, split level house at 62 Briar Hollow (1961) and the contemporary ranch type house at 61 Briar Hollow (1965), both by Wilson, Morris, Crain & Anderson.

J-3
Post Oak Park Townhouses
1317 Post Oak Park Drive
1966, Charles Tapley Associates

Tapley, a landscape architect as well as an architect, grouped these row houses along narrow greenway corridors to preserve existing trees on the heavily wooded site. The developer insisted that house fronts be stylistically varied, but Tapley was able to design their rear elevations as handsomely composed planes of cedar, marked off by light-colored wood trim. This complex was one of the first increments of the 58-acre Post Oak Park, begun in Briar Hollow by Tenneco and the J. V. Dorfman Development Company after the opening of the first segment of West Loop South in the mid 1960s that escalated real estate values, inciting the transformation of Briar Hollow from a country estate neighborhood to an office park, where building complexes chart the cycles of Houston's real estate economy during the last half century.

J-4
U.S. Home Building
[now 1177 West Loop South Building]
1177 West Loop South
1979, Caudill Rowlett Scott

Caudill Rowlett Scott's Paul Kennon was responsible for the design of this doubly faced, 18-story concrete-framed office building. Toward the West Loop it presents a sleek silvery curve that seems to respond to the dynamic rhythm of passing traffic. The opposite side, which faces Memorial Park, is jagged in plan, rather than curved, and clad in dark bronze solar glass. The plan figure derives from the work of the Finnish architect Alvar Aalto; the flashy imagery is pure Houston.

J-5
Caudill Rowlett Scott Building
[now Gulf Coast Veterinary Specialists and Animal Emergency Clinic]
1111 West Loop South
1969, Caudill Rowlett Scott

William W. Caudill led the "design team" (a Caudill Rowlett Scott conceptual innovation) in producing this unusual building to house the Caudill Rowlett Scott architectural practice. The 1-story, 55,000-SF reinforced concrete building lies beneath its parking lot, an arrangement made possible by the site's topographic slope down toward Buffalo Bayou. Only the entry pavilion projects above the rooftop parking court. When CRS Sirrine sold the Caudill Rowlett Scott architectural practice to Hellmuth, Obata + Kassabaum in 1994, the "White House," as it was known within the firm, was also sold.

J-4 U.S. Home Building

J-5 Caudill Rowlett Scott Building

J-6 Four Seasons Inn on the Park

J-7 IBM Building

J-8 Allied Chemical Building

J-9 5000 Longmont

J-6
Four Seasons Inn on the Park
[now Omni Houston Hotel]
4 Riverway
1981, S. I. Morris Associates

Morris's Guy Jackson configured this 11-story, 383-room hotel in a crescent shape in response to the curve of Buffalo Bayou around the promontory on which the building is set. Simply detailed externally, the hotel contains sleekly finished public spaces that are architectural in character and quite elegant. The SWA Group installed the brightly colored wall trough fountains in the swimming pool gardens, borrowing from the Mexican architect Luis Barragán. Unfortunately the grounds go under water when Buffalo Bayou overflows.

J-7
IBM Building
2 Riverway
1980, Caudill Rowlett Scott

For IBM's regional headquarters Caudill Rowlett Scott designed this building with energy conservation as a priority. The 17-story triangular-shaped block has a notched top, and its longest side faces north toward Woodway. The all-glass exteriors contain, ironically, only narrow horizontal window bands at each floor level. The windows were designed to be opened, however.

J-8
Allied Chemical Building
[now 1 Riverway Building]
1 Riverway
1978, S. I. Morris Associates

John Hansen built the 25-story Allied Chemical Building as the first increment of Riverway, a 28-acre, mixed-use complex that he developed on what once were the polo stable grounds of a family who lived in Courtlandt Place. John Bertini and Guy Jackson designed the stepped, faceted tower, which is faced with alternating bands of granite aggregate precast concrete panels and bronze solar glass. Inasmuch as it is visible from the north curve of Post Oak Boulevard, Allied Chemical figures conspicuously on the Post Oak skyline, along with its companion, the 20-story Internorth Building (now 3 Riverway Building, 1980, S. I. Morris Associates).

J-9
5000 Longmont
5000 Longmont Drive
1962, P. M. Bolton Associates

Preston Bolton developed and designed this community of courtyard houses aligned along a private street. The flat-roofed Miesian box, in which Bolton and his ex-partner, Howard Barnstone, specialized in the 1950s, was here faced with textured brick, high paneled wooden doors, and barred windows to give 5000 Longmont a slightly Mexican aspect. Bolton designed most of the houses on Longmont, including his own at No. 1. Hamilton Brown was responsible for 8 and 11, and Robert Sobel designed the house at 16.

J-10
Four-Leaf Towers
5100 San Felipe Road
1982, Cesar Pelli & Associates, Albert C. Martin & Associates, and Melton Henry Architects

Pelli's first Houston project was this pair of 40-story condominium towers built by the Milanese investors, Lorenzo and Giorgio Borlenghi. Pelli designed the curtain wall as a complex grid of rose-, salmon-, and cream-colored spandrel glass, interspersed with solar glass windows to express the spatial organization of the 200 units within each tower. The choice of colors and the provision of faceted caps atop the pent house levels were intended to give the project a domestic aspect. The towers figure prominently as spatial markers, thanks to their defined profiles and static relationship. Poised between them, atop the landscaped podium that conceals extensive underground parking, is Beverly Pepper's 50-foot-tall *Polygenesis* (1981). The 10-acre site was landscaped by The SWA Group.

J-10 Four-Leaf Towers

J-11 Cosmopolitan

J-12 Four Oaks Place

J-13 Southern National Bank Uptown

J-14 Uptown Park

J-15 Post Oak Arches

J-11
Cosmopolitan
1600 Post Oak Boulevard
2008, Brand + Allen

Indicative of the changes wrought in the Post Oak real estate market in the wake of the oil-induced recession of the 1980s and early '90s is this 22-story, glass curtain-wall-faced, setback apartment tower. Its postmodern jukebox profile causes the Cosmopolitan to figure strongly on Post Oak Boulevard. But from the south the tower obtrudes into the visual right-of-way of Pelli's Four Oaks Place, disrupting the urban vista without measuring up to Pelli's architectural sophistication. The problematic design standards that were a marked feature of large-scale architecture in Houston during the 1990s and 2000s are apparent here, although, in comparison to what got built in the Post Oak district during the housing bubble of the 2000s, the Cosmopolitan is competent and stylish. Randall Davis was the developer.

J-12
Four Oaks Place
1300-1400 Post Oak Boulevard
1983, Cesar Pelli & Associates and Melton Henry Architects

Pelli took advantage of the curve of Post Oak to site this group of towers—the 30-story 1330 Post Oak Boulevard Building in the middle, flanked by the 25-story Wells Fargo Tower and the 25-story BHP Billiton Tower, and, off to the west, the 14-story Interfin Building—as an axial terminator. Pelli gave the three tallest buildings flat tops and horizontally banded curtain walls of intense blue spandrel glass and silver reflective vision glass, indicating their open, loft-like, spatial arrangement. The parking structure, which is wrapped around the back of the towers, is surmounted by an arbor, beneath which pedestrians pass between buildings. The Borlenghis' own Interfin Building is in transition between Four Oaks and Four-Leaf; it gets a cap and is colored brown. Just behind it, at 1515 South Post Oak Lane, is Ma Maison (now Chianti), originally the country house of Dr. and Mrs. James Hill (1939, William Ward Watkin), which figured in *Baby Houston*, the novel written by Fanetta Wortham Hill's niece, June Arnold. It was saved and rehabilitated by Giorgio Borlenghi.

J-13
Southern National Bank Uptown
[now Prosperity Bank Uptown Banking Center]
1101 Post Oak Boulevard
2000, Kirksey

Stewart Morris, chairman of the board of the Southern National Bank, displayed his admiration for the architecture of Thomas Jefferson by having Kirksey design the bank's Post Oak branch as a tribute to Jefferson's Farmington in Charlottesville, Virginia of 1803. The image is recognizable, although Jefferson's proportional refinements lost something in the architectural translation.

J-14
Uptown Park
1101 Uptown Houston Park
2000, Brand + Allen

Interfin, developers of the Four-Leaf Towers and Four Oaks Place, is responsible for the 34-acre Uptown Park, which contains the sprawling Uptown Park "lifestyle" shopping center, two high-rise apartment towers (2000 and 2002, Ziegler Cooper), and the 6-story Hotel Granduca (2006, Brand + Allen), all overlooking the West Loop 610 South. The Uptown Park version of the New Urbanism looks suspiciously like business as usual, Houston style c 1965. The shopping center features seven buildings widely separated by gulfs of parking. The apartment towers and the hotel are lined up along the street that cuts through the complex. The architectural distance between Post Oak of the Gerald Hines era (Johnson/Burgee, Pei, Pelli)

and that of the millennium confirms Houston's architectural decline into the realm of the second rate.

J-15
Post Oak Arches
Post Oak Boulevard
1995, Communication Arts

The pairs of parabolic stainless steel arches that span Post Oak Boulevard at intervals, the flying saucers hovering menacingly above major intersections, the sci-fi light standards, and the jokey installations at the bases of some of the arches are an embarrassing, $11 million denial of the need for consistent urban design improvements in the Post Oak-Westheimer retail district. Given the high architectural standards that prevailed here in the 1970s and '80s, it is hard to account for the Uptown Houston Association's lack of confidence in urban designers and landscape architects, who might have endowed the district's public spaces with the coherence and beauty for which the arches are a trivial substitute.

J-16 Blvd Place

J-17 Post Oak Row

J-19 Post Oak Central

J-16
Blvd Place
1800 S. Post Oak Boulevard
2000, DMJM H&N

Retail real estate broker Ed Wulfe sought to make his mark on Houston by constructing a high-density, mixed-use complex that would adhere to the design standards Gerald Hines set along Post Oak in the 1970s and early '80s. The financial crash of 2008 occurred while construction of the first phase of Wulfe's 22-acre, 10-building, low- and high-rise Blvd Place was under construction, slowing the speed with which other components were built. The first increment, the 4-story 1 Blvd Place, is a sleek, neo-modern design by DMJM H&N of San Francisco (now AECOM) that stands with assurance alongside the buildings of Johnson, Pei, and Pelli. Its oversailing profile, cool white lines, and the generous scale of its frontage on Post Oak contrast with the comical styling themes and suburban spatiality that came to stand for postmodern luxe in uptown Houston during the 1990s and 2000s.

J-17
Post Oak Row
1801 Post Oak Boulevard
1972, Skidmore, Owings & Merrill and Wilson, Morris, Crain & Anderson

Gerald D. Hines Interests built this strip center for intermediate use of property in Smith Office Park. The center is faced with a simple but gracefully scaled portico composed of thick, wide-span steel beams and thin steel columns.

J-18
The Warwick Post Oak
[now Hilton Houston Post Oak Hotel]
2001 Post Oak Boulevard
1982, I. M. Pei & Partners and
Richard Fitzgerald & Partners

James Ingo Freed, the Pei partner in charge of the design of the Warwick, treated precast concrete panels as the modern equivalent of dressed stone. The result is a provocative "rusticated" curtain wall screen behind which the hotel's balconies are inserted. The diagonal site planning of Post Oak Central across the street led to the configuration of the 14-story, 460-room hotel, a relationship better appreciated in diagram than in actuality. The great cascade of silver reflective glass that breaks through the front of the hotel contrasts strikingly with the shape and texture of the concrete curtain wall. Pei's office detailed the 6-story lobby beneath the rolled glass vault and the hypostyle anteroom off the ballroom, to the left of the lobby.

Next door at 1901 Post Oak Boulevard is the 351-unit Lofts on Post Oak (2004, Wallace García Wilson and Jackson & Ryan Architects). An 8-story curved slab, faced with banded brick and a grid of bay windows, is the leading edge for an exceptionally dense 4-story mat of apartments organized around six interior light wells.

J-19
Post Oak Central
1980-2000 Post Oak Boulevard
1973, Johnson/Burgee Architects

Thanks to I. S. Brochstein, the custom woodwork manufacturer who owned this 17-acre site, Post Oak Central became Philip Johnson's first project for Gerald D. Hines Interests. The first building, the 24-story One Post Oak Central at 2000 Post Oak (1975, Johnson/Burgee and S. I. Morris Associates) established Johnson's theme: a sleekly banded charcoal and silver tower with faceted corners and two setback terraces. Two Post Oak Central (1978, Johnson/Burgee and Richard Fitzgerald & Partners) was the same building, deflected 45° into a parallelogram. Three (1981, Johnson/Burgee and Fitzgerald) is the most contorted of all, a right triangle in plan, located at the apex of a triangular open space to which all three buildings conform. This exercise in geometric deformation was inspired by Johnson's engagement with Minimalist art of the 1960s and '70s, a fascination expressed simultaneously in his design of Pennzoil Place in downtown Houston.

At 2200 Post Oak is the Redstone Companies' 20-story BBVA Compass Plaza (2013 HKS), a neo-modern block faced with a multitude of curtain walls.

J-18 The Warwick Post Oak (Galleria)

J-20 Dominion Post Oak

J-21 One West Loop Plaza

J-22 3D/International Tower

J-20
Dominion Post Oak
2323 McCue Road
2005, EDI

The twin pediments marking the skyline of this 31-story apartment building are the clue to its design development; they echo the pediments crowning 77 W. Wacker Drive, a 50-story office building in Chicago designed by Barcelona architect Ricardo Bofill's Taller de Arquitectura (1992). Hired by the Chicago developer, Whiteco Residential, to design this building, Bofill was history by the time it was completed. The pediments are the trace of his absence.

J-21
One West Loop Plaza
2425 West Loop South
1980, I. M. Pei & Partners and
Richard Fitzgerald & Partners

The aluminum curtain wall system, scored into panels that depend for effect upon sure proportioning, is more impressive from a distance than close up. The 11-story building, developed by J. C. Helms, is U-shaped in plan and encloses a central atrium lit by north-facing clear glass carried on a vertical steel space frame. The building was to have been the first of several, which explains its orientation away from the freeway. James Freed was the Pei partner in charge of design.

J-22
3D/International Tower
1900 West Loop South
1979, 3D/International

Parsons, the successor firm to 3D/I, is the chief tenant of this building designed for Hines Interests; it is a gleaming compilation of silver stainless steel spandrel and silver reflective glass, offset in plan to give it sculptural interest and additional corner office spaces.

J-23
Control Data Corporation Building
2000 West Loop South
1971, Skidmore, Owings & Merrill and Wilson, Morris, Crain & Anderson

For this 22-story office slab, built by Hines Interests, Skidmore, Owings & Merrill-Chicago's engineering partner, Fazlur R. Khan, devised the first instance of composite steel-concrete construction in the world. The light steel structural frame was erected, precast window units were slotted into its interstices, and these panels served as formwork for poured concrete that encased the steel, creating an economical structural system.

J-24
Stewart Title Building
2200 West Loop South
1974, Skidmore, Owings & Merrill and S. I. Morris Associates

In the wake of Pennzoil Place, even the staid Chicago office of Skidmore, Owings & Merrill shaped up, breaking out of the box (as Philip Johnson put it) with this 10-story, parallelogram office building for Hines Interests. Stewart Title, Control Data, 3D/International, and the Warwick are located in the 41-acre Smith Office Park, Hines' first venture in the Post Oak area, developed with R. E. "Bob" Smith. Replacement of 2200's curtain wall as part of an upgrading in 2000 altered the building's appearance.

J-23 Control Data Corporation Building

J-24 Stewart Title Building

J-25 Galleria interior

J-25 Neiman Marcus

J-25 Marshall Field

J-25
Galleria

5015 Westheimer Road
1969-1971, Hellmuth, Obata + Kassabaum and Neuhaus & Taylor

The Galleria is a Houston typological development of international consequence. It is a 45-acre, 3.9 million-SF mixed use development, a regional-sized shopping mall that concentrates in specialty retailing and also incorporates two hotels, three multi-story office buildings, and an astonishing 11,263 parking spaces. Gerald D. Hines, who built the Galleria, succinctly stated his ambition for it in 1969, when its first increments were opened, "A shopping center it is not. It will be a new downtown." Hines cited the Galleria Vittorio Emmanuele in Milan as the model for the Post Oak Galleria (although Rockefeller Center deserves some credit for suggesting the ice skating rink). But while the glass-vaulted passageways of Milan's Galleria are part of the street network of the central city, the Post Oak Galleria is an object in the landscape, connected to the outside world by automobiles. Its interior is a conditioned and controlled environment and its vision of public life is focused exclusively on consumption and diversion. Ultimately it is a shopping center, not a downtown.

The complex was built from east to west. The Houston branch of the Dallas specialty store, Neiman-Marcus, a free-standing building on Post Oak Boulevard, was the first segment to open (1969), followed by the 22-story Post Oak Tower (1969), the Galleria Mall (1970), and the 20-story, 404-room Houston Oaks Hotel (now Westin Oaks, 1971). The 25-story Transco Tower at 2700 Post Oak was completed in 1973. Galleria II, the 12-story Galleria II Twin Towers, and the 23-story, 500-room Galleria Plaza Hotel (now Westin Galleria) opened in 1977. Marshall Field & Company (now Saks Fifth Avenue) was completed in 1979. Galleria III opened in 1986, and Galleria IV opened in 2003. By the time that Galleria III was completed, the Galleria had led Post Oak in supplanting downtown as the retail center of Houston. It had more hotel rooms than downtown and the second highest concentration of office space in Houston.

Neiman-Marcus remains the most impressive work of architecture in the Galleria. Although the Post Oak store was satirized by Robert Venturi, Denise Scott Brown, and Steven Izenour in 1972 for its glib repackaging of the Brutalist architecture of the pioneer French modernist, Le Corbusier, the building is notable for its generous internal spaces, its use of natural light, and the quality of its interior design, carried out by Eleanor LeMaire & Associates just before Miss LeMaire's death. None of the other specialty stores in the Galleria approaches this level of quality, which must be ascribed in large part to the store's president, Stanley Marcus. Its prettied-up, smoothed-out Brutalism—the symmetrically stationed bustles on the second floor feature inset panels of onyx that are backlit at night—is a bit overwrought for a specialty store. Yet Neiman-Marcus does possess distinct façades, and it is the only part of the Galleria that faces a public street with any show of confidence and style (although in the 1990s the exterior display windows were covered over). Massimo Vignelli's Helvetica graphics once marked the public entrance to the three-level Galleria mall before they were effaced in the late 1990s with crass postmodern facings. (In proper suburban fashion, a significant number of those coming to the Galleria enter through the rear garages, off West Alabama.)

Like the hotel and office towers, the mall avoids making any strong architectural commitment. The interiors are low-key, with dark carpeted floors and unobtrusive "street" furniture. The concept was to let the display windows and the central, skylit, 170-foot-long ice skating rink stand as feature attractions. Galleria II (Hellmuth, Obata + Kassabaum and S. I. Morris Associates) was not impressive until the main floor level of its 10-story atrium was filled with "street" vendors, who populated what had long been a vacuous space. At Galleria III, Hellmuth, Obata + Kassabaum (and Richard Fitzgerald & Partners) abandoned its earlier aesthetic for neo-traditional imagery and tighter spaces. These are not unwelcome after Galleria II. But they fail to impart a sense of urban coherence to the complex. The exteriors of Galleria III, watered down corporate postmodernism at its most tiresome, likewise seem to be starting over again rather than summarizing and concluding what has gone before.

Philip Johnson and John Burgee (with S. I. Morris Associates) designed the curved planar limestone façade of Marshall Field. This was to have been a screen for Claes Oldenburg's giant aluminum, *Paintsplats*, free-form blobs of color that looked like they had come from giant paintbrushes flicked carelessly against the façade. As this proposal did not accord with Marshall Field's Midwestern sense of style, the façade went up without the art.

Galleria IV was designed by Cooper Cary of Atlanta for the Indianapolis-based Simon Property Group, which bought the complex in 2002. The Galleria has become a surrogate for downtown in a city that no longer requires one of the old-fashioned sort. Its success made it the model for many mixed-use complexes, both in the U.S. and abroad, in both center cities and suburbs. Whether it will outlive the set of circumstances that brought it into being and survive to attain the historic distinction that might eventually accrue to it is a serious question. For in Houston low margins of profitability inexorably lead to the disposal of non-performing resources. Not only does anything go here, everything goes.

J-27 The Lake on Post Oak Park

J-28 Mercer West Tower

J-29 Ranger Insurance Company Building

J-30 Guest Quarters Galleria West

J-26
Transco Tower
[now Williams Tower]
2800 Post Oak Boulevard
1983, Johnson/Burgee Architects
and Morris*Aubry Architects

Although the Galleria is the anchor of the Post Oak district, its architectural symbol is the equivocal Transco Tower. At 64 stories, 901 feet in height, this is the third tallest building in Houston. Its isolated setting and tapered profile make it a landmark, one that has attracted a surprising degree of popular awareness and approbation. Johnson/Burgee modeled Transco on the setback Art Deco towers of the late 1920s, but surfaced it entirely in reflective glass (applied, as John Burgee explained, as stone facing would have been in the '20s). It is the ghost image of a skyscraper from the city that Post Oak rejected, an ironic inversion that passively reflects its suburban environment. Crowning the tower is the Transco Beacon, a searchlight that rotates at night. Alongside the building is the 3-acre Transco Park, with the Transco Fountain (1985, Johnson/Burgee Architects and Richard Fitzgerald & Partners), a stunning work of hydraulic engineering built by the Transco Companies and Hines Interests, the building's two principal tenants.

J-27
The Lake on Post Oak Park
3000-3050 Post Oak Boulevard
1978, 1980, 1982, 3D/International

These three towers, built by Hines Interests and surfaced in bronze anodized aluminum and bronze solar glass, exhibit varied plan geometries. They are set in a pastorally landscaped park (Edward D. Stone, Jr. & Associates, landscape architects) containing an emergency storm run-off retention basin (a.k.a. the lake), a publicly mandated site feature. Indicative of the postmodern turn in Houston architecture that persisted into the 21st century are the 9-story Manhattan Lofts (2002, Meeks + Partners) at 3030 Post Oak and the 8-story Empire Lofts and Flats (2006) at 5005 Hidalgo, which Randall Davis developed in partnership with Hines.

J-28
Mercer West Tower
3388 Sage Road
2003, EDI

Rating the 2000's equivalent of immortality—an entry in *Wikipedia*—is the excruciatingly slender 30-story Mercer West condominium tower. The building type of the "sliver" building, associated with the construction of narrow skyscrapers on townhouse-sized lots in Manhattan, made its Houston appearance in the most unlikely of places, the wide open spaces of Post Oak.

J-29
Ranger Insurance Company Building
[now 5333 Westheimer Building]
5333 Westheimer Road
1971, Skidmore, Owings & Merrill and Wilson, Morris, Crain & Anderson

Hines Interests constructed this 10-story building as the first increment of Galleria West, a 15-acre office park adjacent to the Galleria. It is a classic Chicago frame building, its steel structural skeleton sheathed in bronze anodized aluminum and its interstices enclosed with flush set bronze solar glass. Next door, at 5251 Westheimer, is the 11-story Kaneb Building (now Galleria Plaza I, 1976), also by Skidmore, Owings & Merrill-Chicago for Hines, with its structural frame clad in travertine.

J-30
Guest Quarters Galleria West
[now Doubletree Guest Suites Houston]
5353 Westheimer Road
1982, Skidmore, Owings & Merrill

Designed by the Houston office of Skidmore, Owings & Merrill, the 26-story, 349-unit Guest Quarters hotel features the heavy-handed detailing that characterized its work. Rolled tops, fat circular moldings, and ribbed precast concrete spandrels are the decorative details on this offset tower, which is faced with brown Texas granite aggregate precast concrete. Where Guest Quarters excels is at ground level. The Westheimer frontage is planted with a tranquil glade of trees; entrance to the hotel is from a discreetly walled motor court at the back of the building. From Guest Quarters one can look across Westheimer to the extraordinarily long, 9-story Bechtel Building (1981) by the San Francisco office of Skidmore, Owings & Merrill at 5400 Westheimer Court. The site it occupies was part of a 110-acre tract where in 1958 R. E. "Bob" Smith and Judge Roy Hofheinz planned to build a giant shopping mall, Air-Conditioned City, a project that was, in spirit, a precursor to the Galleria.

J-26 Transco Tower

J-31 One Westheimer Plaza

J-32 Memorial Lutheran Church

J-33 J. Frank Jungman Branch, Houston Public Library

J-31
One Westheimer Plaza
[now Capital One Plaza]
5718 Westheimer Road
1982, Morris*Aubry Architects

A deftly inflected 22-story office tower, faced with alternating bands of travertine and bronze solar glass. Its elegant minimalism has been compromised by exhibition of the principal tenant's advertising logo.

J-32
Memorial Lutheran Church
5800 Westheimer Road
1965, Todd Tackett Lacy

Gerald Tackett endowed this church with presence by capping it with a sharply profiled roof culminating in a hooded skylight above the central worship space. Replacement of wood shingles by a raised seam metal roof altered the church's scale and texture.

J-33
J. Frank Jungman Branch, Houston Public Library
5830 Westheimer Road
1974, W. Irving Phillips, Jr. & Robert W. Peterson

Phillips described this sculpturally convoluted building as incorporating something from every building along the Westheimer strip. It's hard to decide whether its straightforward, loft-like interior is a relief or a disappointment.

J-34
Augusta Green Building
2603 Augusta Drive
1984, Morris*Aubry Architects

Houston's speculative office buildings of the late 1970s and early '80s display a range of solutions to the problem of "skinning" what is essentially the same building. Guy Jackson's response at the 16-story Augusta Green is assured and understated: alternating horizontal bands of polished and flame-finished Swedish red granite, set off by thin stainless steel strips that bracket the windows. The vertical notch marks the front door.

J-35
San Felipe Plaza
5847 San Felipe Road
1984, Skidmore, Owings & Merrill

This is the best building that Richard Keating produced during his tenure as head of Skidmore, Owings & Merrill's Houston office. What is perhaps most impressive is the carefully detailed curtain wall of polished granite, in which light pink and gray granites are subtly combined. Built by the Farb Companies, the 45-story San Felipe Plaza presently marks the western boundary of the Post Oak district.

J-36
Emerson Unitarian Church
1900 Bering Drive
1974, MacKie & Kamrath

For a Unitarian congregation, Kamrath turned to one of Frank Lloyd Wright's greatest works, Unity Temple in Oak Park, Illinois, of 1906. His tribute is so literal that it is a little startling to encounter. The church's exterior finish of stucco and wood stripping does not compare favorably with the original, and, internally, its central space tends to leave the architecturally aware a bit deflated. To the north is the church's community building, a vaulted-roof pavilion supported on glue-laminated wood beams, an early Houston work of Caudill Rowlett Scott (1960).

J-36 Emerson Unitarian Church

J-34 Augusta Green Building

J-35 San Felipe Plaza

J-37 The Park Regency Terrace Residences

J-39 St. Michael The Archangel Catholic Church

J-40 Kaim House

J-37
The Park Regency Terrace Residences
2333 Bering Drive
1983, Venturi, Rauch & Scott Brown and McCleary Associates

A seldom-mentioned Venturi project, this is a 2-building, middle-income condominium apartment complex packs 80 units and structured parking onto a constricted 11.5 acre L-shaped site. The Adamesque cutout at the entrance to the complex is the high point. What follows is a cautionary tale about the hazards that high design is apt to encounter in the speculative market.

J-38
Marathon Oil Tower
5555 San Felipe Road
1983, Pierce Goodwin Alexander

The diagonal orientation and vertically ribbed window bays of this 41-story corporate office tower, its deep-set openings, and the density and color of its flame-finished Carmen red granite exterior make the Marathon Oil Tower one of the best tall buildings in the San Felipe corridor. It is located in the 48-acre San Felipe Green office park, developed by Mark Lee & Associates.

J-39
St. Michael The Archangel Catholic Church
1801 Sage Road
1966, Edward J. Schulte with Charles Hightower

Philip Johnson proposed a design for this parish complex in 1953, a brick, barrel-roofed *Rundbogenstil* church, in which the nave was contained beneath a series of freestanding vaults like those in his New Canaan guesthouse. Had it been built, it would have been, as Johnson later exclaimed, "my first Romanesque design." It was rejected as too modern. What the parish got instead was a lavishly detailed quasi-modern church, finished in brick, limestone, and gold-impregnated stained glass by the Cincinnati architect Schulte. Acknowledging the realities of suburban life, Schulte reoriented the church so that its front door faces the back parking lot rather than Sage Road.

J-40
Kaim House
5203 Stamper Way
1955, Harwood Taylor

An exceptionally well-maintained modern house designed in the spirit of the Los Angeles architect, Richard Neutra. The wooden garage nearest the corner of Stamper and Sage (Brand + Allen) is a slightly intrusive, but sympathetically detailed, addition.

J-38 Marathon Oil Tower

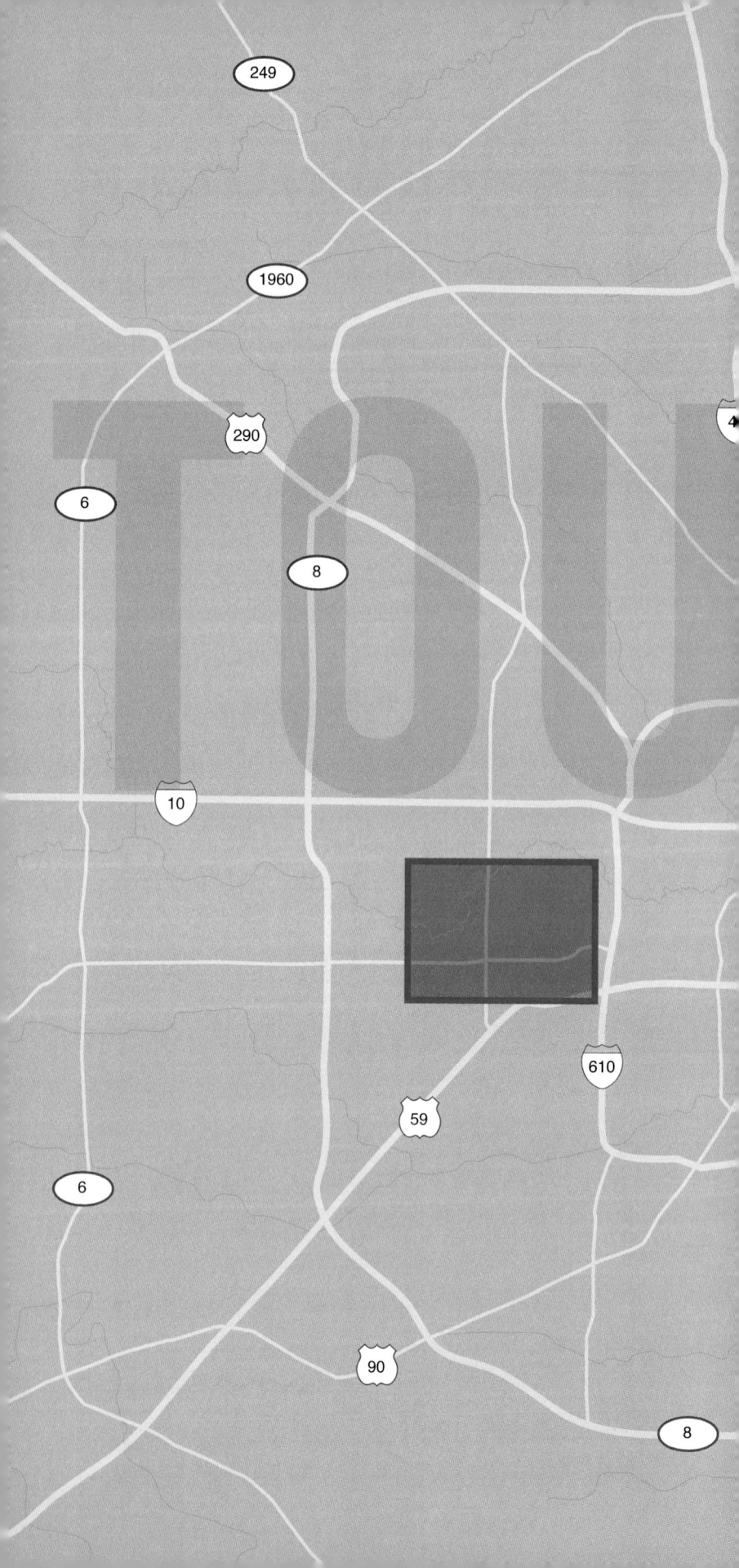

Westheimer / Richmond

59

610

225

45

Westheimer / Richmond

Tour J-2

South of Buffalo Bayou and west of the Post Oak district lies a landscape that preserves the no-zoning, no-planning enthusiasm reflected in Houston real estate development practices in the second half of the 20th century. The large subdivision of Tanglewood, which enticed the Houston Country Club to relocate there from its site in the East End in 1957, was the dominant residential development, but the emphasis of its developer, William G. Farrington, on community planning and tree planting was not widely shared.

Nowhere is Houston's "anything goes" image more blatantly displayed than along the stretch of Westheimer between Chimney Rock and South Gessner. Middle-class subdivisions of the 1950s flank this strip, but they are hidden behind broad bands of commercial development that face Westheimer. Most of this development dates from the 1960s and early '70s, when Houston's suburbanizing ethos was at its least constrained. Not only do shopping centers, gas stations, and fast-food restaurants line up along Westheimer, each with flashing signs or theme-styled inducements to passersby, but also mega-garden apartment complexes compete for attention in a mixture of dimly recognizable "traditional" styles. The order of the strip is economic, rather than visual or experiential—the biggest-grossing land uses get the prime frontage. Movement perpendicular to the strip entails passage through a descending hierarchy of economic generators before arriving at the restricted enclaves of single-family residences that the layers of development insulate. In some instances developers have manipulated values by moving from the inside out, using inner layers of development to stimulate the attractiveness of the prime frontage for some purpose, such as a multistory office building, that might not be feasible otherwise. And one should not be surprised at encountering large tracts of undeveloped land. These exemplify the way in which Houston has grown by distension and subsequent infilling, rather than by a neat process of incremental extension.

41. **House,** 275 Pine Hollow Lane
42. **Tanglewood House,** 5477 Doliver Drive
43. **Park Classic Homes House,**
    5617 Longmont Drive
44. **House,** 5470 Tilbury Drive
45. **House,** 5530 Tupper Lake Drive
46. **Fleming House,** 5517 Sturbridge Drive
47. **St. Martin's Episcopal Church,** 717 Sage Road
48. **Lurie House,** 7 Pine Forest Circle
49. **House,** 5221 Pine Forest Road
50. **Pierce House,** 5211 Green Tree
51. **Bell House,** 5135 Bayou Timber Lane
52. **House,** 5207 Shady River
53. **Wilson House,** 2 Briar Trail
54. **Briar House,** 670 Briar Drive
55. **Bank of Tanglewood Building,**
    500 Chimney Rock Road
56. **Northern Trust Bank of Texas Building,**
    600 Bering Drive
57. **Cook House,** 315 Brown Saddle
58. **House,** 6011 Park Circle Drive
59. **House,** 6006 Park Circle Drive
60. **House,** 6050 Crab Orchard Road
61. **Cantrell House,** 815 Wild Valley Road
62. **Second Baptist Church,** 6400 Woodway
63. **Lindsay House,** 7623 River Point Drive
64. **Golemon House,** 1010 Riverglyn Drive
65. **House,** 2110 Amberly Court
66. **Townhouses,** 2511 Nantucket Drive
67. **House,** 6126 Meadowlake Lane
68. **Trafalgar Place Condominiums,**
    2744 Briarhurst Drive
69. **The Mesa,** 5959 Richmond Avenue
70. **Unity Church of Christianity,** 2929 Unity Drive
71. **Hillcroft Professional Building,**
    3838 Hillcroft Avenue
72. **Great Southern Bank Building,**
    8820 Westheimer Road
73. **Southwestern Bell Telephone Co. Area
    Accounting Center,** 9051 Park West Drive
74. **Esso Eastern of New Jersey Building,**
    2401 South Gessner Road

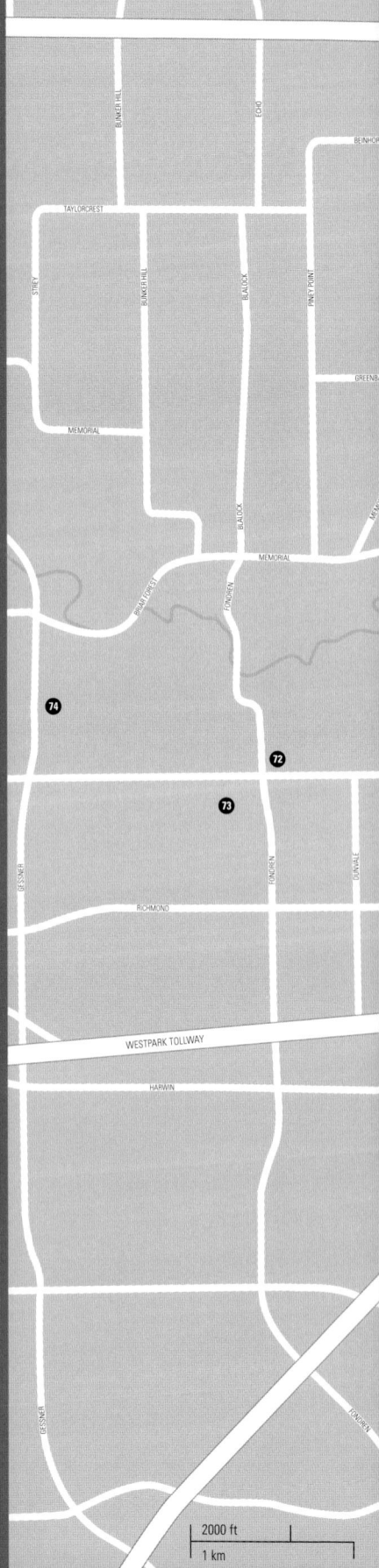

Westheimer / Richmond

Tour J-2

J-41 McCartney House

J-42 Tanglewood House

J-43 Park Classic Homes House

J-44 House

J-45 House

J-41
McCartney House
275 Pine Hollow Lane
1956, Harwood Taylor

Taylor successfully domesticated the strict architectural discipline of the Miesian courtyard house in order to produce single-family houses that accommodated their upper-middle-income occupants without unduly diluting the architecture. Pine Hollow also contains houses by P. M. Bolton Associates (1972) at 266, Wilson, Morris & Crain (1953) at 250, and William N. Floyd (1954) at 226. At the west end of Pine Hollow lies 300 Pinewold (1933, John F. Staub—not visible from the street), an evocation of a colonial farm house that makes one feel as though one had been transported to Connecticut.

J-42
Tanglewood House
5477 Doliver Drive
2000, Richard S. Condon

Tanglewood, where this house is located, was begun by William G. Farrington in 1948 as the postwar successor to River Oaks, a status it never quite attained. This was not because it lacked respectability. Rather, Tanglewood lacked diversity and distinction. The full impact of the Eisenhower era was visible here, matured and well maintained: big, low, one-story houses on large, flat lots. In the 1990s Tanglewood's profile began to change as the postwar houses were replaced by bulkier, stylistically aggressive successors. Condon's evocation of Frank Lloyd Wright's Prairie School stands out amid the overscaled Mediterraneans.

J-43
Park Classic Homes House
5617 Longmont Drive
1993, L. Barry Davidson Architects

Davidson evokes a French Classical precedent in this replacement house.

J-44
House
5470 Tilbury Drive
1996, L. Barry Davidson Architects

Two-story houses changed the Tanglewood community in the 1990s by replacing listless 1-story spatiality with a firmer sense of space. What this transformation has not accomplished is an improvement in the architectural mediocrity of the neighborhood. This gable-fronted picturesque manorial style house is one of the few that transcend such mediocrity.

J-45
House
5530 Tupper Lake Drive
2010, Dillon Kyle

Vertically attenuated proportions activate this salute to the American colonial.

J-46
Fleming House
5517 Sturbridge Drive
1956, C. C. "Pat" Fleming

Although Fleming made his reputation as a landscape architect, he was trained as an architect. This house, one of his few building designs, was constructed for his own family, although they never lived there.

J-47
St. Martin's Episcopal Church
717 Sage Road
2004, Jackson & Ryan Architects

This twin-towered, neo-High Victorian Gothic church faces resolutely onto is parking lot. It is hallucinatory in its suburban setting.

J-48
Lurie House
7 Pine Forest Circle
1956, Joseph Krakower

This house is a Herb Greene production, as can be deduced from the way that the heavy-lidded flat roof curves outward in response to its setting at the end of a cul-de-sac. One street to the north is Green Tree, where a series of houses by well-known architects are located: 5135 Green Tree (1962, Staub, Rather & Howze), 5027 (1968, Ford, Powell & Carson), and 5008 and 5005 (1966, Hamilton Brown).

J-47 St. Martin's Episcopal Church

J-46 Fleming House

J-48 Lurie House

J-49 House

J-50 Pierce House

J-51 Bell House

J-52 House

J-53 Wilson House

J-54 Briar House

J-49
House
5221 Pine Forest Road
2009, Dillon Kyle

Kyle salutes the 20th-century Baton Rouge eclectic architect, Hays Town, in this neo-Creole house, which displays Kyle's distinctively quirky sense of composition.

J-50
Pierce House
5211 Green Tree Road
1956, George Pierce-Abel B. Pierce

The 36-acre Pine Shadows subdivision, where this house is located, was developed in 1948 and quickly became the architects' subdivision. George F. Pierce, Jr. built his family's house here, a 1-story, flat-roofed courtyard house.

J-51
Bell House
5135 Bayou Timber Lane
1969, Howard Barnstone
& Eugene Aubry

In response to the clients' collection of American furniture, Barnstone and Aubry designed a house of many gables, fitted with bay windows and exquisitely finished with wood clapboards. The result is so lovely that it is disconcerting to find that the gables are merely picturesque volumetric protrusions above what is essentially a flat roof. The horizontally battened wood wall screening the motor court is quite striking. This house served as the prototype for most of Aubry's subsequent domestic production.

J-52
House
5207 Shady River
2003, Allen Bianchi

Walls faced with white stucco and a red, shingle roof emphasize the planar simplicity of this house, located in the Bayou Glen subdivision. Next door at 5211 Briar is a closed, 2-story house faced with buff colored concrete block (2004, Val Glitsch).

J-53
Wilson House
2 Briar Trail
1961, Wilson, Morris,
Crain & Anderson

Talbott Wilson designed this house for his family, a low, flat-roofed pavilion of glue-laminated post-and-beam construction surfaced on the street side with stucco-finished, redwood-framed panels and redwood screens. The overhanging roof slabs give the house a floating quality. At 1 Briar Trail (which looks like a driveway but is a street) one can barely glimpse the ski-slope shed roof of an otherwise invisible, but huge, house by Frank Welch & Associates (1972). A block west, off Briar Drive, is Broad Oaks Circle, a cul-de-sac where 102 Broad Oaks (1977, Frank Welch & Associates) and 202 Broad Oaks (1971, Clovis Heimsath Associates) are totally occluded by foliage.

J-54
Briar House
5670 Briar Drive
2010, Dan Shipley

Dallas architect Shipley stacked shed roofs in an ascending array above this house, which he carefully sited beneath the canopies of mature Live Oak trees.

J-55
Bank of Tanglewood Building
[now Bank of Texas]
500 Chimney Rock Road
1997, Jackson & Ryan Architects

The architects paid homage to the 16th-century Vicenza architect, Andrea Palladio, in this symmetrically composed villa; its Tuscan portico is faced with limestone.

J-56
Northern Trust Bank of Texas Building
600 Bering Drive
2000, William T. Cannady & Associates

The clock tower strikes a note of civic authority in this suburban branch bank.

J-57
Cook House
315 Brown Saddle
1961, Lawrence D. Starnes

Dallas architect Starnes produced the ultimate ranch house in this amazingly long, low-slung Tanglewood house, which includes decorative panels of black volcanic rock.

J-58
House
6011 Park Circle Drive
1995, Curtis & Windham

Cleverly adapted to an awkward site, this urbane townhouse is very refined in both composition and detail.

J-56 Northern Trust Bank of Texas Building

J-57 Cook House

J-55 Bank of Tanglewood Building

J-58 House

J-59 House

J-60 House

J-61 Cantrell House

J-62 Second Baptist Church of Houston

J-63 Lindsay House

J-59
House
6006 Park Circle Drive
1989, Virginia Kelsey

The entry alcove-corner, with its window-chimney roof composition, energizes this planar house front. The house at 6022 Park Circle (1987, W. O. Neuhaus Associates) with 6011 Park Circle completes a trio of architecturally assured houses.

J-60
House
6050 Crab Orchard Road
1966, A. Hays Town

This house, an adaptation of a 1-story Greek revival cottage, is so subtle that one could drive by without noticing it. Yet the composition, scale, proportions, pitch of the slate-covered roof, and contrast between the stucco-surfaced front elevation and brick side walls are rendered with cool authority. Town, a Baton Rouge architect, was renowned for his adaptations of traditional Louisiana house types. Up the street at 6058 Crab Orchard is Wilson, Morris, Crain & Anderson's house for their frequent collaborator, the structural engineer, Walter P. Moore (1961).

J-61
Cantrell House
815 Wild Valley Road
1965, Maurice, Wilkins & Associates

Although missing the roof vaults and decorative filigree panels that once screened its courtyard, this delicately scaled modern house persists, despite the mania in Tanglewood for replacing such graceful houses.

J-62
Second Baptist Church of Houston
6400 Woodway
1986, Calhoun, Tungate, Jackson & Dill

When the sociologist of religion, William Martin, described Second Baptist Church as a "superchurch," he did not exaggerate. The congregation's $25 million, 6,000-seat church, built adjacent to its existing neo-Georgian style complex (1961, Wirtz, Calhoun, Tungate & Jackson), defies simple characterization. It is inert externally, yet phantasmagoric inside, where the vast octagonal worship space is decorated with oddly-spaced, quasi-classical pilasters, window walls of stained glass, and a steel dome that rides ambiguously above and outside the container. The earlier church, though not outstanding, is legible architecturally; its super successor is not. It is a blunt, ambivalent object rising awkwardly alongside a big parking lot, an archetype of the self-sufficient, enclosed, suburban environmental package that acknowledges no connections to or responsibility for the outside world.

J-63
Lindsay House
7623 River Point Drive
1958, Bolton & Barnstone

The folded plate roof capping this courtyard-centered house announced the transition in Houston from Miesian discipline to New Formalist experimentation in the late 1950s. The decorative screen shielding the courtyard is made of cast iron, a surreptitious expression of Barnstone's fascination with Southern regionalism. The Lindsay House was built in the River Bend subdivision, which lies in the town of Hunter's Creek Village rather than Houston. Here a number of architect-designed houses exhibit architectural trends of the 1950s and '60s. Also located on this block are notable houses at 7614 (1961, Lloyd, Morgan & Jones) and 7827 (1995, Frank Welch & Associates).

J-64
Golemon House
1010 Riverglynn Drive
1967, Golemon & Rolfe

Architect Harry Golemon built his hyperbolic-paraboloid-roofed house over a below-grade garage, a topographic opportunity afforded by ravines that run through River Bend and once fed into Buffalo Bayou. Still standing in River Bend (at the time of publication) are 1001 River Bend (1959, Cowell & Neuhaus) and 1106 River Bend (1955, Bruce Wallace).

J-65
House
2110 Amberly Court
1988, C/A Architects

Because this house bookends a row of party-wall houses, Ralph A. Anderson, Jr. juxtaposed its thin, gabled section with a long, taut, street wall plane and brilliantly striped surfaces, so that the house stand out dramatically from its prosaic surroundings.

J-64 Golemon House

J-65 House

J-66 Todd Townhouses

J-67 House

J-68 Trafalgar Place Condominiums

J-69 The Mesa: A Better Home and Living Center

J-66
Todd Townhouses
2511 Nantucket Drive
1982, William T. Cannady & Associates and Anderson Todd

Following an amendment to the deed restrictions that permitted construction of up to four houses on one lot, this nondescript neighborhood, Westhaven, was almost entirely redeveloped in the 1970s and '80s for high-density, high-rent housing. The result is singularly dreary. It is amazing that so much building should add up to so little urbanity. One of the few exceptions to this state of affairs is this cluster of white, stucco-surfaced row houses. Their clarity, simplicity, and unpretentiousness make them seem absolutely extraordinary on a street teeming with obnoxious bores.

J-67
House
6126 Meadowlake Lane
1957, William N. Floyd

Like most post-World War II subdivisions along the Westheimer corridor, Briar Grove is long in the north-south direction but relatively narrow in the east-west direction. It is unusual in being heavily wooded and in possessing a collection of modern houses, although these tend to be spaced widely among more conventional models (and have also been candidates for replacement in the 1990s and 2000s). This nifty flat-roofed house features a device seen time and again on modern houses built in this part of Houston during the 1950s: the porte-cochère in place of the front porch. Here it is combined with wall panels of thin Roman brick, lit by thin horizontal clerestory windows slotted between exposed glue-laminated wooden beams. Two other modern houses are located at 2003 Briarmead (1959, Larson & Wingfield; altered) and 6206 Ella Lee (1955, William N. Floyd).

J-68
Trafalgar Place Condominiums
2744 Briarhurst Drive
1976, Jake Williams

Trafalgar West (1963), which occupies this block-long street, was one of the first of the garden apartment mega-complexes built in this part of Houston in the mid 1960s. The condominium building, a later addition, is a fantasy style production (Mexican is the theme), as was common with this building type. It is, however, composed, detailed, and landscaped with sufficient conviction and consistency to make the imagery at least mildly notable. This was rarely the case with the giant complexes.

J-69
The Mesa: A Better Home and Living Center
5959 Richmond Avenue
1985, Arquitectonica

If Houston lay in an earthquake zone, one might well draw the conclusion that some seismic disaster had thrown this 4-story retail and office building seriously out of whack. Rest assured, it's just Arquitectonica. The skewed columns and racked floor plates are all part of the fun, as is the ironically monumental stair facing Richmond and the sinuously parapeted access ramp on the building's back side. Turquoise and red accentuate the positive.

J-70
Unity Church of Christianity
2929 Unity Drive
1975, Rapp Tackett Fash
2004, Ray+Hollington

Gerald Tackett broached the possibility of a pyramid at his Memorial Lutheran Church. Here he went all the way, bestowing the age-old authority of this hieratic shape (surfaced in gleaming gold anodized aluminum) on a suburban New Age congregation. The palm trees in the parking lot appropriately nuance the Unity-on-the-Nile aspirations and serve to remind that, as Houston cultural observer Douglas Milburn has observed, Houston and Cairo both lie on the 30th parallel. In 2002 Albuquerque architect, Antoine Predock, was commissioned to design a larger church building adjacent to the pyramid. But after preparing a design, Predock withdrew from the project. Ray+Hollington altered and adapted Predock's design to achieve a dramatically profiled church whose ascending rooflines peak above the entrances.

J-70 Unity Church of Christianity

J-71 Hillcroft Professional Building

J-72 Great Southern Bank Building

J-73 Southwestern Bell Telephone Company Area Accounting Center

J-71
Hillcroft Professional Building
3838 Hillcroft Avenue
1965, Jenkins Hoff & Heimsath

The programmatic components of this suburban office building are differentiated dramatically. The service core sits to one side of the office block, which is cantilevered far beyond the perimeter of the ground floor. Windows are spaced randomly, an effect enhanced by the rhythmic alternation of concrete fins. The vocabulary is that of the New Brutalism, which William R. Jenkins articulated frequently in the late 1960s.

J-72
Great Southern Bank Building
[now Prosperity Bank]
8820 Westheimer Road
1971, Wilson, Morris, Crain & Anderson

Westheimer is visually appalling. Now almost historically venerable, it is a classic example of what architecture critic Peter Blake, in the title of his 1964 jeremiad, decried as *God's Own Junkyard*. This bank, a thick pavilion of vertically striated cast-in-place concrete, still seeks valiantly to represent the cause of design.

J-73
Southwestern Bell Telephone Company Area Accounting Center
[now AT&T Services]
9051 ParkWest Drive
1978, Caudill Rowlett Scott

Tucked away on a back street adjacent to Piney Point, a small black community encircled by Houston's suburban growth, is this impressive corporate office building. A matte-finished aluminum panel wall system gives the center a taut, planar look, reinforced by flush-set glazing and shallow incisions that reveal the red-clad structural frame within. On the rear (southern) side, windows are recessed in wide bays to provide views of a tree-shaded lawn.

J-74
Esso Eastern of New Jersey Building
[now Exxon Coal and Minerals Company]
2401 South Gessner Road
1971, Charles Tapley Associates
and Robert Husmann & Associates

Tapley was involved in the initial planning of Friendswood Development's Woodlake, a mixed-use office, retail, and residential project, and he was able to carry forward some of his proposals for building responsibly in nature with the design of this three part corporate office building. The buildings, glass pavilions shaded by their exposed concrete structural frames, are set atop a podium above underground parking. The podium level can be approached from the garage below by way of a sunken central courtyard. Esso Eastern is an object in the landscape rather than an extension of it. But it seeks to work with, not in spite of, its surroundings. The Tapley office also designed the Woodlake Recreation Center (1971) at the northwest corner of Tanglewilde and Ella Lee.

J-74 Esso Eastern of New Jersey Building

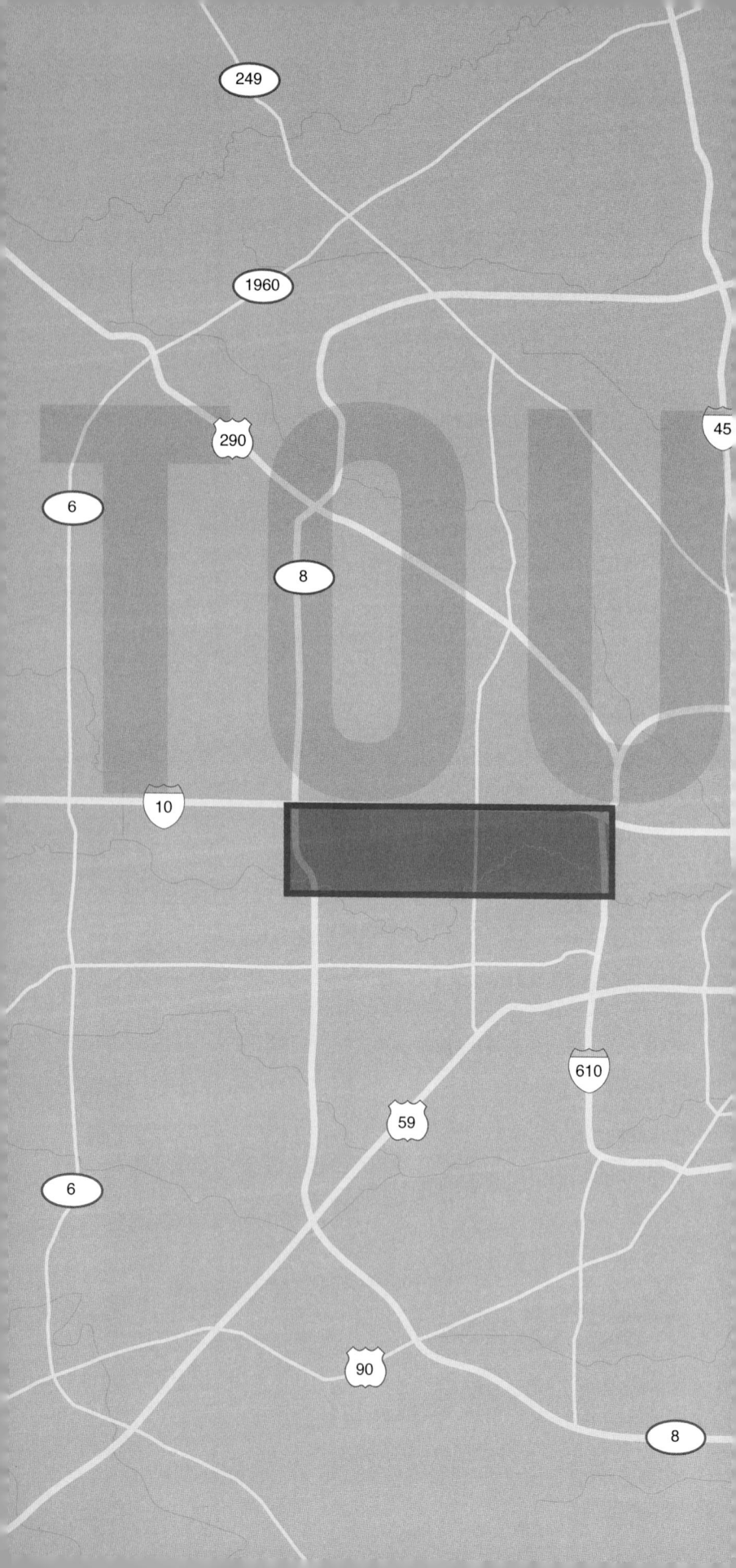

Memorial Villages

Memorial Villages

Tour K

At the end of the 1920s, wealthy Houstonians discovered at their back door the dense pine forest that had captivated Frederick Law Olmsted in 1854, when he passed through it on his way to Houston. There a small number of families established weekend retreats where country pastimes—horseback riding, tennis, polo, and swimming—could be pursued. After the middle 1930s year-round houses, usually on multiple-acre sites, began to be built along Buffalo Bayou near South and North Post Oak lanes. A few isolated subdivisions followed in the late 1930s. Then, at the end of the 1940s, the tidal wave of suburban expansion that engulfed Houston's hinterlands in the succeeding decade broke over this large area. North of the bayou, where the tree cover is denser and much more extensive, the entire area known as Memorial (after Memorial Park, the 1,500-acre forest park on its eastern edge) developed in a random series of small subdivisions tied to Houston by the winding Memorial Drive and Katy Road to the north.

Between 1954 and 1956 the large agglomeration of subdivisions incorporated as six independent municipalities: Spring Valley Village, Piney Point Village, Bunker Hill Village, Hedwig Village, Hilshire Village, and Hunters Creek Village.

The City of Houston acquiesced but in 1957 annexed a strip surrounding all six towns. Zoning codes limit property use within the "Villages," as they are collectively known, almost exclusively to single-family residences, often with minimum plot sizes of an acre or more. Schools and churches are the most visible exceptions to the single-family rule; commercial development is almost all concentrated along the Katy Freeway. As a result Memorial Drive (which has been defiantly kept to a narrow road with a series of right-angle turns and flanked by open drainage ditches,) is lined with expensive, if prosaic, houses. For despite economic affluence and dense vegetation, the Memorial Villages are monotonous. The seemingly infinite repetition of big houses on flat, wooded sites becomes oppressive, the more so since almost all vestiges of Memorial's recent past as a rustic forest have been sacrificed for subdivision development.

1. **McAshan Botanical Hall, Houston Arboretum,** 4501 Woodway
2. **Bayou Club,** 8550 Memorial Drive
3. **Antares Building,** 710 North Post Oak Road
4. **Warren House,** 431 Pinehaven Lane
5. **House,** 8730 Memorial Drive
6. **Reed House,** 111 Carnarvon Drive
7. **Abramowitz House,** 421 Buckingham Drive
8. **House,** 316 Buckingham Drive
9. **Albritton House,** 306 East Friar Tuck Lane
10. **House,** 603 West Friar Tuck Lane
11. **House,** 606 West Friar Tuck Lane
12. **Brogniez House,** 505 Little John Lane
13. **St. Mary's Seminary,** 9845 Memorial Drive
14. **Willard House,** 611 Timber Terrace
15. **Bonner House,** 1 Spring Hollow
16. **Frame House,** 403 Westminster Drive
17. **House,** 412 Lindenwood Drive
18. **Lasher House,** 203 Timberwilde
19. **Greer House,** 108 Timberwilde Lane
20. **Shartle House,** 624 Shartle Circle
21. **House,** 626 Hunters Grove Lane
22. **Block House,** 443 Hunterwood Drive
23. **House,** 414 Thamer Lane
24. **House,** 407 Thamer Circle
25. **Houston Racquet Club,** 10709 Memorial Drive
26. **House,** 315 Teakwood Lane
27. **Conrad House,** 819 Wade Hampton Drive
28. **House,** 845 Pecanwood
29. **Lapin House,** 22 Willowend Drive
30. **Durst-Gee House,** 323 Tynebrook Lane
31. **McFarland House,** 11110 Wickwood Drive
32. **Krajcizek House,** 9 Woods Edge Lane
33. **Straus House,** 8505 San Felipe Road
34. **Johnston House,** 11325 Greenbay
35. **Memorial Drive Presbyterian Church,** 11612 Memorial Drive
36. **Bracht House,** 11626 Monica Street
37. **Lawrence House,** 11715 Timberknoll Drive
38. **House,** 26 Liberty Bell Circle
39. **Bullock House,** 672 Flintdale Road
40. **Goodwin House,** 3 Leisure Lane
41. **St. Cecilia Catholic Church,** 11730 Denise Street
42. **House,** 11914 Knippwood Lane
43. **Baumgardner House,** 7 Robin Lake Lane
44. **Smith-Herzog House,** 21 Robin Lake Lane
45. **House,** 253 Mayerling Drive
46. **Thaxton House,** 12020 Tall Oaks Road
47. **Kayem House,** 12502 Taylorcrest
48. **House,** 12607 Mossycup Drive
49. **Krell House,** 12612 Broken Bough
50. **Interurban Pharmacy,** 12647 Memorial Drive
51. **Caudill House,** 311 Electra Drive
52. **Lawrence House,** 12919 Figaro Drive
53. **House,** 503 Electra Drive
54. **Cropp House,** 12923 Memorial Drive

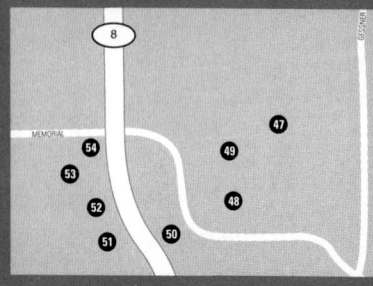

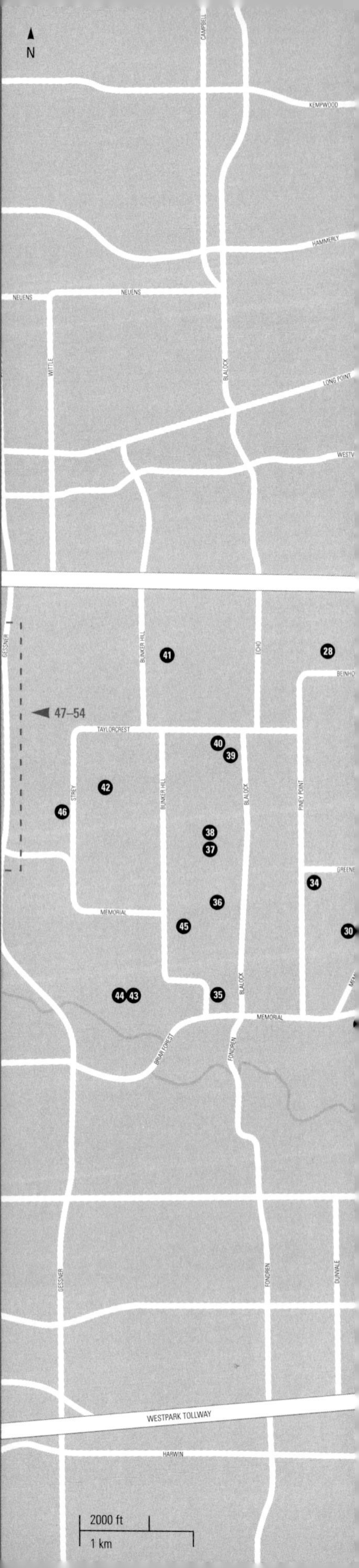

Memorial Villages

Tour K

K-1 Aline McAshan Botanical Hall for Children, Houston Arboretum and Nature Center

K-2 Bayou Club

K-3 Antares Building

K-4 Warren House

K-5 House

K-1
Aline McAshan Botanical Hall for Children, Houston Arboretum and Nature Center
4501 Woodway
1968, Neuhaus-Wingfield Associates

This concrete-framed pavilion is not one of Hugo Neuhaus' most memorable buildings, but it lends a note of urbanity to the 155-acre Arboretum. Exhibitions are set up inside the building, and one can also obtain instructions for a self-guided tour of the grounds, which contain a number of ecological settings characteristic of the Houston region. Alterations and additions (1995) include the glass-roofed east wing. The Houston Arboretum and Nature Center is located in Memorial Park. This forested, 1,500-acre tract was acquired by Will C. Hogg's Varner Realty Company, which sold it at cost and on very generous terms to the City of Houston in 1924 for use as a public park. Prior to Hogg's acquisition of the site, it had been part of Camp Logan, Houston's temporary World War I training base. The park is dedicated to the Houstonians who died in that war. It is the largest park in the center of the city and, despite intensive use, still preserves much of its a original character.

K-2
Bayou Club
8550 Memorial Drive
1940, John F. Staub

This small clubhouse (not visible from the street) is Staub's adaptation of a Louisiana Creole plantation house. It looks very much at home in its forest clearing.

K-3
Antares Building
710 North Post Oak Road
1969, Rapp Tackett Fash

Gerald Tackett explored the aesthetic possibilities of precast concrete construction in this 4-story office building. The canted sunshade panels give a sense of depth to the elevations.

K-4
Warren House
431 Pinehaven Lane
1985, Compendium

Jay Baker designed this postmodern house, faced with a base course of Mexican sandstone, panels of rose-colored stucco, and a roof of slate, with a subtle mix of color. Square-sectioned windows and pyramidal roof shapes give it a picturesque aspect. Baker detailed interior fixtures and was responsible for furniture and fabric design as well. Herbert Pickworth was the landscape architect.

K-5
House
8730 Memorial Drive
2011, MC² Architects

Robust cantilevers mark this house, built of concrete tilt walls. In the midst of grotesque new Mediterraneans, manorials, chateaux, and Georgian wannabes, this house is a resounding vote of confidence in architecture.

K-6
Reed House
111 Carnarvon Drive
1960, Alden B. Dow

The Midland, Michigan architect, Alden Dow, lived in Houston during the 1940s, when he planned the new town of Lake Jackson, 45 miles south of Houston, for the Dow Chemical Company. His only major building in Houston is this large, flat house for a Dow corporate executive. It is organized around a courtyard, visible through the wood lattice screen. The thickness of the porte-cochere canopy suggests the scale of this house (the columns beneath the canopy are not original). Just inside the gated subdivision at the end of Carnarvon is 7 Winston Woods, a magnificent English Regency style country house (1939, John F. Staub) built for James O. Winston, Jr. Winston's brother-in-law, William Stamps Farish, stabled his polo ponies on the tract of land now traversed by Carnarvon Drive, which was subdivided in 1941 to become the neighborhood of Bayou Woods.

K-6 Reed House

K-7 Abramowitz House

K-8 House

K-9 Albritton House

K-11 House

K-7
Abramowitz House
421 Buckingham Drive
1998, Reagan Miller

Reagan Miller's rendition of the picturesque manorial style is tactfully scaled and conscientiously detailed. Alterations and additions are by L. Barry Davidson (2008).

K-8
House
316 Buckingham Drive
2006, Michael Landrum

The rustic stone walls of this house, patterned on the granary of Mission San José in San Antonio, are so vivid that they startle.

K-9
Albritton House
306 East Friar Tuck Lane
1971, Armon E. Mabry

Mabry went all the way on this, his last major work, a limestone-faced, 17th-century French chateau. The garden parterre that leads up to the house is flanked by exposed aggregate-paved driveways. As the street names imply, this house lies in the Sherwood Forest subdivision, developed on what had been the weekend estate of the Houston lumberman, W. T. Carter, Jr. John F. Staub's Carter Lodge (1930) is extant at 331 West Friar Tuck Lane (it actually faces Longbow), but so altered by additions as to be unrecognizable. Down the mysteriously crooked Longbow Lane is a notable collection of houses, but only one is visible from the street. These include 3 Longbow (1968, O'Neil Ford & Associates) and 2 Longbow (1956, Wilson, Morris, Crain & Anderson).

K-10
House
603 West Friar Tuck Lane
1999, L. Barry Davidson Architects

Davidson evokes vernacular houses of the Mediterranean in this stone-faced, tile-roofed house.
* Not pictured.

K-11
House
606 West Friar Tuck Lane
2003, Lake/Flato

San Antonio architects Lake/Flato engaged the woodland setting of this house, which they arranged as a series of parallel bars organized beneath crisply profiled shed roofs. Sheet-steel wall panels are juxtaposed with planes of colored stucco to play off the green tones of the pine forest. The modesty and precision of this refined house contrast markedly with most other new houses in Sherwood Forest.

K-12
Brogniez House
505 Little John Lane
1961, Raymond Brogniez

Brogniez designed this pavilion-like house for his own family. Raised on a podium above its flat site, the house is oriented away from the street and into the trees.

K-13
St. Mary Seminary
9845 Memorial Drive
1954, Maurice J. Sullivan-Charles F. Sullivan

Constructed on a 50-acre site in what was at the time the country, this small complex of classroom and dormitory buildings, a chapel, and a refectory for the Roman Catholic archdiocesan seminary was Maurice Sullivan's last multi-building commission. He carried it out in the Lombard Romanesque style with which he had made his reputation three decades before at the Villa de Matel.

K-14
Willard House
611 Timber Terrace
1954, Philip G. Willard

Architect Willard developed the 15-acre Timber Lane Terrace subdivision in 1950. He designed this contemporary house for his family on a site that, by Houston standards, features dramatic slopes.

K-12 Brogniez House

K-14 Willard House

K-13 St. Mary's Seminary

K-15 Bonner House

K-16 Frame House

K-17 House

K-18 Lasher House

K-19 Greer House

K-20 Shartle House

K-15
Bonner House
1 Spring Hollow Terrace
1958, James C. Morehead, Jr.

A spirited Contemporary design, this house pivots in plan around its sectionally exposed stair. At 3 Spring Hollow is a Contemporary house by Wilson, Morris & Crain (1950). The clients for both these houses were Rice University professors, as was the architect, James Morehead.

K-16
Frame House
430 Westminster Drive
1960, Neuhaus & Taylor

Harwood Taylor carefully fit this large house to a site that slopes dramatically down to Buffalo Bayou (which is not apparent from the street). By building the house right up to the street line on Farther Point, Taylor conserved open space so that the pavilion-like house seems poised between a woodland glade facing the street and bluffs that cascade down to the bayou. Stern and Bucek restored this house to its Modern glory in 2006.

K-17
House
412 Lindenwood Drive
2009, Murphy Mears

This serene manorial style house demonstrates that it is possible to build new houses that are much larger than those they replace without brutalizing the entire neighborhood. The architectural virtues of proportion, restraint, simplicity, and material economy make this house an asset to the Memorial Drive Manor subdivision.

K-18
Lasher House
203 Timberwilde Lane
1958, Thomas M. Price

Price, Galveston's foremost modern architect, was responsible for this large, 1-story house. Masonry solar screens and a dynamically configured porte-cochère canopy give it a light, buoyant aspect. The house lies in the Timberwilde subdivision of Hunter's Creek Village, a classic Memorial landscape of large, flat lots and dense vegetation.

K-19
Greer House
108 Timberwilde Lane
1967, Richard S. Colley

Corpus Christi architect, Richard Colley, produced here one of his finest houses. Colley's aptitude for detailing materials and his precision with linear composition are displayed in the dun-colored brick wall surfaces and the thin projecting roof slab of this 1-story house. The pyramid rising above the center of the house shields an internal courtyard.

K-20
Shartle House
624 Shartle Circle
1941, John F. Staub

Staub's partner, J. T. Rather, Jr., designed this Texas regional style country house on a large site that was redeveloped in the 1960s as Hunters Grove subdivision. Its planar walls and tight, low-pitched roof recall the 19th-century Alsatian buildings of Castroville in central Texas. The lean-to gallery, infilled with big-scaled trellis work, introduces a shallow spatial layering characteristic of Rather's houses. Despite inappropriate alterations and the subtraction of an entire wing, this house radiates quiet superiority in the midst of numbing mediocrity.

K-21
House
626 Hunters Grove Lane
2005, L. Barry Davidson Architects

An Irish country house inspired the design of this house in Hunters Grove.

K-22
Block House
443 Hunterwood Drive
1972, Charles Tapley Associates

Charles Tapley and Joe Mashburn designed this 2-story house, faced with dark-stained cedar siding, for photographer Gay Block. Its angled and inflected wall planes, directed views, and (originally) woodland vegetation were meant to establish a pattern for future residential construction in the Hunterwood subdivision, a pattern that clearly was not followed.

K-21 House

K-22 Block House

K-23 House

K-24 House

K-25 Houston Racquet Club

K-26 House

K-28 House

K-29 Lapin House

K-23
House
414 Thamer Lane
1969, MacKie & Kamrath

The composition and proportions, the handling of materials, and the telling decorative details visible in this house make one aware of how architecturally impoverished many houses in the Memorial Villages are by comparison, and how architecturally rich they might have been. Hunterwood, where this house is located, is a case in point, despite the presence of two distinguished modern houses at 347 Hunters Trail (1968, Ford, Powell & Carson) and a marvelously idiosyncratic house in the spirit of Bruce Goff at 311 Hunters Trail (1976) by Dr. Davey E. Lieb, an amateur architect.

K-24
House
407 Thamer Circle
1974, Raymond Brochstein, Anderson Todd, and William T. Cannady

This white-stucco-surfaced, flat-roofed house plays off the dense green woodland vegetation that enshrouds its site.

K-25
Houston Racquet Club
10709 Memorial Drive
1969, MacKie & Kamrath

In addition to his architectural career, Karl Kamrath was a nationally ranked tennis player and a founding member of the Houston Racquet Club. Thus the disappointing quality of the clubhouse comes as a surprise. The use of white brick robs the walls of the textural richness and density one expects of Kamrath. And the insensitive despoiling of the site to provide space for parked cars and tennis courts leaves the building unrelated to any natural feature.

K-26
House
315 Teakwood Lane
1967, Marvin Gordy

Architect Marvin Gordy liked the design of this, one of his first houses, so much that he virtually reproduced it for his own house in Beaumont.

K-27
Conrad House
819 Wade Hampton Drive
1970, Anderson/Wilson

William J. Anderson and Thomas Redyard Wilson began their careers designing wood-faced, shed-roofed houses such as the Conrad House, which retains its taut profiles.

K-28
House
845 Pecanwood
2006, Pope Design

Lisa Pope Westerman's house for a young family in Hedwig Village is raised on tall concrete piers to preserve mature trees on the site. The house, a series of gabled volumes, possesses a delightful spontaneous quality.

K-29
Lapin House
22 Willowend Drive
1960, Wilson, Morris, Crain & Anderson

Although many of the modern houses built in the Piney Point Village subdivision of Willowick in the 1950s and '60s were demolished in the 2000s, this expansive house has been meticulously restored. Still surviving, but not especially visible, is the M. Arthur Kotch House, designed for his family at 11119 Wickway (1962).

K-30
Durst-Gee House
323 Tynebrook Lane
1960, Bruce Goff with Joseph Krakower
1982, Bruce Goff

This house by the Oklahoma (later Tyler, Texas) architect Bruce Goff is extraordinary. Subtly curved in plan in response to its location on a cul-de-sac, it carries the circular theme to a logical conclusion in the witty round windows that project (volumetrically, inside) above the thin, sloped roof membrane. Molded brick frames these windows. Herb Greene, a former student of Goff's, supervised construction. The two families who succeeded the original clients in residence were so devoted to the house that each had Goff carry out alterations and additions, the last set completed a year before his death in 1982.

K-30 Durst-Gee House

K-31 McFarland House

K-32 Krajcizek House

K-34 Johnston House

K-35 Memorial Drive Presbyterian Church

K-36 Bracht House

K-37 Lawrence House

K-31
McFarland House
11110 Wickwood Drive
1996, Frank Welch & Associates

This redwood clapboard-surfaced house in the Willowick Estates subdivision confounds expectations. Instead of being laid-back, it is tense and edgy as if to make the point that it is a city house despite its suburban location. Herbert Pickworth was the landscape architect. Across the ravine, just north of this house, is a Lloyd, Morgan & Jones-designed house at 11114 Wickwood (1966). Missing is MacKie & Kamrath's immense and extraordinary house for Cynthia and George Mitchell that stood at 11010 Wickwood (1965) before it was demolished and replaced by two big nonentities.

K-32
Krajcizek House
9 Woods Edge Lane
1978, Robert E. Griffin

What this house presents to the street is a taut, stucco-surfaced elevation, containing a row of high-set clerestory windows. These underscore the linear organization of the house, but conceal its internal vistas and a parallel plane of glass through which the interior is opened to the forested landscape. Just up the street, at 13 Woods Edge, is another reclusive modern house by W. O. Neuhaus Associates (1973).

K-33
Straus House
8505 San Felipe Road
1950, Staub & Rather

Not visible from the street, this is a rare remaining Memorial country house, which still preserves its expansive woodland setting. J. T. Rather, Jr. designed the house in the contemporary style, rather than the historical styles associated with him and his partner Staub.
* Not pictured.

K-34
Johnston House
11325 Greenbay
1964, Charles Tapley

This is one of Tapley's earliest independent designs. The side of the house visible from Greenbay displays the sectional overlapping of roofs, through which skylight is brought into the middle of the house. The front yard, facing Piney Point Road, was sold for new development.

K-35
Memorial Drive Presbyterian Church
11612 Memorial Drive
1959, 1972, MacKie & Kamrath

Built of randomly coursed slabs of limestone, this large church complex is a striking sight in Bunker Hill Village. The soaring profile of the steel-framed roof of the church (1972) culminates at its apex in an unconventional carillon, suspended from the tip of the beam. The church, chapel, and educational building, planned around two internal courtyards, display exuberant organic decoration. Its leitmotif, the red square, was Frank Lloyd Wright's architectural insignia. Additions are by Hall/Merriman (1992).

K-36
Bracht House
11626 Monica Lane
1956, Christensen & Cannata

This small house has a big presence thanks to the architect's zany exaggeration of Wrightian motifs. Down the street at 11617 Monica Lane is a Contemporary style house by Bolton & Barnstone (1956).

K-37
Lawrence House
11715 Timberknoll Drive
1969, Caudill Rowlett Scott

Charles E. "Tiny" Lawrence of Caudill Rowlett Scott designed this triangular-plan house set beneath a high-pitched roof. Its glazed perimeter is ringed with a shallow moat.

K-38
House
26 Liberty Bell Circle
1964, MacKie & Kamrath

With this house Karl Kamrath embarked on an exploration of Frank Lloyd Wright's early work that was to mark Kamrath's production of the 1970s. The model here is Wright's Isabel Roberts House in River Forest, Illinois (1908) with its story-and-a-half living room thrust forward of the body of the house.

K-39
Bullock House
672 Flintdale Road
1964, Caudill Rowlett Scott

Caudill Rowlett Scott partner, Tom Bullock, designed this 2-story, hipped roofed, brick house supported on cedar posts for his family.

K-40
Goodwin House
3 Leisure Lane
1955, Edwin J. Goodwin, Jr.

Jim Goodwin, a partner in the firm that eventually became Pierce Goodwin Alexander & Linville (PGAL), designed this 1-story modern house for his family. The street on which it is located preserves the ultimate authenticating trait of "old" Memorial: it is unpaved.

K-38 House

K-40 Goodwin House

K-41 St. Cecilia Catholic Church

K-42 Thompson House

K-43 Baumgardner House

K-44 Smith-Herzog House

K-45 House

K-41
St. Cecilia Catholic Church
11730 Denise Street
1978, Charles Tapley Associates

Built of brick bearing wall construction with structural masonry arches, the square-planned church rises up into a low-pitched pyramidal roof. Additions to the parish complex are by Tapley Lunow Architects (1989); the parish school was designed by the Cincinnati architect Edward J. Schulte (1958).

K-42
Thompson House
11914 Knippwood Lane
1957, Bowles & Bowles

A low monopitch roof containing clerestory side lighting hovers above this 1-story house of load bearing brick construction. Mary Lynn Thompson and Bob Bowles designed this house for her parents.

K-43
Baumgardner House
7 Robin Lake Lane
1960, Lars Bang

This 1- and 2-story modern house in the subdivision of Sandalwood is surfaced with concrete, stone, wood, and masonry solar screens— and a spectacular sectional picture window that reveals an open-riser stair. Rehabilitated by architect Philip C. Ewald.

K-44
Smith-Herzog House
21 Robin Lake Lane
1956, Frank D. Welch;
1974, Howard Barnstone

This house is so self-effacing that it hides its true nature from the street. Barnstone reworked an existing house, the first independent work of Frank Welch, extensively altering the flat-roofed original and adding to it a series of glazed concourses that open out to a lush landscape garden. The sensational effect that results can just barely be experienced vicariously in a view through the front door, which is virtually the only feature that presents itself to the street.

K-45
House
253 Mayerling Drive
2011, Cameron Armstrong

This steel-framed house replaces a '60s ranchburger. Its rotational thrusts and spins and interpenetrating roof planes announce an architectural agenda that differentiates it from most new houses in Memorial.

K-46
Thaxton-Gaw House
12020 Tall Oaks Road
1954, Frank Lloyd Wright

This small concrete-block house in Bunker Hill Village was Frank Lloyd Wright's first built project in Texas and his only work in Houston. Planned on a 30°-60° reflexive grid, it is closed on the south and open to the north. Wright's hand is clearly evident: the prow-shaped master bedroom, for instance, induces an intense sensation of spatial projection, and the subtly battered profiling of the exterior block walls rhythmically counters the horizontal extension of the redwood eaves. Threatened with demolition in 1991, the house was the object of a preservation campaign headed by Vicki List and the Greater Houston Preservation Alliance. Dentists Betty and Allen Gaw rescued the house, which had suffered extensive unsympathetic alterations, and had Kirksey Meyers restore it and design a large, but compatible, annex that wraps around the rear patio (1995).

K-47
Kayem House
12502 Taylorcrest Road
1957, Wylie W. Vale & Associates

The shallow-pitched gabled roof, its ridgeline spanning the short dimension of the house, is a recurring profile among mid-20th-century modern houses in Texas. The house that pipe and steel company founder Hans Kayem built is an expansive example, its glazed central bay anchored by a brick chimney. Vale, a prolific residential architect, was especially identified with the design of Contemporary style ranch type houses.

K-48
House
12607 Mossycup Drive
1957, Joseph Krakower

Herb Greene, while a draftsman for Joe Krakower, designed this distinctive 1-story house. Its panelized wood surfacing and shaped eaves exhibit Greene's special touch.

K-46 Thaxton-Gaw House

K-47 Kayem House

K-48 House

K-49 Krell House

K-50 Interurban Pharmacy

K-52 Lawrence House

K-53 House

K-54 Cropp House

K-49
Krell House
12612 Broken Bough Drive
1958, William N. Floyd

The long, linear spatial organization of this 1-story house is emphasized by the continuous fascia of the flat roof, which plays off the verticality of the giant pine trees that surround it. The Woodland Hollow subdivision, where it was built, is quite picturesque thanks to the way that Hollow Drive undulates around a ravine coursing through the neighborhood.

K-50
Interurban Pharmacy
[now Gulf States Laundry Machinery Company]
12647 Memorial Drive
1960, Don J. Tomasco Associates

Not quite as buoyant or transparent as it was when published in *Arts and Architecture* in 1961, the ex-Interurban Pharmacy also has lost its pine tree-studded landscape setting in the Memorial Bend Shopping Park, developed by architect William N. Floyd in 1956 in conjunction with the adjacent Memorial Bend subdivision.

K-51
Caudill House
311 Electra Drive
1958, William N. Floyd

This low, contemporary house, once occupied by the architect William W. Caudill and his family, is in the subdivision of Memorial Bend. Apart from the fact that street names are derived from the titles of operas (Butterfly, Tosca, Traviata, Figaro), the remarkable thing about Memorial Bend is that many of its houses were designed by the architect William N. Floyd, one of the investors in the subdivision's development in 1954-55. Floyd's crisp, undemonstrative modern style gives Memorial Bend an inherent quality lacking in the surrounding neighborhoods of west Memorial.

K-52
Lawrence House
12919 Figaro Drive
1958, William N. Floyd

When Caudill Rowlett Scott moved its architecture practice from Bryan to Houston in 1959, several of the firm's partners bought houses in Memorial Bend. This flat-roofed house, its blind brick wall plane divided into rhythmic panels, was home to Caudill Rowlett Scott partner Charles E. Lawrence.

K-53
House
503 Electra Drive
1958, William N. Floyd

Michael E. Brichford was so taken by Memorial Bend after moving there in 2001 that he began to investigate its history, made the acquaintance of 91-year-old William N. Floyd, organized the Memorial Bend Architecture webpage, and became a co-founder of Houston Mod in 2003. Brichford's website identifies many of Floyd's houses in Memorial Bend, such as this flat-roofed house with high-set clerestory windows slotted between the roof beams.

K-54
Cropp House
12923 Memorial Drive
1956, David Crockett

Rehabilitated by Jeff Horning, this modern courtyard house turns a blind front toward busy Memorial Drive.

K-51 Caudill House

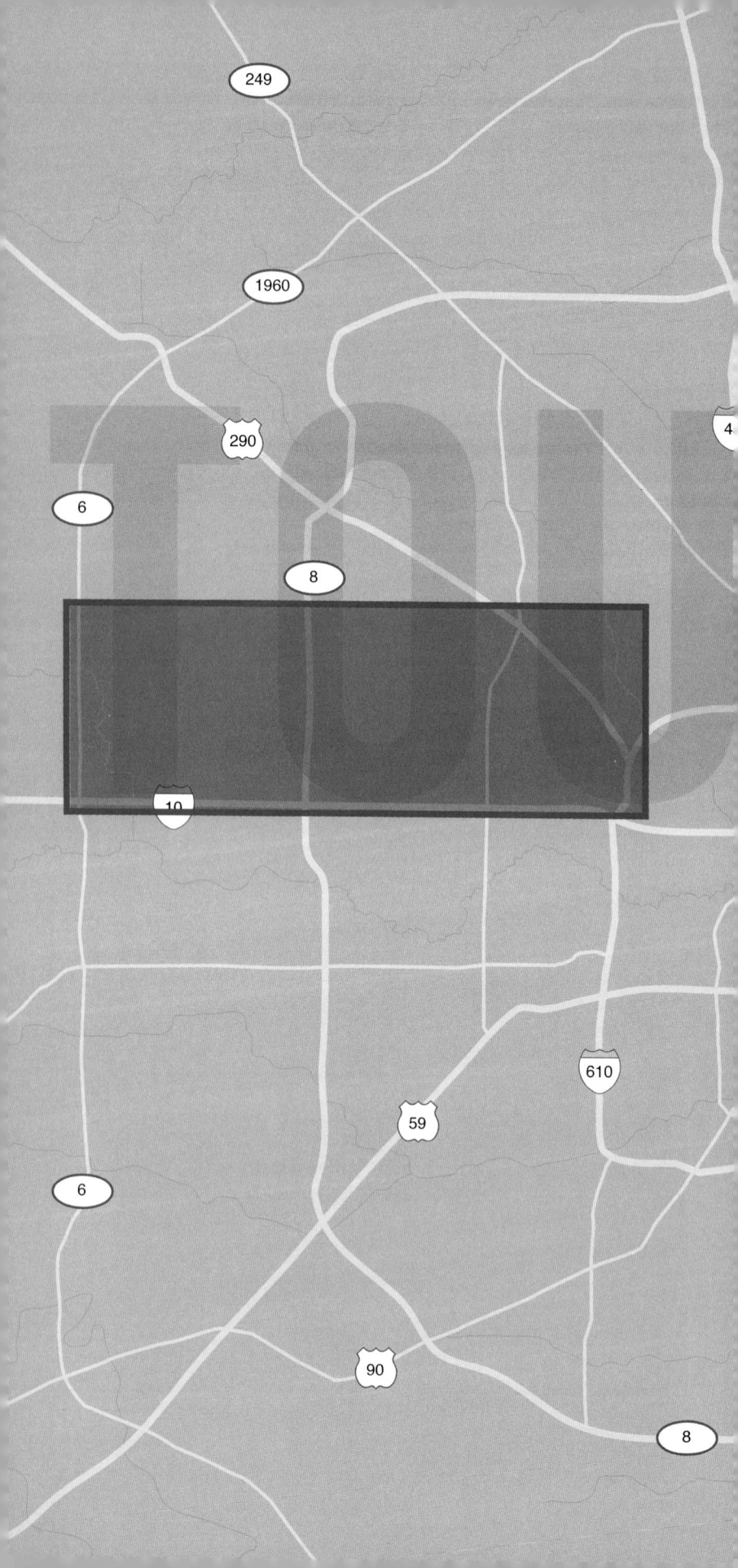

Spring Branch / Energy Corridor / Bear Creek

Spring Branch / Energy Corridor / Bear Creek

Tour L

Houston freeway historian Erik Slotboom notes that the practice of constructing surface-level frontage roads to provide access to freeways is a distinct Texas phenomenon. The impact of this practice on Houston's urban development in the second half of the 20th century is apparent along the Katy Freeway (I-10 West), where the corridor of real estate adjoining the freeway (what Lars Lerup calls the "speedzone") operates at a much different tempo than adjacent layers of real estate not connected to the frontage roads. This sets up a two-tier experience of suburban space, with higher value land uses gravitating to the freeway speedzone, disconnected from the local uses bound to the armature of surface streets.

North of the Katy Freeway lies Spring Branch, named for a tributary of Buffalo Bayou. Here the pine forest, with which the Memorial area south of the freeway is identified, thins out. German place names indicate the one-time presence of German-owned dairy and truck farms in the area that supplied the markets of Houston in the 19th and early 20th centuries. The major east-west streets, such as Long Point Road, exhibit the strip development characteristic of the mid-20th century, with low commercial buildings pushed far back from the street to accommodate parked cars and big signs (now as likely to be in Spanish or Korean as in English). Behind these thoroughfares, the restricted, aging subdivisions remain neat and tidy.

The speedzones along the Katy Freeway and the north-south sector of W. Sam Houston Parkway N. developed as ribbons of high-rise office and intensive retail use. They demonstrate the stratification of architecture in early 21st-century Houston between the "architect's architecture" of corporate office buildings and the thematically styled, strip-planned retail building types. Office park developments additionally mobilize professional landscape design to construct enclaves of visual order amid the otherwise non-design-controlled landscape of the speedzone. Reconstruction of the Katy Freeway in the 2000 decade swelled its capacity to 16 lanes, reinforcing its role as the infrastructural axis of West Houston.

1. **Big Three Industries Building,** 3535 West 12th Avenue
2. **Society for the Prevention of Cruelty to Animals Building,** 900 Portway Drive
3. **Kirksey,** 6909 Portwest Drive
4. **Interior Resources Center,** 7026 Old Katy Road
5. **First Baptist Church,** 7401 Katy Freeway
6. **Proler Family Chapel, Beth Israel Cemetery,** 1101 Antoine Drive
7. **Lawyer House,** 1030 Glourie Circle
8. **Our Lady of Walsingham Catholic Church,** 7809 Shadyvilla Lane
9. **Unitarian Fellowship of Houston,** 1504 Wirt Road
10. **Smith's Lucky 7 Grocery,** 6702–6724 Westview Drive
11. **Holy Cross Lutheran Church Parish Hall,** 7901 Westview Drive
12. **Garage-Workshop,** 8320 Merlin Drive
13. **Spring Branch Savings & Loan Association Building,** 8224 Long Point Road
14. **St. Peter's Evangelical Church,** 9022 Long Point Road
15. **Seismic Exchange Building,** 11050 Capital Park Drive
16. **Satterfield & Pontikes Building,** 11000 Equity Drive
17. **Aquasource Building,** 11100 Brittmoore Park Drive
18. **New Life Church,** 10800 Hammerly Boulevard
19. **Shell Woodcreek Exploration and Production Offices Building,** 200 North Dairy Ashford Road
20. **Conoco Building,** 600 North Dairy Ashford Road
21. **Energy Center I and II,** 585 North Dairy Ashford Road
22. **Addicks United Methodist Church,** 1212 N. State Highway 6
23. **Fat Frank's Grub and Saloon,** 1010 N. State Highway 6
24. **BP Project Rodeo—IST Building Helios Plaza,** 201 Helios Way
25. **The Amoco Center,** 501 Westlake Park Boulevard
26. **Bridgepoint Bible Church,** 13277 Katy Freeway
27. **Three Eldridge Place,** 737 N. Eldridge Parkway
28. **Citycentre,** 600 West Sam Houston Parkway North
29. **Memorial-Hermann Hospital,** 929 Gessner Road
30. **9430 Old Katy Road Building,** 9430 Old Katy Road

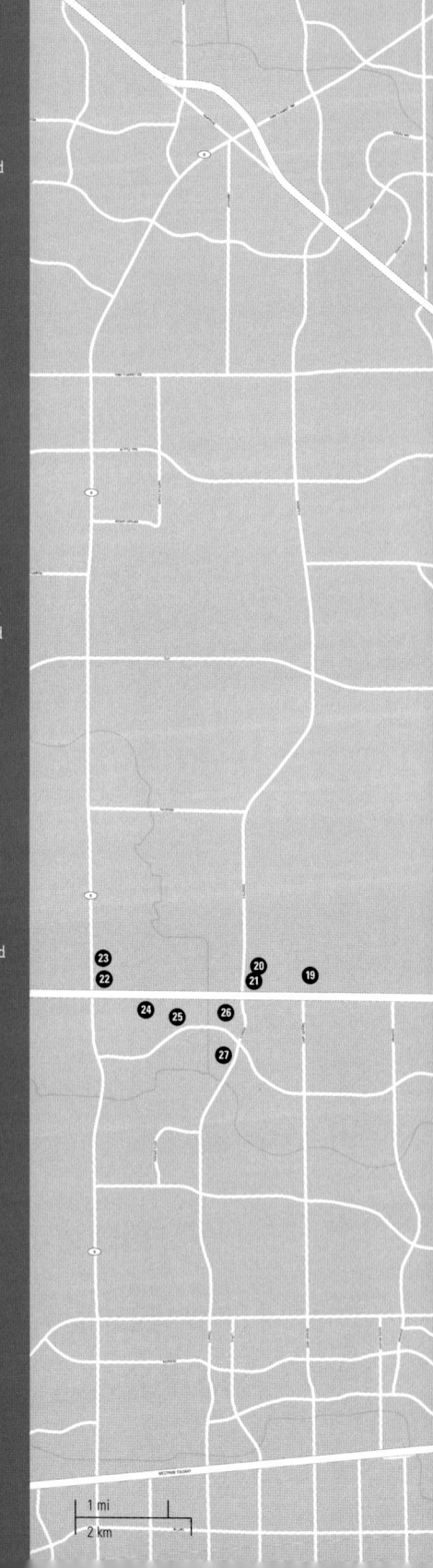

L-1 Big Three Industries Building

L-2 Society for the Prevention of Cruelty to Animals

L-3 Kirksey

L-4 Interior Resources Center

L-5 First Baptist Church of Houston

L-1
Big Three Industries Building
3535 West 12th Avenue
1974, MacKie & Kamrath

This extraordinary corporate headquarters building adapts the formal organizational principles of Frank Lloyd Wright's Unity Temple to the program of a multi-story office building. Both the building and site details are solidly executed in cast-in-place concrete.

L-2
Society for the Prevention of Cruelty to Animals
900 Portway Drive
1993, Jackson & Ryan Architects

The long, low, hipped roof that is the building's foremost characteristic allows it to hold its own in a typical Houston flatland setting.

L-3
Kirksey
6909 Portwest Drive
2000, 2007, Kirksey

Westport Business Park was developed in the early 1980s with generic blocks of office-warehouse space on a tract backing up to I-10. Taking advantage of the big-box building type's flexibility, architect John Kirksey located his firm's studio here: a concrete tilt wall warehouse-loft building expanded with a west wing in 2007. Studio spaces open on the south towards a lushly planted lawn.

L-4
Interior Resources Center
[now Houston Design Center]
7026 Old Katy Road
1984, 1985, House/Reh Associates

Furniture and interior systems showrooms are housed here in a campus-like setting. Two and 3-story buildings, connected by open-air corridors, are arranged around a shallow lake and, inevitably in Houston, a parking lot.

L-5
First Baptist Church of Houston
7401 Katy Freeway
1976, S. I. Morris Associates

From the freeway the only visible part of the First Baptist Church complex is the education wing, which is wrapped around the quarter-circular church—a 5,000-seat auditorium. The adjoining Christian Life Center, visible at the juncture of the Katy Freeway and Loop 610, is by Denny, Ray & Wines (1985).

L-6
Herman and Elaine Proler Family Chapel, Beth Israel Cemetery
1101 Antoine Road
1997, Daniel Solomon with Barry Moore

The San Francisco architect Daniel Solomon and his associate Gary Strang sought to make an open-air public space that is solemn and meditative in feeling, engages its landscape setting, and accommodates Houston's extreme and unpredictable climate. They use shapes in section and plan to slow spatial movement and to enhance visitors' awareness of the phenomenon of transition. The chapel frames views into the cemetery while screening out Antoine Road, against which the complex is built. Proler Chapel represents a too rare effort in Houston to design a place for public spirituality and a space that works with the climate.

L-7
Lawyer House
1030 Glourie Circle
1962, Frank D. Lawyer

The Burkhardt Plaza subdivision in Hilshire Village contains a number of flat-roofed, slab-sided modern courtyard houses. This example was the house of Caudill Rowlett Scott partner Frank Lawyer.

L-8
Our Lady of Walsingham Catholic Church
7809 Shadyvilla Lane
2004, Hoyle, Doran & Berry

Boston architect Ethan Anthony sought to recover the spirit of Cram & Ferguson (predecessors to Hoyle, Doran & Berry) in his design of this Anglican-use Roman Catholic parish church, dedicated to the patroness of England. The stout, staged limestone tower fronts a tall nave flanked by side aisles. The west transept contains a reconstruction of the Holy House, the medieval shrine of our Lady of Walsingham. Houston architect Warren Goulas designed the other components of the parish complex.

L-7 Lawyer House

L-6 Herman and Elaine Proler Family Chapel, Beth Israel Cemetery

L-8 Our Lady of Walsingham Catholic Church

L-9 Unitarian Fellowship of Houston

L-10 Smith's Lucky 7 Grocery

L-11 Parish Hall, Holy Cross Lutheran Church

L-12 Workshop

L-13 Spring Branch Savings & Loan Assoc. Building

L-14 St. Peter's Evangelical Church

L-9
Unitarian Fellowship of Houston
1504 Wirt Road
1993, Val Glitsch and Natalye Appel

Working with a very small budget, the congregation asked the architects to design a worship and educational space that made the most of its wooded site along a busy thoroughfare. Glitsch and Appel's shed-like buildings are in tune with the rusticity characteristic of Spring Branch. James Burnett's landscape design complements the architecture by appearing not to have been designed at all.

L-10
Smith's Lucky 7 Grocery
6702-6724 Westview Drive
1966

The impact of Miesian discipline on Houston architecture is evident in this shopping center, built by grocer Curtis Smith in the mid-1960s. Thin steel canopies above sidewalks attach to panelized, brick-faced building blocks. A brave showing for architecture in the suburbs.

L-11
Parish Hall, Holy Cross Lutheran Church
7901 Westview Drive
1955, Paul H. Elliott

The parish hall, facing Westview, was the first increment of this church complex to be constructed. It exemplifies one of the most popular typologies for modern churches in the post-war period.

L-12
Workshop
8320 Merlin Drive
1993, David Guthrie

This is a backyard workshop and garage, serene and confident.

L-13
Spring Branch Savings & Loan Assoc. Building
8224 Long Point Road
1956, Burdette Keeland
and Clyde Jackson

Burdette Keeland designed this small, steel-framed, flat-roofed Miesian pavilion as a financial institution. Its shallow portico has been filled in to expand interior space, and the building has been joined by companions at 8210 and 8226. The grungy condition of all three suggests the challenge of trying to restrain market-driven urban development in Houston with architecture.

L-14
St. Peter's Evangelical Church
9022 Long Point Road
1864

St. Peter's was a country church built to serve the community of German immigrant farmers and dairymen who first settled the Spring Branch area in the 1830s and '40s. Although it has undergone evident remodeling, it preserves its identity as a rural Southern vernacular church house.

L-15
Seismic Exchange Building
11050 Capital Park Drive
2009, Powers Brown Architecture

Powers Brown's 6-story headquarters for Seismic Exchange features a curtain wall built up with shallow layers of terra cotta cladding, steel tubing, and glass. The building is located in the 150-acre Westway Park office complex, developed by the Wolff Companies in 1998. Westway Park stands out for the consistency of its landscape architecture and building design. Notable neighbors include the 9-story Cameron Building at 4646 W. Sam Houston Parkway N. (2001, Hellmuth, Obata + Kassabaum) and the 10-story DNA Westpark II Building at 4424 W. Sam Houston Parkway N. (2008, Kirksey). The impressive 11-acre park within which the BJ Services Building at 4601 Westway Park is situated was designed by the landscape architects Kudela & Weinheimer (2006).

L-15 Seismic Exchange Building

L-16 Satterfield & Pontikes Building

L-17 Aquasource Building

L-18 New Life Church and Kid's Castle

L-19 Shell Woodcreek Exploration and Production Offices Building

L-20 Conoco Building

L-16
Satterfield & Pontikes Building
11000 Equity Drive
2006, Kirksey

Headquarters of the Satterfield & Pontikes construction corporation, this office building consists of a 4-story east wing framed by thin steel columns supporting a screen of steel louvers that shades recessed curtain walls, and a 3-story west wing faced with a refined aluminum and glass curtain wall that envelops the building's concrete structural frame. Like a number of the buildings in Westway Park, the Satterfield & Pontikes Building was designed to achieve LEED certification.

L-17
Aquasource Building
[now Daniel Measurement and Control]
11100 Brittmoore Park Drive
1999, ArcTec Associates

Architect Israel Grinberg organized this 2-story corporate office building as a rectangular bar. A glazed entrance cube and an offset, aluminum-faced stair cylinder give the building volumetric presence on its street front. The long east elevation is faced with ranks of canopied windows overlooking a retention basin. The site is typical of the corridor along the W. Sam Houston Parkway N—an electrical transmission right-of-way to the west, a trailer park to the northwest, and an array of big-box workshop and warehouse structures, all backing up to the 12,460-acre Addicks flood detention reservoir.

L-18
New Life Church and Kid's Castle
10800 Hammerly Boulevard
1993, Monolithic Constructors

The mega-church occupies the concrete dome facing Alcott. Kids Castle, the congregation's freestanding children's building, is visible from Brittmoore. The uses of architectural imagery here are intriguing. The church, built by Monolithic Constructors of Italy, Texas, makes no effort to advance a religious identity, while Kids Castle is imagery intensive. Both structures stand out in the landscape adjacent to the W. Sam Houston Parkway N., which is dominated by distribution centers housing oil field service and equipment businesses.

L-19
Shell Woodcreek Exploration and Production Offices Building
200 North Dairy Ashford Road
1980, Caudill Rowlett Scott;
2007, Hellmuth, Obata + Kassabaum

West of amazing flyover ramps marking the Katy Freeway interchanges with the Sam Houston Tollway lies the Energy Corridor. In the design of Shell Oil Company's corporate complex, Caudill Rowlett Scott consciously addressed environmental issues in the aftermath of the Energy Crisis of the 1970s. The 4-story, 7-building group consists of triangular-shaped bays, each surrounding an internal courtyard to maximize views to the outdoors without unduly expanding each building's perimeter or internal circulation. Almost all offices have natural light and views out. Precast concrete exterior components were designed to filter and diffuse daylight into the interior. Caudill Rowlett Scott's successor, Hellmuth, Obata + Kassabaum, was responsible for a major expansion in 2007.

L-20
Conoco Building
[now ConocoPhillips]
600 North Dairy Ashford Road
1985, Kevin Roche, John Dinkeloo & Associates
2006, Pickard Chilton, Kendall/Heaton Associates, and PDR

The Connecticut architect Kevin Roche cites the Kellum-Noble House in Sam Houston Park as inspiring the sun-defying architectural treatment of this 3-story, 16-building corporate headquarters complex. Conoco is located on a 62-acre site that backs up to the huge Addicks Reservoir, a flood retention basin encircled by high, grass-lined dikes. Roche's widespread, aluminum-framed fiberglass awnings are the most identifiable elements. They extend so far forward of the buildings that they acquire a strong, gestural quality, especially on faceted end bays. Awnings are joined by a network of second-story pedestrian bridges that encircle the buildings and shade first-floor windows. Because almost all offices have outdoor exposure, controlling sunlight was critical. The bridges also traverse an artificial lagoon, in which the complex is set. Conoco is organized on a circulation diagram that integrates pedestrian and vehicular movement. It has no real front door (the public enters at the middle of the complex from a ground-level parking garage) but doesn't require one since public access is carefully guarded. Conoco represents a high level of technical skill in designing the optimal corporate office environment. But its inevitable repetitiveness, its self-effacement, and its insulation give the complex a slightly oppressive sense of bureaucratic control that undermines the ingenuities and amenities of the architecture. Substantial additions to the west side along North Eldridge were completed in 2006. The Office of James Burnett was the landscape architect.

L-21 Energy Center I and II

L-22 Fat Frank's Grub and Saloon

L-23 Addicks United Methodist Church

L-24 BP Project Rodeo—IST Building Helios Plaza

L-25 The Amoco Center

L-21
Energy Center I and II
585 North Dairy Ashford Road
2007, 2008, Hellmuth, Obata + Kassabaum

This pair of 12-story office buildings were designed for the Trammell Crow Companies as parallel bars of space offset to either side of each building's central core. The corner bays are faced with blue glass curtain walls that contrast with horizontally aligned precast concrete spandrel panels. The offset theme is reiterated in the spacing of exterior verticals. Clark Condon was the landscape architect. Across North Eldridge is the outspread, brightly reflective Hyatt Regency West Houston (now Omni Hotel Westside, 13102 Katy Freeway, 1984, LAN).

L-22
Fat Frank's Grub and Saloon
[now Cattleguard Restaurant and Bar]
1010 N. State Highway 6
1985, Taft Architects

With their customary wit and prowess, Taft deconstructed this western-themed, fast-food restaurant. somewhat the worse for wear, the false-front façade has been remodeled with an off-center covered deck in place of the original shed-roofed front porch.

L-23
Addicks United Methodist Church
1212 N. State Highway 6
1915

This wooden church was built to serve the rural community of Addicks. It now faces the very different world of West Houston: Park Ten, a 550-acre office and industrial park begun in 1970 by Wolff, Morgan & Company. Park Ten established this stretch of the Katy Freeway as the Energy Corridor, an edge-city business center where oil and gas corporations have clustered since the late 1970s.

L-24
BP Project Rodeo—IST Building Helios Plaza
201 Helios Way
2009, Gensler

BP built the 6-story Helios Plaza adjacent to its headquarters in Westlake Park to contain its international supply and trading sections. Designed to be a model of sustainable construction and operation practices, the low-rise building faces the Katy Freeway with big-scaled, stacked, 30-foot high trading floors visible through north-facing curtain walls of high performance clear glass. Horizontal and vertical louver systems screen windows on east- and west-facing walls.

L-25
The Amoco Center
[now BP]
501 Westlake Park Boulevard
1983, Skidmore, Owings & Merrill

This dark gridded, 28-story tower, infilled with light green solar glass, is the tallest building in the Energy Corridor. In addition to a lower unit, it is joined by the 17-story Westlake Park Two Building (1982) and the 20-story Westlake Park Three Building (1983) at 500 and 550 Westlake Park. All were designed by the Houston office of Skidmore, Owings & Merrill for Gerald D. Hines Interests. Richard Keating of Skidmore, Owings & Merrill's Houston office moved to Los Angeles in 1985, but was recalled to design BP Plaza (1993, Keating Mann Jernigan Rottet and Wilson Griffin) at 200 Westlake Park. After BP merged with Amoco in 1998, the Amoco Center became BP's U.S. headquarters. Next door to Westlake Park, at 13501 Katy Freeway, is the ExxonMobil Chemical Company complex (1980, Pierce Goodwin Alexander), which is barely visible from the street. Just beyond Westlake Park's back door, at 15375 Memorial Drive, is the very visible ex-ARCO Oil & Gas District Offices complex (1986, CRS Sirrine). Just around the corner, at 801 North Eldridge Parkway, is the McDermott Engineering Office Complex (1981, Jack Reber), with its pyramidal incline of pre-stressed, precast concrete sun baffles.

L-26
BridgePoint Bible Church
13277 Katy Freeway
2007, Ray+Hollington

This congregation left Spring Branch, where it had been organized as a community church in the 1930s, to move to this 10-acre site facing the Katy Freeway. Emulating adjacent corporate complexes, the church seeks visibility with a freeway location. The architects designed a sequence of wedge-shaped buildings facing Memorial View Drive. These are recessed deeply into the site to accommodate substantial anticipated future growth.

L-26 BridgePoint Bible Church

L-27 Three Eldridge Parkway Building

L-28 Citycentre

L-30 Select Specialty Hospital—Houston West

L-27
Three Eldridge Place Building
737 N. Eldridge Parkway
2009, Gensler

Overlapping and folding planes of curtain wall in shallow layers give this 13-story office building a deconstructed look. Asakura Robinson was the landscape architect.

L-28
Citycentre
600 West Sam Houston Parkway North
2009, Gensler and the Office of James Burnett

Citycentre is a makeover of the site of Town and Country Mall, which opened in 1983 just north of the Town and Country Village retail center (1968, Brodnax Phenix & Associates). Despite its location-location-location site, Town and Country Mall did not prove competitive. It was demolished in 2005 and replaced by Citycentre, a 37-acre mixed-use complex developed by the Midway Companies with planning by Gensler, and landscape architecture by the Office of James Burnett. Gensler worked around Town & Country Mall's three parking garages (not demolished) to implant an inner vehicular street network and a sequence of figural pedestrian spaces framed by mid- and low-rise buildings. Gensler designed the 12-story Hotel Sorella by Valencia (2009, with Remedios Siembieda), three office buildings, and a series of retail blocks. Kirksey designed the Lofts at Citycentre (2009). Citycentre represents the Houston market interpretation of New Urbanism. It demonstrates the dilemmas involved in trying to graft a "traditional neighborhood" spatial order onto hyper-suburban infrastructure. The results are, spatially, slightly claustrophobic. Citycentre retains the persistent sense of interiority associated with shopping malls. Its urbanity comes across as lifestyle make-believe rooted in market segmentation. To the east of Citycentre, at 10505 Town and Country Way, is the Town and Country Station, U.S. Post Office (1978, Clovis Heimsath Associates), originally outfitted with a roof full of solar collectors. The decision to junk the system when the solar collectors required replacement indicates the limits of the architecture of good intentions (as also exemplified by Citycentre) in Houston. Without public regulation to enforce good practices over the long term, design solutions tend to become short-term trends that get replaced (or demolished) when the market needs new attractors.

L-29
Memorial-Hermann Tower
929 Gessner Road
2008, Morris Architects

The wedding cake profile, reflective glass center section, and faceted "crown of thorns" lantern give this 33-story medical professional building, headquarters of the Memorial-Hermann Hospital system, a spectacular, if somewhat ominous, presence along the Katy Freeway—especially at night when it turns blue. In 2009 Katharine Shilcutt, writing in the Houston Press, acclaimed it as one of the ugliest buildings in Houston. Projecting off the east end of the tower, at 945 Gessner, is the 22-story Westin Houston Memorial City (2011, Morris Architects), a mixed use hotel and condominium slab that exudes retro-mod flair. At ground level though, the complex is labyrinthine. Morris Architects designed the 14-story, glass-faced Three Memorial City Medical Plaza (1999) at 840 Gessner. Across Gessner from the Memorial City Hospital complex is Memorial City Mall (1966, 2003), developed by MetroNational, which also operates the medical complex. Memorial City's most high profile components are the 14-story Cemex Center (2009, Morris Architects) at 920 Mcmorial Way, with its wavy roof, and the adjacent Fountains at Memorial City residential slab (2010, Morris Architects).

L-30
Select Specialty Hospital—Houston West Building
9430 Old Katy Road
1981, House/Reh Associates

Stacked trays of office space, underscored with white horizontal banding, endow this 4-story office building with a strong, uncomplicated image.

L-29 Memorial-Hermann Tower

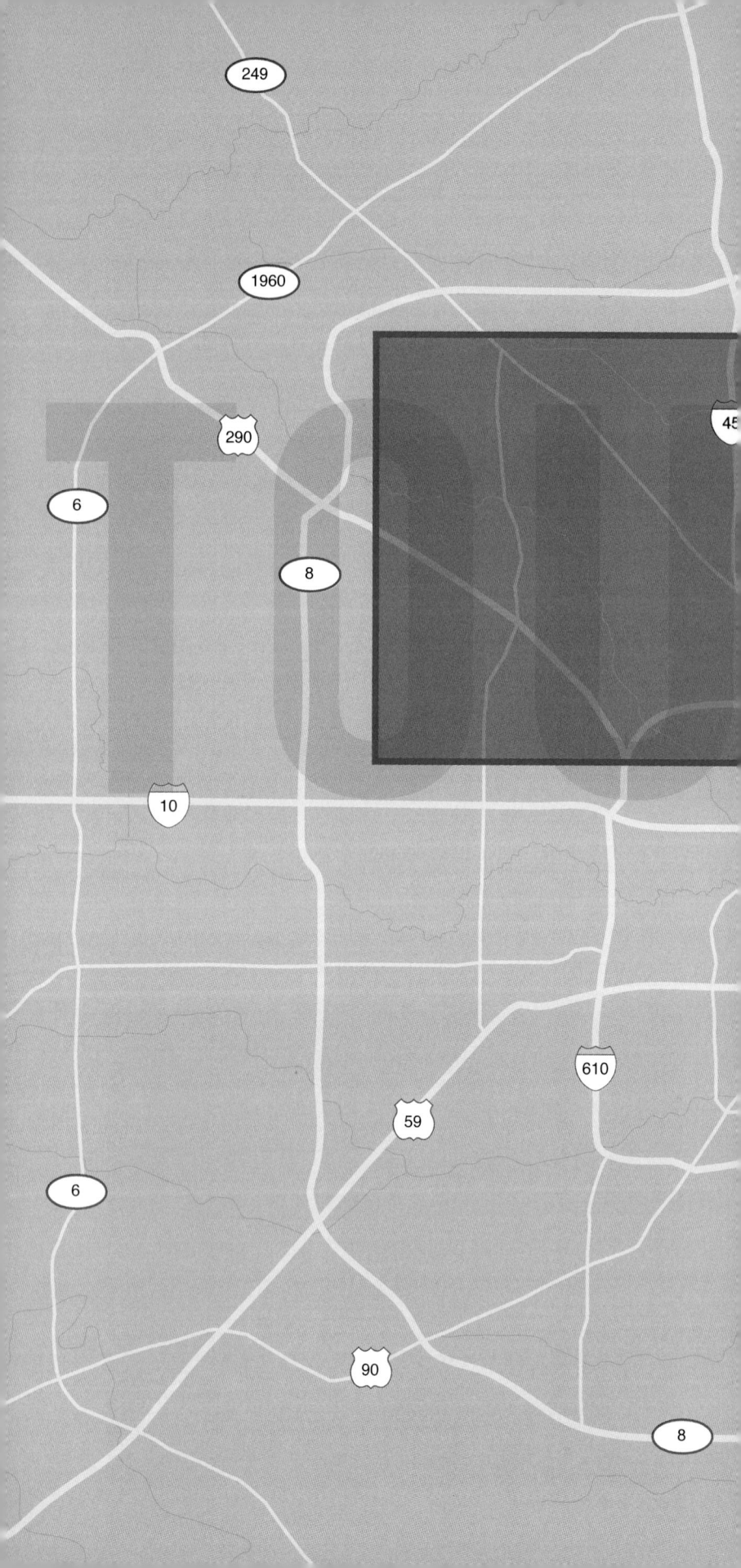

Hempstead Highway / Garden Oaks / Acres Homes

Hempstead Highway / Garden Oaks / Acres Homes

Tour M

The difference between the architecture of the freeway and the architecture of the rest of the city stands out in the northwest quadrant of Houston, which is especially identified with the Houston & Texas Central Railway, its vehicular parallel, the Hempstead Highway, and the highway's successor, the Northwest Freeway (U.S. 290). The freeway, lined by gleaming office buildings, constructs a misleading impression of this sector of Houston.

To either side of the "speedzone" of the freeway lie vast stretches of blue-collar Houston: industrial production zones, lower-income neighborhoods, and thoroughfare streets bereft of the corporate retail brands that signify middle-income suburbia. Northwest Houston is home to a pair of adjoining neighborhoods that stand out in the local history of real estate subdivision: Garden Oaks, developed beginning in 1937, Houston's first Federal Housing Administration-insured residential community, and Oak Forest, developed by Frank W. Sharp in 1946, the largest residential subdivision in the postwar U.S. until surpassed by Levittown. Historical distinction has not spared either the up-and-down cycles to which Houston real estate is subject. Farther north, where W. Montgomery Road diverges from N. Shepherd, is Houston Acre Homes Estates, better known as Acres Homes, a large-lot, subsistence community developed during the New Deal and marketed to African-American families. Acres Homes is the threshold beyond which low-income, minority neighborhoods stretch northward in a discontinuous, low-density sprawl that verges on the upper-middle-income suburban field associated with FM 1960. This is a part of Houston where one keenly senses the extraordinary scale of the suburbanized city, and the extent to which broad swathes of it are areas where newness and prosperity do not prevail.

1. **Memorial Hospital Northwest,** 1635 North Loop West
2. **2550 Brookhollow Building,** 2550 North Loop West
3. **Bridgestone One Building,** 2600 North Loop West
4. **Brookhollow Central II and Brookhollow Central III Buildings,** 2900–2950 North Loop West
5. **Humble Oil & Refining Company Brookhollow,** 4400, 4500, and 4550 Dacoma Road
6. **James M. Delmar Field House,** 2020 Mangum Road
7. **Keystone Plaza,** 10510 Northwest Freeway
8. **Willis Flow Control Division of Cameron Iron Works Building,** 10810 Northwest Freeway
9. **General Services Administration Regional Field Office Building,** 1 Justice Park Drive
10. **J. Everett Collier Branch, Houston Public Library,** 6200 Pinemont Street
11. **Cameron Ironworks World Headquarters,** 13013 Northwest Freeway
12. **Northwest Corporate Park,** 6700 Hollister Road
13. **Reed Rock Bit Drilling Technology Center Building,** 7000 Hollister Road
14. **Our Lady of Lourdes Catholic Church,** 6550 Fairbanks-North Houston Road
15. **Time Warner Building,** 8400 W. Tidwell Road
16. **Texas Steel Processing Building,** 5480 Windfern Road
17. **Katherine Smith Elementary School,** 4802 Chrystell Lane
18. **Oak Forest Branch, Houston Public Library,** 1349 W. 43rd Avenue
19. **Oak Forest Park Pool House,** 2100 Judiway Drive
20. **Revere Quality House Institute House of Expanding Rooms,** 1101 Wakefield Drive
21. **St. Rose of Lima Parish Hall and School,** 3604 Brinkman Road
22. **House,** 806 Fisher Street
23. **Sears, Roebuck & Company Bus Shelter,** 4000 N. Shepherd Drive
24. **Haley House,** 726 W. 43rd Avenue
25. **Our Savior Lutheran Church,** 4425 N. Shepherd Drive
26. **Art Guys World Headquarters,** 5757 Knox Street
27. **Grotfeld Studio-House,** 2007 Paul Quinn Street
28. **Houston Astros Major League Baseball Urban Youth Baseball Academy Training Center, Sylvester Turner Park,** 2801 S. Victory Drive
29. **Houston Police Department North Police Station,** 9455 W. Montgomery Road
30. **Salvation Army Garden City Boys and Girls Club,** 9717 W. Montgomery Road
31. **Our Lady of La Vang Catholic Church,** 12311 Old Foltin Road

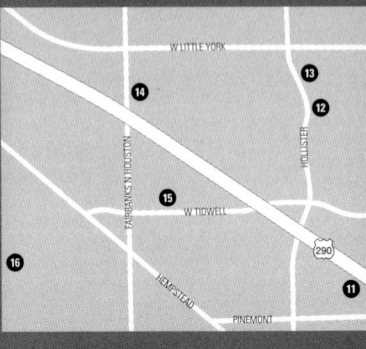

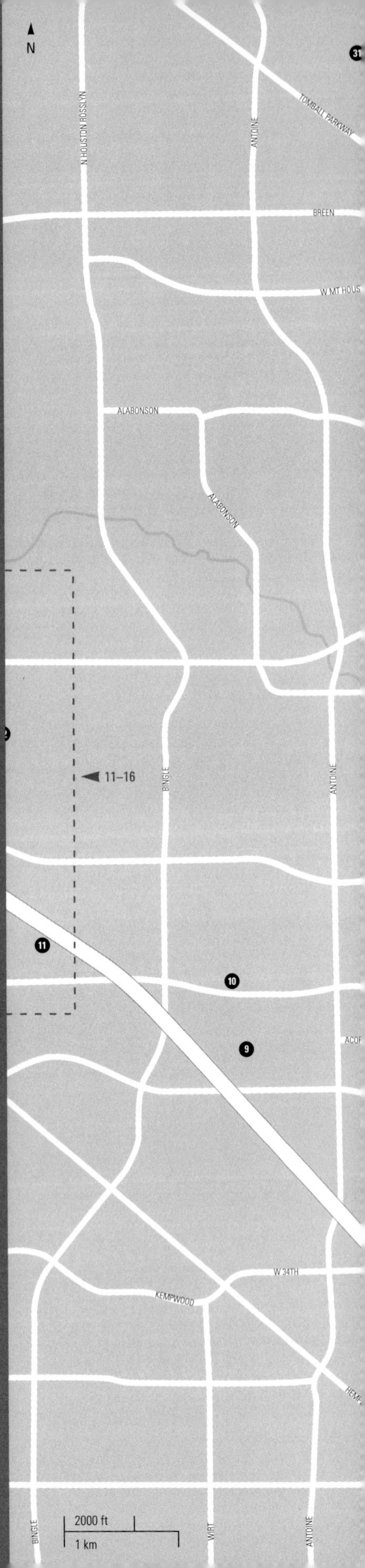

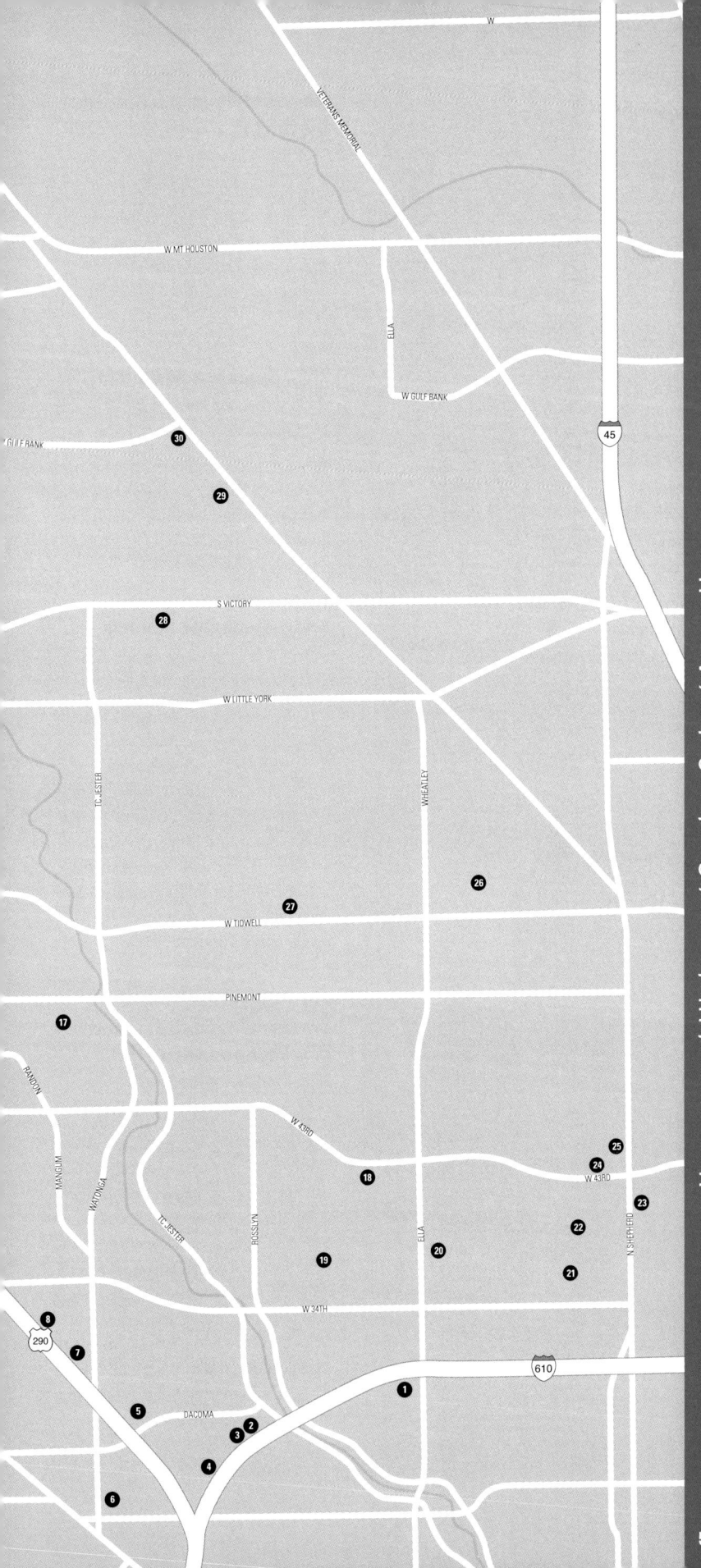

M-1 Memorial-Hermann Hospital Northwest

M-2 2550 Brookhollow Building

M-3 Bridgestone One Building

M-4 Brookhollow Central II and Brookhollow Central III

M-5 Humble Oil & Refining Company Brookhollow

M-1
Memorial-Hermann Hospital Northwest
1635 North Loop West
1988, Falick/Klein Partnership

The elements of this complex exhibit varying degrees of planar relief, which the gridded surfaces subtly highlight.

M-2
2550 Brookhollow Building
2550 North Loop West
1975, Richard Fitzgerald & Partners

The Tenneco Building downtown served as a model for this restrained, 7-story office building built by Russo Properties.

M-3
Bridgestone One Building
2600 North Loop West
1976, Richard Fitzgerald & Partners

On the heels of Pennzoil Place, parallelogram-plan buildings with unconventional fenestration signaled the first step toward more adventurous office building design undertaken by several Houston architectural offices. Here Fitzgerald highlighted the folding back of the wall planes by dropping the sill levels of the window bands.

M-4
Brookhollow Central II and Brookhollow Central III
2900-2950 North Loop West
1980, 1982, 3D/International

The intersection of Loop 610 and the Northwest Freeway provided just the site for the play of oval geometries embodied in these two speculative office buildings, both constructed by P.I.C. Realty Co. The curtain walls of bronze solar glass and bronze anodized aluminum were souped up with red sill-level racing stripes. In 2008 the curtain walls were silverized (Ziegler Cooper), diminishing the buildings' visual impact.

M-5
Humble Oil & Refining Company Brookhollow
[now ExxonMobil Brookhollow Campus]
4400, 4500, and 4550 Dacoma Road
1971, 1972, 1975, Pierce Goodwin Flanagan

Sun control and the expression of cast-in-place concrete construction were the architectural determinants of these three corporate office buildings. They are located in Brookhollow, a 170-acre mixed-use development that was an early scene of design-conscious office building in Houston, where the Humble Brookhollow buildings set the standard.

M-6
James M. Delmar Field House
2020 Mangum Road
1958, Milton McGinty

The thin-shell paraboloid roof canopy of this gymnasium represents a comparatively rare local use of a technology that was quite popular in American architecture during the late 1950s and early 1960s.

M-7
Keystone Plaza
10510 Northwest Freeway
1986, W. O. Neuhaus Associates

Bill Neuhaus developed the design of this strip shopping center from the image of the false-fronted western frontier town, a relevant architectural analogy to the expedient real estate practices that transpire along freeway frontage roads in Texas. It is rendered here with wit and style. Behind the shopping center, at 2855 Mangum Road, is the unconventionally organized Biehl Building, a 5-story office building with integrated parking (1980, W. O. Neuhaus Associates).

M-8
Willis Flow Control Division of Cameron Iron Works Building
[now Cameron Controls]
10810 Northwest Freeway
1980, Lockwood, Andrews & Newnam (LAN)

The diagonally raked sectional cutaway of this small corporate office building gives it considerable presence in its freeway setting.

M-6 James M. Delmar Field House

M-8 Willis Flow Control Division of Cameron Iron Works Building

M-7 Keystone Plaza

M-9 General Service Administration Regional Field Office Building

M-10 J. Everett Collier Branch, Houston Public Library

M-11 Cameron Ironworks World Headquarters Building

M-12 Northwest Corporate Park

M-9
General Service Administration Regional Field Office Building
1 Justice Park Drive
2009, Leo A. Daly/LAN and PageSoutherlandPage

This U.S. government office building is an 8-story slab that commands attention from the Northwest Freeway with its sunscreen of green glass projected out in front of the building's aluminum-clad walls. By varying the size of apertures in the sunscreen and articulating the metal framing system supporting the glass, PSP's Lawrence Speck emphasized scale gradation rather than the building's repetitive grid of windows. Staggering the placement of vertical mullions in the windows further animates the building.

M-10
J. Everett Collier Branch, Houston Public Library
6200 Pinemont Street
1985, MRW Architects

Rotational geometry is combined with the recollection of rural vernacular buildings to enliven this small branch library. Careful articulation of the supporting structure, infilled with glass clerestories and dark tile wall facing, reinforces its presence tectonically and materially.

M-11
Cameron Ironworks World Headquarters Building
[now Harris County Appraisal District]
13013 Northwest Freeway
1978, 3D/International

The original client's role as a major local industrial enterprise specializing in the production of steel components for oilfield and petrochemical equipment is symbolized in the wide-span, white-painted, steel-framed construction of its 7-story office building. The approach is reductivist rather than Miesian, however. The building looks monotonous because no variation in scale is introduced.

The one instance of counterpoint is dissonant: the freestanding brick-faced shafts at the back of the building, in which circulation is clustered, detract from the simplicity of the building by introducing inconsistent sculptural elements. After Cameron left this building, it was acquired by the Midway Companies and remodeled in 2004 by Kirksey and Morris Architects to become headquarters of the Harris County Appraisal District.

M-12
Northwest Corporate Park
[now Reynolds & Reynolds]
6700 Hollister Road
1982, Morris*Aubry Architects

Like most of the widely spaced buildings in Northwest Crossing, a 245-acre mixed-use development begun by Joe A. McDermott and Northwest Hollister Corporation in 1975, this is a speculative office building. Its bifurcated façade of granite aggregate precast concrete panels and dark green reflective glass give it a tense, but cool, image that holds its own in this open landscape.

M-13
Reed Rock Bit Drilling Technology Center
[now Telvent]
7000 Hollister Road
1985, White Budd Van Ness Partnerships

This sleekly skinned complex of low-rise buildings, buoyed by projecting cylindrical circulation stacks, is situated in Northwest Crossing. It projects the vision of suburban neatness, order, and control for which the term "planned" has become the coded expression in Houston real estate parlance. The gleaming hermeticism of the Technology Center encapsulates this ethos architecturally.

M-13 Reed Rock Bit Drilling Technology Center

M-14 Our Lady of Lourdes Catholic Church

M-15 Time Warner Building

M-16 Texas Steel Processing Building

M-17 Katherine Smith Elementary School

M-18 Oak Forest Branch, Houston Public Library

M-14
Our Lady of Lourdes Catholic Church
6550 Fairbanks-North Houston Road
2010, Jackson & Ryan Architects

This triple-towered brick church, built for a Vietnamese parish, comes as a complete surprise amid the array of commercial buildings lining the Northwest Freeway. Material thinness and squat proportions don't support the architecture's Romanesque aspirations, however. Across the south parking lot from the church is the outdoor shrine of Our Lady of Lourdes, which contains life-sized sculptural depictions of the Stations of the Cross.

M-15
Time Warner Building
[now Comcast]
8400 W. Tidwell Road
2003, Archimage

Archimage's Richard Buday emphasized the horizontal in detailing the granite and glass curtain wall of this 4-story corporate office building. Faceted bays project the horizontal lines volumetrically. Archimage also designed the corporation's supporting service buildings along W. Tidwell.

M-16
Texas Steel Processing Building
5480 Windfern Street
2009, Powers Brown Architecture

Located on a 10-acre tract in the Fairbanks Industrial Park, this combination office building and industrial workshop faces Carverdale, a subdivision of single-family houses, in a juxtaposition of land uses typical of unzoned Houston. PowersBrown mitigated the potential for incompatibility (and advertised their client's specialty) with their use of laser cut sheets of weathered steel as sunscreens on the building's 1-story west elevation, which overlooks a moat-like retention basin. The glazed second story is recessed behind the projecting first story.

M-17
Katherine Smith Elementary School
4802 Chrystell Lane
2010, Brave/Architecture

Fernando Brave added this low-key, planar, brick and stucco addition to an existing 1950s-era Houston Independent School District school complex immersed in temporary classroom buildings.

M-18
Oak Forest Branch, Houston Public Library
1349 West 43rd Avenue
1960, Golemon & Rolfe
2011, James Ray, Natalye Appel & Associates Architects, and ArchitectWorks

This is an extraordinarily refined and respectful expansion of Golemon & Rolfe's 1-story original, which faces West 43rd. The architects took advantage of the library's awkward site within a neighborhood shopping center to open the 2-story west addition to a park-like planted lawn on Oak Forest Drive.

M-19
Oak Forest Park Pool House
2100 Judiway Drive
2002, Bricker + Cannady

The pool house is a gateway structure, which the designer, Mark Wamble, emphasized with counterposed roofs above the central entrance; their profile reiterated above the enclosed portions of the building. The yellow-green brick exterior facing intensifies the light and color perceptions of the park's lawn on a hot summer day.

M-20
Revere Quality House Institute House of Expanding Rooms
1101 Wakefield Drive
1948, MacKie & Kamrath

Frank W. Sharp developed the Oak Forest subdivision in 1946-1948. At 1,100 acres, it was the largest subdivision in the U.S. until surpassed by Levittown on Long Island. Sharp teamed up with Revere Copper & Brass to build this 1-story, 1,060-SF demonstration house, one of a series of demonstration houses that Revere built throughout the U.S., all designed by modern architects. MacKie & Kamrath used accordion-fold screens to create the "expanding rooms" concept within the compact house, which is not quite as pristine as it was when new.

M-20 Revere Quality House Institue House of Expanding Rooms

M-19 Oak Forest Park Pool House

M-21 St. Rose of Lima Parish Hall and School

M-22 House

M-23 Sears Roebuck & Company Bus Shelter

M-24 Haley House

M-21
St. Rose of Lima Parish Hall and School
3604 Brinkman Road
1948, Donald Barthelme & Associates

This exquisite parish school and hall (the latter originally served as a temporary church) was the project that brought Barthelme to national attention. Built adjacent to the subdivision of Garden Oaks, it is a diminutively scaled complex of shaped pieces: the rectangular classroom wing blind on the west (parking lot) side, but open to the east (playground) side with its mono-pitch roof and clerestory, and the parish hall, which is splayed in plan and section, yet so subtly as to hardly call attention to its folded wall plane and sloped roof. The precision of the detailing of the crisp, thin-shell canopies to either end of the school wing, the brick wall cross, and the beaten copper entrance doors causes these buildings to resonate with an intensity that their small size would not lead one to anticipate. As Henry-Russell Hitchcock noted in 1959, "With the simplest of means and a wholly secular vocabulary of design, Barthelme has created a serene devotional atmosphere...." Alas, the parish did not turn to Barthelme when it built a permanent St. Rose of Lima Church (1960, George Fasullo). And the addition of the Parish Activity Center (1987, John Martin) to the west side of the parish hall, although well intended architecturally, parodies, rather than complements, the original. The reclining terra cotta figure of St. Rose of Lima (1950) was modeled by Joseph Bulone, a sculptor then connected with Cranbrook Academy.

M-22
House
806 Fisher Street
2011, Donna Kacmar

This 544-SF house was designed to be moved should the property be sold for lot value, a clever response to demolition frenzy that has reshaped Garden Oaks in the 21st century. It is a crisp shed-for-living that includes all the essentials at a sustainable scale.

M-23
Sears Roebuck & Company Bus Shelter
4000 N. Shepherd Drive
1951, George L. Dahl with Cowell & Neuhaus

The most memorable feature of the large Sears in the Garden Oaks shopping strip is the ebullient bus shelter on N. Shepherd Drive. At 3750 N. Shepherd, the ex-Garden Oaks Theater (1949, Pettigrew & Worley) is still identifiable.

M-24
Haley House
726 West 43rd Avenue
1940, W. E. Stokes, designer-builder

This Monterey type house, first occupied by the historian and political activist, J. Evetts Haley, lies in the most affluent section of Garden Oaks. Houston's first Federal Housing Administration-insured subdivision, Garden Oaks was developed by E. L. Crain beginning in 1937 on a 750- acre site planned by the landscape architects Hare & Hare. Crain hired young Houston architects, including his nephew, B. W. Crain, Jr., to design many of Garden Oaks's 1-story, ranch type houses, most of which were considerably more modest in size than the Haley House.

M-25
Our Savior Lutheran Church
[now Kay On-Going Education Center]
4425 N. Shepherd Drive
1960, MacKie & Kamrath

MacKie & Kamrath consistently produced modern buildings that stabilized the landscape of ceaseless suburban flow in postwar Houston. Significant architecture did not prevent the congregation from selling this property to the Houston Independent School District in 2000 and moving even farther out.

M-26
Art Guys World Headquarters
5757 Knox Street
2005, Cameron Armstrong

Jack Massing and Michael Galbreth are The Art Guys, conceptual and performance artists. Cameron Armstrong designed their "world headquarters" as a live/work metal-faced, steel-framed barn in the rustic setting of Acres Homes, a historically African-American, rural-subsistence subdivision developed in 1940. This was the first of a series of artist's studio-houses Armstrong produced in Acres Homes.

M-25 Our Savior Lutheran Church

M-26 Art Guys World Headquarters

M-27 Grotfeldt Studio-House

M-28 Houston Astros Major League Baseball Urban Youth Baseball Academy Training Center, Sylvester Turner Park

M-29 Houston Police Department North Police Station

M-30 Salvation Army Garden City Boys and Girls Club

M-27
Grotfeldt Studio-House
2007 Paul Quinn Street
2007, Cameron Armstrong

Designed for the painter Virgil Grotfeldt, this is an airy steel-framed studio lit by high set windows. The shed roof peaks above the residential portion of the live/work complex. Armstrong also designed live/work studio-houses for artists at 715 Marcella Street (2007) and 404 Thornton Road (2007).

M-28
Houston Astros Major League Baseball Urban Youth Baseball Academy Training Center, Sylvester Turner Park
2801 S. Victory Drive
2011, RdlR Architects

Rey de la Reza's architecture in this public park, built to train young people from Acres Homes and adjacent neighborhoods to excel in baseball, is small but spirited: a shed-roofed field house and concession building faced with ruddy red concrete block interspersed with panels of black and white striped glazed bock.

M-29
Houston Police Department North Police Station
9455 W. Montgomery Road
1997

Bold red and white horizontal stripes make this regional police and municipal court complex a visual standout in a part of Houston with few architecturally distinctive buildings.

M-30
Salvation Army Garden City Boys and Girls Club
9717 W. Montgomery Road
2011, Turner Duran

Turner Duran emphasized the volumetric presence of the center's gym with the curved profile of the steel-framed roof plate. Polychrome spandrel panels further activate this building.

M-31
Our Lady of La Vang Catholic Church
12311 Old Foltin Road
2001

Harking back to churches in Vietnam such as Phat Diem Catholic Cathedral, Our Lady of La Vang Church, dedicated to the patroness of Vietnam, is a fusion of Chinese, Vietnamese, and European architectural traditions with Houston spatial and construction practices. In a city where anything goes, nothing appears improbable. Sauviac & Dang of Baton Rouge were architects of the Shrine of Our Lady of La Vang, across Foltin from the church (2010). It is focused on a 40-foot tall statue of Our Lady of La Vang and includes the ultimate in Houston style piety, a drive-through Stations of the Cross.

M-31 Our Lady of La Vang Catholic Church

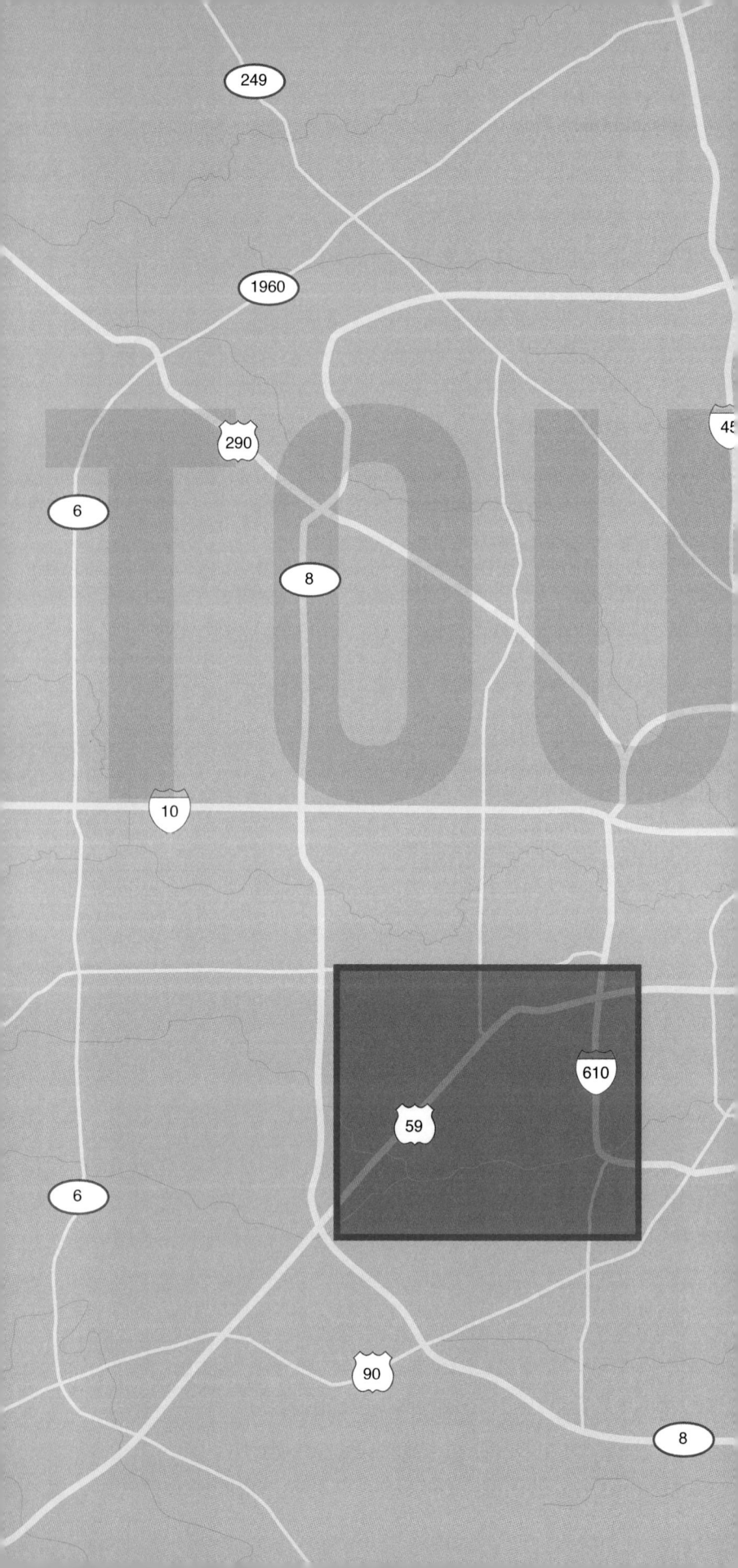

Bellaire / Meyerland / Westbury / Sharpstown

Bellaire / Meyerland / Westbury / Sharpstown

Tour N

Southwest Houston contains a succession of examples of the American suburb as it has evolved during the 20th century. Bellaire, an independent city since 1918, was started as a planned community, an early 20th-century version of Houston Heights, connected to the center of Houston by a long extension of the Main Street streetcar line. Like the Heights, this neighborhood of moderate-income residences was laid out with a central boulevard divided by a wide median as its chief civic feature. Also tied to Main Street and Bellaire Boulevard were the subdivisions developed along Brays and Willow Waterhole bayous in a patchwork array in the 1950s and '60s. Located on the treeless coastal plain, these were the ultimate middle-class white neighborhoods of southwest Houston. The most extensive of Houston's bayou parkways, along Brays Bayou, is an impressive civic achievement for the 1950s, a decade in which public-spirited planning in Houston was simply disregarded. Its existence is a tribute to Ralph Ellifrit, then director of Houston's Department of City Planning, who compelled developers to donate property along the bayou for this parkway as a condition for approval of their plats.

Sharpstown, north of the bayou parkway, is a textbook example of community planning of the 1950s. It is joined to the center of Houston, nine miles distant, by the Southwest Freeway. Sharpstown's developer, Frank W. Sharp, coordinated the donation of a long stretch of right-of-way to ensure that the freeway was built through the middle of Sharpstown. Wide arterial thoroughfares divide neighborhoods, which are focused on schools, parks, and churches. There is a commercial center around the shopping mall, ringed with secondary retail, offices and apartments, a university campus, a large hospital, a medical professional center, office parks, an industrial sector, and a large public golf course. Sharpstown has all the components of a small city, but none of the characteristics—not even the compensatory urban gesture of a grand boulevard like Bellaire's. During the 1960s Houston's middle-class Jewish community relocated upstream along the Brays Bayou Parkway to constitute what was then the most visible ethnic presence within southwest Houston. It is here that Houston's increasing racial and ethnic diversity is becoming evident as middle-class Hispanic and Asian families settle in these neighborhoods. The transformation of entire shopping strips along arterial streets into Chinese and Indian business enclaves exemplifies the quiet, but radical, change in images of middle-class normality that is occurring. The corner of Bellaire and Hillcroft, in the odd, mixed residential and light industrial corridor between Bellaire and Sharpstown, is where an early **Fiesta Mart** store is located. This Houston grocery chain has continued to be developed by responding to emerging demographic trends in southwest Houston and elsewhere. Fiesta stocks an unusually wide array of international products for the increasing numbers of Houstonians for whom these are not exotic specialties, but the necessities of everyday life.

1. **KRIV Channel 26 Fox TV Studio,** 4621 Southwest Freeway
2. **Houston Post Building,** 4747 Southwest Freeway
3. **House,** 4535 Sunburst Street
4. **Texaco Office Building,** 4800 Fournace Place
5. **Smith Photographers Studio,** 5226 Elm Street
6. **Round Valley Texas Office Building and Garage,** 5202 Spruce Street
7. **Harris County Youth Services Center,** 6300 Chimney Rock Road
8. **Amegy Bank Bellaire Building,** 5301 Bissonnet Avenue
9. **House,** 4902 Chestnut Street
10. **Prudential Insurance Company Building,** 6500 West Loop South
11. **Faith American Lutheran Church,** 4600 Bellaire Boulevard
12. **Boulevard Green,** Bellaire Boulevard and Boulevard Green
13. **Albin House,** 645 Mulberry Lane
14. **Lundy House,** 701 Mulberry Lane
15. **House,** 4520 Oleander Street
16. **House,** 7204 Avenue B
17. **House,** 4826 Bellaire Boulevard
18. **House,** 4901 Cedar Street
19. **House,** 4807 Bellview Street
20. **St. Thomas Episcopal Church and School,** 4900 Jackwood Street
21. **House,** 4815 Braesvalley Drive
22. **1955 Parade of Homes House,** 5146 Jackwood Street
23. **Red Elementary School Outdoor Science Classroom,** 4520 Tonawanda Drive
24. **Jenkins House,** 10911 Willowisp Drive
25. **Godine-Hoover House,** 10920 Willowisp Drive
26. **Willowbend Medical and Dental Clinic,** 4910 Willowbend Boulevard
27. **Shell Pipe Line Company Buildings,** 5521 Gasmer Drive
28. **Westbury United Methodist Church,** 5200 Willowbend Boulevard
29. **Stephens Company House of Ideas,** 5103 South Braeswood Boulevard
30. **Fredricks House,** 5111 Contour Place
31. **Zinn House,** 5319 Braesheather Drive
32. **Brooks House,** 5231 Braesvalley Drive
33. **Congregation Beth Israel Temple,** 5600 North Braeswood Boulevard
34. **House,** 8220 Hillcroft Avenue
35. **Kirby Building Systems Building,** 7101 Renwick Drive
36. **Houston Fine Art Press Building,** 7336 Rampart Street
37. **Prototype 180,** 6513 Sharpview Drive
38. **Academic and Student Center Building, Houston Baptist University,** 7502 Fondren Road
39. **Spa Building,** 7255 Clarewood Drive
40. **House,** 8222 Leader Street
41. **Alliance Tower,** 8701 S. Gessner Drive
42. **Centre One Building,** 9800 Centre Parkway
43. **Church of the Epiphany,** 9506 South Gessner Road
44. **Kagan-Rudy Chapel, Emanu El Memorial Park,** 8341 Bissonnet Avenue
45. **Hildebrandt House,** 9314 Lugary Drive
46. **The Crescent,** 7826 Westwind Court
47. **KPRC Channel Two Studio,** 8181 Southwest Freeway
48. **Texas Bank & Trust Tower,** 6161 Savoy Drive

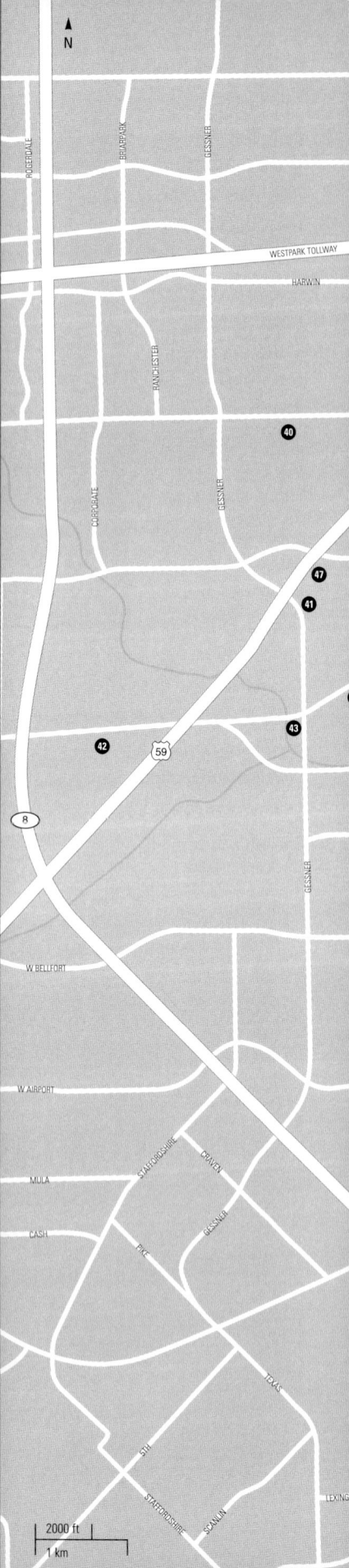

Bellaire / Meyerland / Westbury / Sharpstown

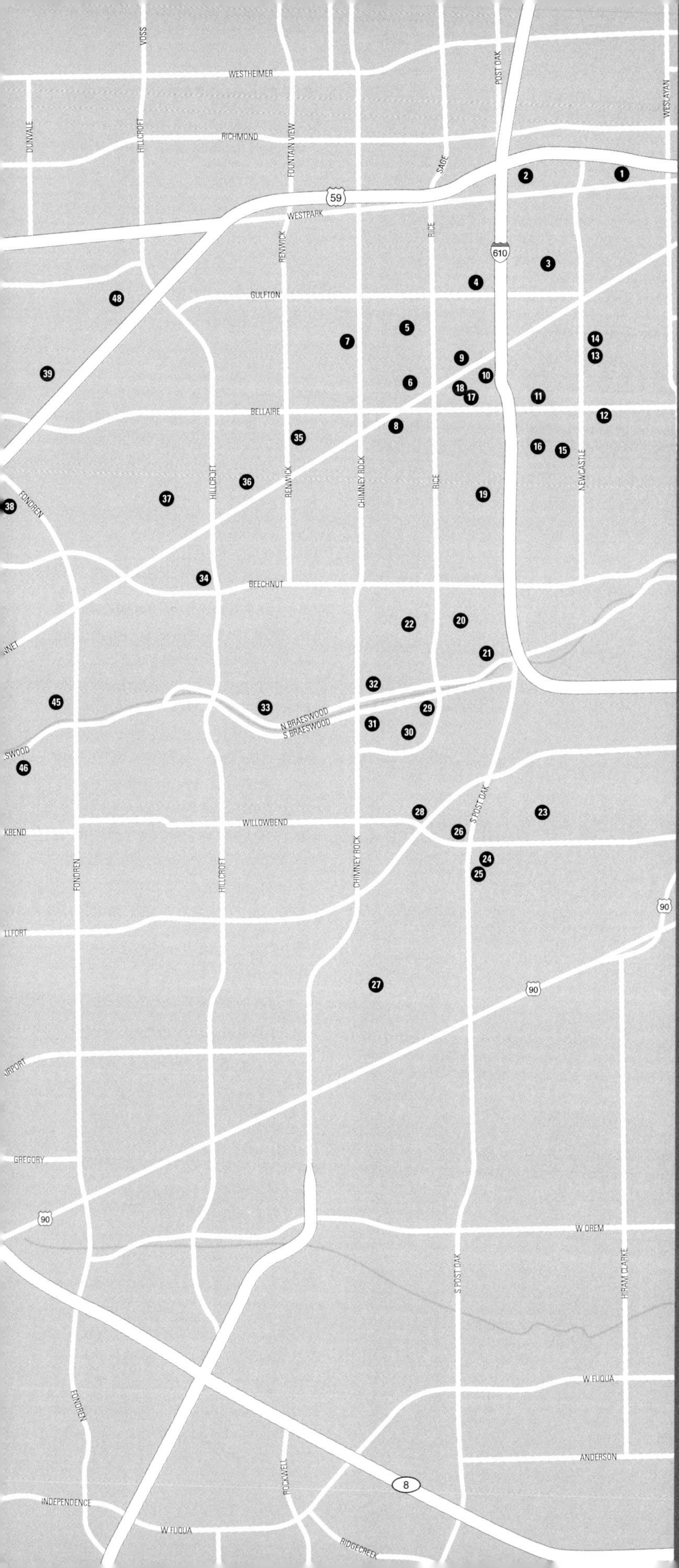

Tour N

553

N-1 KRIV Channel 26 Fox TV Studio

N-2 Houston Post Building

N-3 House

N-4 Texaco Office Building

N-5 Smith Photographers Studio

N-7 Harris County Youth Services Building

N-1
KRIV Channel 26 Fox TV Studio
4621 Southwest Freeway
1998, Dan Taylor & Associates

Fox TV's look is retro-modern, a recycling of 1950s images.

N-2
Houston Post Building
[now Houston Chronicle Building]
4747 Southwest Freeway
1970, Wilson, Morris,
Crain & Anderson

The former office building and production plant of the *Houston Post* appears to be a modern castle. However, as is frequently the case with American buildings designed in the New Brutalist mode, it is a rectangular box around which concrete silos have been picturesquely arrayed. The windowless chamfered turrets contain stairs, toilets, air-conditioning equipment, and photocopying machines. The designer, Ralph A. Anderson, Jr., here devised one of the first examples of "freeway" architecture in Houston: a building that projects a formal image that is strong, yet simple enough to be apprehended from a speeding car.

N-3
House
4535 Sunburst Street
1996, Robert Morris

In staid Bellaire this tin house stands out as a radical exception. Note the sculptural interventions by artist Gertrude Barnstone.

N-4
Texaco Office Building
[now Chevron Oronite]
4800 Fournace Place
1977, S. I. Morris Associates

This 10-story office building, designed by Winton F. Scott, is V-shaped in plan to maximize its north-south exposure. For energy conservation purposes, its horizontal window bands also have a V-profile, which permits the admission of daylight while screening out direct solar penetration. As a result of its symmetrical composition and repetitive window pattern, the building presents a hieratic aspect that is rather overwhelming, especially when seen from Fournace, where the central service core abuts the street.

N-5
Smith Photographers Studio
5226 Elm Street
2000, Natalye Appel

This expansive, steel-framed, steel-panel-faced studio lies on the Houston side of the Bellaire city limit line. The impressive line of oak trees bisecting the parking lot forecasts a series of internal garden courtyards.

N-6
Round Valley Texas Office Building and Garage
5202 Spruce Street
2000, ArchitectWorks and PDR

Donna Kacmar designed this precisely detailed shed-roofed building to function flexibly as a warehouse or office loft. Structural clay tile walls are exposed to give the building material substance and color.

N-7
Harris County Youth Services Building
6300 Chimney Rock Road
2005, PageSoutherlandPage

Wall planes surfaced with corrugated steel siding, a mixed blend of dark brick, green glazed tile blocks, and windows that alternate between vertical and horizontal alignment downplay the institutionality of this mixed-use office, training, and residential complex. The center is set in a county park in a mixed-use corridor filled with heterogeneous operations that separates Bellaire on the east from Sharpstown to the west, introducing, into what should be a consistently middle-class landscape, the land-use equivalent of static.

N-8
Amegy Bank Bellaire Building
5301 Bissonnet Avenue
2006, Kirksey

Replacing a 1960s triangular glass pavilion shaded by a *brise-soleil* superstructure designed by the landscape architect, C. C. "Pat" Fleming, this 2-story bank building reproduces the earlier building's sun-shading theme, materialized in a glass curtain wall featuring different degrees of transparency and reflectivity—and even a *brise-soleil.*

N-6 Round Valley Texas Office Building

N-8 Amegy Bank Bellaire Building

N-9 House

N-10 Prudential Insurance Company Building

N-11 Faith American Lutheran Church

N-12 Boulevard Green

N-13 Albin House

N-14 Lundy House

N-9
House
4902 Chestnut Street
2002, Cameron Armstrong

Armstrong designed this 2-story, metal-faced house as a grounded tree house that makes the most of the extraordinary Live Oak trees that frame its street front.

N-10
Prudential Insurance Company Building
[now AT&T Houston]
6500 West Loop South
1977, S. I. Morris Associates

Eugene Aubry shaped Prudential's ex-regional corporate headquarters with great flair. Its grid of buff-colored, precast concrete fins and lintels is broken to induce shifts in scale that identify the front entrance and emphasize the ends of the 3-block, 665-foot long building. The fins facing the freeway are angled in plan to ward off the east sun. Red porcelain racing stripe headers above each window give the building a special lilt; these running bands of color enliven the building and put it in tune with the flow of traffic on the West Loop. The loop passes here through the suburban city of Bellaire, whose "skyline" is dominated by the work of the Morris office. Across the freeway from Prudential are 6565 and 6575 West Loop South (1978 and 1980), both for McCord Development Company. Farther south are the Sperry Univac Building at 6700 West Loop South (1974), Scientific Design Building at 6750 West Loop South (1977), San Jacinto Savings Building at 6800 West Loop South (1981), and, on Bellaire Boulevard, the 4710 Bellaire Building (1975) and the Crown Central Petroleum Building at 4747 Bellaire (1981), all built by John Hansen.

N-11
Faith American Lutheran Church
4600 Bellaire Boulevard
1959, 1963, Travis Broesche & Associates

During the late 1950s and early 1960s, Broesche's firm produced a number of buildings inspired by the architecture of Frank Lloyd Wright. This church is the finest work from that period. Bellaire Boulevard is the central thoroughfare in the town plan laid out in 1908 by the Kansas City landscape architect Sid J. Hare. Hare also produced a tree-planting plan to conceal the fact that Bellaire sat in the midst of an open prairie, four miles southwest of Houston. The Live Oak trees within the generous medians have done their work. These were planted by the nurseryman Edward Teas, whom the developer of Bellaire, W. W. Baldwin, persuaded to settle in the new community. Teas Nursery Company, established in 1910, operated from its original location at 4400 Bellaire Boulevard until it closed in 2010.

N-12
Boulevard Green
Bellaire Boulevard and Boulevard Green
1981, Alan Hirschfield

Built on a 2-acre lot in Bellaire formerly occupied by a single house, this group of 16 houses refracts, rather than mirrors, conventional signs of domesticity. Hirschfield condensed images from the local scene, then abstracted and reconstituted them. The free-standing white stucco screens are intended to introduce what Hirschfield describes as a "community scale" to the street.

Across Bellaire Boulevard at 4316 Bellaire is a walled modern house designed by Mark D. Musemeche (2011).

N-13
Albin House
645 Mulberry Lane
1999, Albin Vasconcelos Elizalde

Architect Enrique Albin, from Mexico City, was able to take advantage of a half-acre lot in the Westmoreland Farms section of Bellaire to design a brick-faced house that spatially invokes modern Mexican houses.

N-14
Lundy House
701 Mulberry Lane
1988, Victor A. Lundy

Lundy designed this rigorous modern house and studio for himself and his wife, the painter Anstis Manton Lundy. Victor Lundy first gained fame as a member of the Sarasota school of brilliant young Florida architects in the 1950s. From 1960-1976 he practiced in New York, then moved to Houston to teach at the University of Houston and, eventually, to work with the Dallas architects Harwood K. Smith & Partners.

N-15
House
4520 Oleander Street
1952, William N. Floyd
Harwood Taylor and William Jenkins, associate architects

Designed for a European-born naturalist and environmentalist, this flat-roofed house introduced modern architecture to Bellaire. It is preserved in near-original condition.

N-15 House

N-16 House

N-17 House

N-18 House

N-19 House

N-20 St. Thomas Episcopal Church

N-16
House
7204 Avenue B
2011, John Grable

San Antonio architect Grable designed this relaxed, hipped-roofed house as a sequence of rising and receding volumes. Its rustic feel, stone walls, and raised seam metal roofs are San Antonioan attributes.

N-17
House
4826 Bellaire Boulevard
2007, Allen Bianchi

This dramatically configured, white stucco-walled house turns the corner with a sharp diagonal incision, to which adjoining walls and parapets sculpturally adjust. By respecting the scale of neighboring houses, Bianchi ensured that this house "fits in" with more assurance and subtlety than the flashy "traditional" housing with which speculative builders are reshaping Bellaire.

N-18
House
4901 Cedar Street
2002, Duke Fleshman

The overhanging roof eaves of this steel-framed, steel-surfaced house shade the east-side facing North 2nd Street, toward which interior spaces are oriented.

N-19
House
4807 Bellview Street
2011, William T. Cannady and Murphy Mears

This 2-story house, surfaced with a rainscreen, updates a traditional Texas house type with a central, open-air, dogtrot passage.

N-20
St. Thomas Episcopal Church
4900 Jackwood Street
1972, Harvin C. Moore

In the long continuum of Lombard Romanesque style churches in Houston, St. Thomas seemed to represent the last of the line, until Romanesque resurfaced in the 2000s. The church's traditional look had been somewhat at variance with the rest of the parish group, designed in a 1950s contemporary style, which Murphy Mears rectified with its design of the parish school in the 5000 block of Endicott Lane and a new entrance plaza facing Jackwood completed in 2006.

N-21
House
4815 Braesvalley Drive
1957, Lars Bang

Although the novelist Larry McMurtry once characterized Meyerland as the dullest subdivision in Houston, time and the growth of neighborhood trees have made this judgment less definitive (plus: there's no end of competition). What rescues Meyerland from its indistinguishable, 1950s, brick veneer ranch houses is the occasional architect-designed modern house, such as this low-slung Contemporary by Lars Bang. Juxtaposing the open carport with a brick solar screen that shields the entrance courtyard and the shed-roofed east wing spatially animates the street front of the house.

N-22
1955 Parade of Homes House
5146 Jackwood Street
1955, Burdette Keeland

In 1955 these blocks of Meyerland were built out with 30 houses constructed for the Houston Home Builders Association's Parade of Homes. W. K. King broke ranks with the Contemporary style ranch houses and allowed Keeland to produce this flat-roofed, steel-framed, Miesian courtyard house, furnished by the Knoll Planning Unit. It was so much more expensive to build than the other houses that King withheld the sales price. Yet despite flouting suburban conformity, the house is intact and well maintained. It is U-shaped in plan, organized around a small courtyard entered through the side-facing front door. Also surviving from the Parade of Homes are 5127 Jackwood (1955, Harwood Taylor) and the split-level 8710 Pritchard (1955, William R. Jenkins and William N. Floyd).

N-22 1955 Parade of Homes House

N-21 House

N-23 Outdoor Science Classroom, Red Elementary School

N-24 Jenkins House

N-25 Godine-Hoover House

N-26 Willowbend Medical and Dental Clinic

N-27 Shell Pipe Line Company Buildings

N-23
Outdoor Science Classroom, Red Elementary School
4520 Tonawanda Drive
1997, Graduate Design/Build Studio, University of Houston

UH architecture students, directed by Patrick Peters and George Sacaris, designed and constructed this concrete and steel canopy structure sheltering an outdoor classroom.

N-24
Jenkins House
10911 Willowisp Drive
1955, William R. Jenkins and William N. Floyd

Jenkins was responsible for most of the houses in this little enclave of modernity, a cul-de-sac at the end of Willowisp, around which Willow Waterhole Bayou curves. This was his own house, a flat-roofed, steel-framed courtyard house in-filled with concrete block and sliding glass doors. Jenkins also designed 10910 (1955) and 10914 (1957).

N-25
Godine-Hoover House
10920 Willowisp Drive
1956, William R. Jenkins and William N. Floyd

This house emphasizes the thinness and linearity that advanced technology (exposed wood beams and slender steel columns) made possible. The house was beautifully restored in 2007 by Vanessa and Jason Smith. So impassioned did Jason Smith, a musician, become about Jenkins's architecture that he wrote the book *High Style on the Suburbs: The Early Modern Houses of William R. Jenkins, 1951-58*, published by Houston Mod in 2009.

N-26
Willowbend Medical and Dental Clinic
4910 Willowbend Boulevard
1961, Wilson, Morris, Crain & Anderson

This pair of professional buildings, organized around internal courtyards and joined by a multi-lane drive-through, projects the "good design" ethos with which enlightened architects attempted to reform the expanding periphery of the city in the 1950s. The Willowbend Clinic, like the nearby Jenkins houses, is exceptional rather than typical in its milieu. But it demonstrates that, for a time at least, architecture was pursued as a serious response to middle class life in the suburbs.

N-27
Shell Pipe Line Company Buildings
[now Shell Technologies EP]
5521 Gasmer Drive
1961, Cowell & Neuhaus with David Haid, associate architect

The Chicago architect David Haid worked briefly with Hugo V. Neuhaus, Jr. just after he left the office of Ludwig Mies van der Rohe. This pair of small, steel-framed buildings is precisely organized and carefully detailed, in the best Miesian tradition, although their exposed steel framing has been painted brown. What is also remarkable about these buildings is their edge-of-town setting, a residual bit of rural open space that has never been filled in.

N-28
Westbury United Methodist Church
5200 Willowbend Boulevard
1957, Langwith, Wilson & King

In the 1950s church complexes featured as anchors of such new "planned" Houston subdivisions as Westbury. This church paid homage to MacKie & Kamrath's Church of St. John the Divine with its steeply pitched gabled roof, glazed south gable, and limestone facing. Despite socio-economic transitions, the church still figures as a neighborhood landmark. Indicative of the state-of-the-art planning standards of 1950s subdivisions, even in unzoned Houston, was the clustering of non-residential amenities on superblock sites facing major thoroughfares. Westbury Methodist shares its block with St. John's Presbyterian Church at 5020 West Bellfort (1959, Thompson McCleary and Hamilton Brown).

N-28 Westbury United Methodist Church

N-29 Stephens Company House of Ideas

N-30 Fredricks House

N-31 Zinn House

N-32 Brooks House

N-33 Congregation Beth Israel Temple

N-34 House

N-29
Stephens Company House of Ideas
5103 S. Braeswood Boulevard
1964, Walter S. Poage III

Meyerland was unusual among the postwar subdivisions along Brays Bayou in that it was developed on both sides of the bayou. Houses designed by architects were built in greater number in the southern sectors of the neighborhood in the 1960s, one example being this stone-faced demonstration house, notable for its polygonal planning and limestone-faced exterior walls.

N-30
Fredricks House
5111 Contour Place
1962

This modern pavilion type house was designed with Japanese overtones.

N-31
Zinn House
5319 Braesheather Drive
1970, Ressler & Applebaum

The chalky rose color and soft texture of pink St. Joe brick animate this planar, flat-roofed courtyard house.

N-32
Brooks House
5231 Braesvalley Drive
1965, Brooks & Brooks

Architect David Brooks' own house features the carport as a surrogate front porch. Closed on its street side, the house overlooks a south-facing back yard through walls of glass.

N-33
Congregation Beth Israel Temple
5600 North Braeswood Boulevard
1967, Irving R. Klein & Associates

New Formalism was the term coined to describe such buildings as Temple Beth Israel, home of the oldest Jewish congregation in Texas. The peripheral colonnade, which rises to a ceiling of plaster vaults and capped with a flat-lidded roof, has a vaguely classical look, although its immediate antecedents were contemporary, in particular the work of the Michigan architect Minoru Yamasaki. The expressive wing of the Modern movement is given its due with the drum-like bay that protrudes from one side of the building. New Formalism tried to annex the dignity of classical architecture; it aspired to make the new pretty and refined. At Beth Israel this works to some extent because of the building's size and its siting on a large flat lawn around which the boulevard curves. Nonetheless, the temple is at best a period piece. Across Brays Bayou and slightly downstream is the Jewish Community Center at 5601 South Braeswood Boulevard (1969), also by the Klein office.

N-34
House
8220 Hillcroft Avenue
2010, MC² Architects

Chung and Choung Nguyen designed this compact, but immensely clever, house on a cul-de-sac stubbed off from busy Hillcroft. A brick wall plane (brick facing was required by subdivision deed restrictions) conceals an L-shaped plan sheltered beneath a warped roof plane. Interior spaces are focused on a large, spatially layered garden, designed by Asakura Robinson, landscape architects.

N-35
Kirby Building Systems Building
7101 Renwick Street
1975, S. I. Morris Associates

Attached to what was the production plant of a pre-engineered metal buildings manufacturer, this 2-story front office building, designed by Magruder Wingfield, Jr., is a disingenuously simple design of light steel framing infilled with solar glass windowpanes. The glass is deeply recessed along the Renwick frontage, providing space for ample plantings that perceptually dissolve easy distinctions between what is outside and what is not.

N-35 Kirby Building Systems Building

N-36 Houston Fine Art Press Building

N-37 Prototype 180

N-38 Academic and Student Center Building, Houston Baptist University

N-39 Spa Building

N-40 House

N-41 Alliance Tower

N-36
Houston Fine Art Press Building
7336 Rampart Street
1987, Carlos Jiménez

Built to house the studio of an art printing establishment, this building occupies a long and very narrow lot in a mixed neighborhood of warehouses, light industry, and garden apartments between Sharpstown and Bellaire. Jiménez took advantage of the site constraints, extruding a gable-roofed bay, containing exhibition and office spaces, into a rear production area that spans the width of the lot. By cleverly manipulating the section, Jiménez opened a north-facing monitor in the roof to light the production area. The elementary geometries, intense pink stucco finish, and austere high-walled motor court of the building interact with the shaded strip of lawn alongside the front bay and the blue sky to produce an arresting and quite poignant image: "a little outpost of the faith beside its barbaric neighbors," as Wilhelm Hahn has written.

N-37
Prototype 180
6513 Sharpview Drive
1961; 2011, Mary Ellen Carroll, artist

New York-based conceptual artist Mary Ellen Carroll describes her project at 6513 Sharpview as a land art piece. In 2011 she had this 1,300-SF, brick veneer house, which she bought in 2007, lifted, rotated 180 degrees, then lowered onto a new concrete slab whose location mirrors the location of the original slab with respect to the rear property line. The process of securing permissions, permits, financing, neighbors' support, and publicity all play into an ethnographic narrative on public/private relationships that is articulated and "performed" in the transformation of a representative Sharpstown suburban house into a work of art.

N-38
Academic and Student Center Building, Houston Baptist University
7502 Fondren Road
1963, Hermon Lloyd & W. B. Morgan and Milton McGinty

Houston Baptist University occupies a 200-acre campus in Sharpstown, Houston's ultimate 1950s suburban real estate development. Frank W. Sharp, the developer, sold this site to the newly chartered college in 1958. The Academic and Student Center Building, on axis with the entrance, is a local reaction (amusing for doctrinal as well as architectural reasons) to Philip Johnson's campus for the University of St. Thomas. A low, 2-story building, configured around a large central courtyard, HBU's Academic and Student Center is faced with brick and glass, inset in an exposed structural frame, here of concrete rather than steel. As at St. Thomas, the scale is almost domestic, so that the building feels more like a high school than a university. What HBU lacks is the precision of Johnson's Miesian details, the clarity of his proportions, and the ambition to be noble rather than merely nice. The approach drive from Fondren Road is a suburban landscape classic, a divided boulevard spatially modulated by tall, slender, aluminum light standards. The campus entrance is by Langwith Wilson King Associates (1987). Lloyd, Morgan & Jones designed the Edward Durell Stone-like Atwood School of Theology (1964) to the left of the Academic Building. Behind the Academic and Student Center Building is a plaza containing a screen of freestanding columns salvaged from the demolished Galveston County Courthouse in Galveston (1899, Messer, Sanguinet & Messer). Buildings constructed in the 1990s and 2000s try, unsuccessfully, to sound a more "traditional" note. Southwest of the campus lies Houston's Baptist hospital, Memorial Hospital (now Memorial-Hermann Southwest, 1976, S. I. Morris Associates).

N-39
Spa Building
[now Bally Total Fitness]
7255 Clarewood Street
1970

Peter Papademetriou has likened this 4-story building, its curtain wall recessed deeply behind a reticulated grid of square bays, to the Casa del Fascio by Giuseppe Terragni, one of the landmarks of Italian modern rationalism of the 1930s. The Italian original faced the piazza of Como; the Houston homage, its reinforced concrete structural frame now painted dark blue, lies in the Sharpstown Industrial Park near the heart of "downtown" Sharpstown, a loose cluster of multi-story apartment buildings and low-rise office buildings ringing Sharpstown Center (1961, Sidney H. Morris & Associates, reconstructed 1980, Nikita Zukov; and rebranded PlazAméricas in 2010), the first air-conditioned shopping mall in Houston. Conforming to a pattern that became dominant in postwar Houston, Sharpstown is singularly bereft of distinctive architecture. Therefore this, no doubt unintentional tribute to a classic of the Modern movement must suffice as a local monument.

N-40
House
8222 Leader Street
1962, Robert Dyrel Kirk, Jr.

In contrast to the production housing that dominates Sharpstown, this 1-story, modern courtyard house, punctuated by a series of shallow roof vaults, creates a welcome point of difference and distinction.

N-41
Alliance Tower
8701 S. Gessner Drive
1985, Klein Partnership

By pinching the top ends of this dark, red, granite-clad, 13-story office building, designer Robert Sobel gave it a figural presence along S. Gessner as it curves past, as well as from the overpass of the Southwest Freeway.

N-42 Centre One Building

N-43 Church of the Epiphany

N-44 Emanu El Memorial Park, Kagain-Rudy Chapel

N-45 Hildebrandt House

N-46 The Crescent

N-42
Centre One Building
9800 Centre Parkway
1983, Skidmore, Owings & Merrill

The Farb Companies developed the 72-acre Centre, planned by Craig Hartman in the Houston office of Skidmore, Owings & Merrill. Hartman designed the one office building constructed there, the 11-story Centre One. Faced with white precast concrete panels, the building is subdivided vertically into three planes by shallow vertical incisions. Scored planes and delicately modulated surfaces distinguish the Retail Centre, a 2-block-long strip shopping center at Centre Parkway and Bissonnet, also designed by Hartman. Until leasing agents, eager to boost rentals, tarted up its original pristine exteriors, the Retail Centre, with a parking lot full of Washingtonia palm trees (no longer in evidence), was an oasis of architectural sanity along the raucous Bissonnet corridor.

N-43
Church of the Epiphany
9506 South Gessner Road
1973, Clovis Heimsath Associates

Heimsath's interest in geometrical manipulation led to the complex shapes generated by rotating the ridge beam of this church so that it spans the square-planned nave on the diagonal. The roof was treated as a warped plane, folded around the diagonally canted wheel window that is oriented northeast, on the axis of Bissonnet. The result is visually striking. But Epiphany's brick, stone, and shingled surfaces, which totally conceal its acrobatic framing, are architectural non sequiturs.

N-44
Emanu El Memorial Park, Kagan-Rudy Chapel
8341 Bissonnet Avenue
1983, Clovis Heimsath Associates

This hexagonal, domically roofed, open-air pavilion, built of reinforced concrete, is one of Heimsath's best buildings. It embodies a feeling of silence, repose, and gentle loss that is quite moving, yet subtle. Heimsath incorporated Jewish religious symbols and architectural details in the design; Maryann Heimsath was responsible for the stained glass panels in the dome.

N-45
Hildebrandt House
9314 Lugary Drive
1960, Golemon & Rolfe

The architect Mel Hildebrandt designed this 1-story modern house for his family in the subdivision of Bonham Acres.

N-46
The Crescent
7826 Westwind Court
1961, John Robbins Building Company

The crescent-shaped Crescent house encircles an interior courtyard, into which all its windows face.

N-47
KPRC Channel Two Studio
8181 Southwest Freeway
1972, Wilson, Morris, Crain & Anderson

Eugene Aubry adroitly organized this television studio in three distinct elements: a studio block to the left, a long, faceted office wing to the right, and the triangular transmitting tower out front. The double-height, top-lit, glazed spine, a recurring feature in Aubry's work in the 1970s, is KPRC's unifying element.

N-48
Texas Bank & Trust Tower
[now Wells Fargo]
6161 Savoy
1974, Lloyd Jones Associates

Regency Square, developed by Marvin E. Leggett & Associates, is one of a series of office parks along Harwin Drive, on Sharpstown's northern frontier. The formless layout of most of these developments and the bland architecture bespeak the low expectations that attended commercial development in Houston's suburbs through the 1960s. Regency Square represents the beginnings of the great reversal in design apathy. This 12-story precast concrete-faced block and its twin, the Colonial Savings Tower at 6200 (1978), are unassertive but sufficiently considered in their design, detailing, and the spatial relationship they establish between them to attract notice. The faceted and reflective Cowperwood Regency Building at 6001 (1978) and the green Texaco Oil Company Computer Services Building at 6464 (1980), both developed and designed by the New York architects Morse & Harvey, play off the solemnity of the Lloyd Jones buildings.

N-47 KPRC Channel Two Studio

N-48 Texas Bank & Trust Tower

Fifth Ward / Far North Side

Fifth Ward / Far North Side

Tour O

The Fifth Ward and the Far North Side, northeast and north of downtown Houston, are historically lower-income, minority neighborhoods. Crisscrossed by railroad lines and vaulted over by freeways, they exist largely outside the awareness of Houston's middle class. In the 20th century Fifth Ward expanded eastward along the axis of Lyons Avenue. In the 1940s and '50s it was one of the most vibrant African-American sectors of Houston. Today it displays the efforts of local institutions, such as the Fifth Ward Community Redevelopment Corporation, to reverse decades of official neglect and disinvestment. The challenge for grass roots non-profit organizations is to stimulate new investment in the community that benefits residents rather than dispossessing them in order to redevelop property for mythical higher and better uses. Because of the hands-off policy of Houston's city government, community development corporations are left to their own devices to ignite and manage systemic change. Efforts by other Houston non-profits to reinforce such programs are visible in architect-designed, low-cost housing. The checkered history of such projects suggests the limitations of the self-help model. Houston freeways are magnets for architectural production; on the Far North Side they attract the good, the bad, and the outrageous.

Fifth Ward / Far North Side

1. **Lyons Village,** 3300 Lyons Avenue
2. **Phillis Wheatley High School,** 1700 Gregg Street
3. **Fifth Ward Business and Financial Center,** 4300 Lyons Avenue
4. **First Shiloh Baptist Church,** 4420 Lyons Avenue
5. **CORE: The 99K House,** 4015 Jewel Street
6. **Garden House,** 5013 Pickfair Street
7. **Cummins Southern Plains Parts and Services Building,** 7045 North Loop 610 East
8. **House,** 815 Woodard Street
9. **Theodore Roosevelt Elementary School,** 6700 Fulton Street
10. **Houston Community College Northline Campus,** 8001 Fulton Street
11. **Templo Regional de la Luz del Mundo,** 8312 Eastex Freeway
12. **9111 Eastex Freeway Building,** 9111 Eastex Freeway

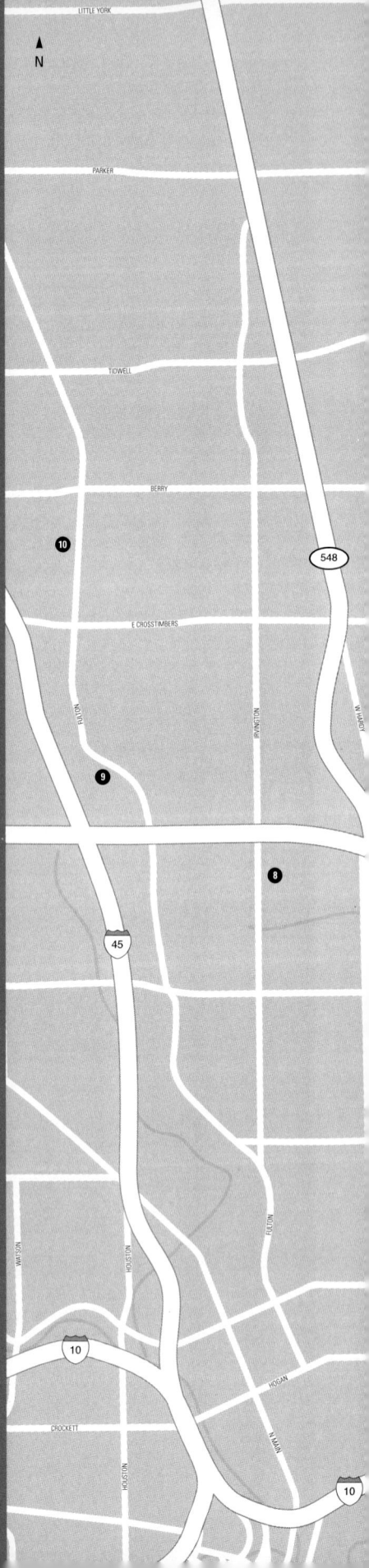

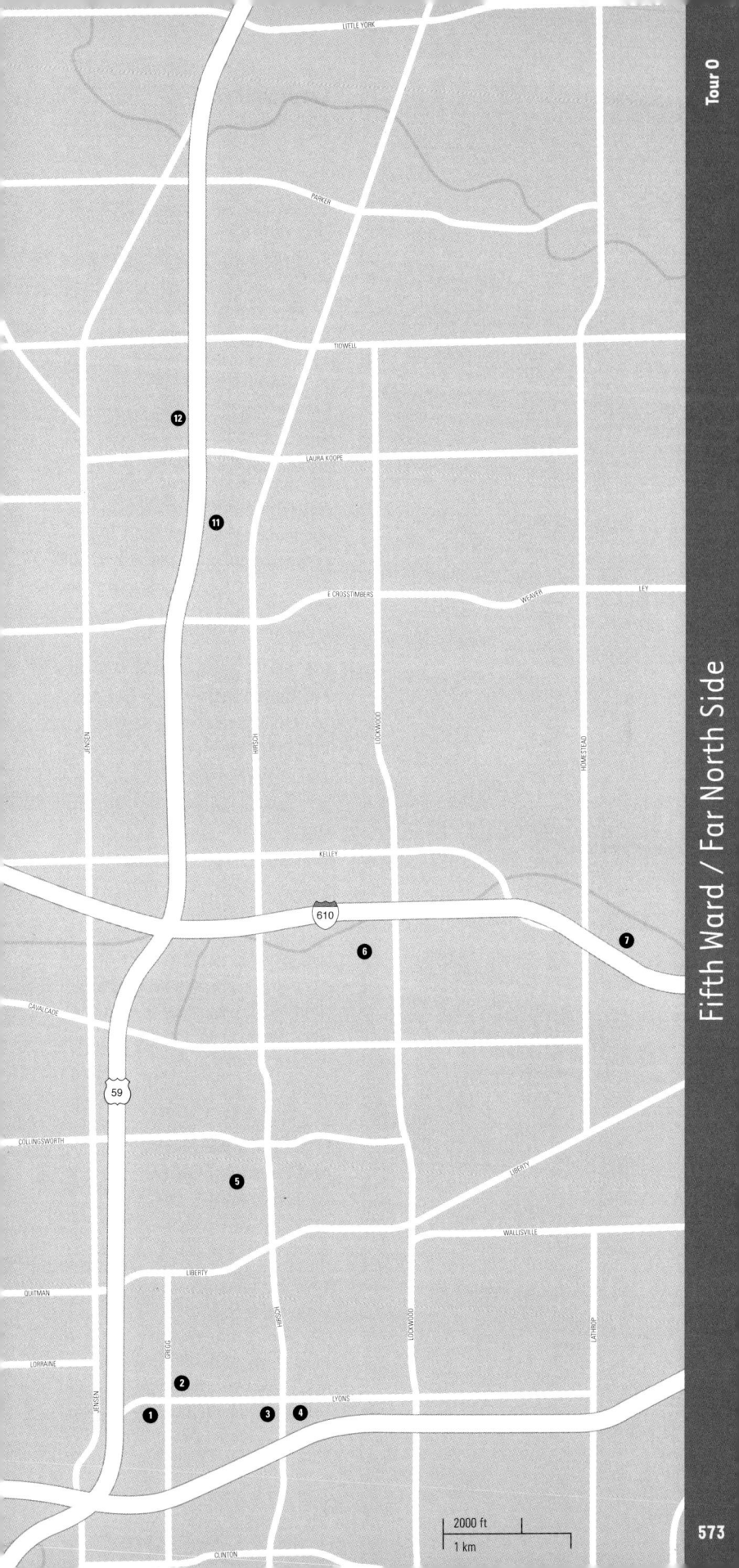

0-1 Lyons Village

0-2 Phillis Wheatley High School

0-3 Fifth Ward Business and Financial Center

0-4 First Shiloh Baptist Church

0-5 CORE: The 99K House

O-1
Lyons Village
3300 Lyons Avenue
2000

Lyons Village is a 3-story mixed-use office, retail, and residential complex built by the Fifth Ward Community Redevelopment Corporation, which, during the 1990s, was the most active community development corporation in Houston. Begun in 1989 by the Rev. Harvey Clemons, Jr., pastor of Mount Pleasant Baptist Church, the Fifth Ward Community Redevelopment Corporation sought, among other projects, to revive the fortunes of Lyons Avenue, the main street of Fifth Ward during the middle decades of the 20th century. Across the street at 3301 Lyons and dating from Lyons's heyday is the Deluxe Theater (1941).

O-2
Phillis Wheatley High School
[now H. P. Carter Career Center]
1700 Gregg Street
1929, Harry D. Payne

In the mid-1920s the Houston Independent School District acknowledged the substantial population growth of Fifth Ward's African-American population by constructing the first public high school open to African-American students in the community. Payne's substantial 3-story building, a landmark on Lyons, is decorated with cast stone Spanish detail.

O-3
Fifth Ward Business and Financial Center
4300 Lyons Avenue
1999

Another project of the Fifth Ward Community Redevelopment Corporation was the construction of this 1-story professional building. In most of its projects the community development corporation followed existing suburban architectural trends.

O-4
First Shiloh Baptist Church
4420 Lyons Avenue
1964, John S. Chase

Chase was only one of the many Houston architects influenced by MacKie & Kamrath's interpretation of Frank Lloyd Wright's Usonian architecture in the 1950s and '60s. The dramatic rising roofline and the church's open frame, steel-and-brick bell tower mark the Shiloh Church architecturally. Next door to the church, at 4514 Lyons, is St. Elizabeth Hospital (1947, Wyatt C. Hedrick), now the Barbara Jordan Healthcare Center.

O-5
CORE: The 99K House
4015 Jewel Street
2009, Hybrid Seattle and ORA

In 2008 the Rice Design Alliance and the American Institute of Architects, Houston Chapter organized an open architectural competition to design an environmentally sustainable, single-family demonstration house that could be built for just under $100,000. The winning design, by two Seattle firms, Hybrid and ORA, was constructed by Harvey Builders on a lot in Fifth Ward donated by the City of Houston's Land Assemblage Redevelopment Authority.

O-6
Garden House
5013 Pickfair Street
2002, Morris Gutiérrez

Rice architecture professor Michael Bell, in collaboration with the Fifth Ward Community Redevelopment Corporation and DiverseWorks, invited teams of architects, most associated with the Rice School of Architecture, to design 16 houses that the Fifth Ward CRC could build. The DiverseWorks exhibition *16 Houses* of 1998 and Bell's book of the same title (2003) documented the results. This house, designed by Deborah Morris and Gabriella Gutiérrez, was the only one of the 16 designs to be built. Like the 99K House, its lack of refinement, as constructed, bespeaks the contradictions involved in attempting to design and build affordable housing incorporating architectural innovations.

O-6 Garden House

0-7 Cummins Southern Plains Parts and Services Building

0-8 House

0-9 Theodore Roosevelt Elementary School

0-10 Houston Community College Northeast Campus

0-12 9111 Eastext Freeway Building

0-7
Cummins Southern Plains Parts and Services Building
7045 North Loop 610 East
2001, Carlos Jiménez Design Studio

The Columbus, Indiana-based diesel engine manufacturer, Cummins, commissioned Jiménez to design a prototype truck engine maintenance and repair workshop, which could be reproduced in other locations. Constructed of concrete tilt-wall panels, the building is divided into two bays. Repainting has destroyed the original architectural color scheme. Moreover Cummins' franchisees decided that a standardized design did not suit their varying requirements so the prototype was the only one built to Jiménez's design.

0-8
House
815 Woodard Street
2009, Brett Zamore Design

Brett Zamore's kit house system is adapted to a lot in the 1930s Lindale Park neighborhood.

0-9
Theodore Roosevelt Elementary School
6700 Fulton Street
1929

Roosevelt Elementary, with its spare Spanish style ornament, is a landmark along Fulton. Completion of the Houston Independent School District's adjacent replacement school (2011, RWS Architects) will entail demolition of this school, one of the neighborhood's oldest, most historic buildings.

O-10
Houston Community College Northeast Campus
8001 Fulton Street
2008, Hellmuth, Obata + Kassabaum and Archi*Technics/3

Built adjacent to the now-demolished Northline Mall, HCC's Northeast College is a 4-story building faced with patterned brickwork, a transparent glass curtain wall, and lath-like solar screens. In a depressed part of the city, it stands out as architecturally assured.

O-11
Templo Regional de la Luz del Mundo
8312 Eastex Freeway
2005, Enrique González

A startling site along the Eastex Freeway, this Mexican-Texan version of the neoclassical Church of la Madeleine in Paris astonishes with its marble Ionic portico, storiated pediment, and brazen gilded dome. The flanks of the church bespeak its complex interior spatial organization; the curved quadrants embracing the freeway frontage road add a Baroque frisson.

O-12
9111 Eastex Freeway Building
9111 Eastex Freeway
1984, Dyal & Babendure

Dyal & Babendure paid homage to the postmodern Rationalism of Italian architect Aldo Rossi in this speculative office building.

O-11 Templo Regional de la Luz del Mundo

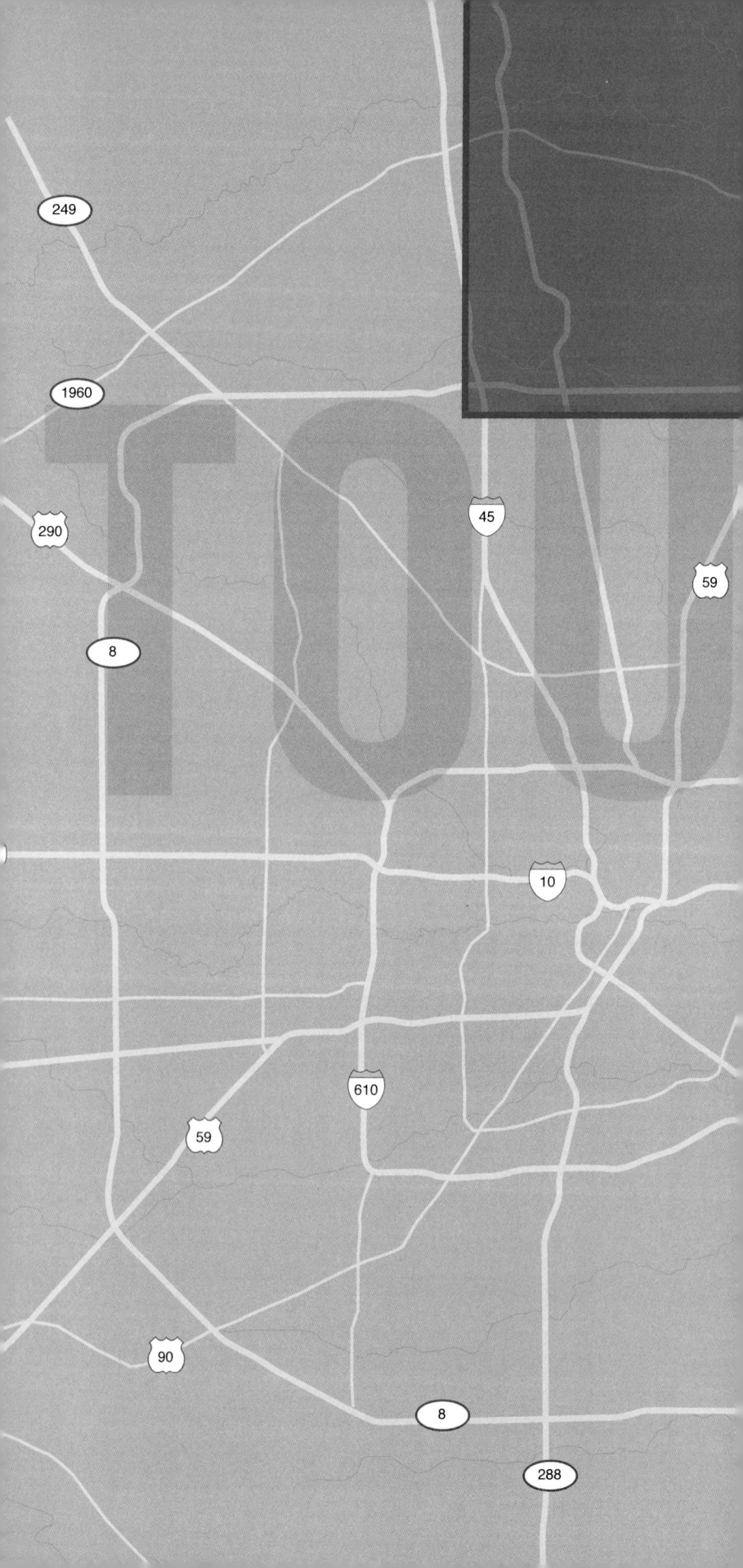

IAH / Kingwood / Humble / Spring

IAH / Kingwood / Humble / Spring

Tour P

The sector of north-central Harris County that encompasses Bush Intercontinental Airport (IAH), the planned community of Kingwood and its neighbor, the town of Humble, as well as the community of Spring demonstrates just how rapidly the "new" in Houston gets transformed into the "old." I-45 (North Freeway) constructed in the early 1960s and US-59 (Eastex Freeway) in the 1960s and '70s along with

Houston Intercontinental Airport (George Bush Intercontinental since 1997), begun in 1961 and completed in 1969, were the infrastructural operations that encouraged suburbanization of this immense slice of territory, bordered on the east by the San Jacinto River and the reservoir it feeds–Lake Houston, completed in 1953. The compact historic cores of Humble and Spring, both railroad towns with the scale and density of early 20th-century railroad-related development, contrast markedly with the car-related suburban sprawl of the second half of the century. This unevenness stands out today. Greenspoint Mall, which opened in 1976 and was for a time larger than the Galleria, began to lose ground in the late 1980s once it was outflanked by newer malls located even farther from the center of Houston. Although adjacent to the Greenspoint office corridor, the mall struggles to survive. The office buildings along the oldest stretch of North

Sam Houston Parkway East, between I-45 and US-59, still share freeway frontage with less prestigious uses and vacant real estate. Bush Airport's extensive grounds are an example of the kind of civic landscape Houston might have if it were not for the irrational hostility to public planning. Here is a beautiful reminder that alternatives to the visual dissonance of suburban Houston do exist. Kingwood, reached after navigating a stretch of the Eastex Freeway, where every surface seems to be paved, was developed in 1970-71 by the Friendswood Development Co. and the King Ranch as an antidote to Houston. Now covering over 15,000 acres, it is nearly built out. In contrast to the planned communities of The Woodlands and First Colony in Sugar Land, Kingwood did not develop a major office and institutional sector, nor was a regional mall built there. In 1996 the City of Houston annexed Kingwood despite the opposition of its residents and its 22-mile distance from downtown Houston. Humble (pronounced: 'Umble), resists absorption into the blur of suburban Houston chiefly because of the survival of its historic center. Barely a mile to the west of this center, along Humble-Westfield Road, lies Bordersville, a historically African-American rural settlement that the City of Houston annexed in 1965, but did not provide with city utilities until 1981. In Bordersville the landscape of uneven development correlates with historic patterns of official neglect. Spring is both a tiny historic town and a sprawling "census designated place" bounded by I-45 to the west, Spring Creek to the north and east, and Cypress Creek to the south. The City of Houston has been much more selective about annexing new territory west of Bush Intercontinental than to the east, so Spring lies in unincorporated Harris County but within the City of Houston's Extra Territorial Jurisdiction. Old Town Spring, as the historic townsite brands itself, is an island of charm in the midst of suburban anonymity. Here the new/old opposition is made to work in favor of the old, because distinctiveness of the old offers respite from the bland and undistinguished sameness of the no-longer-new.

1. **Wyndham Hotel Greenspoint,** 12400 Greenspoint Drive
2. **First City Bank-North Belt Building,** 400 North Sam Houston Parkway East
3. **Gateway I Building,** 3663 North Sam Houston Parkway East
4. **Houston Intercontinental Airport,** 2800 North Terminal Road
5. **Light Spikes,** John F. Kennedy Boulevard and Will Clayton Parkway
6. **King's Crossing Town Center,** 1 North Main Street, Kingwood
7. **Pangburn Building,** 200 E. Main Street
8. **Three H Services Center,** 19300 block Hightower Lane
9. **Wunsche Brothers Café and Saloon,** 103 Midway Street

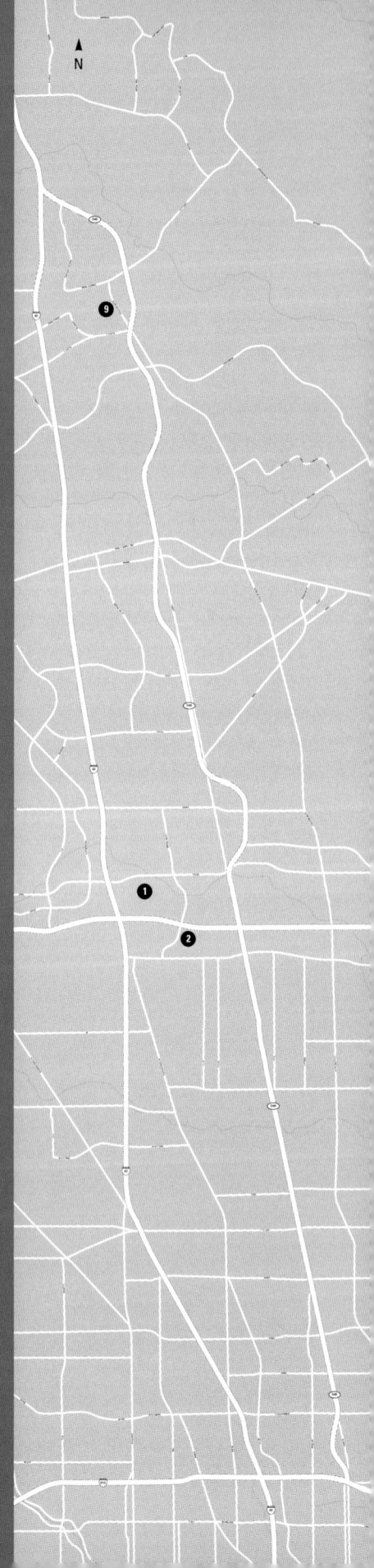

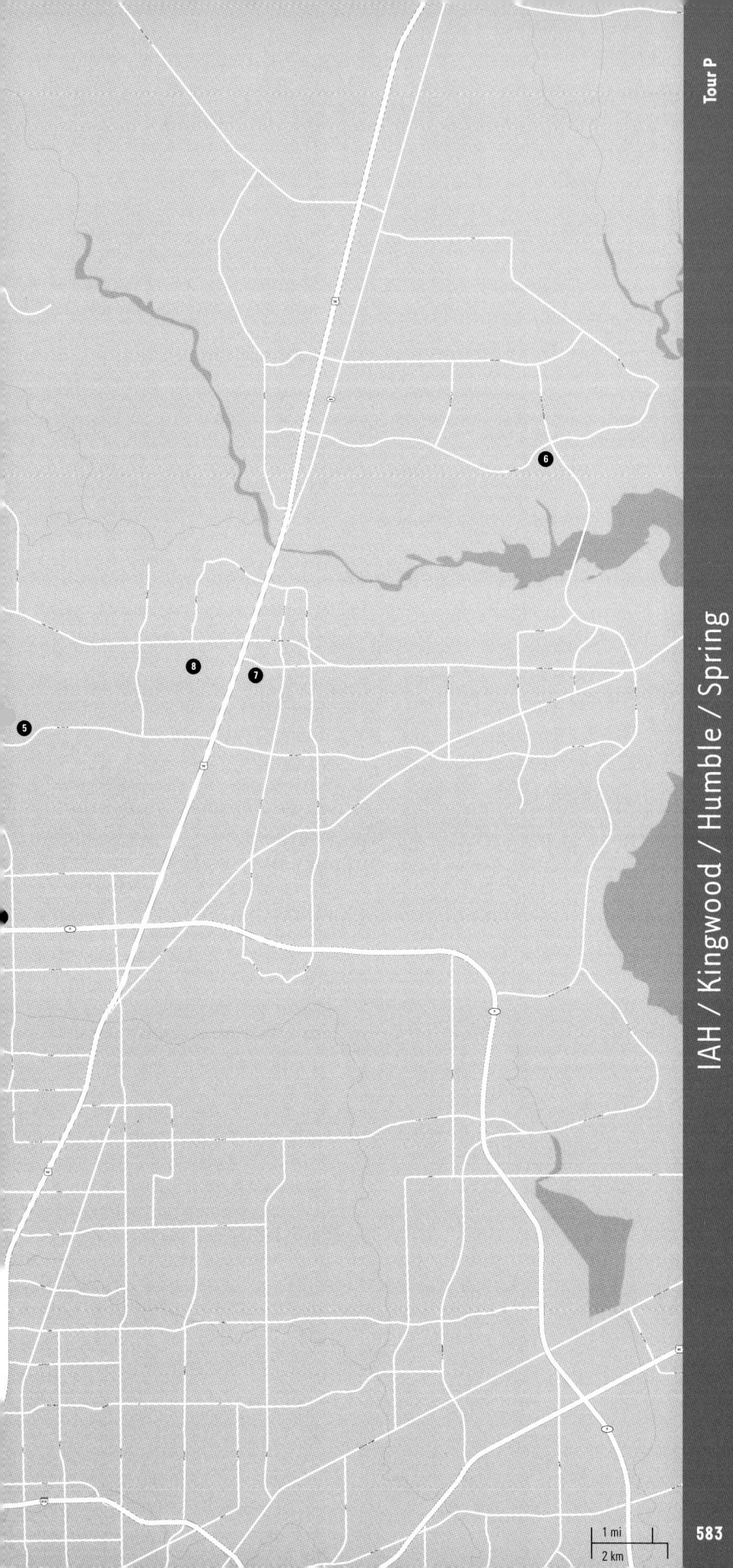

P-1 Wyndham Hotel Greenspoint

P-2 First City Bank-North Belt Building

P-3 Gateway I Building

P-1
Wyndham Hotel Greenspoint
[now Hilton Houston North]
12400 Greenspoint Drive
1984, Morris*Aubry Architects

The gabled parapets and banded brick wall surfaces of this 15-story hotel are more impressive at a distance than on close inspection, where the perceptible thinness of what is, after all, a curtain wall clashes with its architectural conception as a masonry bearing wall. The Wyndham Hotel is located in Greenspoint, a 220-acre mixed-use development begun by Exxon's Friendswood Development Co. in 1976 near the intersection of North Sam Houston Parkway and the North Freeway, and in proximity to Bush Intercontinental Airport. Buildings in Greenspoint are spaced out between parking garages, although a retail strip connects the hotel and several buildings along Greenspoint Drive. Six Greenspoint (1987, Pierce Goodwin Alexander) at 12450 Greenspoint exhibits deft planar massing and the contrast of two shades of granite aggregate precast concrete panels. PGAL also designed Five Greenspoint (1992) at 17001 Northchase Drive. The PetroLewis Tower (1983, Sikes Jennings Kelly), 16945 Northchase Drive, just behind the Wyndham, is, at 23 stories, the tallest building in Greenspoint. The 8-story One Greenspoint Plaza at 16855 Northchase and the 16-story Two Greenspoint Plaza at 16825 Northchase (1978, 1980, S. I. Morris Associates) display Eugene Aubry's predilection for designing buildings in series, exploring here the random cantilevering of shallow window bays to fragment the boxy shapes of the buildings and provide multiple corner office spaces.

P-2
First City Bank-North Belt Building
[now Amegy Bank of Texas Greenspoint South]
400 N. Sam Houston Pkwy. E.
1983, Gwathmey, Siegel & Associates and Urban Architecture

The New York architects Gwathmey Siegel produced a series of speculative office buildings along North Sam Houston Parkway—the 2-story Internorth Energy Building (1978) at 256, the 3-story Damson Oil Building (1978) at 260, and the 4-story Northpoint Building (1979) at 262, all for Ronald Bouchier—that culminated in this 12-story building for Treptow, Murphree & Company. Like the shorter buildings, First City is organized programmatically. Circulation and services are differentiated from the trays of office space by being collected into a tower on the west side of the building. The arrangement of windows varies from side to side according to solar orientation. Whereas Charles Gwathmey faced the earlier buildings with precast concrete, he sheathed First City in an all-glass curtain wall, horizontally banded with iridescent pearl and ivory spandrel glass and reflective window glass that is wrapped expressively around the building's curved northeast corner. Farther east on Sam Houston Parkway, which began to emerge as a major office corridor in the mid-1970s, are two large corporate complexes, NL Industries North Belt Complex at 3000 (now Halliburton: 1979, 1981, Pierce Goodwin Alexander) and Hydril Technology Center at 3300 (now GE Oil and Gas: 1980, Albert C. Martin & Associates).

P-3
Gateway I Building
3663 North Sam Houston Pkwy. East
1982, Richard Fitzgerald & Partners

This 6-story, brick-surfaced speculative office building asserts its presence by virtue of its knife-edged angled corners and a shift from the scale of the structural grid (expressed in the horizontal bands of flush-glazed windows) to the big-scaled, deep-set notches at either end of the building, a feat that the Fitzgerald office duplicated with the eight-story Gateway II (1984), around the corner at 15333 Drummet. Crossing Greens Road on John F. Kennedy Boulevard, one enters the 11,000-acre grounds of Bush Intercontinental Airport. Their park-like appearance is an indication of what Houston's public landscapes could become if they were designed instead of merely developed. On the east side of JFK Boulevard are the Federal Aviation Administration Air Traffic Control Center (1965, Golemon & Rolfe and George Pierce-Abel B. Pierce) at 16600 JFK and Intercontinental Bank (now Chartway Federal Credit Union: 1972, MacKie & Kamrath) at 16830 JFK. The three freestanding metal sculptures are *Radiant Fountains* by Dennis Oppenheim (2010).

P-4 Houston Intercontinental Airport

P-4 Houston Intercontinental Airport

P-4 Houston Intercontinental Airport interior

P-4 Houston Intercontinental Airport terminal

P-4 Houston Intercontinental Airport interior

P-4
Houston Intercontinental Airport
[now George Bush Intercontinental Airport]
2800 North Terminal Road
1969, Golemon & Rolfe and George Pierce-Abel B. Pierce

Houston Intercontinental Airport (IAH) was the second airport in the U.S. designed especially for jet traffic and the first to employ an arrangement of linked unit terminals. IAH, as Reyner Banham acknowledged, "is recognized as a conceptual breakthrough, where movement patterns were finally allowed to dominate the whole design concept." The airport complex reduced neatly to a flow diagram that operated both laterally and vertically to minimize the distance travelers had to walk within a terminal or between terminals. To that end not only did cars and public transportation pick up and deliver at each unit terminal, but cars also can be parked directly in each terminal. There is also a subterranean tram that shuttles between terminals that is now supplemented by the above-grade TerminaLink automated people mover. The architectural design of Terminals A, B, and C was a slick rendition of the New Brutalism. Externally the design articulated the spatial organization of the terminals. These had no real facades, but since one never had the opportunity to contemplate the buildings as isolated objects, it didn't really matter. Generous dimensions, muted colors, and variations in texture and lighting allowed the interiors of the two original terminals, A and B, to age gracefully. (Expropriation of public spaces to accommodate retail expansion is another matter.)

The weakest point in the site organization was, as William T. Cannady noted soon after completion, the right-angle turn that incoming cars must negotiate around the 7-story, flying saucer-shaped Airport Hotel (now Houston Airport Marriott: 1971, William B. Tabler & Associates; Annex, 1981, Golemon

& Rolfe Associates), which broke the continuity of movement and induced uncertainty about which direction to take. The master plan called for the addition of new terminals to the east of the hotel, duplicating A and B. Instead of orderly phased growth, however, plans for expansion were shelved due to political considerations, and then revived when Terminal C (1982, Golemon & Rolfe Associates and Pierce Goodwin Alexander) was built especially for Continental Airlines. Its much larger size reflected the specific requirements of the prime tenant, but it adhered in concept to the master plan. This is not true of the International Terminal (now Mickey Leland Terminal D: 1990, Harry Golemon Architects and PGAL). Golemon's Mario Bolullo produced a handsome and spirited building with a public presence that Terminals A, B, and C lack. But the ease with which the architects who devised the original master plan rejected the logic and discipline of that plan was typical of Houston, where even a public body dealing with one of the most important public buildings in the city seems unable to make long-term commitments to environmental order and clarity. Terminal E (2003–04, Corgan Associates) is an eastward extension of Terminal C and lies parallel to Terminal D). It is all interior, focused on a shopping mall and food court. Terminals A and B were substantially altered in the early 2000s to accommodate many more passengers. Houston transportation expert Christof Spieler observes that none of this should matter: the City of Houston Airport System's long-range plan is to tear everything down and start over.

The original 6,000-acre site of what was popularly called Jetero (jet era) airport is 21 miles north of downtown, a significant distance when property acquisition began in 1960. IAH lies midway between two radials, the North Freeway and the Eastex Freeway, and is now directly served by a third, the Hardy Toll Road, all of which are connected by the Sam Houston Parkway ring road. This conjunction of air and auto routes made the airport a major node for real estate development of the Houston variety: commercial strips along the freeways backed by a patchwork of residential subdivisions. This patchwork does not closely tail the commercial corridors, but is instead dispersed on a scale more regional than local, and by the mid-1970s was already spilling northward into Montgomery County.

P-5 Light Spikes

P-6 King's Crossing Town Center

P-7 Pangburn Building

P-8 Three H Services Center

P-9 Wunsche Brothers Café and Saloon

P-5
Light Spikes
John F. Kennedy Boulevard
and Will Clayton Parkway
1990, Llewellyn-Davies Sahni
and Jay Baker

Baker designed the *Light Spikes* as a temporary installation to celebrate the 1990 World Economic Summit held in Houston during the administration of President George Bush. Eight feet high, the internally lit spikes are adaptations of the flags of the nations that participated in the international conference. The installation was such a hit that the Spikes were reinstalled permanently at IAH. Motorists proceeding east along Will Clayton Parkway pass through an outlier of the East Texas Piney Woods. Along this stretch of parkway, near its intersection with Col. Fisher Street, is the blazing yellow suspended steel piece *West of the Pecos* by Rolf Westphal (1975).

P-6
King's Crossing Town Center
1 North Main Street
1998, Palmer Brook Schooley,
I. Phillips and EDI, planners

Stationed deep within Kingwood, a 13,000-acre planned community developed on the north bank of the San Jacinto River, just outside Humble, is King's Crossing Town Center, a retail lifestyle center. Schooley designed the buildings in accordance with Irving Phillips and EDI's master urban design plan for a suburban shopping precinct fashioned in terms of the New Urbanism. The effort to recreate the spatiality of late 19th- and early 20th-century small town urbanism, invoke regional architectural precedents, and mix retail, institutional, and residential uses, rather than segregate them, is commendable, although the result seems to be trapped within quotation marks. The surface parking lots that engulf the buildings give the center the feeling of a stage set. Schooley exercised considerable architectural restraint; the buildings do evoke the architecture of a small Texas town of the turn of the 20th century. Unfortunately Kingwood has sacrificed its own genuine historical landmarks. Gone are both the original Kingwood Sales Pavilion (1971, Charles Tapley Associates) and its successor (1986, 3D/International) at 810 Kingwood, Tapley's Trailwood Village community swimming pool and bath house (1971) in the 2100 block of Running Springs no longer exists, nor does the Kingwood Fire Department Station #1 at 1863 Kingwood. A pair of 2-story office buildings by Tapley at 1801 Kingwood (1976) do survive—for now.

P-7
Pangburn Building
[now Humble City Café]
200 E. Main Street
1914

About six miles southwest of King's Crossing lies the real thing: downtown Humble, laid out in 1904 alongside the tracks of the Houston East & West Texas Railway. Its mixture of 1- and 2-story wood and brick buildings, and its proximity to surrounding neighborhoods, schools, and churches explain the appeal of the New Urbanism and of Traditional Neighborhood Design. This appeal has not saved downtown Humble from being usurped by the daunting retail landscape that unfolds to either side of the Eastex Freeway between the Townsen and F.M. 1960 overpasses. Will future developers seek to build nostalgic re-creations of this "downtown" Humble to evoke the turn of the 21st century? In the real downtown Humble the Pangburn Building is a small town classic, with its second-story shed-roofed balcony built out over the sidewalk. The 1-story brick buildings at 214 (1912), 218 (1907), and 302 (1912) E. Main bespeak the impact of the opening of the Humble Oil Field in January 1905. At 309 E. Main is another 2-story building with double-level porch (1916).

P-8
Three H Services Center
19300 block Hightower Road
1975, John Zemanek
with Alexander MacNab and
Charles Keith Associates

This community center is located in Bordersville, a low-income, African-American rural settlement that has existed here, on the edge of Humble, since the early 1900s. Zemanek's building group is of wood post-and-lintel construction, surfaced with cement asbestos panels, stock aluminum window sash, and corrugated composite sheet roofing. The feeling is Japanese, but tough and gritty, rather than delicate or precious. Isolated in a clearing in the midst of an East Texas Piney Woods landscape, the Three H Services Center was built to compensate residents for the neighborhood's lack of public services. It now backs up to a thriving commercial corridor along the Eastex Freeway.

P-9
Wunsche Brothers Café and Saloon
103 Midway Street
1902; 1983, Graham B. Luhn

Like Humble, Spring was tied historically to a rail line, the International & Great Northern. Its current incarnation dates from the restoration of the Wunsche Brothers Café and Saloon in 1983 by G. Scott Mitchell, a son of the Houston oilman George Mitchell, developer of The Woodlands. This sparked the revival of what is now called Old Town Spring as a quaint shopping district, with its narrow, somewhat irregular streets, consoling scale, minimal surface parking lots, and weekend bustle. It proclaims amid the post-1970 hyper-suburban landscape of north Harris County that there is a there-here.

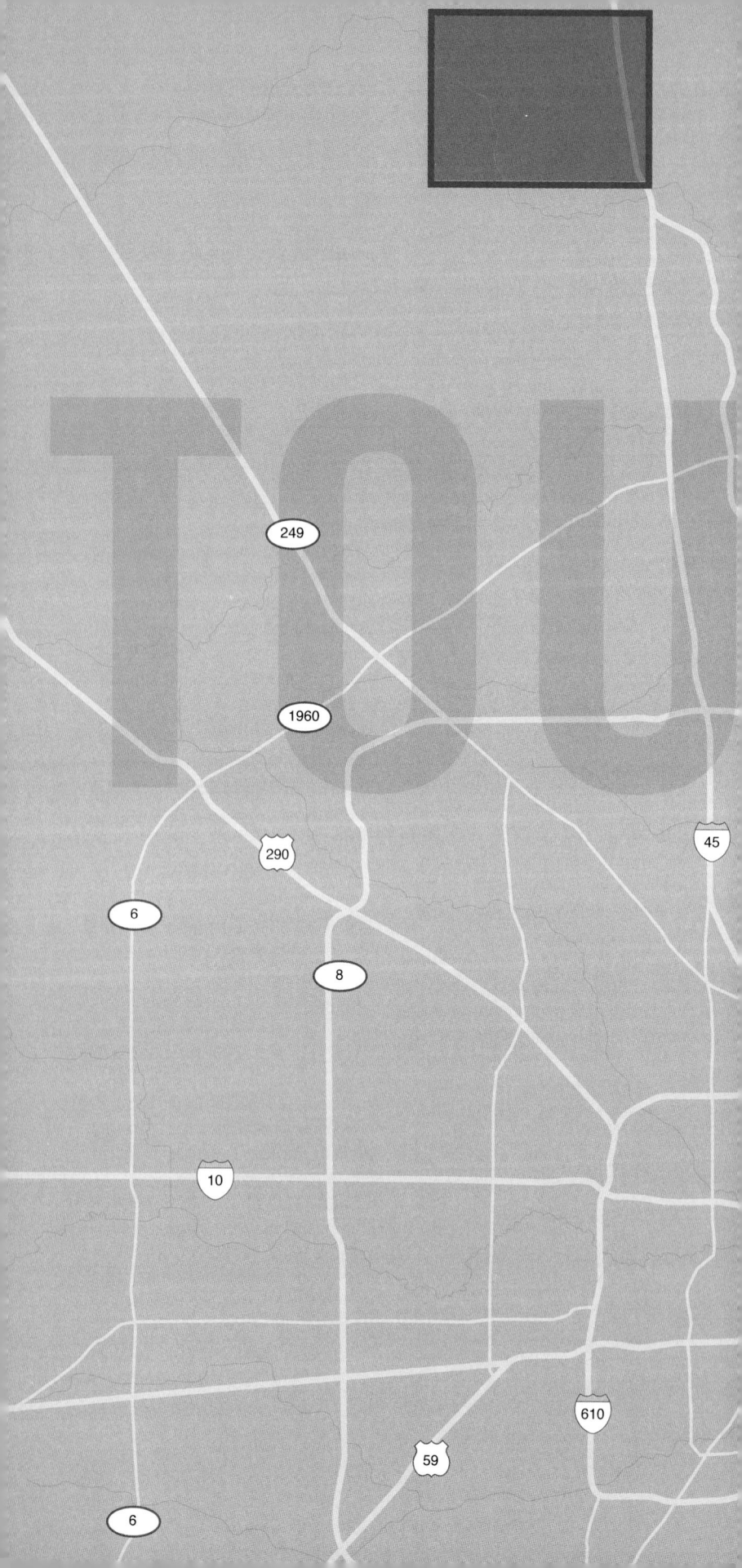

The Woodlands

The Woodlands

Tour Q

The Woodlands was envisioned by its developer, Houston oilman George P. Mitchell, as an alternative to suburban sprawl. It is a 17,000-acre new town, 28 miles north of downtown Houston, opened in 1975—the only one of 13 such communities developed under the U.S. Department of Housing and Urban Development's Title VII new towns program that did not fail economically. Its success is due in part to the fact that The Woodlands was developed according to conventional suburban real estate practices. Aside from the eerie screens of pine trees that oppressively mask all signs of human occupation, The Woodlands is not essentially different from the other planned communities on Houston's periphery. Mitchell paid special attention to environmental factors in the initial planning. The Philadelphia landscape architects Wallace, McHarg, Robert & Todd planned its extensive system of flood control waterways and forest preserves. Architecture was not as high a priority, and the result is a lack of distinction, especially in residential construction. The obsessive woodsiness of Grogan's Mill has been relaxed in Panther Creek and Cochran's Crossing, newer villages west of Lake Woodlands on the Woodlands Parkway, and Research Forest, the office park district along Research Forest Drive, west of the north end

of Grogan's Mill Road. But as the scabrous strip along the North Freeway at the very gates of The Woodlands indicates, there is no escape. High-minded private munificence is simply no match for the freewheeling real estate dynamics of a city without planning controls.

By 2010 the population of The Woodlands rose to just under 94,000. In 2007 the community's legislative representatives in Austin negotiated an agreement with the City of Houston to extricate The Woodlands from Houston's Extra Territorial Jurisdiction and enable it to seek incorporation as a city in 2014. George Mitchell sold The Woodlands Corporation in 1997, and, since 2003, it has been owned by the Rouse Company and its parent, General Growth Properties. Rouse has concentrated on development of the Town Center, the most consistently developed example of New Urbanism planning principles in the Houston area. The Woodlands has been the subject of two serious analyses: *The Woodlands: New Community Development, 1964–1983* by George T. Morgan, Jr., and John O. King (1987) and Ann Forsyth's excellent *Reforming Suburbia: The Planned Communities of Irvine, Columbia, and The Woodlands* (2005). As an alternative to Houston patterns of suburbanization though, The Woodlands still seems problematic. It exchanges the monotony that results from unregulated suburban development for a monotony of engineered nature that is inoffensive, but also can be suffocating. What makes Town Center seem promising is that architecture has been introduced there (alongside pedestrian examples of thematic styling) to strike a new balance, suggesting that urban design can be a positive force in constructing desirable community.

1. **Anadarko Tower,** 1201 Lake Robbins Drive
2. **U.S. Oncology Building,**
   10101 Woodloch Forest Drive
3. **The Fountains at Waterway Square,**
   Waterway Square Place and Waterway Avenue
4. **The Woodlands Mall,** 1201 Lake Woodlands Drive
5. **Market Street and The Woodlands Town Center,**
   9595 Six Pines Drive
6. **Cynthia Woods Mitchell Pavilion,**
   2005 Lake Robbins Drive
7. **The Woodlands Water Resources Building,**
   2455 Lake Robbins Drive
8. **Woodlands Peace Palace,**
   10210 Grogan's Mill Road
9. **The Woodlands United Methodist Church,**
   2200 Lake Woodlands Drive
10. **St. Anthony of Padua Catholic Church,**
    7801 Bay Branch Drive
11. **The Woodlands High School,**
    6106 Research Forest Drive
12. **Fellowship of The Woodlands,** 1 Fellowship Drive
13. **The Woodlands College Park High School,**
    3701 College Park Drive
14. **Portofino Center,** 19705 Interstate 45 North
15. **Pinecroft Center II,** 9301 Pinecroft Drive
16. **WoodsEdge Community Church,**
    25333 Gosling Road

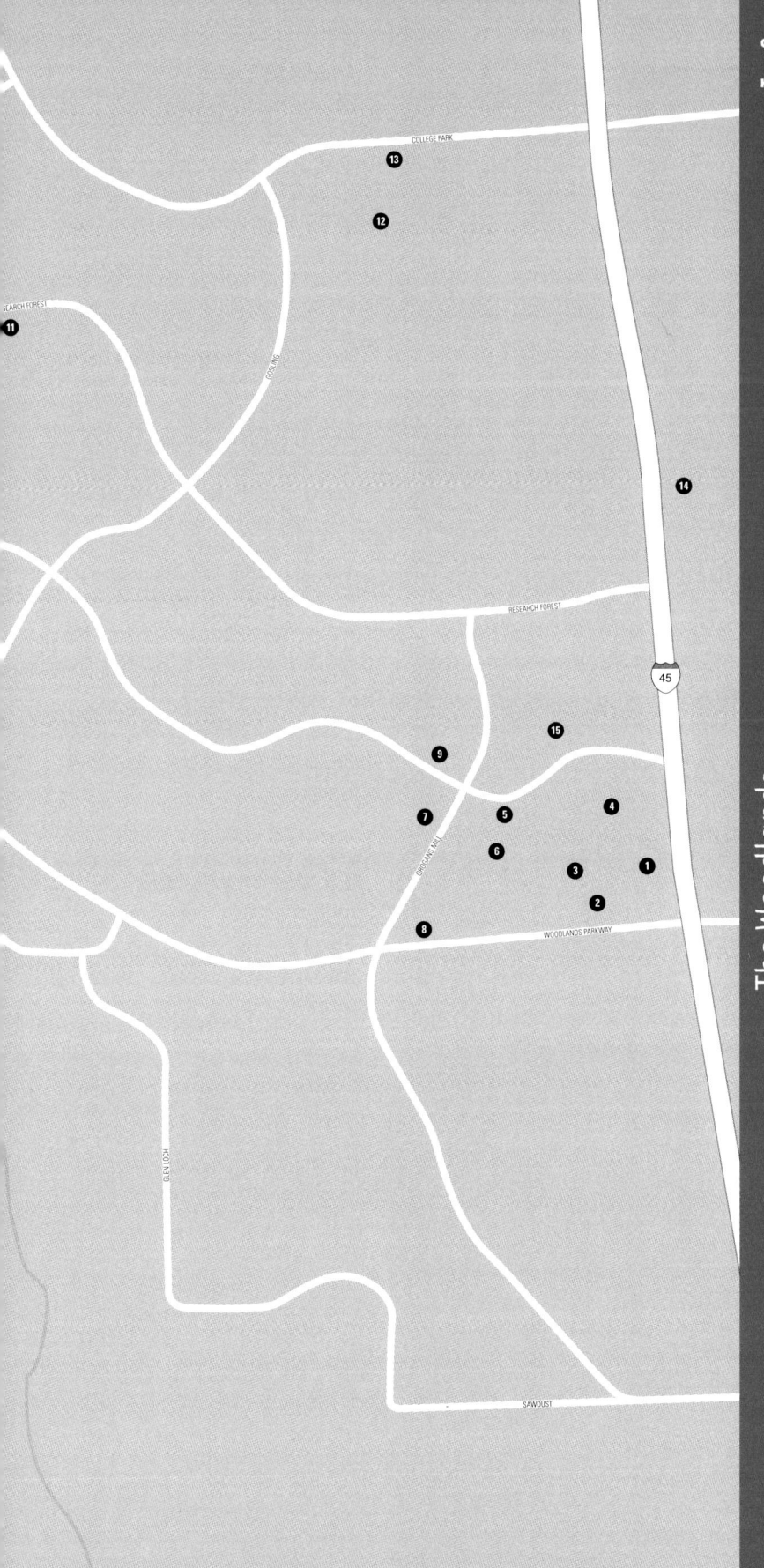

Q-1 Anadarko Tower

Q-2 U.S. Oncology Building

Q-1
Anadarko Tower
1201 Lake Robbins Drive
2002, Gensler

From I-45, the 30-story Anadarko Tower, which bills itself as the tallest building between Houston and Dallas, is The Woodlands' architectural icon. The southeast face of the building is stratified between a projecting, stair-stepped façade and the curved, glass-curtain-walled slab to which it is attached. A "supergrid" of precast concrete, superimposed on the stair-stepped section, imparts a sense of scale gradation and monumentality to the building. At ground level, the tower is set on the shore of Lake Robbins, a scenic flood retention basin. The lake is part of The Woodlands' extensive system of flood control waterways that double as landscape amenities. Lake Robbins Drive crosses the lake on a picturesquely engineered bridge (1999) designed by Ford, Powell & Carson of San Antonio and CBM Engineers.

Q-2
U.S. Oncology Building
10101 Woodloch Forest Drive
2009, Elkus Manfredi

The Boston architects Elkus Manfredi designed this 8-story corporate office building as part of a larger plan developed for The Woodlands Development Company. The red brick curtain wall with precisely gridded openings spanned by cast stone lintels gives this building a sense of material solidity and distinction.

Q-3
The Fountains at Waterway Square

Waterway Square Place and Waterway Avenue
2009, Sasaki Associates

Waterway Square is part of Town Center built out in the 2000s. Stepping down to the south channel of the Woodlands Waterway, it is a 1-acre square configured around an illuminated (at night) fountain that, at regular intervals, plays music in concert with specially programmed water displays. Artist Dixie Friend Gay is responsible for the terrazzo-paved fountain court titled *Treasures from Grandma's Purse*. That The Woodlands Company markets space here on the basis of its urban design plan bespeaks not just the company's ambitions, but also its successes. The Woodlands Waterway corridor is a case study of New Urbanist planning principles applied with consistency and intelligence. Narrow streets accommodate cars but favor pedestrians. Buildings enclose space rather than punctuating it. Open space is public space, not surface parking lots. The passing of time will diminish the initially inescapable stage-set feel. Framing Waterway Square to the north is the 12-story 24 Waterway Avenue office building (2008, Elkus Manfredi). East of Waterway Square lie 4 Waterway Square (2009, Elkus Manfredi) at 9901 Woodloch Forest and the 9-story Waterway Plaza I (2001) and 6-story Waterway Plaza II (2002), both by Gensler at 10003 and 10001 Woodloch Forest, respectively. West of the square are the 12-story Woodlands Waterway Marriott Hotel and Convention Center (2003, Gensler) and at 1 and 3 Waterway Court on the south shore the 6-story Waterway Lofts I and the 7-story Waterway Lofts II (2003 and 2004, Ziegler Cooper).

Q-3 The Fountains at Waterway Square

Q-4 The Woodlands Mall

Q-5 Market Street and The Woodlands Town Center

Q-6 Cynthia Woods Mitchell Pavilion

Q-4
The Woodlands Mall
1201 Lake Woodlands Drive
1994, ELS/Elbasani Logan

The retail heart of The Woodlands is its mall, the last regional shopping mall to be built in the Houston area. Typical of planned communities, the surrogate "downtown" that it anchors does not lie in the geographical center of The Woodlands, but abuts I-45 on its east edge to facilitate access by the maximum number of cars. The Woodlands Corporation has sought to amend the original everything-in-its-place pattern of good suburban planning of the 1970s to reprogram real estate to achieve the mixture of uses promoted by the New Urbanism in the 1990s, now elevated to marketing doctrine for up-scale retail projects. To achieve this, an open-air lifestyle center was added to the south flank of the mall (2004, RTKL of Dallas; MESA Design Group of Dallas, landscape architect), connecting it to the north channel of the Woodlands Waterway.

Q-5
Market Street and The Woodlands Town Center
9595 Six Pines Drive
2003, Development Design Group, Runyon Architects, and Gensler

Market Street, a smaller, more upscale retail center, was constructed just west of the Woodlands Mall. Of the New Urbanist traditional town centers in the Houston area, Market Street joins Waterway Square in being the most consistently designed. The incorporation of an unpretentiously landscaped central square (TBG Partners of Austin, landscape architect), the low height of the surrounding retail blocks, and the inclusion of moving and parked cars work to make this seem like a real place, although the architecture is of the nostalgic Americana stage-set variety. Banishing the unavoidable giant surface parking lot to the west side (and therefore keeping it out of the picture) and integrating the complex with Lake Robbins Drive by making pedestrian portals through a parking garage mean that Market Street is not spatially isolated from the rest of The Woodlands' Town Center.

Q-6
Cynthia Woods Mitchell Pavilion
2005 Lake Robbins Drive
1990, Sustaita Architects and Horst Berger Partners

George Mitchell, the developer of The Woodlands, built this open-air performance center in honor of his wife. Horst Berger designed the three-peaked fabric structure containing 3,000 of the pavilion's 10,000 seats. The fabric structure was badly damaged during Hurricane Ike in September 2008, but has been repaired and expanded by RdlR Architects (2009).

Q-7
The Woodlands Water Resources Building
[now The Woodlands Joint Powers Agency]
2455 Lake Robbins Drive
1985, Taft Architects

Somewhat overwhelmed by the neighboring, mid-rise, residential Village at Woodlands Waterway (2011, Ambrose & House and Muñoz and Albin), this little building is still one of the architectural highlights of The Woodlands. Its portico typologically identifies it as a public building, for it is as close as The Woodlands comes to having a city hall. The building contains the administrative offices of the eight Municipal Utility Districts that serve the presently developed parts of The Woodlands. Developers finance the installation of water and sewer services in unincorporated areas in Texas by creating Municipal Utility Districts to sell construction bonds, which tax new property owners within the service area to pay off the bonds. Taxpayers do elect the governing boards of MUDs. Therefore this building houses the only institution of local governance in The Woodlands. Taft combined brick, split-faced concrete block, and panels of scored stucco with keen attentiveness to the affective properties of color and texture. The dark green anodized aluminum mullions contrast piquantly with the gold-green vegetation and the brown-green water in the drainage ditch, whose diagonal alignment prompted the building's stepped plan, visible on the south side. The interior is arranged around a double-volume civic hall. By resorting to architecture rather than to pseudo-environmental camouflage, Taft has made a building that engages its setting far more profoundly than do other buildings in The Woodlands. The ingenuity, intelligence, and articulateness of their work give this little building big presence.

Q-7 The Woodlands Water Resources Building

Q-8 Woodlands Peace Palace

Q-9 The Woodlands United Methodist Church

Q-10 St. Anthony of Padua Catholic Church

Q-11 Woodlands High School

Q-8
Woodlands Peace Palace
10210 Grogan's Mill Road
2005, Truitt Architectural Services

Tucked deep in an office park, this 3-story office building is most visible from the westbound lanes of the Woodands Parkway as it bridges Grogan's Mill Road. The building's Vedic architectural detail reflects the client's devotion to Hindu spiritual practices.

Q-9
The Woodlands United Methodist Church
2200 Lake Woodlands Drive
2001, Lancaster & Associates

The magnitude of The Woodlands is brought home by this enormous church-and-school complex, centered on the church's dome. Thomas Lancaster used symmetry, centrality, and figuration to bring spatial clarity and order to the church. But the extent to which the sprawl of buildings and parking lots in the contemporary suburb undermines the quest for traditional hierarchies of order, stability, and legibility is apparent here. Crossing Lake Woodlands going westbound on Lake Woodlands Drive, one sees to the right the silvery, slightly bowed, 4-story Chicago Bridge & Iron Building (2003, Hellmuth, Obata + Kassabaum) at 2103 Research Forest Drive and the two-building, 6-story Hewitt Associates Building (now AonHewitt: 2000, Gensler) at 2601 Research Forest Drive.

Q-10
St. Anthony of Padua Catholic Church
7801 Bay Branch Drive
2004, Jackson & Ryan Architects

Massive religious complexes are a recurring feature of The Woodlands. Yet rather than standing out as neighborhood landmarks that orient people by virtue of their location in the landscape, they too are sequestered behind dense screens of trees that deny the presence of the city.

Jackson & Ryan reiterate gabled profiles to identify this complex as a church.

Q-11
Woodlands High School
6106 Research Forest Drive
1996, Perkins + Will and
PBK Architects

The architects consolidated academic spaces within a ¾ circle; the athletic and community spaces project outside this circle toward the community. Continuous additions have eroded the clarity of the original.

Q-12
Fellowship of The Woodlands
[now Woodlands Church]
1 Fellowship Drive
1996, Studio Red

While mainstream religious congregations in The Woodlands adopt outsized architectural symbols of "traditional" identity, non-denominational megachurches exhibit a more flexible attitude. The Woodlands Church (its *Wikipedia* entry describes it as the 12th largest church in the U.S.) could just as plausibly be a low-rise corporate headquarters. Its most overtly religious component is a chapel, which pays homage to the work of Fay Jones, lying west of the main parking lot. Kudela & Weinheimer was the landscape architect. Like other churches in The Woodlands (but unlike corporate headquarters), the Woodlands Church is hidden behind dense screens of trees.

Q-12 Fellowship of The Woodlands

Q-13 The Woodlands College Park High School

Q-14 Portofino Center

Q-15 Pinecroft Center II

Q-13
The Woodlands College Park High School
3701 College Park Drive
and Honor Roll Drive
2005, PBK

With its red brick and light-toned concrete classical portico and cupola, and its frontality and symmetry, College Park High tries very hard to revert to a 1920s architectural image of American civic virtue. Although not entirely satisfactory as classical architecture, the building makes the point that The Woodlands' landscaping practices are oppressive because they deny architecture the opportunity claim civic place. College Park High School must assert itself from the back side of a tree-screened retail strip facing College Park Drive.

Q-14
Portofino Center
19075 Interstate 45 North
2001, Hermes Architects

The real estate that George Mitchell assembled for The Woodlands lies on the west side of I-45. Consequently the freeway's east side has become the Achilles heel of The Woodlands' ambition to represent a socially responsible alternative approach to suburbanization. No place mocks The Woodlands' earnestness more raucously than Portofino Center, a strip mall that is a Las Vegas style re-enactment of the Piazza San Marco in Venice, where a retention basin fills in for the Grand Canal.

Q-15
Pinecroft Center II
9301 Pinecroft Drive
2007, Browne McGregor

The reflective glass skylights on the front of this 2-story medical professional building rhythmically punctuate its long elevation, contrasting with the reddish-brown sandstone facing. This group of buildings (all designed by Browne McGregor) illustrates one of The Woodlands' abiding contradictions as a model of alternative suburban spatial practices. Once the obligatory screen of trees is penetrated, it's life as usual in Houston, with the surface parking lot tyrannically dominating all other spatial arrangements. Reflecting the 1970s when it was conceived, The Woodlands is car-dependent, making automobile use and storage an absolute necessity.

Q-16
WoodsEdge Community Church
25333 Gosling Road
2008, Morris Architects

Flintridge Drive follows the course of Spring Creek. The creek valley was set aside by The Woodlands Company in 2007 as the 1,700-acre George Mitchell Nature Preserve, one increment of a 12,000-acre linear park along both sides of Spring Creek. The creek valley's undulating topography makes Flintridge one of the most visually rewarding streets in The Woodlands. The Woodlands has developed additional "villages" on the south side of Spring Creek in Harris County. Abutting one of these is the WoodsEdge mega-church, which adopts The Woodlands' landscape formula of recessing buildings (and surface parking) behind a thick screen of vegetation. Morris Architects used counterthrust shed roofs to break down the scale of the complex and disguise its boxy plan configuration.

Q-16 WoodsEdge Community Church

Klein / Cypress / Fairbanks / Satsuma

Klein / Cypress / Fairbanks / Satsuma

Tour R

This enormous area of northwest Harris County lies between I-45 (North Freeway) on the east and I-10 (Katy Freeway) on the south, and following the curving axis of Farm-to-Market Road (FM) 1960 and its north-south continuation as Texas Highway 6. Historically this territory was a mixed landscape of dense stands of trees and coastal plain first populated by German immigrant farm families beginning in the middle decades of the 19th century. Its absorption into Houston's suburban empire began during the 1970s, undeterred even by the contraction of Houston's energy economy in the 1980s, when new sources of wealth production, notably the Compaq Computer Corporation, came to the rescue. Community development in the Klein-Cy-Fair district has occurred in smaller-scale real estate increments that did not seek total control, in contrast to Kingwood and The Woodlands. These give the suburban landscape more diversity, but also less spatial coherence, notably along FM 1960, where age and the ups-and-downs of the business cycle have created a landscape of alternating affluence and shabbiness that seems out of place so far from the center of Houston. Architecture ranges from hidden pockets of rural heritage to cool corporate modernism to thematic styling that can be amusing or

appalling, or both simultaneously. Occasionally architecture and landscape architecture do connect poetically with the places they were built. These instances demonstrate that design does play an emotionally captivating role in the interpretation of place—a fragile message overwhelmed by the sheer volume of careless, prosaic, and superficial construction that is the norm in suburban Houston. The construction of Segments E, F, and G of the Grand Parkway (Texas Highway 99), a 180-mile circumferential toll way that pivots around downtown Houston at a 22- to 25-mile radius, especially serves major economic interests, such as the 365-acre tract where ExxonMobil, abandoning downtown Houston, will consolidate all 15,000 employees in a new North American headquarters (2015, Pickard Chilton, Gensler, PDF). Approval of construction of this segment of the Grand Parkway in 2011 clarified the intimate connection between publicly funded infrastructure, corporate investment, and real estate development, underlining the crucial role infrastructure plays in opening up undeveloped countryside, much of it already owned by canny investors, for increased urbanization, adding yet another ring to the infinitely expanding circumference of metropolitan Houston.

1. **Northside Christian Church,** 20250 Kuykendahl Road
2. **Adam Frederick Klein House,** 6970 Spring Cypress Road
3. **Klein Independent School District Technology Center,** 7200 Spring Cypress Road
4. **Peter Wunderlich Farm Stead,** 18128 Theiss Mail Route Road
5. **Vintage Park,** 110 Vintage Park Boulevard
6. **Compaq Computer Corporation Administration Building,** 20555 Tomball Parkway
7. **St. Mary's Episcopal Church,** 15415 North Eldridge Parkway
8. **Cypress Creek Family YMCA,** 19915 Tomball Parkway
9. **Houston Texas Temple,** 15725 Champion Forest Drive
10. **Pearl Fincher Museum of Fine Arts,** 6815 Cypresswood Drive
11. **Northwoods Presbyterian Church,** 3320 Farm-to-Market Road 1960 West
12. **Sandtrap Office and Retail complex,** 7840–7908 N. Sam Houston Parkway W.
13. **Christ The Redeemer Catholic Church,** 11507 Huffmeister Road
14. **Texas Department of Public Safety Region Two Headquarters,** 12230 West Road
15. **SpawGlass Construction Company Headquarters,** 13800 West Road
16. **St. Cuthbert's Episcopal Church,** 17020 West Road
17. **Lone Star College Cy-Fair,** 9191 Barker-Cypress Road
18. **Richard E. Berry Educational Support Center,** 8877 Barker-Cypress Road
19. **St. Mary and Archangel Michael Coptic Orthodox Church,** 7030 Lakeview Haven Drive
20. **St. John's Lutheran Church,** 7934 Highway 6 North

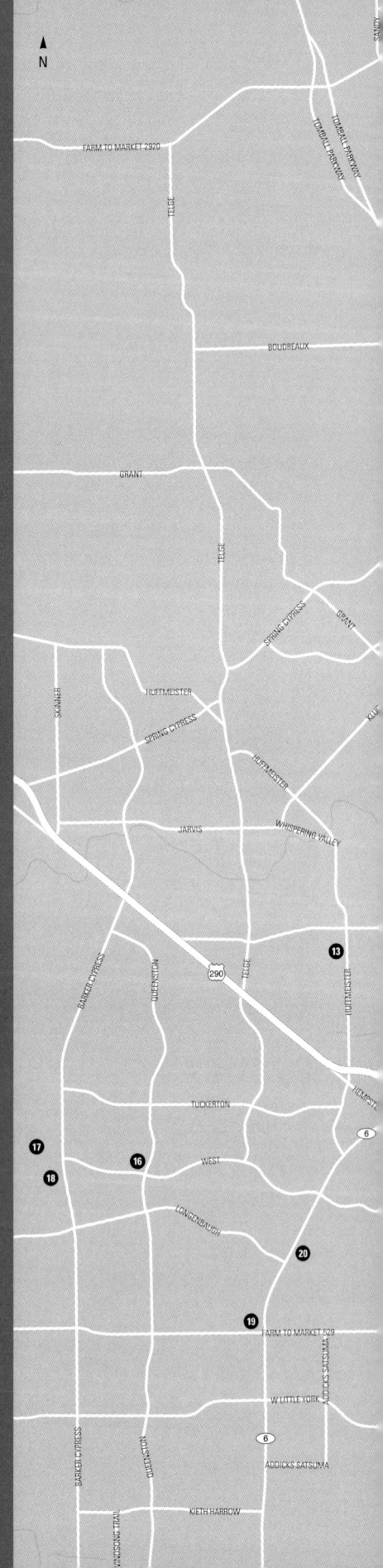

Tour R

Klein / Cypress / Fairbanks / Satsuma

R-1 Northside Christian Church

R-3 Klein Independent School District Technology Center

R-4 Peter Wunderlich Farmstead

R-1
Northside Christian Church
20250 Kuykendahl Road
2009, Visioneering Studios

Visioneering Studios, based in Irvine, California, designed the Grove, the first phase of Northside Christian Church's complex, to attract visitors by looking like a row of trendy townhouse lofts rather than a church. Shed roofs and siding of different materials and colors are collaged onto the building to visually reduce its scale and give it a non-institutional appearance. The retention basin is treated as a lagoon and the grounds as "woods." In the exploding suburban landscape of north Houston, churches function as sources of community association and identity to socialize newcomers.

R-2
Adam Frederick Klein Farm House
6970 Spring Cypress Road
1930

Before suburbanization lapped at, then flooded, Klein in the late 1960s, it was a dispersed community thinly populated by farm and ranch families, many descended from German immigrants. This house, which is not visible from the street, was built by a grandson of one of those immigrants, Adam Klein, who in 1854 settled the community that came to bear his name. Along Spring Cypress Road are other remnant ranch and farmsteads, many marked by 1950s brick veneer "ranch" houses.
* Not pictured.

R-3
Klein Independent School District Technology Center
7200 Spring Cypress Road
2008, Powers Brown Architecture

Powers Brown applied a paper-thin, Venturi-like classical false front to the Klein Independent School District's technology center to identify it as a civic building. Since Klein possesses neither a historic townsite nor visually obvious boundaries, community identity is bound up with the public school district, organized in 1938. Decorating the shed, as Power Brown has done, architecturally acknowledges the ambivalent status of the architectural landmark in Houston's suburban universe: its presence is desired, but not with sufficient ardor to inspire significant investment.

R-4
Peter Wunderlich Farmstead
[now Klein Museum]
18218 Theiss Mail Road
1891

The campus of Doerre Intermediate School, set deep within the Memorial Northwest subdivision, contains, along its east flank, the Texas Historical Foundation's open-air Klein Museum. Architectural components include nine buildings preserved from the Peter Wunderlich farmstead, which occupied this site, as well as additional buildings moved here by the foundation. As visitors enter the site from Theiss Mail Road, the buildings they encounter are the 1-story, wood, Maria Katherina Hofius Wunderlich House, a Gulf Coast cottage built by the widowed mother of Peter Wunderlich in 1874 at another location; the 1-story Kohrville School, a wooden, rural, public school built to serve African-American students in the Kohrville community near the intersection of Louetta and Jones; and the 1-story, wood, Peter Wunderlich Farmhouse (1891) and associated out-buildings. As with Old Town Spring, the Wunderlich farmstead asserts the antiquity and historical depth of a landscape that otherwise seems to have arrived fully formed in the 1970s.

R-5
Vintage Park
110 Vintage Park Boulevard
2007, Brand + Allen

The current 21st century vogue for open-air lifestyle centers rather than enclosed, air-conditioned shopping malls is evident at Vintage Park, developed by Interfin, which also built Brand + Allen's Uptown Park in the Post Oak area. Although inoffensive, Vintage Park's architecture fails to evoke Italy, as the Italianate street names posted on the sides of buildings suggest was intended. Clark Condon was the landscape architect.

R-5 Vintage Park

R-6 Compaq Computer Corporation Administration Building

R-7 St. Mary's Episcopal Church

R-8 Cypress Creek Family YMCA

R-10 Pearl Fincher Museum of Fine Arts

R-11 Northwoods Presbyterian Chruch

R-6
Compaq Computer Corporation Administration Building
20555 Tomball Parkway
1998, Hellmuth, Obata + Kassabaum

Between its founding in 1982 and its absorption into Hewlett Packard in 2002, Compaq emerged as a major producer of personal computers. The Spencer Partnership of Houston designed most of the numerous office buildings, manufacturing plants, and parking garages Compaq constructed between 1984-1988 on its 80-acre site at Cypress Crossing. The office buildings, clusters of cubes rotated so that their corners touch, are linked by an extensive network of air-conditioned, elevated pedestrian bridges. SLA was the landscape architect. Compaq's 10-story headquarters by Hellmuth, Obata + Kassabaum, facing the Tomball Parkway-Louetta intersection on the diagonal, is a sleekly detailed pair of 10-story slabs joined at the middle. The entire "campus" is insulated by vegetation; even interior streets within the corporate park seem blank because the buildings are all inward turning. In 2010 HP sold much of the Spencer-designed portion of the complex to Lone Star College, which adapted it to become its University Park campus. Trammell Crow Properties bought the administration building and its garage. Just south of the ex-Compaq campus, facing Tomball Parkway, is Chasewood Technology Park. The 5-story 4 Chasewood Building (2008, Ziegler Cooper) at 20329 Tomball Parkway reiterates the horizontal sleekness of Compaq's Administration Building.

R-7
St. Mary's Episcopal Church
15415 North Eldridge Parkway
1988, Gregory Harper Associates
with Gerald Moorhead

The parish house of this suburban church consists of a relaxed collision of shapes and low-budget materials.

R-8
Cypress Creek Family YMCA
19915 Tomball Parkway
2010, Brave/Architecture

Fernando Brave's building, closest to the Tomball Parkway-Maranatha intersection, is an annex to a large, much-added-to YMCA complex. Buff brick and dark metal siding articulate different programmatic components.

R-9
Houston Texas Temple, Church of Jesus Christ of the Latter Day Saints Church
15725 Champion Forest Drive
2000, Spencer Partnership

This temple, a Mormon administrative and cult center, steps forward and rises up in symmetrical tiers to a three-staged tower and spire 159 feet tall. Its cast stone and granite facing reflects the sunlight, enhancing a sense of stateliness. However the nervous verticality, improvised classical detail, and hermeticism of the temple's architecture give it a stage-set quality shared with other contemporary architectural efforts to evoke the solemnity and dignity of historical models.

R-10
Pearl Fincher Museum of Fine Arts
6815 Cypresswood Drive
2008, Stern and Bucek Architects

The Pearl Fincher Museum of Fine Arts, a non-collecting museum, opened in 2008 in an ex-Harris County library branch amid a complex of county-owned buildings shared with the Barbara Bush Branch of the Harris County Public Library (2002, Morris Architects), Cypress Creek Christian Church, and the Centrum, a performance space. The metal panel infill system with which Stern and Bucek faced the recessed front of the museum stands out when juxtaposed to the 1976 building by Clovis Heimsath Associates that frames it.

R-11
Northwoods Presbyterian Church
3320 FM 1960 West
1983, Charles Tapley Associates

Farm-to-Market Road (FM) 1960 merges with Texas Highway 6 to loop from Humble, on the northeast, around and through Sugar Land on the southwest, at a distance of about 18 miles from the center of Houston. In the late 1970s it became the axial ring of what was then Houston's most recent phase of concentric expansion. As the main street of northwest Harris County (only a small segment presently lies within Houston's city limits), FM 1960 has attracted the usual mad array of shopping centers, public institutions, mid-rise office buildings, and convenience stops. In the midst of this very evidently non-master-planned setting, Northwoods Presbyterian, designed by Tapley and Gerald Moorhead, introduces a welcome note of calm. Its rust-colored stucco walls, steeply-pitched copper roof, greenish-gray pine-shingled gables, and rotated square windows, cleverly filled with diagonal arrays of gray, bronze, and gold reflective solar glass instead of stained glass, are quietly but intensely colorful. The effect is serene and unsentimental; the interior is spacious and austere.

R-9 Houston Texas Temple, Church of Jesus Christ of the Latter Day Saints Church

R-12 Sandtrap Office and Retail Complex

R-13 Christ The Redeemer Catholic Church

R-14 Texas Department of Public Safety Region Two Headquarters

R-15 SpawGlass Construction Company Headquarters

R-12
Sandtrap Office and Retail Complex
7840-7908 N. Sam Houston Parkway W.
2002-2007, M. Nasr & Partners

Architect Mohammed Nasr and his associates developed Heron Lake Estates, a golf course subdivision at Sam Houston Parkway and Gessner Road. They developed the frontage along the Sam Houston feeder road with this strip of mid-rise office buildings and retail blocks that exuberantly indulge retro-mod styling themes.

R-13
Christ The Redeemer Catholic Church
11507 Huffmeister Road
2009, Hall Barnum Lucchesi

Houses of worship stand out in the landscape of Houston's 21st-century suburban sprawl, which seems to endlessly reproduce the same building types, materials, and site plan formulas with disquieting profusion. Yet too often the desire to mobilize architecture to assert the specificity of place in this depressing environment is compromised by expediency and hubris, as the 1,600-seat church of Christ the Redeemer attests. A 100-foot tall version of the tower of Mission San José in San Antonio is glommed onto a postmodern triumphal arch entry portal. The long nave culminates in an 80-foot-high cylindrical drum and dome, with low-roofed extensions protruding from this crossing. Internally, however, the church is organized not on a cruciform plan, as the exterior implies, but in an arena configuration requiring lateral breadth with no intervening columns. This breadth is achieved with steel structural truss framing that enables the crossing to be completely cantilevered above the worship space. Rather than make architecture out of the contradictory desire for combining traditional architecture with modern liturgical planning, engineering is deployed (and masked with drywall) to pretend that there is no contradiction between Mission San José and contemporary Catholic liturgical requirements. As a result architecture is reduced to scenography, and what was intended to be a monumental exception to the monotonous spatiality of suburban Houston is efficiently absorbed back into the system of suburban spatial production. Christ the Redeemer dwarfs the 1983 parish group designed by Charles Tapley Associates, which extends to the south facing Huffmeister.

R-14
Texas Department of Public Safety Region Two Headquarters
12230 West Road
2002

Located in the suburban town of Jersey Village, the Texas Department of Public Safety's Houston regional headquarters building is a 1-, 3-, and 4-story complex of offset slabs. Externalizing the building's concrete structural frame and infilling the interstices of the frame with blue and white glazed tile economically impart a sense of scale and proportion that enables the building to figure strongly on its open site when seen from the Northwest Freeway.

R-15
SpawGlass Construction Company Headquarters
13800 West Road
2003, Kirksey

The headquarters of SpawGlass is economically built and imaginatively designed to achieve sustainability goals. Constructed of concrete tilt-wall panels, the 1-story building has both extensive north facing windows at the rear and rooftop monitors to bring daylight into work spaces. Construction is externalized inside as well as outside. Kudela & Weinheimer was the landscape architect.

R-16
St. Cuthbert's Episcopal Church
17020 West Road
2009, James Ray

The first phase of St. Cuthbert's parish complex consists in a wide octagonal, 1-story building that differentiates between a ground-level band of windows and doors, interspersed with wood screening, and an upper zone of white stucco that emphasizes the building's geometric creases. Ray's design is heartening because it doesn't try to substitute sentimental imagery for architectural invention and rigor.

R-16 St. Cuthbert's Episcopal Church

R-17 Lone Star College Cy-Fair Campus

R-18 Richard E. Berry Educational Support Center

R-20 St. John's Lutheran Church

R-17
Lone Star College Cy-Fair Campus
9191 Barker-Cypress Road
2003, Gensler and Cobourn, Linseinsen & Ratcliff

The Cypress-Fairbanks campus of Lone Star College is especially impressive for its site planning and landscape architecture by The SWA Group. It reintroduces wetlands to the environmentally sensitive Katy Prairie in the form of an extensive retention basin around which both the campus and auto circulation are organized. Gensler sited academic buildings close to the linear portion of the basin, setting them back at irregular intervals to shape intimately scaled outdoor spaces. The buildings also shield the central campus from surface parking lots to the north and south. SWA planted native trees and grasses to restore the natural vegetation of the prairie, historically used first for cattle grazing, then rice cultivation, and then subdivision development. Lone Star Cy-Fair demonstrates that the careless development patterns that prevail in Houston are not inevitable or done without awareness of alternatives.

R-18
Richard E. Berry Educational Support Center
8877 Barker-Cypress Road
2006, PBK Architects and Hellmuth, Obata + Kassabaum Sports Venue Event

The late 20th-century French philosopher Jean Baudrillard coined the term "simulacrum" to describe a phenomenon he saw as pervasive in contemporary culture: the production of copies for which there are no originals. This would seem to describe the Cypress-Fairbanks Independent School District's Berry Educational Support Center, which combines an 11,000-seat football stadium, an 8,300-seat basketball arena, and a 456-seat theater with a 4,000-car surface parking lot. It is not the Berry's mixed-use athletic and entertainment program but its neo-Jeffersonian architecture that makes it such an unnerving spectacle on the Katy Prairie, just across West Road from the Lone Star campus. As elsewhere in suburban Houston, the desire to use architecture to proclaim that there is a here here goes awry when historical models are invoked but not rigorously adjusted to spatially address the design issues of siting, construction, materials, scale, proportion, and economy. The results suggest a society that idolizes "tradition" while operating on a flawed and superficial understanding of what that might constitute.

R-19
St. Mary and Archangel Michael Coptic Orthodox Church
7030 Lakeview Haven Drive
2004, Awad Youssef Eskander

The Church of St. Mary and the Archangel Michael in Copperfield is one of three Egyptian parishes in Houston and one of only five in Texas. The architect, Awad Youssef Eskander of Dallas, valiantly strives to reproduce a Byzantine prototype fronting on a West Houston parking lot. The proportions are attenuated and there is a lack of depth. Mosaics set within the entry portico enliven the façade. The adjoining parish hall is the work of PDG Architects.

R-20
St. John's Lutheran Church
[now Heritage Presbyterian Church]
7934 North Highway 6
1916

The tall, thin steeple of this wood-frame country church is a distinctive landmark on the prairie. The Heritage Presbyterian congregation saved the building and moved it to this site with the assistance of Friendswood Development Company, whose extensive Copperfield residential community lies across Highway 6.

R-19 St. Mary and Archangel Michael Coptic Orthodox Church

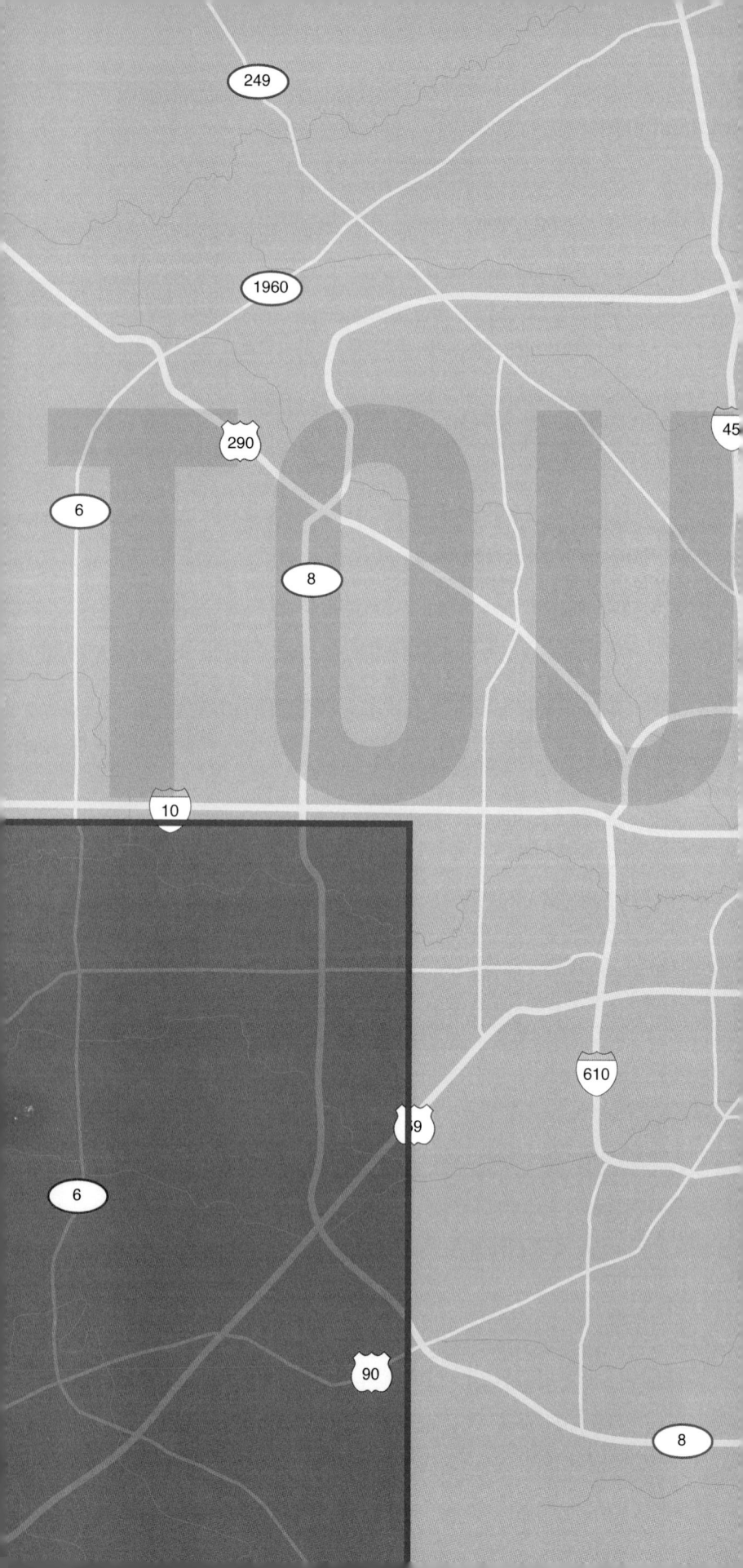

Addicks / Alief / Stafford / Missouri City

Addicks / Alief / Stafford / Missouri City

Tour S

The flat, coastal plain landscape of West Houston derives its identifying place names from such historical settlements as Addicks (developed 1884) and Alief (1894). Alief's 27-block townsite south of the Westpark Tollway (formerly the right-of-way of the San Antonio & Aransas Pass Railway) between S. Kirkwood and Cook Road survives, but it has been submerged by late 20th-century suburban sprawl. The diversity visible here hints at the velocity with which development trends occur in Houston, and the equally astonishing rapidity with which economic contractions arrest these patterns, stalling development out until the next cycle swings into action. City maps show this sector of Houston as thickly covered with a matrix of residential subdivisions. But the view from the long east-west thoroughfare streets (Briar Forest, Westheimer, Richmond, Bellaire, Beechnut, Bissonnet, West Bellfort, West Airport) traversing this plain tell more complex spatial stories, especially in the volumes of lightly developed or undeveloped land that creep in between the subdivisions, apartment complexes, and strip malls. One of the most fascinating of these landscape narratives involves the Chinese and Vietnamese business corridor along Bellaire Boulevard, where thematic styling architecturally

capitalizes on exoticism. The exotic is also apparent in the architecture of places of worship built by immigrants of many faiths from many parts of Asia. Between W. Bellfort and W. Airport, one crosses from Harris County into Fort Bend County and into the adjacent towns of Stafford and Missouri City, incorporated suburban cities that have grown with the same frantic intensity as Houston. Emerging in the early 2010s along an otherwise nondescript stretch of W. Bellfort in southwest Houston is a corridor of Asian national cultural centers. Rather than locate in the center of Houston, these institutions collectively form an international district in the suburbs, demonstrating the fluidity with which "centrality" is defined in the Houston metropolitan area.

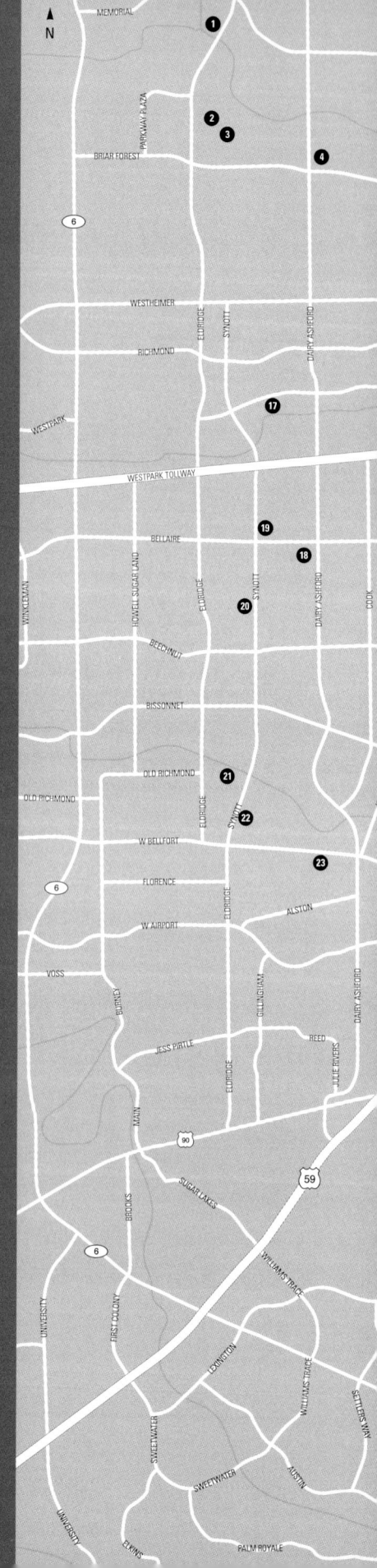

1. **Belle Sherman Kendall Community Library and Neighborhood Center,** 609 N. Eldridge Parkway
2. **Cardinal Health Care Building,** 1330 Enclave Parkway
3. **Sysco Corporate Headquarters,** 1370–1390 Enclave Parkway
4. **Schlumberger Building,** 1325 South Dairy Ashford Road
5. **Chevron Geosciences Building,** 2811 Hayes Road
6. **BMC Software Corporate Headquarters,** 2101 Citywest Boulevard
7. **One BriarLake Plaza,** 2000 W. Sam Houston Parkway S
8. **Enserch Building,** 10375 Richmond Avenue
9. **ImageNet Houston Building,** 6050 North Course Drive
10. **American First National Bank Building,** 9999 Bellaire Boulevard
11. **Texas First National Bank Building,** 9315 Bellaire Boulevard
12. **Dynasty Plaza,** 9600 Bellaire Boulevard
13. **Brown & Root Southwest Houston Office Building,** 10200 Bellaire Boulevard
14. **Texas Teo Chew Temple,** 10600 Turtlewood Drive
15. **Saigon Houston Plaza,** 10613 Bellaire Boulevard
16. **Hong Kong City Mall,** 11201–11215 Bellaire Boulevard
17. **Chong Hua Sheng Mu Gong Holy Palace,** 3695 Overture Drive
18. **Jade Buddah Temple,** 6969 Westbranch Drive
19. **Apple Dentist Headquarters,** 13194 Bellaire Boulevard
20. **Killough Middle School,** 7600 Synott Road
21. **Vietnamese Buddhist Center,** 10002 Synott Road
22. **Chinmaya Prabha,** 10353 Synott Road
23. **St. Thomas Aquinas Catholic Church,** 12635 West Bellfort Avenue
24. **Robert D. Cummings Elementary School,** 10455 South Kirkwood Drive
25. **Masjid AlRasool AlAkram,** 9300 South Course Drive
26. **Nathdwara Hindu Temple, Shri Vallabh Priiti Seva Samaj,** 11715 Bellfort Village Drive
27. **Raindrop Turkish House,** 9301 W. Bellfort Boulevard
28. **India House O. P. Jindal Community Center,** 8888 West Bellfort Avenue
29. **Jenard Gross Elementary School,** 12583 S. Gessner Road
30. **Congregation Beth Messiah Synagogue,** 9001 West Airport Boulevard
31. **International Buddhist Progress Society,** 12606 Jebbia Lane, Stafford
32. **Stafford Centre,** 10505 Cash Road, Stafford
33. **Century Oaks Business Park,** 10601–10631 S. Sam Houston Parkway W. S
34. **Missouri City Branch, Fort Bend County Library,** 1530 Texas Parkway
35. **Robinson House,** 3033 Hampton Drive
36. **BAPS Shree Swaminarayan Mandir,** 1150 Brand Lane, Stafford
37. **Texas Instruments,** 12201 Southwest Freeway

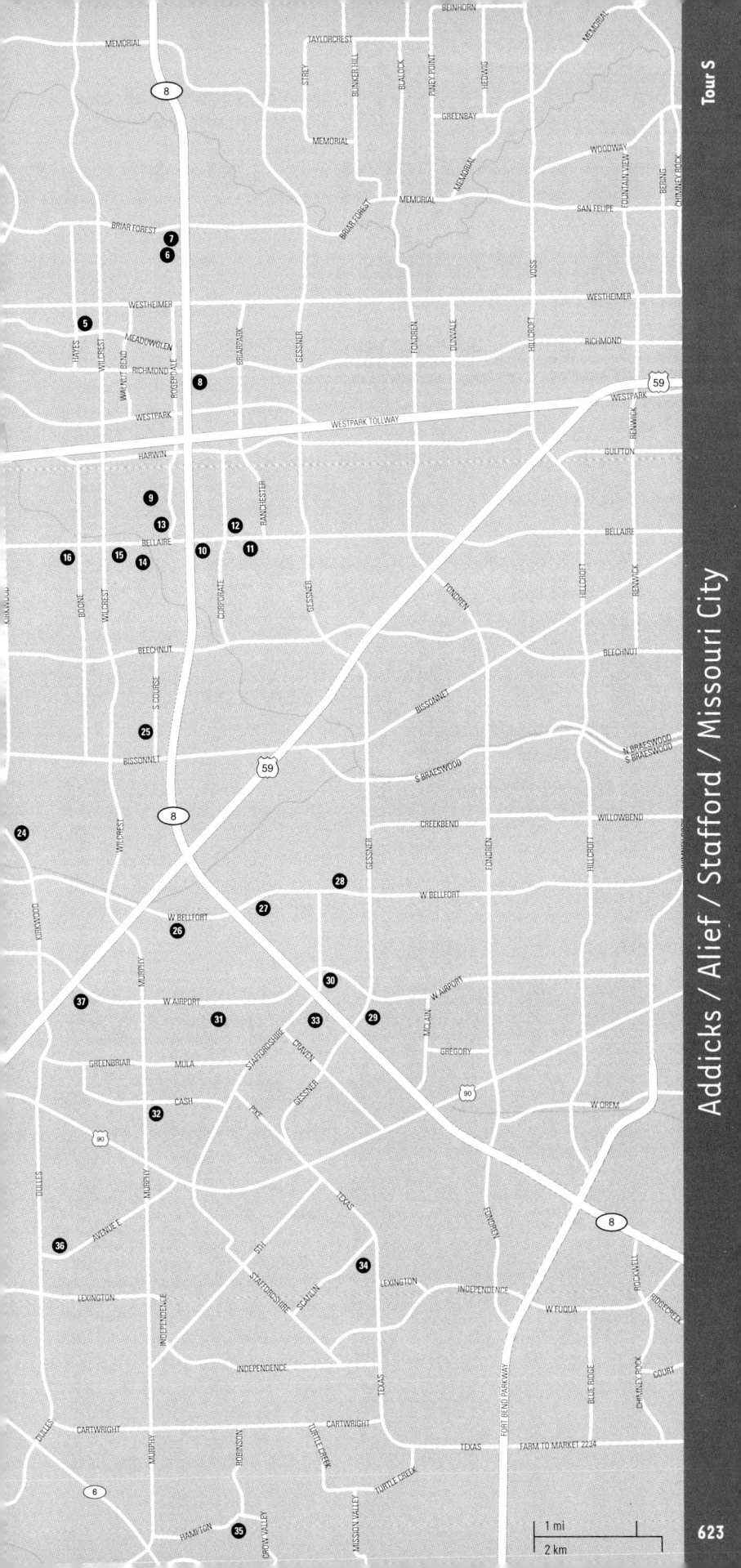

S-1 Belle Sherman Kendall Neighborhood Library and Community Center

S-2 Cardinal Health Care Building

S-3 Sysco Corporate Headquarters

S-4 Schlumberger Building

S-5 Chevron Geosciences Building

S-1
Belle Sherman Kendall Neighborhood Library and Community Center
609 N. Eldridge Parkway
2009, English + Associates Architects

The Houston Public Library and the City of Houston Parks and Recreation Department constructed this joint-use building adjacent to Terry Hershey Park, a linear green space that follows the course of Buffalo Bayou. Designed to achieve LEED certification, the building is faced with polished concrete block and a horizontally striped rainscreen. Landscape architects Asakura Robinson installed native grasses instead of a lawn and underlaid the parking lot with a water retention system that turns runoff into irrigation.

S-2
Cardinal Health Care Building
1330 Enclave Parkway
1999

Enclave Business Park is a 100-acre office park developed in a bend of Buffalo Bayou. This 4-story office building faces north toward a curve in the parkway, overlooking its front lawn with a startlingly transparent glass curtain wall.

S-3
Sysco Corporate Headquarters
1370 and 1390 Enclave Parkway
2008, Hellmuth, Obata + Kassabaum and Kendall/Heaton Associates

Hellmuth, Obata + Kassabaum designed this pair of glass-faced office slabs as headquarters for Sysco, a foodservice distribution corporation. Glazing patterns vary according to orientation, with vertical fins on the north and horizontal trays on the south contrasting with the flat profile of east-facing surfaces. Clark Condon was the landscape architect. Sysco contributes to the ambiance of the Enclave, an island of designed tranquility in the raucousness of west Houston.

S-4
Schlumberger Building
1325 South Dairy Ashford Road
1983

This 5-story office building, stepped in plan at each end, is faced with concrete spandrel panels whose depths vary depending on solar orientation as they step out in front of a glass curtain wall. At 1685 S. Dairy Ashford the Smaller Scholars Montessori School by W. O. Neuhaus Associates (1996).

S-5
Chevron Geosciences Building
[now Houston Community College Alief Campus]
2811 Hayes Road
1983, Caudill Rowlett Scott
2007, HarrisonKornberg Architects

The design of this corporate office and research complex reflects specific programmatic requirements, so that it differs considerably from the surrounding speculative office buildings. An angular geometry reconciles the office slab with a large rear block. The two are connected with a high, glazed circulation spine directly accessible from a porte cochère inserted beneath the office slab with much structural ado. A facing of horizontal bands of precast concrete in different finishes introduces color, texture, and relief into the land of reflective glass. HarrisonKornberg transformed the building into the Alief campus of Houston Community College after HCC acquired the property in 2006.

S-6
BMC Software Corporate Headquarters
2101 CityWest Boulevard
1993, Keating Mann Jernigan Rottet and Ziegler Cooper

Symbolizing the impact that computer and software production had on Houston's economy in the 1980s and '90s, this sleek 20-story office building for BMC Software was the first of a sequence of office buildings and conscientiously designed parking garages, all by Los Angeles architect Richard Keating. Phase two, a 9-story office building (1995); phase three, a visitor and conference center (1997); and phase four, a 21-story office building (2001), were designed by DMJM Keating. BMC joined the 25-story ParkWest Tower at 2500 CityWest and Westheimer (1983, Sikes Jennings Kelly) in the 83-acre CityWest Place office park.

S-6 BMC Software Corporate Headquarters

S-7 One BriarLake Plaza

S-8 Enserch Tower

S-11 Texas First National Bank Building

S-12 Dynasty Plaza

S-7
One BriarLake Plaza
2000 West Sam Houston Parkway South
2000, Kirksey

Just north of the BMC complex, the 20-story BriarLake Plaza office building juxtaposes a glass curtain wall of various finishes with the building's expressed structural frame.

S-8
Enserch Tower
[now Millennium Tower]
10375 Richmond Avenue
1982, Lloyd Jones Brewer & Associates

Sam Houston Parkway splits in two the 1,347-acre Westchase complex, a mixed-use development begun in 1975 by Westchase Company and Tenneco Realty on what was then the western edge of Houston. The broad, flat tract is now dotted with gleaming midrise office buildings, condominium apartment complexes, two large hotels, and a big, clumsily picturesque shopping center, Carillon West (1976, Charles Lanclos) at 10001 Westheimer. Westchase illustrates the standards for ambitious commercial real estate developments that prevailed in Houston in the mid-1970s: strict development and building controls exercised through deed restrictions, comprehensive improvements and landscaping, and provisions for mixed use. The most visually striking of the buildings along Richmond, the principal office corridor in Westchase, is the 21-story Enserch Tower, a compilation of gray solar glass and flashing stainless steel stripes that Lloyd Jones Brewer's designer, Robert Fillpot, sent over the top with a giant, rolled soffit. Enserch's high profile, reflective finishes, and flamboyant composition are attributes shared by other office buildings along Richmond and Wilcrest.

S-9
ImageNet Houston
6050 North Course Drive
2007, Elliott + Associates

Located in Town Park at Rogerdale, an office park along the west side of the Sam Houston Parkway, this 1-story office and warehouse building is constructed of concrete tilt-wall panels. Oklahoma City architect Rand Elliott used the simplicity of this constructional system to emphasize phenomenal experience—shadow patterns, controlled views, degrees of translucence—to invest the building with perceptual depth. Blue glass panels externalize interior divisions.

S-10
Texas First National Bank Building
9999 Bellaire Boulevard
2007, EDI

The tallest peak in Chinatown is the 12-story Texas First National Bank, a bowed glazed tower that rises out of a precast concrete-clad base. The tiered glass bays facing west terminate the vista along Bellaire. The stretch of Bellaire from the west edge of Sharpstown to the Sam Houston Parkway began to emerge as "new" Chinatown in the 1990s, superseding a tiny Chinatown on the east edge of downtown and a concentration of Asian-owned businesses clustered in Midtown dating from the 1980s. Here the Old World mainstreams with undisguised enthusiasm into the new world of suburban Houston.

S-11
Texas First National Bank Building
[now Golden Bank]
9315 Bellaire Boulevard
1995, STOA International

The Texas First National Bank's previous headquarters is a low, glass-faced office building that discreetly juxtaposes elements of Chinese identity with an architectural assertion of technological modernity.

S-12
Dynasty Plaza
9600 Bellaire Boulevard
1986, Ray Bailey Architects

The Dynasty Plaza shopping center was one of the first outposts of Chinese business in the west Bellaire corridor.

S-10 Texas First National Bank

S-9 ImageNet Houston

S-13 Brown & Root Southwest Houston Office Building

S-14 Texas Teo Chew Temple

S-15 Saigon Houston Plaza

S-16 Hong Kong City Mall

S-13
Brown & Root Southwest Houston Office Building
[now Halliburton]
10200 Bellaire Boulevard
1980, S. I. Morris Associates

Brown & Root, Houston's largest engineering and heavy construction company, selected as a site for this expansive, 3-story office building a large tract along the Sam Houston Parkway, almost midway between Katy Freeway and the Southwest Freeway, 13 miles southwest of its headquarters near downtown Houston. Accessibility by white-collar employees sent Brown & Root, as it has so many other large corporate employers in Houston, to a new kind of exurban settlement where the concept of center has been superseded by the desire for individual, personal connection, with the landscape rearranged accordingly. That the parkway was not completed until eight years after the Brown & Root Building opened merely served to confirm the corporation's prescience. By the time they are finally built, public infrastructure improvements in Houston have already generated the sorts of uses that they were projected to serve. Eugene Aubry provided Brown & Root with a low-rise building configured in plan like a bow tie, with cylindrical service and circulation stacks lined up along its north and south faces. The central arced opening indicates the location of a skylit, vertical spine that cuts through the center of the building. As an image Brown & Root is compelling, especially because of the way its light-colored, horizontal mass seems to ride the undulating berms installed by Charles Tapley Associates, the landscape architect. Halliburton, which divested itself of Brown & Root in 2006, added a front building facing Bellaire that now obscures the Morris building.

S-14
Texas Teo Chew Temple
10600 Turtlewood
1996, STOA International

Nothing symbolizes the extraordinary rise to prominence of Chinese and Vietnamese Houstonians in the 1980s and '90s as dramatically as this Chinese and Vietnamese Confucian temple. It is an open-air pavilion, capped by a tiered, orange tile roof. Its concession to Houston is a big parking lot. The complex backs up to Brays Bayou.

S-15
Saigon Houston Plaza
10613 Bellaire Boulevard
2005, 2007, TKYL and
Mitchell Carlson Stone

East of the Sam Houston Parkway lies Chinatown; west of the parkway on Bellaire lies an amazing retail strip identified by its Vietnamese-owned businesses. Saigon Houston Plaza is one of the architectural anchors. Its three building blocks frame a central parking lot, focused on an axial entrance drive lined with palm trees. The architectural theme is Vietnamese Palladian.

S-16
Hong Kong City Mall
11201-11215 Bellaire Boulevard
1999

Built by Vietnamese investor Hai Du Duong, the Hong Kong City Mall set the standard for subsequent ambitious retail development in the Bellaire Asian retail corridor. Landscape amenities in the parking lot and liberal use of green reflective glass give the complex a distinctive presence.

S-17
Chong Hua Sheng Mu Gong Holy Palace
3695 Overture Drive
2002, Cho Design Force
and Cisneros Design Studio

Built for a Taoist sect headquartered in Hong Kong, this was to have been the first of a large complex of buildings occupying the flat, open site. The building's dramatic, stair-step section, cradling a gold anodized aluminum geodesic globe, 4 stories in diameter, imbues it with a science fiction aspect in the midst of a partially developed multi-family housing community dating from the early 1980s.

S-17 Chong Hua Sheng Mu Gong Holy Palace

S-18 Jade Buddah Temple

S-18
Jade Buddah Temple
6969 Westbranch
1988, David Tan

A tank, thick with aquatic plants, civilizes the front parking lot and gives this Taiwanese Buddhist temple an authoritative presence.

S-19 Apple Dentists Headquarters

S-19
Apple Dentists Headquarters
13194 Bellaire Boulevard
2008, Dan Design

This tiered, 4-story, apple green office building, flanked by a lower retail wing to the east, is forceful and bold. It is the work of Vietnamese-trained Houston architect Doanh Hoang.

S-20 Killough Middle School

S-20
Killough Middle School
7600 Synott Road
1977, McKittrick Drennan Richardson Wallace

During the 1970s, McKittrick Drennan Richardson Wallace of Houston designed multiple schools for the Alief Independent School District and other Houston area school districts. Killough Middle School stands out for its crisp lines, generous proportions, and cast-in-place concrete construction.

S-21 Vietnamese Buddhist Center

S-21
Vietnamese Buddhist Center
10002 Synott Road
1991, 1995

Dominated by a 72-foot tall standing figure of Guanyin, bodhisattva of compassion, this Vietnamese worship center, set in a bend of Keegan's Bayou, was established by disciples of the Venerable Thich Nguyen Hahn. Buildings are focused on landscaped exterior spaces.

S-22
Sri Saumyakasi Siva Temple of Houston, Chinmaya Prabha
10353 Synott Road
2007, Mahendra Viashnav

Houston architect Mahendra Vaishnav designed this Hindu temple, dedicated to Shiva, as a modern, glass-walled, octagonal pavilion, raised a full story above grade within the symmetrically organized temple compound. The polished black cupola arising on axis above the temple is the lingam, the symbol of Shiva. Next door, at 10415 Synott Road, is the Islamic Society of Greater Houston's Synott Masjid.

S-23
Aquinas Hall, St. Thomas Aquinas Catholic Church
12627 West Bellfort Avenue
1982, Charles Tapley Associates

This parish hall and office complex, the first increment of St. Thomas Aquinas center, is a strong figural and spatial presence in the landscape. Tapley and his associate, Gerald Moorhead, used boldly scaled alternating bands of red and buff brick to give the small building visual impact. Its shallow, concave south front, which peaks at the center, seems to be informed spatially by the panoramic vista that it faces across the treeless coastal plain. This face, behind the building's street front, bounds one side of a garden atrium.

S-24
Robert D. Cummings Elementary School
10455 South Kirkwood Drive
1984, MRW Architects

This handsomely detailed elementary school, faced with ribbed concrete block and bright blue banding, was designed to use daylight rather than shut it out. Thus the monitors, which MRW pulled out at intervals and expressed as volumetric extrusions in order to articulate the spatial organization of the building.

S-22 Sri Saumyakasi Siva Temple of Houston, Chinmaya Prabha

S-22 Aquinas Hall, St. Thomas Aquinas Catholic Church

S-24 Robert D. Cummings Elementary School

S-25 Masjid AlRasool AlAkram

S-26 Nathdwara Hindu Temple,
Shri Vallabh Priiti Seva Samaj

S-27 Raindrop Turkish House

S-28 India House O.P. Jindal Community Center

S-29 Jenard M. Gross Elementary School

S-30 Congregation Beth Messiah Synagogue

S-25
Masjid AlRasool AlAkram
9300 South Course Drive
2005

The predilection of suburban Asian religious congregations for Houston distribution centers is borne out by the Masjid AlRasool AlAkram, the first Shia mosque built in the United States. The slender minarets and the tapered dome rise amid big box warehouses.

S-26
Nathdwara Hindu Temple, Shri Vallabh Priiti Seva Samaj
11715 Bellfort Village Drive
2005, Llewelyn Davies Sahni

Much of the commercial real estate in this corner of Houston, where it bumps up against Stafford and where the Sam Houston Parkway and the Southwest Freeway intersect, consists of business parks of flex buildings, distribution centers, and parking lots. Hemmed in by one such cluster is the Villages of Bellfort, which was intended to be a subdivision of apartments. Instead it was built out as a subdivision of Asian religious institutions, of which the Nathdwara Hindu Temple by Houston architect Randhir Sahni is the most architecturally distinctive. Instead of employing folkloric imagery, Sahni produced a complex of modern buildings that reference, without exoticizing, Hindu identity. At 11935 Bellfort Village Drive is Our Lady of the Cedars Maronite Catholic Church (2003, Shawn Kashou).

S-27
Raindrop Turkish House
9301 W. Bellfort Boulevard
2008, 2011

Raindrop Turkish House is a foundation promoting Turkish culture in the U.S. and sponsoring events of interest to Turkish immigrants and Turkish-Americans. Its buildings, the Turquoise Center (2008) and the Istanbul Convention and Exhibition Center (2011), present

Turkish culture as an exotic pastiche of Ottoman historical images rather than in terms of contemporary Turkish architecture.

S-28
India House O. P. Jindal Community Center
8888 W. Bellfort Avenue
2009, RdlR Architects

Rey de la Reza avoided folkloric clichés in the design of this community and cultural center oriented to Houston's Indian expatriate and Indian-American communities.

S-29
Jenard M. Gross Elementary School
12583 S. Gessner Road
2001, PDG Architects

PDG revamped and added to the ex-Emory Weiner School, which they transformed from a private school into an elementary school for the Houston Independent School District. Strong color and striking shapes cause the complex to figure strongly in its suburban setting.

S-30
Congregation Beth Messiah Synagogue
9001 W. Airport Boulevard
2004, Cisneros Design Studio

For a Jewish-Christian fusion congregation, Tim Cisneros incorporated mildly exotic architectural references into this economical institutional complex.

S-31
International Buddhist Progress Society
12550 and 12551 Jebbia Lane
2001; 2004, Ray+Hollington

The city of Stafford has attracted the worship centers of many Asian religious traditions. One of the most expansive is the International Buddhist Progress Society's complex, straddling property on Jebbia Lane that still seems to be in transition from country to suburbia. The gabled and hipped roofs of the temple (12550) and columbarium (12551), both clad with orange tile, appear to float above the flat, green, ground plane on which each is set.

S-31 International Buddhist Progress Society

S-32 Stafford Centre

S-33 Century Oaks Business Park

S-34 Fort Bend County Library, Missouri City Branch

S-37 Texas Instruments Building

S-32
Stafford Centre
10505 Cash Road
2004, Gensler

Receding planes of red brick and glass cause the city of Stafford's municipal auditorium, its one major work of civic architecture, to stand out when seen across the broad grass lawn that fronts it. The Office of James Burnett was the landscape architect. At 10041 Cash Road is the Stafford campus of Houston Community College Southwest (2011, Hermes Architects and Llewelyn Davies Sahni).

S-33
Century Oaks Business Park
10601-10631 S. Sam Houston Parkway W.
2004, Powers Brown Architecture

Trammell Crow Company's Century Oaks Business Park represents a building type pervasive in Houston's suburban commercial real estate landscape, the "flex" building available for use as office, warehouse, or assembly space, here tied to the Sam Houston Parkway.

S-34
Fort Bend County Library, Missouri City Branch
1530 Texas Parkway
1992, Hall/Merriman Architects

Missouri City shares with its neighbor, Stafford, the problem of not having a strong municipal identity. This branch library sets out to correct that deficiency at a modest scale with a low, 1-story building that encompasses the landscape and a driveway in Missouri City's public sector complex.

S-35
Robinson Desert House
3033 Hampton Drive
1959, William F. Cody & Associates
with Hightower & Moreland

Houston physician Hampton Robinson built this expansive 1-story house as a weekend retreat on what had once been his family's plantation in northeast Fort Bend County. He retained Palm Springs architect William F. Cody to produce what the *Houston Post* described as a "desert villa," combining the space planning of Richard Neutra and the materiality of Frank Lloyd Wright. As Ben Koush noted in writing about the house, it embraces its flat site spatially, using architecture to poeticize the experience of being on the coastal plain. The site is now surrounded by the golf course of the Quail Valley Country Club and is not visible from a public road.
* Not pictured.

S-36
BAPS Shree Swaminarayan Mandir
1150 Brand Lane
2004

Raised on a marble plinth, this temple for a Gujarat-based Hindu sect is completely open air. Italian marble and Turkish limestone were employed to build the load-bearing stone pavilion; the decorative carving was executed by teams of stonecutters brought from India. Outbuildings continue to be erected to complete the enclosure. Asakura Robinson was the landscape architect.

S-37
Texas Instruments Building
12201 Southwest Freeway
1968, Ford, Powell & Carson
and Richard S. Colley

Although San Antonio architect O'Neil Ford and Corpus Christi architect Richard S. Colley initiated their 25-year-long sequence of production plants for Texas Instruments with the Houston Technical Laboratories on Richmond (1957; demolished), it was with their semiconductor plant for the company in the Dallas suburb of Richardson that they established the architectural vocabulary that Colley reproduced in many of the subsequent plants. The characteristic attributes visible here at TI's complex in Stafford are gray Georgia marble panels (revetted with exposed clips) and pink Mexican brick as facing materials on the south, facing the freeway, and the expression of the servicing stacks, alternating with panels of bronze solar glass, on the side facing Airport Boulevard, all capped by a flat-lidded concrete roof. Colley's tectonic assembly of materials and straightforward ordering of elements give this large manufacturing plant the quiet refinement of a corporate office building.

S-36 BAPS Shree Swaminarayan Mandir

Sugar Land / First Colony

Sugar Land / First Colony

Tour T

Sugar Land began as a slave plantation established in 1838, which became an early 20th-century rural-industrial company town and, in the last quarter of the 20th century, a planned suburban city whose development was financed by global investment capital. This sequence of disjunctive transformations is only dimly perceptible in the landscape, as each succeeding episode tended to efface what preceded it. The company town that succeeded the plantation is today "old" Sugar Land along US Highway 90-A, between Eldridge Road and Ulrich Street. It was developed by W. T. Eldridge, co-founder and managing partner of the Imperial Sugar Company, beginning in the first decade of the 20th century to house the families of workers employed in the company's sugar refinery, one of the largest in the U.S. Supplying sugar cane to the refinery were nearby state-owned prison farms, occupying what before the Civil War had been slave plantations. Local sugar cane cultivation ceased in 1928 when Imperial Sugar began to process imported raw sugar instead. In the 1950s the company began to dispose of its extensive real estate holdings, including all property in the Sugar Land town site, which was incorporated as a city in 1959. The extension of the Southwest Freeway (US 59) from Houston into

Fort Bend County in the 1970s accelerated the scale and intensity of real estate development. In 1976 Imperial Sugar sold 9,700 acres of its former cane fields to Gerald D. Hines Interests and the Royal Dutch/Shell Pension Fund, on which they developed the planned community of First Colony, opened in 1978. The city of Sugar Land incrementally annexed First Colony during the decade of the 1990s and, in so doing, nearly tripled the city's population by 2000. In the 21st century, Sugar Land (now primarily First Colony and such other planned communities as New Territory and Telfair, developed on what had been the state prison system's plantations) emerged as the third largest city in the Houston metropolitan region, with a population of just under 80,000. Old Sugar Land is an uneasy combination of early 20th-century workers' housing, scattered 1950s' subdivisions, and a few Imperial Sugar Company structures that survived demolition of the refinery site after the company went bankrupt in 2001. New Sugar Land is the architecturally coordinated First Colony. As in Kingwood and The Woodlands, master planning imbues First Colony with a reassuring sense of ordinariness unmarred by the rude disjunctions of unzoned Houston. The "Sugar Land style" of First Colony's red brick strip malls, banded with precast concrete, reappears not only throughout the Houston region but in other parts of Texas also as a symbol of enlightened development practices.

1. **Casa de Mañana,** 806 Lakeview Drive
2. **Sugar Land School Auditorium,** 300 Lakeview Drive
3. **St. Theresa Catholic Church Education and Office Building,** 705 St. Theresa Boulevard
4. **Imperial Sugar Company Char Filter House,** 198 Kempner Street
5. **Texas Department of Criminal Justice Central State Farm Main Building,** 1 Circle Drive
6. **Houston Museum of Natural Science at Sugar Land,** 13016 University Boulevard
7. **University of Houston/Wharton County Junior College at Sugar Land,** 14000 University Boulevard
8. **University Branch, Fort Bend County Library,** 14010 University Boulevard
9. **Williams Trace Baptist Church,** 16755 Southwest Freeway
10. **Methodist Hospital Sugar Land,** 16655 Southwest Freeway
11. **First Colony Church of Christ,** 2140 First Colony Boulevard
12. **Ismaili Jamatkhana and Center,** 1700 First Colony Boulevard
13. **St. Luke's Health System Hospital and Sugar Land Medical Plaza,** 1317 Lake Pointe Parkway
14. **One SugarLand Office Park,** 15200 Southwest Freeway
15. **First Colony Commons,** 15375 Southwest Freeway
16. **Fort Bend Independent School District Athletic Complex,** 16403 Lexington Boulevard
17. **First Colony Branch, Fort Bend County Library,** 2121 Austin Parkway
18. **Sweetwater Country Club,** 4400 Palm Royale Boulevard
19. **First Colony Mall,** 16535 Southwest Freeway
20. **Sugar Land City Hall,** 2700 Town Center Boulevard
21. **Sugar Land Marriott Town Square,** 16090 City Walk
22. **Minute Maid Building,** 2150 Town Square
23. **Unocal Building,** 14141 Southwest Freeway
24. **House,** 9 Regent Court
25. **Southern National Bank Building,** 14060 Southwest Freeway
26. **Museum of Southern History,** 14080 Southwest Freeway
27. **Southern National Bank Corporation Headquarters,** 80 Sugar Creek Center Boulevard

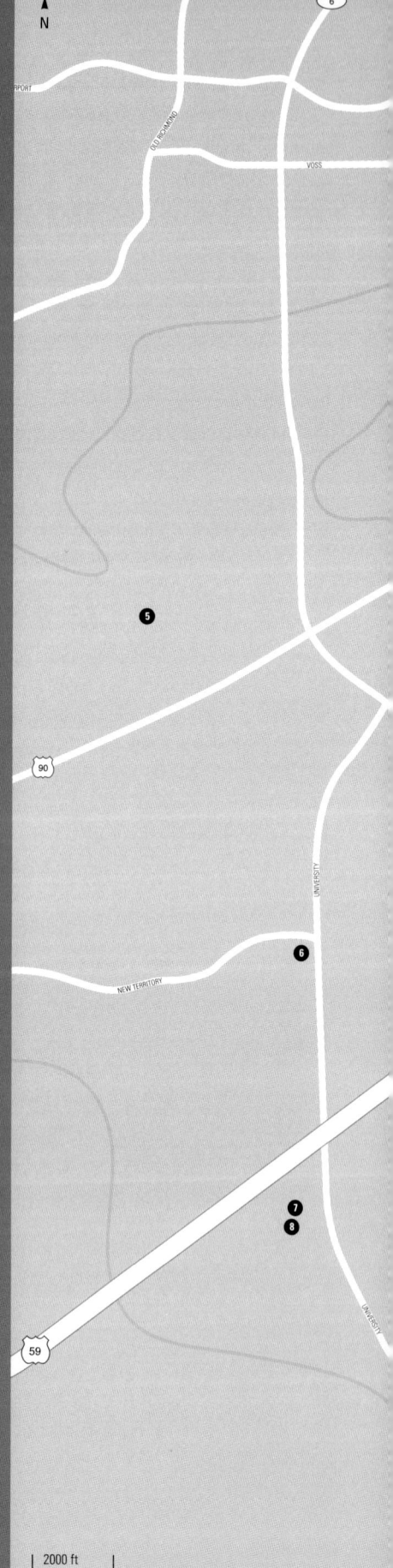

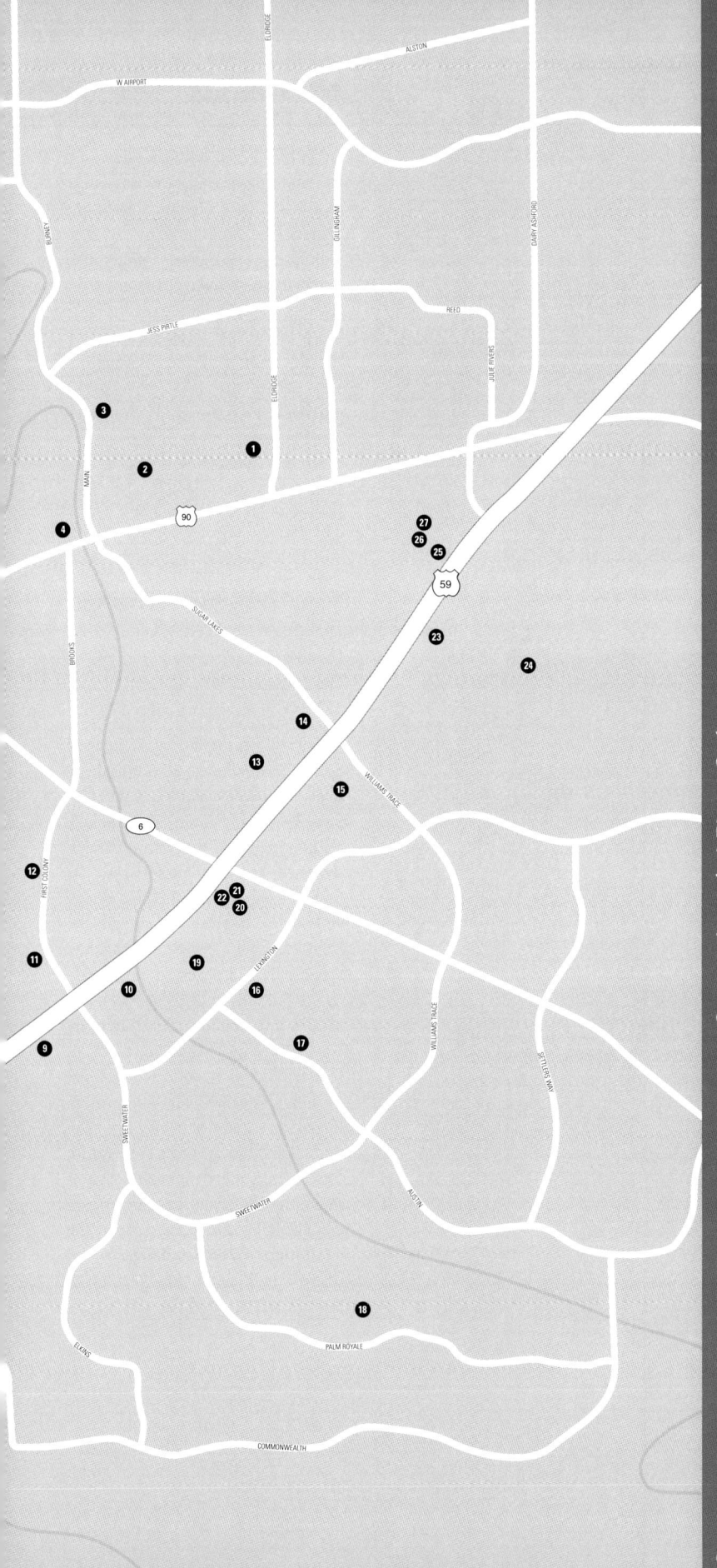

T-1 Casa de Mañana

T-2 Sugar Land School Auditorium

T-3 St. Theresa Catholic Church, Education, and Office Buildings

T-4 Imperial Sugar Company Char Filter House

T-1
Casa de Mañana
806 Lakeview Drive
1928, William Ward Watkin

W. T. Eldridge, for whom this house was built, was a cofounder of the Imperial Sugar Company, a subsidiary of Sugarland Industries, which wholly owned the town of Sugar Land. Eldridge built the only large house in his company town, a true country house, although it now sits in the midst of suburbia. Watkin's stucco-faced, tile-roofed Mediterranean style design is an expanded version of his Cohen House on the campus of Rice University.

T-2
Sugar Land School Auditorium
[now Sugar Land Cultural Arts Foundation Lakeview Auditorium]
300 Lakeview Drive
1918, M. R. Wood, engineer

Because Sugar Land was Imperial Sugar's company town, it subsidized construction of a public school complex for white children in the neighborhood north of the railroad tracks, where the company built housing for its white employees. M. R. Wood, the company's engineer, designed the school complex based on bungalow schools he had observed on a study trip to California. The 500-seat auditorium and administration building was flanked by 10 (no longer extant) freestanding classroom blocks, five to either side of the auditorium, linked by canopied walkways. The Sugar Land Cultural Arts Foundation raised funds for the rehabilitation of the auditorium and manages it as a civic theater and event space. The auditorium was rehabilitated in two phases by Houston architect Mark Stewart (2004, 2011).

T-3
St. Theresa Catholic Church, Education, and Office Buildings
705 St. Theresa Boulevard
2009, Duncan G. Stroik

Tucked into the old factory neighborhood is the sprawling complex of St. Theresa Catholic Church. The pastor, Fr. Stephen Reynolds, retained Notre Dame, Indiana-based classical architect Duncan Stroik to design a 2-story addition to the parish school as part of an ambitious master plan that would lead to construction of a new church in the parking lot across from the education building. Classical details distinguish what is otherwise a typical institutional building.

T-4
Imperial Sugar Company Char Filter House
198 Kempner Street
1926, Dwight P. Robinson & Company

Sugar cane was first grown in the fertile Brazos River lowlands of Fort Bend County in the 1820s and producing sugar plantations had been established along Oyster Creek by the time of the Texas Revolution in 1836. From the 1890s through the 1910s, Sugar Land (the name dates from the 1850s) was the center of the Texas "sugar bowl," its fields worked by convict labor contracted from the State of Texas. In 1908 the largest producer was bought out by W. T. Eldridge and the Galveston investor I. H. Kempner, who formed Sugarland Industries and began the Imperial Sugar Company in the 1920s. The Char Filter House was built to refine West Indian sugar, after cane ceased to be grown locally. The town of Sugar Land was developed on company property to the north of the refinery and it was not until the late 1940s that Sugarland Industries began to sell real estate to residents of the town. Since the late 1950s Sugarland Industries has sold its former fields for transformation into the bedroom suburbs of Houston, including the 1,000-acre Sugar Creek and First Colony. The Imperial Sugar Company merged with another corporation in 1988, expanded rapidly in the 1990s, declared bankruptcy in 2001, and closed the refinery in 2002. The Char Filter House is one of the few refinery buildings to escape demolition. It will be preserved as part of Imperial, a redevelopment of the 165-acre refinery site by the Johnson Development Corp. of Houston.

T-5
Texas Department of Criminal Justice Central State Farm Main Building
1 Circle Drive
1930, Giesecke & Harris

The white-painted, tiered main building of this prison farm was designed by Austin architects Giesecke & Harris as part of a reformation of state prison facilities. In 1895 the State of Texas opened the first of its prison farms in the Brazos River valley. These supplied sugar planters in Fort Bend and Brazoria counties with convict labor. The abuses that resulted led the state to end convict leasing in 1910. Instead convicts were put to work in the state's own sugar cane fields to pay for their incarceration. In 1985 the Texas Department of Criminal Justice began to sell its properties in Fort Bend County for suburban redevelopment. In 2011 the department announced that the last remnant of the Central Farm, containing the Central Building, would be closed and sold.

T-6 Texas Department of Criminal Justice Central State Farm Two Camp

T-7 University of Houston / Wharton County Junior College Academic Building

T-8 University Branch, Fort Bend County Library

T-9 Williams Trace Baptist Church

T-10 Methodist Hospital Sugar Land

T-6
Texas Department of Criminal Justice Central State Farm Two Camp
[now Houston Museum of Natural Science at Sugar Land]
13106 University Boulevard
1930, Giesecke & Harris;
2011, Gensler

The ominous looking, red brick Two Camp was built to house African-American prisoners. Now surrounded by the planned community of Telfair, the barn-like structure has been recycled by Gensler as the Sugar Land branch of the Houston Museum of Natural Science.

T-7
University of Houston / Wharton County Junior College Academic Building
14000 University Boulevard
2009, Archi*Technics and PageSoutherlandPage

This 3-story academic building is a collage of right-angled and splayed planes and visually overlapping fields of brick. It joins Albert and Mamie George Hall (2002, B2HK) on the suburban campus shared by Wharton County Junior College and the University of Houston. Built in what is now the planned community of Telfair, this flat plain on the northeast bank of the Brazos River was formerly part of the prison's fields.

T-8
University Branch, Fort Bend County Library
14010 University Boulevard
2011, Bailey Architects

The county public library is also the university library. Bailey Architects treated the building as a lively array of shapes clad in brick or metal siding that reflect internal program variations.

T-9
Williams Trace Baptist Church
[now Sugar Land Baptist Church]
16755 Southwest Freeway

Facing the frontage road of the Southwest Freeway, the Sugar Land Baptist Church is in the official First Colony style of light red brick with light colored trim. The pentagonal church and the adjacent educational building are designed in an impressionistic mixture of traditional and contemporary themes meant to make it identifiable as a church.

T-10
Methodist Hospital Sugar Land
16655 Southwest Freeway
1998; 2008, Hellmuth, Obata + Kassabaum

Houston's major hospitals sought to maintain a profitable client base by aggressively building medical complexes in peripheral communities in the 1990s and 2000s. Methodist Hospital's cluster of buildings uses postmodern devices (framed glazed center bays) and a modern interpretation of the Sugar Land style to stand out alongside the Southwest Freeway.

T-11
First Colony Church of Christ
2140 First Colony Boulevard
2009, Turner Durán

It's the tall, slender, banded brick bell tower that identifies this bulky complex as a church.

T-12
Ismaili Jamatkhana and Center
1700 First Colony Boulevard
2002, Arcop Group

Departing from the ways that other institutions architecturally advertise their presence in First Colony, the Ismaili mosque and community center dispenses with declarative architecture. It recedes into its site along a canal and makes a virtue of its suburban setting with gardens, courtyards, and shade structures. Exposed steel members are used to frame panels of patterned brickwork, constructing an allusive dialogue on cultural identity and modernity. The Indian- and German-trained Montréal architect Ramesh Khosla designed the complex.

T-11 First Colony Church of Christ

T-12 Ismaili Jamatkhana and Center

T-13 St. Luke's Health System Hospital and Sugar Land Medical Plaza

T-14 One SugarLand Park Building

T-15 First Colony Commons Shopping Center

T-16 Fort Bend Independent School District Athletic Complex

T-17 Fort Bend County Library, First Colony Branch

T-13
St. Luke's Health System Hospital and Sugar Land Medical Plaza
1317 Lake Pointe Parkway
2008, PageSoutherlandPage

Curvilinear profiles and stacked ribbons of lustrous porcelain enamel panels and dark reflective glass are a welcome respite from the officially sanctioned banded brick Sugar Land style. Dispensation for this departure from the First Colony style code came from the architectural centerpiece of First Colony's office park, the Fluor Houston Operations Center at 1 Fluor Drive (1984, Welton Becket & Associates). This 4-building complex, which ascends in height from one to seven floors, looks like an array of silver icebergs.

T-14
One SugarLand Park Building
15200 Southwest Freeway
1982, Johnson/Burgee Architects
and Richard Fitzgerald & Partners

Only one of a projected cluster of 3-story speculative office buildings designed by Johnson/Burgee for a site on Oyster Creek was built by Hines Interests. Philip Johnson claimed the Feilner House in Berlin by the 19th-century Prussian architect, Karl Friedrich Schinkel, as his historic source for the banded façades of buff and red brick. A companion building at 15300 Southwest Freeway is by Watkins Carter Hamilton (1995).

T-15
First Colony Commons Shopping Center
15375 Southwest Freeway
1992, Hermes Reed Hindman

Because of its size and demographics, First Colony supports an extensive retail economy. The distribution of various kinds of retail trade is accommodated in a hierarchy of shopping center types. Hermes Reed Hindman used a Louis Kahn-like arrangement of shallow arched openings to organize the lines of lease spaces in this community center, which backs up to the Southwest Freeway and Oyster Creek.

T-16
Fort Bend Independent School District Athletic Complex
16403 Lexington Boulevard
1979, Cavitt McKnight Weymouth

First Colony's emergence as the new Sugar Land first became apparent when the public school district, which serves Sugar Land and Missouri City, located its district sports complex here rather than in either of its two towns of origin. Cavitt McKnight Weymouth of Houston inserted the building components of the complex into the landscape by constructing mounds around the field house, which faces Lexington, topographically modulating the unrelenting flatness of Sugar Land. Their crisp, laconic design has aged well amid the too-eager-to-please stylisms of First Colony. Cavitt McKnight Weymouth were also architects of the adjoining Fort Bend Independent School District Administration Building (1985) at 16431 Lexington.

T-17
Fort Bend County Library, First Colony Branch
2121 Austin Parkway
1993, Brooks Association for Architecture and Planning

One reason that houses of worship stand out so forcefully in First Colony and Houston's other planned communities is because these communities lack public institutions and public (as opposed to community-only) spaces that architecturally offset commercial and residential construction. First Colony's public library illustrates the architectural dilemmas public institutions face. It is a relatively small, 1-story building that needs to incorporate a substantial amount of parking. Brooks designer, Mark Stewart, architecturally oriented the library toward Austin Parkway (even though entrance is from the rear-facing parking lot), giving it a simple, dignified appearance. A postmodern, gabled bay centers the building visually.

T-18 Sweetwater Country Club

T-19 First Colony Mall

T-20 Sugar Land City Hall

T-21 Sugar Land Marriott Town Square

T-22 Minute Maid Building

T-18
Sweetwater Country Club
4400 Palm Royale Boulevard
1983, MLTW/Turnbull Associates, Charles Moore, and Richard Fitzgerald & Partners

The architectural crown jewel of First Colony in its early days was Charles Moore and William Turnbull's country club, a pyramidally roofed, brick-faced mass sculpturally eroded by (what else?) the driveway entrance to the building. Raised on an artificial mound, the clubhouse is a relaxed, expansive, and benign presence. Beginning in the early 2000s, the clubhouse was challenged for visual dominance by an amazing array of a type of Houston house that the *Houston Chronicle* columnist, Maxine Mesinger, first identified in the 1960s—the "swankienda"—built along Palm Royale Boulevard. These 10,000+-SF Mediterranean extravaganzas bear the same relation to architecture that drag show queens bear to women: not the real thing, perhaps, but entertaining nonetheless in their bold and hilarious voluptuousness.

T-19
First Colony Mall
16535 Southwest Freeway
1996, RTKL

Handsome, dignified, light-filled interior passages originally marked the First Colony Mall. Subsequent expansion has diluted its initial architectural clarity.

T-20
Sugar Land City Hall
2700 Town Center Boulevard
2004, PGAL

Business and real estate cycles since World War II have focused especially on suburban development. The associated building type is the enclosed, air-conditioned regional shopping mall, of which First Colony Mall is a classic example. At the turn of the 21st century, though, the mall was declared outdated. Its successor is the "lifestyle center," an open-air collection of retail shops that mixes in entertainment and leisure uses and, here at Town Square, residential and civic uses. As a sign of its demographic triumph over the old company town of Sugar Land, First Colony moved Sugar Land's city government to Town Square and into a purpose-designed City Hall facing a ceremonial plaza focused on Bob Pack's impressionistic bronze statue of Stephen F. Austin on a rearing stallion (more like John Wayne than the deliberate and statesman-like Austin) set in a fountain, with extensive historical narration inscribed in the plaza (Smith Locke Asakura, landscape architects). The 3-story City Hall is a postmodern spin on a neo-Classical public building. However the liberties it takes with Classical architecture are so scandalous that they deprive it of the decorum for which it yearns.

T-21
Sugar Land Marriott Town Square
16090 City Walk
2004, Cooper-Cary

Planned Community Developers, the operational and management affiliate of Sugarland Properties, a joint venture of Hines and the Royal Dutch/Shell Pension Fund, which developed First Colony, planned Town Square to fit into a 32-acre tract facing the Southwest Freeway and bracketed by First Colony Mall to the west, the Market at Town Center power center to the south, and the Creekside at Town Center mixed-use center to the east. With planning assistance from Smith Locke Asakura and architects Ambrose, McEnany & House, PCD envisioned the complex according to New Urbanist principles as a walkable downtown center. The 300-room Marriott and its attached convention center and parking garage (both paid for by the City of Sugar Land as part of a public-private venture), anchor Town Square.

Cooper-Cary's architecture is late postmodern, making the hotel look like it could fit interchangeably into any one of the many lifestyle centers constructed in affluent U.S. suburbs in the 2000s. People-watching at the hotel's corner Starbucks does disclose that Sugar Land's affluent demographic is multi-racial, multi-ethnic, and multi-national.

T-22
Minute Maid Building
2150 Town Square
2009, Ambrose, McEnany & House

Although the postmodern styling of Town Square is scripted to support a narrative of small-town neighborliness and familiarity, the underlying mechanics of its business transactions are thoroughly modern. The City of Sugar Land granted the Minute Maid division of Coca Cola a $2.4 million direct incentive to locate its corporate headquarters in Sugar Land. Publicly subsidized free enterprise complements the neo-Conservative imagery the Town Square projects.

T-23
Unocal Building
[now One Sugar Creek Place]
14141 Southwest Freeway
1982, C. Jackson Wisdom

Wisdom positioned this corporate office building as overlapping slabs that step up from 6 to 8 to 10 stories. External precast concrete spandrels horizontally band the sloping glass curtain wall, creating a high-contrast juxtaposition between the light-toned concrete and the dark glass.

T-23 Unocal Building

T-24 House

T-25 Souther National Bank Building

T-26 Museum of Southern History

T-24
House
9 Regent Court
1984, William R. Jenkins Associates

Built in the community of Sugar Creek, developed in 1968, and now part of Sugar Land, this house, backing onto the Sugar Creek Country Club golf course, is one of the highlights of postmodern residential architecture in the Houston area. Jenkins and his designer, Peter Jay Zweig, project triangular pediments supported on single columns forward of overlapping planes of glass and banded brick.

T-25
Southern National Bank Building
[now Prosperity Bank Sugar Land]
14060 Southwest Freeway
1997, Kirksey Architects

For Stewart Morris, chairman of the Southern National Bank and a connoisseur of Southern history, Kirksey designed the bank's headquarters as Thomas Jefferson's Monticello—with drive-in windows.

T-26
Museum of Southern History
14080 Southwest Freeway
2002, Kirksey

Stewart Morris, a supporter of the Museum of Southern History, retained Kirksey to design the museum building, modeled on Thomas Jefferson's Poplar Forest (1806). To recreate the Virginia house's sloped site, the museum sits on top of an artificial hillock in the parking lot behind the bank.

T-27
Southern National Bank
[now Prosperity Bank El Campo]
80 Sugar Creek Center Boulevard
2005, Kirksey

Adjacent to the bank and the Museum of Southern History is what was to have been the bank's corporate headquarters. Here Kirksey began to reproduce the lawn of Jefferson's University of Virginia (1817). After completion of the first phase, however, the Southern bank corporation was sold to Prosperity Bank, casting doubt on whether the rest of the lawn, including the rotunda, will ever be realized.

T-27 Southern National Bank

South / Southwest Houston

South / Southwest Houston

Tour U

The south/southwest quadrant of Houston is not the upbeat development frontier of West and Northwest Houston or of north Harris County. This landscape, along the highway extension of Main Street (U.S. Highway 90-A), was bypassed by prosperity after the early 1960s as its population shifted from white and middle class to African American and working class. In the 21st century, new development began to occur once again. But south/southwest Houston is still characterized by extensive real estate "voids" between Main Street and the South Sam Houston Parkway that underscore the correlation between uneven development and the racial and economic demography of this sector of Houston. Yet these voids support the perpetuation of traditional lifeways. This is the part of Houston where cattle ranching and cowboys survive, carried on by African-American Houstonians. Toll roads built in the 2000s (the Sam Houston Parkway and the Fort Bend Parkway along the line of Hillcroft) sail over or around this sector, causing the expansion of services to some constituencies, while insulating and isolating others. Architecture correlates with these asymmetries: buildings that stand out are institutional buildings rather than commercial or residential ones.

1. **Nichols House,** 14410 Minetta Street
2. **The Fountain of Praise,** 13950 Hillcroft Avenue
3. **West Orem Family YMCA Building,** 5801 West Orem Drive
4. **Jean Hines Caldwell Elementary School,** 5515 West Orem Drive
5. **Windsor Village United Methodist Church Kingdom Builders Center,** 6011 West Orem Drive
6. **City of Houston Fire Station #59,** 13925 South Post Oak Road
7. **Verges House,** 4421 Simsbrook Drive
8. **House,** 13904 Hiram Clarke Road
9. **William Vinson Branch, Houston Public Library,** 3810 W. Fuqua Street
10. **Minnitex Community Church,** 13233 Cullen Boulevard
11. **Christia V. Adair mural,** 15107 Cullen Boulevard

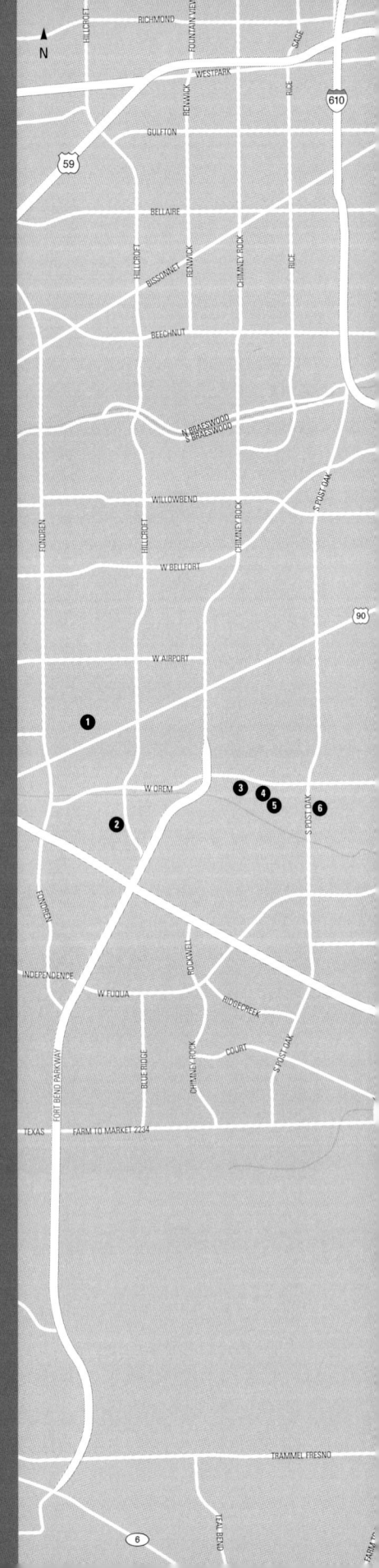

U-1 Nichols House

U-2 The Fountain of Praise

U-3 West Orem Family YMCA Building

U-4 Jean Hines Caldwell Elementary School

U-1
Nichols House
14418 Minetta Street
1934, F. McM. Sawyer

Roy B. Nichols, then postmaster of Houston, developed this subdivision, Main Street Gardens, 12 miles outside Houston on the Main Street highway. Nichols had Sawyer design for him this diminutive, picturesque Mediterranean style house, which is built of reinforced concrete block. *All* components are concrete.

U-2
The Fountain of Praise
13950 Hillcroft Avenue
2003, Morris Architects

Pete Ed Garrett designed the 2,500-seat Fountain of Praise as a performance-like arena inset within the serpentine curved front of the church's freestanding building.

U-3
West Orem Family YMCA Building
5801 W. Orem Drive
2007, Brave/Architecture

Fernando Brave volumetrically expressed the building's program in a series of offset spatial containers that aggregate around the recessed entrance bay.

U-4
Jean Hines Caldwell Elementary School
5515 W. Orem Drive
2005, PBK Architects

The diagonal alignment of classroom blocks and the rotational spin-offs visible in the school's entrance bay seek to compensate with architectural exuberance for evident construction economies.

U-5
Windsor Village United Methodist Church Kingdom Builders Family Life Center
6011 W. Orem Drive
2007, Morris Architects

The Kingdom Builders Family Life Center, a 191,000-SF multi-purpose community center, is part of the community revitalization project launched by the Rev. Kirbyjon Caldwell, a Houstonian who gave up a career in investment banking to become an ordained Methodist minister then, between 1982-2011, transformed the nearly defunct Windsor Village United Methodist Church into the largest United Methodist congregation in the U.S. The church's non-profit Pyramid Community Development Corporation developed the 220-acre Corinthian Pointe subdivision of affordable houses during the late 1990s (R. C. Johnson Architects and Hermes Reed, planners). The western extension of W. Orem created frontage for the subdivision and the array of community institutions (the YMCA and the school) that Rev. Caldwell was able to attract. Still to come is a projected 7,000-seat worship arena, to be built next to the Family Life Center. What this effort lacks is any vision of an architectural alternative to the characteristic Houston suburban landscape of widely spaced, inexpensively built buildings isolated behind surface parking lots and strung out along thoroughfare streets.

U-6
Fire Station No. 59
13925 South Post Oak Road
1968, Todd Tackett Lacy

The precision of Anderson Todd's Miesian detail was brought to bear with authority on this suburban steel, brick, and glass fire station. Street widening has brought Post Oak Road right up to the building's front apron. Just north of the station, at 13855 South Post Oak Road, is Hugo V. Neuhaus's ex-Madison Southern National Bank Building (1970), which is also a steel-framed, brick-faced pavilion.

U-6 Fire Station No. 59

U-5 Windsor Village United Methodist Church Kingdom Builders Family Life Center

U-7 Verges House

U-9 William Vinson Branch, Houston Public Library

U-10 Minnitex Community Church

U-7
Verges House
4421 Simsbrook Drive
1965, Mike G. Verges

A late Usonian house designed by the architect for his family on the banks of Sims Bayou.

U-8
House
13904 Hiram Clarke Road
2008, Environment Associates

Architect Laverne Williams went "green" during the Energy Crisis of the 1970s, and he has been a consistent proponent of environmentally sustainable design during the course of his career. This shed-roofed green house (it really is green) is hidden from the street by thick vegetation.

U-9
William Vinson Branch, Houston Public Library
3810 W. Fuqua Street
1967, Clovis Heimsath Associates

Heimsath and Irving Phillips designed this compact, complexly layered branch library. Superseded by a newer library branch, the building now sits vacant, a relic of times past when public library branches were treated as works of architecture.

U-10
Minnitex Community Church
[now Cullen Baptist Church]
13233 Cullen Boulevard
1965, Travis Broesche & Associates

Built to serve the rural Minnitex community, this modern church still stands out by virtue of its sweeping gabled entrance flanked by a cantilevered porte-cochère to one side and a wafer-thin pylon tower to the other. Extensive additions defer to the small-scaled original.

U-11
Christia V. Adair Mural, Adair Park
15107 Cullen Boulevard
1984, John Biggers, painter

Located in a small pavilion at the far east end of the entrance road to this Harris County park is a concave panel on which Biggers painted a series of layered, architecturally resonant images drawn from the life and work of Christia V. Adair, a Houston civil rights leader who was instrumental in challenging racial segregation beginning in the 1910s.

U-11 Christia V. Adair Mural, Adair Park

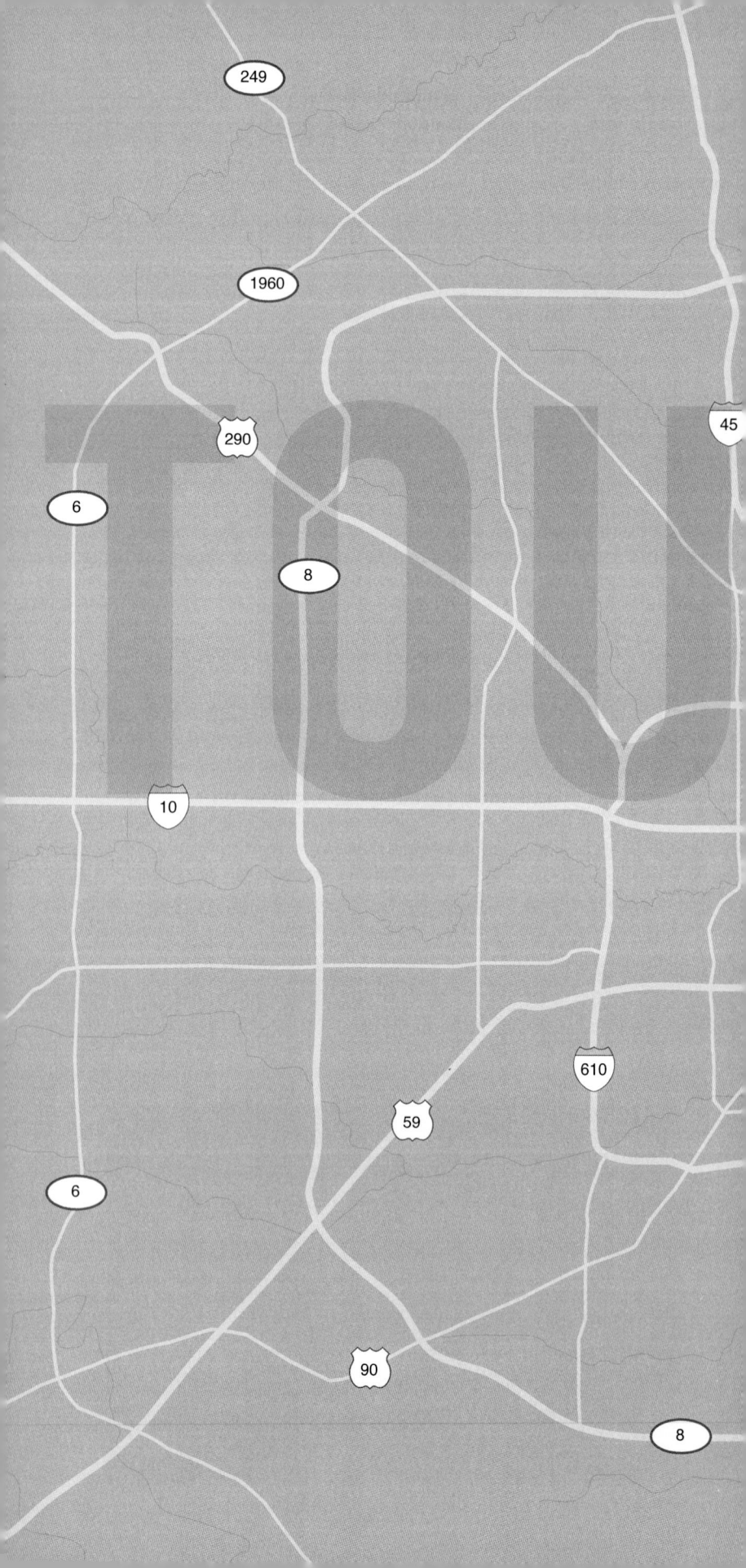

Southeast Houston / Pasadena / Harrisburg

Southeast Houston / Pasadena / Harrisburg

Tour V

Southeast Houston and the adjoining City of Pasadena represent spatial overlays of the 1910s, the 1920s, and the postwar 1940s through early '60s. Suburban development first crept east of Houston along the line of the Galveston, Houston & Henderson Railroad (paralleled by Old Galveston Road, TX Highway 3) and the Galveston-Houston Electric Co.'s high-speed interurban streetcar that commenced in 1911. The streetcar line became the pathway of the Gulf Freeway (I-45), Houston's first freeway, in 1948. Other types of transportation infrastructure affected this sector as well. The U.S. Army Air Service opened Ellington Field in 1917 as a flight training school. Closed in 1920, it was reactivated in 1940 by the U.S. Army Air Corps and continued to operate in various capacities as Ellington Air Force Base until 1984. In 1937 the City of Houston opened the Houston Municipal Airport after it acquired W. T. Carter, Jr.'s 10-year-old private airfield. Today it is the City of Houston's Hobby Airport, with both domestic and international flights as well as facilities for private airplanes.

The 52-mile-long Houston Ship Channel opened in 1914 after Buffalo Bayou was dredged for deep-draft vessels, not only turned Houston into an inland seaport, but also it was a critical factor in the location of oil refineries beginning in the 1910s. During World War II an entire new industry based on the refining and distribution of petrochemicals was developed along the Houston Ship Channel. The construction of the National Aeronautics and Space Administration's Manned Spacecraft Center (now Johnson Space Center) at Clear Lake, 25-miles southeast of downtown Houston in the first half of the 1960s, added interplanetary space flights to Houston's repertory of transportation modes. This transit infrastructure supported chronological layers of urbanization. The suburban town of Park Place , the country place community of Garden Villas, developed in 1926, and the subdivision of Glenbrook Valley, developed in 1954, represent three phases of 20th-century suburbanization. Pasadena, founded in 1893 as an agricultural settlement on Buffalo Bayou, was transformed when the Houston businessman, Jesse H. Jones, as chairman of the Reconstruction Finance Corporation and Federal Defense Coordinator during the Franklin D. Roosevelt administration, subsidized the construction of an American petrochemical industry during the years of World War II. This caused Pasadena to become a city in its own right in the second half of the 20th century, with a population of just under 150,000 by 2010. Yet what is apparent in southeast Houston and Pasadena is the extent to which infrastructure investment and economic good fortune have not been translated into long-term community stability and urban improvements. This is especially apparent in Harrisburg, the oldest townsite on Buffalo Bayou, founded in 1826, ten years before the establishment of Houston but part of Houston since 1926. These largely working class sectors of the Houston metropolitan region have been marginalized by disinvestment, despite the impressive durability, and continued economic productivity, of their infrastructure. Architecture survives as a testament to the faith that these communities once evoked from those who lived there.

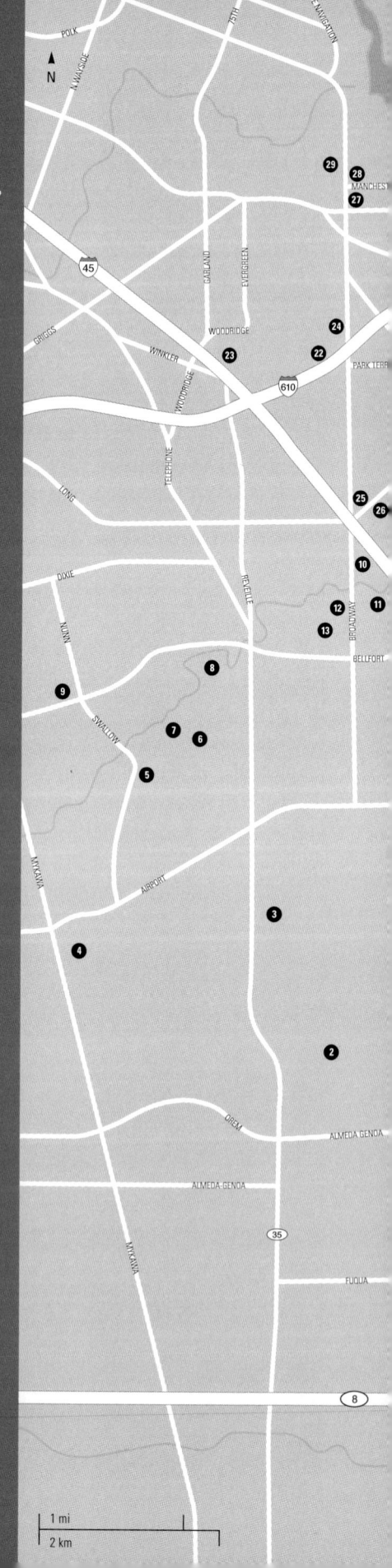

1. **Bracewell Neighborhood Library, Houston Public Library,** 9002 Kingspoint Road
2. **City of Houston Firemen's Training Academy,** 8030 Braniff Street
3. **Houston Municipal Airport Terminal,** 8325 Travelaire Road
4. **Emsco Derrick and Equipment Company Building,** 7600 South Santa Fe Drive
5. **Garden Villas United Methodist Church,** 7155 Ashburn Avenue
6. **Garden Villas Park Recreation Building,** 6720 South Haywood Drive
7. **Patterson House,** 7370 Sims Drive
8. **Hess House,** 6410 North Haywood Drive
9. **Bellfort Square Office Building,** 6711 Bellfort Street
10. **Park Place Baptist Church,** 4101 Broadway
11. **Richardson House,** 7911 Santa Elena Drive
12. **Montalbano House,** 8035 Glenforest Court
13. **Kirkland House,** 8210 Colgate Street
14. **C. C. Bell Construction Company House,** 8202 Glenview Drive
15. **White House,** 5226 Berry Creek Drive
16. **Stein House,** 2305 Redwinn Drive
17. **First Pasadena State Bank Building,** 1001 E. Southmore Avenue
18. **Pasadena Town Square,** 181 Pasadena Town Square Drive
19. **St. Pius V Catholic Church,** 824 South Main Street
20. **Capitán Theater,** 1001 Shaw Avenue
21. **Pasadena State Bank Building,** 107 Shaw Avenue
22. **YMCA East End Branch Building,** 7903 South Loop East
23. **Office City Building One,** 7135 Office City Drive
24. **James W. Deady Junior High School,** 2500 Broadway
25. **Park Place United Methodist Church,** 3827 Broadway
26. **St. Christopher Catholic Church,** 8150 Park Place Boulevard
27. **Harrisburg National Bank Building,** 1007 Broadway
28. **John R. Harris Elementary School,** 801 Broadway
29. **Holy Cross Episcopal Church,** 710 Medina Street

Tour V

Southeast Houston / Pasadena / Harrisburg

V-1 Bracewell Neighborhood Library, Houston Public Library

V-2 Houston Firemen's Training Academy

V-3 Houston Municipal Airport Terminal

V-4 Emsco Derrick & Equipment Company Building

V-5 Garden Villas United Methodist Church

V-1
Bracewell Neighborhood Library, Houston Public Library
9002 Kingspoint Road
2009, mArchitects

Architect Michael Morton took advantage of a highly visible site adjoining the South Sam Houston Parkway when he designed this branch library, a modest, economical, and delightful loft space sheltered beneath a rising roof plate carried on internally exposed steel joists and columns. Ample daylight illuminates the spacious, simply finished interior. The building is faced with ruddy clay tile blocks and corrugated steel panels. Located nearby are Blackhawk Park at 9401 Fuqua and Blackhawk (2006, Clark Condon Associates, landscape architect; RdlR, architect) and the Pasadena Independent School District's Laura Welch Bush Elementary School at 9100 Blackhawk (2006, Dansby & Miller).

V-2
Houston Firemen's Training Academy
[now Houston Fire Department Val Jahnke Training Facility]
8030 Braniff Street
1967, Jenkins Hoff Oberg Saxe

The training academy comprises a campus of widely scattered, tough-looking buildings framed with thick, cast-in-place concrete members infilled with buff brick panels. The Drill Tower and the smoke-blackened Fire Building at the back of the site stand out.

V-3
Houston Municipal Airport Terminal
[now 1940 Air Terminal Museum]
8325 Travelaire Road
1940, Joseph Finger

In 1937 W. T. Carter, Jr. sold an airfield that he and his family had operated for 11 years to the City of Houston, which built this passenger terminal and a concrete hangar complex three years later with a grant from the Public Works Administration. Finger's pyramidal sky-city gateway is a modernistic delight, as is the architecturally coordinated hangar at Travelaire and Nelms. In 1988 the City's Department of Aviation demolished a series of crude additions to the terminal and had Barry Moore Architects rehabilitate the exterior. The non-profit Houston Aeronautical Heritage Society, organized in 1998, leased the terminal and raised funds for its phased restoration as an aeronautical museum (2004, 2009, Howard Hill). The 1940 terminal was superseded by a new terminal (now William P. Hobby Airport) on the north side of the field at the head of Broadway (1954, Wyatt C. Hedrick). All the 1954 components of the Hobby Airport terminal, except the entrance pavilion, were demolished following completion of a new concourse and gates (2005, 2008, Lockwood Andrews & Newnam).

V-4
Emsco Derrick & Equipment Company Building
7600 South Santa Fe Drive
1942, Fooshee & Cheek

The architects, a Dallas firm, designed this restrained, very dignified suburban office building with a smooth skin of limestone and glass-block window panels. It has been respectfully maintained despite subsequent additions (1959, Golemon & Rolfe).

V-5
Garden Villas United Methodist Church
7155 Ashburn Avenue
1941, 1946, 1952, Edward A. Bodet

Bodet's limestone-faced, suburban Gothic church complex sits near the northern terminus of Garden Villa's radial cross streets, Villa, Kopman, and Prentiss. Garden Villas was laid out in 1925 by the architect Edward Wilkinson for the developer, W. T. Carter, Jr., on the south bank of Sims Bayou. Wilkinson devised the radial street plan focused on a pivotal site now occupied by Garden Villas Elementary School (7185 Santa Fe Drive, 1932, Stayton Nunn and Edward Wilkinson). Belying the incipient monumentality of the town plan, Garden Villas initially was proclaimed a garden community, where families of modest means could supplement their incomes with produce raised in their own back yards. Because of plentiful open land nearby, Garden Villas still seems very much on the edge of Houston. It is a characteristic Texan place—uncurbed streets lined with pecan trees, rambling wooden houses with multiple additions, open yards—just the sort of neighborhood for people who probably prefer not to live in neighborhoods. Garden Villas lets them have it both ways. On an historical note, in 1926 Garden Villas advertised one of Wilkinson's 1-story houses as a "ranch type house," the first known use of that term in Houston.

V-6 Garden Villas Park Recreation Building

V-7 Patterson House

V-8 Hess House

V-9 Bellfort Square Office Building

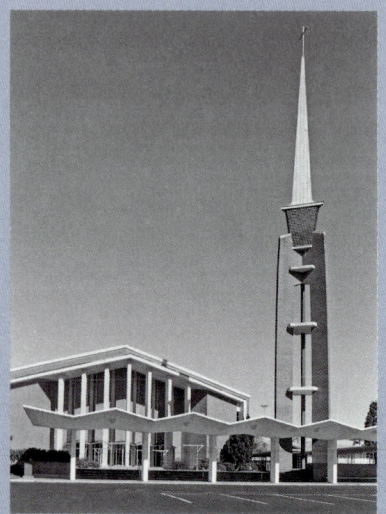
V-10 Park Place Baptist Church

V-6
Garden Villas Park Recreation Building
6720 South Haywood Drive
1959, William R. Jenkins

The big scale of the steel-framed basketball court canopy makes for an impressive open-air space. The adjoining recreation building, based on a 9-square, neo-Palladian grid (a bit stretched in the middle), is a very mannered interpretation of the architecture of Mies van der Rohe.

V-7
Patterson House
7370 Sims Drive
1937, H. A. Salisbury & T. G. McHale

Salisbury and McHale brought their best River Oaks manner to Garden Villas in this precisely composed and detailed American colonial farmhouse. To the left of the main house is a smaller version, the guest house.

V-8
Hess House
6410 North Haywood Drive
1950

The Hess House is a fine example of the Garden Villas contemporary look: low slung, with low-pitched roofs, clerestory strip windows, and a dramatically glazed bay juxtaposed with the obligatory chimney pylon.

V-9
Bellfort Square Office Building
6711 Bellfort Street
1966, Arthur D. Steinberg

This is one of the zaniest buildings in Houston. As if the warped penthouse weren't enough, the building is faced with green aggregate, precast concrete panels and gold anodized aluminum mullions.

V-10
Park Place Baptist Church
[now Southwestern Seminary]
4101 Broadway
1961, Ben F. Greenwood with
E. Gene Hines

A contemporary rendition of the pointed style, executed at large scale.

V-11
Richardson House
7911 Santa Elena Drive
1955, Doughtie & Porterfield

An exuberant '50s Contemporary with splayed structural bents supporting a broadly projecting carport porte-cochère canopy, this expansive house is nestled into one of the hollows that give the subdivision of Glenbrook Valley its topographical distinction. Planned by the landscape architects Hare & Hare for Detering Interests, Glenbrook Valley opened in 1954. Because of the number of mid-20th-century Contemporary houses it possesses, Glenbrook Valley became the City of Houston's first modern historic district in 2011.

V-12
Montalbano House
8035 Glenforest Drive
1958, John D. Dansby, Jr.

This angled and curved Contemporary style house is one of a several similar designs Dansby produced in Houston in the 1950s. Its plan geometry is keyed to the configuration of the lot.

V-13
Kirkland House
8210 Colgate Street
1960, Paul Wahlberg

A flat-roofed, glass-walled pavilion, this Glenbrook Valley house is set back on the downslope of its expansive lot, the better to contrast with its more conventional ranch type neighbors.

V-11 Richardson House

V-12 Montalbano House

V-13 Kirkland House

V-14 C. C. Bell Construction Company House

V-15 White House

V-16 Stein House

V-17 First Pasadena State Bank Building

V-14
C. C. Bell Construction Company House
8202 Glenview Drive
1926, C. C. Bell Construction Company, designer-builder

The subdivision of Meadowbrook was developed in 1926 by George F. Howard and the San Jacinto Trust Company as a country club community focused on the Glenbrook Country Club golf course and connected to Houston by the Galveston-Houston Electric Company's Interurban light rail (its right-of-way became the right-of-way of the Gulf Freeway). Howard and the builder, C. C. Bell, Jr., traveled to Florida in the mid-1920s to inspect the latest examples of Spanish Mediterranean architecture, which Bell reproduced in several of the original Coral Gables-inspired bungalows, such as this one. Also surviving from the community's early days is Melinda Bonner Elementary School (1930, Charles A. Dieman) at 5110 Arizona.

V-15
White House
5226 Berry Creek Drive
1969, MacKie & Kamrath

Because Houston's East End was the 20th-century industrial production and distribution, it was not an attractive location for middle-income neighborhoods. Among exceptions to this rule was Meadowbrook Village, planned alongside Berry Gully, a tributary of Sims Bayou, in 1950 by architect-developer R. W. Clemens. At the head of a cul-de-sac off Berry Creek Drive, this late example of MacKie & Kamrath's residential work architecturally distinguishes its setting.

V-16
Stein House
2305 Redwinn Drive
1958, Brooks & Brooks

Tucked into the otherwise unexceptional Fenwood neighborhood along Vince's Bayou in the city of Pasadena is this neatly detailed

1950s modern house. Its front elevation consists of planes of wood and brick relieved by volumetric intrusions and projections, and a raised band of clerestory windows.

V-17
First Pasadena State Bank Building
1001 East Southmore Avenue
1962, MacKie & Kamrath with Lloyd Borget and Doughtie & Porterfield

Pasadena's only skyscraper is this distinctive 14-story tower, a glass-curtained shaft that appears to project forward from a brick-faced spine containing stairs, elevators, and toilets. The sculptural shaping of offset volumes and masses is quite effective. First Pasadena State is remarkable. In a decade in which the design of American tall buildings was especially conformist, it stands out as a spirited alternative developed on principles derived from the work of Frank Lloyd Wright. In 2002 Bank One, successor to First Pasadena State Bank, vacated the building, and it has not been occupied since. Its deterioration bespeaks only too clearly the alarming disinvestment in the resources and infrastructure of Pasadena.

V-18
Pasadena Town Square
1001 East Southmore Avenue
1982, Caudill Rowlett Scott

About 1960 the center of Pasadena shifted from the compact (and now deserted) downtown at South Main and the La Porte Freeway to the corner of Southmore and Tatar, 1.5 miles to the southeast. In the 1990s it slid an additional 2.75 miles south to the Fairmount Parkway corridor, a process that construction of this small shopping mall by Federated Stores Realty failed to arrest. Pasadena Town Square was designed to function as the city center that Pasadena literally left behind. The public space is generously dimensioned, well lit, and furnished with numerous amenities. Still it was an insulated environment rather than a downtown turned inward, not making any attempt to connect to any of the public buildings around it. Pasadena Town Square sums up Pasadena's post-downtown predicament. It has no public face, projects no public image, and thus cannot function as the representative center it was intended to be.

V-18 Pasadena Town Square

V-19 St. Pius V Catholic Church

V-20 Capitán Theater

V-21 Pasadena State Bank Building

V-22 YMCA East End Branch Building

V-23 Office City Building Two

V-19
St. Pius V Catholic Church
824 South Main Street
1959, T. G. McHale

After the First Pasadena State Bank Building, St. Pius V is Pasadena's outstanding public building. McHale's blocky tower, a late rendition of the Bertram Goodhue style of planar set-back composition, is an emphatic spatial marker in this flat, predominantly domestic, go-as-you-please landscape. Cantoned piers of rough-faced limestone bracket inset screens filled with anagrammatic Christian ornament. Contrasting with the monumental bulk of the tower are the attenuated copper flèche and the thin, stepped nave.

V-20
Capitán Theater
1001 Shaw Avenue
1949, Richard F. Smith

Facing an elevated stretch of the La Porte Freeway (TX Highway 225), the Capitán Theater is the most imageable survivor of the first downtown Pasadena, whose heyday was the 1940s, the decade that the U.S. government, through the Reconstruction Finance Corporation's Defense Plant Corporation, funded construction of a petrochemical empire along the Houston Ship Channel. The City of Pasadena restored the Capitán's exterior and the pylon light mast in 2005, but the interior is a shell.

V-21
Pasadena State Bank Building
[now Harris County Courthouse Annex]
101 Shaw Avenue
1950

It is dismaying to see how decayed and abandoned the real downtown of Pasadena is. Government agencies now account for its few occupants, preserving what little is left of its urban infrastructure, such as the handsome (and deserted) ex-U.S. Post Office at 102 S. Munger.

V-22
YMCA East End Branch Building
[now Cossaboom Branch YMCA]
903 South Loop East
1955, Milton McGinty

One of a series of neighborhood YMCAs that the McGinty office designed in the mid-1950s, this 4-story building consists of a slab, programmatically organized to display horizontal window bands, a vertical service and circulation tower, and the exposed fire stair that projects off one end of the building as an architectural exclamation mark.

V-23
Office City Building Two
[now Houston Community College Cosmetology]
7015 Gulf Freeway
1961, MacKie & Kamrath

The brothers Carl A. and Herman E. Detering developed this tract, located in a quadrant of the Gulf Freeway-South Loop 610 East interchange, as Office City, a suburban office park, with MacKie & Kamrath as architects. The Gulf Freeway benefitted from NASA's location on Clear Lake during the early 1960s, where the Johnson Space Center was under construction. MacKie & Kamrath's office buildings (including 7007 of 1963) are L-shaped in plan and feature solar screens. The ex-Texas American Bank Building [now Enterprise Bank] at 7125 Gulf Freeway also lies in Office City. The original pavilion, with its space-framed drive-in canopy, is by Kenneth Bentsen Associates (1976). On the south side of the Gulf Freeway was Gulfgate Shopping City (1956, John Graham Company and Irving R. Klein & Associates), Houston's first regional shopping mall. Built by Theodore Berenson and Allied Stores Corporation at Houston's first freeway interchange, it was demolished in 2001 and replaced by a lifestyle center (Hermes Architects). The Gulfgate pylon facing the South Loop East is the site's only mid-century survivor.

V-24
James W. Deady Junior High School
2500 Broadway
1928, Louis A. Glover

The Glover family was involved in real estate development in this section of Harrisburg, which perhaps accounts for the fact that Glover designed both Charles H. Milby Senior High School (1601 Broadway) and Deady Junior High. Deady displays resplendent terra cotta decoration, a type of ornament popular in the 1920s but comparatively rare in Houston. Glover also was responsible for the tile-faced modern wing added in 1950.

V-24 James W. Deady Junior High School

V-25 Park Place United Methodist Church

V-26 St. Christopher Catholic Church

V-27 Harrisburg National Bank Building

V-28 John R. Harris Elementary School

V-25
Park Place United Methodist Church
[now Servants of Christ United Methodist Church]
3827 Broadway
1960, Edward A. Bodet

Pivoted on its site near the Park Place-Broadway intersection, this conservatively designed brick church is a local landmark because of its imposing scale and the height of its copper-clad spire. The congregation acquired the site from Park Place Baptist Church after it moved three blocks south on Broadway. Park Place was served by the Houston-Galveston Interurban light rail line, which ran along the right-of-way of the Gulf Freeway.

V-26
St. Christopher Catholic Church
8150 Park Place Boulevard
1952, Maurice J. Sullivan

The brick façade and campanile of St. Christopher, striated with limestone bands, dignify Park Place's main street, Park Place Boulevard.

V-27
Harrisburg National Bank Building
[now Frost Bank]
1001 Broadway
1964, George Pierce-Abel B. Pierce

This is an example of the glass-walled pavilion building type of the 1960s, constructed with thick concrete piers and a heroically cantilevered roof slab. The bank is a mid-20th-century modern addition to Harrisburg, the oldest town in Harris County. Surveyed in 1826, the Mexican *ayuntamiento* of Harrisburg was founded by John R. Harris of Cayuga, New York, a member of Stephen F. Austin's original Old 300 colony of Anglo-American settlers, the man for whom Harris County is named, and the great-grandfather of the architect Birdsall P. Briscoe.

V-28
John R. Harris Elementary School
801 Broadway
1971, Clovis Heimsath Associates

This addition to an existing building consists of the anti-gravitational projection of deep, brick-faced soffits above the classroom windows. Architecturally it is the only bright spot along Broadway. No trace of Harrisburg's comparatively ancient past has been allowed to remain, and what is left, principally business buildings of the 1930s and '40s, is falling into decay. At the east end of East Magnolia Street is Glendale Cemetery, in which the plots of such pioneer families as Harris, Briscoe, Milby, Tod, and Allen are located.

V-29
Holy Cross Episcopal Church
710 Medina Street
1920, John McLelland

This is a handsomely maintained Craftsman style church. Nearby at 8001 E. Elm Street is a 1.5-story wood house of late 18th-century origin, one of the oldest surviving buildings in Harrisburg.

V-29 Holy Cross Episcopal Church

Bay Area

Bay Area

Tour W

The Houston metropolitan region does not extend all the way to the Gulf of Mexico, but it does have its own shoreline along Galveston Bay, into which Buffalo Bayou and its tributaries discharge and, in turn, empty into the Gulf. Although it is largely a working class sector because of the industrial and refining corridor along the Houston Ship Channel, the Bay Area possesses, like the rest of Houston, disparate landscapes that (also like the rest of Houston) tell many stories rather than contributing to a unified spatial narrative. The East Freeway (I-10) grazes the Houston Ship Channel at Channelview, where the San Jacinto River empties into Buffalo Bayou. Here the San Jacinto Monument is visible from the freeway and is especially impressive at night when lit. At San Jacinto, site of the 1836 battle that led to Texas's independence from Mexico, this sector's economic and political history is apparent. But it is the awesome petrochemical network that dominates all views from the monument's observation deck. The Fred Hartman Bridge, which spans the ship channel to connect La Porte and Baytown, is one of the few works of monumentally scaled infrastructure designed to impress visually as well as perform economically. What is not immediately apparent about the bay shore is the survival

of landscapes associated with its late 19th- and early 20th-century role as an upper-income summer resort. Bay Ridge in the town of Morgan's Point and portions of the coast along Todville Road in Seabrook preserve discrete elite enclaves with distinctive architecture. Clear Lake, which is formed by Clear Creek and marks the boundary between Harris and Galveston counties, is characterized by intensive suburbanization that began in the 1960s with construction of the Lyndon B. Johnson Space Center and associated development of the planned community of Clear Lake City, now part of the City of Houston. Like other sectors of metropolitan Houston, the Bay Area is a crazy quilt of landscapes strung together by infrastructure networks. Architecture punctuates this amalgam with landmarks that attest to the various economic cycles and historical episodes that continue to produce the suburban metropolis.

1. **John E. Codewell Hall, HCC, Northeast College,** 555 Community College Drive
2. **Nira Park,** 12443 Market Street Road
3. **Northshore Dental Clinic,** 2 Evanston Street
4. **Old River Terrace United Methodist Church,** 16102 East Freeway
5. **San Jacinto Monument,** 3800 Park Road 1836
6. **Fred Hartman Bridge,** State Highway 146 and Houston Ship Channel
7. **Cottage,** 119 Bay Ridge Road
8. **Bullock House,** 311 Bay Ridge Road
9. **Irvin House,** 431 Bay Ridge Road
10. **Sterling House,** 515 Bay Ridge Road
11. **Reynaud House,** 1520 Roscoe Avenue
12. **St. Mary of the Immaculate Conception Catholic Church,** 816 Park Avenue
13. **St. John's Episcopal Church,** 815 S. Broadway
14. **Sylvan Beach Pavilion,** 554 N. Bayshore Drive
15. **Harris House,** 4700 Oleander Street
16. **House,** 606 Baywood Drive
17. **House,** 319 Lakeshore Drive
18. **West Ranch House,** 3303 E. NASA Parkway
19. **NASA Manned Spacecraft Center,** 2101 E. NASA Parkway
20. **First State Bank Building,** 1055 Bay Area Boulevard
21. **University of Houston Clear Lake,** 2700 Bay Area Boulevard
22. **IBM Federal Systems Division Regional Office Building,** 3700 Bay Area Boulevard
23. **Armand Bayou Nature Center Interpretive Building,** 8600 Bay Area Boulevard
24. **Wetcher House,** 14303 Harvest Glen Court
25. **Webster High School,** 400 S. Walnut Street
26. **Pipers Meadow Community Center,** 15920 Piper's View Drive and Elder Vista Drive
27. **NASA Value Center,** 20710 Gulf Freeway
28. **Crenshaw Professional Plaza,** 5150 Crenshaw Road
29. **First United Methodist Church,** 1062 Fairmont Parkway

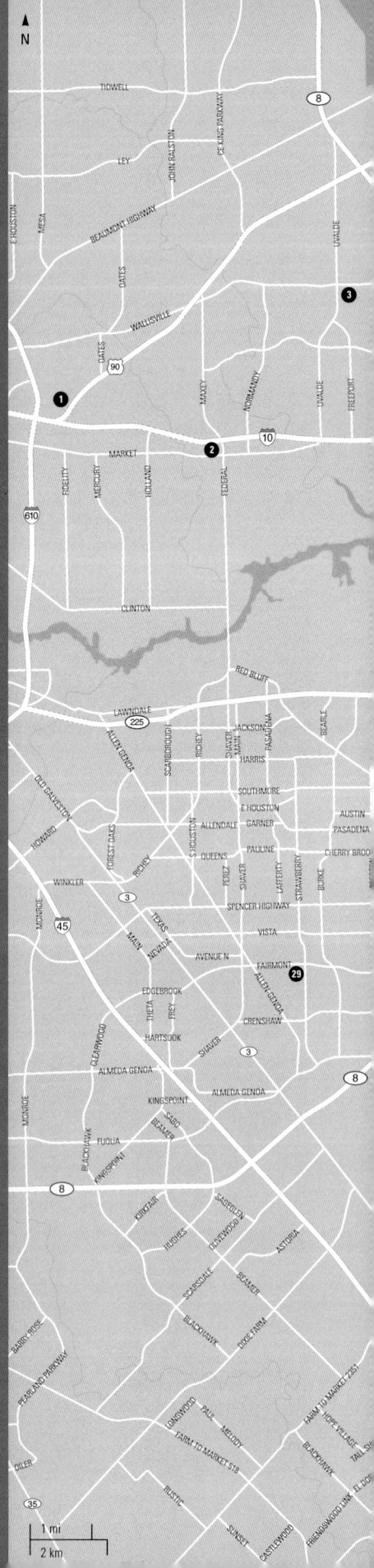

Bay Area

Tour W

683

W-1 John E. Codewell Hall, Houston Community College, Northeast College

W-2 Nira Park

W-3 Northshore Dental Clinic

W-4 Old River Terrace United Methodist Church

W-5 San Jacinto Monument

W-1
John E. Codewell Hall, Houston Community College, Northeast College
555 Community College Drive
1999, Golemon/Bolullo

Mario Bolullo's sure hand is visible in the articulately assembled curtain wall with which he faced this 3-story academic building. Located in the midst of the industrial and distribution sector tied to the Houston Ship Channel, I-10, and Loop 610, the northeast branch of Houston Community College teaches such specialized skills as 18-wheel truck driving.

W-2
Nira Park
12443 Market Street Road
1934, Maurice J. Sullivan

As architecturally unimpressive as this small 1-story house appears (in part because of an addition glommed onto its front), it was one of the few houses (100 were planned) built in Nira Park, a limited dividend suburban resettlement community developed during the early years of the New Deal by the oilman and philanthropist J. S. Cullinan. Cullinan had Sullivan design the houses with steel stud construction.

W-3
Northshore Dental Clinic
2 Evanston Street
2007, Enter Architecture

Karen Lantz compensated for uninspired surroundings in the Woodforest area by splitting this medical professional building into two bars, which look into a serene interior courtyard through which patients enter the complex. Light-colored polished concrete block give the complex its radiant quality.

W-4
Old River Terrace United Methodist Church
16102 East Freeway
1955

Although overshadowed by a prosaic church school building next door, the Old River Terrace Methodist Church is a lithe modern building that opens confidently toward the East Freeway (I-10). Note the white-painted steel cross architecturally integrated into the wing wall.

W-5
San Jacinto Monument
San Jacinto Battleground State Park
3800 Park Road 1836
1938, Alfred C. Finn

In the midst of the petrochemical corridor along the Houston Ship Channel stands the San Jacinto Monument, a reinforced concrete obelisk, 570 feet tall, faced with Texas fossilized limestone and capped by a three-dimensional Lone Star. The obelisk was erected by the State of Texas with assistance from the Public Works Administration. It commemorates the Battle of San Jacinto, April 21, 1836, when a small force of Anglo-Texians led by Sam Houston surprised and routed the Mexican army, which had camped on this plain opposite the confluence of the San Jacinto River and Buffalo Bayou, and captured its leader, Mexican general Antonio López de Santa Anna. Santa Anna was forced to concede the independence of Texas from Mexico and April 21st has ever since been celebrated in Texas as San Jacinto Day. The State of Texas commenced site acquisition at the battlefield in 1883, but not until 1909 did the legislature designate the site as a state park. Preparation for the centennial of Texas independence in 1936 led Jesse H. Jones, then chairman of the federal government's Reconstruction Finance Corp., to propose construction of this monument in 1935. Jones's perennial architect, Alfred C. Finn, got the job and tradition has it that Jones sketched the obelisk, with its 3-D star, that Finn's office obligingly produced. High, raised terraces surround the base of the monument, which contains the San Jacinto Museum of History and an elevator that carries sightseers to an observation deck at the top of the shaft. The relief carving at the base of the shaft, the modeling of the bronze entrance doors, and the crowning star are the work of William M. McVey. At the water end of the principal axis is the U.S.S. Texas, a 1914 vintage battleship involved in World Wars I and II. It was restored in 1990. At the channel end of Park Road 1836 one can take the Lynchburg Ferry across the Houston Ship Channel to Crosby-Lynchburg Road, which leads to I-10. In its heroic scale, radical symmetry, frontality, and isolation, the San Jacinto Monument is the only work of architecture that stands up to the intimidating, impersonal engineering operations that dominate the landscape of oil and gas production along the Ship Channel. Its elementary geometry is extended laterally across the prairie by the 1,750-foot-long reflecting basin, which stretches out in front of the monument. The ritual character of this approach sequence was undermined in 1985, however, when the Texas Parks and Wildlife Dept. demolished the flanking driveways in order to use the basin as a flood retention pond. Thus one now approaches the monument from its side flank rather than frontally. There is something unsettling about this monument. Its hieratic character, and the ceremonial conception of public life that this implies, are so disconnected from its landscape and from visiting tourists that the monument seems meant for some other place, some other culture, and to have ended up here by mistake. It bespeaks epic deeds and heroic stature, attributes that here have manifestly passed from people to objects of processing and production.

W-6 Fred Hartman Bridge

W-7 Cottage

W-8 Bullock House

W-9 Irvin House

W-10 Sterling House

W-6
Fred Hartman Bridge
State Highway 146 and
Houston Ship Channel
1992, State Dept. of Highways and
Public Transportation, District 12

The Hartman Bridge spans the Ship Channel to connect La Porte and Baytown. Two roadways are carried 178 feet above the channel on cables suspended from two pairs of reinforced concrete "double diamonds," one pair to each side of the channel. The diamond-shaped towers are 440 feet high; the bridge itself is 1,250 feet long.

W-7
Cottage
119 Bay Ridge Road
1898

In classic Bay Ridge fashion, the 2-story front of this board-and-batten cottage faces Galveston Bay, leaving the 1-story rear wing backed up to the road.

W-8
Bullock House
311 Bay Ridge Road
1928, John F. Staub

Bay Ridge, a high promontory at the rim of Galveston Bay just south of Morgan's Point where Buffalo Bayou merges with the bay, is a place to which well-to-do Houstonians began to retreat in the 1890s. The constant breeze blowing off the water provided the only antidote to the steaminess of coastal summers before the introduction of air-conditioning. Staub's bay house for a Houston family was more elaborate than most of the simple cottages along Bay Ridge Road, but he acknowledged the local carpenters' vernacular with its 2-over-2 windows. Major rooms look out across the wooded downhill slope toward the water.

W-9
Irvin House
431 Bay Ridge Road
1928, Joseph Finger

This pink stucco-surfaced, tile-roofed Mediterranean house is indicative of the suburbanization that Bay Ridge began to undergo in the late 1920s. Like earlier houses, however, it is entirely open on the bay side behind a screened loggia with full-width sleeping porch above. Mr. and Mrs. W. H. Irvin, the original owners, maintained their private zoo across the street at 430, one of the sights along Bay Ridge in the 1930s.

W-10
Sterling House
515 Bay Ridge Road
1928, Alfred C. Finn

When Ross S. Sterling decided to leave his Houston house on Rossmoyne and live year-round at the bay, he had Finn's designer, Robert C. Smallwood, produce this Newport-sized, limestone-faced, neo-Georgian country house, patterned rather closely on the work of the New York architect Charles A. Platt (especially the imposing semi-circular Ionic portico on the water side). The expansive grounds are bare of trees, so that the huge house is clearly silhouetted against the water and the sky. The balustraded roof terrace provides a splendid prospect point for viewing the immensely tall ships that traverse the Ship Channel, which lies just beyond the Bay Ridge beach. Across the street at 514 are the garage and servants' quarters. Farther south on Bay Ridge, although not always clearly visible from the street, are a house by Birdsall P. Briscoe (615), a delightful Victorian cottage built by an original member-family of the Bay Ridge Park Association (811), and a house by Sanguinet & Staats (835).

W-11
Reynaud House
1520 Roscoe Avenue
1927

Sallie Wynne Reynaud designed this shingled cottage, a bundle of tense shapes with a marvelously improvised air, for her own family. It is located on the bay shore in La Porte, Texas.

W-11 Reynaud House

W-12 Kirwin Memorial Chapel

W-13 St. John's Episcopal Church

W-14 Sylvan Beach Pavilion

W-15 Harris House

W-12
Kirwin Memorial Chapel
[now St. Mary of the Immaculate Conception Catholic Church]
816 Park Avenue
1927, Maurice J. Sullivan

This brick-faced, tile-roofed Lombard Romanesque style church was built as the chapel of St. Mary's Seminary, which was located here until it was moved to Sullivan's new campus in Houston in 1954. Prior to 1901, when the Diocese of Galveston acquired the property, it had been the site of the Sylvan Beach Hotel, a Victorian resort hotel on the bay shore, around which the town of La Porte was laid out by the La Porte Improvement Company in the 1890s.

W-13
St. John's Episcopal Church
815 S. Broadway
1953, Henry Steinbomer

The San Antonio architect Steinbomer, like his Houston counterparts, Hiram A. Salisbury and T. George McHale, produced modestly scaled, but conscientiously detailed, parish churches such this one into the 1960s. Nearby is La Porte's small downtown. The 2-story wood commercial building at 406 W. Main (c. 1900) with a 2-story wood veranda is what one would expect of a bay front community.

W-14
Sylvan Beach Pavilion
554 N. Bayshore Drive
1956, Greacen & Brogniez

Embraced by grass berms, the Sylvan Beach Pavilion is a glass-walled octagonal dance hall elevated above the low-lying shore of Galveston Bay on a ring of concrete columns that rise through the building to support a thin shell concrete roof 135 feet in diameter, which is curved in section to stiffen it. The flat-roofed wing contains a foyer and, facing the bay front, an expansive terrace deck. Thomas E. Greacen and Raymond H. Brogniez organized the building according to functionalist practices, evident in its assembly of purpose-specific shapes. The octagonal plan of the dance hall relates this modern pavilion to a series of 19th-century Texas vernacular dance halls. Strenuous opposition by bay area residents in 2009-10 caused Harris County, which built the pavilion, to back down on plans to demolish it and instead to restore the complex. Kirksey is restoration architect.

W-15
Harris House
4700 Oleander Street
c. 1832, 1872

This 3-bay wooden Gulf Coast cottage is only visible to the left of the house at 210 Park in Seabrook's El Jardín subdivision. It sits on Red Bluff Point overlooking Galveston Bay. The front portion of the house was constructed in 1872 by Glenn Morgan Harris, but its rear, hipped roofed wing is part of the house that Harris's father, William P. Harris, occupied at Red Bluff after he was granted the property by the Mexican government in 1832. Harris family papers suggest it was originally built to house the Mexican customs agent on Galveston Island and was moved to this site by Harris in 1833. William Harris was the brother John R. Harris of Harrisburg, for whom Harris County is named, and the great-great-uncle of architect Birdsall P. Briscoe. The house is still occupied by Harris descendants.

W-16
House
606 Baywood Drive
1960, F. Carrington Weems

Houston engineer Carrington Weems developed the Baywood subdivision in Shoreacres and designed a number of modern houses along its one street. This flat-roofed, planar-walled house is the best preserved of Weems's houses; the house at 514 (1959) is still recognizable as his work.

W-17
Lakeshore House
319 Lakeshore Drive
2008, Miró Rivera

Backing onto Taylor Lake in Seabrook, this sophisticated 2- and 3-story house is faced with gleaming white limestone and brilliant copper. Austin architects Juan Miró and Miguel Rivera set the house in a constructed landscape that combines water, planting, and paved terraces.

W-16 House

W-17 Lakeshore House

W-18 West Ranch House

W-19 National Aeronautics and Space Administration Manned Spacecraft Center (NASA)

W-20 First State Bank Building

W-18
West Ranch House
3303 E. NASA Parkway
1929, Joseph Finger

NASA Parkway is the nightmarish antithesis of Clear Lake City and the other "planned" communities that it skirts (Nassau Bay, Taylor Lake Village, and El Lago)—a chaotic strip along the north shore of Clear Lake where all the action is, and all the traffic too. Its foremost architectural sight is this sprawling, Mediterranean style country house built by the lumberman, oilman, cattleman, and banker J. M. West on his 35,000-acre ranch assembled in the 1920s midway between Houston and Galveston. Like the Sterling House at Bay Ridge, the West House was larger and much more pretentious than houses Houstonians had built previously on Clear Lake. The exterior detailing of the stucco-surfaced, tile-roofed, U-shaped villa is superlative, especially the cast-concrete, classical decoration. Most of the reception rooms were restored in 1968 by Brown & Root when the house (which had been unoccupied and vandalized) was adapted for use as a research and conference center for the Lunar Science Institute. Unfortunately the most distinctive space, the magnificent Art Deco playroom that occupied the angled wing, has lost its specially designed furniture and fountain. Only the zigzag marble floor paving and a Cubist relief panel above the fireplace remain. Mason C. Coney laid out the gardens. A swimming pool and classical bathhouse pavilion survive at the rear as does a small formal garden on axis with the angled wing. In 1995 Rice University sold the house with a time-limited preservation easement. Successive owners have failed to maintain the house.

W-19
National Aeronautics and Space Administration Manned Spacecraft Center (NASA)
[now Lyndon B. Johnson Space Center]
2101 NASA Parkway
1964, Brown & Root with Manned Spacecraft Center Architects (Brooks & Barr, MacKie & Kamrath, Harvin C. Moore, and Wirtz, Calhoun, Tungate & Jackson), Charles Luckman Associates, planning and design consultants.

Constructed between 1962-1964 the initial buildings of NASA illustrate the trivialization that the Modern movement underwent in the 1960s at the hands of architects employed by the American power elite. The Luckman office and Lyndon B. Johnson's favored builder and architects—Brown & Root and Brooks & Barr of Austin—imposed their version of modernist order on this flat 1,600-acre site. Visually weightless freestanding buildings, faced with white precast concrete and dark solar glass, are widely dispersed in a sea of green turf. Numerous parking lots and an extensive street grid were pragmatic insertions. On oppressively humid days the trek from one air-conditioned building to another can be wilting: the landscaping only provides visual relief. Space Center Houston, the Johnson Space Center's visitor center (1992, Walt Disney Imagineering) at 1601 NASA Parkway, replaced the original visitor center. From Saturn Lane, one can see the space center's sleek Building 20 (2009, Hellmuth, Obata + Kassabaum), a long, 3-story, LEED platinum-certified office building.

W-20
First State Bank Building
[now Baja Party Bar]
1055 Bay Area Boulevard
1966, Welton Becket & Associates

This concrete and glass pavilion, designed for the Humble Oil & Refining Company and the Del E. Webb Corporation, developers of Clear Lake City, dates from the community's inception. Clear Lake City was planned in 1962 on 10,000 acres excerpted from the ex-West ranch, which Humble acquired in 1938. Clear Lake City is a classic version of the American suburban dream, 1960s-Southwestern style. Single-family houses dominate. The entire community is built around a golf course, laid out to function as a system of greenway "fingers." Commercial buildings are segregated along major thoroughfares and multi-family housing is located to serve as a buffer. It doesn't look all that much different from the rest of Houston, except for its compulsive tidiness. The isolated, clean-lined, structurally expressive pavilion was the preferred public building type; the Becket office's bank is a case-study example. Nearby at 16511 Diana Lane is the Community Recreation Center (1964, Caudill Rowlett Scott). Subsequent additions have diluted the clarity of its original organizational scheme but not its architectural blandness, which is all too typical of Clear Lake City as a whole. As can be seen from the present condition of this building (its glass curtain wall has been replaced by a solid wall pierced by Islamic pointed arched windows), Clear Lake City is very Houston in dishonoring its historic landmarks.

W-21 University of Houston, Clear Lake Campus, Bayou Building

W-22 IBM Federal Systems Division Regional Office Building

W-24 Wetcher House

W-21
University of Houston, Clear Lake Campus, Bayou Building
2700 Bay Area Boulevard
1976, S. I. Morris Associates, Golemon & Rolfe, and Pitts, Phelps & White

John Bertini and Guy Jackson of S. I. Morris conceived this laterally expansive, 3-story, aluminum and glass-faced building as a machine in the garden—a precise, technologized object that contrasts maximally with its wooded surroundings. Across Horsepen Bayou to the south are the Arbor Building, the first on the Clear Lake Campus, of concrete tilt-wall construction (1971, Van Ness & Mower), and the Developmental Arts Building (1979, S. I. Morris Associates), the athletic center. The latter was designed as an experiment in energy conservation techniques. Faced with porcelain-enameled insulated metal panels, it was equipped with roof-mounted, flat-plate solar collectors intended to power fuel heating, air-conditioning, and water heating for the building.

W-22
IBM Federal Systems Division Regional Office Building
[now Boeing Company]
3700 Bay Area Boulevard
1986, CRS Sirrine

This is an authoritative building. Its crescent-shaped, 6-story mass spatially defines the broad curve of Bay Area Boulevard. Its centered composition and restrained coloration–gray granite base course, pink granite walls, reflective glass punched windows, and blue metal trim–give it a strong, but subtle, presence. Here a postmodern vocabulary has been intelligently articulated not just to project a corporate image, but to discharge a civic responsibility. The IBM Building creates a sense of place by addressing its site in a spatially positive, architecturally urbane manner. The channel gardens on the concave side of the building were laid out by the San Francisco landscape architects Peter Walker and Martha Schwartz.

W-23
Armand Bayou Nature Center, Interpretive Building
8600 Bay Area Boulevard
1977, Pierce Goodwin Alexander

This building is reached via a raised wooden boardwalk that traverses a small portion of the low-lying, marshy landscape characteristic of parts of the bay area. The 1-story building, raised on piers and surrounded by a veranda, pays homage to the Gulf Coast Cottage type, although literalism is avoided. The Natural Plant Greenhouse is by W. O. Neuhaus Associates (1983). This 1,800 acre park is being selectively restored to its aboriginal prairie condition with the removal of later tree growth and its replacement with prairie grasses.

W-24
Wetcher House
14303 Harvest Glen Court
1992, Peter Waldman

Clear Lake City does not have its fair share of vanguard architecture. Therefore the presence of Peter Waldman's uninhibited exercise in mythic narrative is all the more startling. Architect-designed houses in Clear Lake City are rare, giving this house in the Bay Oaks subdivision and, only a block away, the Chen House at 2106 Orchard Country Lane (1990, Jay Baker Architects) special significance.

W-23 Armand Bayou Nature Center, Interpretive Building

W-25 Webster High School

W-26 Piper's Meadow Community Center

W-27 NASA Value Center

W-28 Crenshaw Professional Plaza

W-25
Webster High School
[now Clear View Education Center]
400 S. Walnut Street
1939, R. G Schneider

As was true of many small town public schools constructed with PWA grants in the 1930s and early '40s, Webster High was a conventional 1-story brick building organized along a double-loaded corridor. Its one moment of architectural exuberance is the entrance pavilion. Schneider invoked the full array of streamlined modernistic devices to imbue the high school with civic distinction. Across Walnut is Webster Elementary School (1955, George Pierce-Abel B. Pierce), an important mid-century Modern building published in the national architectural press when new, but now sadly oppressed by postmodernization.

W-26
Piper's Meadow Community Center
15920 Piper's View Drive
1984, William R. Jenkins Associates

The community center of the Piper's Meadow subdivision in Webster is this stark, cross-gabled postmodern pavilion by Jenkins and his designer Peter J. Zweig.

W-27
NASA Value Center
20710 Gulf Freeway
1989, Hermes Reed Hindman

Hermes Reed Hindman's designer, Mark Boucher, added considerable zip to this strip with this exuberant shopping center, originally anchored by a Fiesta Mart. The flying bowstring trusses, curved parapets, and perforated fascias brought wit, postmodern style, and an appropriately big scale to a highly visible location.

W-28
Crenshaw Professional Plaza
5150 Crenshaw Road
2009, MC²

Houston architects Chung and Choung Nguyen designed this medical office complex in suburban Pasadena as a series of long, thin, 1½-story lofts constructed of concrete tilt wall. Buildings are spaced close together to frame intermediate planted courts. Wall panels are scored and articulated with different finishes and colors. MC² took a prosaic commission—a speculative office building facing a freeway frontage road—and, with imagination, reinterpreted it spatially to make a sense of place architecturally.

W-29
First United Methodist Church
1062 Fairmont Parkway
1986, PBK

Calvin Powitzky and Mark R. French made bold use of unpatinated copper, folded around rising roof shapes that penetrate the brick wall planes of Pasadena's First Methodist Church. The roof flares out to encompass the diamond-shaped plan.

W-29 First United Methodist Church

Late Additions

This section consists of entries for buildings discovered too late to be included in the lettered tours. Sites are identified to indicate where they would fall in each of the lettered tours. For example: C-103B would fall in Tour C after the site numbered 103.

B-41B Louise J. and W. T. Moran Center, Magnificat House

B-82B Sicardi Gallery

B-83B House

B-101B House

B-41B
Louise J. and W. T. Moran Center, Magnificat House
1410 Elgin Avenue
2011, Leslie Elkins

A multi-use facility serving the non-profit Magnificat House, this is a one-story clapboard and concrete block building, animated by its shallow pitched roofs.

B-82B
Sicardi Gallery
1506 W. Alabama Avenue 2012, Brave/Architecture

For a gallery specializing in contemporary Latin American art, Fernando Brave organized this compact, two-story building as a sequence of stacked volumes. Big-scaled openings and the contrast between horizontally ribbed steel panel siding on the second floor and a stucco-finished ground floor make the gallery a stand out. Architect Dillon Kyle's studio is located next door at 1500 W. Alabama.

B-82C
HEB Montrose Market
1701 W. Alabama Avenue
2011, Lake/Flato

To placate neighborhood indignation over demolition of the Wilshire Village Apartments (1940), the HEB grocery corporation retained Lake/Flato of San Antonio to design this large supermarket. Clerestory roof monitors, broad roof overhangs, wood lathe screens, and wood rain-screens give the store a designed appearance unusual among Houston grocery markets. Nine mature Live Oak trees were preserved from the 7-acre grounds of Wilshire Village.

B-83B
House
1850 Norfolk Street
2012, Suyama Peterson Deguchi

Developer Carol Isaak Barden is from Seattle, which has led her to import hometown architectural talent for her Houston projects. Architects George Suyama and Jay Deguchi produced this serene courtyard house, sheltered beneath a mature Live Oak tree.

B-101B
House
1200 Bomar Street
2011, John Zemanek

Near another house at 1122 Willard he designed, Zemanek produced this asymmetrically roofed, shed-like house, raised on an elevated wood platform. Sliding screens open the exterior to an east-facing side porch sheltered beneath a solar collector canopy.

B-82C HEB Montrose Market

C-53B House

C-84B Handmade House

C-103B Southampton House

C-103C House

C-109B Brice-Davidson House

C-53B
House
1314 South Boulevard
2011, Jay Baker Architects

Baker enlisted an array of picturesque compositional techniques to scale this expansive house to its neighborhood setting.

C-83B
House
1648 Vassar Street
2012, Guthrie+Strasser

Architects David Guthrie and Scott Stasser designed and built this vertical house to demonstrate the feasibility of affordable design.
* Not pictured.

C-84B
Handmade House
1916 Banks Street
2010, Olson Sundberg Kundig Allen

Seattle architect Richard Sundberg designed this house for developer Carol Isaak Barden. It is a two-story bar that recedes into its lot, positioning the garage (with roof deck above) to screen the rear garden from the street. Gray-green painted stucco gives it a tranquilizing aspect that Sundberg carries inside with a Northwestern sensibility, evident in his subtle handling of daylight and use of wood finishes. OSKA designed a related house for Barden at 2316 Bartlett (2008).

C-103B
Southampton House
2110 Tangley Road
2011, Content

Architect Jesse Hager shaped this 2-story, U-plan courtyard house as an assembly of austere brick planes sliced by regularly spaced rectangular window openings. The entrance bay and a wood-sheathed skylight above the stair mitigate the austerity of the architecture with shallow planar recession and changes of material.

C-103C
House
2362 Tangley Road
2011, Shirat Mayligit

A modern intervention in this traditional interwar neighborhood, this house is an assembly of volumes attached to a central spine.

C-109B
House
2001 Wroxton Road
2011, L. Barry Davidson Architects

This gable-fronted traditionally designed house is crisply rendered in white stucco and accented with a base course of stone and stone chimneys.

D-22B
Twilight Epiphany
Rice University
2012, James Turrell, artist,
Thomas Phifer & Partners

Artist James Turrell's second skyspace in Houston is located in the Susanne Deal Booth Centennial Pavilion, which contains an inner chamber designed to accommodate musical performances. Thomas Phifer designed the chamber within a pyramidal grass berm, which encloses the pavilion, and the 72-foot-square canopy above that contains the 14-foot-square skyspace.

Late Additions

D-22B *Twilight Epiphany*

N1-42B DuZar

H-57B Tulane Townhouses

H1-84B Row on 25th

H1-92B Studio

N-73B House

G-22B
BBVA Compass Stadium
2200 Texas Avenue
2012, Populous

The diagrid-like triangular framework of this 22,000-seat open-air stadium, home to the Houston Dynamos professional soccer team, is sheathed with a sculptural skin of expanded metal that emphasizes profile and transparency. Populous (formerly HOK Sport) keeps up with the times; their stadiums in Houston represent a checklist of the formal preoccupations of American architecture since the 1990s.

H1-42B
DuZer
1601 Northwood Street
2012, Palmer Brook Schooley

Architect Schooley designed and built this homage to the ZeRow house at Project Row Houses as his effort to formulate an environmentally sustainable minimal house type that feels spatially expansive.

H1-57B
Tulane
730 Tulane Street
2007, Esplanade Homes

Designer-developers Tina and Matt Ford grouped five 3-story houses on a pair of lots in a corner of the Heights undergoing transition from industrial to residential uses. Wood rainscreens are inset in planar exteriors of stucco-surfaced concrete block to achieve reduction in energy use and offset, rather than overwhelm, smaller scaled historical dwellings. Next door at 734 Tulane are the buildings the Fords call American Gothic (the 2-story house) and a rear building, the Flex Barn.

H1-84B
Row on 25th
226 West 25th Avenue
2011, Esplanade Homes

Tina and Matt Ford may well rehabilitate postmodernism with this austere, gable-fronted, clapboard house, the first of a projected nine that will be built in a staggered row facing W. 25th Avenue. Large-scaled apertures and sure proportions abstract the familiar form of the gabled house front, satisfying community design critics who might otherwise decry the effect of abrasive new construction on the fragile historical fabric of the Heights

H1-92B
Studio
1528 West 24th Avenue
2010, John Blackmon and Ian Glennie

This white-painted, metal-surfaced shed, raised on concrete piers, is a private library and gallery. It is purposefully unassuming in a neighborhood rapidly transitioning from working class cottages to aggressively scaled rowhouse complexes.

N-73B
House
3931 Inverness Drive
2011, Roger M. Cooner

This house is an architectural homage to the 20th-century Baton Rouge architect A. Hays Town, who retrieved historic Louisiana house types as models for new suburban houses. Rather than designing a mega-mansion, Cooner organized program spaces in a series of connected buildings based on Louisiana Creole prototypes. The result is a very large house that does not overwhelm its site.

G-22B BBVA Compass Stadium

Index

1010 Lamar Building 35, 50
1100 Milam Building 4, 16
13 Celsius 118
1600 Smith Building 4, 12
2550 Brookhollow Building 536, 538
2990 Richmond Building 432, 452-53
3D/International 16, 22, 28, 45, 47, 56, 70, 281, 458, 470-71, 474, 538, 540, 589
3D/International Tower 458, 470
500 Jefferson Building 4, 12-13
5000 Longmont 458, 464-65
9111 Eastex Freeway Building 572, 576-77
99K House 572, 574-75
Abercrombie Laboratory, Rice University 196, 202-03
Abercrombie, J. S. 321
Abramowitz House 500, 504
Academic/Student Life Building, UH Downtown 89
Acres Homes 534-35, 545-46
Act II House 154, 180
Adair Park 656, 661
Adams Architects 100, 107, 445, 447
Adams Architects Studio and House 100, 107
Adams, Gail and Joe 107
Adams, S. N. 426
Addicks United Methodist Church 520, 528
Aeschbacher, Carl 172
African-American Library at the Gregory School 109
Agnes Arnold Hall, UH 268, 294
Aichler, Kurt 75
Airport Hotel, Bush Intercontinental Airport 586
Ake House 236, 250
Alamo Plaza Motel 268, 290-91
Albans Townhouses 236, 242
Albert C. Martin & Associates 465, 585
Albert F. Keller Grocery Store 336, 346-47
Albert Thomas Convention Center 4, 25, 28-29
Albert, Larry, AIA 366
Albin, Enrique House 552, 556-57
Albritton House 500, 504
Alden Houston Hotel 63
Alexan Lofts 314
Alice Pratt Brown Hall, Rice University 196, 206-07
Alkek Building, Baylor College of Medicine 198, 226
Alkek Building, Discovery Green 47
Alkek Eye Center, Baylor College of Medicine 198, 228, 229
All Saints Catholic Church 336, 357
Allen Center 10-12
Allen Parkway 392-93, 398
Allen Parkway Village 104-05
Allen, A. C. Addition 311
Allen, Augustus C. 10, 71, 90
Allen, John Kirby 10, 71, 90, 110
Allen, L. D., House 236, 260
Allen, Richard 11
Allen's Landing 86, 90
Alley Theatre 4, 26
Alliance Tower 552, 564-65
Allied Bank Plaza 4, 16-17
Allied Chemical Building 458, 464

Alquimia 146
Ambrose & House 599
Ambrose, McEnany & House 649
Ambrose/McEnany 204
Amegy Bank, Bellaire 552, 555
American General Building 100, 106
American General Life Building 106
American Institute of Architects v, x, 29, 192, 217, 575,
Amoco Center 520, 528-29
Anadarko Tower 594, 596
Anderson Hall, Rice University 204
Anderson House 154, 177, 183, 185-87, 396, 415, 418
Anderson, Clayton & Company 63, 158
Anderson, Jr., Ralph A., AIA 183, 285
Anderson, William J., AIA 187, 509, 430, 443
Anderson, William J., House and Shop 430, 443
Anderson/Wilson 250, 443, 509
André Emmerich Gallery 117
Angel, John, *William Marsh Rice Statue* 212
Anna Mod x, 79, 453,
Annunciation Catholic Church 35, 61
Annunciation Greek Orthodox Cathedral 102, 126-27
Antares Building 500, 502-03
Anthony, Ethan (Boston) 523
Antioch Baptist Church 4, 8, 10-11, 109
Antoine Predock Architects 205
Appel, Natalye, + Associates Architects 25, 159, 351, 356, 382, 543
Appel, Natalye, FAIA 179, 376, 382, 385, 524
Appelbaum, Ralph, Associates 157
Apple Dentist Headquarters 622, 630
Aquasource Building 520, 526
Arbor Building, UH Clear Lake 692
Archi*Technics 3, 577, 644
Archimage 542
Architecture Building, UH 268, 294-95
Architecture Center Houston 29
Architecture Center Houston Foundation vi
ArchitectWorks 388, 543, 555
ArchiTexas 77
ARCO Oil & Gas District Offices 529
Arcop Group 645
ArcTec Associates 526
Arlington Court 338, 363
Armand Bayou Nature Center 682, 693
Armor Building 68, 70
Armstrong, Cameron 144, 347-48, 356, 379-80, 381, 383-84, 423, 513, 545-46, 556
Arnold, Scott 80
Arquitectonica 48, 179, 183, 376, 406, 445, 493
Art Car Museum 336, 343
Art Guys World Headquarters 536, 545
Art League of Houston Building 102, 146-47
Artspace USA 351
Asakura Robinson 158, 313, 330, 427, 445, 530, 563, 624, 635
Asakura, Keji 158, 313, 330, 427, 445, 530, 563, 624, 635, 649
Asia Society Texas Center 152, 158-59
Associated Housing Architects of Houston 104, 278
Association for the Advancement of Mexican Americans Learning Center 306, 324-25
Astrodomain 220-31
Astrodome 36, 63, 151, 198, 230-31, 252
Atwood School of Theology, Houston Baptist University 565

Aubry, Eugene, FAIA 7, 49, 135-36, 188-89, 398, 416-17, 488, 556, 567, 628
Aubry, Eugene, House 154, 188-89
Auditorium Hotel 4, 23
Audubon Place 448
Augusta Green Building 458, 477
Austin House 396, 417
Austin Senior High School 304, 318-19
Autry House 102, 128-29, 213
Avalon Place 434, 444
Avalon Place Projects 374, 389
Avenue Community Development Corp. 351
B2HK 644
Bachelors Club 154, 189
Baer, David C. 273
Bailey Architects 213, 255, 644
Bailey Architects, Ray 6, 56, 59, 115, 125, 162, 164, 166, 177, 192, 213, 226, 258, 311, 359, 411, 420, 438, 440, 627
Bailey, James Ruskin 39, 82, 91, 112, 315, 320
Bailey, Ray, FAIA 6, 56, 59, 115, 125, 162, 164, 166, 177, 192, 213, 226, 255, 258, 311, 359, 411, 420, 438, 440, 627, 644
Baker Addition 334, 345, 351
Baker, Jay Architects 168, 186, 253, 401, 409, 421-24, 426, 693, 698
Baker, Jay, FAIA 168, 186, 253, 401, 407, 409, 421-24, 426, 503, 588, 693, 698
Baldwin, Bill 353
Ballantyne, A. J. 399
Ballard, Scott 188, 409, 441
Bang, Lars 256, 512, 559
Bank Building Corporation of America 244
Bank of Houston 152, 160
Bank of Tanglewood 484, 489
Bank of the Southwest 35, 51
Bankhead, Daniel, AIA vi
Banta, Jonathan E., House 338, 360-61
BAPS Shree Swaminarayan Mandir 622, 635
Barbara Jordan Healthcare Center 575
Barber, George F. 132, 358,
Barden, Carol Isaak viii, 108, 142, 697-98
Barglebaugh & Whitson 70
Barglebaugh, Charles Erwin 77
Barker Brothers Studio 161
Barkley, Joel (Ike Kligerman Barkley) 399
Barnstone, Gertrude 183, 385, 554,
Barnstone, Howard & Eugene Aubry 135-36, 207, 398, 417, 488
Barnstone, Howard, FAIA 60, 134-38, 179-80, 183, 207, 261, 291, 398, 412, 417, 421, 462, 465, 488, 491, 511-12
Barnum, Daniel, FAIA 119, 614
Barovier & Toso (Murano) 48
Barrick, Nolan 133
Barry Moore Architects, 70, 77, 80, 134, 143, 244, 292, 327, 669
Barthelme & Associates, Donald 544
Batchelor, Kevin 438
Bates College of Law, UH 268, 296-97
Battelstein's 35, 52-53
Baumgardner House 500, 512
Bay Architects 309
Bay Ridge 681, 686-87
Bay Ridge Cottage 682, 686
Baylor Clinic and Hospital 229
Baylor College of Medicine 198, 226, 228-29
Bayou Bend x, 378, 394, 402

Bayou Club 500, 502
Bayou Lofts 73
BBVA Company Plaza 469
BBVA Compass Stadium 700
Beaconsfield, The 35, 38
Beardsley, John 327
Bechtel Building 475
Beck Building, Museum of Fine Arts, Houston 152, 171
Beckett, Cheryl vi
Beckmann, Williams & Williams 273
Beeby, Tom 208
Beer Can House 374, 378-79
Bell House 484, 488
Bell, C. C., Construction Company 672
Bell, C. C., Jr. 182, 672
Bell, Michael 575
Bellaire 550-51, 554-58, 564
Bellfort Square Office Building 666, 670
Belt House 394, 414-15
Ben Taub General Hospital 198, 227
Benedit House 236, 256
Benjamin Apartments 113
Benner, Lee 72
Bentsen House 430, 436-37
Bentsen, Kenneth, Associates 77, 294, 437, 675
Berenson, Theodore 675
Berg & Androphy Building 120
Berlin & Swern 214
Berry, C. R., & Company 314
Bertini, John 160
Best, David 343
Bethany United Methodist Church 236, 258
Bethel Baptist Church 110
Bettis Apartments 396, 427
BG Group Place front cover, 35, 53
Bianchi, Allen 141, 191, 245-46, 445, 448, 488, 558
Biehl Building 539
Bienvenue, Rusty vi, vii
Biering, Robert O. 19
Biesel House 266, 283
Big Three Industries Building 520, 522
Biggers, John 273, 276, 280, 661
BioScience Research Collaborative, Rice University 196, 213
Bishkin House 268, 288
BJ Services Building 525
Blackmon, John 701
Blayney, T. Lindsey, House 152, 158-59
Blessed Sacrament Catholic Church 306, 322
Block, Gay, House 500, 507
Bloomer, Kent, Studio (New Haven) 208-09
Blue Triangle Y.W.C.A. 266, 273
Bluebox Architekten Rösch Schubert Hanisch 114
Blvd Place 458, 468
BMC Software Corporate Headquarters 622, 625
BNIM 219, 220, 293
Bodet, Edward A. 669, 676
Bodmer, Luis 314
Boesel, Minnette 72
Bofill, Ricardo 207, 470
Bohmfalk, Gordon & Troy Kennedy 297
Bolton & Barnstone 134, 261, 291, 421, 462, 491, 511
Bolton, P. M., Associates 405, 486
Bolton, Preston M., FAIA 134, 261, 291, 405, 421, 462, 465, 486, 491, 511
Bolullo, Mario 47, 295, 587, 684

Bonner House 154, 185, 500, 506
Bonner Elementary School 672
Booth Pavilion, Rice University 699
Bordeaux, W. D. 123, 282
Bordersville 581, 589
Borget, Lloyd 673
Borgstrom Grocery Co. Building 311
Borlenghi, Giorgio 465
Borlenghi, Lorenzo 465
Bossom, Alfred C. 60
Bouchard Architects 308
Bouchier, Ronald 585
Boulevard Green 552, 556-57
Boulevard Oaks 150-51, 185-86
Bouraine, Marcel 344
Bourgois, Laurent (Paris) 420
Bowles & Bowles 512
Bowles, Bob 512
BP Center 529
BP Plaza 529
BP Project Rodeo-Helios Plaza 520, 528-29
Bracewell Branch, Houston Public Library, 666, 668
Bracht House 500, 510-11
Bradfield, Richards & Associates 279
Bradley, Barrie Scardino vi, vii
Brady Addition 322
Brady House 306, 321
Brady, John Thomas 303, 321
Brady, Sherman 321
Braes Heights 254, 256
Braes Manor 259
Braeswood 235. 260-61
Braeswood Corporation House 236, 260
Brand + Allen 466-67, 479, 611
Brashear Building 68, 83
Brave, Alejandro House 236, 247
Brave, Fernando L., FAIA 140-41, 247, 299, 382, 543, 613, 658, 696
Brave/Architecture 140-41, 247, 299, 382, 543, 613, 658, 696
Brays Bayou 210, 219, 234-35, 256, 259, 265, 282, 291, 303, 327, 550-51, 562-63, 629
Brays Crossing 306, 325
Briar Grove 492
Briar Hollow 462-63
Briar House 484, 488-89
Brice-Davidson House 696
Brichford, Michael E. 515
Bricker + Cannady Architects 25, 258, 543
Bridgepoint Bible Church 520, 529
Bridgestone One Building 536, 538
Briscoe & Dixon 60, 168-69, 177, 310, 354, 408, 414
Briscoe, Birdsall P. 130-31, 158, 169, 177-78, 260, 273, 283, 319, 402-03, 407-08, 411, 415, 417-19, 439, 676, 689
Broadacres 176-78
Brochstein Pavilion, Rice University 196, 210-11
Brochstein, I. S. 257, 469
Brochstein, Raymond, FAIA 508
Brochsteins, Inc. Building 236, 256-57
Brockman Hall for Physics, Rice University 196, 206
Brodnax, Phenix & Associates 230
Broesche, Travis, & Associates 349, 557, 660
Brogniez, Raymond H. 114, 410, 505, 688
Brogniez, Raymond, House 500, 505
Broker, Karin 387
Brooke-Smith Addition 335, 354
Brookhollow Central 536, 538

Brookline School 306, 324-25
Brooks & Barr 691
Brooks & Brooks 258-59, 367, 562, 672
Brooks Association 647
Brooks House 552, 562
Brooks, Barr, Graeber & White 214
Brooks, David G. 259
Brooks, E. B. 259
Brooks, Patton W. 408
Brooks/Collier 205
Brown & McKim 191
Brown & Root 628, 690-91
Brown & Root Building 622, 628
Brown METRO Administration Building 35-36
Brown, Alice Pratt and George R., House 394, 413
Brown, Alice Pratt Hall, Rice University 196, 206-07
Brown, Ann Bohnn vi
Brown, George R. 47, 166, 413
Brown, Hamilton, FAIA 191, 452, 465, 487, 561
Brown, Lee P., Mayor 36, 48
Brown, Peter H., FAIA 41, 165, 174
Brown, Russell, Company 124, 158
Browne McGregor 602
Brune, Geoffrey, FAIA (GBA Architecture) 296, 441-42
Brunner Addition 372, 387-88
Brunsting, Carl 369
Bruton House 394, 404
Bryan House 394, 410-11
Bucek, David, FAIA 190, 206, 209, 327, 364, 412, 446, 613
Buckley Lofts 100, 108-09
Buffalo Bayou 3, 7, 11, 28-31, 81, 88-93, 104, 109, 302-03, 314, 321-22, 324, 328, 344, 377-78, 398-400, 402, 462-64, 482, 491, 498, 506, 518, 624, 664-65, 680, 685-86,
Buffalo Bayou Partnership viii, 31, 90
Buffalo Bayou Sabine-to-Bagby Promenade 4, 30-31
Buffalo Soldiers National Museum 123
Bullington House 394, 407
Bullock House (Morgan's Point) 682, 686
Bullock, Tom, House 500, 511
Bulone, Joseph 544
Burdette Keeland & Associates 442
Burgan House 236, 250
Burgee, John 20-21, 218, 295, 467, 469, 473-74, 644, 646
Burke Baker Planetarium 164
Burke House 394, 396, 404-05, 424
Burnett, James, Office of 17, 159, 202, 206-07, 210, 228-29, 254, 257, 342, 376-77, 426, 442, 527, 530, 634
Burnham, Daniel H. 81
Burns & James 185, 282-83, 400, 405, 413
Burrell, Seymour 56
Burrow, Robert 275
Burrows, Robert 365
Burt Hill Kossar Rittlemann Associates 219
Burton, Scott 295
Bush Branch, Harris County Public Library 613
Bush Elementary School 668
Bush Intercontinental Airport 580-82, 585-88
Bute, Martha B., AIA 412-13
Butler Brothers-Union Terminal Warehouse 336, 350
Butler House 266, 286-87
Butler, Hiram 369
Butler, Hiram Gallery 374, 388

Buxton, Fred 293, 462
Buxton, Fred, & Associates 19, 292
Byne, Arthur 414
Byrd's Department Store 68, 82
Byzantine Fresco Chapel 102, 137
C. C. Bell Construction Company House 666, 672
C. D. Hill & Co. 93
C/A Architects 491
Cade, James R., House 304, 310-11
Cadillac Fairview Corporation 45, 47
Cage Elementary School 304, 319
Caldwell Elementary School 656, 658
Caldwell, William C. 443
Calhoun, Harold, FAIA 124, 260, 491, 691
Calhoun, Tungate, Jackson & Dill 491
Callis, Joan 353
Cambridge Seven Associates 204, 449
Camburas, Peter E. 127
Cameron Building 525
Cameron Controls 539
Cameron Fairchild & Associates 447
Cameron Iron Works 306, 321, 536, 539-40
Cameron, Harry 321
Camp Logan 502
Camp Logan Addition 376
Campanile, Rice University 196, 203
Campbell & Keller 185
Campbell House 266, 282
Canal Street Apartments 304, 312-13
Candra Scott & Associates (San Francisco) 76
Cannady, Jackson & Ryan 174-75
Cannady, William T. & Associates 116, 173, 189, 244, 439, 489, 492
Cannady, William T. House 152, 154, 172-73, 189
Cannady, William T., FAIA 116, 152, 154, 172-73, 189, 242, 244, 439, 489, 492, 508, 558, 586
Cannata, Fred V. 345
Cantrell House 484, 490
Capital One Plaza 476
Capitán Theater 666, 674
Capitol Hotel 57
Capitol of the Republic of Texas 57
Cardinal Health Care Building 622, 624
Cargill, David Our Lady Seat of Wisdom 135
Carillon West 626
Carlon, Rocio vi
Carnegie Branch, Houston Public Library 304, 310-11
Carowitz, Jeff vii
Carpenter, J. E. R. 54
Carroll, J. J. House 102, 130
Carroll, Mary Ellen 564
Carson, Chris, FAIA 293, 409, 487, 508, 596, 635
Carter, Jr., W. T, Lodge 504
Carter, Jr., W. T. 130, 504, 664, 669
Carter, W. T. 130-31
Casa de Amigos 309
Casa de Amigos Community Health Center 304, 308
Casa de Amigos Health Center 304, 310
Casa de la Amistad 304, 311
Casa de Mañana 640, 642
Casbarian, John J., FAIA vi, 245, 249, 253, 259, 343, 352, 378, 389, 400, 420, 437, 440, 528, 599
Casita 236, 250-51
Castanié-Fromm House 4, 10
Cato, Lamar Q. 279
Caudill Rowlett Scott 15-16, 24-25, 29, 45, 49, 166, 217, 223, 292, 425, 451, 463, 464, 477, 494, 511, 515, 523, 527, 625, 673, 691
Caudill, William House 500, 514-15
Caudill, William W., FAIA 15-16, 24-25, 29, 45, 49, 166, 217, 223, 292, 425, 451, 463-64, 477, 494, 511, 514-15, 523, 527, 625, 673, 691
Cavitt McKnight Weymouth 134, 280, 647
Cemex Center 531
Cemo Lecture Hall, Bauer College of Business 268, 293
Central Church of Christ 101, 124-25
Central Library, Houston Public Library 4, 6-7
Central Presbyterian Church 432, 448-49
Central Warehouse and Forwarding Company 91
Centre One Building 552, 566
Centrum 613
Century Development Corporation 11, 15, 42, 216, 449, 451-52
Century Oaks Business Park 622, 634
Cerracchio, Enrico F. 163
César Pelli & Associates 12, 209, 217, 465-66
Chadwick, Susan, House 336, 357
Chancery of the Episcopal Diocese of Texas 35, 58, 59
Chaneyville 344
Chapel of St. Basil, University of St. Thomas 135
Charles Keith Associates 189, 415, 589
Chase III, Charles S. 65
Chase, John S., FAIA 47-48, 273, 280-82, 285-86, 575
Chase, John S., House 266, 285
Chasewood Technology Park 612
Cheek-Neal Coffee Company Building 304, 314-15
Chelsea Market 154, 181
Chemistry Building, Rice University 196, 202-03
Chen House 693
Cherry, Emma Richardson 9, 122
Chevron Geosciences Building 622, 624-25
Chew House 394, 412, 413
Chicago Bridge & Iron Building 600
Children's Museum of Houston 152, 156-57
Children's Nutrition Research Center 198, 222
Childress House 394, 410
Chilton Court Apartments 430, 434, 435
Chin, Mel, *Manila Palm* 173
Chin, Mel, *Seven Wonders* 28
Chinatown 627-29
Chinese American Citizens Alliance Hall 315
Chinmaya Prabha 622, 631
Cho Design Force 629
Chong Hua Sheng Mu Gong Holy Palace 622, 629
Christ Church Cathedral 35, 58-59
Christ The King Lutheran Church 236, 244
Christ The Redeemer Catholic Church 608, 614
Christensen & Cannata 511
Christia V. Adair Mural 656, 661
Christian Life Center 523
Christie House 394, 412-13
Christie, Theodosia Campbell 413
Church of the Epiphany 552, 566
Church of the Redeemer, Episcopal 306, 320
Church, Thomas D. 261
Cirincione, J. B. 243
Cisneros Design Studio 94, 172, 369, 629, 633
Citizens State Bank Building 336, 342
City Beautiful Movement 65, 163, 170
City Hall and Market House 71
City National Bank Building 35, 43
City of Houston Dept. of Public Health Building 198, 226

City of Houston Permitting Center 350
City of Houston, Public Works 304, 318
City of Houston, Firemen's Training Academy 666, 668
City of Houston, Water Customer Service Building 304, 318
City of Houston, Willow Street Pump Station 86, 92
CityCentre 520, 530-31
Civitello, Rob, Local Architect 255, 366, 369, 379, 381
Cizik House 396, 420
Clark Condon Associates 25, 49, 105, 668
Clark, Dick (Austin) 244
Clarke & Courts Building 100, 108
Clayton, N. J. 37, 61, 349
Clayton, Susan Vaughn 414
Clayton, Will, House 152, 158
Clayton, Will, Summer House 394, 414
Clayton, William L. 158, 414
Clear Lake Campus, UH 682, 692
Clear Lake City 325-26, 681, 690-91, 693
Clear View Education Center 694
Clemens, R. W. 672
Clemens, Robert W. & Associates 444
Clemons, Harvey 574
Cleveland, A. Sessums, House 102, 128-29
Clinton & Russell 40
Clovis Heimsath, FAIA 59, 133, 192, 280, 489, 531, 566, 613, 660, 677
Club Quarters Hotel 64
Co-Cathedral of the Sacred Heart 35-36
Cobourn, Linseinsen & Ratcliff 616
Coburn, I. W., & Associates 443
Cochran & Cochran 379
Cochran, Catherine 379
Cochran, Stephen 379
Cockrell Butterfly Center 164
Codewell Hall, HCC, Northeast College 682, 684
Cody, William F., & Associates 635
Coe, Herring 6, 162, 166
Coffee Pot Building 91
Cohen Building 100, 118-19
Cohen House, Rice University 102, 132-33, 196, 236, 248, 642
Cohen, Ben 118
Cohen, George, House 133
Colby, Rudolph 415, 436
Coleman House 152, 176
Collaborative Designworks ix, 134, 142, 184, 246
Collaborative Projects 442
Colley, Richard S. 293, 507, 635
Collier Branch, Houston Public Library 536, 540
Collignon, G. W. 63
Colonial Savings Tower 567
Colquitt Court 441
Columbia House 338, 362-63
Comcast Building 542
Commerce Building 51-52
Commerce Towers 52
Commercial Buildings 304, 314-15
Commercial National Bank Building 38, 74
Communication Arts 467
Community Recreation Center 691
Compaq Computer Corporation 606, 608, 612
Compendium 126, 503
Condon, Richard S. 486
Coney, Mason C. 690
Congregation Adath Emeth Synagogue 266, 278, 349

Congregation Beth Israel Temple 552, 562-63
Congregation Beth Messiah Synagogue 622, 632-33
Congregation Beth Yeshurun Synagogue 266, 284
Congregation Emanu El Temple 154, 192
Conn House 102, 140-41
Connick, Charles J. (Boston) 61
Conoco Building 520, 526-27
ConocoPhillips 527
Conopio, Kathy vi
Conrad House 500, 509
Container House 336, 354
Contemporary Arts Museum 152,171-73, 221
Content 698
Control Data Corporation Building 458, 471
Cook House 484, 489
Cooke & Company 88, 132, 327
Cooke, Henry C. 345
Cooke, W. A., House 306, 327
Cooley, Denton A., Building, St. Luke's Hospital 198, 223
Cooner, Roger M. 701
Cooper-Cary (Atlanta) 473, 649
Cooper, Keith D. 202
Coover, Gary 128
Copley House 152, 174
CORE Design Studio 219
CORE: The 99K House 572, 574-75
Corgan Associates 587
Corinthian Pointe 659
Corinthian, The 74-75
Cornell, Bridges & Troller 292
Coryell, Ross 212
Cosmopolitan 458, 466
Cotswold 2000 68, 80-81
Cotswold Manor 154, 182
Court at Museum's Gate 101, 126
Courtlandt Place 102, 128-29
Courtney Harper & Partners 114
Covenant Church 152, 159
Cowell & Neuhaus 400-01, 412, 561
Cowperwood Regency Building 567
Craig, Christopher 379
Crain Ready-Cut Building Company 141
Crain, B. W., Jr. 545
Crain, E. L. 545
Cram & Ferguson 6, 119, 203, 212-13, 414, 523
Cram, Goodhue & Ferguson 150, 200-01, 203, 211
Cram, Ralph Adams 6, 119-21, 150, 162, 170, 119, 200-01, 203, 211-13, 414, 523
Crane Company Building 316
Crane House 336, 356-57
Crate & Barrel Building 396, 426
Crenshaw Professional Plaza 682, 694-95
Creole Design 353, 355
Crescent, The 552, 566-67
Criner, Sanford 343
Crispin Company 347
Crockett, David Addition 446-47, 515
Cropp House 500, 514-15
Crotty House 152, 169
Crown Central Petroleum Building 556
CRS 15-16, 24-25, 29, 45, 49, 166, 217, 223, 292, 425, 451, 463, 464, 477, 494, 511, 515, 523, 527, 625, 673, 691
CRS Building 458, 463
CRS Sirrine 55, 227, 463, 529, 692
Culbertson, Margaret 132, 358
Cullen Building, Baylor College of Medicine 198, 226

Cullen Family Plaza, UH 268, 292
Cullen Hall, University of St. Thomas 135
Cullen House 394, 412
Cullen Sculpture Garden, Museum of Fine Arts 152, 170-71
Cullen, Hugh Roy 171, 215, 412,
Cullinan, Craig, House 152, 168-69
Cullinan, J. S. 60, 167-69, 277, 684
Cummings Elementary School 622, 631
Cummins Southern Plains Building 572, 576
Cummins, Robert J. 323
Cuney Homes 264, 266, 278
Curry Boudreaux 255
Curry, Kemo vi
Curry, Steven, AIA vii, 255-56
Curtis & Windham 110, 177, 253, 404, 416-17, 419-21, 437, 489
Curtis, William 110, 177, 253, 404, 416-17, 419-21, 437, 489
Cy Twombly Gallery 102, 138-39
Cyclone Anaya's Mexican Kitchen 381
Cynthia Woods Mitchell Center for the Arts, UH 268, 296-97
Cynthia Woods Mitchell Pavilion 594, 598-99
Cypress Creek Christian Church 613
Cypress Creek Family YMCA 608, 612-13
D. H. Burnham & Co. 81
DaCamera of Houston 137
Dahl, George L. 545
Dahlstrand, Kevin 149, 185
Damascus Baptist Church 336, 344
Damson Oil Building 585
Dan Design 630
Dansby & Miller 668
Dansby, Jr., John D. 671
Dargan House 154, 178-79
Daughters of the Republic of Texas 227
David Crockett Addition 446-47, 515
David House 154, 186-87
David, Dorman 437
Davidson Architects, L. Barry 146, 189, 248-50, 252, 349, 417, 423, 486, 487, 504, 507, 699
Davila, Morgana vi
Davis, Larry S., & Associates 382, 384
Davis, Randall 56-57, 70, 76, 93, 108, 466, 475
De la Reza, Rey, Architects 81, 89, 105, 219, 325, 361, 546, 633
De la Reza, Rey, FAIA 89, 325, 361, 546, 633
De Menil, Dominique Schlumberger 134-38, 207, 412
De Menil, François 108, 137,180, 245,
De Menil, John 134, 136-37, 207, 412
De Santos Gallery 102, 140
Deady, James W. Junior High School 666, 675
Deal Centennial Pavilion, Rice University 699
Dean House 394, 408-09
DeBakey, Michael E., Veterans Affairs Medical Center 227
Deborah Nevins & Associates 420
Deguchi, Jay 697
Delia's Lounge 277
Dell Butcher Hall, Rice University 196, 204-05
Denny, Ray & Wines 523
Denny*Ray*Wines Associates 144
DePelchin Faith Home 100, 110-11
Detering Interests 671
Detering, Carl A. 675
Detering, Herman E. 675

Detherage, Roger 347
Development Design Group 598
Dewane, David 275
Di Suvero, Mark 139
Dickey, George E. 76, 133, 349
Dickey, William M. 444
Dickey, William T. 444
Dielmann, Leo M. J. 313, 317
Dieman, Charles A. 283
Dinkeloo, John, & Associates 527
Discovery Green 17, 35, 46-48
DiverseWorks 71, 575
Dixon & Greenwood 161
Dixon, Jr., Sam H. 319
DMJM H&N 468
DMJM Keating 16, 625
DNA Westpark 525
Doerre Intermediate School 611
Dogwoods 403
Doherty Library, University of St. Thomas 135-36
Dominion Post Oak 458, 470
Don J. Tomasco Associates 514
Donoghue, Thomas J., House 102, 130-31
Donovan Park 357
Dorfman, J. V., Development Company 463
Dormant, F. L. 90-91
Dorrance House 102, 129
Dotson, H. S. 368
Doubletree Guest Suites Houston 475
Doughtie & Porterfield 671, 673
Douglas, J. Herbert 260
Dow Chemical Company 503
Dow Elementary School 336, 346
Dow, Alden B. 503
Dowdy, W. A. 351
Dowling, Dick, Statue 227
Down and Up House 154, 179
Downtown Houston Association 71
Downtown Redevelopment Authority 57, 71
Draut, Joel vi
Dreef, Ferenc 367
Drink Milner Architects 191
Drumheller House 338, 364
Du Ross, James L., House 142
Dubuffet, Jean, *Monument au Fantôme* 16, 47
Duell, Randall & Associates 230
Duff, R. C., House 100, 116
Dumas, Steven Paul 387
Duncan College, Rice University 202
Duncan Hall, Rice University 196, 202
Dunn Memorial Chapel 223
Dunn Outreach Center at the Beacon 35, 58-59
Dunne, W. Scott 143
Dupree, C. W. 274
Durán, Turner 547, 645
Durham Center 381
Durst-Gee House 500, 509
DuZer 700
Dvořák House 338, 368
Dwight P. Robinson & Company 643
Dwyer, Laney McAdow vi
Dy, Kathy 277
Dyal & Babendure 577
Dynasty Plaza 626, 627
Eades, Gary 364
Eamon, Anne 299, 425
East End State Bank Building 316
Eastwood Elementary School 306, 320-21

707

Eberson, John 55
Eckbo, Dean, Austin & Williams (Los Angeles) 399
EDI 470, 475, 588, 627
Edmundson, Jesse 73
Edward D. Stone, Jr. & Associates 474
Ekrenkrantz, Eckstut & Kuhn 41
El Jaral 430, 437
Elder Street Artists Lofts 351
Eldorado Ballroom 266, 274
Eldridge, W. T. 638, 642-43
Electric Tower 4, 19
Elizalde, Albin Vasconcelos 557
Elkins, Leslie K., AIA 191, 122, 369, 378, 696
Elkins, Leslie, Architecture 191, 122, 378, 696
Elkus Manfredi (Boston) 596-97
Eller Wagon Works Building 95
Ellifrit, Ralph S. 258, 550
Ellington Field 664
Elliott + Associates 627
Elliott, Paul H. 524
ELS/Elbasani Logan 598
Emancipation Park 274
Emerson Unitarian Church 458, 477
Emmerich Gallery 117
Emory Weiner School 633
Empire Lofts and Flats 475
Emsco Derrick and Equipment Co. Building 666, 668-69
Enclave Business Park 624
Energy Center I and II 520, 528
English + Associates Architects 624
English, Kathleen, AIA vi, 624
Enron Center 4, 12
Enron Field 62-63
Enserch Building 622, 626
Enter Architecture 179, 684
Environment Associates 119, 660
Erie City Iron Works 86, 92-93
Ernest S. Sterling Student Center, Rice University 266, 280-81
Ernst, Carter 349
Eskander, Awad Youssef 617
ESPA Group 330
Esperson, Mellie Keenan 55, 522
Esplanade Homes 700-701
Essinger, Catherine vi
Esso Eastern of New Jersey Building 484, 495
Eubanks/Bohnn Associates 128-29, 167, 174
Euclid House 430, 440-41
Eugene Werlin & Associates 164
Evans, James M., AIA ix, 134, 142, 184, 246, 342
Ewald, Philip C. 512
Exxon Coal and Minerals Company 495
ExxonMobil Brookhollow Campus 539
ExxonMobil Chemical Company 529
ExxonMobil North American Headquarters 607
ExxonMobil Research Center 451
Ezekiel W. Cullen Building, UH 268, 292
F. S. Glover & Son 73, 325
Fabre, Rodolfo 359
Fairchild, Cameron D. 407, 436, 447
Faith American Lutheran Church 552, 556-57
Falick/Klein Partnership (FKP) 50, 215, 538
Farb Companies 477, 566
Farfel House 396, 420-21
Farish, Libbie Rice 152, 168
Farish, William Stamps, House 152, 168
Farish, William Stamps, Stables 503

Farnsworth & Chambers Building 306, 326
Farrington, William G. Company 229, 410
Farrington, William G. 482, 484
Farris, Kirk, *McKee Street Bridge* 93
Fasulllo, George 544
Fat Frank's Grub and Saloon 520, 528
FdM: Arch 108, 180
Federal Office Building and U. S. Courthouse 4, 28-29
Federal Reserve Bank of Dallas (1922) 35, 60
Federal Reserve Bank of Dallas (2005) 100, 105
Fehr, Bruce 79
Fellheimer & Wagner 190
Fellowship of The Woodlands 594, 601
Fergus, Daniel 439
Ferndale Addition 443, 446-47
Ferrara, Jackie 295
Fifth Ward Business and Financial Center 572, 574
Fifth Ward Community Redevelopment Corporation 570, 574-75
Fifth Ward Hotel 92
Finger & Bailey 315
Finger & Rustay 284, 315
Finger Companies 47, 182
Finger House 268, 288
Finger, Joseph, 6, 23, 52-53, 63-64, 82, 91, 94, 108, 110, 118, 121, 139, 143, 159, 161, 173, 182, 282, 287-89, 315, 319, 322, 342, 352, 669, 687, 690
Finley, Dawn 140, 434
Finn, Alfred C., FAIA 9, 30, 38, 41, 43, 50, 52-54, 57, 80, 82, 95, 113, 124-25, 127, 131, 162, 168, 214, 227, 292, 310, 316, 360, 362, 685, 687
Finnegan Park Recreation Building 330
Finnell House 154, 184
Fire Station No. 7 100, 115
Fire Station No. 9 304, 308-09
Fire Station No. 59 656, 659
First Baptist Church 520, 522-23
First Christian Church 154, 191
First City Bancorporation 49
First City Bank, North Belt Building 582, 584-85
First City Motor Bank Building 100, 112-13
First City National Bank Building 19, 35, 42-43, 51
First City Tower 35, 48-49
First Colony Branch, Fort Bend County Library 640, 646-47
First Colony Church of Christ 640, 645
First Colony Common 640, 646-47
First Colony Mall 640, 648-49
First Congregational Church 152, 161
First Evangelical Church 121-22, 161
First Evangelical Lutheran Church 100, 120-21
First International Plaza 4, 16
First National Bank Building 68, 74
First Pasadena State Bank Building 666, 672-74
First Presbyterian Church 152, 162
First Shiloh Baptist Church 572, 574-75
First State Bank Building 682, 690-91
First Unitarian Church 152, 160
First Unitarian Universalist Church 160
First United Methodist Church 35, 38-39, 682, 695
Fitzgerald, Richard & Partners 138, 218, 402, 469-70, 473-74, 538, 585, 646, 648
Five Houston Center 45
Five Post Oak Park Building 458, 462
FKP Architects 191, 203, 213, 217-18, 220, 222-23
Flato, Malou 70
Flatow, Max, House 268, 289

Flatow, Moore, Bryan & Fairburn 289
Flavin, Dan 139
Fleming & Sheppard 178, 402, 404,
Fleming, C. C. "Pat" 177-78, 401-02, 404, 487, 555
Fleming, C. C., House 484, 487
Fleming, Will 186, 252, 437
Fleshman, Duke 558
Flint, Howard, Ink Company Building 306, 330
Flower Man, The 266, 274-75
Floyd, William N. 444, 486, 492, 514-15, 557, 559, 560
Fluor Houston Operations Center 646
Focke, Wulf 441
Fogel, Seymour 191
Foley Brothers 133
Foley's 41, 53
Folger, J. A., Coffee Company Building 306, 322-23
Fondren Library, Rice University 211-12
Fondren, Walter W., House 102, 126-27
Fooshee & Cheek 669
Forakis, Peter 294
Ford Motor Company Building 306, 328-29
Ford, O'Neil, FAIA (San Antonio) 293, 409, 418, 487, 504, 508, 596, 635
Ford, Powell & Carson 293, 409, 487, 508, 596, 635
Ford, Tina and Matt 700-701
Forest Hill 327
Forster, Frank J. 416
Fort Bend ISD Administration Building 647
Fort Bend ISD Athletic Complex 640, 646-47
Fort-Brescia, Bernardo 48
Forty-eight Foot House 102, 140
Forum of Civics Building 430, 438-39
Founders Memorial Park 110
Fountain of Praise 656, 658
Fountains at Memorial City 531
Fountains at Waterway Square 594, 597
Four Allen Center 4, 11-12
Four Oaks Place 458, 466-67
Four Seasons Hotel-Houston Center 49
Four Seasons Inn on the Park 458, 464
Four-Leaf Towers 458, 465, 467
Fox, Stephen vi, vii
Frame House 500, 506
Frank Welch & Associates 418, 436, 489, 491, 510
Frankfurt, H. D. 272
Franzen, Ulrich & Associates, 26
Franzheim, Kenneth, FAIA 13, 39-41, 51-52, 54, 57, 65, 128, 214-15, 220, 345, 410
Fred Hartman Bridge 680, 682, 686
Fred Winchell Studio 430, 441
Frederick, Anthony E. 137, 139, 178, 248, 250, 312, 364, 408, 415, 418, 437
Fredricks House 552, 562
Freed Memorial Tower 121
Freed, Eleanor Montrose Branch Library 125
Freed, James 470
Freedmantown 109
Freedmen's Town Historic District 109
Freeman, Jr., John H. 215
Freeman, Van Ness & Mower 297
Freeway Baptist Church 306, 326
French, Mark R. 695
Fretz, Robert 82
Freuhling, George 116
Friedlander House 266, 283
Friedman Clock Tower 71
Friendswood 495, 581
Friendswood Development Co. 584, 617
Frost Office Building 430, 440
Frothingham, Louis 403
FS Partners 207
Fulbright Tower 45, 49
Fuller & Sadao 171
Fullerton School 306, 322-23
Gabert, Lenard 192, 257, 274, 282, 287
Gabert, Lenard & W. Jackson Wisdom 259, 286
Gables Residential (Atlanta) 439
Gabriel Architects 73, 83,
Gabriel, Ange-Jacques 120-21
Gaenslen, Frederick B. 310, 322, 357
Gaertner, Michael & Associates 346
Gaffney, E. Kelly 349
Galbreth, Michael 545
Galea, Edward Z. 117, 215, 226
Galleria Plaza Hotel 472
Galleria, The (I, II, III,IV) 458, 472-475
Gallery Sonja Roesch 100, 114
Gamma Construction Company Building 430, 448
Garcín, Peter 72, 116, 469
Garden Club of Houston Park 198, 224-25
Garden House 572, 575
Garden Oaks 534, 544-45
Garden Oaks Theater 545
Garden Villas 665, 669-70
Garden Villas Elementary School 669
Garden Villas Park Recreation Building 666, 670
Garden Villas United Methodist Church 666, 668-69
Garrett, Pete Ed (Studio Red) 243, 350, 451-52, 601, 658
Garrow, J. W., House 102, 130-31
Garvey, Frank 75
Garza, Carmen Lomas 325
Gateway I Building 582, 584-85
Gateway Lofts 143
Gaw, Betty and Allen 512-13
GBA Architects 296
GE Oil and Gas 585
Gehring & Reichert 258
General Growth Properties 593
General Mercantile Store Building 338, 368
General Services Administration Regional Field Office Building 536, 540
Gensler 6-7, 17-18, 27, 29, 42, 45, 48, 50, 55, 90, 92, 117, 164, 342, 529-30, 596-98, 600, 607, 616, 634, 644
Gensler & Associates 8, 20, 29, 51, 73
George Hall, UH/Wharton Jr. College 644
George Pierce-Abel B. Pierce Professional Building 430, 436
George R. Brown Convention Center 9, 17, 29, 35, 46-47
George R. Brown Hall, Rice University 196, 204
Gerald D. Hines College of Architecture vi, x, 295-96, 312
Geyer, Charles E 444
Gianukos, Sam 355
Gibbs Wellness Center 196, 207
Gibraltar Building 100, 114
Giesecke & Harris 89, 643-44
Giffels & Vallet 329
Gillette, R. W. 246
Gilmer House 154, 178
Giurgola, Romaldo 50
Glassell Junior School, Museum of Fine Arts 152, 172

Glassell School of Art 152, 172
Glassman Shoemake Maldonado 152, 156, 158, 179, 191, 249, 260, 325, 410, 414
Glenbrook Valley 671
Glendale Cemetery 677
Glendower Court 436
Glennie, Ian 386, 701
Glenwood Cemetery x, 334, 336, 344-45
Glesby House 236, 261
Glitsch-Inman House 430, 444
Glitsch, Val, FAIA 141, 160, 253, 313, 330, 355, 365, 380, 417-18, 427, 443-45, 488, 524
Glover, F. S., & Son 73, 325
Glover, J. M. 283, 359
Glover, Louis A. 6, 675
Glover, Tim 79
Godine-Hoover House 552, 560
Goff, Bruce 508-09
Goldberg, Brad 81
Golding Memorial Chapel, Christ Church Cathedral 59
Golemon & Rolfe 14, 37, 47, 162, 216, 413, 491, 543, 567, 585-87, 669, 692
Golemon House 484, 491
Golemon, Harry Architects 295, 587, 684
Golemon, Harry, FAIA 14, 37, 47, 162, 216, 295, 413, 491, 543, 567, 585-87, 669, 692
Golemon/Bolullo 684
González House 394, 400
González, Enrique 577
Gonzalez, Jose 353
Good, Fulton & Farrell (Dallas) 426
Goode Gallery 430, 445
Goodhue, Bertram G. 120, 123, 150, 200-01, 203, 211, 674
Goodman, Charles M. 38
Goodwin, Jr., Edwin J 205, 511
Goodwin, Jr., Edwin J. (Jim), House 500, 511
Gordon House 236, 260-61
Gordon, Sewall & Company Building 91
Gordy, Marvin 509
Gorlin, Alexander 403
Gose House 287
Gottlieb, R. D. 7, 58, 60, 63, 74-75, 109, 121, 124, 132, 310,
Goulas & Associates 83
Goulas, Warren 523
Gould, Lenya 242
Grable, John 558
Graduate Design/Build Studio, UH 187, 560
Graham, John Company 675
Graustark Family Townhouses 154, 178-79
Graves House 162, 174-75
Graves, Michael 29, 105, 201
Graves, Michael, & Associates 105
Greacen & Brogniez 114, 688
Greacen II, Thomas E. 114, 160, 688
Great Southern Bank Building 484, 494
Greater Houston Preservation Alliance ix, 345, 349, 513
Greater Zion Missionary Baptist Church 266, 272-73
Green & Briscoe 322
Green & Finger 53, 80, 159
Green & Svarz 74
Green Conservancy viii, 46
Green House 394, 403
Green, Lewis Sterling 53, 74, 80, 159, 322
Green, Mark 351
Greenberg, Allan 211
Greene, Herb 113, 133, 256, 487, 509, 513,
Greenspoint 580, 584-85
Greenway Plaza 38, 328, 432, 449-51
Greenwood, Ben F. 671
Greer House 500, 506-07
Greeven 208
Gregory Elementary School 100, 109
Gregory Harper Associates 612
Gregory House 268, 290
Gregory, Jr., O'Neil 290
Grenader, Nonya, FAIA 190, 277, 367, 386
Gribble Stamp and Stencil Company Building 304, 314
Griffin, Robert E. 510
Griffin, Walter Burley 70
Griffith Associates, Lauren 46, 71
Grinberg, Israel 526
Grocer's Supply Company Building 86, 94
Gross Elementary School 622, 632-33
Grotfeld, Virgil, Studio-House 536, 546
Grotfeldt, Deborah 276
Grott, James 384
Grove Court Townhouses 374, 388-89
Grove, The, Discovery Green 47
Guadalupe Plaza 304, 314
Guaranty National Bank 80
Guardian Trust Company 55
Guastivino tile 62, 65, 200-01, 324
Guest Quarters Galleria West 458, 475
Gulf Building 22, 35, 54-55
Gulf Tower 35, 44-45
Gulfgate Shopping City 675
Gund, Graham, Associates 424
Gunn, Ralph Ellis 191, 401
Gunnar Birkerts & Associates 172
Gus S. Wortham Theater Center 4, 26-27
Guthrie, David 143, 244, 524, 698
Guthrie+Strasser 698
Gutierrez, Gabriella 255, 575
Guy Thornton Design (Denver) 58
Gwathmey Siegel & Associates 585
Gwathmey, Charles 585
Habitat for Humanity Demonstration Houses 304, 312-13
Habitat for Humanity Jimmy Carter Work Project Houses 306, 328
Hager, Jesse 698
Hagstette, Guy, FAIA 28, 46, 73, 83
Hai Du Duong 629
Haid, David (Chicago) 561
Hail House 152, 174
Haley, J. Evetts, House 536, 544-45
Hall Barnum Lucchesi (HBL) 614
Hall, Jr., William H., AIA 119, 124, 510, 614, 634
Hall/Barnum Architects 119
Hall/Merriman Architects 119, 124, 244, 511, 634
Halliburton 585, 628
Hamilton Middle School 360
Hamman Exploration Company Building 434, 435
Hamman Hall, Rice University 205-06
Hamman, John, House 102, 128
Hamman, Kendall 448
Hamman, Laura R. 437
Hammond Beeby Babka 208
Hamrick, Rebecca vi
Hanbury Evans Wright Vlattas 202, 211
Handmade House (Strasser-Ragni) 102, 142

Handmade House (Olson Sundberg Kundig Allen) 696
Hanna/Olin Associates 163
Hannah, David 73
Hansen, John 125, 464, 556,
Harding, Steve 165
Hare & Hare 6, 104, 163, 166, 171, 254, 260, 278, 291-92, 392, 545, 671
Hare, Sid J. 327, 557
Hargreaves Associates 46
Harithas, James 343
Harley & Ellington 330
Harold's 338, 366-67
Harper Associates, Gregory 612
Harper, Courtney & Partners 114
Harris County Administration Building 77
Harris County Center for the Retarded 394, 398
Harris County Courthouse 68, 77
Harris County Criminal Justice Center 68, 78
Harris County Family Law Center 68, 78
Harris County Youth Services Center 552, 554-55
Harris County-Houston Sports Authority 48, 62
Harris County, Anderson Clayton Building 63
Harris County, Civil Courthouse 78-79
Harris County, Peden Correction Facility 91
Harris Elementary School 666, 676-77
Harris House 682, 688-89
Harris, Glenn Morgan 689
Harris, John R. 322, 676, 689
Harris, William P. 689
Harrisburg 303, 322, 344, 475-77, 665, 689
Harrisburg National Bank Building 666, 676
Harrison & Associates, Price (Nashville) 248
Harrison, Price 248
HarrisonKornberg Architects 187, 326, 423, 425, 625
Harry Golemon Architects 295, 587
Hartman Bridge 680, 682, 686
Hartman, William 245
Hartmann, Craig 213
Harvey Builders 575
Harwood K. Smith & Partners 557
Hassebroek, Dan, AIA vi
Hatch Partnership 440
Haven restaurant 430, 442
Hayes, Bruce 224
Haywood Jordan McCowan 47, 281, 284, 287
Health and Physical Education Building, TSU 266, 280-81
Heard, Ethel Lyon 344
Heard, Kathy Design 441
Hearsay restaurant 72
HEB Buffalo Market, 236, 250-51
HEB Montrose Market 696
Hebert House 336, 354-55
Hebrew Cemetery 110
Hedrick & Gottlieb 7, 75, 109, 121, 124, 310
Hedrick & Lindsley 226
Hedrick, Wyatt C. 7, 58, 75, 109, 121, 124, 214-15, 226, 280, 310, 575, 669
Heger, Wendy Teas, AIA vi
Heights Branch, Houston Public Library 338, 359
Heights Christian Church 338, 360
Heights Church of Christ 338, 362
Heights High School 338, 360
Heights Playground 336, 356-57
Heights State Bank Building 336, 342
Heights Theater 338, 366

Heights Transit Center 338, 360-61
Heights Venture Architects 406
Heights Women's Club 361
Heimsath, Clovis, Associates 59, 133, 192, 280, 489, 531, 566, 613, 660, 677
Heimsath, Maryann 567
Heinen Theater, Houston Community College 121
Heiner, Eugene T. 72-73, 80, 83, 345
Heizer, Michael 139, 203
Hellmuth, Obata + Kassabaum (HOK) 23, 39, 48, 62-63, 208, 229, 231, 463, 472-73, 525, 527-28, 577, 600, 612, 616, 624, 645, 691
Helmet House 152, 174-75
Helms, J. C. 470
Henke's Fifth Ward Store 86, 92
Henry Brashear Building 68, 83
Henry Henke's Fifth Ward Store 86, 92
Henry, Melton 165, 465
Henry, Melton, Architects 165, 465-66
Herbert Voelcker & Associates 317
Heritage Plaza 4, 6-7
Heritage Presbyterian Church 617
Heritage Society 7-10
Hermann Estate Building 73
Hermann Hospital 196, 214, 531, 538
Hermann Hospital Pavilion 214
Hermann Park viii, 36, 150-52, 163-66, 214-15, 227, 291
Hermann Park Clubhouse 152, 164
Hermann Park Conservancy viii, 163-65
Hermann Professional Building 196, 214-15, 217
Hermann, George H. 6, 163, 214
Hermes Architects 602, 634, 675
Hermes Reed Hindman 647, 694
Hermon Lloyd & W. B. Morgan 54, 207, 419, 565
Herolz, Jr., Robert A. 123
Herolz, Trudy Hutchings 123
Herring Hall, Rice University 196, 208-09, 227
Hershey, Olive 99
Hershey, Terry Park 624
Herzog House 236, 261
Herzstein Hall (Physics Building), Rice University 201
Hess House 666, 670
Hess Tower 35, 45
Hester, Paul 71
Hewitt Associates Building 600
Hewlett Packard 612
Heyer House 394, 404
Heymann, David 252
HHN Homes 111
Hicks, Jackson 75
Hidalgo Park Kiosk 306, 324
High School for the Performing and Visual Arts 102, 134
Highland Village 426-27
Hightower & Moreland 635
Hightower, Charles 478
Hildebrandt House 552, 566-67
Hill, Ben vii
Hill, C. D. & Co. 93
Hill, Howard 669
Hill, James, Country House 467
Hillcroft Professional Building 484, 494
Hille, Karl, House 102, 128
Hilton Americas Hotel 35, 48
Hilton Houston North 584
Hines College of Architecture vi, x, 295-96, 312

711

Hines, E. Gene 671
Hines, Gerald D. ix, 18, 425, 452, 467, 472
Hines, Gerald D. Interests (Hines) 17, 18-22, 26, 42, 51, 53, 217, 425, 452-53, 468-75, 529, 639, 649,
Hiram Butler Gallery 374, 388
Hirschfield, Alan 557
Hispanic Consortium 314
HKS Architects (Dallas) 45, 223, 469,
Hoang, Doanh 630
Hobby Airport 664, 669
Hobby Center for the Performing Arts 4, 30-31
Hobby Family Foundation 435
Hobby House 394, 409
Hobby, Oveta Culp 409
Hoffman Hall, UH 268, 294
Hoffman, Gilbert 295
Hofheinz, Roy 230, 475
Hogg Palace Lofts 70
Hogg, Ima 402, 408
Hogg Junior High School 336, 354
Hogg, Mike 70, 398, 402
Hogg, Will C. 70, 353, 398, 402, 439, 502,
HOK 23, 39, 48, 62-63, 208, 229, 231, 463, 472-73, 525, 527-28, 577, 600, 612, 616, 624, 645, 691
HOK Sport 48, 62, 63, 208, 231, 616, 700
Holland House 102, 132-33
Holland Lodge No. 1 154, 182
Holland, H. C. 80
Hollington, Richard 204, 209, 284, 493, 529
Hollis, Doug 47, 71
Holmes Shopping Center 236, 256-57
Holocaust Museum Houston 152, 157
Holtz, B. W. 156, 319
Holy Cross Episcopal Church 666, 677
Holy Cross Lutheran Church Parish Hall 520, 524
Holy Name Catholic Church 304, 310
Holy Rosary Catholic Church 100, 120
Homeyer, Paul, AIA 50
Hong Kong City Mall 622, 628-29
Hood, Jr., Lucian T. 288-90
Hooton, Claude E. 246, 404
Hoover, Sharon Tyler 444
Hopkins Architects (London) 202, 211
Hopkins, Michael 202, 211
Horning, Jeff 515
Horst Berger Partners 599
Horton, Sallie Sewall House 122
Hotel Icon 76
Hotel Sorella by Valencia 530
Houchins, John F. 436
House 2045 236, 246-47
House of Expanding Rooms 536, 543
House X2 154, 184
House, C. L., House 129
House, Gladys 109
House/Reh Associates 522, 531
Houston Academy site 65
Houston Aeronautical Heritage Society 669
Houston Aeros 49
Houston Architecture Foundation vi
Houston Area Urban League 60
Houston Astros 230
Houston Astros Baseball Academy Training Center 536, 546
Houston Ballet Center for Dance 4, 27
Houston Baptist University 552, 564-65
Houston Belt & Terminal Railway 62

Houston Cardiac Association Clinic 236, 258
Houston Center 3, 47
Houston Center for Contemporary Craft 161
Houston Chronicle Building 554
Houston City Hall 4, 6
Houston Community College, Administration Building 118
Houston Community College, Alief Campus 625
Houston Community College, Cosmetology 675
Houston Community College, Heinen Theater 121
Houston Community College, Learning Hub and Science Building 121
Houston Community College, Learning Resources Center 120
Houston Community College, Northeast Campus 572, 576-77
Houston Community College, Northeast College 684
Houston Community College, Southwest 634
Houston Convention Center Architects & Engineers 47
Houston Convention Center Hotel Corporation 48
Houston Cotton Exchange 68, 72-73
Houston Cotton Exchange and Board of Trade 35, 62-63
Houston Country Club 303, 324-5, 327, 482
Houston Design Center 522
Houston Downtown Management District 42, 71, 79, 81
Houston Downtown Park Corporation 46
Houston Fine Art Press Building 552, 564
Houston Heights 334-35, 355, 358, 368-69, 372, 550
Houston Heights Association 358
Houston Heights City Hall and Fire Station 338, 358
Houston House 35, 38
Houston Housing Finance Corporation 57
Houston Light Guard Armory 101, 122-23
Houston Lighting & Power Company Substation 304, 316
Houston Lighting & Power, Hyde Park Substation 102, 144
Houston Livestock Show and Rodeo 231
Houston Metropolitan Research Center vi, 7, 50,
Houston Mod vii, x, 515, 560,
Houston Municipal Airport 664, 66, 668-69
Houston Museum of Natural Science 152, 164
Houston Museum of Natural Science, Sugar Land 644
Houston National Bank Building 68, 75
Houston Negro Hospital 266, 276-77
Houston Oaks Hotel 472
Houston Parks and Recreation Department 46, 71, 163, 165-66, 624
Houston Pavilions 35, 39
Houston Police Department, North Police Station 536, 546
Houston Post Building 304, 316-17, 552, 554
Houston Public Elevator 306, 328-29
Houston Public Library vi, 6-7, 109, 125, 158, 310-11, 359, 476, 540, 542-43, 624, 660, 668,
Houston Racquet Club 500, 508
Houston Rockets 49
Houston Schutzen Verein 312
Houston Ship Channel 303, 322, 328-29, 664-65, 674, 680, 684-86,
Houston Stadium Consultants 231
Houston Telephone Employees Federal Credit Union 100, 118-19

Houston Terminal Warehouse and Cold Storage Building 91
Houston Texans 231
Houston Texans YMCA 268, 299
Houston Texas Temple 608, 613
Houston Typewriter Exchange Building 100, 112-13
Houston Zen Center 360
Houston Zoo 152, 165-66, 171
Howard, George F. 185, 672
Howard, George F., House 154, 185
Howard, Russell vii
Howell & Thomas 107
Howell House 107
Howell House 154, 184-85
Hoyle, Doran & Berry (Boston) 523
Hruska, Rame and Russell ix, 159, 251, 426
Hubbard House 394, 406-07
Hughes, Howard R., House 135
Hull, Kurt, AIA 37
Humanities Building, Rice University 196, 210-11
Humble Building 35, 40
Humble City Café 589
Humble Oil & Refining Company 14, 40, 127, 192, 344-45, 451, 538-39, 691
Humble Oil & Refining Company, Brookhollow 536, 538-39
Humble Oil & Refining Company, Station No. 179 336, 344-45
Humble Oil Field 589
Humble Research Center 432, 450-51
Humble Tower 4, 14
Hunt House 266, 286
Hunt, Jarvis 73
Hunter, Frederica 386
Huntingdon, The 430, 434
Hurwitz House 236, 258-59
Husmann & Associates, Robert 495
Hutcheson House 154, 178
Hutsell Speculative House 268, 288-89
Hutsell, A. E. 289
Hutsell, C. D. 289
Hyatt Regency Houston 4, 14-15
Hyatt Regency West Houston 528
Hybrid (Seattle) 575
Hyde Park Double 102, 142
Hydril Technology Center 585
I. M. Pei & Partners 22, 56, 70, 469-70
I. W. Coburn & Associates 443
IBM Building 458, 464
IBM Federal Systems Division Regional Office Building 682, 692
Idylwood 327
Ike Kligerman Barkley 377, 399
ImageNet Houston Building 622, 627
Immanuel Lutheran Church 338, 364
Imperial Sugar Company 638-40, 642-43
Incarnate Word Academy 61
Independence Heights 335, 368
India House O. P. Jindal Community Center 622, 632-33
Indochinese Cultural Center 122
Inman, Gary 444
Innova 430, 448-49
Institute Commons and South Hall, Rice University 196, 210-11
Intercontinental Bank 585
Interior Resources Center 520, 522
Interloop A/D 140
Interloop Architecture 434

International Buddhist Progress Society 622, 633
International Coffee Company Building 90
Internorth Building 465
Internorth Energy Building 585
Interurban Pharmacy 500, 514
Intexure Architects ix, 159, 251, 426
Inwood Manor 396, 421
Ironcraft Studio Building 123
Irvin House 682, 686-87
Irvin, W. H., House 687
Irvine & Hoyt 315
Irving R. Klein & Associates 38, 121, 166, 278, 299, 316, 563, 675
Irving R. Klein & Associates 38, 166, 278, 299, 316, 563, 675
Isabella Court 101, 123, 408
Isis Theater Building 83
Ismaili Jamatkhana and Center 640, 645
Istanbul Convention and Exhibition Center 632
Ittner, William B. 186
J. A. Folger Coffee Company Building 306, 322-23
J. K. Wagner & Company 76
J. P. Morgan Chase Center 56
J. P. Morgan Chase Motor Bank 70
Jackson & Ryan Architects 47, 95, 157, 206, 208, 224, 411, 469, 487, 489, 522, 542, 600
Jackson, Clyde 525
Jackson, Guy, AIA 47, 95, 157, 206, 208, 224, 411, 469, 487, 489, 522, 542, 600
Jacobs, Karrie 299
Jade Buddah Temple 622, 630
James A. Baker III Institute, Rice University 196, 208-09
James Bute Paint Company Warehouse 86, 92-93
James M. Delmar Field House 536, 539
Jay Baker Architects 168, 186, 253, 401, 409, 421-24, 426, 693, 698
Jefferson Chemical Company Building 432, 450-51
Jefferson Davis Hospital 336, 350-51
Jefferson Davis Senior High School 304, 310
Jenkins Hoff & Heimsath 494
Jenkins Hoff Oberg Saxe 126, 668
Jenkins House 552, 560-61
Jenkins William R., Associates 650, 694
Jenkins, William R., FAIA 126, 444, 494, 557, 559, 560, 670
Jennings Cleaning and Dyeing Building 100, 118
Jessen Jessen Millhouse 208
Jewish Community Center 563
Jiménez Design Studio 102, 144, 145, 257, 576
Jiménez, Carlos 139, 145, 157, 172, 180, 186, 248, 253, 356, 357, 418, 437, 445, 447, 564
Jiménez, Luis 308
Jimenez, Luis, *Vaquero* 304, 308
John Dinkeloo & Associates 527
John R. Dunn Outreach Center at the Beacon 35, 58, 59
Johnson Development Corp. 643
Johnson Space Center 325, 665, 675, 681, 691
Johnson, Bernard 47, 222
Johnson, J. M., House 416
Johnson, Lyndon B. 691
Johnson, Mark 389
Johnson, Philip C., 20-21, 126, 134-36, 295, 380, 412, 421, 468-69, 471, 473, 478, 565, 646
Johnson, Philip C., Associates 134, 412
Johnson, R. C. Architects 659
Johnson/Burgee Architects 20-21, 295, 467, 469,

713

473-74, 644, 646
Johnston House 500, 510-11
Jonas & Tabor 156, 319, 350
Jonas, Henry F. 156, 319, 350
Jones Hall for the Performing Arts 4, 24
Jones Plaza 4, 25
Jones School of Business, Rice University 266, 279
Jones, Arthur E., FAIA 11, 15, 17,106, 212, 230, 252, 296, 449-51, 491, 510, 565, 567
Jones, Jesse H. 24, 42, 52, 54, 57-58, 76, 665, 685
Jones, Margo, *Synchronicity of Color* 47
Jones, Mary Margaret (San Francisco) 46
Jones, Murray B. 131
Jones, Robert 11
Jones, Sarah Brashear, House 102, 130-31
Jordan, Barbara, Healthcare Center 575
Jordan, Willie, AIA 47, 281, 284, 287
Julia Ideson Building, Houston Pubic Library back cover, 4, 6-7
Jungman Branch, Houston Public Library 458, 476
Junior League of Houston Building 462
JV III 15-16
Kacmar, Donna, FAIA 379, 388, 545, 555
Kagan-Rudy Chapel 552, 566
Kaim House 458, 478-79
Kaldis Development Interests 74, 81, 111
Kamrath, Karl House 394, 399
Kamrath, Karl, FAIA 26, 104, 161, 182, 192, 221-23, 226, 278, 284, 287, 294-95, 298, 326, 330, 399-400, 411, 424-25, 443, 451, 477, 508, 510-11, 522, 543, 545, 561, 575, 585, 672-73, 675, 691
Kaneb Building 475
Kaplan McLaughlin Díaz 220
Kashou, Shawn 632
Kay On-Going Education Center 545
Kayem, Hans, House 500, 513
Keating Mann Jernigan Rottet 529, 625
Keating, Richard, FAIA 16, 181, 477, 529, 625
Keating, Richard, House 154, 181
Keeland Design Exploration Center, UH 268, 296
Keeland, Burdette 257, 441-42, 525, 559
Keith Associates, Charles 189, 415, 589
Keith-Wiess Geological Laboratories, Rice University 196, 205
Keller, Theo G. 121, 185,
Kellum-Noble House 4, 8, 10, 417, 527
Kelly, Frank, FAIA 55, 113, 216, 584, 625
Kelly, Lee, Waterfall, Stele, and River 292
Kelsey, Virginia, AIA 490
Kelvin Design Group Studio 236, 243
Kempner, I. H. 643
Kendall Community Library 622, 624
Kendall/Heaton Associates iv, 2, 12, 16, 20, 23, 53, 159, 171-72, 186, 202, 207, 217, 257, 295, 318, 378, 527, 624
Kennedy Bakery Building 68, 70-71
Kennedy Corner Building 68, 72
Kennedy, John 71
Kennedy, Troy 297
Kennon, Paul 463
Kessler, George E. 150, 163, 167
Keystone Plaza 536, 539
Khan, Fazlur R. 19, 471
Khosla, Ramesh (Montreal) 645
Kiam Building 68, 80
Kieran Timberlake Associates (Philadelphia) 206
Killough Middle School 622, 630
Kilper, Dennis 310

Kilroy Visitor and Education Center, Bayou Bend 374, 378-79
Kinder Lake, Discovery Green 46
King, Robert L. 412-13
King's Crossing Town Center, Kingwood 582, 588
Kingwood 581-82, 588-89, 606, 639
Kipling Academy 141
Kipling Townhouses 430, 442
Kipp Aquarium 166,
Kipp, Herbert A. 398, 407
Kirby Building Systems Building 552, 563
Kirby Court Apartments 430, 444
Kirby, John Henry 112
Kirby, John Henry, House 100, 112-13
Kirk, Jr., Robert Dyrel 565
Kirkland House 666, 671
Kirksey & Partners 19, 70, 650
Kirksey-Meyers Architects 181, 448
Kirksey 13, 121, 135, 209, 215, 218, 229, 279, 467, 520, 522, 525-26, 530, 541, 555, 615, 626, 650-51, 689
Kirksey, John H., FAIA 181
Kittleson, Paul 349
Klein Independent School District Technology Center 608, 610
Klein Musuem 611
Klein Partnership 565
Klein, Adam Fredrick, House 608, 610
Klein, Irving R., & Associates 38, 121, 166, 278, 299, 316, 563, 675
Knapp Chevrolet Company Building 336, 349
Knapp, Carl. M. 286
Knapp, Christopher 441
Knoll 115, 223, 261, 559
Knoll Building Houston 100, 114-15
Knoll, Florence 261
Knox, W. R. 368
Koch Building 449
Koelsch Gallery 338, 358-59
Koerber, Edward 326
Koetter, Tharp & Cowell 15-16, 223
Kohn Pederson Fox 224
Kohrville School 611
Kollectiv 367
Kopriva, Gus 366
Kopriva, Sharon 363, 366
Kotch, M. Arthur, House 509
Koush, Ben vii
KPRC Channel Two Studio 552, 567
Krajcizek House 500, 510
Krakower, Joseph 113, 122, 256, 487, 509, 513
Krell House 500, 514
KRIV Channel 26 TV Studio 552, 554
Krull House 266, 286-87
Krumwiede, Keith 187
Krupp & Tuffly 50
KTRK Channel 13 TV Studio 236, 252
Kudela & Weinheimer 525, 601, 615
Kuhl-Linscomb 430, 440
Kuhlman, Theo H., House 268, 289
Kuldell House 154, 176
Kurth House 268, 288
Kyle, Dillon 246, 355, 359, 363, 422, 435, 441, 446, 487-88
Kyser, A. C. 328
L. Barry Davidson Architects 146, 248, 249, 250, 252, 349, 417, 423, 486, 487, 504, 507, 699
L'Encore 102, 144-45

La Carafe 71
La Colombe d'Or 127
La Mont Apartments 100, 120
La Nueva Casa de Amigos 304, 309
La Porte Improvement Company 688
Laguarda.Low 39
Lake on Post Oak Park 458, 474
Lake Plaza, Hermann Park 152, 165
Lake Robbins, The Woodlands 596
Lake Street Apartments 430, 444
Lake, Sarah 179, 447
Lake/Flato (San Antonio) 207, 220, 251, 296, 505, 696
Lakeshore House 682, 689
Lakewood Church 451
Lamar House 266, 284
Lamar Senior High School 394, 410
Lamar-River Oaks Community Center 394, 410
Lamar, Mirabeau B. 142
Lamb House 394, 405
Lancaster & Associates 600
Lancaster Hotel 23
Lancaster, Thomas 600
Lanclos, Charles 626
Lander, David 63
Landrum, Michael 179, 343, 447, 504
Lane, E. 439
Lang & Witchell 77, 327
Langwith Wilson King & Associates 561, 568
Lanier Public Works Building 19
Lanier, Bob, Mayor 157, 62, 109
Lantrip, Dora, Elementary School 320
Lantz, Karen vii, 179, 684,
Lapin House 500, 508-09
Lard Investment Company Community Center 304, 319
Larson & Wingfield 492
Lasher House 500, 506
Lassig, Oswald J. 119-20, 201
László, Paul 261
Latham Memorial Hall, Christ Church Cathedral 59
Lauren Griffith Associates 46, 71
Lauricella Grocery Store Building 374, 388
Lawing, Doug 72
Lawndale Art and Performance Center 161
Lawrence, Charles E., House (1958) 500, 514-15
Lawrence, Charles E., House (1969) 500, 510-11
Lawyer, Frank D., House 520, 523
Layton & Smith 120-21
Le Blanc, W. Jude 251
Le Voisinage 430, 447
Leathers & Associates 324, 357
Leathers, Robert 324, 357
Ledoux, C.-N. 295
Lee, Mark, & Associates 478
Leggett, Marvin E., & Associates 567
Leibrock House 236, 248, 249
Lemmon, Mark 447
Lenarduzzi, Nino 410
Leo A. Daly/LAN 59, 540
Leon House 266, 282
Lerup, Lars vi, x, xi, 518
Leslie Elkins Architecture 191, 122, 378, 696
Lester House 154, 178
Letzerich House 394, 409
Levan, George 117
Levy House 336, 352
Levy, Abe M. Community House 121
Levy's 52
Lewis, Fred L. 344
Lewis, J. Vance 110
Lewter, Michael E. vi
Liao, Jeffrey vi
Library Service Center, Rice University 236, 257
Liddell, Alice Y. 383
Lieb, Davey E. 508
Light Spikes 582, 588
Lightfoot, Ewart H., House 102, 133
Lighthouse, Henry R., House 336, 345
Linbeck, Leo F. III 81
Lindeberg, Harrie T. 128, 167, 168-69, 192, 409
Lindsay House 484, 490-91
Lindsey House 154, 181
Linesch & Reynolds 230
Link House 102, 126
Linkwood Community Center 236, 258
Linkwood Park 258
Linnstaedter, W. Herbert 90, 117, 347
Littlefield, Lee 385
Live Oak Friends Meeting House 338, 368-69
Live-Work Studio 93, 152, 158-59
Llewelyn Davies Sahni, 227, 588, 632, 634
Lloyd & Morgan 54, 207, 318, 419, 565
Lloyd Jones Associates 106, 450-51, 567
Lloyd Jones Brewer & Associates 11, 17, 106, 449, 450, 626
Lloyd Jones Fillpot & Associates 216
Lloyd, Hermon, FAIA 54, 189, 207, 318, 410, 419, 435, 565
Lloyd, Hermon & W. B. Morgan 54, 207, 419, 565
Lloyd, Jones & Associates 296
Lloyd, Morgan & Jones 15, 106, 212, 230, 252, 450, 491, 510, 565
LNG-Liberty Tower 106
Lo/Kester 308
Lockwood, Andrews & Newnam (LAN) 59, 539-40
Loew's State Theater 42, 81
Lofts at Citycentre 530
Lofts on Post Oak 469
London, Ruth 177, 402
Lone Star College, Cy-Fair 608, 616
Lone Star College, University Park 612
Long, Bert L., Jr., *Field of Vision* 274
Looney Ricks Kiss 439
Lord, Aeck & Sargent 226
Lorehn, Olle J. 37, 93, 115, 130
Lottman Manufacturing Company 314
Loughman, Mandy vi
Love, Jim, *Area Code* 26
Love, Jim, *Giant Bird House* 386
Love, Jim, House 374, 386
Loveless, I. E. 37
Lovett Hall, Rice University 200-01, 212
Lovett Square 100, 116-17
Lovett, Edgar Odell 200
Lowe, Rick 276
Loy House 394, 405
Lozano, Vidal 324
Lucchesi, Stephen A., AIA 614
Luckman Associates, Charles 691
Luhn, Graham B., FAIA 73, 439, 589
Lundy, Anstis Manton 557
Lundy, Victor A., FAIA 557
Lundy, Victor, House 552, 556-57
Lurie House 484, 487
Lusk House 266, 282-83

Luvin' Canada 448
Lynn Goode Gallery 430, 445
Lyons Village 572, 574
Lyons, Scott (Dallas) 421
M. D. Anderson Biological Laboratories, Rice University 196, 205
M. D. Anderson Cancer Center 220, 222
M. D. Anderson Foundation 251
M. D. Anderson Hospital and Tumor Institute 198, 222
m+a architecture studio 299, 425
M2L Associates 36, 41, 79
Ma Maison 467
Mabry, Armon E. 407, 504
MacAgy, Jermayne 135
MacGregor Park Clubhouse 268, 291
MacGregor, Henry F. 291, 358,
MacGregor, Peggy Stevens 291
Machado & Silvetti Associates 209
Machado, Rodolfo 209
Macham Building 432, 452
MacKenzie, H. Jordan 124
Mackenzie, James C. 403
MacKie & Kamrath 26, 104, 161, 182, 192, 221-23, 226, 278, 284, 287, 294-95, 298, 326, 330, 399, 400, 411, 424-25, 443, 451, 477, 508, 510-11, 522, 543, 545, 561, 575, 585, 672-73, 675, 691
MacKie & Kamrath Building 330, 430, 443
MacKie, Fred 26, 104, 161, 182, 192, 221-23, 226, 278, 284, 287, 294-95, 298, 326, 330, 399, 400, 411, 424-25, 443, 451, 477, 508, 510-11, 522, 543, 545, 561, 575, 585, 672-73, 675, 691
MacLean, Alex S. 49
MacNab, Alexander 589
Madison Southern National Bank 659
Magnificat House 100, 122
Magnolia Ballroom 86, 88
Magnolia Cafe Building 86, 88
Magnolia Grove 387
Magnolia Hotel Houston 58
Magnolia Park 303
Mahlangu, Esther 277
Main Street Gardens, Sugar Land 658
Main Street Square 35, 41-42
Main Street Viaduct 90-91
Main Street-Market Square Historic District 57
Mainland Building and Development Group 106
Majestic Metro 81
Majestic Theater 55
Malarkey, Brian, FAIA vi
Maldonado, Ernesto, AIA 152, 156, 158, 179, 191, 249, 260, 325, 410, 414
Maloney, Martin & Mitchell 107
Mandell Residences 154, 182-83
Manhattan Lofts 475
Manley, John 135
Manned Spacecraft Center Architects 691
Mansbendel, Peter 158
Mansfield House 338, 361
Maragliotti, Vincent Modern Houston 55
Marathon Oil Tower 458, 478-79
mArchitects 92, 668
Marck, Gerhard 297
Marichal, Albert 445
Maris, Stelios 127
Mark Lee & Associates 478
Market Square Park 68, 71
Market Street, The Woodlands Town Center 594, 598

Marshall Field & Company Building 472-73
Marshall Junior High 310
Martel College, Rice University 196, 201
Martha B. Bute-Robert L. King 413
Martin and Oskouie 308
Martin Luther King Humanities Center, TSU 266, 280-81
Martin, Albert C., & Associates 465, 585
Martin, John 544
Martin, Paul E. 308, 384
Marvin E. Leggett & Associates 567
Mary Gibbs Jones Hall, Texas Women's University 198, 224-25
Mashburn, Joseph W., FAIA vii, 507
Masjid AlRasool AlAkram 622, 632
Mason Park Shelter House 306, 328
Masonic Temple Building 35, 38
Massing, Jack 545
Masterson, Carroll Sterling 401
Masterson, Harris, III 401
Mathes Group, The 71, 296
Mauer, Michael P. 79
Mauran & Russell 111
Mauran, Russell & Crowell (St. Louis) 57, 76
Maurice, Robert W. 419, 490
Maurice, Wilkins & Associates 490
Maxwell, Isaac (San Antonio) 296
Mays Clinic, M. D. Anderson Cancer Center 198, 220
Mc Neal House 306, 326-27
MC^2 Architects ix, 350, 369, 381-82, 403, 503, 563, 695
McAshan Botanical Hall, Houston Arboretum 500, 502
McAshan House 430, 442-43
McBee, Silas 58
McCall House 266, 282
McCartney House 484, 486
McClain, Robert, Gallery 430, 442
McCleary Associates 478
McCleary, Thompson 452, 561
McCord Development Company 556
McCowan, Haywood Jordan 47, 281, 284, 287
McCutchen, Sims vii
McDermott Engineering Office Complex 529
McDermott, Joe A. 541
McDougal, Steph 122
McDugald-Steele 189, 378, 400, 410, 413, 439,
McDugald, Jr., William H. 388
McFarland House 500, 510
McGehee Hall, Christ Church Cathedral 59
McGinty, Milton 181-82, 207, 224, 329, 539, 565, 675
McGinty, Milton 181, 278, 406
McGovern Branch, Houston Public Library 236, 254-55
McGovern Campus, Texas Medical Center 228
McGovern Lake, Hermann Park 165
McGovern Texas Medical Center Commons Building 198, 224
McHale, T. G. 405, 411, 670
McHale, T. George 176, 185, 328, 405, 411, 670, 674, 688
McIntyre/Robinowitz 355
McKee Street Bridge 86, 93
McKenzie, James Gordon 93
McKinney Place Garage 52
McKissack, Jeff D. 326
McKittrick Drennan Richardson Wallace 630

McLelland, John 677
McMillin, George G. 348
McMurtry, Deedee and Burton College, Rice University 202
McNair Campus, Baylor College of Medicine 229
McNair Hall, Rice University 196, 208-09
McReynolds Junior High School 306, 330
McReynolds, James 136
McVey, William M. 182, 203, 685
McWhorter, Thomas 312
Meadowbrook Village 672
MECA (Multi-Ethnic-Cultural Arts Committee) 346, 348
Mecom Fountain 163
Medical Clinic of Houston Building 191
Medical Towers Building 196, 216
Meeks + Partners 475
Melcher Hall, UH 293
Mellie Esperson Building 55
Mellinger House 394, 414-15
Melrose Building 35, 54
Melton Henry Architects 165, 465-66
Melton Henry/Maurice Robison 165
Memorial Bend 514-15
Memorial Bend Shopping Park 514
Memorial City Mall 531
Memorial City Medical Plaza 531
Memorial Drive Presbyterian Church 500, 510-11
Memorial Hermann Medical Plaza 215
Memorial Hospital Northwest 536, 538
Memorial Lutheran Church 458, 476, 493
Memorial Park 372, 376-77, 463, 498, 502
Memorial-Hermann Hospital 520, 531
Memorial-Hermann, Southwest Hospital 565
Menil Collection, The viii, x, 102, 138-39, 180, 312, 412
Menil Foundation 137, 412
Menil Foundation Business Office 102, 136-37
Menil House 394, 412, 421
Mercado del Sol 314
Mercer West Tower 458, 474-75
Merchants and Manufacturers Building 86, 89
Meredith Long & Company 430, 434-35
Merkel, Joseph, House 304, 312
Merkel's Grove 312
Merriman Holt 135, 162, 191, 244
Merriman Holt Architects 135
Merriman, William, AIA 119, 124, 135, 162, 191, 244, 511, 634
Mesa: A Better Home and Living Center 484, 492-93
Methodist Hospital 216, 225
Methodist Hospital Research Institute 198, 224-25
Methodist Hospital, Outpatient Center 215
Methodist Hospital, Sugar Land 640, 644-45
Metro Downtown Transit Center 35-36
Metro, Texas Medical Center Transit Facility 196, 218-19
Metropolitan Design Group 111, 245, 441, 445
Metropolitan Transit Authority (Metro) 3, 36, 41-42, 53, 78, 79, 81, 218-19, 361
Metrorail Red Line, Preston Station 68-78, 79
Meyer, David 218
Meyer, Sterling House 129
Meyerland 559, 562
MGP2 Studio 336, 351
Michael Gaertner & Associates 346
Michael Graves & Associates 105
Michael Wilford & Associates 204

Michael, Pierre D. 123
Michael, Pierre L., House 394, 408
Mid City Shops 51
Midtown Redevelopment Authority 112
Midway Companies 530, 541
Milam, Terry 384
Milby Senior High School 675
Milford Live/Work 154, 184
Milford Townhomes 154, 179
Milkovisch, John 378
Millennium Tower 626
Miller Dahlstrand 149, 185
Miller Outdoor Theatre 152, 164
Miller, Reagan 149, 185, 504
Miller, Tim 63
Milroy, John A., House 336, 358
Milton Foy Martin & Associates 217, 286
Minnitex Community Church 656, 660
Minor Design vi
Minor, Craig vi
Minor, Suzy vi
Minute Maid Building 640, 648-49
Minute Maid Headquarters 649
Minute Maid Park at Union Station 35, 62-63, 315
Mirabeau B. at Hyde Park 102, 142
Mirador 438
Miró Rivera 689
Miro, Juan 689
Miss, Mary, 100 Chairs 268, 296-97
Mission German Methodist Episcopal Church, South 304, 309
Missouri City Branch, Fort Bend County Library 622, 634
Mitchell Carlson Stone 76, 629
Mitchell Center for the Arts, UH 296-97
Mitchell, Cynthia Woods 296, 599
Mitchell, G. Scott 589
Mitchell, George P. 286, 510, 589, 592-93, 599, 602-03
Mix Contemporary 430, 444, 445
Mixon House 236, 249
Mize, Jamie 72
MLTW/Turnbull Associates 648
Mo Mong 143
Moeller, Frederick House 338, 365
Molina & Associates 47
Moneo, Rafael 171, 209
Monolithic Constructors 527
Monotech Gallery 101, 124
Monotech House 374, 380
Montalbano House 666, 671
Monteith House 152, 176
Montrose Elementary School site 134
Montrose Townhouse Lofts 102, 142-43
Montrose Veterinary Clinic 102, 146
Moore, Barry, FAIA x, 70, 77, 80, 134, 143, 244, 292, 327, 453, 523, 669
Moore, Charles 648
Moore, Harvin C. & Hermon Lloyd 189
Moore, Harvin C., FAIA 9-10, 29, 70, 71, 286, 410, 417, 435, 559, 691
Moore, Henry, Large Spindle Piece 105
Moores School of Music, UH 268, 296
Moorhead, Gerald, FAIA vi, 244, 261, 328, 612
Moran Center, Magnificat House 696
Moran Center, University of St. Thomas 135
Moravian Pottery and Tile Works 201
Morehead, Jr., James C. 506

Moreland, Payson W. 286
Morgan House 154, 186
Morgan, W. B. 54, 207, 318, 419, 565
Morgan's Point 681, 686-87
Morningside Square 244
Morningside Townhomes 242
Morris Architects 30, 48-49, 51, 52, 91, 208-09, 210, 223-24, 424, 451, 531, 541, 603, 613, 658, 659
Morris Associates, S. I., 7, 21, 45, 135-36, 172, 216, 398, 406, 416, 464-65, 469, 471, 473, 523, 554, 556, 563, 565, 584, 628, 692
Morris Gutiérrez 255, 575
Morris House (1927) 154, 191
Morris Zax Grocery Building 304, 311
Morris, Deborah 255, 575
Morris, Robert 366, 385, 554
Morris, S. I., FAIA 7, 21, 45, 135-36, 172, 216, 398, 406, 416, 424, 435, 464-65, 469, 471, 473, 523, 554, 556, 563, 565, 584, 628, 692
Morris, S. I., House (1952) 152, 174,
Morris, Sidney H., & Associates 565
Morris, Stewart 467, 650
Morris*Aubry Architects 12, 26, 27, 49, 189, 295, 462, 474, 476-77, 541, 584
Morse & Harvey (New York) 567
Morton, Michael, AIA (mArchitects) 92, 668
Moseley Associates 47
Moss-Vreeland, Patricia and Robert 157
Moss, Arthur 440
Mott houses 185, 394, 413
Mott, Harry 283
Mott, Katharine 185, 283, 405, 413
Mount Pleasant Baptist Church 574
MRW Architects 540, 631
Mucasey, Mark S., AIA 157
Multicultural Education and Counseling Arts Center 346
Mulvey, Carl A. 260
Munoz and Albin 599
Murphy Mears 157, 254, 350, 366, 385, 439, 506, 558-59
Murrell, Russell 366
Museum of Fine Arts Administration Building 152, 172
Museum of Fine Arts, Houston viii, x, 150, 152, 170-72, 378, 401-02
Museum of Southern History 640, 650-51
Myers, J. Allen, Jr. 104
Nabisco 94-95, 228
NASA 326, 675, 682, 690-91, 694
NASA Value Center 682, 694
Nash House 102, 132
Nasr & Partners, M. 7, 38-39, 614
Nasr Penton & Associates 50
Nasr, Mohammed 7, 38-39, 50, 382, 614
Natalye Appel + Associates Architects 25, 159, 351, 356, 382, 543
Natex Corporation 89
Nathdwara Hindu Temple 622, 632
National Art Services Company Building 374, 383
National Bank of Commerce 55
National Biscuit Company Building (1910) 86, 94-95
National Biscuit Company Building (1949) 198, 228
National Cash Register Company 63
National Steel Products Company Building 306, 329
Nations, Howard L. Law Office 124

Nazro House 102, 132
Neal, J. Robert, House 394, 402-03
Neiman-Marcus 53, 472-73
Nelms House 396, 416
Nelson, C. N. 360
Neuhaus & Taylor 13, 15-16, 117, 401, 421, 425, 451-53, 472, 506
Neuhaus House (1994) 430, 437
Neuhaus III, J. Victor, FAIA 114
Neuhaus-Wingfield Associates 409, 502
Neuhaus, Hugo V., House 152, 168-69
Neuhaus, Jr., Hugo V., FAIA 26, 169, 345, 400-01, 561
Neuhaus, Jr., Hugo V., House 394, 400-01
Neuhaus, W. O., Associates 106, 228, 351, 414, 422, 490, 510, 539, 625, 693
Neuscheler, Kim 277
Neville, Daphne Palmer 130
Neville, Edwin L., House 102, 130
Nevins, Deborah & Associates 420
New Arts gallery 117
New Hope Housing 86, 94-95, 313, 325, 330
New Life Church 520, 526-27
New Territory 639
New World Museum 374, 380-81
Newman Hall 266, 280
Nguyen, Choung (MC^2 Architects) ix, 350, 369, 381-82, 403, 503, 563, 695
Nguyen, Chung, AIA (MC^2 Architects) ix, 350, 369, 381-82, 403, 503, 563, 695
Nguyen, Su 111, 184
Nichols House 656, 658
Nichols-Rice-Cherry House 4, 8-10, 78
Nichols, Katie 354
Nichols, Roy B. House 658
Niels Esperson Building 21, 35, 55
Nira Park 682, 684
NL Industries North Belt Complex 585
Noguchi, Isamu 171
Nordheimer, Clyde 27
Norhill 353-54
Norhill Esplanades 336, 353
North San Jacinto Café 92
Northern Trust Bank of Texas Building 430, 438, 439, 484, 489
Northpoint Building 585
Northrop, Jr., Joseph W. 114, 121, 161, 163, 174, 185, 188, 415, 439
Northshore Dental Clinic 682, 684
Northside Christian Church 608, 610
Northwest Corporate Park 536, 540-41
Northwest Hollister Corporation 541
Northwoods Presbyterian Church 608, 612-13
Numen Development 354
Nunn, Stayton & Milton McGinty 181, 278, 406
Nunn, Stayton, FAIA 181, 278, 330, 406, 414, 669
Nutter, Arthur E. 164, 291, 328
O'Connor, Ann 343
O'Neil Ford & Associates 504
OA+D/Office for Architecture+Design 252
Oak Forest Branch, Houston Public Library 536, 542, 543
Oak Forest Park Pool House 536, 543
Oakdale Modern Dwellings 152, 156
Oberholzer, Mark 142, 183, 258, 387, 441, 446,
Odell Associates (Charlotte) 214
Office City Building Two 666, 674-75
Office of James Burnett 17, 159, 202, 206-07, 210,

228-29, 254, 257, 342, 376-77, 426, 442, 527, 530, 634
Oittenen, Mauno 215
Olajuwon, Hakeem 75
Old Place 4, 9
Old River Terrace United Methodist Church 682, 684-85
Olin Partnership 165
Olin, Laurie 163, 165, 173
Oliver House 394, 406-07
Oliver, Charles W. 398, 400-01, 403, 407-09, 413
Oliver, Patricia Belton, FAIA vii
Olivewood Cemetery 343
Olmsted Brothers 403
Olson Sundberg Kundig 698
Omni Hotel Westside 528
Omni Houston Hotel 464
On Leong Chinese Merchants Association 304, 314-15
One Allen Center 4, 10-11
One BriarLake Plaza 622, 626
One Shell Plaza 4, 14, 18-19, 21, 453
One SugarLand Park Building 640, 646
One West Loop Plaza 458, 470
One Westheimer Plaza 458, 476
One-Two Townhouses 100, 108
Openshop Studio (New York) 246
Oppenheim, Dennis 585
ORA (Seattle) 575
Orange Show Center for Visionary Art 378-79
Orange Show Foundation 327, 343
Orange Show, The 306, 326-27, 343, 379
Oriental Textile Mill 338, 367
Orozco, Sylvia 349
Oshman Engineering Design Kitchen, Rice University 196, 206
Oskouie, Hossein 119
Our Lady of Guadalupe Catholic Church 304, 312-13
Our Lady of La Vang Catholic Church 536, 547
Our Lady of Lourdes Catholic Church 536, 542
Our Lady of the Cedars Maronite Catholic Church 632
Our Lady of Walsingham Catholic Church 520, 523
Our Savior Lutheran Church 536, 545
Outram, John 202
Overland Partners 165
Owsley House 458, 462
P. M. Bolton Associates 405, 465, 486
P.I.C. Realty 538
Pace, Randle 10, 83
Pacific Mutual Life Insurance Company Building 100, 117
Pack, Bob Stephen F. Austin Statue 649
Paddock House 394, 408
Padilla Associates 274
Padilla, John 274
Page, C. H. & Company 91
Page, C. H. & Brother 346
PageSoutherlandPage (PSP) 17, 46-47, 52, 57, 59, 64, 74, 78, 451, 540, 555, 644, 646
Palace Hotel, 68, 79
Palacios, Armando 381
Palmer Brook Schooley Design 359, 383, 588, 700
Palmer Memorial Episcopal Church 213
Palms Center 299
Pan America Ballroom 308
Pangburn Building 582, 588-89
Parc IV and Parc V 102, 126-27

Parade of Homes (1955) 552, 559
Park at Midtown 116
Park Classic Homes House 484, 486
Park in Houston Center 35, 48, 49
Park Place 665, 676
Park Place Baptist Church 666, 670-71, 676
Park Place United Methodist Church 666-76
Park Regency Terrace Residences 458, 478
Park Ten 528
Parker Brothers & Company Building 306, 322
Parker, J. W., House 129
ParkWest Tower 625
Parkwood Apartments 229
Parque Amistad 324
Parra Design Group 142, 365
Parra, Camilo 142, 365
Parsons 470
Parsons, David G. 205
Pasadena State Bank Building 666, 674
Pasadena Town Square 666, 673
Pasternak House 268, 288-89
Patchen, Jerry 79
Patio Shops 152, 156, 319
Patout, Timothy 383
Patterson House 666, 670
Payne, Harry D. 186, 320, 410, 434, 574
PBK Architects 601-02, 616, 658, 695
PDF 607
PDG Architects 617, 633
PDR 527
Pearl Fincher Museum of Fine Arts 608, 612-13
Peden Company Building 88, 90-91
Peden House 152, 169
Peden Iron & Steel Company 91
Peden Wholesale Building 91
Pei, I. M., & Partners 22, 56, 70, 469-70
Pelli, César, & Associates 12, 209, 217, 465-66
Pelli Clarke Pelli 295
Penguin Arms Apartments 430, 440
Pennzoil Place viii, 4, 21-22, 45, 52, 469, 471, 538
Pepper, Beverly, *Polygenesis* 465
Peranteau, Michael 276
Pereira Associates, William L. 44
Pereira, Melanie 442
Perkins + Will 206, 213, 601
Perry, Malcolm M. 257
Pershing Middle School 255
Peter Walker & Partners (San Francisco) 81, 692
Peter Wunderlich Farm Stead 608, 610-11
Peters, Anna vi
Peters, Patrick 187, 346, 560
Peterson, Jacob 46
Peterson, Robert W. 309, 476
Peterson's Pharmacy Building 236, 246-47
Petroleum Building 35, 60, 556
Petroleum Club 14, 57
Pettigrew & Worley 545
PGAL 36, 41, 77-79, 89, 105, 201, 255, 257, 279, 511, 584, 587, 648
Phifer, Thomas, & Partners 210, 699
Philip C. Johnson Associates 134, 412
Phillips Jr., W. Irving, FAIA 101, 124-25, 140, 143, 146, 280, 309, 388, 476, 588
Phillips Studio and Townhouses 101, 124-25
Phillips/Ryburn 388
Phillips/Wild Design 140, 143
PhiloWilke Partnership 214
Phoenix Insurance Company of Hartford Building

719

432, 452-53
Piano, Renzo 138
Pickard Chilton (New Haven) 53, 527, 607
Pickworth, Herbert 503
Pierce Goodwin Alexander 478, 511, 693
Pierce Goodwin Flanagan 539
Pierce, George-Abel B. Pierce 14, 118, 164, 205, 276, 293, 436, 488, 585-86, 676, 694
Pierce, Grace 441
Pierce, Jr., George F., House 484, 488
Pigg, Alonzo C. 38, 358
Pillot Building 77
Pillot House 4, 8-9
Pinckney House 396, 415
Pincoffs House 154, 178
Pine Shadows 488
Pinecroft Center II 594, 602
Pioneer Memorial Log House 227
Piper, F. Stanley 182
Piper's Meadow Community Center 682, 694
Pirtle, Jim 80
Pittman House 430, 436
Pittman, W. Sidney 272
Pitts, Phelps & Mebane 297
Pitts, Phelps & White 692
Pittsburgh Plate Glass Company 306, 328-29
Pitzman, Julius 132
Planned Community Developers 649
Platt, Charles A. 418, 687
Playhouse, The, 152, 160-61
Plaza Apartment Hotel 172
Plaza del Oro 229
Poage III, Walter S. 562
Poe Elementary School 154, 186
Pontiac Motor Division Building 452
Pope + Sherman 242
Pope Design 509
Pope, Albert 242
Populous 700
Porcher, George S. 314
Porcher, Nananne 27
Portofino Center 594, 602
Post Midtown Lofts 100, 112
Post Oak Arches 458, 466-67
Post Oak Central 458, 468-69
Post Oak Park Townhouses 458, 462-63
Post Oak Row 458, 468
Post Oak Tower 472
Post Rice Lofts 57
Post-Dispatch Building 35, 58
Potter, Alexander 92
Powell, Ian, AIA vi
Powers Brown Architecture 29, 525, 542, 610, 634
Powers, Joe, AIA vi
Powitzky, Calvin, AIA 695
Prairie View A&M, School of Nursing Building, 196, 214-15
Predock, Antoine 205, 210, 493
Preservation Houston ix, 345, 349, 513
President's House, Rice University 192
Price, Thomas M. 506
Price, William 146
Primary Data Center, Rice University 236, 257
Proctor, Frederick C. 403
Progressive Amateur Boxing Assn. Community Center 266, 274
Progressive New Hope Baptist Church 266-276, 277
Project for Public Spaces 46, 71

Project Row Houses 266, 274-77
Proler Family Chapel, Beth Israel Cemetery 520, 523
Proler House (1952) 268, 288
Proler, Ben, House (1936) 266, 284
Proler, House (1949) 268, 290
Prosperity Bank, El Campo 651
Prosperity Bank, Sugar Land 650
Prototype 180, 552, 564
Prozign Architects 7, 48
Prudential Building 198, 220-21
Prudential Insurance Company Building 552, 556
PSP (PageSoutherlandPage) 17, 46-47, 52, 57, 59, 64, 74, 78, 451, 540, 555, 644, 646
Pulaski House 266, 287
Pulido, Pio 349
Pullum, Ned P. 110
Pyramid Community Development Corporation 659
QMET Architects 297
Quebedeaux, Walter A., Plaza 78
Rabinowitz House 268, 290
Rabitt, Patrick S. 349
Radetzki House 306, 327
Ragni, Erik, AIA 142, 180, 190, 245, 359, 387-88, 419, 446
Raindrop Turkish House 622, 632
Randall Duell & Associates 230
Ranger Insurance Company Building 458, 475
Ransom, Harry 310
Rapp Tackett Fash 503
Rather, Jr., John T., FAIA 29, 181, 185, 203, 315, 411, 413, 507, 510
Ravenna 394, 404
Ray Bailey Architects 6, 56, 59, 115, 125, 162, 164, 166, 177, 192, 213, 226, 258, 311, 359, 411, 420, 438, 440, 627
Ray, James 543, 615
Ray+Hollington 28, 71, 82, 161, 209, 284, 493, 529, 633
RdlR Architects 81, 89, 105, 219, 325, 546, 599, 633
Reagan Senior High School 338, 362-63
Reber, Jack 529
Reckling Park 196, 208
Red Bluff 689
Red Elementary School 552, 560
Red, David D. 243
Redbird House 394, 408
Redstone Companies 469
Reed House (1960) 500, 503
Reed Rock Bit Drilling Technology Center 536, 541
Reed, Frank. R., House (1910) 336, 354
Reese, Donald C. 442
Regency House 444
Regency Square 567
Reid, Marshall L. 146, 254, 442
Rein Company Building 100, 106-07
Reliant Astrodome 220-31
Reliant Energy Plaza 35, 42
Reliant Park 36, 161
Reliant Stadium 198, 231
Remington Hotel 462
Renteria, Kim Clark 325
Renzo Piano Building Workshop 138
RepublicBank Center 4, 20, 26
Ressler & Applebaum 562
Revere Quality House Institute 536, 543
Rey de la Reza Architects (RdlR) 81, 89, 105, 219, 325, 546, 599, 633
Reynaud House 682, 687

Reynaud, Sallie Wynne, House 687
Reynolds & Reynolds 541
Rice Building Workshop 157, 275, 277
Rice Children's Campus 236, 244-45
Rice Design Alliance vii, x, 28, 165, 575,
Rice Hotel 35, 57, 83
Rice Media Center 196, 206-07
Rice School-La Escuela Rice 236, 259
Rice Stadium 196, 205-07
Rice University vii, x, xi, 36, 150, 170, 187, 192, 197, 200-13, 227, 245, 257, 275, 277, 321, 330, 439, 506, 642, 690,
Rice, Allen 162
Rice, William M. 212
Richard E. Berry Educational Support Center 608, 616
Richard Fitzgerald & Partners 138, 218, 402, 469-70, 473-74, 538, 585, 646, 648
Richard Roeder Associates 347
Richardson House (1955) 666, 671
Richardson, Charles E., House 142
Richardson, E. R., House 100, 122
Richardson, J. Perkins 122
Richmond Hall, Menil Collection 139
Rienzi 394, 401
Ritchie & Fiore 135
Ritz Theater 68, 81
River Oaks 70, 104, 106-07, 265, 372, 378, 670, 392-427
River Oaks Apartments 447
River Oaks Bank & Trust Building 434
River Oaks Community Center 394, 406
River Oaks Corporation 398, 400-01, 406-08, 410
River Oaks Country Club 413
River Oaks Court 394, 406-07
River Oaks Elementary School 430, 434
River Oaks Garden Club Building 439
River Oaks Gate Piers 394, 398
Rivera, Miguel 489
Riverside General Hospital 277
Riverside National Bank Building 266, 280
Riverside Service Station 266, 280-81
Riverside Terrace 264-65, 282-83, 287-89
Riviana Building 106
Robbins, John, Building Company 567
Robert McClain Gallery 430, 442
Roberts, Catherine 110
Robertson Design 169, 247, 254, 354
Robertson Hall, University of St. Thomas 135
Robertson House (Gramercy) 236, 254
Robertson House (Main Street) 152, 169,
Robertson, Christopher 169, 247, 254, 354
Robinson & Company, Dwight P. 643
Robinson, Hampton, Desert House 622, 635
Robinson, Margaret 158, 313, 330, 427, 445, 530, 563, 624, 635
Robison, Maurice 165
Roche, Kevin 527
Rockefeller Hall 342
Roeder, Richard, Associates 347
Roemer House 336, 346
Roemer, Frederick 346
Rogers + Labarthe 159, 357, 367, 381
Rohde Partners 142
Romano, Joey 142
Ron, Avi 79
Ronk, Timothy vi
Roosevelt Elementary School 572, 576

Rosenberg, Ian 118
Rosenthal House 268, 290-91
Rosenthal, Tony Bronco 50
Rother's Bookstore 268, 296-97
Rothko Chapel x, 102, 135-37, 139
Rothko, Mark 136
Rothman, Stuart L. 82
Rottet, Lauren, FAIA 55, 529, 625
Round Valley Texas Building 552, 555
Rouse Company 593,
Row House Community Development Corporation 277
Row on 25th 701
Rowe, Colin 125
Roy Avenue Townhouses 386
Royalton at River Oaks 107
Royden Oaks 422
RTKL Associates (Dallas) 49, 112, 223, 598, 648
Rubenstein Group Building 336, 347
Rubenstein, Larry 347
Runyon Architects 598
Rupe, Don D. 244
Russell Brown Company 124, 158
Russo Properties 538
Rustay & Martin 29
Rustay, George W. 29, 53, 223, 419
Rustay, Martin & Vale 223
RWS Architects 204, 576
Ryan, Jeff, AIA 47, 95, 157, 206, 208, 224, 411, 469, 487, 489, 522, 542, 600
S. H. Kress & Company Building 35, 56
S. I. Morris Associates 7, 21, 45, 135-36, 172, 216, 398, 406, 416, 464-65, 469, 471, 473, 523, 554, 556, 563, 565, 584, 628, 692
Sacaris, George 560
Sacred Heart Catholic Church 35, 37
Sacred Heart CoCathedral 35, 36, 37
Saigon Houston Plaza 622, 628, 629
Saint Street Swim Club 430, 448
Sakowitz Brothers 41, 53-54, 82
Sakowitz Housing 306, 330
Saks Fifth Avenue Building 472-73
Sales, Jill vi
Salisbury, H. A. & T. G. McHale, 405, 411, 670
Salisbury, Hiram A. 123, 176, 185, 223, 244, 273, 328, 688
Salvation Army Garden City Boys and Girls Club, 536, 546, 547
Sam Houston Equestrian Statue 152, 162-63, 165
Sam Houston Hotel 35, 62-63
Sam Houston Park 4, 6-10, 78, 104, 417, 527
Sammons, Doug 118
Samuels, Danny, FAIA 245, 249, 253, 259, 343, 352, 378, 389, 400, 420, 437, 440, 528, 599
San Felipe Cottage 4, 8
San Felipe Courts 100, 104-05, 109
San Felipe Green 478
San Felipe Plaza 458, 477
San Jacinto Monument 680-82, 684-85
San Jacinto Museum of History 685
San Jacinto Savings Building 556
San Jacinto Street Bridge 91
San Jacinto Trust Company 672
Sánchez, Chula Ross 296
Sanchez, Roque 275
Sanders & Sanders 119
Sandtrap Office and Retail Complex 608, 614
Sanford, H. M. 156

Sanguinet & Staats 39, 74, 75, 129, 132, 687
Sanguinet, Marshall R. 39, 58, 60, 63, 74, 75, 91, 126, 129, 132, 687
Sanguinet, Staats & Barnes 39, 91, 126, 129
Sanguinet, Staats & Gottlieb 132
Sanguinet, Staats, Hedrick & Gottlieb 58, 60, 63, 74
Sargent, Elizabeth vi
Sarmiento, Wenceslao A. 244
Sarofim Building, UT, Houston Health Science Center 196, 219
Sasaki & Associates 208, 597
Satterfield & Pontikes Building 520, 526
Satterfield, Blair 52
Sauer House 394, 405
Sauviac & Dang (Baton Rouge) 547
Savino Architecture 380
Savino, Monica 380
Sawyer, F. McM. 405, 658
Scanlan Building 68, 81
Scanlan, Kate 81
Scanlan, T. H. 81
Schatz, Mark, AIA 299, 425
Schauer Filling Station 363
Schleser, Joseph, House 338, 362
Schlumberger Building 622, 624-25
Schlumberger Well Services Headquarters 268, 298
Schmidt, Garden & Erickson 222
Schneider, R. G. 694
Schnitzer, Kenneth 452
Schoeppl, Carlos B. 181
Scholibo Building 83
Schooley, Palmer Brook, AIA 359, 383, 588, 700
Schulte, Edward J. (Cincinnati) 478, 512
Schwarz, Conrad 387
Schwarz, Martha 218
Science and Engineering Building, UH 268, 295
Science and Research Center, UH 268, 294
Science Building, Houston Community College 121
Science Building, TSU 266, 280-81
Scientific Design Building 556
Scurlock Tower 216
Scurry House 396, 416-17
Seabrook 681, 689
Sears Roebuck & Co. Bus Shelter 536, 544-45
Second Baptist Church 484, 490-91
Second Church of Christ, Scientist 338, 362
Seeberger, Perry, AIA vi
Seismic Exchange Building 520, 525
Select Specialty Hospital—Houston West 520, 530-31
Self, Ronnie 275
Selser Schaefer Architects 251
Sesquicentennial Park 4, 28-29, 38
Sewall Hall, Rice University 196, 212
Sewall, Blanch Harding 212, 414
Sewall, Cleveland House 394, 414
Shade restaurant 366
Shadow Design Studio 374, 384
Shady Acres Village 338, 368-69
Shadyside 128, 167-70, 173-74, 409,
Shamrock Hotel 151, 167-69, 218, 220,
Shanley, Kevin 31, 49, 90,
Sharp, Frank W. 426, 446, 534, 543, 551, 565
Sharpstown 551, 555, 564-65, 567, 627
Sharpstown Center 565
Shartle House 500, 506-07
Shaw, Clarence, Architects 451
Shea Street Building 89

Shell Information Center 198, 228, 229
Shell Oil Company 18, 198, 228-29, 254, 520, 526-27, 552, 560-61
Shell Pipe Line Company Buildings 552, 560-61
Shell Woodcreek 520, 526-27
Shepherd Square 438
Shepherd+Boyd 462
Sheridan Apartments 116
Sheridan, Christian, AIA 275
Sherman Brady Brick Company 321
Sherman, William 242
Sherwood Forest 504
Shipley, Dan 489
Shipman, Ellen B. 177, 403, 414
Shirat Maylight 699
Shoemake, Carrie, FAIA 152, 156, 158, 179, 191, 249, 260, 325, 410, 414
Shorthand House 236, 244-45
Shot-Trot House 306, 318-19
Shotgun Houses 108
Shrine of Our Lady of La Vang 547
Shriners Hospital for Children 218
Shultz, Steven vi
Sicardi Gallery (2001) 430, 442
Sicardi Gallery (2012) 696
Sidney H. Morris & Associates 565
Sidney Sherman Bridge 306, 328
Siewerssen and Hogan-Allnoch Buildings 86, 88
Sikes Jennings Kelly 55, 113, 216, 584, 625
Silverman, Melvin A. 54
Silvetti, Jorge 209
Simms, Carroll, *African Queen Mother* 281
Simms, Carroll, *Man and the Universe* 280
Simms, E. F. 326
Simon Hubig Company Building 336, 348
Simon Property Group 473
Sing, Emily 245
Sisters of Charity of the Incarnate Word 37, 324
Six Square House 266, 277
Sixth Ward Community Park 336, 348
Sixth Ward Historic District 345, 348
Skidmore, Owings & Merrill 16-19, 43, 78, 181, 213, 216, 468, 471, 475, 477, 529, 566
Skogland, Herbert 439
SLA 612
Slaney Santana Group 348-49
Slaney, Scott 163, 348-49
Slaughter, S. R. 327
Small House and Small House 2 268, 298-99
Smaller Scholars Montessori School 625
Smallwood, Robert C. 687
Smart Shop, The 35, 50
Smith & Company Architects 109
Smith County School 439
Smith Elementary School 536, 542-43
Smith House (1948) 266, 285
Smith House (1970) 154, 188
Smith Locke Asakura 649
Smith Office Park 468
Smith Photographers Studio 552, 554-55
Smith Tower 196, 216
Smith-Herzog House 500, 512
Smith, Claire 366
Smith, Harlan 348
Smith, Harwood K., & Partners 557
Smith, Ken 218
Smith, Michael John, FAIA 257
Smith, R. E. "Bob" 471, 475

Smith, Richard F., 674
Smith, Terry, AIA 109
Smith, Vanessa and Jason 560
Smith's Lucky 7 Grocery 520, 524
Sobel, Robert 565
Society for the Prevention of Cruelty to Animals 520, 522
Solar Decathlon 275
Solomon House 236, 258
Solomon, Daniel 523
SOM 16-19, 43, 78, 181, 213, 216, 468, 471, 475, 477, 529, 566
South End Junior High School 100, 120
South Main Baptist Church 101, 124
South Plant 196, 210
Southampton Court Townhomes 236, 242
Southampton House 698
Southampton Place 187-190
Southcorp Realty Advisors 107
Southern National Bank Building 640, 650, 659
Southern National Bank Headquarters 640, 651
Southern National Bank, Uptown 458, 466-67
Southern Pacific Building 68, 72-73
Southgate 245-247
Southgate House 236, 246-47
Southmore Addition 156, 159-60
Southmore Terrace 159
Southside Place 235, 253
Southside Place Bath House 236, 253
Southside Place Club House 253
Southwestern Bell Telephone Co. Accounting Center 484, 494
Southwestern Bell Telephone Company Building 100, 118, 122
Southwestern Seminary 671
Spa Building 552, 564-65
SpawGlass Construction Company Headquarters 608, 614-15
Spear, Laurinda 48
Speck, Lawrence W., FAIA 46-47, 59
Spencer Partnership 111, 612-13
Sperry Univac Building 556
Spire Realty Group 53, 73
Spring Branch Savings & Loan Assn. 520, 524-25
St. Anne Catholic Church 430, 438
St. Anthony of Padua Catholic Church 594, 600
St. Cecilia Catholic Church 500, 512
St. Christopher Catholic Church 666, 676
St. Cuthbert's Episcopal Church 608, 615
St. Elizabeth Hospital 575
St. Emanuel House 266, 275
St. George Syrian Orthodox Church 309
St. Germain Lofts 56
St. James Episcopal Church 266, 284
St. John Baptist Church 266, 272
St. John Church 4, 8
St. John Missionary Baptist Church 266, 273
St. John The Divine Church 394, 411, 424
St. John's Episcopal Church 682, 688
St. John's Lutheran Church 608, 616-17
St. John's Presbyterian Church 561
St. John's School 424-25
St. Joseph Catholic Church 336, 348-49
St. Joseph Hospital, South Wing 35, 37
St. Luke's Evangelist Church 280
St. Luke's Health System Hospital 640, 646
St. Luke's Hospital 217-18, 223, 646
St. Luke's Medical Tower 196, 217

St. Luke's United Methodist Church 430, 447
St. Martin's Episcopal Church 484, 487
St. Mary and Archangel Michael Coptic Orthodox Church 608, 617
St. Mary of the Immaculate Conception Catholic Church 682, 688
St. Mary's Episcopal Church 608, 612
St. Mary's Seminary 505, 688
St. Matthew Lutheran Church 161
St. Michael The Archangel Catholic Church 458, 478
St. Nicholas Catholic Church 304, 316-17
St. Paul's Methodist Church 116
St. Paul's United Methodist Church 152, 162-63
St. Peter's Evangelical Church 520, 524-25
St. Pius V Catholic Church 666, 674
St. Regis Houston Hotel 462
St. Rose of Lima Church 544
St. Rose of Lima Parish Hall and School 536, 544
St. Theresa Catholic Church Education and Office Building 640, 642-43
St. Thomas Aquinas Catholic Church 622, 631
St. Thomas Episcopal Church and School 552, 558-59
Staats, Carl G. 39, 58, 60, 63, 74-75, 91, 126, 129, 132, 687
Stafford Centre 622, 634
Staiti House 4, 8-9
Standard Brass & Manufacturing Co. 304, 315
Standard Sanitary Manufacturing Co. 304, 316
Stapley, Mildred 414
Star Engraving Company Building 100, 106
Starnes, Lawrence D. 489
State Dept. of Highways and Public Transportation, District 12, 686
State National Bank Building 68, 82
Staub & Rather 203, 204, 212, 223, 315, 443, 510
Staub & Rather Building 430, 443
Staub, John F. House 174, 177, 394, 412, 414-15
Staub, John F., FAIA 29, 40, 57, 129, 164, 167, 170, 174, 176-78, 181, 192, 213, 223, 260, 278, 345, 363, 398, 401-04, 409-10, 412-13, 415, 417-18, 439, 486-87, 502-04, 507, 686
Staub, Rather & Howze 29, 57, 164, 170, 223, 401, 418, 487
Stayton Nunn & Milton McGinty 181
Stedman Studio 107
Steele, R. D. 106, 116, 128
Steffy, Linda 382
Stegeman Building 83
Stein House 666, 672
Steinberg Design Collaborative 107
Steinberg, Arthur D. 670
Steinbomer, Henry 688
Stella Link Redevelopment Association 255
Stella, Frank 296
Stephens Company House of Ideas 552, 562
Sterling Building 58
Sterling Heights 336, 356
Sterling Victorian Homes 356
Sterling, Ross S. House 101, 124-25, 682, 686-87
Stern and Bucek Architects 190, 206, 209, 327, 364, 412, 446, 613
Stern, Robert A. M. 30, 125, 209
Stern, William F. & Associates 120, 173, 180, 184, 186, 242-43, 363, 409, 446
Stern, William F., House 154, 180
Sterne Building 80
Stewart Service Station 438

Stewart Title Building 458, 471
Stewart, Mark 642, 647
Stinson Design Group 81
Stirling & Wilford (London) 204-05
Stirling, James 204
STOA International 627, 629
Stokes, W. E. 545
Stone, Jr. Edward D., & Associates 474
Stone, Marracini & Patterson, 227
Stowers Building 53
Strasser Ragni Architecture 142, 180, 190, 245, 359, 387-88, 419, 446
Strasser, Scott 142, 180, 190, 245, 359, 387-88, 419, 446, 697
Straus House 500, 510
Straus-Frank Company Building 304, 318
Straus, Robert D. 317
Streetman House 154, 181
Stroik, Duncan G. 643
Strombom, Dean, AIA 251
Stuart Buildings 80
Stubee, Henry A. 288
Stude, Henry W., House 152, 168, 394, 400
Student Life Plaza, UH 268, 292-93
Studio 333 109
Studio Red 350, 451-52, 601
Studio-Shed Building 338, 364
StudioMET 184
Style-in-Steel Townhouses 236, 256
Sugar Creek 650
Sugar Land 638-639
Sugar Land Baptist Church 645
Sugar Land City Hall 640, 648
Sugar Land Cultural Arts Foundation 642
Sugar Land Marriott Town Square 640, 648-49
Sugar Land Medical Plaza, Sugar Land 640, 646
Sugar Land School Auditorium 640, 642
Sugarland Industries 642-43
Sugarland Properties 649
Suit House, 154, 188
Sullivan, Maurice J., FAIA 59, 60-61, 120, 160, 162, 277, 310, 319-20, 322, 324, 354, 360, 438, 505, 676, 684, 688
Sullivan, Maurice J.-Charles F. Sullivan 505
Sullivan, Maurice J., House 152, 160
Summit, The 451
Sundberg, Richard 698
Sunnystones 154, 189
Sunset Hospital 304, 308
Sunset Terrace Houses 242
Surls, James 71
Sustaita Architects 320, 599
Suyama Peterson Deguchi 697
Suyama, George 697
SWA Group, The 11-12, 27, 31, 37, 39, 49, 81, 90, 126, 165, 177, 226, 464-65, 616
Swan, Simone 386
Sweeney & Coombs Building 80
Sweeney, Coombs & Fredericks Building 68, 76
Sweetwater Country Club 640, 648
Swenson & Linnstaedter 117
Swenson Studio 100, 116-17
Swenson, Bailey A. 117, 161, 247, 284, 287-88, 290
Swenson, Kathryn 117
Swift, Hill 253
Sylvan Beach Hotel 688
Sylvan Beach Pavilion 682, 688
Sylvan, Linda vii

Sylvester Turner Park 536, 546
Synott Masjid 631
Sysco Corporate Headquarters 622, 624
Tabler, William B. & Associates 586
Tabor, J. Rodney 156, 319, 350
Tackett, Gerald, AIA 476, 493, 503, 659
Taft Architects 245, 249, 253, 259, 343, 352, 378, 389, 400, 420, 437, 440, 528, 599
Taggart Park Townhouses 374, 376
Tall Timbers, Hogg Brothers Camp 420
Taller de Arquitectura 207, 470
Tamayo, Rufino, *America* 51
Tamminga, William 186
Tan, David 630
Tanaguchi, Yoshio, & Associates 159
Tanglewood 482, 484
Tanglewood House 484, 486-89
Tanguma, Leo, *The Rebirth of our Nationality* 306, 323
Tapley, Charles, Associates 30, 89, 107, 172, 186-87, 225, 244, 414, 463, 495, 507, 512, 589, 613, 615, 628, 631
Tapley Lunow Architects 512
Tapley, Charles, FAIA 30, 89, 107, 172, 186-87, 225, 244, 296, 414, 463, 495, 507, 511-12, 589, 613, 615, 628, 631
Tate, Ken 377
Tatham Fine Arts Center, St. John's School 396, 424
Tax Increment Reinvestment Zone No. 2 112
Taylor, Dan, & Associates 554
Taylor, Harwood 421, 441, 444, 453, 479, 486, 506, 557, 559
Taylor, Jessie Carter 131
Taylor, Judson, House 102, 130-31
TBG Partners (Austin) 135, 598
TeamHou 28
Teas Nursery 557
Teas, Edward 557
Teich & Gideon 128
Telfair 639, 644
Tellepsen Construction Company 13, 320
Tellepsen Family Downtown YMCA Building 4, 13
Telvent 541
Tempest, J. Arthur 58
Tempietto Zeni 374, 383
Temple Beth Israel 100, 121, 563
Temple of Rest, Beth Israel Cemetery 100, 110
Templo Jerusalen 309
Templo Regional de la Luz del Mundo 572, 576-77
Ten-Ten Garage 51
Tennant House 154, 177
Tenneco Building 4, 18, 538
Terry Hershey Park 624
Texaco 45, 130, 167, 554
Texaco Computer Services Building 567
Texaco Office Building 552, 554, 567
Texas A&M, Landscape Architecture Studio 348-49
Texas American Bank 675
Texas Bank & Trust Tower 552, 567
Texas Children's Hospital 196, 198, 217-18, 222
Texas Children's Hospital, Clinical Care Building 198, 222
Texas Commerce Bank Motor Bank 68, 70
Texas Commerce Center 35, 56
Texas Commerce Tower 4, 22, 39, 56
Texas Company Building 35, 64-65, 73, 130
Texas Department of Criminal Justice, Central State Farm 640, 643-44

Texas Department of Public Safety, Region Two Headquarters 608, 614-15
Texas Eastern Corporation 45, 47
Texas First National Bank Building 622, 626-27
Texas Heart Institute 198, 223
Texas Instruments Building 622, 634-35
Texas Medical Center 36, 150-51, 213-29
Texas Packing Company Building 86, 90-91
Texas Southern University 266, 278-81
Texas State Hotel 35, 64
Texas Steel Processing Building 536, 542
Texas Teo Chew Temple 622, 628-29
Texas Woman's University Institute of Health Sciences 196, 218
Textile restaurant 367
Thaxton-Gaw House 500, 513
The 505 102, 134
The Woodlands 581, 589, 592-603, 606-07
Third Church of Christ, Scientist 152, 156
Thomas, James M. 272, 344
Thompson + Hanson 448
Thompson House 500, 512
Thompson-Frater Associates 353
Thompson, Mary Lynn 512
Thompson, Thomas C. 113
Thomsen, Charles B., House 236, 246
Thornhill-Craver Company Building 330
Thornton, Guy Design (Denver) 58
Three Eldridge Place 520, 530
Three H Services Center 582, 588-89
Thurgood Marshall School of Law Building, TSU 266, 280-81
Tidwell, Dan 72
Tien Hou Temple 304, 317
Tiffany Studios 59
Tigerman Fugman McCurry 115, 439
Tigerman, Stanley 115
Timber Crest 286
Timber Crest Corporation House 266, 286
Timber Lane Terrace 505
Timberlake, James (Philadelphia) 206
Time Warner Building 536, 542
Tin Houses 374, 386-87
TJK Investments Building 113
TKYL 629
Todd Tackett Lacy 476, 659
Todd Townhouses 484, 492
Todd, Anderson, FAIA 175, 188, 242, 476, 484, 492, 508, 592, 659
Todd, Iris G. 188
Tomasco Associates, Don J. 514
Toomey, Charles 109
Tovar, Rodrigo 111
Tower Community Center 143
Tower Lofts 143
Tower Theater 102, 143
Town & Country Mall 530
Town Center, The Woodlands 594, 598
Town Square, Sugar Land 649
Town, A. Hays 490
Trafalgar Place Condominiums 484, 492-93
Trammell Crow 45, 612, 634
Tranquility Park 4, 30-31
Transco Fountain 474
Transco Tower 135, 458, 472, 474
Transcontinental Gas Pipeline Building 100, 116-17
Transportation Plaza 78
Travis Elementary School 336, 352

Treptow Murphree & Company 585
Trinity Episcopal Church 100, 118-19
Trinity Lutheran Church 349
Trinity United Methodist Church 276
Truitt Architectural Services 600
Truxillo, Bart 88, 361
Tudor Field House, Rice University 196, 208
Tulane Townhouses 699, 700
Turner House 396, 418-19
Turner, Cleveland 275
Turner, Drexel 312
Turner, Harry A. 444
Turner, Richard 71
Turquoise Center, Raindrop Turkish House 632
Turrell, James 171, 369, 699
Tutt, Courtney vi
Twilight Epiphany 699
Two Houston Center 35, 44-45
Tycer, Scott 367
U.S. Home Building 458, 463
U.S. Oncology Building 594, 596
U.S. Post Office 35, 65, 86, 89, 531
UH Energy Research Park 298
UH Graduate Design/Build Studio 186-87, 346, 560
Ullberg, Kent, *The Guardian* 105
Ulrich Franzen & Associates, 26
Underhill, Michael 261
Underwood House 394, 407
Union National Bank Building 68, 76
Union Station 62-63, 315
Uniroyal 123
Unitarian Fellowship of Houston 520, 524
United Gas Building 4, 15
United Methodist Church Kingdom Builders Center 656, 659
United Way Center 336, 342
Unity Church of Christianity 484, 493
University Branch, Fort Bend County Library 640, 644
University Center, UH 268, 292-93
University of Houston vi, x, 89, 114, 187, 226, 265, 279, 292-99, 346, 453, 557, 560, 644, 692
University of Houston / Wharton County Junior College 640, 644
University of Houston-Downtown 89, 90, 92
University of Houston, Clear Lake 682, 692
University of St. Thomas 102, 126, 134-35, 207, 565
University of Texas, M. D. Anderson Hospital and Tumor Institute 198, 222
University of Texas, School of Nursing viii, 196, 220
University Savings Association Building 236, 244
Unocal Building 640, 649
Upjohn, Hobart 162
Upjohn, Richard M. 162
Upstream Technical Training Center 451
Uptown Park 458, 467
Urban Architecture 52, 79, 119, 308, 386, 585
Urban Investment & Development Company 49
Urban Meridian Group Building, 374, 386-87
Urban Partners (Dallas) 439
Valdez, Alice M. 346
Vale & Associates, Wylie W. 513
Van Alstyne, W. A. Building 76-77
Van Buren, Ralph 388
Van Court 110
Van der Rohe, Ludwig Mies, 134, 160, 170, 412, 561
Van Ness & Mower 225, 297, 692
Van Pelt, Patrick 113

725

Vaquero 304, 308
Varela, Alfonso 248
Varner Realty Company 354, 502
Vassar Place Apartments 154, 182-83
Vassar Place Townhouses 154, 184
Vaughan House 396, 418
Venturi, Rauch & Scott Brown 478
Venturi, Scott-Brown & Associates 157, 312
Verges, Mike G., House 656, 660
Verlinder, Jacques 426
Veterans Administration Medical Center 198, 226-27
Viashnav, Mahendra 631
Vietnamese Buddhist Center 622, 630
Villa de Matel 306, 324, 438
Village Square 244
Village State Bank Building 244
Vinson Branch, Houston Public Library 656, 660
Vintage Park 608, 611
Virginia Point 430, 445
Virginia Townhouses 442
Visioneering Studios 610
Voelcker & Associates, Herbert 317
Volz & Associates 59, 115
W. L. Foley Dry Goods Company Building 68, 72
W. O. Neuhaus Associates 106, 228, 351, 414, 422, 490, 510, 539, 625, 693
Waggaman House 100, 114
Wagner Hardware Building 247
Wagner House 54, 190
Wagner, J. K. & Company 76
Wagner, Stewart 190
Wahlberg, Paul 671
Wald Transfer & Storage Company Building 304, 316
Waldman, Peter D. 26, 27, 353, 693
Waldo House 102, 132-33
Waldo, Wilmer 133
Walker, John 354
Walker, Peter, & Partners (San Francisco) 81, 692
Walker, Randall, AIA vi
Walker@Main Garage 35, 52
Wallace Garcia Wilson 469
Wallace McHarg Robert & Todd 592
Wallace, Bruce 491
Wallace/Garcia & Associates 116
Walne House 154, 177
Walsh, Sally Sherwin 7, 441
Walt Disney Imagineering 691
Walter Kidde Company 298
Wamble, Mark 25, 140, 258, 434, 543
Ward House 336, 352
Ward, Cinda 381
Warren & Wetmore 62, 65, 130, 132
Warren House 500, 502-03
Warwick Post Oak 458, 469
Warwick Towers 152, 162
Warwick, Gary 81
Washington Cemetery 334
Washington Colorado Townhouses 336, 350
Washington Plaza 374, 381
Waters, Camille 385
Waters, R. Newell 349
Waters, Steve 356, 362
Waterway Lofts 597
Waterway Square, The Woodlands 597
Watkin, Nunn, McGinty and Phenix 224
Watkin, William Ward 6, 59, 81, 119, 125, 133, 135, 170, 174-76, 178, 192, 203-04, 212-13, 224, 274, 291, 310, 354, 363, 467, 642

Watkins Carter Hamilton 438, 646
Waugh, Scott 312
Weatherford, Hal 256
Weaver, Harry 227
Webster Elementary School 694
Webster High School 682, 694
Webster, Frederick Leon 144
Weekley Family YMCA Building 255
Weems, F. Carrington 689
Weingarten, Joe, House 266, 268, 287, 289
Welch City Residences 102, 146
Welch, Frank, & Associates 418, 436, 489, 491, 510
Welch, Frank D., FAIA 418, 436, 489, 491, 510, 512
Weldon's Cafeteria 152, 160-61
Welton Becket & Associates 13-14, 77, 128, 229, 646, 691
Werlin, Eugene & Associates 164
Werlin, Eugene, FAIA 142, 164, 415
Wesley Chapel A.M.E. Church 266, 272
West Ave 430, 438, 439
West House 236, 246
West Orem Family YMCA Building 656, 658
West Ranch House 682, 690
West University Place 234-35, 243, 245-54
West, J. M., Ranch 690
West, Virginia and R. C., House 246
Westbury 561
Westbury United Methodist Church 552, 561
Westchase 626
Westerman, Lisa Pope 509
Western Electric Company Building 86, 94-95
Westfall House 102, 132
Westheimer Building 63
Westheimer House 127
Westin Galleria Hotel 472
Westin Houston Memorial City 531
Westlake Park 529
Westphal, Rolf 588
Wetcher House 682, 692-93
Wharton, Earl, House 152, 168
Wheatley High School (1929) 572, 574
Wheatley Senior High School (1949) 306, 330
Whitaker, Alfred 344
Whitco Residential (Chicago) 470
White Budd Van Ness Partnership 293, 295, 541
White House 396, 419, 666, 672
White Memorial Plaza, University of St. Thomas 126
White Oak Bayou 90-91, 302, 343-4, 351, 369
White Oak Studio 165
White, Bill, Mayor 7, 46, 345
Whiting, Sarah M., AIA vi
Whitney & Whitney 63
Whitney Bank Main Street 160
Whole Foods Market 440
WHR Architects 214-15, 224
Wier House 154, 177
Wiess College, Rice University 196, 208-09
Wiess, Harry C. House 154, 192
Wilford & Associates, Michael 204
Wilkins, Richard M. 419, 490
Wilkinson, Edward 669
Willard House 500, 505
Willard, Philip G. 288
Willard, Philip G. & Lucian T. Hood, Jr. 288, 289, 290
William A. Wilson Company 320, 352
William B. Tabler & Associates 586
William F. Stern & Associates 120, 173, 180, 184, 186, 242-43, 363, 409, 446

William L. Pereira Associates 44
William R. Jenkins Associates 650, 694
Williams House 430, 434
Williams Tower 474
Williams Trace Baptist Church 640, 644-45
Williams, Jake 493
Williams, Laverne (Environment Associates) 119, 660
Willis Flow Control Building 536, 539
Willis, Bricker & Cannady 215, 243, 318
Willow Street Pump Station 86, 92
Willowbend Medical and Dental Clinic 552, 560-61
Willowick, The 396, 425, 510
Wilsford, Larry 72
Wilshire Village Apartments 696
Wilson & Associates 48
Wilson Griffin Architects 529
Wilson House (1959) 285
Wilson House (c 1907) 266, 272
Wilson, F. Talbott, FAIA 256, 424, 434-35, 449, 489
Wilson, F. Talbott, House 484, 489
Wilson, Morris & Crain 174, 285, 486, 506
Wilson, Morris, Crain & Anderson 19, 256, 468, 567
Wilson, Robert 427
Wilson, Thomas Redyard, AIA 187, 189, 250, 252, 254, 509
Wilson, Thomas, House 236, 250
Wilson, William A., Company 320, 352
Wilson, William, House 336, 353
Wilson/Crain/Anderson/Reynolds 88
Windham, Russell 110, 177, 253, 404, 416-17, 419-21, 437, 489
Windsor Village Builders Center 656, 659
Wingfield, Jr., Magruder 563
Winkler, Paul 138
Winlow-Westheimer District 430, 438, 439
Winslow Court 152, 158
Winston, Jr., James O. 503
Winston, Oliver C. 406
Wirtz & Calhoun 124, 260
Wirtz, Calhoun, Tungate & Jackson 491, 691
Wirtz, L. M 124, 260, 691
Wisdom, C. Jackson 649
Wisdom, W. Jackson 259, 286
Wittenberg Architects 247
Wittenberg Associates 438
Wittenberg Oberholzer 183, 387
Wittenberg Oberholzer Architects 258
Wittenberg Oberholzer Partnership 441, 446
Wittenberg Partnership Architects 184
WLS Interests 107
Woitena, Ben 450
Wolf, Matt vi
Wolff Companies 525
Wolff, Morgan & Company 528
Womack House 152, 167
Womack, Kenneth E. House 167
Wood, M. R. 642
Woodlake 495
Woodlake Recreation Center 495
Woodland Heights 320, 335, 352-53
Woodlands Church 601
Woodlands College Park High School 594, 602
Woodlands High School 594, 600-01
Woodlands Mall 594, 598
Woodlands Peace Palace 594, 600
Woodlands, The 581, 589, 592-603, 606-07
Woodlands United Methodist Church 594, 600
Woodlands Water Resources Building 594, 599
Woodlands Waterway Marriott Hotel and Convention Center 597
WoodsEdge Community Church 594, 603
Woodson Research Center, Rice University vi
Woodward House 338, 360
Woodward, Emerson F. House 360
Workshop 520, 524
Wortham Fountain 196, 218
Wortham IMAX Theater 164
Wortham Theater Building, UH 296
Wortham Tower 106
Wortham, Elena Cusi 83
Wortham, Gus S. Park 303, 325, 327
Wortham, Pia 353
Wray, Andrew Jackson, House 152, 167
Wray, Margaret Cullinan 167
Wright, Frank Lloyd 513
Wroxton Road Residences 236, 242, 243
Wroxton Townhouses 236, 242
Wunderlich, Maria Katherina Hofius, House 611
Wunsche Brothers Café and Saloon 582, 588-89
Wylie W. Vale & Associates 513
Wyndham Hotel Greenspoint 582, 584
X-Small House 266, 274-75
Yamasaki, Minoru (Michigan) 563
Yates Homestead 4, 8
Yates, Jack, House 100, 110
Yates, Rutherford B. H. 110
YMCA East End Branch Building 666, 674-75
Young House 394, 404
Young, Mary Ann 379
Zagst, Stephen R. House 338, 366-67
Zamore, Brett ix, 156, 319, 389, 576
Zemanek House 102, 138-39, 144-45
Zemanek, John 139, 145, 293, 589, 697
Zeni, Frank 382-84
Zephyr, The 430, 444-45
ZeRow House 266, 274-75
Ziegler Cooper 15, 36, 190, 242, 422, 425, 439, 467, 538, 597, 612, 625
Ziegler, Scott, AIA 15, 36-37, 190, 242, 422, 425, 439, 467, 538, 597, 612, 625
Zimmerman & Bible 117
Zimmerman, A. G. 94, 117
Zinn House 552, 562
Zorach, William, The New State of Texas 51
Zukov, Nikita 565
Zumwalt, Frank 228
Zweig, Peter Jay, FAIA 124, 380, 650, 694